The Definitive Guide to SOA

Oracle® Service Bus

SECOND EDITION

Jeff Davies, David Schorow, Samrat Ray, and David Rieber

Apress®

The Definitive Guide to SOA: Oracle Service Bus, Second Edition

Copyright © 2008 by Jeff Davies, David Schorow, Samrat Ray, and David Rieber

ISBN-13 (pbk): 978-1-4302-1057-3

ISBN-13 (electronic): 978-1-4302-1058-0

Printed and bound in the United States of America (POD)

Lead Editor: Steve Anglin
Technical Reviewer: Jay Kasi
Editorial Board: Clay Andres, Steve Anglin, Ewan Buckingham, Tony Campbell, Gary Cornell, Jonathan Gennick, Matthew Moodie, Joseph Ottinger, Jeffrey Pepper, Frank Pohlmann, Ben Renow-Clarke, Dominic Shakeshaft, Matt Wade, Tom Welsh
Project Manager: Richard Dal Porto
Copy Editor: Marilyn Smith
Associate Production Director: Kari Brooks-Copony
Production Editor: Laura Esterman
Compositor/Artist: Kinetic Publishing Services, LLC
Proofreader: Nancy Sixsmith
Indexer: Broccoli Information Management
Cover Designer: Kurt Krames
Manufacturing Director: Tom Debolski

Distributed to the book trade worldwide by Springer-Verlag New York, Inc., 233 Spring Street, 6th Floor, New York, NY 10013. Phone 1-800-SPRINGER, fax 201-348-4505, e-mail orders-ny@springer-sbm.com, or visit http://www.springeronline.com.

For information on translations, please e-mail info@apress.com, or visit http://www.apress.com.

Apress and friends of ED books may be purchased in bulk for academic, corporate, or promotional use. eBook versions and licenses are also available for most titles. For more information, reference our Special Bulk Sales–eBook Licensing web page at http://www.apress.com/info/bulksales.

The source code for this book is available to readers at http://www.apress.com.

Contents at a Glance

Contents

Foreword

The enterprise service bus (ESB) is a hot topic today. Many vendors are either building new products in this category or dressing up their existing products to pitch as ESBs. However, there is no clearly accepted definition of what an ESB is, what its architecture should be, or what its programming paradigm should be. Definitions range from saying that it is nothing and wholly unneeded to saying it is everything and has all the capabilities of a full integration suite with built-in orchestration, data aggregation, and web services management capabilities. Architectures range from being embedded in the clients and endpoints to being a central intermediary to being a decentralized intermediary. Programming paradigms for the ESB range from writing Java to being completely configuration-driven and pliable with graphical interfaces.

BEA Systems, the original creator of what is now the Oracle Service Bus, did not dress up one of its existing products and pitch it as an ESB. It built an ESB from scratch (first introduced in the summer of 2005), with a razor-sharp focus on where it is positioned as a component in an end-to-end service-oriented architecture (SOA). It complements a business process management or orchestration service, but serves a different and distinct role. Much of SOA is about componentization, interconnectivity, and reuse. The ESB is a component that serves as an intermediary, with the clear and distinct role of providing loose coupling between clients and services, a routing fabric, connectivity, and a central point of security enforcement, contributing to the manageability of your SOA network. It can be a central intermediary or a decentralized network of intermediaries. It is completely configuration-based with browser-based graphical interfaces.

In this book, the authors introduce you to ESBs in general and Oracle Service Bus in particular, with many examples and clear and understandable explanations of the product and its implementation in a number of ESB use cases. This book takes the very practical and useful approach of picking one of the leading products in the ESB category and does a show-and-tell, instead of dwelling on a lot of philosophical discussions and arguments of various contrasting architectures or definitions of an ESB. It is a very readable and instructive book. As one of the architects of the first release of the product, I feel this book is a fine introduction to Oracle Service Bus.

Jay Kasi
Director, Product Management,
Oracle Corporation

About the Authors

 **JEFF DAVIES** has more than 25 years of experience in the software field. This includes developing retail applications, such as Act! for Windows and Macintosh, and a number of other commercially available applications, principally in the telecommunications and medical fields. His background also includes the development, design, and architecture of enterprise applications. Previous to joining BEA, Jeff was Chief Architect at a telecommunications company and ran his own consulting company for a number of years. Now at Oracle, Jeff is focused on the SOA.

 **DAVID SCHOROW** has more than 20 years experience working on enterprise software. David is currently the Director of Software Development, leading the Oracle Service Bus team. Previously, he was the Chief Architect for BEA AquaLogic Service Bus. He has guided the product's development and evolution from the first release through five (and counting) subsequent releases. Prior to joining BEA, David was the chief Java architect at the NonStop division of Hewlett-Packard, overseeing the development of a wide variety of Java projects, including the NonStop Java Virtual Machine, NonStop SQL JDBC drivers, the port of WebLogic Server to the NonStop platform, and other demanding Java products. David has extensive experience in high-performance, transaction-processing systems—the application environments used by the most demanding customers, such as stock exchanges, airline reservations, health care, and banking.

 **SAMRAT RAY** has more than 10 years of experience in the architecture, design, and implementation of Java/J2EE-based enterprise software. Samrat is a Product Manager at Oracle, where he is responsible for RASP (Reliability, Availability, Scalability, Performance) aspects of multiple products in the SOA Suite. As the Performance Architect for AquaLogic Service Bus at BEA Systems, Samrat has been a key contributor to the architecture and design of the product. He is responsible for multiple innovative features that enable users to build scalable and flexible SOAs using Oracle Service Bus. Samrat has extensive experience in the areas of high-volume transaction processing and high-performance message-oriented systems.

DAVID RIEBER has more than 12 years of experience working on software development. David was a member of the BEA AquaLogic Service Bus team since its inception. As the Security Architect for AquaLogic Service Bus, he designed and implemented its security model and made major contributions to OSB's core runtime. Prior to joining BEA, David was a senior software developer at Sun Microsystems, where he worked on Sun's Java HotSpot Virtual Machine. David has a Master's Degree in Computer Science from Stanford University. David is now a software engineer at Google Inc.

About the Technical Reviewer

JAY KASI has been a software architect for about 20 years. He has worked for Hewlett-Packard as a relational database management system kernel architect, high-availability architect, and distributed OLTP architect. He was the Chief Architect at Commerce One for orchestration and ESB technologies, as well as B2B e-commerce infrastructure. He was the architect for the first few releases of OSB at BEA Systems, and later worked on designing and coordinating the integrations of OSB with other products. He is currently one of the Product Managers at Oracle for the SOA Suite.

Acknowledgments

Many people have helped me to make this book a reality. I want to thank my wife, Roberta, for her love and understanding as I spent hours on my computer, mumbling incoherently about "namespaces" and the like. There is no finer wife in the world. Similarly, I'd like to thank my children, Eric and Madeline, for putting up with my highly distracted nature while writing this book. Of course, I'd like to thank my parents and my aunt and uncle for enabling me to get to this point in my life with their constant love and support.

I'd like to thank Jay Kasi at Oracle for his help and tutelage while writing this book. I have never met a person with such a deep understanding of any software product in my life. Many times when I was stuck on a problem, Jay would quickly look at the code and deliver an exact analysis of the problem within moments.

I'd also like to thank the many folks who helped review the book and to provide me with technical answers to the more unusual scenarios. Specifically, I want to recognize (in alphabetical order) Deb Ayers, Stephen Bennett, Naren Chawla, George Gould, David Groves, Dain Hansen, Gregory Haardt, Karl Hoffman, Ashish Krishna, Usha Kuntamukkala, Saify Lanewala, Denis Pilipchuk, Michael Reiche, Kelly Schwarzhoff, Chris Tomkins, Tolga Urhan, Jeremy Westerman, Mike Wooten, and Bradley Wright.

Finally, I'd like to thank the great mentors in my life, Mark Russell and Gerry Millar. They taught me everything from how to tie a necktie to how to "listen to what they are feeling." They both taught me that it's the people that are important; the software is incidental. That's a hard but invaluable lesson for a natural-born geek.

Jeff Davies

Chapter 17 describes how to extend OSB to communicate with additional applications by writing a custom transport using the Transport SDK. This useful extensibility mechanism was designed and implemented by Greg Fichtenholtz, a Senior Engineer on the OSB team. It is his design that enables OSB to be used in new and different environments not addressed in the original implementation. The usefulness of the Transport SDK is due to his good design work.

Greg is only one member of a very talented team that created the OSB product; however, their names are too numerous to mention (and I'd be afraid of leaving someone out). This group, with its engineering prowess and creative energy, working under the management of Ashok Aletty, who fosters a productive, cooperative, and enjoyable atmosphere, is responsible for making OSB such a fantastic product. I consider myself fortunate to have the opportunity to work with such a great team on this exciting product.

I'd like to thank my sister, Stephanie Schorow, for her thorough review of an early draft of the chapter. She is the real writer of the family. Chapter 17 is much more readable due to her efforts.

Lastly, I'd like to thank my wife, Mona, and my son, Marcus, for their understanding and support when working on this book required my nights and weekends (and a canceled ski trip).

David Schorow

My contributions to this book have been derived from my real-world experiences of developing OSB and enabling customer success with the product. It has been my privilege to be part of a great team that has created and nurtured an outstanding product like OSB.

There are a number of very talented and supportive individuals who directly or indirectly have helped me become an effective contributor to OSB and to this book. Special thanks go to Jay Kasi for being there whenever I have needed his guidance and his wisdom.

I would like to thank Ashok Aletty, David Schorow, and Deb Ayers for their unstinting support and encouragement. I would also like to thank Naren Chawla, Boris Chen, and Dain Hansen for their belief in me during my initial years with OSB. I want to thank Jeff Davies for giving me the opportunity to contribute to this book.

I would like to thank my wife, Devyani, for her support and understanding during all those weekends and nights that I spent on this book. Finally, I would like to thank my parents for being an immense source of inspiration throughout my life.

Samrat Ray

There are many people at BEA I'd like to thank for their support throughout the years. First of all, I'd like to thank David Schorow for being such a great manager and friend. I'd also like to thank Ashok Aletty for keeping OSB on track in the early years and for giving me the opportunity to play a bigger role in OSB security. Thanks to Jay Kasi for his thoughtful insights and to Kelly Schwarzhoff for his invaluable feedback. Special thanks go to Jeff Davies for giving me the opportunity to contribute the security chapter and for his immense patience.

I had the privilege of collaborating with a lot of bright people throughout BEA, beyond the OSB team. Special thanks go to Neil Smithline, John Herendeen, Craig Perez, Juan Andrade, David Garrison, and Denis Pilipchuk

I'd like to thank my wife, Astrid, for her love and support; my kids, Noemi, Joshua, and Raquel, for making me such a proud dad. Finally, I'd like to thank my parents, who taught me that everything is possible.

David Rieber

Introduction

Service-oriented architecture (SOA) is rapidly becoming the new standard for today's enterprises. A number of books discuss various aspects of SOA. Most (if not all) are high level in their discussions, providing some strategies for you to consider but very little tactical information. As software professionals, we are able to grasp these abstract concepts fairly quickly, as we're sure you can. However, the devil is always in the details. We know that once we begin to implement a new technology, we will discover a whole new dimension of bugs, design issues, and other problems that are never discussed in those strategy books.

SOA is not a technology; it is architecture and a strategy. In order for you to implement your own SOA, you will need to learn a new way of thinking about your enterprise and managing software assets. SOA is generally implemented using newer technologies—not a single new technology, but a whole series of different technologies. We thought we knew XML pretty well before we began walking the path to SOA. It didn't take long for us to figure out that there was a lot more to XML than we had previously thought. You can expect to need to learn the details of XML, XML Schema, Web Services Description Language (WSDL), XQuery, and XPath before you can begin to make informed design judgments.

While we enjoy reading about new strategies, we enjoy realizing them in code just as much. Code keeps you honest. A lot of things work very well on paper, but once you start flipping bits, the truth will emerge in all of its intolerant glory. What we really wanted to read was a detailed book on SOA development. Since we could not find one, we wrote one. We wrote this book under the assumption that there were thousands of other software developers like ourselves—people who enjoy writing code and love to put theory into practice.

This book is a mix of theory and working code samples. One of the reasons there are so few books on writing real code for an SOA is because there are so few SOA platforms that the average developer can download and use. Most SOA (and more specifically, enterprise service bus) vendors keep their software locked away, demanding that you purchase it before you can use it. This is like purchasing a car you have never seen or driven based solely on the description provided to you by the salesperson.

Fortunately, Oracle provides an enterprise-class service bus that anyone can download for free, called Oracle Service Bus. This book will walk you through many detailed examples of connecting Oracle Service Bus to legacy systems, show common design patterns for web services, and generally increase both your development and architectural expertise in enterprise service bus (ESB) and SOA.

About the Oracle Service Bus

The Oracle Service Bus (OSB) is a rebranded version of the AquaLogic Service Bus (ALSB) from BEA Systems. Readers of the first version of this book learned about ALSB version 2.6 in depth. ALSB was released by BEA Systems in 2005. In mid-2008, Oracle Corporation acquired BEA Systems. The ALSB product was rebranded to OSB.

The initial release of OSB is version 10.3, in compliance with Oracle naming standards. As we write this, the rebranding of the ALSB product to become OSB is still in progress. As a result, you may see differences in the text and the screenshots of the live product. The screenshots were taken from the "prebranded" version of ALSB. Wherever possible, we have used the new product name in an effort to avoid confusion over the long term.

Oracle had an ESB before the acquisition of BEA. That product is now called Oracle Enterprise Service Bus (OESB). OESB continues to be supported by Oracle.

What's New in OSB 10.3?

In late 2007, version 3.0 of ALSB was released. Now branded as OSB 10.3, it boasts a number of significant enhancements over its earlier versions. OSB incorporates new functionality and enhancements in many areas. Some of the key enhancements include the following:

New development environment: OSB now uses an Eclipse-based IDE called WorkSpace Studio. WorkSpace Studio provides software developers with a more traditional IDE and development life cycle. Oracle has not removed the web-based configuration environment; that is still in place and is a great tool for software quality assurance professionals and operations people. Oracle WorkSpace Studio provides a unified, collaborative design experience across development teams and Oracle products, promoting higher development productivity.

Advanced service pooling and endpoint failover: If a service endpoint is not responding, you can take that service endpoint URI offline automatically and route service requests to alternate service endpoints. When the endpoint URI comes back online, it can be automatically returned to the endpoint pool to handle requests.

Support for Web Services Reliable Messaging (WS-RM): Built on top of the proven WebLogic Server product, OSB 10.3 provides support for the WS-RM standard specified by OASIS.

Business service overload protection (aka throttling): You can limit the amount of throughput to business services to prevent overloading of those services.

Optimized transports for reliability and security propagation: Optimized transports are available when connecting different types of server technologies that are colocated on the same physical machine. These optimized transports are able to reduce the overhead associated with making distributed calls, thereby increasing their performance.

Navigational and metadata sharing in WorkSpace Studio: When working with the Oracle Enterprise Repository (OER) Service Assembly Modeler, you can quickly navigate from a Service Component Architecture (SCA) resource to the design view for an OSB service. OSB also supports the sharing of metadata with OER in WorkSpace Studio. This simplifies the process of ensuring that the metadata from each project is kept in sync with the OER.

Who This Book Is For

This book is for software professionals who are working in an SOA environment, or want to work in an SOA environment. It contains real-world information on SOA best practices, working code samples, and more than 10 years of combined experience from the authors solving real SOA problems.

How This Book Is Structured

This book contains a total of 18 chapters. We've written most of the chapters so that they may be read individually. However, we do recommend reading Chapters 2 and 3, which cover setting up your development environment and understanding the basic principles of an ESB.

Here's a brief summary of what you'll find in this book:

Chapter 1, Why Use a Service Bus?: This chapter describes the functions and benefits of an ESB.

Chapter 2, Installing and Configuring the Software: This chapter guides you through installing and configuring OSB and setting up a development environment. By installing the software as described in this chapter, you will be able to run all of the sample code contained in this book.

Chapter 3, Creating a Hello World Service: In the grand tradition of programming books, we write a web service, test it, and integrate it with OSB. Along the way, you'll get a quick tour of the WorkSpace Studio development environment.

Chapter 4, Message Flow Basics: In this chapter, you will learn how to create message flows and how they are used in OSB.

Chapter 5, A Crash Course in WSDL: WSDL is the language of modern web services. Creating (or just reading) a WSDL file requires a fair bit of skill beyond what is necessary for simple XML. This chapter teaches you the core of what you need to know about WSDL and leaves out the fluff!

Chapter 6, Intermediate Message Flows: In this chapter, we really put OSB through its paces, with sample code for almost every feature available.

Chapter 7, Asynchronous Messaging: In this chapter, you will learn how to loosely couple services with regard to time.

Chapter 8, Service Types and Transports: This chapter walks you through the many different service types and transports supported by OSB, and provides you with information on how to select the correct service type and transport for your needs.

Chapter 9, Advanced Messaging Topics: In this chapter, we cover the advanced messaging capabilities of OSB.

Chapter 10, Reporting and Monitoring: There is more to OSB than just messaging. It can keep you informed about the health of your enterprise, providing automated alerts and sophisticated status reports on both your services and the servers that host them. The chapter describes OSB's reporting and monitoring features.

Chapter 11, SOA Security: This chapter covers a topic that is often discussed but seldom understood. It will provide you with a solid understanding of how to implement security within your service bus.

Chapter 12, Planning Your Service Landscape: The move to SOA requires considerable planning. This chapter introduces a methodology that will simplify this planning process and provide you with a taxonomy by which you can quickly classify your services.

Chapter 13, Implementing Your Service Landscape: In this chapter, we put into action the service landscape methodology introduced in the previous chapter.

Chapter 14, Versioning Services: This is possibly the most controversial chapter in the book! Forget everything you've heard about versioning web services and brace yourself for some heresy!

Chapter 15, Performance: Tuning and Best Practices: This chapter provides tips on how to tune OSB for maximum scalability and performance.

Chapter 16, Administration, Operations, and Management: There is more to a service bus than just development. This chapter covers some best practices for managing your service bus.

Chapter 17, Custom Transports: While OSB provides many useful transport protocols out of the box, it also contains an API that allows you to create your own customer transports so it can integrate with any legacy system. This chapter describes how to create your own custom transport and details the Transport SDK.

Chapter 18, How Do I . . . ?: In this chapter, we answer some common questions about using OSB in the real world.

Downloading the Code

The code presented in this book is available for download in ZIP file format. You can download it from the Downloads section of this book's page on the Apress web site (http://www.apress.com).

Contacting the Authors

Readers can contact the authors as follows:

- For questions regarding security, please direct your e-mail to David Rieber at drieber@gmail.com.

- For questions on performance tuning, please contact Samrat Ray at samrat.ray@oracle.com.

- For questions on using the Transport SDK, please contact David Schorow at david.schorow@oracle.com.

- For all other questions, please contact Jeff Davies at jeff.x.davies@oracle.com. You can also visit Jeff's web site at http://jeffdavies.org.

## CHAPTER 1

Why Use a Service Bus?

Enterprise service buses (ESBs) are all the rage in modern software development. You can't pick up a trade magazine these days without some article on ESBs and how they make your life wonderful. If you're a software development veteran, you'll recognize the hype immediately. ESBs aren't going to be the magic answer for our industry any more than were XML, web services, application servers, or even ASCII. Each of the aforementioned technologies started life with a lot of fanfare and unrealistic expectations (the result of the inevitable ignorance we all have with any emerging technology), and each technology ended up becoming a reliable tool to solve a specific set of problems.

The same is true for the ESB. Putting the hype aside, let's focus on a bit of software history so we can better understand the problems that the ESB is designed to address.

The Problems We Face Today

Software development is a tough business. We expect modern software systems to have exponentially more functionality than we expected from them only a few years ago. We often develop these systems with ever-dwindling budgets and sharply reduced timeframes, all in an effort to improve efficiency and productivity. However, we cannot lament these issues. These very issues drive us to deliver software that's better, faster, and cheaper.

As we've raced to develop each generation of software system, we've added significantly to the complexity of our IT systems. Thirty years ago, an IT shop might have maintained a single significant software system. Today, most IT shops are responsible for dozens, and sometimes hundreds, of software systems. The interactions between these systems are increasingly complex. By placing a premium on delivering on time, we often sacrifice architecture and design, promising ourselves that we'll refactor the system some time in the future. We've developed technologies that can generate large quantities of code from software models or template code. Some of the side effects of this race into the future are a prevalence of point-to-point integrations between software applications, tight coupling at those integration points, a lot of code, and little configuration.

Point-to-Point Integrations

Software development today is tactical and project-oriented. Developers and architects frequently think in terms of individual software applications, and their designs and implementations directly reflect this thinking. As a result, individual applications are directly integrated with one another in a *point-to-point* manner.

A point-to-point integration is where one application depends on another specific application. For example, in Figure 1-1, the CustomerContactManager (CCM) application uses the BillingSystem interface. You can say that the CCM application "knows" about the BillingSystem application. You also hear this kind of relationship referred to as a *dependency*, because one application depends on another application to function correctly.

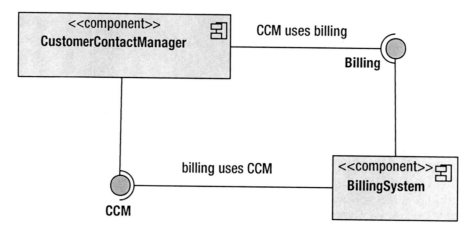

Figure 1-1. *Early point-to-point integrations*

Figure 1-1 illustrates a trivial IT environment, with only two applications and two point-to-point integrations. Just to be clear, the first integration allows the CCM system to call the BillingSystem application. The second integration point allows the BillingSystem application to call the CCM system. When your information technology (IT) department is this small, point-to-point integration is fairly easy to manage.

Figure 1-2 expands on the problem a bit. The IT shop is now home to 8 software systems and a total of 11 integration points. This illustrates a common pattern in integration: the number of integration points grows faster than the number of systems you're integrating!

Even Figure 1-2 is, by modern standards, a trivial IT system. A midsized service provider where Jeff once worked had 67 business systems and another 51 network systems—118 software systems integrated in a point-to-point manner is unmanageable. We know of telephone companies that have 12 or more billing systems. Having duplicates of certain software systems (such as billing) or having a large number of software systems in general is quite common; large companies can acquire smaller companies (and therefore acquire the software systems of the smaller companies) faster than most IT shops can integrate the newly acquired systems.

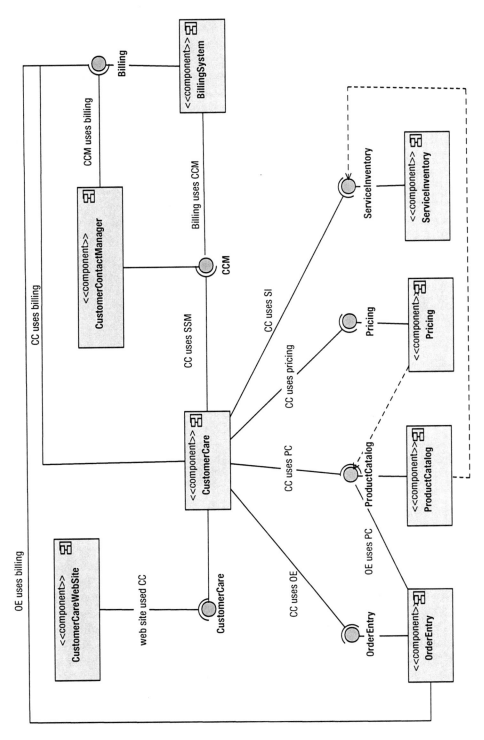

Figure 1-2. *Increasing point-to-point integration*

Tight Coupling

Tight coupling is often a by-product of point-to-point integrations, but it's certainly possible to develop tightly coupled applications no matter what your integration environment looks like. Loose coupling is desirable for good software engineering, but tight coupling can be necessary for maximum performance. Coupling is increased when the data exchanged between components becomes larger or more complex. In reality, coupling between systems can rarely be categorized as "tight" or "loose." There's a continuum between the two extremes.

Most systems use one another's Application Programming Interfaces (APIs) directly to integrate. For Enterprise JavaBeans (EJB) applications, you commonly create a client JAR file for each EJB application. The client JAR file contains the client stubs necessary for the client applications to call the EJB application. If you make a change to any of the APIs of the EJB application, you need to recompile and deploy the EJB application, recompile the client JAR, and then recompile and redeploy each of the client applications. Figure 1-3 illustrates this set of interdependencies among the software components and the file artifacts that realize them.

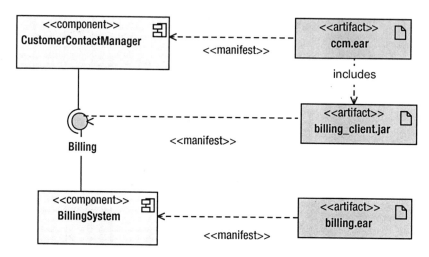

Figure 1-3. *EJB coupling model*

Tight coupling results in cascading changes. If you change the interface on which other components depend, you must then recompile the client applications, often modifying the client code significantly.

It's a common (and false) belief that you can use interfaces to reduce the coupling between systems. Interfaces are intended to abstract out the behavior of the classes that implement the interfaces. They do provide some loosening of the coupling between the client and the implementation, but their effect is almost negligible in today's systems. This is not to say that interfaces aren't useful; they most certainly are. But it's important to understand the reasons why they're useful. You still end up tightly coupled to a specific interface. Here is an example:

```
package com.alsb.foo;
public interface SampleIF {
    public int getResult(String arg1);
}
```

A client that depends on this interface is tightly coupled. If you change the getResult() method to take another argument, all clients of the interface must be recompiled. It's precisely this level of intolerance to change that tightly couples the code. The problem isn't so much in the design of the interface, but with the technology that implements the interface.

Enterprise Application Integration

Commonly referred to as EAI, enterprise application integration reached its peak in the 1990s. EAI now suffers the fate of many older technological approaches: being relegated to the category of "yesterday's" architecture. This reflects a bad habit we technologists have—any idea that seems smart today will be considered foolish or stupid tomorrow.

Contrary to popular belief, there is nothing wrong with EAI, and it remains a viable tool in our problem-solving tool chest. The only real problem with EAI is that it is misnamed; it is not really fit for enterprise-level architecture. EAI is fine for departmental-level integration or for simply deriving greater business value by integrating several software applications together so that they behave as a single meta-application.

The downside to EAI is twofold. First, EAI systems tend to employ a point-to-point approach to integrating applications. There is little or no abstraction of the component systems. This makes EAI systems just as brittle as any other point-to-point integration. The second flaw in the approach (from an enterprise perspective) is that all of the integration logic and any additional business logic are defined and maintained in the EAI tool, which lies at the center of the integration. EAIs are sometimes referred to as "spoke-and-hub" architecture because the EAI tool lies in the center of the integrated systems, like the hub of a great wheel, as illustrated in Figure 1-4.

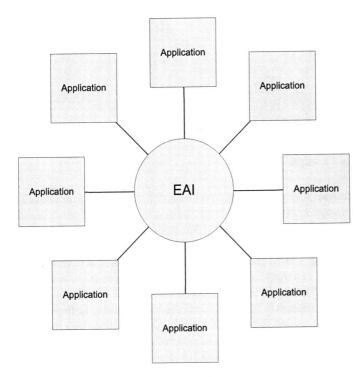

Figure 1-4. *EAI's "spoke-and-hub" architecture*

We are often asked how EAI differs from service-oriented architecture (SOA). The answer is simple. With EAI, all integration is done in the center—the hub. With SOA, the integration logic occurs at the edges of the architecture, not the heart. The integrations are pushed outward, toward the applications themselves, leaving the bus to "speak" a standardized language. Figure 1-5 illustrates the ESB/SOA architecture.

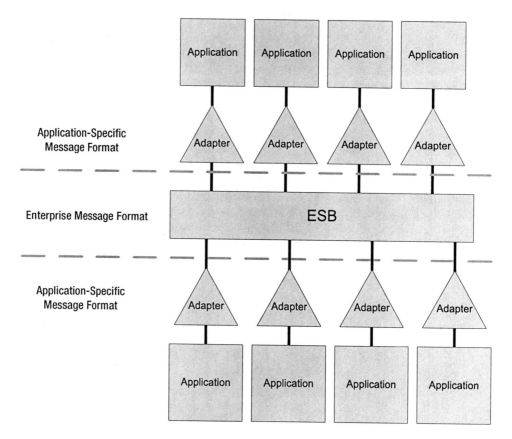

Figure 1-5. *ESB/SOA integrates at the edges.*

Every application "speaks its own language." By that, we mean that every application has its own way of representing information and working with that information. This language takes the form of an API. SOA recognizes that every enterprise also speaks its own language, which is why most applications are customized to meet the specific needs of the company. SOA uses an ESB to route and exchange messages at a high level of abstraction. Application-specific adapters are used to convert message formats from application-specific formats to enterprise-specific formats. SOA integrates at the edges of the applications, not in the heart of the enterprise.

This is not only an architectural approach, but also an architectural pattern. Enterprises have their own language, but so do the various departments within the enterprise. Each department has its own needs and way of doing business. Increasingly, we are seeing a hierarchical use of service buses to allow different departments, subsidiaries, or other business units to provide an abstraction layer between their applications and the interfaces they support. Figure 1-6 illustrates hierarchical ESB usage.

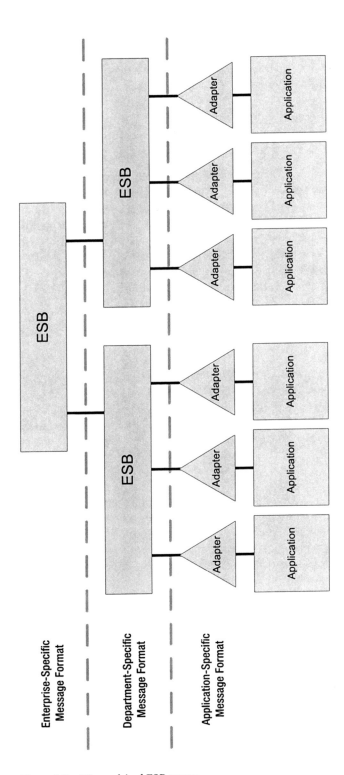

Figure 1-6. *Hierarchical ESB usage*

In Chapters 12 and 13, we will go into detail on the architectural principles used to achieve the specific goals of agility, resilience, and manageability, but the crux of the matter is hinted at in Figures 1-5 and 1-6. You must define formal layers of abstraction in order to have loose coupling and agility. Point-to-point integration approaches can never achieve these goals, no matter what technologies they may employ.

Early ESBs

Early ESBs were primarily concerned with making web services available to service consumers. Their implementation was clunky (as new technologies usually are) and didn't embrace many open standards, simply because those standards didn't exist at the time. Furthermore, the developers of early ESBs could only try to predict how web services would affect enterprise computing and IT organizations.

The early ESBs were "ESBs" in name only. As the industry has matured, so has our understanding of the role of an ESB in modern architecture. Today's ESBs must go far beyond simply "service-enabling" functionality. An ESB must also provide robust solutions for today's IT challenges.

Modern Solutions

The IT industry is constantly evolving. Our understanding of the issues that surround the management of large IT systems matures on a daily basis. Modern ESBs are simply the latest tools to help us manage our IT problems. They benefit from real-world examples of how SOA is changing the face of today's advanced corporations. Although early ESBs could only address a handful of the following issues, modern ESBs need to address them all.

Loose Coupling

You might have heard that web services provide you with loose coupling between systems. This is only partially true. Web services, by the very nature of Web Services Description Language (WSDL) and XML Schema Definition (XSD) document, can provide some loose coupling because they formalize a contract between the service consumer and the service provider. This is a "design-by-contract" model, and it does provide tangible benefits. If you're careful, you can create a schema that's platform-neutral and highly reusable.

However, if you take a look at any WSDL, you'll see that the service endpoints are written into the WSDL, as you can see in Listing 1-1.

Listing 1-1. *HelloWorld Service Definition*

```
<service name="HelloWorldService">
   <port binding="s1:HelloWorldServiceSoapBinding"
      name="HelloWorldPortSoapPort">
      <s2:address location="http://www.bea.com:7001/esb/Hello_World" />
   </port>
</service>
```

By specifying a specific machine and port (or a set of machines and ports), you're tightly coupling this service to its physical expression on a specific computer. You can use a Domain Name Server (DNS) to substitute portions of the URL, and therefore direct clients into multiple machines in a server farm. However, DNS servers are woefully inadequate for this, due to their inability to understand and manage the status of the services running on these servers.

So, loose coupling isn't achieved by WSDL or web services alone. A more robust solution is to provide some mediation layer between service clients and service producers. Such a mediation layer should also be capable of bridging transport, message formats, and security technologies. For example, a service might be invoked through a traditional HTTP transport mechanism, but it can then invoke lower-level services through Java Message Service (JMS), e-mail, File Transfer Protocol (FTP), and so on. This approach is often effectively used to "wrap" older services and their transports from the newer service clients.

Location Transparency

Location transparency is a strategy to hide the physical locations of service endpoints from the service clients. Ideally, a service client should have to know about a single, logical machine and port name for each service. The client shouldn't know the actual service endpoints. This allows for greater flexibility when managing your services. You can add, move, and remove service endpoints as needed, without needing to recompile your service clients.

Mediation

An ESB is an intermediary layer, residing between the service client and the service providers. This layer provides a great place for adding value to the architecture without changing the applications on either end. An ESB is a service provider to the service clients. When clients use a service on the service bus, the service bus has the ability to perform multiple operations: it can transform the data or the schema of the messages it sends and receives, and it can intelligently route messages to various service endpoints, depending on the content of those messages.

Schema Transformation

The web service published by the service bus might use a different schema from the schema of the business service it represents. This is a vital capability, especially when used in conjunction with a canonical taxonomy or when aggregating or orchestrating other web services. It's quite common that a service client will need to receive its data using a schema that's significantly different from that of the service provider. The ability to transform data from one schema to another is critical for the success of any ESB.

Service Aggregation

The service bus can act as a façade and make a series of web service calls appear as a single service. Service aggregation follows this pattern, making multiple web service calls on behalf of the proxy service and returning a single result. Service orchestration is similar to service aggregation, but includes some conditional logic that defines which of the lower-level web services are called and the order in which they are invoked.

Load Balancing

Due to their position in any architecture, ESBs are well suited to perform load balancing of service requests across multiple service endpoints. When you register a business web service with Oracle Service Bus (OSB), you can specify the list of service endpoints where that business service is running. You can change this list, adding or removing service endpoints without needing to restart the OSB server.

Enforcing Security

You should enforce security in a centralized manner whenever possible. This allows for a greater level of standardization and control of security issues. Furthermore, security is best enforced through a policy-driven framework. Using security policies means that the creation and application of security standards happen outside the creation of the individual web services.

Monitoring

An ESB plays a vital role in an SOA. As such, you must have a robust way to monitor the status of your ESB, in both proactive and reactive manners. The ability to proactively view the performance of the service bus allows you to help performance-tune the service bus for better performance. Tracking the performance over time can help you plan for increasing the capacity of your ESB.

Reactive monitoring allows you to define alerts for specific conditions. For example, if a specific service doesn't complete within a given timeframe, the ESB should be able to send an alert so that a technician can investigate the problem.

Configuration vs. Coding

A modern service bus should be configuration-based, not code-based. For many engineers, the importance of that statement isn't immediately obvious. It took us some time before we appreciated the configuration-oriented capability of OSB. Most software systems in use today are code-based. Java EE 5 applications are a great example of this. In a Java EE 5 application, you write source code, compile it into an EAR or WAR file, copy that EAR or WAR file onto one or more Java EE 5 application servers, and then deploy those applications. Sometimes it's necessary to restart the Java server, depending on the nature of your deployment.

Configuration-based systems work differently. There's nothing to compile or deploy. You simply change the configuration and activate those changes. We would argue that your telephone is configuration-based; you configure the telephone number you want to call, and your call is placed. There's no need to restart your phone. Similarly, network routers and switches are configuration-based. As you make changes to their configuration, those changes take effect. There's no need for a longer software development life cycle to take place.

Configuration and coding are two different strategies. Neither is superior to the other in all situations. There are times when the Java EE 5 approach is the most appropriate, and other times when the configuration-based approach is best.

Enter Oracle Service Bus

BEA released AquaLogic Service Bus in June 2005. With the Oracle acquisition of BEA in mid-2008, the product was rebranded to Oracle Service Bus (OSB). OSB runs on Windows, Linux, and Solaris platforms. OSB is a fully modern ESB and provides functionality for each of the capabilities expected from today's enterprises, as described in the following sections.

Loose Coupling

Aside from the loose coupling benefits from WSDL and XSD, OSB adds the ability to store WSDL, XSD, eXtensible Stylesheet Language Transformation (XSLT), and other information types within the OSB server as "resources." These resources are then made available throughout the OSB cluster of servers, allowing you to reuse these resources as needed.

The benefit of this might not be immediately clear, so we'll give an example. Many companies define and manage enterprise-wide data types using an XML document schema. Because OSB can store an XML document schema as a resource in the service bus, that schema can easily be reused by any number of WSDLs or other XSDs. This enables you to create and enforce enterprise-wide standards for your data types and message formats.

Location Transparency

One of the capabilities of OSB is to register and manage the locations of various web services within the enterprise. This provides a layer of abstraction between the service client and the service provider, and improves the operational aspect of adding or removing service providers without impact to the service clients.

Mediation

One of the roles for which OSB is specifically designed is that of a service mediator. OSB uses the paradigm of "proxy services" and "business services," where the proxy service is the service that OSB publishes to its service clients, and the business services are external to OSB. In between the proxy service and the business service is the layer where service mediation takes place. Schemas can be transformed, as can the data carried by those schemas. Intelligent or content-based routing also takes place in this mediation layer.

Schema Transformation

Schema transformation is a central capability of OSB. OSB provides a number of ways to transform schemas, depending on your specific needs. You can use XSLT to transform XML data from one schema to another. Similarly, you can use XQuery and XPath to perform XML document schema transformations. Additionally, OSB supports the use of Message Format Language (MFL) to format schemas to and from non-XML formats, such as comma-separated value (CSV) files, COBOL copy books, Electronic Data Interchange (EDI) documents, and so on.

Service Aggregation

OSB doesn't match a single proxy service to a single business service. Instead, OSB allows you to define a many-to-many relationship between proxy services and business services. This approach allows for service aggregation, orchestration, and information enrichment.

Load Balancing

Because OSB registers the service endpoints of all business services, it's ideally situated for operating as a load balancer. This is especially true because OSB is configuration-based, not code-based. As a result, you can add or remove service endpoints from a business service and activate those changes without needing to restart your service bus.

Enforcing Security

OSB, as a service mediator, is ideally situated to enforce the security of the web services because it operates on the perimeters of the enterprise. OSB is designed to enforce security through the use of explicit security policies. Using OSB, you can propagate identities, mediate, and transform between different security technologies, such as Basic Authentication, Secure Sockets Layer (SSL), and Security Assertion Markup Language (SAML).

Monitoring

OSB provides a robust set of features around monitoring. The service bus console allows you to look proactively at the state of your entire ESB.

For reactive monitoring, OSB allows you to define alerts for conditions that you define. Alerts can be delivered via e-mail to specified recipients. We'll discuss monitoring more fully in Chapter 10.

Configuration vs. Coding

OSB is a configuration-based service bus. You don't write Java code for OSB, although OSB can recognize and make use of Java code in some circumstances. Instead, you configure OSB through its web-based console.

One handy feature of the OSB console is that your configuration changes don't take effect when you make each change. Instead, your configuration changes are grouped together, similarly to a database transaction, and take effect only when you tell OSB to activate your changes. This is a critical capability, because many times you'll make multiple changes that are interdependent.

Of course, creating these changes by hand can be an error-prone process. To avoid mistakes, OSB allows you to make changes in one environment (a development or a test environment), and then export those changes as a JAR file. You can then import that JAR file into your production environment as a set of configuration changes, and further customize the configuration file for a specific deployment environment upon import. This process allows you to script your changes and activate them as if you had entered those changes directly into the OSB console by hand.

Won't This Lock Me into Oracle Technologies?

OSB is entirely standards-based. You configure OSB through the use of XQuery, XPath, XSLT, and WSDLs. The only aspect of OSB that might be deemed "proprietary" is the implementation of the message flows (see Chapter 4). However, these message flows are simply graphical constructs for common programming logic, and they're easy to reproduce in just about any programming language. The real heavy lifting in OSB is done using the open standards for functionality, and WebLogic Server for reliability and scalability.

Because OSB is standards-based, it's designed to integrate with and operate in a heterogeneous architecture. Using OSB as a service bus doesn't preclude you from using other technologies in any way. OSB is used to integrate with .NET applications, TIBCO, SAP, JBoss, WebSphere, Siebel, and many more technologies. Oracle didn't achieve this level of heterogeneity by accident; it's all part of the company's "blended" strategy, which involves using open standards and open source to achieve the maximum amount of interoperability.

Why Buy an Enterprise Service Bus?

We come across this question frequently. The truth is that an ESB contains no magic in it at all. It's possible to build your own ESB from scratch. In fact, one of the authors has done it twice before joining Oracle. There's nothing that the engineers at Oracle can write that you cannot write yourself, given enough time, money, and training. This principle holds true for all software. You don't need to use Microsoft Word to write your documents; you could create your own word processor. In the same way, HTML standards are publicly available, and you could use your engineering time to develop your own web browser.

Naturally, few of us would ever consider writing our own word processor or web browser. It's a far better use of our time and money either to buy the software or to use an open source version. This is especially true if your company isn't a software company. If you work in an IT shop for a company whose primary line of business isn't software, you'll recognize the fact that building software from scratch is a difficult sell to your executive staff. There simply is no return on investment for such development efforts. Your time and skills are better spent solving problems specific to your company.

There are a number of benefits to purchasing OSB. First is the fact that it comes from a dyed-in-the-wool software company. Oracle has been in business for more than three decades and has a long history of delivering innovative, successful products. Furthermore, Oracle supports those products for many years.

A number of open source ESBs are available today. Most are in the early stages of development and functionality. Although we love open source and advocate its use in many areas, we would be hesitant to use an open source ESB. An ESB will become the central nervous system of your enterprise. You should exercise caution and diligence when selecting an ESB. You want one with a proven record of success, from an organization that works hard to keep itself ahead of current market demands.

OSB is built on Oracle's WebLogic Server technology. This gives you enterprise-quality reliability and scalability. On top of this, OSB is built on open standards for maximum interoperability in a heterogeneous environment. It's an ESB that will carry your company into the future.

Summary

In this chapter, we reviewed the features and functions that a modern ESB should have, and we've described each feature's importance to the organization. OSB implements all these features, and it possesses many more advanced features that we'll cover in this book. But we've talked enough about OSB. It's time to start to demonstrate, in working code, exactly how to use these features to their fullest.

CHAPTER 2

■ ■ ■

Installing and Configuring the Software

This chapter will walk you through the procedures for installing OSB and configuring your development environment. By the end of this chapter, you'll be able to compile and run the sample code that comes with this book.

To begin with, you need a computer that runs Java. Specifically, it needs to run Java Development Kit (JDK) version 1.5 or later. All the examples are written using JDK 1.5 (though they will work with JDK 1.6), and OSB requires that you have JDK 1.5 installed. Fortunately, OSB ships with two different JDKs that meet this requirement. One is the JRockit JDK, which is intended for use on production systems that run on Intel (or compatible) CPUs. The second is the Sun JDK, which is recommended for use with development versions of OSB or production versions that are not running on Intel-compatible CPUs.

Naturally, you need to install the OSB software. You can download OSB from http://dev2dev.bea.com/alservicebus/. You will also be able to access OSB directly from Oracle's web site at http://www.oracle.com. It's a good idea to download the most recent documentation as well, so you can stay informed about recent changes.

OSB ships with WorkSpace Studio, an integrated development environment (IDE) based on Eclipse 3.2 (http://www.eclipse.org), and comes with a suite of Eclipse plug-ins that are preconfigured to make your development with OSB much faster.

You'll sometimes use Ant (http://ant.apache.org) to build your software. You'll need Ant version 1.6 or later. Like most of the software used by OSB, Ant is included with the OSB installer and is preconfigured in the WorkSpace Studio environment.

Finally, you'll need two software packages for some of your more advanced work with the service bus. The first is an FTP server that you'll use to demonstrate integrating the service bus with legacy systems via FTP. You can use any FTP server that you like. We selected the FileZilla FTP server (http://filezilla.sourceforge.net/). Also, you'll need access to an e-mail server when testing the e-mail integration. Because your company might not appreciate you sending test e-mail messages over its e-mail server, we recommend installing your own Simple Mail Transfer Protocol (SMTP) server. We selected Java Mail Server, which is available at http://www.ericdaugherty.com/java/mailserver. Because both FTP and SMTP are based on well-defined standards, feel free to substitute your own FTP and e-mail servers. However, we do provide a detailed configuration walk-through of both these programs, so if you aren't accustomed to setting up these types of servers, you're better off using the same ones we've used.

You'll find all the software you need for this book in the Source Code/Download area of the Apress web site at http://www.apress.com.

Installing the Software

OSB comes with most of the software you'll need to compile and deploy the applications you create in this book: Ant, Workspace Studio, WebLogic 10, and JDK 1.5.

Installing OSB is a breeze. For the most part, you can safely accept the default values provided by the installation program. However, we do recommend creating a new home directory if you have a previous version of WebLogic installed. Because we work with multiple Oracle products, we've created a C:\Oracle directory. We installed OSB into C:\Oracle\osb30 to keep the installations separate. In the future, as OSB becomes fully integrated with the rest of the Oracle product suite, the installation process will become rationalized with the installation process for other Oracle products.

Once you have the software installed, you need to do a little configuration to complete the setup. If you are just using OSB and don't care about integrating it with an existing Eclipse or AquaLogic installation, you can skip to the "Configuring WorkSpace Studio" section. On the other hand, if you do want to integrate OSB with an existing installation, continue reading to discover how to do that.

Using a Single WorkSpace Studio IDE

OSB uses WorkSpace Studio as its IDE. This includes OSB itself, AquaLogic Data Services Platform (ALDSP), and Oracle Enterprise Repository. However, if you accept the default values while installing each of these products, you will get three different IDE environments installed. It's preferable to create a single IDE for your work with OSB. You do this by specifying a custom installation when you are installing OSB 3.*x*. You can then choose to use Eclipse as the host for WorkSpace Studio, update an existing ALDSP installation, or install other AquaLogic products into your existing version of WorkSpace Studio.

Using Eclipse 3.2 to Host WorkSpace Studio

If you don't have Eclipse installed on your system and you want to use a single instance of Eclipse to support WorkSpace Studio, the easiest thing to do is to download the "all-in-one" version of Calisto (that's the name for the 3.2 release of Eclipse), which includes the Web Service Tools package. You can download that from http://download2.bea.com/pub/callisto/wtp154/wtp-all-in-one-sdk-R-1.5.4-win32.zip.

If you already have Eclipse 3.2 installed on your computer, you need to be sure that you have the Web Standard Tools (WST) plug-in installed also. The WST plug-in, in turn, requires several other libraries. You will also need to install the Graphical Editing Framework (GEF), the Eclipse Modeling Framework (EMF), the XML Infoset Model, and the Java EMF Model (JEM) first. You can install these from the Eclipse IDE by selecting Help ➤ Software Updates ➤ Find and Install from the Eclipse menu bar. Select the "Search for new features to install" option. Then choose the Calisto Discovery Site and select a mirror close to you. Once this is done, you will be presented with an Updates dialog box, as shown in Figure 2-1. Select the appropriate libraries and choose to install them.

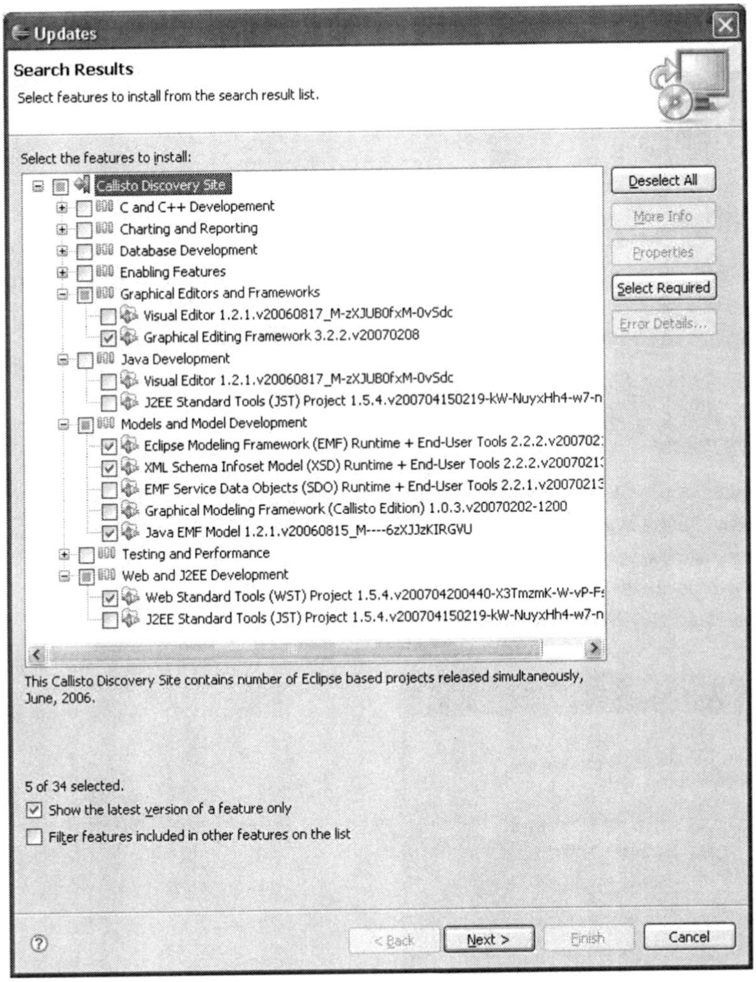

Figure 2-1. *Selecting the correct plug-ins to support WorkSpace Studio*

After you have these basic libraries installed into Eclipse, you can install the OSB software. When the installation wizard starts, select the custom installation option. The installation wizard will give you the opportunity to use an existing Eclipse installation. Choose that option, and then specify the directory where you've installed Eclipse (commonly in C:\Eclipse).

Updating an Existing ALDSP 3.0 Installation

If you already have ALDSP 3.0 installed, you can install the OSB 3.0 WorkSpace Studio plug-ins into the existing ALDSP WorkSpace Studio instance. Select a custom installation of OSB, and then select the option to use an existing Eclipse installation. In the ALDSP directory, you can find the Eclipse directory at ORACLE%\tools\eclipse_pkgs\1.1\eclipse_3.2.2\eclipse.

Updating an Existing OSB WorkSpace Studio Installation

The process for installing other AquaLogic products into an existing instance of OSB WorkSpace Studio is generally the same as for updating an existing ALDSP installation. The location of the Eclipse directory in OSB is %ORACLE%\tools\eclipse_pkgs\1.1\eclipse_3.2.2\eclipse.

Configuring WorkSpace Studio

OSB ships with a customized version of Eclipse known as WorkSpace Studio. This customization is achieved by using Eclipse's plug-in capability to extend Eclipse. WorkSpace Studio comes entirely preconfigured and ready to run. However, you will need to do a bit of setup for the examples in this book.

Selecting a Workspace

When you start WorkSpace Studio for the first time, it will ask you to select a *workspace*, as shown in Figure 2-2. A workspace is a directory where your WorkSpace Studio projects will be created. WorkSpace Studio allows you to create as many workspaces as you like. For now, we recommend that you name your new workspace osb30_book, and use that workspace as the home for all the projects you'll create in this book.

Figure 2-2. *Creating a workspace in WorkSpace Studio*

Once you're happy with the name of your workspace, click the OK button, and the Work-Space Studio IDE loads.

If you're familiar with the Eclipse IDE, learning WorkSpace Studio will be a breeze for you. If this IDE is new to you, you can quickly get up to speed. We'll review the major capabilities of WorkSpace Studio in the following section. Also, the first project in Chapter 3 walks you through the IDE in detail, making it much easier to learn the WorkSpace Studio IDE as you go.

A Quick Tour of WorkSpace Studio

WorkSpace Studio is a modern IDE for developing modern applications. Much of the functionality of WorkSpace Studio is directly inherited from Eclipse. Developers using WorkSpace Studio enjoy the features they've come to expect from a modern IDE: code completion, code refactoring, project awareness, built-in Ant and JUnit, and much more. WorkSpace Studio is even aware of a wide variety of application servers, and you can easily configure it to start and stop application servers from within the IDE. A robust debugger is included.

When you run WorkSpace Studio for the first time, the IDE will resemble Figure 2-3. The left side of the IDE is dedicated to project information and the Design Palette. The right side shows an outline of the current file. The bottom portion of the IDE provides access to information about code problems, tasks, properties, servers, Database Explorer, and snippets. The center of the IDE is dedicated to editing source code and other file types.

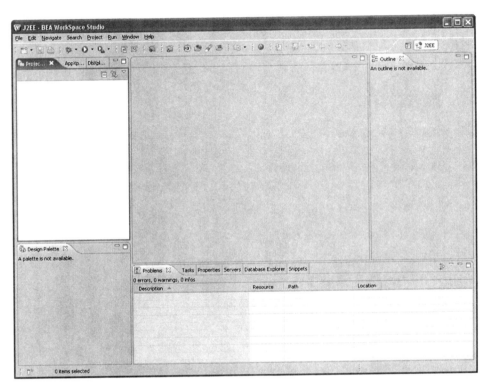

Figure 2-3. *WorkSpace Studio's first run*

You might have noticed that WorkSpace Studio makes liberal use of tabs. Every window in the IDE has a tab, allowing you to switch quickly between different views of information. This helps to make the most of your screen real estate. The real star of the show is the icon with each window. Those of you moving to WorkSpace Studio from WebLogic Workshop 8 will also love this little icon. Clicking this icon causes the associated window to expand to fill the entire IDE application window. The claustrophobic days of Workshop 8 are now a distant memory!

Creating Libraries

You also want to configure WorkSpace Studio to be aware of the specific libraries you'll need to use, especially for some of your client code that doesn't execute within a WebLogic container. To this end, you need to create several libraries in WorkSpace Studio. A *library* is just a named collection of JAR files that you can add to your projects.

Begin by selecting Windows ➤ Preferences from the main menu bar of WorkSpace Studio. When the Preferences window appears, select the Java ➤ Build Path ➤ User Libraries path in the tree. Click the Add button and specify the name of the library. Your first library will be designed for web service test clients, so name the library **WebLogic Web Service Client**, as shown in Figure 2-4.

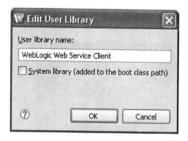

Figure 2-4. *Naming the new library*

Next, click the Add JARs button. You need to navigate into your C:\Oracle\osb30\wlserver_ 10.0\server\lib directory to find the JAR files you need. Select the following JAR files:

- %WEBLOGIC_HOME%\server\lib\weblogic.jar

- %WEBLOGIC_HOME%\server\lib\webserviceclient.jar

Creating the Service Bus Domain

For the purposes of this book, you'll create a new WebLogic 10 domain for OSB. Follow these steps to create the domain:

1. On a Windows system, select Start ➤ BEA Products ➤ Tools ➤ Configuration Wizard.

2. Ensure the "Create a new WebLogic domain" radio button is selected and click the Next button.

3. Ensure the "Generate a domain configured automatically to support the following BEA Products" radio button is selected. Also ensure the OSB and the Workshop for WebLogic Platform check boxes are checked. Click the Next button.

4. Set the password to something simple, such as weblogic. Be sure Caps Lock isn't set on your keyboard. Click the Next button.

5. Select Development Mode and the BEA-supplied JDK radio buttons. Select the Sun SDK from the associated list box. The JDK must be version 1.5.0 or later. Click the Next button.

6. In the Customize Environment and Service Settings page, ensure the No radio button is selected and click the Next button.

7. Set the domain name to osb30_book and click the Create button.

8. In the Creating Domain page, check the Start Admin Server check box, and then click the Done button.

You have now created and started the osb30_book domain that you'll use for the rest of this book.

Configuring Ant

The Ant plug-in in WorkSpace Studio needs a slight configuration to enable it to recognize the WebLogic-specific Ant tasks you'll use in this book. Furthermore, some WebLogic Ant tasks simply won't work unless you tell Ant about the weblogic.jar file. Follow these steps:

1. From the main menu in WorkSpace Studio, select Window ➤ Preferences.

2. In the Preferences window, navigate to the Ant ➤ Runtime category, and then click the Classpath tab.

3. You need to add the weblogic.jar file to the Ant classpath. Click Ant Home Entries, as shown in Figure 2-5, and then click the Add External JARs button.

Figure 2-5. *Configuring the Ant plug-in in WorkSpace Studio*

4. Navigate to your C:\Oracle\osb30\wlserver_10.0\server\lib directory and select the weblogic.jar file.

5. Click OK to save your changes.

This enables Ant to recognize the WebLogic-specific Ant tasks listed in Table 2-1.

Table 2-1. *WebLogic-Specific Ant Tasks*

Task	Description
ClientGenTask	Web service client generator Ant task
JwscTask	Java web service compiler Ant task
WLDeploy	WebLogic deployment Ant task
WsdlcTask	WSDL compiler Ant task

You'll use these tasks in each of your project Ant files.

Setting Up an OSB Server in WorkSpace Studio

Next you want to configure WorkSpace Studio so you can manage your OSB server from the IDE. Follow these steps:

1. In WorkSpace Studio, select File ➤ New ➤ Server from the main menu bar.

2. The New Server dialog box appears, and the Server's host name field should be set to localhost, as shown in Figure 2-6. Click the Next button.

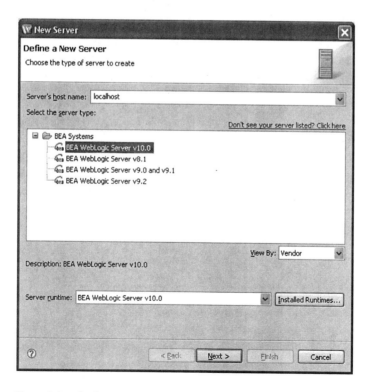

Figure 2-6. *The first step in creating a new server is to specify the hostname and runtime.*

3. Specify the server name, and then select the domain that you created earlier in this chapter. We also recommend checking the "Always start WebLogic server in debug mode" check box, since this is for a development environment, not a production server. Once your dialog box looks like the one shown in Figure 2-7, click the Next button.

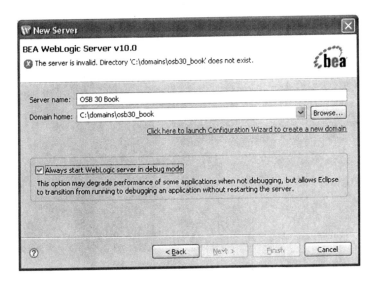

Figure 2-7. *Specifying the server details*

4. The last step of configuring a server is to define the projects that are deployed on the server. Because you don't have any projects defined yet, just click the Finish button. At this point, your new server should appear in the Servers window of the WorkSpace Studio IDE, as shown in Figure 2-8.

Figure 2-8. *The Servers window in the WorkSpace Studio IDE*

If you haven't already started the osb30_book server, you can do so now by right-clicking the server name in the Servers window and selecting Start from the pop-up menu, or by selecting the server and clicking the start button ▶ . If you've previously started the server, WorkSpace Studio automatically detects that the server is running.

Importing the Sample Code

This book comes with a significant amount of sample code. Your first step is to copy the projects you downloaded from the Source Code/Download area at http://www.apress.com into the workspace that you created when you first started WorkSpace Studio (see Figure 2-1). Next, you need to import those projects into the IDE, as follows:

1. Right-click in the Project Explorer window and select Import from the pop-up menu. This brings up the Import dialog box.

2. Select Existing Projects into Workspace from the dialog box, as shown in Figure 2-9, and then click the Next button.

Figure 2-9. *Importing the existing projects into WorkSpace Studio*

3. Select the root directory and browse to the workspace directory you created earlier in this chapter, as shown in Figure 2-10. Your project list might not match the one shown in Figure 2-10 exactly, but that's okay. Click the Finish button to import all these projects into WorkSpace Studio.

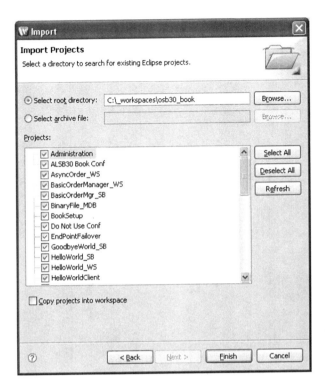

Figure 2-10. *The final step in importing the sample projects into WorkSpace Studio*

Summary

When the steps covered in this chapter complete, your WorkSpace Studio IDE will be fully configured to use with the following chapters of this book. The ease with which you can interact with the OSB server will improve your coding experience and productivity. You're now ready for the fun part. In the next chapter, you'll get right down to business by creating a Java web service, then using OSB to exercise the web service.

CHAPTER 3

■ ■ ■

Creating a Hello World Service

In the tradition of computer-learning books of the past several decades, you'll get started by writing a quick Hello World service. In this chapter, you'll gain a fundamental understanding of the WorkSpace Studio interface for OSB. You'll learn how to create and deploy projects from WorkSpace Studio. You'll also learn how to create automated test clients and use the OSB test console for testing to ensure that your services are working as desired.

However, before we get to the exercise, we'll cover business services and proxy services, because they are important concepts in OSB.

Service Mediation

The term *service mediation* means the ability to inject logic between the service consumer and the service provider. Service mediation is a key capability of any ESB. From the point of view of OSB, services are divided into two categories: business services and proxy services. You can think of proxy services as the services published by OSB. Instead of your service clients calling the services directly, they call OSB proxy services instead. This might seem odd at first glance, but we promise it will make sense by the time you finish reading this section.

Business services are defined in OSB to represent services that are *external* to OSB. For example, the HelloWorld_WS service you will create in this chapter is external as far as OSB is concerned. For OSB to be able to call the HelloWorld_WS service, you need to create a business service in OSB. Business services are really just metadata about an external system or service.

So let's answer the question that we're sure you're asking yourself: "Why shouldn't my service clients just call the services they need?" There are five reasons.

Location transparency: One of the features of OSB is the ability to proxy multiple endpoints for the same service. If you have the same service running on five different machines, OSB can load-balance the calls among those servers. Location transparency allows you to add, remove, and change service endpoints without needing to recompile your clients or perform some DNS trickery.

Service aggregation: Not every proxy service in OSB must represent a single business service. A proxy service can invoke any number of business services, and it can apply additional logic to select the proper subset of business services, depending on the needs of the caller. This also abstracts out the routing logic from the client and places it inside the service bus, where it belongs.

Abstraction layer: Another reason to use OSB is to provide a layer of abstraction between your service clients and your service providers. For example, let's say your company has a customer management system, and you've created a number of service providers that provide services based on a set of XML document schemas that you've defined. At some point, your company decides to replace your old customer management system with a newer system. This new system has web services built in. The problem is that the new system uses its own set of XML document schemas that are different from yours. What's a developer to do? Rewrite all your existing service clients? Madness! With OSB, you can simply create transformations that modify the new XML documents into the form expected by your current clients.

Centralized logging or metrics collection: OSB provides a centralized area for logging or collecting service invocation metrics. It allows you to create your own Service-Level Agreements (SLAs) that help you monitor service performance, display statistics, and provide a reporting platform. OSB does all this without requiring you to modify or otherwise instrument the services themselves.

Centralized security policies: OSB provides a centralized platform for security policies. Even if the external web service isn't robust enough to provide security, the fact that OSB "proxies" those services gives you the ability to apply industry-standard, robust security policies.

Creating and Deploying a Web Service

In the remainder of this chapter, you'll create and deploy the sample Hello World web service, by following these steps:

1. Use WorkSpace Studio to create and deploy a web service that implements the business logic.

■**Note** OSB supports interoperability between heterogeneous systems. It can connect to .NET, Apache Axis, WebSphere, and other web service platforms. However, for ease of development, you'll develop your web services using WebLogic Server.

---

2. Create an OSB configuration project in WorkSpace Studio.

3. Create a Hello World OSB project in WorkSpace Studio.

4. Create a business service definition in WorkSpace Studio that represents the web service you created in step 1.

5. Create a proxy service in WorkSpace Studio based on the business service.

6. Deploy the project onto the server.

7. Test the proxy service to confirm that everything runs properly, end to end.

Your first step is to create a web service that implements the business logic. Your requirements for this service are simple. The service will contain one operation named getGreeting. This operation takes a String argument that is a name of a person. The service returns a String greeting.

```
getGreeting(String name) : String
```

You'll implement this web service using WorkSpace Studio to create your project. You need to have completed the installation process outlined in Chapter 2 before you begin. You'll find the complete source code for this exercise in the Source Code/Download area at http://www.apress.com.

Creating the Web Service Project

To create the web service project, follow these steps:

1. Start the WorkSpace Studio IDE by selecting Start ➤ BEA Products ➤ WorkSpace Studio 1.1. If it prompts you to select a workspace, select the workspace that you created in Chapter 2.

2. Right-click in the Project Explorer window (on the left side of the IDE) and select New ➤ Project from the pop-up menu. This will bring up the New Project dialog box.

3. Select the Web Service Project in the Web Services folder, as shown in Figure 3-1, and then click the Next button.

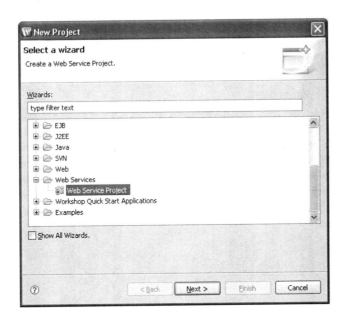

Figure 3-1. *WorkSpace Studio's New Project wizard*

4. Name the project HelloWorld_WS. The Target Runtime should default to BEA WebLogic 10.0 (or later). Click the Next button.

5. On the Project Facets page of the New Project wizard, you can select the "facets" of your project, as shown in Figure 3-2. For your purposes, the defaults are fine. Click the Next button.

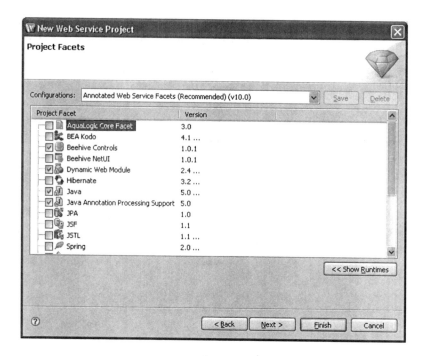

Figure 3-2. *Hello World project facets*

6. The next window allows you to configure the web module. Change the Context Root field from HelloWorld_WS to business/hello, as shown in Figure 3-3. A context root is part of the overall URI to the web service. The basic pattern for service URIs is http:// <server:port>/<context root>/<service name>. Context roots must be unique across projects within a server. The business prefix of the root allows you to group all your "business" services together, making it easier to navigate the web services later on. Click Next to continue.

■Tip If you want to change the context root of an existing web service project, just right-click the project name and select Properties from the pop-up menu. Then select Web Project Settings in the Properties window. You will see a text-entry box that shows the context root, which you can edit.

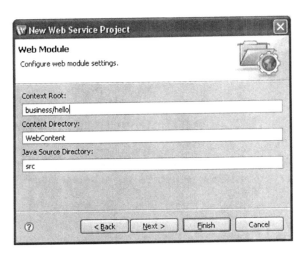

Figure 3-3. *Specifying the Hello World context root*

7. The next several pages in the wizard allow you to either use the WebLogic J2EE libraries installed on the server or to copy those libraries into the web-inf directory of your project. Using the WebLogic J2EE libraries simply tells that application to use the libraries already installed on the server, and this is generally the best approach. If you copy the libraries into the web-inf directory, your application is then guaranteed to use the libraries it was compiled with, which makes the application a little more tolerant to change if you deploy it onto a WebLogic Server that uses a slightly different version of those libraries. For our purposes, you can safely accept the default values and click the Finish button to complete the wizard.

■Caution Copying the libraries into the application's web-inf directory will greatly increase the size of the resulting EAR and WAR files. For example, if you do not copy the libraries into the project and export the web service project as a WAR file, the resulting file will be 9KB in size. If you do copy all of the libraries into the project, the resulting WAR file will be 1.5MB.

8. WorkSpace Studio will then create your project. If it prompts you to change to the J2EE Perspective, click the Yes button. The HelloWorld_WS project appears in the Project Explorer window, as shown in Figure 3-4.

Figure 3-4. *The HelloWorld_WS project in Project Explorer*

Creating the Web Service

Writing a web service for WebLogic Server 10 is a snap. You'll write your web service as a POJO (that is, a Plain Old Java Object), because that's the simplest way to create a web service.

Creating the Java Package

First, you need to create a Java package for your web service, as follows:

1. Open the Java Resources folder in the Project Explorer window. Right-click the src folder and select New ➤ Package from the pop-up menu.

2. Name the package com.alsb.hello.

3. Right-click the newly created package and select New ➤ WebLogic Web Service from the pop-up menu.

4. Enter HelloWorld for the file name and click the Finish button.

WorkSpace Studio creates a HelloWorld.java file for you and displays it in the design view. The design view provides a simple, graphical view of the web service class.

Click the source view link to view the source code. The generated code contains two annotations: @WebService and @WebMethod. This is just a skeleton web service; you need to put some meat on the bones before it becomes useful.

First, change the default operation name from hello to getGreeting. You also need to change the signature of the operation so that it takes a String argument and returns a String value.

Working with Source Code Properties

WorkSpace Studio allows you to work either directly with the source code or via the Properties window. One of the great things about the Properties window is that it gives you a menu of options, making it simple to see what's available. Each of these properties translates directly into an annotation in the source file, so there's no hidden code. The source files are still the source of "truth," reflecting all the property and annotation settings.

With the `HelloWorld.java` file selected in WorkSpace Studio, look at the Properties window. As shown in Figure 3-5, at the top of this window is a group of properties under the title of WebService (if this group isn't open, click the plus sign next to the group name to show the child properties). You can see that the `name` attribute is set to [HelloWorld]. The square brackets are an idiom specific to WorkSpace Studio, and they indicate that the default value that will be used.

Note If the Properties window is not visible in WorkSpace Studio, open it by selecting Window ➤ Show View ➤ Properties.

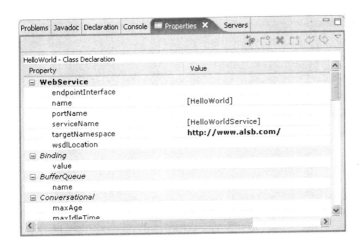

Figure 3-5. *Viewing WebService properties*

Maybe it's just our nature, but we've never trusted default values, so we prefer to set them explicitly. Remove the square brackets around the `name` property setting, so that it is now set to `HelloWorld`. Notice how the `@WebService` annotation in your source code has been modified to include the `name` attribute. Now set the `serviceName` attribute to `HelloWorldService` and the `targetNamespace` attribute to `http://www.alsb.com/`.

Tip It's a best practice to standardize on the format of the namespaces used in your enterprise. Either end all namespaces with a slash or never end them with a slash. No matter which way you choose, this will save you tons of time in debugging later on. In this book, we have chosen to end all namespaces with a trailing slash character.

Next, scroll down to the `WLHttpTransport` property. This property is worthy of some description. Setting this property defines the transport protocol used by your web service. Every web service needs to have a protocol specified to function. You'll set the `portName` property to HelloWorldSoapPort to indicate that you're using a SOAP binding for the web service port.

Next, set the serviceURI property to HelloWorldService. The service URI is appended to the context path for the web service, which brings up an interesting point. When you created this web service project, the wizard prompted you for a context root, which you set to business/hello. If you set a value in the contextPath property of the WLHttpTransport property group, it will override the value that you set when you first created the project. However, it's best to use this property to record the context path instead of relying on the value that you specified when you created the service. Why? Because using this property records in the source code, for all to see, what the context path is. Otherwise, you are relying on a person's memory for this information. Set the contextPath property to business/hello.

Next, modify the WSDL property, at the bottom of the Properties window. Set its exposed property to true. You want to be able to see the WSDL in a web browser. You also need to set the SOAPBinding property. Set parameterStyle to WRAPPED, style to DOCUMENT, and use to LITERAL.

■**Note** Where you place your cursor in the source code will affect the properties that you see in the Properties window of WorkSpace Studio. If you place the cursor on an annotation, you will see only the properties for that annotation. If you place the cursor outside an annotation, all possible properties are shown.

Writing the Web Service Code

Next, you need to write some code for this web service. Your HelloWorld_WS service needs to have one operation: getGreeting(). This operation will take a String argument that contains a name, and will return a String that contains a customized greeting. See Listing 3-1 for the implementation details of this method.

Listing 3-1. *The Hello World Web Service*

```
package com.alsb.hello;

import javax.jws.*;
import weblogic.jws.WLHttpTransport;
import weblogic.jws.WSDL;
import javax.jws.soap.SOAPBinding;

@WebService(targetNamespace="http://www.alsb.com/")
@WLHttpTransport(portName="HelloWorldSoapPort", ➥
serviceUri = "HelloWorldService", contextPath = "business/hello")
@WSDL(exposed=true)
@SOAPBinding(parameterStyle=SOAPBinding.ParameterStyle.WRAPPED)
public class HelloWorld {
    @WebMethod
    public String getGreeting(String name) {
```

```
      return "Hello " + name;
    }
}
```

In this web service, you use only the fundamental annotations to achieve your goal, so it's worth your time to better understand these annotations, which include @WebService, @SoapBinding, @WLHttpTransport, and @WebMethod.

@WebService

The @WebService annotation denotes the Java class as defining a web service. This annotation takes at most five arguments, shown in Table 3-1. In general, we recommend that you always specify at least the name and targetNamespace attributes. To use this annotation, you need to import javax.jws.WebMethod in your Java source code.

Table 3-1. *@WebService Annotation Attributes*

Attribute	Description	Required
name	The name of the port type of the WSDL that will be generated for this service.	No
targetNamespace	The XML namespace that will be used in the generated WSDL. The default value is specified by the JAX-RPC specification (http://java.sun.com/xml/jaxrpc/index.jsp).	No
serviceName	The name of the service. This maps to the <wsdl:service> element of the WSDL file. The default value is the unqualified name of the Java class with the string Service appended.	No
wsdlLocation	The relative or absolute URL of a predefined WSDL file that this web service will implement. If you leave this undefined, a WSDL file will be generated for you by the jwsc Ant task. If you do enter a value here, the jwsc Ant task will return errors if the Java class is inconsistent with the port types and bindings specified in the WSDL file.	No
endpointInterface	The fully qualified name of an existing service endpoint interface file. If you specify this value, the jwsc Ant task won't generate the interface for you, and you're required to have the interface file in your classpath. If this value is undefined, the jwsc Ant task will generate the interface for you.	No

@SoapBinding

The @SoapBinding annotation allows you to specify the information that's contained in the <wsdlsoap:binding> section of a WSDL file. Its attributes are shown in Table 3-2. In general, we recommend specifying all these attributes explicitly to communicate your intention clearly for how the code will operate. To use this annotation, you need to import javax.jws.SOAPBinding in your Javasource code.

Table 3-2. *@SoapBinding Annotation Attributes*

Attribute	Description	Required
style	Specifies the encoding style of the SOAP messages. Valid values are SOAPBinding.Style.Document and SOAPBinding.Style.RPC. The default is SOAPBinding.Style.Document.	No
use	Specifies the formatting style of the SOAP messages. Valid values are SOAPBinding.Use.Literal and SOAPBinding.Use.Encoded.a The default is SOAPBinding.Use.Literal.	No
parameterStyle	Defines if method parameters represent the entire body of a message or if they are elements wrapped inside a top-level element named after the operation. Valid values are SOAPBinding.ParameterStyle.Bare and SOAPBinding.ParameterStyle.Wrapped. The default is SOAPBinding.ParameterStyle.Wrapped.	No

aYou should generally avoid using the Encoded SOAP binding. It isn't WS-I compliant and therefore reduces your ability to reuse encoded web services.

@WLHttpTransport

The @WLHttpTransport annotation specifies the URI information for the resulting web service. Its attributes are shown in Table 3-3.

Table 3-3. *@WLHttpTransport Annotation Attributes*

Attribute	Description	Required
contextPath	The context root of the web service.	No
serviceURI	The web service URI portion of the URL used by the client. WorkSpace Studio IDE will provide a default service URI for you if you don't use this annotation.	Yes
portName	The name of the <wsdl:port> value. If you don't specify this value, the jwsc Ant task and WorkSpace Studio will generate a default port name based on the name of the class that implements the service.	No

@WebMethod

You use the @WebMethod annotation to identify a Java method as a web service operation. Table 3-4 lists the @WebMethod attributes.

Table 3-4. *@WebMethod Annotation Attributes*

Attribute	Description	Required
operationName	The name of the operation. This maps to a <wsdl:operation> tag in the WSDL file. The default value is the name of the Java method.	No
action	The action for this operation. For SOAP bindings, the value of this attribute determines the value of the SOAPAction header in the SOAP messages. This attribute appears in the WSDL file that is generated for the web service.	No

Testing the Web Service

At this point, you need to test the web service. However, web services need to run on a server. In Chapter 2, as part of setting up for the exercises in this book, we walked through creating a server in WorkSpace Studio. If you have not created a server yet, follow the instructions in Chapter 2 to create one before continuing here.

In the Servers window, you should see the osb30_book server listed, as shown in Figure 3-6. This window shows that status and state of the server. To make life even more convenient, you can start and stop that server from within the WorkSpace Studio IDE itself. You'll notice that the state of your server is listed as Republish. This is because the HelloWorld_WS project needs to be published (that is, deployed onto) to the server. This occurs for two reasons:

- You've never published the project to that server before.

- You've made changes to the project and now it's out of sync with the server.

Figure 3-6. *The configured osb30_book server*

Publishing a project to the server is a simple process. Just right-click the server name and select Publish from the pop-up menu. If the state of the server changes to Synchronized, as shown in Figure 3-7, then you know the server is running the latest compiled versions of all your projects.

■**Tip** If you get a "failed to deploy" message from WorkSpace Studio, open the server by clicking the plus sign next to the OSB server in the Servers window, right-click the HelloWorld_WS project, and select Remove from the pop-up menu. Then you can republish the project.

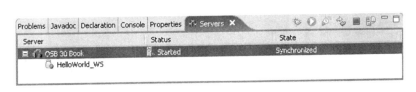

Figure 3-7. *The osb30_book server state after publishing the project to the server*

You can quickly confirm the deployment of the web service by pointing your web browser to the URL http://localhost:7001/business/hello/HelloWorldService?WSDL. The WSDL that was generated for your HelloWorld POJO is displayed. It should look identical to Listing 3-2.

Listing 3-2. *WSDL for the Hello World Web Service*

```
<?xml version='1.0' encoding='UTF-8'?>
<s0:definitions name="HelloWorldServiceDefinitions"
                targetNamespace="http://www.alsb.com/" xmlns=""
                xmlns:s0="http://schemas.xmlsoap.org/wsdl/"
                xmlns:s1="http://www.alsb.com/"
                xmlns:s2="http://schemas.xmlsoap.org/wsdl/soap/">
  <s0:types>
    <xs:schema attributeFormDefault="unqualified"
               elementFormDefault="qualified"
               targetNamespace="http://www.alsb.com"
               xmlns:s0="http://schemas.xmlsoap.org/wsdl/"
               xmlns:s1="http://www.alsb.com"
               xmlns:s2="http://schemas.xmlsoap.org/wsdl/soap/"
               xmlns:xs="http://www.w3.org/2001/XMLSchema">
      <xs:element name="getGreeting">
        <xs:complexType>
          <xs:sequence>
            <xs:element name="name" type="xs:string"/>
          </xs:sequence>
        </xs:complexType>
      </xs:element>
      <xs:element name="getGreetingResponse">
        <xs:complexType>
          <xs:sequence>
            <xs:element name="return" type="xs:string"/>
          </xs:sequence>
        </xs:complexType>
      </xs:element>
    </xs:schema>
  </s0:types>
  <s0:message name="getGreeting">
    <s0:part element="s1:getGreeting" name="parameters"/>
  </s0:message>
  <s0:message name="getGreetingResponse">
    <s0:part element="s1:getGreetingResponse" name="parameters"/>
  </s0:message>
  <s0:portType name="HelloWorld">
    <s0:operation name="getGreeting" parameterOrder="parameters">
      <s0:input message="s1:getGreeting"/>
      <s0:output message="s1:getGreetingResponse"/>
    </s0:operation>
  </s0:portType>
  <s0:binding name="HelloWorldServiceSoapBinding" type="s1:HelloWorld">
    <s2:binding style="document"
                transport="http://schemas.xmlsoap.org/soap/http"/>
    <s0:operation name="getGreeting">
```

```
      <s2:operation soapAction="" style="document"/>
      <s0:input>
        <s2:body parts="parameters" use="literal"/>
      </s0:input>
      <s0:output>
        <s2:body parts="parameters" use="literal"/>
      </s0:output>
    </s0:operation>
  </s0:binding>
  <s0:service name="HelloWorldService">
    <s0:port binding="s1:HelloWorldServiceSoapBinding"
            name="HelloWorldSoapPort">
      <s2:address location="http://localhost:7001/business/ ➥
hello/HelloWorldService"/>
    </s0:port>
  </s0:service>
</s0:definitions>
```

Creating an OSB Configuration Project

An OSB configuration project is a special kind of project in WorkSpace Studio. It represents the configuration information associated with an OSB domain (a group of servers, all similarly configured and providing identical functionality). For example, Java Naming Directory Interface (JNDI) provider details and SMTP server information are not specific to individual OSB projects; rather, they are a part of the system configuration of the OSB domain and are available for use by all of the individual OSB projects within the OSB domain, much like a configured Java Database Connectivity (JDBC) connection can be shared among multiple EJB applications on a Java 5 EE server. An OSB configuration project is also an umbrella project that will contain all of the other OSB projects that you wish to deploy onto a specific OSB domain.

You create an OSB configuration project in the same manner as any other project in WorkSpace Studio:

1. Right-click in the Project Explorer window of WorkSpace Studio and select OSB Configuration Project within the AquaLogic Service Bus group of project types. Then click Next.

2. Name the project OSB30 Book Conf. We will use this configuration project as the parent project for almost all of the rest of the OSB projects we create in this book.

3. Leave the other fields in the New Project wizard blank. Click the Finish button to create the project.

Creating the Hello World OSB Project

Next, we will create an OSB project. This type of project is used to contain proxy services and business services. Create another new project, but this time select OSB Project as the project type. In the New AquaLogic Service Bus Project dialog box, set the project name to HelloWorld_SB and ensure that OSB30 Book Conf is selected as the OSB configuration, as shown in Figure 3-8.

■**Tip** We have adopted the custom of using the suffix SB on our service bus projects. This practice helps us to quickly differentiate between OSB projects and the various other project types that we have in our WorkSpace Studio environment. Similarly, you may have noticed our earlier web service project was entitled HelloWorld_WS, and the OSB configuration project was named OSB30 Book Conf. A naming convention for projects, while not essential to a development organization, can certainly make it a lot easier to quick distinguish among the various project types without needing to memorize what all of the different icons mean.

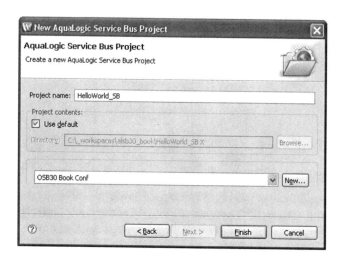

Figure 3-8. *Creating an OSB project in WorkSpace Studio*

Now that our HelloWorld_SB project has been created, the interesting part begins. First, we need to create a business service.

Creating the Business Service

A business service is really just metadata about an external service. That means that creating a business service is fast and simple, since we can usually introspect the external service to generate the business service.

We need to create a business service that represents the HelloWorld_WS service we created and deployed earlier in this chapter.

1. Open the HelloWorld_WS project and navigate to the HelloWorld.java file in the Java Resources/src/com.alsb.hello section of the project.

2. Right-click the HelloWorld.java file and select Web Services ➤ Generate WSDL from the pop-up menu. This will create a HelloWorldService.wsdl file in the same package as the HelloWorld.java file.

3. Click to drag the new WSDL file, and drop it into the HelloWorld_SB project. Now you are ready to create a business service.

4. Right-click the HelloWorld_SB project in the Project Explorer window and select New ➤ Business Service from the pop-up menu.

5. In the New AquaLogic Business Service dialog box, make sure that the HelloWorld_SB project is selected, and then set the file name field to HelloWorldBiz, as shown in Figure 3-9. Click the Next button to continue.

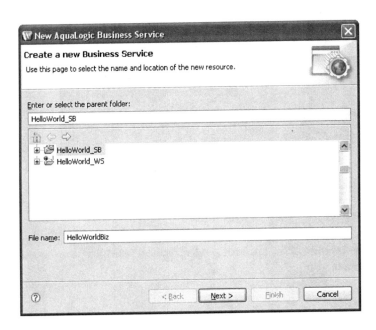

Figure 3-9. *Naming the business service*

6. The next page of the wizard allows you to specify the general type of business service and to provide a description of the service. We are going to create this service based on the WSDL file we just copied into this project. Select the WSDL Web Service radio button, and then click the associated Browse button. Select either the binding or the port from the HelloWorldService.wsdl file.

7. Your dialog box should look like the one shown in Figure 3-10. Click the Finish button to skip the rest of the configuration details; the defaults will serve us perfectly.

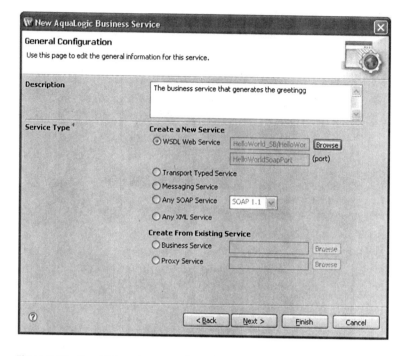

Figure 3-10. *Specifying the general configuration*

That completes the creation of the business service. Now let's create a proxy service to invoke the business service.

Creating the Proxy Service

You create a new proxy service in the manner to which you have become accustomed:

1. Right-click the project and select New ➤ Proxy Service from the pop-up menu.

2. Name the proxy service HelloWorld, and then click the Next button.

3. In the Service Type section on the next page of the wizard, select the Business Service radio button under the Create From Existing Service header. Click the Browse button and select the HelloWorldBiz business service that you just created. Click the Next button to continue.

4. You are now able to define some of the transport information for the proxy service. The default values are fine for the most part, but you do need to change the Endpoint URI field. By default, the endpoint URI for any proxy service takes the form /<project name>/<proxy service name>. Although you can specify pretty much any URI value you want, it's best to have a naming strategy and not just rely on the project name. Change the Endpoint URI field to contain the value /esb/HelloWorld, as shown in Figure 3-11. Then click Finish.

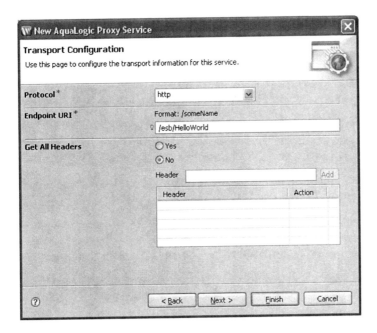

Figure 3-11. *Defining the transport for the proxy service*

The project is complete. Let's get it deployed onto our OSB server.

Deploying the Projects

We need to deploy two projects onto the OSB server. First, be sure that your server is up and running. You should see it in the Servers tab of the WorkSpace Studio IDE.

Right-click the server and select Add and Remove Projects from the pop-up menu. Be sure to add the OSB30 Book Conf and HelloWorld_WS projects to the server configuration. The HelloWorld_SB project is part of the OSB30 Book Conf project, so you do not need to add it explicitly. Just click the Finish button, and WorkSpace Studio will deploy the projects. You know when WorkSpace Studio is finished with the deployment when the server status changes to Synchronized.

Testing the Project

There are two main ways to quickly test your OSB projects. The more labor-intensive method is to create a test client. The advantage of writing a test client is that you can begin to write sophisticated, automated tests. The second method is to use the web-based test console. We will go over both methods here.

Creating a Test Client

Creating a test client in WorkSpace Studio is now much easier than in previous versions. Perform the following steps:

1. Create a Java project in WorkSpace Studio. Name it HelloWorldClient. Click the Next button several times until you get to the Java Settings step in the New Project wizard.

2. Select the Libraries tab, and then click the Add External JARs button. Locate the webservicesclient.jar file, which is in the %BEA_HOME%/wlserver_10.0/server/lib directory, and add it to the project. Click the Finish button to create the project.

3. Right-click the HelloWorldClient project and create a new folder for the source code. Name the folder src.

4. Right-click the HelloWorldClient project and select New ➤ Other from the pop-up menu. In the New dialog box, check the Show All Wizards check box. Then select the Web Service Client wizard, located in the Web Service folder. Click the Next button.

5. In the Service Definition field, enter the URL to the proxy service WSDL: http://localhost:7001/esb/HelloWorld?WSDL. Click the Next button.

6. The Output Folder field should default to /HelloWorldClient/src. This value is fine. Click the Finish button.

7. WorkSpace Studio will create a package named com.alsb.www in the src/ folder. In this package, create a new Java class and name it HelloWorldClient.java.

8. Edit the client code so that it matches the code in Listing 3-3.

Listing 3-3. *Client Code for the HelloWorld Proxy Service*

```java
package com.alsb.www;

import java.rmi.RemoteException;
import javax.xml.rpc.ServiceException;

public class HelloWorldClient {
    public static void main(String[] args) {
        HelloWorldServiceLocator locator = new HelloWorldServiceLocator();
        try {
            HelloWorld port = locator.getHelloWorldSoapPort();
            String greeting = port.getGreeting("Test");
            System.out.println("Greeting returned was: " + greeting);
        } catch (ServiceException ex) {
            ex.printStackTrace();
        } catch(RemoteException ex) {
            ex.printStackTrace();
        }
    }
}
```

To run this client, right-click in the source code and select Run As ➤ Java Application.

As you can see, with a little effort, you could easily use this approach to write JUnit tests and begin to produce traditional unit tests to ensure that any changes you make to the services you define in OSB remain true to their contracts.

Testing Using the OSB Test Console

Usually, when you are developing services. and especially when you are first learning how to use OSB, you really just want a fast way to test a service to ensure that it works the way you intended. The test console was created for this reason.

Follow these steps to open the test console:

1. Open the HelloWorld proxy service and click the Message Flow tab at the bottom of the proxy service window. This displays the message flow for the proxy service (Chapter 4 covers message flows), as shown in Figure 3-12.

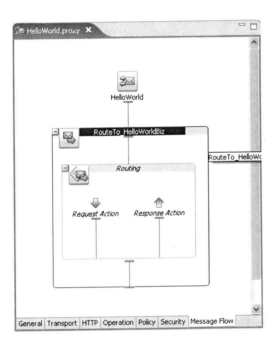

Figure 3-12. *The message flow for the proxy service*

2. Right-click anywhere inside the message flow window and select Run As ➤ Run on Server from the pop-up menu.

3. Make sure that the correct server is selected, and then click the Finish button. WorkSpace Studio will ensure that the projects are compiled and deployed to the server, and then it will bring up your default browser and show the Proxy Service Testing web page that is hosted by the OSB server, as shown in Figure 3-13.

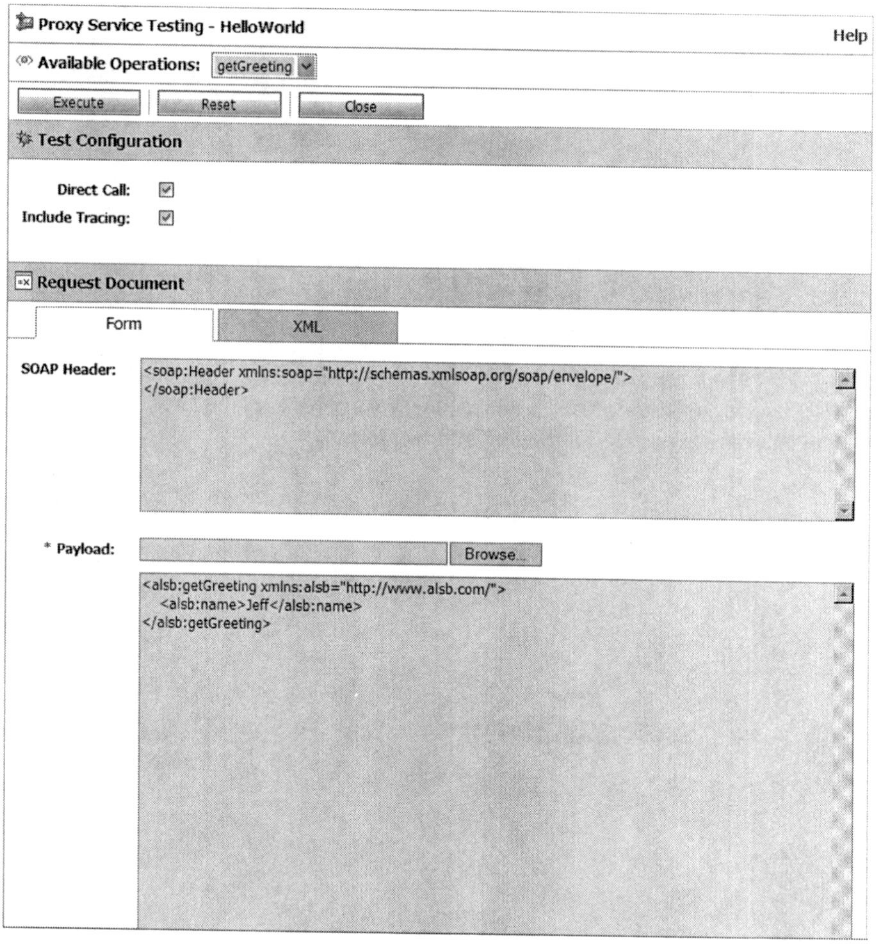

Figure 3-13. *The OSB test console*

Using the test console is simple. In the Payload section is a default SOAP message payload that matches the format expected by the proxy service. Just edit the contents of the `<alsb:name>` tags and click the Execute button. This will invoke the proxy service and then display the result of the service call, as shown in Figure 3-14.

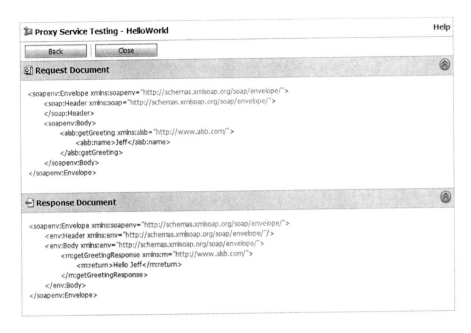

Proxy Service Testing - HelloWorld   Help

Back   Close

Request Document

```
<soapenv:Envelope xmlns:soapenv="http://schemas.xmlsoap.org/soap/envelope/">
    <soap:Header xmlns:soap="http://schemas.xmlsoap.org/soap/envelope/">
    </soap:Header>
    <soapenv:Body>
        <alsb:getGreeting xmlns:alsb="http://www.alsb.com/">
            <alsb:name>Jeff</alsb:name>
        </alsb:getGreeting>
    </soapenv:Body>
</soapenv:Envelope>
```

Response Document

```
<soapenv:Envelope xmlns:soapenv="http://schemas.xmlsoap.org/soap/envelope/">
    <env:Header xmlns:env="http://schemas.xmlsoap.org/soap/envelope/"/>
    <env:Body xmlns:env="http://schemas.xmlsoap.org/soap/envelope/">
        <m:getGreetingResponse xmlns:m="http://www.alsb.com/">
            <m:return>Hello Jeff</m:return>
        </m:getGreetingResponse>
    </env:Body>
</soapenv:Envelope>
```

Figure 3-14. *The result screen of the test console*

One of the great things about the test console is that it shows you the contents (and format) of the documents involved in the web service interaction. You will find this tool to be invaluable later when you need to transform a message from one format to another.

You can also access the test console outside the WorkSpace Studio environment. Open your web browser and point it to http://localhost:7001/sbconsole (sbconsole is for the service bus console application). You may need to log in to the console using the username and password that you gave when you created the osb30_book domain (most likely the username and password are both weblogic, if you followed the installation and configuration instructions in Chapter 2).

Once you have logged in to the web console, you will see the Operations page by default. This page is used to show the health of the servers in the OSB domain. Since we have a single server in our osb30_book domain and it is running fine, there is not a lot to see on the Operations page.

In the navigation pane on the left side of the page, scroll down toward the bottom and click the Project Explorer link. This will show you a list of projects that are deployed on your OSB server. At this time, only two projects should appear: the default project, which was created when you created your OSB domain, and the HelloWorld_SB project, which you deployed onto the OSB server. Click the HelloWorld_SB project link to open it. Your browser window should look like Figure 3-15.

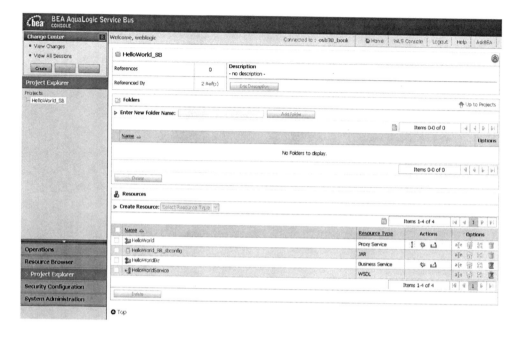

Figure 3-15. *The project view for HelloWorld_WS*

The little bug icon 🐞 is a link to the built-in test console. Clicking it will bring up the web-based test console that we used in earlier in this chapter (see Figure 3-13). As you can see, you can test either the proxy service or the business service from this interface. The other icons on this screen are links to the message flow ⚡ and export 📤 features of the web console. We will cover message flows more extensively in the next chapter.

We recommend that you spend a little time getting used to the web console of OSB. All of the development work that you can do in WorkSpace Studio can also be done directly in the web console. The web console is intended primarily for use by operations personnel, but developers will also find this to be a handy tool when debugging problems with OSB projects for which their full development environment is not immediately handy.

Summary

You did quite a lot quickly in this chapter. Let's review what you've accomplished.

- You learned how to create and deploy a web service (the HelloWorld_WS project) for WebLogic Server 10.

- You learned the basics of project creation in WorkSpace Studio and of business services and proxy services. OSB acts as an intermediary between the service provider (HelloWorld_WS in this case) and the service consumer, providing a layer of abstraction between the two.

- You gained a basic understanding of the OSB interface.

- You learned how to create several of the most common resources in any OSB project: business services, proxy services, and WSDLs.

- You learned how to create web service test clients to verify that your code behaves as expected and the deployments were successful.

- You learned how to use the test console to quickly test the proxy and business service that you created.

Now you know the basics of developing for OSB. It is time to move onto greater challenges. In the next chapter, you'll learn more about the message flows and how to use them effectively.

■ ■ ■

## CHAPTER 4

Message Flow Basics

Messaging is at the heart of OSB. Messages are handled by *message flows*: a set of instructions on what to do with each message. In Chapter 3, you created your first message flow automatically. Although trivial in nature, that message flow shares the same basic set of components that even the most advanced message flows possess.

In this chapter, we will introduce the basic of message flows, and then reuse the `HelloWorldBiz` business service we created in the previous chapter to demonstrate how message flows work.

Message Flow Overview

A proxy service is defined by its message flow. Each message flow is constructed from one or more *nodes*. If no nodes are added to a message flow, then OSB simply echoes the request message back to the caller.

Message flows may contain four main types of nodes: Start, Pipeline Pair, Branch, and Route. Each type of node is used for a specific purpose, as noted in Table 4-1.

Table 4-1. *Main Message Flow Node Types*

Node Type	Description
Start	Every message flow begins with a Start node. A Start node cannot be modified. It exists only to mark the entry point of the message flow.
Route	This is a leaf node that handles the request/response dispatching of the message to a business service. No other nodes can follow a Route node.
Branch	This node is used to make decisions in the message flow, based on the contents of the message. You can make two types of decisions in a Branch node: operational branches or conditional branches.
Pipeline Pair	A Pipeline Pair node explicitly represents both the request and the response message paths in the node, making it easier to customize transformations and other operations on either the request or response side of the node. This type of node can be followed by at most one other node type.

As you can see from Table 4-1, there are rules concerning each node type, specifically about the number of nodes that might follow. Figure 4-1 is a graphical representation of a sample message flow that demonstrates some of these node rules. The Pipeline Pair nodes are followed by, at most, one other node. The Branch nodes can make decisions to route the message among any number of other nodes. Though the diagram shows Branch nodes routing to only at most two nodes, there is no limit on the number of nodes that a Branch node can reference. Last, the Route nodes make up the leaves of this message flow tree, because their job is to route messages to external services.

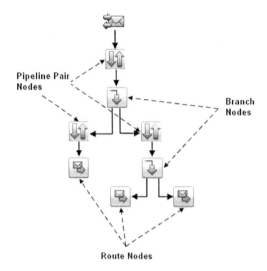

Figure 4-1. *Sample message flow structure*

Pipeline Pairs

As its name implies, a Pipeline Pair node is a pair of pipelines. Each pipeline is a sequence of stages representing a nonbranching, one-way processing path. The left pipeline is the request pipeline. This pipeline is dedicated to request processing only. The right pipeline is the response pipeline, dedicated solely to the handling of the response.

Pipeline Pair nodes are composed of stages. A *stage* is simply a group of actions. An *action* is an instruction, similar in nature to a line of code in a traditional programming language. However, unlike with traditional programming languages, an action isn't source code that is compiled, but rather configuration information that's stored in the message bus. Actions aren't written in Java, C++, or even in a scripting language such as Python or Ruby. Instead, actions are created graphically, with the occasional mix of XQuery, XPath, and/or XSLT. Each stage in a Pipeline Pair or an error handler pipeline can contain any number of actions. Route nodes also contain actions.

The Pipeline Pair node contains a request pipeline and a response pipeline. You can create error handlers at the stage level. Additionally, you have the option of adding an error handler to each of the two pipelines. This error handler will catch any errors generated in the pipeline that aren't already handled by a stage error handler.

Figure 4-2 shows this relationship graphically. By the way, both the Request Pipeline Start ⬇ and Response Pipeline Start ⬆ icons are not modifiable. The only things you can do with Start nodes is to add stages or add a pipeline error handler.

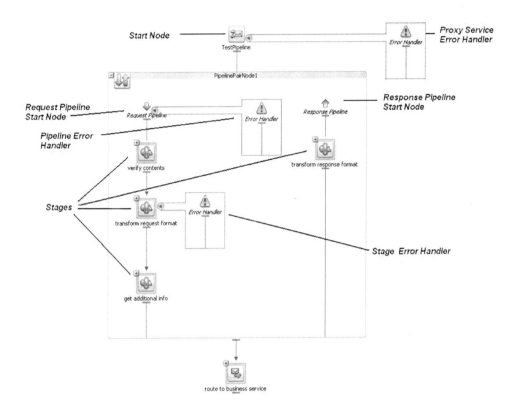

Figure 4-2. *Pipeline Pair details*

Let's focus on the request pipeline side. The warning symbol ⚠ indicates that an error handler is associated with the request pipeline. This means that if any of the stages within the pipeline generate an error, the request pipeline will handle the error. However, you also see that the "transform request format" stage has a stage error handler associated with it, so any errors that are generated in that stage will be handled by the stage error handler, not the overall request pipeline error handler. One interesting thing to note: if the stage error handler raises an error, the pipeline error handler will then handle that error. This nesting of error handlers is reminiscent of Java's exception-handling approach.

On the other side of the pipeline, the response pipeline has no error handlers at all. Any errors that arise in this pipeline will be handled by the proxy service error handler attached to the Start node. If an error handler for the proxy service is not present, or if the error handler raises its own error, the system error handler will handle the error.

Branch Nodes

Branch nodes provide decision-making capability to the message flow. Each Branch node is capable of enforcing a single decision only. If your decision logic requires multiple decisions, you'll need to use multiple, nested Branch nodes.

There are two subtypes of Branch nodes: conditional and operational. A conditional Branch node makes decisions based on comparing values. For example, Figure 4-3 shows the design environment for a conditional Branch node. The Branch node can take three possible paths, depending on the contents of the variable testValue. If the testValue is less than zero, then the less-than-zero branch will be taken. If the testValue is greater than zero, then the greater-than-zero branch will be taken. Of course, if the testValue is zero, the default branch will be taken.

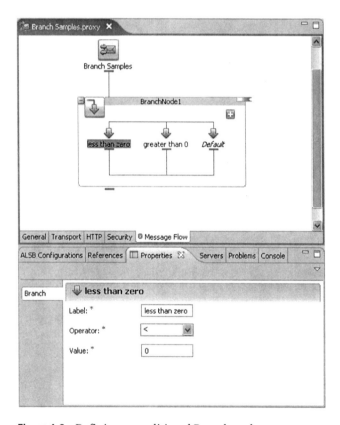

Figure 4-3. *Defining a conditional Branch node*

An operational Branch node works similarly, but it uses operations defined in a WSDL, not string values. This is handy if your WSDL defines multiple operations and you need to perform some additional logic based on the operation that is being invoked, as shown in Figure 4-4.

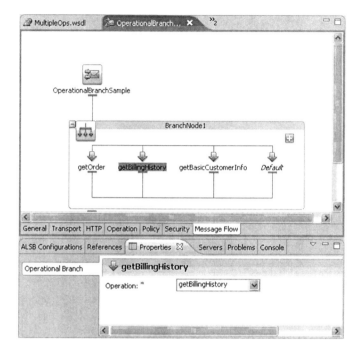

Figure 4-4. *Defining an operational Branch node*

Route Nodes

Route nodes are the nodes that handle the request and response communication between the message flow and another service. The other service might be a business service, or it might be another proxy service within OSB itself.

The Route node represents the boundary between the request and response processing for the proxy. Like a Pipeline Pair node, the Route node has an intrinsic understanding of both the request and response values of its messages. Also, as with the Pipeline Pair node, you can perform specific request and response functions on the messages. However, unlike the Pipeline Pair node, the Route node isn't divided into stages. From an error handling point of view, it's an all-or-nothing construct. You can add an error handler to the entire Route node, but that's the extent. No error handling is possible within a Route node.

Finally, because the Route node communicates with other services directly, there can be no other nodes in the message flow that follow a Route node. A Route node is composed of a series of actions that are performed on the request and/or response portions of the message.

Goodbye World!

Let's put this newfound knowledge to use by creating a variant of your HelloWorld proxy service. In this exercise, you'll create a new project and a new proxy service. However, you'll reuse the existing HelloWorldBiz business service from the previous chapter. The purpose of this project is to take the string response from the HelloWorldBiz business service and translate its contents to say "Goodbye" instead of "Hello." Though modest in scope, this simple project will demonstrate the value of data transformation and service reuse.

Creating the Goodbye World Project and Proxy Service

Follow these steps to create the new project and proxy service for this example:

1. In WorkSpace Studio, create a new OSB project and name it GoodbyeWorld_SB.

2. In the new project, create a folder named ProxyServices.

3. In the ProxyServices folder, create a proxy service named GoodbyeWorld. This proxy service is based on the existing HelloWorldBiz business service in the HelloWorld_SB project. Click the Next button in the New Proxy Service wizard.

4. Set the endpoint URI for the service to /esb/GoodbyeWorld. Click the Finish button.

5. Open the GoodbyeWorld proxy service in WorkSpace Studio.

6. Click the Message Flow tab for the GoodbyeWorld proxy service.

7. Click the Routing node (within the Route node) in the Message Flow window. The Properties window at the bottom of WorkSpace Studio shows that the Routing node will use the inbound operation name for the outbound service. This is exactly what we want. The GoodbyeWorld proxy service will provide a getGreeting operation, and all calls to the proxy's getGreeting operation will be routed directly to the business service. Your Message Flow window should look like Figure 4-5.

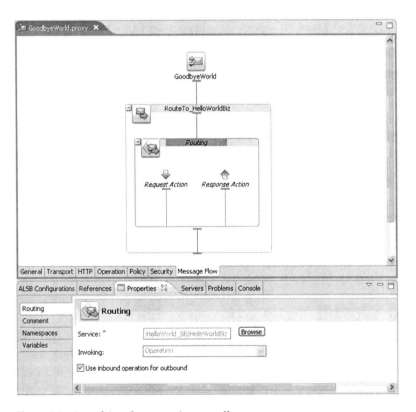

Figure 4-5. *Specifying the operation to call*

Configuring the Route Response

Now you'll work some magic. You know that the HelloWorldBiz business service takes a name argument and returns a greeting result that contains the string with the format: Hello <name>. You need to intercept and translate the response from the business service and change the "Hello" to a "Goodbye." Therefore, you need to add some actions in the *response* portion of the Route node. You need to perform a minimum of two steps. The first step is to get the greeting string from the response and store it in a local variable. The second step is to replace the "Hello" portion with "Goodbye," and then put the new string back into the response value.

TRANSLATION AND TRANSFORMATION

The words *translation* and *transformation* are thrown around a lot today, especially in the SOA world. At the risk of being pedantic, we use these words to indicated specific actions. Clear communication is probably the single most important aspect of software architecture, and using words judiciously is an important part of communicating clearly.

- *Translation:* The act of changing the content of a message. If you think about our Goodbye World example, we are changing only the contents of the <alsb:return> tag. We are not changing the message format itself. Changing the content of a message is translation.

- *Transformation:* The act of changing the format of the message itself. If we need to change the return document format from <alsb:return>Goodbye some-name</alsb:name> to <ns2:greeting> Goodbye some-name</ns2:greeting>, we are transforming the message.

Of course, it is possible to perform both translation and transformation within a proxy service.

Storing the Response String in a Variable

Perform the following steps to complete the response processing for this node:

1. In the Design Palette window, open the Stage Actions ➤ Message Processing category.

2. Drag the Assign action and drop it onto the Response section of the Routing node. Notice that when you drag an action around in the Message Flow window, little circles appear, indicating valid areas to drop the action. Your message flow should look like Figure 4-6.

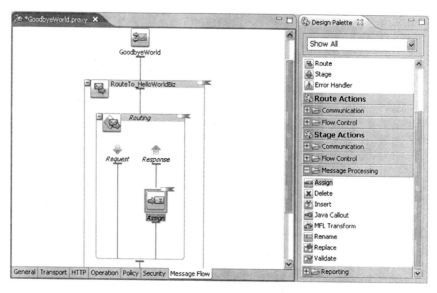

Figure 4-6. *Adding an Assign action to the message flow*

Note Red flags on a message flow are used to indicate errors. The source of the error is usually in the most deeply nested part of the message flow. In Figure 4-6, the error flags point to the Assign action. The errors exist because the Assign action is not yet properly configured.

---

3. Click the Assign icon in the message flow.

4. The Properties window allows you to specify the expression to execute and the local variable to which the expression results will be assigned. Click the Expression link, and the XQuery/XSLT Expression Editor appears.

5. The Expression Editor is an immensely useful tool in WorkSpace Studio. The Variable Structures tab makes it easy to see the schemas of different messages. In the Variable Structures tab, open the body item and continue to open the child items until you reach the return element under getGreetingResponse. Drag and drop the return element into the text area of the Expression tab on the left side of the Expression Editor. Dragging and dropping the elements greatly reduces the chances of introducing errors, which is easy to do when you're typing in XPath expressions.

6. Modify the expression so that it reads as follows, as shown in Figure 4-7:

```
replace($body/alsb:getGreetingResponse/alsb:return, 'Hello', 'Goodbye')
```

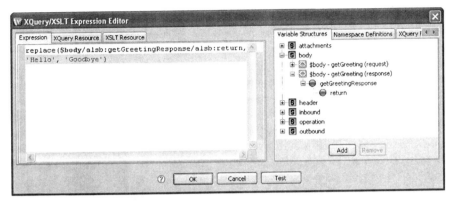

Figure 4-7. *The XQuery/XSLT Expression Editor window with the modified expression*

7. Click the OK button once you are satisfied with the expression. The Properties window for the Assign action should look like the one shown in Figure 4-8.

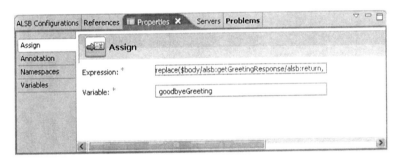

Figure 4-8. *Say "Goodbye" to "Hello"!*

■**Caution** The XQuery `replace()` method is case dependent!

A bit of explanation is due here. You just created an XQuery script that calls the XQuery `replace()` function. It searches through the first string argument, finding all instances of the second string argument (`'Hello'` in this case) and replaces all those instances with the third string argument, `'Goodbye'`. It then returns the resulting string, which is stored in the variable `goodbyeGreeting`.

■**Note** You don't need to declare variables in advance. Simply enter the variable name, and OSB takes care of the rest.

Putting the String in the Response Variable

Now that you have the 'Goodbye' string stored in the goodbyeGreeting variable, you need to insert that data back into the message response variable, $body. To do this, you need to create a Replace action to follow your existing Assign action.

Drag the Replace action from the Design Palette and drop it just below the Assign action in the message flow. A Replace action has three required fields: the XPath, the variable you are modifying, and the expression that will provide the new value. Think of this method as an equation: *<variable>/<XPath> = <expression>*. The variable we need to change is the body variable, which contains the message that will be returned to the caller. The XPath that we need to modify on the body variable is ./alsb:getGreetingResponse/alsb:return. The expression that contains the new value is $goodbyeGreeting.

Also, be sure that the "Replace node contents" radio button is selected, since we want to overwrite only the contents of the alsb:return node, not the node itself. The Properties window for your Replace action should look like Figure 4-9.

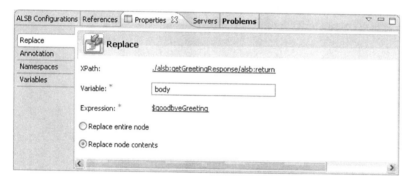

Figure 4-9. *The Replace action properties*

■**Note** When entering variable names into the Properties window in WorkSpace Studio, do not enter the $ character. The $ character is necessary only when using variable names in XPath script expressions.

The GoodbyeWorld proxy service is now functionally complete, but we are going to add one more action to the message flow, a Validate action.

Adding a Validate Action

A Validate action validates a message, or even a part of a message, against a known schema. Using the Validate action will save you a lot of time that you would otherwise spend chasing down minor message-formatting problems.

■**Tip** Always use Validate actions while developing proxy services.

Drag and drop a Validate action beneath the Replace action in the message flow. We want to validate that the message we are returning in the body variable conforms to the message format specified by the HelloWorldService.wsdl. The XPath expression is ./* and the variable name is body. This results in the overall XPath expression of $body/*, meaning "the contents of the body variable."

For the Against Resource field, click the Browse button and select the getGreetingResponse (element) of the HelloWorldService.wsdl file. Select the "Raise error" radio button.

You have just told OSB to check the entire contents of the body variable and ensure that it matches the getGreetingResponse message format. If the response does not match the expected format, OSB will raise an error.

Testing the Service

Save the project in WorkSpace Studio. Go to the Servers tab and synchronize the changes with the osb30_book server. Now, open your web browser to http://localhost:7001/sbconsole and navigate to the GoodbyeWorld proxy service. Use the test console to test it, as described in Chapter 3. You can also access the test console from within WorkSpace Studio by right-clicking the proxy service and selecting Run As from the pop-up menu. When you test the service, you should get a "Goodbye" message instead of a "Hello" message.

What we love about the test console is the incredibly rich detail that it provides. You don't just get the response string—you get so much more! The test console provides you with the following details:

- The request document

- The response document

- The response metadata

- A detailed invocation tree

You'll quickly come to love and rely on the test console. It lays open to you all the messaging to make your life as a service developer easier.

How Does All This XQuery Work?

Did you find the Goodbye World exercise a little confusing? Does it seem like you've stepped into an alien world where nothing makes sense? Good—that's normal, unless you have a strong background in XML and XQuery.

We felt the same way when we got started with OSB. We thought we had a good understanding of XML, but it turns out that our knowledge only scratched the surface. OSB does a great job of making much of the work quick and easy. However, there's no masking XML or XQuery. These are important technologies that will be with us for a long time to come. The difficulty is that if you come from a traditional programming background, XML and XQuery often seem like alien languages; they just don't map well to procedural or object-oriented programming models.

The good news is that with a little practice, and a bit of explanation, this will become clear and simple. We'll walk you through the XQuery you just entered and do our best to explain some of the basics so that this becomes a simple process when you're working on your own projects. On top of what we'll cover here, Chapter 5 is all about WSDL, and that discussion will also help to give you some clarity.

Let's begin with the replace statement you used in the GoodbyeWorld proxy. The replace function itself is easy to understand if you have a background in software engineering. The part of the statement you're probably confused by is the first argument in that function: $body/alsb:getGreetingResponse/alsb:return. How did we know what the first argument should be? More important, how will *you* know which argument to use when you're working through this in the real world?

To begin, it's important to understand that OSB breaks down all request and response messages into several components, and makes these components available to you through the use of XQuery variables. The $body variable is a prime example of this. The $body variable holds the main payload (also known as the *body*) of the message. You'll find that most of your message translations and transformations involve the $body variable of the message. The other standard XQuery variables of a message are $attachments, $fault, $header, $inbound, $operation, and $outbound.

■**Note** OSB uses SOAP as the canonical message format. Whenever non-SOAP messages are used, OSB will transform the messages into SOAP format. The $body variable contains the <soap:body> element, and the $header variable contains the <soap:header> element.

The $body is composed of XML. To know the format of that XML, you need to know the type of message you're dealing with. In this case, you know that you're dealing with a response message from the HelloWorldBiz business service. In OSB, navigate to the HelloWorldService.wsdl file that you created in Chapter 3. Start by looking for the operation declaration in the <portType> tag. You know you're dealing with the getGreeting operation. For convenience, we've included this declaration in Listing 4-1.

Listing 4-1. *The getGreeting Operation Definition*

```
<sO:operation name="getGreeting" parameterOrder="parameters">
    <sO:input message="s1:getGreeting" />
    <sO:output message="s1:getGreetingResponse" />
</sO:operation>
```

As you can see in Listing 4-1, the operation takes an input message and returns an output message. Because you're modifying the greeting that's returned by the business service, you know that you need to know the structure of the response message. From Listing 4-1, you can determine that the message you need to modify is named getGreetingResponse (ignore the sO: and other namespace prefixes for now). Your next step is to find the getGreetingResponse message declaration in the WSDL file, shown in Listing 4-2.

Listing 4-2. *The getGreetingResponse Message Definition*

```
<sO:message name="getGreetingResponse">
    <sO:part element="s1:getGreetingResponse" name="parameters" />
</sO:message>
```

There isn't a lot to see here. The format of this message is defined by the getGreetingResponse element. Your next step is to find that element definition, which is conveniently located in Listing 4-3.

Listing 4-3. *The getGreetingResponse Element Definition*

```
<xs:element name="getGreetingResponse">
    <xs:complexType>
        <xs:sequence>
            <xs:element name="return" type="xs:string" />
        </xs:sequence>
    </xs:complexType>
</xs:element>
```

Finally, you've discovered the structure of the return message. You now know that the $body variable in the return message will contain the structure in Listing 4-4 (namespaces omitted for now).

Listing 4-4. *The getGreetingResponse Return*

```
<getGreetingResponse>
    <return>greeting goes here</return>
</getGreetingResponse>
```

Now that you know the structure of the return document, you can create an XPath expression to represent it:

```
$body/alsb:getGreetingResponse/alsb:return
```

Here, we've inserted the namespaces again for completeness. This XPath expression instructs OSB to get the contents of the alsb:return node. Now, if you return to Figure 4-7, the entire XQuery function call should make sense to you. The real benefit here is that you've learned how to determine the contents of the $body variable for any message you process.

One last note about namespaces: like all programming paradigms, they're brutally intolerant of errors. In Java, if you omit the package name of a class (and don't explicitly import the class), most modern IDEs will detect this and prompt you at design time to import the class, import the entire package, or specify a fully qualified class name when you use it. Due to its interpretative nature, OSB doesn't validate namespace usage at this level of detail. The best it will do is to tell you if you've used a namespace prefix that hasn't been defined. If you omit the namespace when you should have included it, OSB won't detect a problem until runtime. Even at runtime, errors are rarely recognized and reported. Usually your expressions are simply evaluated to null and no value is returned at all. For example, the following are three (invalid) variations of the proper XPath expression from Listing 4-4.

```
$body/alsb:getGreetingResponse/return
$body/getGreetingResponse/alsb:return
$body/getGreetingResponse/return
```

As you can see, it would be easy to omit a namespace inadvertently and difficult to spot the problem when looking at the code. If your expressions are coming back null or empty, look at the namespace usage first.

■**Caution** Namespaces are as fundamental to modern XML communications as package names are in Java. Once you're comfortable with XQuery and XPath, the most common reason for your XQuery and XPath code not to work correctly will be due to using the wrong namespace.

Reusing an XQuery Resource

Your GoodbyeWorld_SB project runs like a rocket, but did you notice the subtle design flaw? The flaw isn't in the service itself, but in how you assembled it. Remember that reuse is a core concept of any ESB and is central to SOA. Your proxy service is certainly reusable, but you missed the opportunity to reuse something within the proxy service itself: the XQuery function that changes "Hello" to "Goodbye."

OSB has the ability to store XQuery, WSDL, XML Schema, XSLT, WS-Policy files, and more as reusable resources. The ability to store these resources (sometimes referred to as *assets* or *artifacts*) along with proxy services makes OSB a lightweight *service repository*. It's certainly a best practice to reuse these resources whenever possible.

Let's take a moment to see how you can make XQuery a reusable resource in your ESB. For this exercise, you'll create a new proxy service inside your GoodbyeWorld_SB project. You'll name this new proxy service GoodbyeWorldXF (the XF indicates it uses an XQuery function). You won't overwrite your GoodbyeWorld service because it will be handy to compare the two when you're finished.

Creating an XQuery Resource

You should be familiar with the process of creating a proxy service by now, so we'll skip over the boring details. The process is essentially the same as the one you followed when you created the GoodbyeWorld proxy service. Set the endpoint URI to /esb/GoodbyeWorldXF. Before you create the actions in the Route node for your new GoodbyeWorldXF proxy service, you need to create your XQuery resource. Creating the XQuery resource is similar to creating a proxy service:

1. Create a folder named XQuery in the GoodbyeWorld_SB project.

2. In the XQuery folder, create an XQuery transformation and name it Hello_to_Goodbye.xq.

3. Click the Simple radio button when prompted for the source type, and select String from the list box.

4. Set the Parameter Name to helloStr and click the Add button. Then click the Next button.

5. Define the parameters for the target type. Again, select the Simple radio button and then select String in the list box. Click the Add button, and then click the Finish button. The XQuery resource will be created.

6. When your new Hello_To_Goodbye.xq resource is created, it will look similar to Figure 4-10, but it won't have the green arrow that indicates the mapping. Create that green arrow by dragging the helloStr element on the left and dropping it onto the string element on the right. This creates a simple transformation in the script that will return the value of helloStr to the caller.

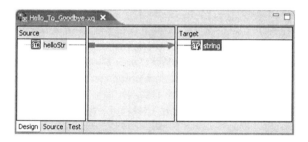

Figure 4-10. *Creating an XQuery transformation*

7. Now you will need to customize the transformation and create the scripting code that will search for all occurrences of "Hello" and replace it with the string "Goodbye." Click the Source tab at the bottom of the Hello_To_Goodbye.xq window (see Figure 4-10). This tab allows you to modify the XQuery script directly. Change the existing script so that it matches Listing 4-5.

Listing 4-5. *Sample XQuery Function Performing a String Replacement*

```
xquery version "1.0";
declare namespace xf = ➥
"http://tempuri.org/GoodbyeWorld_SB/XQuery/Hello_to_Goodbye/";
declare function xf:Hello_To_Goodbye($helloStr as xs:string)
    as xs:string {
        replace($helloStr, 'Hello', 'Goodbye')
};
declare variable $helloStr as xs:string external;
xf:Hello_To_Goodbye($helloStr)
```

Let's look at this XQuery script resource in more detail. It's a good guide for other XQuery resources that you might create. The first line is a declaration of the type of data contained in this resource. It's optional in OSB to include this line. We like to include it for completeness, and because other, external tools require the line to exist, so including it makes it easier to copy and paste the script between tools.

The second line of text is your namespace declaration. This places your function in a specific namespace, which helps to avoid naming collisions. Immediately after the namespace declaration, you declare your XQuery function. Note that you prefix the function name by the namespace. This function takes a single xs:string argument named $helloStr and returns an xs:string. The body of the function is pretty straightforward. The return value of the replace function is returned by the function.

The next line of code is interesting. Here, you formally declare a variable, which you haven't done before. You must explicitly define a variable because you're using an *external* XQuery variable. Later, when you use this script resource, OSB will prompt you to provide a value for this external variable. Declaring external variables is the mechanism for passing data from OSB to the XQuery script.

The last line of code in this script calls the function you've defined, passing in the external variable as the argument. This last line is necessary to "hook up" the caller to the script. Without this line, the XQuery script would still run, but the method would never be invoked. The caller of this script has no knowledge of the xf:Hello_To_Goodbye function. It only knows about the XQuery script resource itself. When OSB invokes the script, it runs the entire script; it doesn't invoke a method. This is similar in nature to how other scripting languages are invoked.

You can also test XQuery scripts very easily within the WorkSpace Studio environment. Click the Test tab at the bottom of the Hello_To_Goodbye.xq window. Enter a string in the Source Data window, and then click the green start button in the Result Data window to run the script. The resulting string is then displayed. Figure 4-11 shows a sample test run and its output.

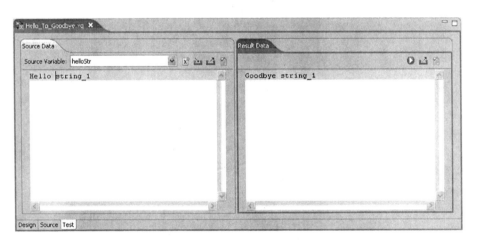

Figure 4-11. *Testing the XQuery script*

Let's get back to defining the proxy service. Save your XQuery script. If you made a typo, WorkSpace Studio will give you a warning and let you correct the problem.

Editing the Route Node

Now it's time to edit the Route node for your GoodbyeWorldXF proxy service.

1. Click the Routing node. It should default to using the inbound operation name for the outbound service, which again is what we want.

2. Add an Assign action to the Response section of the Routing node.

3. Edit the Assign action properties. In the XQuery/XSLT Expression Editor, click the XQuery Resource tab.

4. Use the Browse button next to the XQuery text box to search for the XQuery expression you want to invoke. In this case, select GoodbyeWorld_SB/XQuery/Hello_To_Goodbye. In the Bind Variables section of this window, set the helloStr field to string($body/alsb:getGreetingResponse/alsb:return), as shown in Figure 4-12. This tells OSB to set the XQuery script's external variable to the value you need to modify.

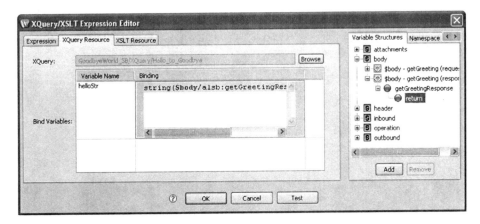

Figure 4-12. *Invoking an XQuery resource*

5. Click the OK button when you are satisfied with the variable binding in the Expression Editor.

6. Set the variable name for the Assign action to greeting.

7. Add a Replace action. Set the XPath to ./alsb:getGreetingResponse/alsb:return, and set the variable field to body.

8. Set the expression to string($greeting) and select the "Replace node contents" radio button.

9. Again, we should validate the response message just to be sure everything is correct. The Validate action is exactly the same as the one we added to the GoodbyeWorld proxy service. However, instead of going through all of the steps that we did for the GoodbyeProxy service, you can just copy the Validate action from the GoodbyeWorld proxy and paste it into the Response section of the GoodbyeWorldXF Routing node.

10. Save everything and publish your changes to the server.

Test the new service using the OSB test console. You should see the "Goodbye" message instead of "Hello."

While you probably wouldn't want to reuse such trivial functionality in the real world, you would use this same process to create and store your "real" XQuery scripts.

Summary

In this chapter, you were introduced to the basics of message flows. You also reused the HelloWorldBiz business service you created in Chapter 3. Reuse is one of the core concepts of ESBs and SOA, and here we've demonstrated the power of that concept. You also saw an example of data transformation, where you intercepted data in flight and modified it to suit your needs. You learned how to create, use, and store XQuery scripts as reusable resources within OSB, again promoting the reusability of the services in your ESB. You also gained familiarity with a powerful tool in OSB: the test console. Your skills are rapidly growing, and you're now ready to tackle more advanced topics.

CHAPTER 5

■■■

A Crash Course in WSDL

In this chapter, you'll learn the basics of creating a Web Services Description Language (WSDL) file by hand. Our goal in this chapter is to provide you with some best practices and quickly get you up to speed with the language. If you're already comfortable with WSDL, you can safely skip this chapter. If you're a WSDL/XML Schema purist, then reading this chapter will only upset you, because we won't take the time to cover the esoteric capabilities of the language here.

WSDL is a nontrivial language. To express the depth and breadth of the language fully is beyond the scope of this book. In this chapter, we'll focus on a WSDL format that's most amenable to creating highly interoperable web services: document-centric and unencoded (also known as *bare* or *literal* encoding). Don't worry if these terms are meaningless to you now. By the end of this chapter, they'll make perfect sense.

Why Learn About WSDL?

In Chapter 3, you learned how to use the Java annotations to have WorkSpace Studio generate a WSDL file for you. This is a handy feature, especially when learning how to write web services in Java. WorkSpace Studio also provides the ability to generate code in the other direction: to generate Java code from a WSDL file.

You should be aware of the subtle differences in these approaches. They both have their strengths and their weaknesses. We've heard it proposed that if you're a Java-centric shop, you should just use the WSDL-generation feature and not worry about the details of WSDL creation and syntax. This is patent nonsense.

We remember the days when the C language was introduced to the personal computing world. At the time, BASIC was the dominant language. Some vendors created BASIC-to-C language converters, making the claim that you didn't need to waste time learning C; you could continue to write your BASIC programs and then push a button to convert the programs into C. These programs did work, especially for very small projects, but they weren't viable in the long run. By using this code-generation approach, you rob yourself of the ability to use more powerful, language-specific capabilities. As a result, you guarantee that you'll write mediocre software at best. The one saving grace of these BASIC-to-C converters was that they did work as a learning tool to help BASIC programmers understand how to write C programs.

We live in an increasingly web service–oriented world. WSDL is the language of web services, and it will serve you well to become conversant in WSDL, especially if you're striving to create excellent systems. You can fall into a subtle mental trap when you generate WSDL from your Java code: you might find yourself generating Java API–oriented web services. If you look at the world through Java-colored glasses, the work you produce will be similarly colored; if you look at the world through the prism of web services, your work will naturally become more service-oriented. It's vital to adopt the new mindset as soon as possible.

WSDL Basics

Listing 5-1 shows a sample WSDL file for a simple web service that returns customer information based on the ID of the customer. Even though it describes a simple service, the sample WSDL includes all the necessary principles that you need to understand. We'll use this listing as a reference throughout our discussion on WSDL basics.

Listing 5-1. *A Basic WSDL File*

```
<?xml version="1.0" encoding="UTF-8"?>
<wsdl:definitions xmlns:soap="http://schemas.xmlsoap.org/wsdl/soap/"
xmlns:tns="http://www.alsb.com/Sample/"
xmlns:wsdl="http://schemas.xmlsoap.org/wsdl/"
xmlns:xsd="http://www.w3.org/2001/XMLSchema" name="Sample"
targetNamespace="http://www.alsb.com/Sample/">
<wsdl:types>
    <xsd:schema targetNamespace="http://www.alsb.com/Sample/">
        <xsd:complexType name="Customer">
            <xsd:sequence>
                <xsd:element name="customerID" type="xsd:int" minOccurs="1"/>
                <xsd:element name="firstName" type="xsd:string" minOccurs="1"/>
                <xsd:element name="lastName" type="xsd:string" minOccurs="1"/>
            </xsd:sequence>
        </xsd:complexType>

        <xsd:complexType name="CustomerQuery">
            <xsd:sequence>
                <xsd:element name="customerID" type="xsd:int" minOccurs="1"/>
            </xsd:sequence>
        </xsd:complexType>

        <!-- Map our types into elements  -->
        <xsd:element name="getCustomer" type="tns:CustomerQuery"/>
        <xsd:element name="getCustomerResponse" type="tns:Customer"/>
    </xsd:schema>
</wsdl:types>

<wsdl:message name="GetCustomerRequest">
    <wsdl:part element="tns:getCustomer" name="customerQuery" />
</wsdl:message>
```

```
<wsdl:message name="GetCustomerResponse">
   <wsdl:part element="tns:getCustomerResponse" name="customer"/>
</wsdl:message>

<wsdl:portType name="Sample">
   <wsdl:operation name="getCustomer">
      <wsdl:input message="tns:GetCustomerRequest" />
      <wsdl:output message="tns:GetCustomerResponse" />
   </wsdl:operation>
</wsdl:portType>

<wsdl:binding name="SampleSOAP" type="tns:Sample">
   <soap:binding style="document"
      transport="http://schemas.xmlsoap.org/soap/http" />
   <wsdl:operation name="getCustomer">
      <soap:operation
         soapAction="http://www.alsb.com/Sample/Customer" />
         <wsdl:input>
            <soap:body use="literal" />
         </wsdl:input>
         <wsdl:output>
            <soap:body use="literal" />
         </wsdl:output>
   </wsdl:operation>
</wsdl:binding>

<wsdl:service name="Sample">
   <wsdl:port binding="tns:SampleSOAP" name="SampleSOAP">
   <soap:address location="http://www.alsb.com/" />
   </wsdl:port>
</wsdl:service>
</wsdl:definitions>
```

XML Namespaces

Before we get too far into our discussion of WSDL, we'll take a moment to discuss XML namespaces. The namespace concept is used extensively both by WSDL and XML Schema. Namespaces can make reading a WSDL file difficult unless you understand what a namespace is and how it affects the document.

A namespace is a way to categorize or group element, data type, and attribute names within an XML document. This is especially handy when combining multiple XML vocabularies into a single document. An XML namespace is analogous to a Java package or a C# namespace keyword. Namespaces help to protect against naming collisions. Let's examine a concrete example of a naming collision and learn how XML namespaces help. Examine both Listing 5-2 and Listing 5-3 and notice the difference in how the Address data types are defined.

Listing 5-2. *Shipping.xsd Snippet*

```
<xsd:complexType name="Address">
    <xsd:sequence>
        <xsd:element name="street" type="xsd:string" minOccurs="1"/>
        <xsd:element name="city" type="xsd:string" minOccurs="1" maxOccurs="1'"/>
        <xsd:element name="state" type="xsd:string" minOccurs="1" maxOccurs="1"/>
        <xsd:element name="zipCode" type="xsd:string" minOccurs="1" maxOccurs="1"/>
    </xsd:sequence>
</xsd:complexType>
```

Listing 5-3. *Customer.xsd Snippet*

```
<xsd:complexType name="Address">
    <xsd:sequence>
        <xsd:element name="street1" type="xsd:string" minOccurs="1" maxOccurs="1"/>
        <xsd:element name="street2" type="xsd:string" minOccurs="1" maxOccurs="1"/>
        <xsd:element name="street3" type="xsd:string" minOccurs="1" maxOccurs="1"/>
        <xsd:element name="city" type="xsd:string" minOccurs="1" maxOccurs="1'"/>
        <xsd:element name="state" type="xsd:string" minOccurs="1" maxOccurs="1"/>
        <xsd:element name="zipCode" type="xsd:string" minOccurs="1" maxOccurs="1"/>
    </xsd:sequence>
</xsd:complexType>
```

Both Address types are valid, but their structure varies significantly. If you try to use both these schemas in an Order web service, there will be a naming conflict because they share the same name. To correct this problem, you would declare two namespaces: one for each of the schemas that you want to use. The following XML snippet shows how to declare a namespace:

```
xmlns:shp="http://www.alsb.com/shipping/"
```

In this case, the namespace you declare is http://www.alsb.com/shipping. This namespace uses the prefix of shp to represent the namespace. A namespace is defined by a URI string, not the prefix. You can think of the prefix as a variable that holds the namespace "value." Alternatively, you can think of a namespace prefix as a pointer that represents a namespace. For example, Listing 5-4 shows what might appear to be two namespace declarations. In reality, it is a single namespace referred to by two different namespace prefixes. The string is the namespace, not the prefix.

Listing 5-4. *Two Prefixes Can Represent the Same Namespace*

```
xmlns:shp="http://www.alsb.com/shipping/"
xmlns:foo="http://www.alsb.com/shipping/"
```

Note that the URI doesn't need to point to anything in particular or even be a URL. It's simply a string within the document. The xmlns: that appears before the prefix is simply the notation that tells the XML parser that an XML namespace is about to be declared.

Listing 5-5 shows how namespaces allow you to use two different data types with the same name (Address, in this case) in the same WSDL file. The <CustomerAddress> element takes the form of the <Address> type that you defined in Listing 5-3, while the <ShippingAddress> takes the form of the <Address> type you defined in Listing 5-2.

Listing 5-5. *The Order.wsdl Snippet*

```
<?xml version="1.0e" encoding="UTF-8"?>
<wsdl:definitions xmlns:soap="http://schemas.xmlsoap.org/wsdl/soap/"
       xmlns:tns="http://www.alsb.com/Sample/"
       xmlns:wsdl="http://schemas.xmlsoap.org/wsdl/"
       xmlns:xsd="http://www.w3.org/2001/XMLSchema" name="Sample"
       xmlns:shp="http://www.alsb.com/shipping/"
       xmlns:customer="http://www.alsb.com/customer/"
       targetNamespace="http://www.alsb.com/order/">
   <wsdl:types>
       <xsd:schema targetNamespace="http://www.alsb.com/customer/">
           <xsd:element name="CustomerAddress" type="customer:Address>
           <xsd:element name="ShippingAddress" type="shp:Address>

           ...

       </xsd:schema>
   </wsdl:types>
</wsdl:definitions>
```

If you've been paying close attention, you might be wondering how these namespaces map to the data types; how does the computer know that a customer:Address has the definition that you provided in Listing 5-3? The answer is that it doesn't. You need to provide that mapping in a separate XML import statement when you import the Customer.xsd schema.

You'll find that namespaces are used frequently in XML Schema and WSDL documents. Knowing how to use them is critical for understanding these documents.

The Default Namespace

Every element and attribute in an XML document or XSD belongs to a namespace. The default namespace is the namespace applied to all nodes in the document that don't have an explicit namespace associated with them. Defining a default namespace is similar to defining a namespace with a prefix; you just don't define a prefix. There can be only one default namespace for each element. There's a fair bit of subtle detail to that last sentence, so let's explore it further.

Listing 5-6 shows how to define a default namespace for an entire WSDL file. Namespaces are inherited by each subelement in an XML document. Because this is a WSDL document, it's a common practice to define the WSDL namespace as the default namespace. As a result, the WSDL-specific elements don't need to have a namespace prefix. You can see this in action in Listing 5-6. The <types> element has no namespace prefix defined for it, so the XML parser uses the default namespace, whereas the <schema> elements all have the xsd: prefix explicitly defined, because the <schema> element isn't part of the WSDL namespace.

Listing 5-6. *Defining and Using a Default Namespace*

```
<?xml version="1.0" encoding="UTF-8"?>
<wsdl:definitions name="Sample"
xmlns="http://schemas.xmlsoap.org/wsdl/"
xmlns:wsdl="http://schemas.xmlsoap.org/wsdl/"
xmlns:xsd="http://www.w3.org/2001/XMLSchema"
targetNamespace="http://www.alsb.com/order/">
```

```
<types>
   <xsd:schema targetNamespace="http://www.alsb.com/customer/e">
      <xsd:element name="CustomerAddress" type="customer:Address>
      <xsd:element name="ShippingAddress" type="shipping:Address>
      ...
   </xsd:schema>
</types>
```

You can override default namespaces in subelements. This allows you to simplify your documents (at least for human readers) by providing a new default namespace in a section of the document where that new namespace is commonly used. You see an example of this in Listing 5-7. The elements <definitions> and <types> are both part of the WSDL namespace. Because <definitions> declares the WSDL namespace as its default namespace, it doesn't need to specify a namespace prefix. Furthermore, the child <types> element inherits the default namespace of its parent <definitions> element.

However, the <schema> and <element> tags are part of the XML Schema namespace, yet they don't have a namespace prefix in their tags. This is because the default namespace is overridden by the <schema> element: it declares its own default namespace, and this new default namespace is inherited by its child <element> tags.

Listing 5-7. *Overriding the Default Namespace*

```
<definitions
name="DefaultNamespaceSample"
xmlns="http://schemas.xmlsoap.org/wsdl/"
xmlns:tns="foo"
xmlns:xsd="http://www.w3.org/2001/XMLSchema"
targetNamespace="foo">
<types>
   <schema xmlns="http://www.w3.org/2001/XMLSchema" targetNamespace="foo">
      <element name="Response" type="xsd:string"/>
      <element name="Request" type="xsd:string"/>
   </schema>
</types>
```

Some people feel this makes the resulting XML easier to read. Other folks argue that it makes it harder to read, especially if you don't know which tag belongs in which namespace. You'll need to decide for yourself how you want to use namespaces in your XML. Just as with the old arguments about where to place the curly braces in your C, C++, and Java code, it's a matter of style and personal preference.

The Target Namespace

Aside from a default namespace, you can define a target namespace. Initially, we found this confusing. Like all things technical, it becomes simple once you understand its usage. In your WSDL and XML Schema files, you're often creating new data types. These new types should belong to a namespace. Technically, you can define new elements that don't belong to a namespace, but remember that you're concerned with real-world usage here, not every fringe usage. You should always define a target namespace.

Listing 5-7 shows the `targetNamespace` attribute in action. The `<schema>` element defines a `targetNamespace` with the value `"foo"`. Nested inside the `<schema>` element are two element definitions: Request and Response. These new elements are created as members of the `"foo"` namespace. For example, the proper way to use the Request element in an XML document is as follows:

```
<Response xmlns="foo">Some string here</Response>
```

Alternatively, you could do the following:

```
<ParentElement xmlns:tns="foo"
   <tns:Response>Some string here</tns:Response>
</ParentElement >
```

■**Caution** Earlier, we mentioned that XML namespaces are analogous to Java and C# package names. It's true that they're similar in many ways, but it's important to know where they're different. When you create a package name in a Java application, you're creating a namespace that affects the organization of software within the scope of that application. When you're defining an XML namespace, you may be creating a namespace that will affect the organization of data types and services throughout your entire organization! As a result, it's important to consider carefully how you'll organize and manage namespaces as a company.

WSDL Definitions

A WSDL file is composed of five sections contained by the `<definitions>` root element:

- `<types>`: You define the data types used by your WSDL here. Data types in a WSDL are expressed as XML Schema elements.

- `<portType>`: This is the abstract interface definition of your web service. It's similar to an interface definition in Java or C#. If you want a quick understanding of the functionality provided by a web service, this is the section of the WSDL to read.

- `<message>`: This section defines the format of the messages (think documents) that the web service uses.

- `<binding>`: This section describes how the `portType` is mapped into a concrete expression of data formats and protocols.

- `<service>`: This section contains a collection of port elements. This allows you to specify the fact that a web service might live on multiple endpoints.

The <types> Section

WSDL files use XML Schema to define data types. Therefore, learning some basics of XML Schema will be our first topic. XML Schema is a large topic. To facilitate things, we'll assume that you have a basic understanding of object-oriented principles. With that background in mind, we'll focus on how to map object-oriented concepts into XML Schema data types. Traditionally, XML Schema files use the `.xsd` file extension.

Native Data Types

XML Schema provides for a fair number of native data types (also known as *primitives*) that you can use in your schemas: strings, integers, dates, times, and so on. Using a native data type is pretty simple. For example, declaring an object of type string looks like the following:

```
<element name="MyString" type="xsd:string" />
```

You can find a complete list of these native data types at http://www.w3.org/TR/xmlschema-2/#built-in-datatypes.

Custom Data Types

Let's move to the next level and create some data types that are much more useful. For this example, you'll create a Customer data type. Your customer has the attribute's first name, last name, and customer ID. Listing 5-8 shows how you would define the customer object.

Listing 5-8. *The Customer Type Definition*

```
<xsd:complexType name="Customer">
    <xsd:sequence>
        xsd:<element name="customerID" type="xsd:int" minOccurs="1" />
        <xsd:element name="firstName" type="xsd:string" minOccurs="1" />
        <xsd:element name="lastName" type="xsd:string" minOccurs="1" />
    </xsd:sequence>
</xsd:complexType>
```

As you can see, you define the Customer object as a complexType. This is roughly equivalent to defining a Customer class in Java or C++/C#. You name the complex type using the name attribute.

■**Note** It's possible to define data types as being anonymous within a named element. This isn't a good practice within the XSD file itself. This type of design pattern is acceptable within the WSDL file, though. Name your complex types in your XSD files, and then refer to them via <element> tags within your WSDL.

Next, you add properties to your Customer data type. In XML Schema, add the properties using the <sequence> tag. The <sequence> tag means that a series of elements or types will follow, in a specific sequence. In this example, you have three properties in this sequence: customerID, firstName, and lastName.

Although you use the <sequence> tag to define a sequence of object attributes, you can use two other tags here, depending on your needs: the <choice> and <all> tags. You use those tags when defining more complicated data types. For our purposes, a <complexType> will always contain a <sequence> of attributes.

Notice that each of the attributes in your Customer data type is defined as an element. You use the <element> tag when referring to an existing data type. In the case of our attributes, the existing data types are of type string and int. Inside the Customer data type, you can also reference other custom data types. For example, you can create an Address data type and then use it within your Customer data type, as shown in Listing 5-9.

Listing 5-9. *Nesting Complex Data Types*

```
<xsd:complexType name="Customer">
    <xsd:sequence>
    <xsd:element name="customerID" type="xsd:int" minOccurs="1" />
        <xsd:element name="firstName" type="xsd:string" minOccurs="1" />
        <xsd:element name="lastName" type="xsd:string" minOccurs="1" />
        <xsd:element name="homeAddress" type="Address"/>
    </xsd:sequence>
</xsd:complexType>
<xsd:complexType name="Address">
    <xsd:sequence>
        <xsd:element name="street" type="xsd:string" minOccurs="1" />
        <xsd:element name="city" type="xsd:string" minOccurs="1" />
        <xsd:element name="state" type="xsd:string" minOccurs="1" />
        <xsd:element name="postalCode" type="xsd:string" minOccurs="1" />
    </xsd:sequence>
</xsd:complexType>
```

minOccurs and maxOccurs

You might have noticed that all the listings so far use the `minOccurs` attribute in the element definitions. This specifies the minimum number of times the element can occur within the sequence. By setting the `minOccurs` value to 1, you're specifying that the element must occur at least once in the sequence. If you set the value to 0, then you're specifying that the element is optional.

The complement to `minOccurs` is the `maxOccurs` attribute. It specifies the maximum number of times the element can occur in the sequence. The `maxOccurs` value must be a positive integer, or it might be the specified as "unbounded" to indicate that there's no limit on the number of times it might occur. These attributes are often used in conjunction. For example, the combination of `minOccurs="1"` and `maxOccurs="1"` specifies that the element must appear only once. The default value of both `minOccurs` and `maxOccurs` is "1".

Importing XML Schemas

As mentioned previously, you can import existing schemas into your XML or WSDL documents. This is an excellent way to reuse these assets, allowing you to make broad changes to your enterprise definitions in a centralized manner. Importing a schema into your WSDL file is done within the `<types>` section. The general format of an `import` statement is as follows:

```
<import namespace="[the URI to the namespace]" schemaLocation= ➥
"[file path or URI to your .XSD file]" />
```

For example, in your WSDL, if you wanted to use the `customer.xsd` and the `shipping.xsd` schemas, you would use the following `import` statements:

```
<xsd:import namespace="http://www.alsb.com/customer/" ➥
schemaLocation="customer.xsd" />
<xsd:import namespace="http://www.alsb.com/shipping/" ➥
schemaLocation="shipping.xsd" />
```

Notice that the URI for the namespace matches exactly the URIs you used in Listing 5-5 when you defined the namespaces. Now, when you declare an element to be of type `customer:Address` or `shp:Address`, the web service is able to determine exactly which `Address` definition to use.

The <message> Section

A message describes the abstract form of the input, output, or fault messages. Messages are composed of one or more `<part>` elements. The `<part>` elements describe the composition of the `<message>`.

Because you're using the document-centric style of WSDL, the `<part>` elements of the `<message>` must refer to data structures using the `element` attribute. For document-centric WSDL, it's common practice to use the operation name as the name of the request message and to append `Response` to the operation name and use that as the name of the response message. Listing 5-10 demonstrates this naming approach with the `GetCustomerResponse` message.

Listing 5-10. *Sample Document-Style Message Definition*

```
<wsdl:message name="GetCustomerResponse">
   <wsdl:part element="tns:getCustomerResponse" name="customer"/>
</wsdl:message>
```

The <portType> Section

The `<portType>` section of the WSDL file describes the abstract interface of the web service. Listing 5-11 provides an example of a simple `portType` definition. This section of the WSDL is often compared to an abstract Java interface because it defines, at a high level, how the operations of the service work (that is, what arguments are expected and what results are returned).

Listing 5-11. *An Example of the <portType>*

```
<wsdl:portType name="CustomerPortType">
   <wsdl:operation name="findCustomer">
      <wsdl:input message="tns:findCustomer" />
      <wsdl:output message="tns:findCustomerResponse" />
   </wsdl:operation>
</wsdl:portType>
```

The `<portType>` element is made up of `<operation>` elements. The `<operation>` elements, in turn, are composed of `<input>` and `<output>` elements that map directly to the `<message>` elements. The `<operation>` elements might also contain `<fault>` elements to indicate the SOAP faults that the operation might throw. However, for the purposes of our crash course, you'll ignore the `<fault>` element.

The <binding> Section

The `<binding>` section is used to define how the `<portType>` (that is, the abstract interface of the web service) is bound to a transport protocol and an encoding scheme. A single `portType` may be bound to many transports and encoding scheme combinations. The most commonly used encoding scheme and transport protocol combination these days is SOAP over HTTP. The most common bindings other than HTTP/SOAP are HTTP/POST and HTTP/GET, especially when dealing with web services that were developed before HTTP/SOAP gained popularity.

As you can see from Listing 5-12, the <binding> is mapped to a <portType>. Each operation of the <portType> is defined in the binding, including the mapping of the operation's input and output to specific message types.

Listing 5-12. *An Example of the HTTP/SOAP Binding*

```
<wsdl:binding name="CustomerServiceSOAP" type="tns:CustomerPortType">
   <soap:binding style="document"
      transport="http://schemas.xmlsoap.org/soap/http" />
   <wsdl:operation name="findCustomer">
      <soap:operation soapAction="" style="document" />
         <wsdl:input>
            <soap:body parts="findCustomer" use="literal" />
         </wsdl:input>
         <wsdl:output>
            <soap:body parts="findCustomerResponse" use="literal" />
         </wsdl:output>
   </wsdl:operation>
</wsdl:binding>
```

The <service> Section

A service is simply a collection of <port> elements. A WSDL might contain multiple <service> definitions, one for every distinct binding type that's supported by the web service.

A <port> describes the physical locations of a binding. Listing 5-13 shows a sample web service that exists at a single SOAP address endpoint. If you are using SOAP for your web services, then there can be only a single <soap:address> entry for each port.

> ■**Note** The term *endpoint* is commonly used when discussing web services. An endpoint is simply a URI that points to a location where a service exists.

Listing 5-13. *Sample <service> and <port> Tags*

```
<wsdl:service name="CustomerService">
   <wsdl:port binding="tns:CustomerServiceSOAP" name="CustomerServiceSOAP">
      <soap:address location="http://server1:7001/customer/CustomerService" />
   </wsdl:port>
</wsdl:service>
```

That's it for the basics of WSDL. Like many technical topics, it's conceptually simple. Also, like many technical topics, "the devil is in the details." Fortunately, this technology has existed long enough for some best practices to emerge. We'll go over some of those best practices in the next section.

WSDL Best Practices

Once you begin creating your own services, the flexibility of WSDL can cause some confusion and even arguments among service designers, especially when they're brand new to services and don't have any experience to draw on. At Oracle, we have the advantage of speaking with numerous members of our Professional Services Group, who help customers design not only individual services, but entire SOAs on a daily basis. This provides us with a great source of real-world experience. In this section, we'll share the best practices that we use to help simplify designs and ensure success.

Reference Types from XML Schema Files

Some of the sample WSDLs you've seen so far used several different mechanisms to create data types. The first is to use <elements> to wrap anonymous data types. Listing 5-14 shows how this is done.

Listing 5-14. *Using an <element> to Wrap a <complexType>*

```
<xs:element name="findProduct">
    <xs:complexType>
        <xs:sequence>
            <xs:element name="id" type="xs:int"/>
            <xs:element name="name" type="xs:string"/>
            <xs:element name="family" type="xs:string"/>
        </xs:sequence>
    </xs:complexType>
</xs:element>
```

This approach provides considerable flexibility, allowing the service designer to define any data type needed by the service.

A second, closely related approach is to define separate, named <complexType> types and then create <elements> of the required type. Listing 5-15 provides a concise example of defining a complexType and then using an element to refer to it.

Listing 5-15. *Using Named Types and Elements*

```
<xs:complexType name="ProductRequestType">
    <xs:sequence>
        <xs:element name="id" type="xs:int"/>
        <xs:element name="name" type="xs:string"/>
        <xs:element name="family" type="xs:string"/>
    </xs:sequence>
</xs:complexType>
<xs:element name="findProduct" type="ProductRequestType"/>
```

This approach is an improvement over the first approach. It gives the service designer the same level of flexibility as the first approach, but now the service designer has the ability to reuse the named complexType. In large, real-world services, documents (defined by data structures) become increasingly complex, and the ability to reuse data types becomes increasingly important. This reuse also eases maintenance of the service, because if a complexType needs to change, having a separate definition of that type will make the change simpler to perform. Also, you can be sure that all the elements of that type will automatically inherit the change.

By defining a complexType by name, you gain the ability to reuse it in your document. However, this principle also operates at a higher level: the enterprise. Many data types are the property of the enterprise. If you define these data types as externally available resources, you gain the ability not only to reuse them across multiple WSDLs, but also to provide enterprise-wide standards and a control point for your SOA governance group.

Listing 5-16 shows how this is done. You create your complexTypes in one or more external XML schema files and then import them into your WSDLs for use. This approach sacrifices some flexibility for the sake of reuse, standardization, and control.

Listing 5-16. *Define Enterprise Data Types Outside Your WSDLs*

```
<schema xmlns:prd=" http://www.alsb.com/product/">
<xs:import namespace="http://www.alsb.com/product/" schemaLocation="product.xsd" />
<xs:element name="findProductRequest" type="prd:ProductRequestType"/>
</schema>
```

Ideally, you would store and publish your XML Schema documents in an enterprise service repository. However, because service repositories are relatively new, you can also simply publish the XSDs on a set of web servers to achieve some of the same benefit. The one benefit that a service repository provides over a simple web server is that a repository can cross-check any changes that you make to your XSDs with any services that import those schemas.

OSB provides you with some repository behavior out of the box. If you are using the web console when you create a WSDL file or a service that uses a specific XSD, OSB keeps track of the resulting dependencies. In fact, OSB will go so far as to give you a warning when you remove a resource that's used by existing services and resources. This protection does not extend to the WorkSpace Studio environment, because it is a traditional developer tool that does not try to protect the developer from making dramatic changes to a project.

In summary, the best practice is to define your types in separate and distinct XML Schema files and reference those types from within your WSDL files.

One thing to note, however: you must exercise moderation when importing various schemas into each other, lest you fall into the dependency trap.

Avoid the Dependency Trap

When you import a schema, you're creating a fairly tight coupling between the imported schema and the WSDL or XSD that imports it. You can create an enterprise-wide set of schemas that are all interdependent, allowing you to more easily "inherit" changes made in lower-level schemas. However, this becomes difficult to manage at scale. It's better to create clusters of related schemas and WSDLs and then use a tool such as OSB to loosely couple them via transformation.

If you examine Figure 5-1, you can see how the dependency trap can manifest itself. In the lower-right section of the figure is a legacy EJB application called ContractManager. This application was developed in-house several years ago to handle the contract management needs of the company. The IT department has service-enabled the ContractManager application by creating the ContractManagerAppService, a web service wrapper. The ContractManagerAppService is invoked via an HTTP over SOAP protocol, and is defined by the ContractManagerApp WSDL, which imports the ContractManagerAppTypes XML Schema.

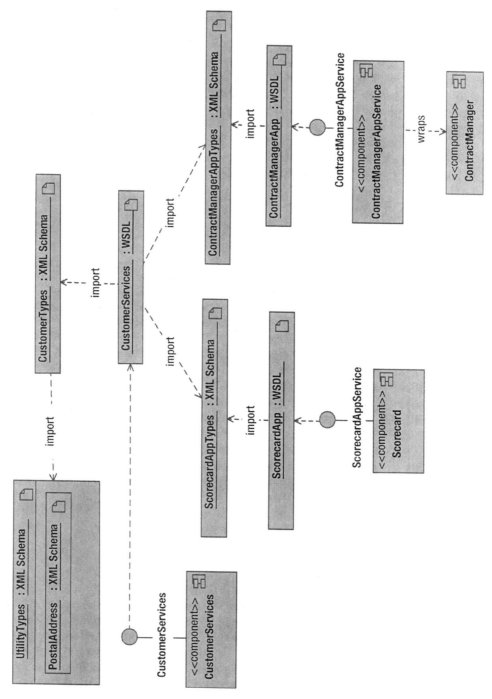

Figure 5-1. *The dependency trap in action*

To the left of the legacy ContractManager application is the Scorecard application. This application is newer, and therefore comes with a prebuilt web service interface. The Scorecard web service also follows the best practice of having the WSDL import its XML Schema types from a separate XML Schema file.

So far, everything seems to be fairly standard. There are no problems yet, simply because we're looking at only stand-alone web service implementations. At this point, the IT department has matured its SOA thinking beyond mere service enablement, and it has begun to realize the value of service aggregation. It decides to create a CustomerService component that will act as a façade for all customer-centric information. This service uses the CustomerServices WSDL as its contract, which in turn imports the CustomerTypes XML Schema file. The CustomerTypes schema also imports a UtilityTypes schema, because the architects and developers have begun to identify some utility types used across the entire organization, namely the PostalAddress type.

Also, the architects have embraced the concept of reuse, so they design the CustomerService WSDL to import the XML Schemas used by the ContractManager and the Scorecard applications. The CustomerServices web service is then coded and placed into production. Everything seems fine on the surface, but the dependency trap is now fully set and is about to be sprung!

The trap is unknowingly sprung by the business leaders of the company when they decide that their homegrown contract management application no longer meets their increasing needs. The business purchases a commercial, off the shelf (COTS) application and asks the IT department to install this new application while the company decommissions the ContractManager application. The business sees this as a simple operation: unplug the old application and plug in the new one—what could be hard about that?

Of course, the architects and developers can now see why this change of applications won't be easy. The new COTS contract management application is already web service-enabled. That means that it comes with its own WSDL and one or more XSDs that define the types specific to itself. Because the CustomerService WSDL imported the older ContractManagerAppTypes directly, it needs to be updated. Furthermore, you can bet that those types have been exposed directly to the consumers of the CustomerService web service, and now they might all need to be recompiled.

In its simplest form, the dependency trap occurs when you allow low-level implementation details, such as application-specific schemas, to bubble up through your services by directly importing them. The way you avoid this trap is through architecture: by defining specific layers of abstraction and then breaking the direct dependencies among each layer. We'll talk about layers of architecture in Chapter 12, when we introduce the concept of a "service landscape." For now, let's see how you could use OSB to defeat the dependency trap and achieve the agility you need.

Figure 5-2 shows the proper usage of OSB to avoid the dependency trap and provide an opportunity to stop the ripple effect of changing the contract application from affecting the service clients. OSB acts as a layer of abstraction between the ContractManagerAppService and the CustomerServices. Inside the service bus, you create a project that defines a proxy service, with its own WSDL and XSD. This helps to decouple the proxy service from the physical service implementation. There has also been another slight change, due to the introduction of OSB. The business service in the OSB project is dependent on the WSDL of the ContractManagerAppService, and is now only indirectly dependent on the schema objects that the ContractManagerAppService defines.

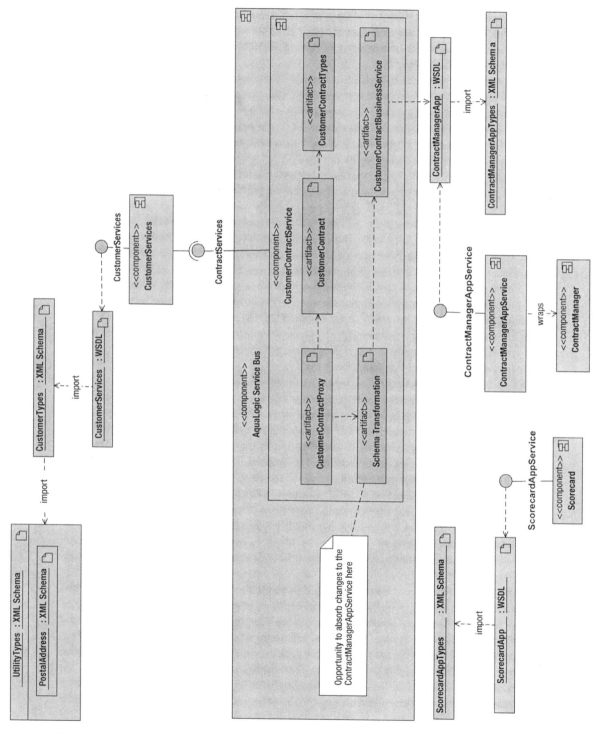

Figure 5-2. *Using OSB to disarm the dependency trap*

So how does this help us achieve the flexible, change-absorbing architecture we desire? Let's go back to our scenario and see how this affects the architects and developers who are tasked with replacing the legacy `ContractManager` application. First, they would need to update the business service definition in OSB to match that of the new COTS application. Second, they would change the message flow of the proxy service, mapping the new message and schema formats into the existing logical formats defined within the proxy service itself. There would be no need to change the `CustomerServices` component at all.

Of course, in the real world, it might be that the changes between the legacy application and the new application are so significant that the message flow of the proxy service won't be sufficient to encapsulate the entire change. However, this approach will give your systems the resilience they need to absorb the majority of system changes without affecting the service clients. When you couple this simple example with the methodology described in Chapter 12, you'll see how you can use multiple layers of abstraction to control the effects of changes within your SOA.

Figure 5-2 shows just the solution for the contract management system. A similar approach would be used to mediate between the Scorecard application and its service consumers. In fact, even the `CustomerServices` component should be abstracted from its service consumers using this same approach. In this small example, the approach may seem like overkill, but imagine the levels of coupling when you consider an entire enterprise with hundreds of software components. *Mediation is the only thing between your enterprise and a service-enabled point-to-point integration.*

Use Document-Centric, Literal Style

Although WSDL allows considerable flexibility when designing web services, emerging standards promote greater interoperability between different web service implementations. The two main approaches are often referred to as *document-centric* and Remote Procedure Call (RPC). Within each of these major approaches is the use of encoded or unencoded (also known as *literal*) data.

RPC History and Issues

RPC style was the first style in use by web service designers. In the early days of SOAP, there was a strong desire to use RPC as a vehicle for invoking remote procedures. The common thinking at that time in the evolution of our industry was to treat a network of computers as if it were one giant, virtual computer. Because the programming paradigm at the time was to make procedure calls, this thinking was carried over into the realm of distributed computing.

As a direct result of this thinking, RPC-style web services usually take multiple arguments. For example, a web service that allowed the caller to create a simple customer record and returned the ID of the new customer record might look like this:

```
createCustomer(String firstName, String lastName) : int orderID
```

At first glance, this seems simple enough and completely harmless. However, problems began to arise as service developers increased the level of abstraction employed in their web services. As the abstraction level increased, the associated data payload also increased. Imagine a service that accepts an order on behalf of a customer, such as a typical shopping cart implementation on a modern web site. A typical order carries a lot of information: customer name, billing information, lists of products and their costs, customer address information, and possible tax implications. Using an RPC approach to such a service might look like the following:

```
submitOrder(Customer customer, Address shipAddr, Address billAddr, Product[] ➥
products) : int orderID
```

As you can see, as services became more abstract and broader in scope, they had to deal with more information. That additional information added arguments to each service. In extreme cases, a dozen or more arguments would appear in the operational signature of a web service. This demanded that the service consumer understand the ordering of the arguments and whether or not it was acceptable to use null values for some arguments. Furthermore, if the service provider changed the service's operational signature to ask for an additional argument, all existing service consumers were immediately obsolete. RPC was simply too brittle an approach for use at the enterprise level.

The advantage that RPC has over the document-centric style is that the RPC WSDLs are generally easier to read. This is because there is less "wrapper" code around the arguments for each operation.

Document-Centric Style Emerges

The document-centric design approach for web services was created to address some of the problems evident in the RPC approach. The primary difference between the RPC and document-centric styles is that the document-centric approach always uses a single argument in its operational signatures, as in this example:

```
submitOrder(OrderDocument orderDoc) : int
```

This change in design might seem trivial, but it has a number of beneficial side effects. First and foremost, it makes your designs more message-oriented. Because you're passing a single argument that contains all the necessary information for the service to perform its duties, service designers will naturally begin to think more in terms of the document (read: message) that they are passing around, and less about individual service operations. A byproduct of this change in thinking is that more thought is given to the interface and less to the functional composition of the service. In turn, services become less "chatty."

We hasten to point out that creating document-centric services doesn't immunize you from bad design. It's still possible to create document-oriented services that are chatty, fine-grained, and so on. However, this design style encourages good design habits, whereas RPC style does not.

Encoded vs. Literal

Whether you use RPC or document-centric services, you have another design decision to make: whether or not to encode the data of the service calls (that is, the operational arguments) or to leave them in their literal form.

■**Note** Using the Literal or Encoded styles applies only to SOAP services.

Here, the decision is easy. The WS-I organization was created to clarify issues regarding the various web service specifications in an effort to improve the interoperability of different web service implementations (commonly referred to as *web service stacks*). WS-I compliance clearly states that encoding is never to be used. Therefore, you're left with using the literal style in your SOAP messages.

Wrapping

At this point, it's obvious that you're going to use the document-centric, literal style in your SOAP bindings. In the past, this design style wasn't sufficient to ensure maximum interoperability. An additional step, called *wrapping*, was taken in the design of WSDLs. Wrapping is the process of naming operations and their request and return values. As an example, an operation named getCustomer would accept a message, also named getCustomer, and it would return a response document named getCustomerResponse.

For a while in web services history, this was an accepted way of improving web service interoperability, especially in the Java community. However, with the advent of the WS-I mandate that the root element of the document must be unique across all operations defined in the WSDL, the use of wrapping is fading into history.

We've seen some WSDL generation tools that define a targetNamespace in several sections where you might not be accustomed to seeing them. The best fix for this problem is to manually define a single targetNamespace for a document, wherever possible.

Visualizing Documents from Schemas

At this point, you're ready to put all this information to good use. It's one thing to know how to define document structures using WSDL and XML Schema. However, it's a different skill to then visualize how instances of these XML documents will appear in the real world. Being able to look at a document definition and then know, unambiguously, how that definition will be realized as a document instance is a critical skill for your success with web services and OSB.

In this section, you'll learn by doing. We'll show you some WSDL files and XML Schemas, and then ask you to choose the correct XML document instance from a choice of several sample documents.

In our experience, most of the trouble in accurately visualizing document instances is centered around XML namespaces. Namespace errors can be subtle (as we just saw), but they fall into a small number of specific problems. We'll examine the most common namespace problems here. Also, because we're concerned with document instances, when we show the WSDL files that define the structures of the documents, we'll skip over the port and binding information because it isn't important for this discussion.

Qualified and Unqualified Elements

Visualizing a document is complicated by the use of the elementFormDefault attribute in the <schema> tag. This attribute is optional and has two possible values: qualified or unqualified. This attribute specifies whether or not the elements in the document must have their namespaces explicitly specified. The default value for this attribute is unqualified.

At this point, we're not willing to declare a best practice around the use of this attribute. Using unqualified elements give you a far more forgiving environment. It doesn't take a lot of skill to create document instances for unqualified elements, and they are usually shorter documents than their fully qualified counterparts. Of course, using fully qualified elements leads to more precise WSDLs and XSDs. We'll focus on qualified element form documents.

Our first exercise uses the schema defined in Listing 5-17 and the WSDL shown in Listing 5-18. The WSDL imports the schema.

Listing 5-17. *The common.xsd File*

```
<?xml version="1.0" encoding="UTF-8"?>
<schema xmlns="http://www.w3.org/2001/XMLSchema"
    targetNamespace="http://www.bea.com/RefArch/common/"
    xmlns:tns="http://www.bea.com/RefArch/common/
    elementFormDefault="qualified">
    <complexType name="PostalAddressType">
        <sequence>
            <!-- Unique ID for this address -->
            <element name="id" type="int" />
            <element name="streetAddress" type="string" maxOccurs="unbounded"/>
            <element name="city" type="string" />
            <element name="state" type="string" />
            <element name="postalCode" type="string" />
        </sequence>
    </complexType>
</schema>
```

Listing 5-18. *Snippet of the SimpleImport1.wsdl File*

```
<wsdl:definitions xmlns:soap="http://schemas.xmlsoap.org/wsdl/soap/"
    xmlns:tns="http://www.bea.com/simple/"
    xmlns:wsdl="http://schemas.xmlsoap.org/wsdl/"
    xmlns:xsd="http://www.w3.org/2001/XMLSchema"
    xmlns:cmn="http://www.bea.com/simple/common/"
    name="simple"
    targetNamespace="http://www.bea.com/simple/">
    <wsdl:types>
        <xsd:schema targetNamespace="http://www.bea.com/simple/"
            elementFormDefault="qualified">
            <xsd:import namespace="http://www.bea.com/simple/common/" ➥
schemaLocation="common.xsd" />
            <xsd:element name="FindAddressResponse">
                <xsd:complexType>
                    <xsd:sequence>
                        <xsd:element name="address" type="cmn:PostalAddressType" ➥
minOccurs="0" maxOccurs="unbounded" />
                    </xsd:sequence>
                </xsd:complexType>
            </xsd:element>
```

```
        <xsd:element name="FindAddress" type="xsd:string" />
    </xsd:schema>
</wsdl:types>
<!-- Messages -->
<wsdl:message name="FindAddressResponse">
    <wsdl:part element="tns:FindAddressResponse" name="FindAddressResponse" />
</wsdl:message>
<wsdl:message name="FindAddress">
    <wsdl:part element="tns:FindAddress" name="FindAddress" />
</wsdl:message>
```

Each <message> in a WSDL file is an XML document. Take a look at the FindAddress message in the WSDL (see Listing 5-18). Which of the following XML documents conforms to the message format defined by the WSDL?

```
<sim:FindAddress xmlns:sim="http://www.bea.com/simple/">Harold</sim:FindAddress>
```

or

```
<FindAddress>Lucy</FindAddress>
```

or

```
<FindAddress><String>Lucy</String></FindAddress>
```

The answer is the first example. It defines and uses the same namespace that's defined in the WSDL file. The namespace prefix is changed to sim, but that's just a prefix and is perfectly acceptable. As you learned earlier in this chapter, the namespace is defined by the literal string, not by the prefix name.

The second example could be correct if the following line appeared near the top of the document:

```
xmlns="http://www.bea.com/simple/"
```

This code line simply defines the default namespace to be the same namespace needed by the <FindAddress> element.

Let's try a slightly more ambitious example. Looking at Listings 5-18 and 5-19 again, select the correct instance of the FindAddressResponse document.

```
<sim:FindAddressResponse xmlns:sim="http://www.bea.com/simple/">
    <cmn:address xmlns:cmn="http://www.bea.com/simple/common/">
        <cmn:id>279</cmn:id>
        <cmn:streetAddress>100 Main Street</cmn:streetAddress>
        <cmn:city>San Jose</cmn:city>
        <cmn:state>CA</cmn:state>
        <cmn:postalCode>95131</cmn:postalCode>
    </cmn:address>
</sim:FindAddressResponse>
```

or

```
<sim:FindAddressResponse xmlns:sim="http://www.bea.com/simple/">
   <sim:address xmlns:cmn="http://www.bea.com/simple/common/">
      <cmn:id>279</cmn:id>
      <cmn:streetAddress>100 Main Street</cmn:streetAddress>
      <cmn:city>San Jose</cmn:city>
      <cmn:state>CA</cmn:state>
      <cmn:postalCode>95131</cmn:postalCode>
   </sim:address>
</sim:FindAddressResponse>
```

or

```
<sim:FindAddressResponse xmlns:sim="http://www.bea.com/simple/">
   <sim:address xmlns:cmn="http://www.bea.com/simple/common/">
      <sim:id>279</ sim:id>
      < sim:streetAddress>100 Main Street</ sim:streetAddress>
      < sim:city>San Jose</ sim:city>
      < sim:state>CA</ sim:state>
      < sim:postalCode>95131</ sim:postalCode>
   </sim:address>
</sim:FindAddressResponse>
```

The correct example is the second one. The point of confusion usually centers on the
<address> element. The <address> element is defined in the WSDL under the targetNamespace
http://www.bea.com/simple/. However, it represents the PostalAddressType defined in the XML
Schema file under the http://www.bea.com/simple/common/ namespace. The rule is to always
use the namespace in which the element is defined, not the type. Therefore, your <address>
element must use the http://www.bea.com/simple/ namespace.

The second common area of confusion has to do with the elements defined in the
PostalAddressType. By applying the rule that you always use the namespace in which the
<element> was defined, you can easily determine that the <id>, <streetAddress>, and other
elements in the PostalAddressType were defined in the http://www.bea.com/simple/common/
namespace. Therefore, you must declare those elements to be in that same namespace when
used in a document instance.

If you examine the WSDL, you'll see that the <address> type is defined as an element in
the WSDL under the targetNamespace http://www.bea.com/simple/. However, the elements
contained by the PostalAddressType are defined under the http://www.bea.com/simple/common/
namespace in the common.xsd file. As a result, all the elements that appear inside the <address>
element must have the cmn: namespace prefix.

Just for completeness, Listing 5-19 shows a version of the FindAddressResponse document
that uses unqualified elements.

Listing 5-19. *Sample Unqualified Document Instance*

```
<sim:FindAddressResponse xmlns:sim="http://www.bea.com/simple/">
   <address xmlns="http://www.bea.com/simple/common/">
      <id>279</id>
      <streetAddress>100 Main Street</streetAddress>
      <city>San Jose</city>
```

```
      <state>CA</state>
      <postalCode>95131</postalCode>
  </address>
</sim:FindAddressResponse>
```

Notice that only the outermost element in Listing 5-19 has a namespace declared. The `<address>` element declares a default namespace that is then inherited by its child elements. The real choice between the qualified and unqualified approaches is whether you want strongly typed documents or loosely typed documents. That's a choice you'll need to make for yourself.

Qualified and Unqualified Attributes

Attributes, like elements, also exist within namespaces. The `attributeFormDefault` attribute is defined in the `<schema>` tag and can have a value of "qualified" or "unqualified". The default value for the `attributeFormDefault` is "unqualified". This attribute value is *not* overridden when its schema is included into a new schema. Listing 5-20 shows a schema that defines the `InnerType` complex type using a qualified attribute namespace. The important lines of the XML Schema have been highlighted in bold.

Listing 5-20. *XML Schema That Defines an Attribute in a Namespace*

```
<?xml version="1.0" encoding="UTF-8"?>
<schema xmlns="http://www.w3.org/2001/XMLSchema"
targetNamespace="http://www.example.org/inner/"
xmlns:tns="http://www.example.org/inner/"
attributeFormDefault="qualified">
    <complexType name="InnerType" mixed="false">
        <sequence>
            <element name="quantity" type="int" />
        </sequence>
        <attribute name="foo" type="string" />
    </complexType>
</schema>
```

Listing 5-21 shows a portion of a WSDL that imports the schema object and uses it in an element. Note that the `attributeFormDefault` in the `<schema>` section of the WSDL is set to unqualified.

Listing 5-21. *Snippet of a WSDL File That Imports the XML Schema*

```
<wsdl:definitions xmlns:soap="http://schemas.xmlsoap.org/wsdl/soap/"
    xmlns:tns="http://www.bea.com/innere/"
    xmlns:wsdl="http://schemas.xmlsoap.org/wsdl/"
    xmlns:xsd="http://www.w3.org/2001/XMLSchema" name="inner"
    xmlns:inner="http://www.example.org/inner/"
    targetNamespace="http://www.bea.com/inner/">
    <wsdl:types>
```

```
    <xsd:schema attributeFormDefault="unqualified"
        targetNamespace="http://www.bea.com/inner/">

        <xsd:import namespace="http://www.example.org/inner/" ➥
schemaLocation="inner.xsd" />

        <xsd:element name="GetInner" type="inner:InnerType" />
        <xsd:element name="GetInnerResponse" type="inner:InnerType" />
    </xsd:schema>
  </wsdl:types>
```

In Listing 5-22, you can see a sample XML document that uses the WSDL from Listing 5-21. Even though the WSDL states that the `attributeFormDefault` is set to `unqualified`, it doesn't override the `"qualified"` declaration in the XML Schema file. Therefore, any reference to the attribute must be qualified by a namespace.

Listing 5-22. *Sample XML Document Showing the Use of a Qualified Attribute*

```
<inn1:GetInner inn:foo="string" xmlns:inn="http://www.example.org/inner/" ➥
xmlns:inn1="http://www.bea.com/inner/">
    <quantity>3</quantity>
</inn1:GetInner>
```

The `elementFormDefault` and `attributeFormDefault` attributes give you a lot of control over when and where namespaces are used. Once again, we aren't prepared to define any best practices around the use of the `attributeFormDefault` attribute. However, declaring all your attributes to be qualified can certainly complicate your XML documents. This additional complexity then increases the complexity of the XML document transformations in your message flows. Therefore, we discourage the use of qualified attribute names unless you see a clear benefit in your specific project or enterprise.

Summary

In this chapter, we haven't gone into detail with samples of document-centric, literal WSDLs, simply because that's the only style used in this book. Instead, we focused on why this is the best approach for creating modern, highly interoperable web services. We also examined the details of a WSDL file, and provided you with a number of best practices on how to create your own WSDLs. Perhaps most important, we've also shown you how to take a WSDL and visualize exactly how the various messages of that WSDL would appear in the form of XML documents.

Now that you've completed this chapter, the WSDLs and XML Schemas that you'll see in the rest of the book should make perfect sense to you. The way is now cleared for you to gain a real expertise with OSB.

CHAPTER 6

■ ■ ■

Intermediate Message Flows

In this chapter, you'll work though a couple of fun and interesting projects to help you get accustomed to creating message flows. Before long, you'll intuitively understand when to use each type of message flow node and exactly how to get the maximum benefit.

We'll design for two use-case scenarios. The first use case will return a product catalog to the caller. The contents of the product catalog will contain only products the customer is qualified to buy, based on the customer's credit rating. The second use case allows the customer to submit an order. The order will be processed differently depending on the customer's credit rating.

In the course of addressing these use cases, we'll also demonstrate some more core principles of SOA: service orchestration (calling services either in a specific order or based on dynamic information carried by the initiating message) and service aggregation (creating a façade over lower-level services to hide their interaction details).

Scenario 1: User Requests a Product Catalog

In the first use case, the user wants to contact a service and get a customized product catalog. The service first gets the credit score for the customer, and then builds a catalog of products that are appropriate for the customer's credit score. For this scenario, you need to create two new operations:

getCreditRating(): This operation takes the customer's first name and last name and returns the credit score. Obviously, credit scores aren't determined this way in the real world, but the implementation isn't important here, so we'll keep things as simple as possible.

getProductCatalog(): This operation takes a credit rating as the argument and returns a list of products that the customer can order.

Both these service implementations are included in the WSDL file you'll create for this project, which is shown in Listing 6-1.

■Note You can find the completed code for this project in the `BasicOrderMgr_WS` project, which is included with the rest of the downloadable code for this book in the Source Code/Download section of the Apress web site (`http://www.apress.com`). Compile this code and deploy it to your WebLogic Server by building the project in WorkSpace Studio. Be sure to assign the `BasicOrderMgr_WS` project to the service bus server that you created.

Listing 6-1. *The BasicOrderMgr.wsdl for the BasicOrderMgr_WS Project*

```
<?xml version='1.0' encoding='UTF-8'?>
<definitions name="BasicOrderMgrDefinitions"
   targetNamespace="http://www.alsb.com/"
   xmlns="http://schemas.xmlsoap.org/wsdl/"
   xmlns:alsb="http://www.alsb.com/"
   xmlns:soap="http://schemas.xmlsoap.org/wsdl/soap/">
   <types>
      <xs:schema attributeFormDefault="unqualified"
         elementFormDefault="qualified" targetNamespace="http://www.alsb.com/"
         xmlns:order="http://www.alsb.com/order/"
         xmlns:xs="http://www.w3.org/2001/XMLSchema">

         <xs:import namespace="http://www.alsb.com/order/" ➥
schemaLocation="./order.xsd" />
         <!-- TIP: Start your element names off lowercase. This will
              more closely match the Java naming conventions when you
              generate the code
         -->
         <xs:element name="getCreditRating">
            <xs:complexType>
               <xs:sequence>
                  <xs:element name="firstName" type="xs:string" />
                  <xs:element name="lastName" type="xs:string" />
               </xs:sequence>
            </xs:complexType>
         </xs:element>

         <xs:element name="getCreditRatingResponse">
            <xs:complexType>
               <xs:sequence>
                  <xs:element name="return" type="xs:int" />
               </xs:sequence>
            </xs:complexType>
         </xs:element>
```

```xml
    <xs:element name="getProductCatalog">
        <xs:complexType>
            <xs:sequence>
                <xs:element name="creditRating" type="xs:int" />
            </xs:sequence>
        </xs:complexType>
    </xs:element>

    <xs:element name="getProductCatalogResponse">
        <xs:complexType>
            <xs:sequence>
                <xs:element name="productList"
                    type="order:ProductList" />
            </xs:sequence>
        </xs:complexType>
    </xs:element>

    <xs:element name="processOrder">
        <xs:complexType>
            <xs:sequence>
                <xs:element name="order" type="order:Order" />
            </xs:sequence>
        </xs:complexType>
    </xs:element>

    <xs:element name="processPreferredOrder">
        <xs:complexType>
            <xs:sequence>
                <xs:element name="order" type="order:Order" />
            </xs:sequence>
        </xs:complexType>
    </xs:element>
    </xs:schema>
</types>

<message name="getCreditRating">
    <part element="alsb:getCreditRating" name="getCreditRating" />
</message>

<message name="getCreditRatingResponse">
    <part element="alsb:getCreditRatingResponse"
        name="getCreditRatingResponse" />
</message>

<message name="getProductCatalog">
    <part element="alsb:getProductCatalog" name="getProductCatalog" />
</message>
```

```xml
    <message name="getProductCatalogResponse">
        <part element="alsb:getProductCatalogResponse" ➥
name="getProductCatalogResponse" />
    </message>

    <message name="processOrder">
        <part element="alsb:processOrder" name="processOrder" />
    </message>

    <message name="processPreferredOrder">
        <part element="alsb:processPreferredOrder"
            name="processPreferredOrder" />
    </message>

    <portType name="BasicOrderMgrPort">
        <operation name="getCreditRating"
            parameterOrder="getCreditRating">
            <input message="alsb:getCreditRating" />
            <output message="alsb:getCreditRatingResponse" />
        </operation>
        <operation name="getProductCatalog"
            parameterOrder="getProductCatalog">
            <input message="alsb:getProductCatalog" />
            <output message="alsb:getProductCatalogResponse" />
        </operation>
        <operation name="processOrder" parameterOrder="processOrder">
            <input message="alsb:processOrder" />
        </operation>
        <operation name="processPreferredOrder"
            parameterOrder="processPreferredOrder">
            <input message="alsb:processPreferredOrder" />
        </operation>
    </portType>
    <binding name="BasicOrderMgrServiceSoapBinding"
        type="alsb:BasicOrderMgrPort">
        <soap:binding style="document"
            transport="http://schemas.xmlsoap.org/soap/http" />
        <operation name="processPreferredOrder">
            <soap:operation soapAction="" style="document" />
            <input>
                <soap:body parts="processPreferredOrder" use="literal" />
            </input>
        </operation>
        <operation name="getCreditRating">
            <soap:operation soapAction="" style="document" />
            <input>
                <soap:body parts="getCreditRating" use="literal" />
```

```
        </input>
        <output>
            <soap:body parts="getCreditRatingResponse" use="literal" />
        </output>
    </operation>
    <operation name="getProductCatalog">
        <soap:operation soapAction="" style="document" />
        <input>
            <soap:body parts="getProductCatalog" use="literal" />
        </input>
        <output>
            <soap:body parts="getProductCatalogResponse" use="literal" />
        </output>
    </operation>
    <operation name="processOrder">
        <soap:operation soapAction="" style="document" />
        <input>
            <soap:body parts="processOrder" use="literal" />
        </input>
    </operation>
  </binding>
  <service name="BasicOrderMgrService">
      <port binding="alsb:BasicOrderMgrServiceSoapBinding"
          name="BasicOrderMgrSoapPort">
          <soap:address location= ➡
"http://localhost:7001/business/basicOrderMgr/BasicOrderMgrService" />
      </port>
  </service>
</definitions>
```

Creating the Basic Order Manager Web Service

Here is the procedure for creating the web service for this project:

1. In WorkSpace Studio, create a new Web Service project (by selecting it from the Web Services folder of WorkSpace Studio's New Project wizard). Name the project BasicOrderMgr_WS. Set the context root to business/basicOrderMgr. Accept the default values for the rest of the wizard.

2. In the src folder of the project, create a package called com.alsb.www.

3. Create a folder in the root directory of the project and name the folder WSDL. In this folder, you can either copy in the BasicOrderMgr.wsdl and order.xsd files from the sample BasicOrderMgr_WS project that accompanies this book, or you can undergo the painstaking process of creating the WSDL file from scratch. If you do opt to create the WSDL file yourself (using Listing 6-1 as your guide), we recommend that you try to do most of the work using the WSDL editor that comes with WorkSpace Studio. It allows you to view the WSDL in a graphical format and a text format, depending on your needs.

■**Note** Although you've generated your web service (and its WSDL) from Java code in the past, this is not a best practice. When dealing with web services, the contract (that is, the WSDL) is of highest importance. The code that implements the contract defined in the WSDL is incidental. By defining the WSDL first, you can plan your architecture up front, without needing to wait for the code to be created. It allows your company to focus on what's most important (the contract), and defer the details (the code) until implementation time.

---

4. Right-click the `BasicOrderMgr.wsdl` file in the `WSDL` folder and select Web Services ➤ Generate Web Service from the pop-up menu. The Source folder field should default to `BasicOrderMgr_WS/src`. For the Package field, enter (or browse to) the value `com.alsb.www`.

5. Click the Finish button. When the wizard finishes, a file named `BasicOrderMgrPortImpl.java` is generated in the `com.alsb.www` package in the `src/` folder.

Because your WSDL is document-oriented, your generated source code is also document-oriented. Instead of passing multiple arguments into each method, only a single argument appears in each method signature. Listing 6-2 illustrates what we mean by "document-oriented source code."

Listing 6-2. *The Complete BasicOrderMgrPortImpl Class File*

```java
package com.alsb.www;
import java.util.Vector;
import javax.jws.WebService;
import com.alsb.order.Product;
import com.alsb.order.ProductList;
import weblogic.jws.*;


/**
 * BasicOrderMgrPortImpl class implements web service endpoint interface
 * BasicOrderMgrPort
 */

@WebService(serviceName = "BasicOrderMgrService", targetNamespace = ➥
"http://www.alsb.com/", endpointInterface = "com.alsb.www.BasicOrderMgrPort")
@WLHttpTransport(serviceUri = "BasicOrderMgrService", portName = ➥
"BasicOrderMgrSoapPort")
public class BasicOrderMgrPortImpl implements BasicOrderMgrPort {

    private static Product[] productCatalog = { new Product(),
        new Product(), new Product(), new Product() };

    public BasicOrderMgrPortImpl() {
        productCatalog[0].setName("Television");
        productCatalog[0].setCreditNeeded(610);
        productCatalog[1].setName("Microwave");
        productCatalog[1].setCreditNeeded(500);
```

```java
    productCatalog[2].setName("Automobile");
    productCatalog[2].setCreditNeeded(710);
    productCatalog[3].setName("Paper Hat");
    productCatalog[3].setCreditNeeded(440);
}

public int getCreditRating(java.lang.String firstName,
        java.lang.String lastName)
{
    int rating;
    if (lastName.compareToIgnoreCase("X") > 0) {
        // If the last name starts with an X or later in the alphabet
        // the person has a bad credit rating.
        rating = 200;
    } else if (lastName.compareToIgnoreCase("S") > 0) {
        // Names starting with S or later have a poor credit rating
        rating = 600;
    } else {
        // Everyone else has a great credit rating
        rating = 750;
    }
    System.out.println("Business: The credit rating for " + firstName + " "
            + lastName + " is " + rating);
    return rating;
}

public com.alsb.order.ProductList getProductCatalog(int creditRating)
{
    // Iterate over the product catalog and return the products that the
    // customer can purchase
    ProductList productList = new ProductList();
    Vector<Product> customerCatalog = new Vector<Product>();

    for (int x = 0; x < productCatalog.length; x++) {
        if (productCatalog[x].getCreditNeeded() <= creditRating) {
            // Add this product to the list because the customer can buy it
            customerCatalog.add(productCatalog[x]);
        }
    }

    Product[] customerProducts = new Product[customerCatalog.size()];
    customerCatalog.copyInto(customerProducts);
    productList.setProduct(customerProducts);
    return productList;
}

public void processOrder(com.alsb.order.Order order)
```

```
    {
        System.out.println("Received a regular order from "
            + order.getFirstName() + " " + order.getLastName()
            + " for product "
            + order.getLineItem()[0].getProduct().getName()
            + " in quantity of " + order.getLineItem()[0].getQuantity());
        return;
    }

    public void processPreferredOrder(com.alsb.order.Order order)
    {
        System.out.println("Received a PREFERRED order from "
            + order.getFirstName() + " " + order.getLastName()
            + " for product "
            + order.getLineItem()[0].getProduct().getName()
            + " in quantity of " + order.getLineItem()[0].getQuantity());
        return;
    }
}
```

Of course, the generated source file won't contain any method implementations. You need to add them yourself. Compile and deploy the BasicOrderMgr_WS web service to WebLogic Server. You've successfully created your web service.

Creating the Basic Order Manager Business Service

Now we get to the heart of the matter. You need to create a new project in OSB that uses the web service you just created. You will create a business service that represents the BasicOrderMgr_WS web service and a proxy service that will aggregate the two business service operations, hiding them from the user. This pattern of hiding underlying complexity is called the Façade pattern. In SOA, it's more commonly known as *service mediation*: using one service to hide the complexity and interrelationships of lower-level services.

■**Note** This exercise demonstrates the best practice for separating the data types used by a WSDL into an XML Schema document. This enhances the ability to reuse fundamental data types. If you were to define these types (such as the Order type) within the WSDL itself, you would be forced to redefine these types if you ever needed to use them in a different WSDL. This is akin to copying and pasting code, and should be avoided whenever possible.

Creating the Business Service

Let's get started. You will create a new project for the business service, copy the WSDL files from the BasicOrderMgr_WS project, and then create the BasicOrderMgrBiz business service based on the BasicOrderMgr.wsdl file.

1. Create a new project in OSB. Name the new project BasicOrderMgr_SB.

2. Create a new folder in the project called WSDL.

3. Open the WSDL folder. Copy and paste the BasicOrderMgr.wsdl and order.xsd files from the BasicOrderMgr_WS project.

4. Right-click the BasicOrderMgr_SB project in the Project Explorer window of WorkSpace Studio and select New ➤ Business Service from the pop-up menu. As you move through the Create a Business Service wizard in WorkSpace Studio, be sure to base the web service on the BasicOrderMgr.wsdl (you'll need to select either the port or the binding during this step).

5. Click the Next button and examine the endpoint URI of the service, as shown in Figure 6-1. If you see that the URI includes a specific IP address, you might wish to change the URI to use the alias *localhost* instead of the physical IP address. This is especially important if your computer is occasionally connected to a virtual private network (VPN), because that might change your physical IP address and make your web service unavailable.

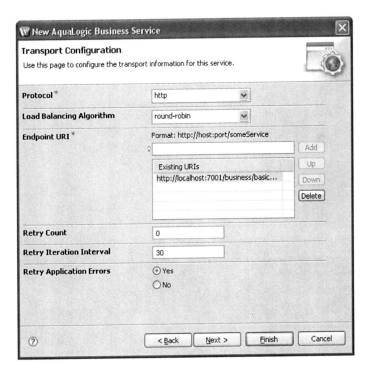

Figure 6-1. *It's best to replace literal IP addresses with DNS names or "localhost" for the examples in this book.*

6. Click the Finish button to accept the default values for your business service.

CONSUMING SERVICES

So far, we have been copying and pasting WSDL files in our project. This is not a bad practice, but there are other ways to get information about external (to OSB) services loaded into WorkSpace Studio. OSB provides a way to consume service information from URIs, UDDI registries, file systems, a WorkSpace Studio workspace, and enterprise repositories. To consume a service from one of these sources, in WorkSpace Studio, first define the service as being based on a WSDL. Then click the Browse button next to the WSDL Web Service radio button. This will bring up the standard Select a WSDL dialog box.

If you click the Consume button in the Select a WSDL dialog box, the Service Consumption dialog box will appear. Here, you can specify the service resource type and location.

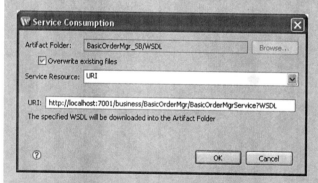

Consuming a service in this manner really just copies the service resource information (a WSDL file in this case) into the selected artifact folder. Whether you copy the file manually or use the Service Consumption dialog box of WorkSpace Studio is really just a matter of personal preference.

Creating the Proxy Service

Now we get to the new and fun part of the exercise. You'll create a proxy service that will take a customer name and return a list of products that the customer can purchase. Previously, your proxy services simply published the WSDL file of the business service it represented (as in the Hello World example in Chapter 3). However, in this case, you have no such luxury. You need a new WSDL file that represents your aggregate service.

Now, we find that creating a WSDL file by hand is about as much fun as hand-coding EJB deployment descriptors (that is to say, no fun at all). Fortunately for us, we can quickly put a WSDL file together based on the two operations we're aggregating (getCreditRating and getProductCatalog).

1. Create a file called BasicOrderMgrProxy.wsdl that defines the proxy service. Place this new WSDL file in the WSDL folder of the project. This proxy service has two operations: getProducts(CustomerName): ProductList and submitOrder(Order). The truly bold can create this WSDL file. If you would prefer to skip that exercise, just copy the BasicOrderMgrProxy.wsdl file you downloaded for the sample project (from the Source Code/Download section of http:www.apress.com).

2. In the root directory of your project, create a new proxy service resource named BasicOrderMgr. Base the service type on the BasicOrderMgrProxy.wsdl resource that you just created. Be sure to specify the endpoint URI as /BasicOrderMgr _SB/BasicOrderMgr. Click the Finish button to save the new proxy service.

So far, so good. You have created a proxy service that uses the WSDL you need for the service. Your next step is to "hook up" the proxy service so that it calls the supporting business services.

Designing the Proxy Service Message Flow

Click the Message Flow tab for the proxy service. You'll see that the current message flow for your proxy service contains only a Start node. You want to use a Pipeline Pair node for this message flow, because it naturally breaks its work processing down into a series of stages. You'll use a stage for the call to the getCreditRating() business service and a second stage for the getProductCatalog() business service.

Now, you could do all this work in a single Route node, but that would be a poor design decision, similar in nature to taking multiple methods in your Java code and making them just one big method. You can do it, but it's not very modular. Modularity of design is important, even within a message flow.

Adding a Pipeline Pair Node

Here's the procedure for adding the Pipeline Pair node to the proxy service message flow:

1. In the Message Flow window, click and drag the Pipeline Pair icon from the Design Palette window and drop it on the line directly underneath the BasicOrderMgr Start node. (The Design Palette window is on the far right side of the WorkSpace Studio interface, and the Pipeline Pair icon is located in the Nodes folder of the OSB Message Flow category.) Your message flow should look like the one in Figure 6-2.

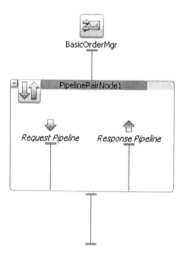

Figure 6-2. *An empty Pipeline Pair*

2. Add the first stage beneath the Request Pipeline icon (on the left, with the green arrow pointing down). There are a couple of ways you can do this. You can drag and drop the Stage icon from the Design Palette window (within the Nodes folder of the OSB Message Flow category). Alternatively, you can right-click the Request Pipeline icon in the message flow and select Insert Into ➤ Stage from the pop-up menu.

3. Click the newly created stage to select it, and then click the Properties tab.

4. In the Properties window, select the nested Stage tab. You will see the Name and Description properties. Set the Name property to assign variables. You can leave the Description property blank.

■**Tip** Give your stages meaningful names. It will help when you need to make changes in the future!

---

5. You now need to edit the request pipeline's assign variables stage to retrieve the firstName and lastName parameters that were passed into your proxy service, and store them in local variables. You do this because later on, when you use the Service Callout actions, those actions cannot use XPath expressions. A Service Callout action expects to see local variables only. Right-click the assign variables stage and select Insert Into ➤ Message Processing ➤ Assign to add the first of two Assign actions within this stage.

6. Click the new Assign action. In the Properties window, set the Variable property to firstName.

7. As in Chapter 4's example, rather than typing an expression directly into the Properties window, risking errors, it's much safer to use the XQuery/XSLT Expression Editor to build the expression. Click the Expression link in the Properties window to open the Expression Editor.

8. In the Variable Structures tab on the right side of the Expression Editor, open the body item (because the data you're looking for is carried in the body of the SOAP message) and drill down to the `body/$body - getProducts (request)/CustomerName/firstName` element. Drag and drop the `firstName` element into the text area of the Expression tab on the left side of the Expression Editor. Because you want only the actual text from the `firstName` node, you need to append the `/text()` command to the end of the expression, so it reads as follows, as shown in Figure 6-3. Then click OK.

```
$body/alsb:CustomerName/alsb:firstName/text()
```

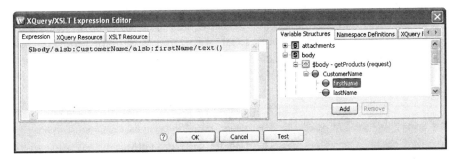

Figure 6-3. *Using the Expression Editor to add the firstName expression*

9. Right-click the `assign variables` stage and select Insert Into ➤ Message Processing ➤ Assign to add the second Assign action immediately after the first.

10. In the Properties window, set the Variable property to `lastName`.

11. Repeat the procedure outlined in steps 7 and 8 to assign the following expression to the `lastName` variable. Be sure to append the `/text()` method to the Assign action for the `lastName` variable also.

```
$body/alsb:CustomerName/alsb:lastName/text()
```

12. Click the `assign variables` stage and select Insert After ➤ Stage from the pop-up menu. Set the name of the node to `get credit rating`.

13. Now it's time to hook up this stage to make the call to the `getCreditRating()` operation of the business service. Using the techniques you've learned so far, insert an Assign action into the `get credit rating` stage. Set the variable name to `soapRequestBody`. Set the expression of the Assign action to the code shown in Listing 6-3. You can see in Listing 6-3 that you are creating a SOAP request document and inserting the `firstName` and `lastName` variables into the request document.

Listing 6-3. *Creating the SOAP Body for the getCreditRating Request*

```
<soap:Body xmlns:soap="http://schemas.xmlsoap.org/soap/envelope/">
<alsb:getCreditRating xmlns:alsb="http://www.alsb.com/">
    <alsb:firstName>{$firstName}</alsb:firstName>
    <alsb:lastName>{$lastName}</alsb:lastName>
</alsb:getCreditRating>
</soap:Body>
```

14. To add the Service Callout action, click the existing Assign action and select Insert
    After ➤ Communication ➤ Service Callout from the pop-up menu. The Service Callout
    action allows you to make a call to an existing service.

15. In the Properties window for the Service Callout action, click the Browse button to
    select the service you are going to call. Choose the BasicOrderMgr.biz service, and
    then click the OK button. Select the getCreditRating() operation from the Invoking
    property's combo box. Select the Configure Soap Body radio button and enter the
    value soapRequestBody for the Request Body property. Similarly, enter the value of
    soapResponseBody for the Response Body property. Your Service Callout Properties
    window should look like Figure 6-4.

> ■**Note** If you chose the Configure Payload Document option instead of the Configure Soap Body option, you
> do not need to construct the <soap:Body> element. You can instead pass in the arguments directly. Since
> we are using document-centric SOAP messages, there is only one parameter in this example. However, if
> you are using RPC style web services, the Configure Payload Document option is often easier to use.

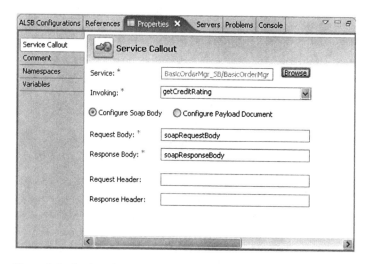

Figure 6-4. *Setting the properties for calling the getCreditRating service*

16. After the Service Callout action, add an Assign action that retrieves the customer's credit rating. Give this Assign action to the Variable property `creditRating` and assign the expression `$soapResponseBody/getCreditRatingResponse/alsb:return/text()`.

Note If you get an error in the Expression Editor complaining that the static `alsb` namespace is not recognized, you can just click the Namespace Definitions tab in the Expression Editor and add the `alsb` prefix with a URI of `http://www.alsb.com/`.

Adding a Route Node

As you learned in Chapter 4, a Pipeline Pair can have at most one node following it. What we didn't point out is that if the Pipeline Pair doesn't have a node following it, then OSB will create an "echo" response for you. This response will just echo the SOAP request back to the caller, which is definitely not what you want here. For this reason, you must add a Route node after the Pipeline Pair node. It's in the Route node that you'll make your call to the `getProductCatalog` operation of the business service.

1. To add a Route node, click the Pipeline Pair node (near the top of the node, not down in the area that shows the stages) and select Insert After ➤ Route. Rename the Route node to `get product catalog`.

2. Right-click the new Route node and select Insert Into ➤ Communication ➤ Routing. This will create the Route action.

3. Select the Route action, and in the Properties window, select the `BasicOrderMgr.biz` business service. Select the `getProductCatalog` operation from the Invoking combo box.

Now things get a little murky here, so we'll take a moment to shed some light on what is happening. By default, all a Route node does is route the request message to a service. In this case, the body of the request message is what the node will route to the `getProductCatalog` operation. However, the body of the original request message to your proxy service isn't what the service is expecting to see, as shown in Figure 6-5.

Figure 6-5. *The request $body of the proxy service*

You know that the `getProductCatalog` operation couldn't care less about receiving the `firstName` and `lastName` arguments. It demands that you send it the customer's credit rating. As a result, you must transform the request to match the format expected by the `getProductCatalog` operation. To perform this transformation, you'll use the Replace action. You need to replace the contents of the `getProductCatalog` element (that is, the `firstName` and `lastName` nodes) with the credit rating.

You need to transform the contents of the request message from this:

```
<alsb:getProducts xmlns:alsb="http://www.alsb.com/">
    <alsb:firstName>John</alsb:firstName>
    <alsb:lastName>Doe</alsb:lastName>
</alsb:getProducts>
```

to this:

```
<alsb:getProductCatalog xmlns:alsb="http://www.alsb.com/">
    <alsb:creditRating>600</alsb:creditRating>
</alsb:getProductCatalog>
```

So, let's continue.

4. Right-click the Request action of the Route node and select Insert ➤ Message Processing ➤ Replace to create the Replace action.

5. Click the <XPath> link. In the Properties window, enter the XPath expression ./*. Set the Variable property to body (no $). This XPath notation means "all children relative to the current (body) node." You need to replace everything in the SOAP body element, represented by the $body variable. Click the Expression link to enter the expression that will replace the contents of the $body variable. The expression you'll use is shown in Listing 6-4. As you can see, you manually construct the XML structure that you want to send to the business service. Most of this is static XML. The curly braces are escape characters, used to denote the section in which dynamic XQuery can be found.

Listing 6-4. *The Expression for the Replace Action in the Route Node*

```
<alsb:getProductCatalog xmlns:alsb="http://www.alsb.com/">
    <alsb:creditRating>{$creditRating}</alsb:creditRating>
</alsb:getProductCatalog>
```

6. Select the "Replace entire node" radio button. Your Replace action Properties window should look like Figure 6-6.

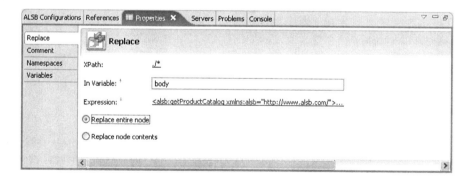

Figure 6-6. *Defining the message body for retrieving the product list*

Because the return message format of the getProductCatalog service matches exactly the format of your proxy service, you allow the return message from the Route node to flow through the Pipeline Pair node without any transformation. Or, to put it more plainly, you're finished with this message flow; no more work is necessary. Your message flow should now look like Figure 6-7.

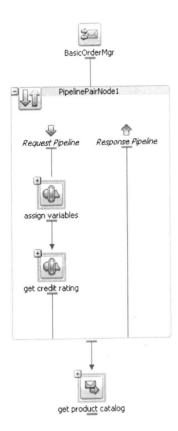

Figure 6-7. *Message flow after stage 2*

That completes the creation of the proxy service. Save all your work and publish the project to the server.

Testing the Scenario 1 Service

Let's test the new web service to ensure that everything is running as expected. Using the OSB web console, navigate to the proxy service in the BasicOrderMgr_SB project and click the testing icon. Enter the name **Bob Aaron** and click the Execute button. You should see the name you entered in the request document section, and you should see a list of four products in the response document section of the page.

Try it again with the name **Tom Zanka**, and you should see that no products show up in the response document. The getCreditRating operation returns the credit rating based on the last name of the customer (our apologies to those of you with last names in the second half of the alphabet), and then the getProductCatalog operation in the business service makes a decision about which products the customer can order.

What if you wanted to make a decision in your proxy service instead of in a business service? For example, suppose that when a customer with good credit orders from you, you want to process that order ahead of the orders from other customers. You would also like to place this decision logic in your proxy service so that you might be able to change it quickly, if necessary. This brings us to our second scenario.

Scenario 2: User Orders a Product

In this scenario, the customer submits an order to your submitOrder operation in your proxy service. The proxy service invokes the getCreditRating operation in the business service. It then checks the credit rating of the customer, and if the customer's credit rating is high enough, it will route the order to the processPreferredOrder operation in the business service. Otherwise, the order will be routed to the processOrder operation in the business service. This routing decision is performed in a Branch node.

■**Tip** Place business decisions into proxy services instead of compiled code. Doing so allows you to change business logic without recompiling any code. This increases your IT and business agility.

The bulk of the infrastructure that you need for this exercise has already been created in the previous sections. However, instead of adding a new proxy service, you are going to extend your existing proxy service to include the submitOrder operation. It is possible to create a new proxy service based on the same WSDL file that was used for the first scenario, but it's more logical to have a single proxy service implement all operations defined in a WSDL file.

Adding Decision Logic

Let's begin by inserting an operational Branch node just after the Start node of the BasicOrderMgr message flow. You may want to collapse the existing Pipeline Pair node first, since you are finished with that for now.

When you insert the operational Branch node, you will get a warning that this will force the existing logic into the default branch, but that is okay. You can easily correct this. Just click and drag the existing Pipeline Pair node so that it is in the getProducts branch. Do the same with the get product catalog Route node, dropping it below the Pipeline Pair node. Your message flow should now look like Figure 6-8.

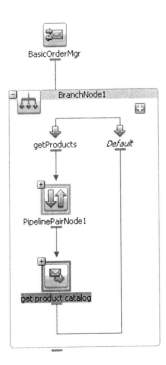

Figure 6-8. *Moving existing nodes within an operational Branch node*

Now, you could just add the new message flow logic into the default path of the operational Branch node. Technically, there is nothing wrong with that. However, we prefer to create a new Branch node that is specific to each operation. We can then use the default Branch node to throw an exception if it is ever invoked. This allows us to monitor whether people are trying to access the proxy service, but are using bad operation names. The benefit of this approach is primarily during development time. Imagine that a customer/partner/supplier is integrating with your proxy service. Your support group gets a call from one of the developers, complaining that she can't hit your service. If she were not using a valid operation name, the default branch would be activated, and you could have it send an alert or log a message, making it far easier to troubleshoot the problem and get the service developer back on the right track.

To create a branch for the submitOrder operation, click the plus sign ⊞ in the upper-right corner of the operational Branch node. This will create a new branch, also for the getProducts operation. WorkSpace Studio defaults all new operational branches to the first operation in the proxy service. Select the new getProducts branch and then, using the Properties window, select the submitOrder operation.

Now you are ready to define the message flow for the submitOrder operation. The submitOrder operation will route the order to either the processOrder or processPreferredOrder operation in the business service, based on the customer's credit rating. So, the first thing you need to do is to determine the customer's credit rating.

Place a Pipeline Pair node into the submitOrder branch. As in our previous scenario, you need to have two stages in this Pipeline Pair node. However, we're going to share a time-saving trick here, so don't race off and create both stages yet. You can copy and paste stages and actions within a message flow, and from one message flow to another. To do so, right-click the `assign variables` stage in the getProducts Pipeline Pair node and select Copy from the pop-up menu. Next, right-click the Request Pipeline icon in the Pipeline Pair node of the submitOrder branch and select Paste from the pop-up menu.

This will give you a stage in your submitOrder Pipeline Pair node that contains two Assign actions to derive the customer's first name and last name from the request. However, the request document for the submitOrder operation is different from the one you used for the getProducts operation, so you will need to examine the properties for each of these Assign actions and change the expressions.

For the `firstName` variable, change the expression to this:

```
$body/alsb:Order/ord:FirstName/text()
```

For the `lastName` variable, change the expression to this:

```
$body/alsb:Order/ord:LastName/text()
```

If you use the Variable Structures tab of the Expression Editor, be sure to browse the body of the submitOrder operation, not the getProducts operation.

Now you need a service callout to the getCreditRating operation of the business service. If you were to create this stage by hand, it would look *almost exactly* like the same stage you defined in the previous example. Again, you can simply copy and paste the get credit rating stage from the getProducts branch into the submitOrder branch. When pasting the stage into the submitOrder branch, right-click the `assign variables` stage and select Paste from the pop-up menu. OSB will paste in the new stage after the selected `assign variables` stage.

We said the Service Callout action will look almost exactly like the one you defined in the first scenario. However, you do need to make a small modification to the Assign action after the Service Callout action. Change it from this:

```
$soapResponseBody/alsb:getCreditRatingResponse/alsb:return/text()
```

to this:

```
$soapResponseBody/alsb:getCreditRatingResponse/alsb:return
```

The reason for this slight change is that the conditional Branch node needs to run an XPath expression on a variable, so you need to change the creditRating variable to an XML node instead of simple text.

Next, you need to add a conditional Branch node after the Pipeline Pair node. Name this new node decide order processing type, set the XPath expression to ./text(), and the variable name to creditRating. When you create a conditional Branch node, you get one named branch (named branch1 by default) and a default branch, similar to the operational Branch node. Click the branch1 branch and set its name to preferred customer in the Properties window. Set the Operator property to >=, and the Value property to 700. This defines a business rule that says that any customer with a credit rating of 700 or higher is a preferred customer, at least as far as order processing is concerned.

Now, add a new branch by clicking the plus sign in the upper-right corner of the conditional Branch node. In the Properties window, name the new branch standard customer, and set the Operator property to < and the Value property to 700. Leave the default branch empty. We won't use it in this exercise, but it's good to have a default branch that can be used to catch any weird anomalies in your conditional processing. For example, it would be easy to mistak-enly set the preferred customer rule to > 700 and the standard customer rule to < 700, leaving customers with a credit rating of exactly 700 with no processing at all. The default branch can catch these oversights, if you provide the necessary reporting or logging actions.

Routing Orders

Now that you have the decision logic in place, it's time to route the submitOrder messages to the appropriate business service operations. Add a Route node to the preferred customer branch and name it route preferred order. Add a Routing action to the new Route node.

In the Properties window, select BasicOrderMgr.biz for the Service property. Select processPreferredOrder as the operation. Leave the "Use inbound operation for outbound" check box unchecked.

The message format expected by the processPreferredOrder operation in the business service is different from the message format received by the submitOrder operation in the proxy service, so you will need to do some transformation. You will need to transform the original message received by the proxy from this:

```
<alsb:Order xmlns:ord="http://www.alsb.com/order/" ➥
xmlns:alsb="http://www.alsb.com/">
    <ord:FirstName>string</ord:FirstName>
    <ord:LastName>string</ord:LastName>
    <!--Zero or more repetitions:-->
    <ord:LineItem>
        <ord:Product>
            <ord:CreditNeeded>3</ord:CreditNeeded>
            <ord:Name>string</ord:Name>
        </ord:Product>
        <ord:Quantity>3</ord:Quantity>
    </ord:LineItem>
</alsb:Order>
```

to this:

```
<alsb:processPreferredOrder xmlns:alsb="http://www.alsb.com/">
    <alsb:order xmlns:ord="http://www.alsb.com/order/">
        <ord:FirstName>string</ord:FirstName>
        <ord:LastName>string</ord:LastName>
        <!--Zero or more repetitions:-->
        <ord:LineItem>
            <ord:Product>
                <ord:CreditNeeded>3</ord:CreditNeeded>
                <ord:Name>string</ord:Name>
            </ord:Product>
            <ord:Quantity>3</ord:Quantity>
        </ord:LineItem>
    </alsb:order>
</alsb:processPreferredOrder>
```

If you examine the two message formats, you'll see that they are pretty darned similar. With a little thinking, you can perform a quick transformation. Remember that the $body variable already contains the initial message received by the submitOrder operation, so you can just manipulate the contents of $body to the format you need before you execute the actual routing to the business service. That means that you need to make some changes in the Route node's Request action.

Let's start with the preferred customer branch. Add an Assign action to the Request action. Set the variable name to bizRequest. The expression for the Assign action is as follows:

```
<alsb:processPreferredOrder xmlns:alsb="http://www.alsb.com/">
   <alsb:order xmlns:ord="http://www.alsb.com/order/">
      {$body/alsb:Order/*}
   </alsb:order>
</alsb:processPreferredOrder>
```

Since the only difference between the message that was sent to submitOrder and the message you need to send to processPreferredOrder is in the first two XML element names, you can simply copy the "interior" of the original request message and place it into the "interior" of the message you need to send to the business service.

After you have the Assign action defined properly, add a Replace action immediately after it. Configure the Replace action so that the XPath is . (a period), the variable is body, and the expression is $bizRequest. Be sure to select the "Replace node contents" radio button.

Of course, you need to take similar action for the standard customer branch. However, in the Route node for this branch, you will add only the Replace node and not the Assign node. You are going to use a "shorthand" approach in this branch and perform the same function that the Assign action did in the first branch within the Replace node itself. Configure this Replace node exactly the same as the first one, but with one important difference: set the expression to the following:

```
<alsb:processOrder xmlns:alsb="http://www.alsb.com/">
   <alsb:order xmlns:ord="http://www.alsb.com/order/">
      {$body/alsb:Order/*}
   </alsb:order>
</alsb:processOrder>
```

Can you see in the expression how you perform the same function in this Replace action as you did in the Assign action earlier? This is an important concept, because each time you include an Assign, Insert, Rename, or Replace action in your message flows, the associated expressions are then run by the XQuery engine in OSB. There is some overhead to initializing the engine. So, the fewer actions that you put into your message flows, the faster they will run.

■**Tip** The fewer actions you put into your message flow, the faster your message flow will execute.

Save all of your work. Take a look at the Outline window in WorkSpace Studio. As shown in Figure 6-9, this window displays the entire message flow, including the Branch node and the branches that you just created. You can use this message flow map to navigate through your message flows.

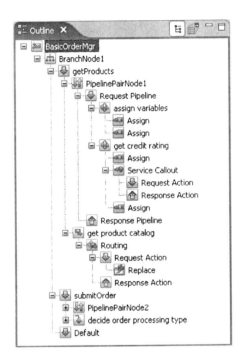

Figure 6-9. *Map of message flow control in the Outline window*

That's it for this message flow. Be sure to publish your changes to the server. It's time to test the changes.

Testing the Scenario 2 Service

Using the OSB web console, navigate to the submitOrder proxy service and click the testing icon to test this service. Click the submitOrder link at the top of the test console.

Notice the field where you can enter your order. You know from your schema that an Order is a complex object, containing the customer's first name, last name, and an array of line items. The test console knows the format of the document and provides you with a simple version that contains sample data. You can leave the sample data in place, or replace it with more specific data, as needed.

To ensure that the service is working as intended, set the last name to Anderson to get a customer with a high credit score, as shown in Figure 6-10, and click the Execute button. Because submitOrder is a one-way call, you won't receive a meaningful response from the web service. However, the test console will show you the invocation trace of the web service. Scroll down to the bottom of the test console and ensure that the route preferred order node was executed, as shown in Figure 6-11.

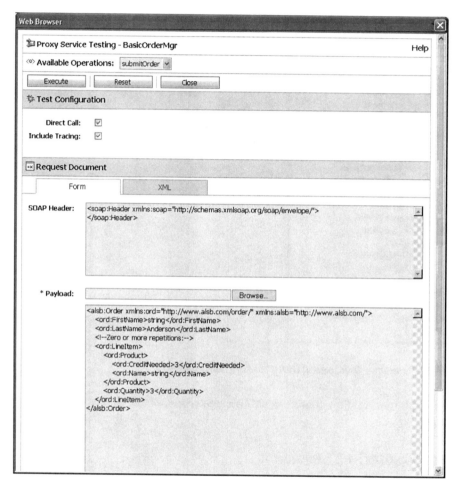

Figure 6-10. *Test console for the submitOrder proxy service*

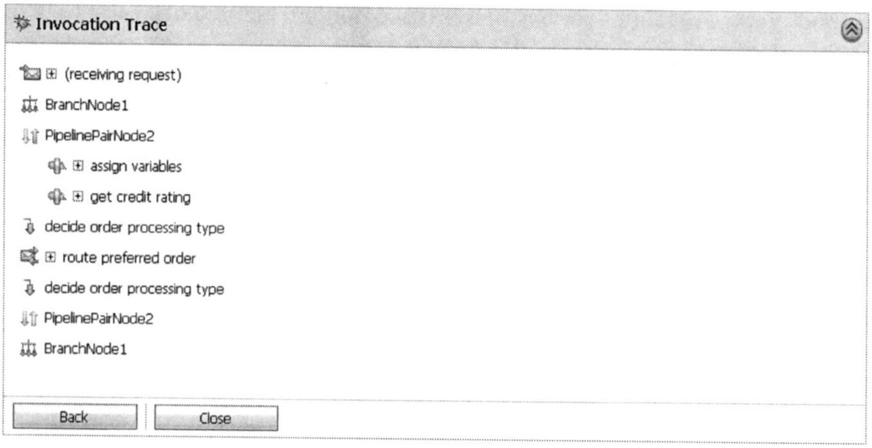

Figure 6-11. *Invocation trace for preferred orders*

Now click the Back button and try the test again, but this time change the name to Zimmerman. The invocation trace for that call should be routed to the route standard order node via the default branch. You can also examine the console output of the OSB server to see the debugging messages from the processOrder and processPreferredOrder Java methods to confirm that everything is working correctly.

Summary

In this chapter, you became more familiar with the three message-flow-processing node types. They might appear a little confusing at first, but now that you've used them, their purposes should be much more evident. Route nodes are used to transfer the processing to external services. Pipeline Pair nodes are used to provide you, the service composer, with an additional level of detail and control over the service proxy, especially in the area of error handling. The Branch nodes make runtime decisions within your proxy services. You can assemble these three node types to meet the needs of any proxy service.

CHAPTER 7

■■■

Asynchronous Messaging

Messages are at the heart of an ESB, and OSB is no exception. Therefore, it's worthwhile to ensure you have a solid understanding of the principles of messages and invocation models. Much of this chapter is more specific to WebLogic Server than it is to OSB. It's important to know both sides of the "services equation," and creating WebLogic web services will figure prominently in your OSB work.

Synchronous Invocation

Synchronous messaging is by far the most common messaging model in use today. A synchronous call is one where the caller waits for the called operation to complete before the caller can take another action. Synchronous calls are often the norm because they're easier to understand and easier to perform (from a developer's point of view).

At times, you might hear people disparage synchronous calls, mistakenly believing that asynchronous calls are somehow "better." Such zealotry should be avoided. Synchronous calls are just another tool in your toolchest and are often the appropriate choice. For example, if a customer logs onto your web site and requests to see his billing details for the last month, you would most likely implement this function synchronously; your customer is waiting for a response, and you don't want to keep the customer waiting for an indeterminate amount of time.

You've already used synchronous messaging in the `HelloWorld_SB` project in Chapter 3. You'll implement another synchronous service here to help illustrate the benefit of using asynchronous services (which we'll cover in the next section). Your synchronous service will accept an order for processing. Order processing (also known as *fulfillment*) often takes an extended amount of time. For our purposes, the process will take 30 seconds to complete, though real-world implementation often requires days to complete, depending on the nature of the products and services ordered.

As in the previous chapter, we begin our service definition with a WSDL file and then generate code from this service contract. You can find the web service for this first exercise, shown in Listing 7-1, in the `SyncBusiness_WS` project in WorkSpace Studio (download the source code from the Source Code/Download area at `http://www.apress.com`). We've deliberately kept the web service simple, in order to illustrate clearly what's important to us in this chapter: the mechanics of synchronous and asynchronous messages, and how to best employ them using OSB.

Listing 7-1. *A Synchronous Web Service*

```java
package com.alsb.syncbusiness;

import javax.jws.WebService;
import weblogic.jws.*;

/**
 * SyncBusinessPortTypeImpl class implements web service endpoint interface
 * SyncBusinessPortType
 */

@WebService(serviceName = "SyncBusinessService",
        targetNamespace = "http://www.alsb.com/",
        endpointInterface = "com.alsb.syncbusiness.SyncBusinessPortType")
@WLHttpTransport(serviceUri = "SyncBusinessService",
        portName = "SyncBusinessService")
public class SyncBusinessPortTypeImpl implements SyncBusinessPortType {

    private static long thirtySeconds = 30000;
    private static long timeDelay = thirtySeconds;
    private static int orderID = 100;

    public SyncBusinessPortTypeImpl() {
    }

    public com.alsb.Order submitOrder(com.alsb.Order order) {
        // Assign an order ID to the order
        order.setOrderID(orderID++);
        System.out.println("Starting to process the SYNC order id "
                + order.getOrderID());
        com.alsb.Order result = new com.alsb.Order();
        result.setOrderID(order.getOrderID());

        try {
            Thread.sleep(timeDelay);
        } catch (InterruptedException ex) {
            ex.printStackTrace();
        } finally {
            System.out.println("Completed processing the SYNC order id "
                    + order.getOrderID());
        }
        return result;

    }
}
```

If you examine the web service source code, you'll see where we put in a `Thread.sleep (timeDelay)` call to force the call to take 30 seconds to complete. This is to simulate a long-running process. Certainly, asking your users to wait for 30 seconds or more is unreasonable by today's standards. Such a length of time should make you either think of a way to optimize this process so that it runs faster or to implement the process asynchronously. In the next section, you'll see how you can take this synchronous process and wrap it in an asynchronous wrapper.

Asynchronous Invocation

A strong component of all loosely coupled systems is *asynchrony*: the ability for a caller to start a process (work) without needing to wait for that process to complete before the caller moves on to its next task. For example, a web site may gather the details of an order for customers. When customers are finished shopping, they click the Submit Order button, and the web site then submits the order to the back-end order-processing system for fulfillment. The order fulfillment process might take days to complete. It isn't reasonable to ask the client to wait for that order to be fully processed before the client can do anything else. You don't want to tie up the execution threads of your web server waiting for back-end systems to complete long-running processes.

In fact, such a situation demands asynchronous processing. The client just wants to submit the order and get on with its life. The client wants to tell the back-end system to "do this unit of work and don't bother me again." That's an asynchronous call. In missile terminology, this is referred to as "fire and forget." Lock the missile onto the target, click the fire button, and the missile does the rest. You can think of asynchronous calls as "fire and forget" technology.

Odds are that if you have a long-running process, like the `submitOrder` operation, you have implemented it asynchronously already, probably as a message-driven bean (MDB) using JMS technology. The challenge with JMS is that it requires a fair bit of technical knowledge to use properly. Should you rewrite your MDB as a web service? That may not be the best approach. We'll demonstrate a couple of solutions in the following sections.

Wrapping an MDB with a Proxy Service

Certainly, one of the fastest and easiest approaches would be to write a web service that simply service-enables (wraps) your existing MDB. Listing 7-2 shows our sample MDB, which you can find in the `OrderManager_MDB` project in the sample code for this book.

Listing 7-2. *A Sample MDB (OrderManager_MDB.java)*

```
package com.alsb.ordermanager;

import javax.ejb.MessageDrivenBean;
import javax.jms.MessageListener;
import javax.jms.Message;
import javax.jms.TextMessage;
import weblogic.ejb.GenericMessageDrivenBean;
import weblogic.ejbgen.MessageDriven;
import java.util.Date;
```

```java
import java.util.Enumeration;
import javax.jms.JMSException;

/**
 * GenericMessageDrivenBean subclass automatically generated by
 * WorkSpace Studio.
 *
 * Please complete the onMessage method and review the MessageDriven
 * annotation to ensure that the settings match your bean's intended use.
 */
@MessageDriven(ejbName = "OrderMananger_MDB",
    destinationJndiName = "jms.WebServiceQueue",
    destinationType = "javax.jms.Queue")
public class OrderMananger_MDB extends GenericMessageDrivenBean implements ➥
        MessageDrivenBean, MessageListener {
    private static final long serialVersionUID = 1L;
    private static long thirtySeconds = 30000;

    /* (non-Javadoc)
     * @see javax.jms.MessageListener#onMessage(javax.jms.Message)
     */
    public void onMessage(Message msg) {
        Date now = new Date();
        try {
          // Send the txtMsg to the XMLBeans constructor if you
          // need to parse this message in the real world.
           TextMessage txtMsg = (TextMessage)msg;
           System.out.println("Message: " + txtMsg.getText());
           Thread.sleep(thirtySeconds);
        } catch(JMSException ex) {
           ex.printStackTrace();
        } catch(InterruptedException ex) {
           ex.printStackTrace();
        } finally {
           now = new Date();
           System.out.println("Finished processing the async order at " + ➥
               now.toLocaleString());
        }
    }
}
```

Service-enabling an existing MDB is pretty easy. We'll go through the process now. First, you need to create an OSB project and name it SyncWS2AsyncMDB_SB. In this project, you will create a synchronous proxy service that will make an asynchronous call to the MDB by posting onto a JMS queue a text message that contains the SOAP message body.

Creating the Business Service

Your next step is to create a folder named WSDL, and then define the WSDL that the business service will use. If you are creating the files yourself, refer to Listing 7-3 for the AsyncBusiness.wsdl file. This file should be placed in the WSDL folder that you just created. You will also need to include the order.xsd file that we used in the previous chapter. Copy and paste the order.xsd file into the WSDL folder.

Listing 7-3. *The AsyncBusiness.wsdl File*

```
<?xml version="1.0" encoding="UTF-8"?>
<definitions name="AsyncBusiness"
   targetNamespace="http://www.alsb.com/AsyncBusiness/"
   xmlns="http://schemas.xmlsoap.org/wsdl/"
   xmlns:wsdl="http://schemas.xmlsoap.org/wsdl/"
   xmlns:soap="http://schemas.xmlsoap.org/wsdl/soap/"
   xmlns:tns="http://www.alsb.com/AsyncBusiness/"
   xmlns:xsd="http://www.w3.org/2001/XMLSchema">
   <types>
      <xsd:schema targetNamespace="http://www.alsb.com/AsyncBusiness/"
          xmlns:xs="http://www.w3.org/2001/XMLSchema"
          xmlns:order="http://www.alsb.com/order/">
         <xs:import namespace="http://www.alsb.com/order/"
             schemaLocation="order.xsd"/>
         <xsd:element name="submitOrder" type="order:Order"/>
      </xsd:schema>
   </types>

   <message name="submitOrder">
      <part element="tns:submitOrder" name="submitOrder"/>
   </message>

   <portType name="AsyncBusiness">
      <operation name="submitAsyncOrder">
         <input message="tns:submitOrder"/>
      </operation>
   </portType>

   <binding name="AsyncBusinessSOAP" type="tns:AsyncBusiness">
      <soap:binding style="document"
          transport="http://schemas.xmlsoap.org/soap/http"/>
      <operation name="submitAsyncOrder">
         <soap:operation
             soapAction="http://www.alsb.com/AsyncBusiness/submitOrder"/>
         <input>
            <soap:body parts="submitOrder" use="literal"/>
         </input>
      </operation>
```

```
    </binding>
    <service name="AsyncBusiness">
        <port binding="tns:AsyncBusinessSOAP" name="AsyncBusinessSOAP">
            <soap:address
                location="http://localhost:7001/advmessage/AsyncBusiness"/>
        </port>
    </service>
</definitions>
```

Now it's time to create a business service based on the AsyncBusiness.wsdl file. When you come to the Transport Configuration page in the New Business Service wizard, be sure to set the protocol to JMS, and then set the endpoint URI to jms://localhost:7001/jms.wsConnectionFactory/jms.WebServiceQueue, as shown in Figure 7-1.

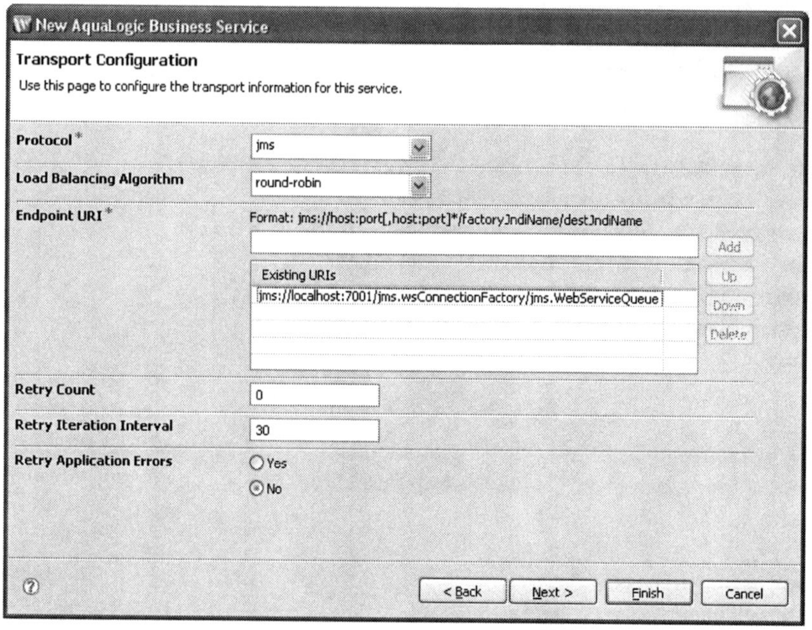

Figure 7-1. *Filling in the JMS transport information*

In the next wizard page, set the Destination Type field to Queue, and set the Message Type field to Text. You can safely ignore the rest of the fields and complete the wizard. You now have a business service that will send SOAP messages to the specified JMS queue.

■**Tip** Even though a WSDL may define a `<binding>` element as using the HTTP transport (as shown in Listing 7-3) the Transport Configuration page of the New Business Service wizard (Figure 7-1) allows you to override the WSDL binding. You can then generate an "effective WSDL" for the proxy or business service that shows your modification by right-clicking the service and selecting Oracle Service Bus ➤ Generate Effective WSDL or by viewing the dynamically generated WSDL at `http://<host>:<port>/sbresource?<BIZ or PROXY>/<Project Name><folder path to service>`. For example, the effective WSDL for the business service `AsyncOrder` in the `SyncWS2AsyncWS_SB` project can be found at `http://localhost:7001/sbresource?BIZ/SyncWS2AsyncWS_SB/AsyncOrder`.

Creating the Proxy Service

Now you need to create the synchronous proxy service that will call the MDB via the business service. As usual, start by defining the WSDL for the proxy service. The proxy's WSDL file looks very much like the `AsyncBusiness.wsdl` file (Listing 7-3), but with some minor differences. The WSDL file for the proxy service is shown in Listing 7-4.

Listing 7-4. *The Sync2AsyncProxy.wsdl File*

```
<?xml version="1.0" encoding="UTF-8"?>
<definitions name="SyncProxy"
    targetNamespace="http://www.alsb.com/SyncProxy/"
    xmlns="http://schemas.xmlsoap.org/wsdl/"
    xmlns:wsdl="http://schemas.xmlsoap.org/wsdl/"
    xmlns:soap="http://schemas.xmlsoap.org/wsdl/soap/"
    xmlns:tns="http://www.alsb.com/SyncProxy/"
    xmlns:xsd="http://www.w3.org/2001/XMLSchema">
    <types>
        <xsd:schema targetNamespace="http://www.alsb.com/SyncProxy/"
            xmlns:xs="http://www.w3.org/2001/XMLSchema"
            xmlns:order="http://www.alsb.com/order/">
            <xs:import namespace="http://www.alsb.com/order/"
                schemaLocation="order.xsd" />
            <xsd:element name="submitOrder" type="order:Order" />
        </xsd:schema>
    </types>

    <message name="submitOrder">
        <part element="tns:submitOrder" name="submitOrder" />
    </message>

    <message name="submitOrderResponse">
        <part element="tns:submitOrder" name="submitOrder" />
    </message>

    <portType name="SyncProxy">
```

```
      <operation name="submitSyncOrder">
        <input message="tns:submitOrder" />
        <output message="tns:submitOrder" />
      </operation>
    </portType>

    <binding name="SyncProxySOAP" type="tns:SyncProxy">
      <soap:binding style="document"
          transport="http://schemas.xmlsoap.org/soap/http" />
      <operation name="submitSyncOrder">
        <soap:operation
            soapAction="http://www.alsb.com/SyncProxy/submitOrder" />
        <input>
          <soap:body parts="submitOrder" use="literal" />
        </input>
        <output>
          <soap:body parts="submitOrder" use="literal" />
        </output>
      </operation>
    </binding>
    <service name="SyncProxy">
      <port binding="tns:SyncProxySOAP" name="SyncProxySOAP">
        <soap:address
            location="http://localhost:7001/advmessage/SyncProxy" />
      </port>
    </service>
</definitions>
```

The proxy service will simply echo the submitted order back to the caller, after it has invoked the MDB via the JMS queue.

After you have defined the WSDL file, create a new proxy service named Sync2Async.proxy and base it on the WSDL file.

■**Note** A web service operation that does not have an output message defined is referred to as a *one-way service*. This type of service is used for asynchronous messages. In the case of one-way services, the response message in the message flow is taken to be the same as the request message with regard to its format.

When configuring the proxy service, set the endpoint URI to /Sync2Async_SB/Sync2Async. You can safely accept the default values in the rest of the New Proxy Service wizard.

The message flow for this proxy service is exceedingly simple. First, add a Route node after the Sync2Async Start node in the message flow. Inside the Route node, create a Routing action. In the Routing action, be sure to call the AsyncOrder business service, invoking the operation submitAsyncOrder.

Configuring the JMS Server in WebLogic

The last step is to configure WebLogic Server so that it will contain the correct JMS queue information. OSB will publish text messages to this queue, and the MDB will subscribe to this queue to receive the messages. To speed things along, we have provided a script that will configure the JMS queue for you automatically.

■**Note** You can find plenty of technical articles online for details on configuring a JMS queue in WebLogic Server. A good place to start is at `http://dev2dev.bea.com/jms/`, where you will find a wealth of articles regarding JMS and WebLogic Server.

In WorkSpace Studio, if you haven't done so already, import the BookSetup project. Then open the build.xml file in the root directory of the project. This is an Ant build script. You may need to modify two of the properties in this file before you can run it: bea.home and workspace.dir. The third property, weblogic.home should not need modification (unless you really did some advanced, custom installation).

After you have the properties in the build.xml file set properly, run the configureServerResources target. This Ant target will then execute the configureServerResources.py script and configure the JMS server for you. You may also wish to examine this script, as it is a good example of how to automate work in WebLogic Server.

Testing the Proxy Service

At this point, you can test the proxy service using the test console. Be sure that you have added the projects, especially the MDB, to the OSB server list in WorkSpace Studio, so that it will be deployed when you start the OSB server.

Start the OSB server from within WorkSpace Studio, and then right-click the server and select Launch the OSB Administration Console from the pop-up menu. In the OSB administration console, select the SyncWS2AsyncMDB_SB project and click the little bug icon to the right of the Sync2Async proxy service to bring up the test console. Test the submitAsyncOperation. In the Console window of WorkSpace Studio, you should see something like the following output:

```
Message: <?xml version="1.0" encoding="UTF-8"?>
<soapenv:Envelope xmlns:soapenv="http://schemas.xmlsoap.org/soap/envelope/">
    <soap:Header xmlns:soap="http://schemas.xmlsoap.org/soap/envelope/">
    </soap:Header>
    <soapenv:Body>
        <syn:submitOrder xmlns:syn="http://www.alsb.com/SyncProxy/">
            <orderStatus>Submitted</orderStatus>
            <id>3</id>
            <FirstName>string</FirstName>
            <LastName>string</LastName>
            <!--Zero or more repetitions:-->
            <LineItem>
                <Product>
                    <CreditNeeded>3</CreditNeeded>
```

```
                    <Name>string</Name>
                </Product>
                <Quantity>3</Quantity>
            </LineItem>
        </syn:submitOrder>
    </soapenv:Body>
</soapenv:Envelope>
Found a message property: SOAPAction
Found a message property: JMSXDeliveryCount
Finished processing the async order at Nov 13, 2008 12:19:34 PM
```

■**Note** We did not take the extra step to transform the message sent from the proxy into the correct format defined by the `AsyncBusiness.wsdl` file. We felt that taking the time to perform the transformation did not add any clarity to this exercise. Obviously, you will want to perform these types of transformations for your real projects.

That's all there is to it. Using a proxy service to send JMS messages to existing MDBs is very simple.

Wrapping an Asynchronous Web Service with a Proxy Service

It is also possible to create asynchronous web services. The steps for this approach are very similar to the steps for wrapping an MDB with a proxy service, as described in the previous section. The only real differences between the two techniques are some annotations that you will need to use in the asynchronous Java Web Service (JWS) file and the fact that you need to pass two headers from the proxy service to the asynchronous JWS via the JMS queue. Here, we will walk through the steps for creating an asynchronous web service.

Creating the Asynchronous Web Service

In WorkSpace Studio, create a new Web Service project and name it `AsyncOrder_WS`. Set the context root to `AsyncOrder_WS` (this should be the default). Create a WSDL folder in this new project.

As always, we will begin with the WSDL. You need to modify the `AsyncBusiness.wsdl` file from the previous example to show that it uses JMS instead of HTTP. To keep things simple, copy and paste the `AsyncBusiness.wsdl` and `order.xsd` files from the SyncWS2AsyncMDS_SB project into this project's WSDL folder. Then modify the `AsyncBusiness.wsdl` file so that it matches the one shown in Listing 7-5. We've used boldface in the listing to highlight the lines that you need to change.

Listing 7-5. *Modifying the AsyncBusiness.wsdl File for Use with JMS*

```
<?xml version="1.0" encoding="UTF-8"?>
<definitions name="AsyncBusiness"
   targetNamespace="http://www.alsb.com/AsyncBusiness/"
```

```
  xmlns="http://schemas.xmlsoap.org/wsdl/"
  xmlns:wsdl="http://schemas.xmlsoap.org/wsdl/"
  xmlns:soap="http://schemas.xmlsoap.org/wsdl/soap/"
  xmlns:tns="http://www.alsb.com/AsyncBusiness/"
  xmlns:xsd="http://www.w3.org/2001/XMLSchema">
  <types>
    <xsd:schema targetNamespace="http://www.alsb.com/AsyncBusiness/"
      xmlns:xs="http://www.w3.org/2001/XMLSchema"
      xmlns:order="http://www.alsb.com/order/">
      <xs:import namespace="http://www.alsb.com/order/"
        schemaLocation="order.xsd" />
      <xsd:element name="submitOrder" type="order:Order" />
    </xsd:schema>
  </types>

  <message name="submitOrder">
    <part element="tns:submitOrder" name="submitOrder" />
  </message>

  <portType name="AsyncBusiness">
    <operation name="submitAsyncOrder">
      <input message="tns:submitOrder" />
    </operation>
  </portType>

  <binding name="AsyncBusinessSOAP" type="tns:AsyncBusiness">
    <soap:binding style="document"
      transport="http://www.openuri.org/2002/04/soap/jms" />
    <operation name="submitAsyncOrder">
      <soap:operation
        soapAction="http://www.alsb.com/AsyncBusiness/submitOrder" />
      <input>
        <soap:body parts="submitOrder" use="literal" />
      </input>
    </operation>
  </binding>
  <service name="AsyncBusiness">
    <port binding="tns:AsyncBusinessSOAP"
      name="AsyncBusiness">
      <soap:address location= ➥
"jms://localhost:7001/AsyncOrder_WS/AsyncBusiness?URI=jms.WebServiceQueue" />
    </port>
  </service>
</definitions>
```

As you can see in Listing 7-5, there are two areas of the WSDL file that you need to modify if you are going to use SOAP over JMS. The first is the `binding/soap:binding` element, where you need to set the `transport` to `http://www.openuri.org/2002/04/soap/jms`. That line alone defines the service as using SOAP over JMS. Further down in the file, in the service/port/soap: address element, you need to modify the address and add a URI argument that points to the JNDI name of the JMS queue that the web service will read.

Next, create a package named com.alsb.async.ws in the Java Resources/src/ folder.

Now you are ready to create the web service from the WSDL. Right-click the AsyncBusiness. wsdl file and select Generate Web Service from the pop-up menu. Select com.alsb.async.ws as the package where you want to generate the web service.

The wizard will have created the AsyncBusinessImpl.java file for you. Open this file and view the source code. You need to make some changes to the file to make it fully functional. In Listing 7-6, we have highlighted the important lines in boldface.

Listing 7-6. *Source Code for AsyncBusinessImpl.java JWS*

```java
package com.alsb.async.ws;

import java.util.Date;
import javax.jws.WebService;
import weblogic.jws.*;

/**
 * AsyncBusinessImpl class implements web service endpoint interface
 * AsyncBusiness
 */

@WebService(serviceName = "AsyncBusiness",
        targetNamespace = "http://www.alsb.com/AsyncBusiness/",
        endpointInterface = "com.alsb.async.ws.AsyncBusiness")
@WLJmsTransport(serviceUri = "AsyncBusiness",
        queue = "jms.WebServiceQueue",
        connectionFactory = "jms.wsConnectionFactory",
        portName = "AsyncBusiness")
public class AsyncBusinessImpl implements AsyncBusiness {

    private static long thirtySeconds = 30000;

    public AsyncBusinessImpl() {

    }

    public void submitAsyncOrder(com.alsb.order.Order submitOrder) {
        Date now = new Date();
        System.out.println("JWS: Starting to process the async order id:  "
                + submitOrder.getId() + " at " + now.toLocaleString());
        try {
            Thread.sleep(thirtySeconds);
        } catch (InterruptedException ex) {
            ex.printStackTrace();
        } finally {
```

```
        now = new Date();
        System.out.println("JWS: Finished processing the async order id:  "
            + submitOrder.getId() + " at " + now.toLocaleString());
    }
  }
}
```

The key thing to notice in Listing 7-6 is that the WLHttpTransport annotation is replaced with a WLJmsTransport annotation. Other than that, it's a perfectly average JWS file.

■**Caution** The portName attribute of the @WLJmsTransport annotation must match exactly the service/port/@name attribute in the WSDL file.

Creating the Service Bus Project

It is time to move back into the world of OSB and create a new OSB project. Name the new service bus project SyncWS2AsyncWS_SB. Create a WSDL folder in this project and copy the AsyncBusiness.wsdl and order.xsd files from the AsyncOrder_WS project and paste them into the WSDL folder you just created. You will also need to copy the Sync2AsyncProxy.wsdl file from the WSDL folder in the previous SyncWS2AsyncMDB_SB project and paste it into the WSDL folder for this project.

Creating the Business Service

Your next step is to create the business service that contains all of the necessary connectivity information to allow your proxy service to call the JWS. Right-click the project and select New ➤ Business Service from the menu. Base the new business service on the AsyncBusiness.wsdl file. Set the transport protocol to JMS and specify the endpoint URI as jms://localhost:7001/jms.wsConnectionFactory/jms.WebServiceQueue. Set the Destination Type field to Queue and the Message Type field to Text.

Creating the Proxy Service

Next, right-click the project and create a new proxy service. Name the proxy service Sync2Async and base the proxy service on the Sync2AsyncProxy.wsdl file. Be sure the protocol for the proxy service is HTTP and that the endpoint URI field defaults to /SyncWS2AsyncWS_SB/Sync2Async.

Now you need to create a message flow for the proxy service. This message flow will be a little different from the one you created earlier in the SyncWS2AsyncMDB_SB project. When you send a SOAP message over a JMS queue, you need to use the Publish action, not the Routing action. Open the Message Flow window for the proxy service and follow this procedure:

1. Add a Pipeline Pair node just after the Start node of the message flow.

2. In the request pipeline, add a Stage node. In the Stage node, add a Publish action.

3. In the Properties window for the Publish action, set the Service property to SyncWS2AsyncWS_SB/AsyncOrder. Set the Invoking property to submitAsyncOrder.

4. Add a simple Rename action inside the Publish action to change the namespace of the root element from `http://www.alsb.com/SyncProxy/` to `http://www.alsb.com/AsyncBusiness/`.

5. Add a Transport Header action to the Request action *inside* the Publish action.

6. In the Transport Header action's properties, set the Direction property to Outbound Request. You also need to create two custom headers for the message. The first header is named `URI` and needs to point to the URI of the JWS that will receive the SOAP message (`"/AsyncOrder_WS/AsyncBusiness"`). The second header is named `_wls_mimehdrContent_Type` and should be set to `"text/xml; charset=UTF-8"`. It is important to add single or double quotes around the values in the Expression Editor to denote them as string literal values.

Figure 7-2 shows the message flow and the completed Transport Header action's Properties window.

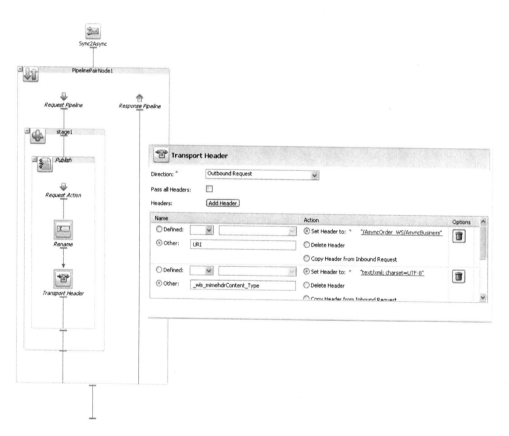

Figure 7-2. *The proxy service message flow and the Transport Header action's properties*

Testing the Asynchronous Web Service

To test the asynchronous web service, you will need to remove the `OrderManager_MDB` project from the server. If you do not remove the MDB project, you will find that the MDB, not the asynchronous web service, will receive all of the messages. Another interesting thing to note is that the asynchronous web service will process messages serially. For example, if you quickly submit three orders through the proxy service, the proxy service will return very quickly. However, if you observe the OSB server console, you will see that as each message is pulled from the queue, it is processed during the 30-second wait time, then the next message is removed from the message queue, and so forth.

Parallel Calls with Split-Join

Split-join is the name given to a new feature in OSB 3 that allows your proxy service to make multiple service calls in series or in parallel, and then aggregate the results into a single return message to the caller. For example, suppose that you had an order-processing proxy service that needed to call an external service to get customer information based on a customer ID, then make a call to the billing system to get the current account status of the customer, and finally contact the order-management system to get the order history for the customer. If each of these external services took 5 seconds to complete, the overall time of the proxy service to execute would be 15 seconds, plus a few milliseconds of overhead.

The split-join feature allows you to make these service calls to the back-end systems in parallel, reducing the processing time of the proxy service from 15 seconds to just over 5 seconds. To demonstrate how to use this feature, we will implement the scenario outlined in the preceding paragraph. To keep things simple, we will create a single JWS that will implement the three operations—`getCustomerInfo`, `getBillingInfo`, and `getOrderInfo`—all based on a customer ID. Each of these operations will have a built-in delay of 5 seconds. We won't go into the details of how to build these back-end web services because it should be trivial to you by now.

The JWS code is implemented in the `SplitJoin_WS` project with the source code that accompanies this book. You can see the working example in the `SplitJoin_SB` project in this book's source code. We will walk you through the process that we took to create that project. Most of the steps will be familiar to you by now.

Adding a Split-Join

To begin the project, create a `WSDL` directory, and in that directory, placed your two WSDL files: `SplitJoin_WS.wsdl`, which represents the back-end web service, and `SplitJoinFlow.wsdl`, which defines the web service that your `SplitJoin_SB` project will implement.

Next, create a business service named `SplitJoin_WS.biz`. The business service is based on the `SplitJoin_WS.wsdl` file, of course. Nothing special is needed by the business service, since you are dealing with straight SOAP over HTTP.

Now things begin to get a little more interesting. Split-joins are not stand-alone services; the split-join is actually internal functionality that you will need to wrap in a business service and, ultimately, a proxy service. Split-join services are often referred to as *flows*.

First, create a split-join, as follows:

1. Right-click the SplitJoin_SB project and select New ➤ Split-Join from the pop-up menu.

2. In the New Split-Join wizard's first page, name the new flow SplitJoin.flow (the .flow suffix is appended for you automatically). Click the Next button.

3. You will be prompted to choose an operation from a WSDL file. Split-joins are limited to a single operation from within a WSDL file. Open the SplitJoinFlow.wsdl file and select the only operation within it, getAllCustomerInfo, as shown in Figure 7-3.

Figure 7-3. *Selecting an operation for the split-join flow*

4. Click the Finish button. The wizard will create the SplitJoin.flow file for you and open it for editing.

Designing the Split-Join Flow

By default, the flow will have a Start node, a Receive action, and a Reply action. Click the gray arrow next to the Start node, and you will see the global variables, request and response, which were automatically created for the flow, as shown in Figure 7-4. A list of external services (services called by the flow) is also shown. Of course, since this is a new flow, no external services are listed yet. You can also create new variables in this window by right-clicking the Variables icon. Variables created here have a global scope; all other nodes within the entire message flow are able to reference these global variables.

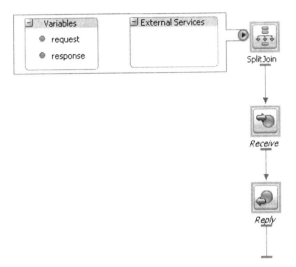

Figure 7-4. *Split-Join Start node components*

This concept of variable scope is especially important in a split-join flow. The general process for creating a flow is to identify the various message parts that the flow will need to either pass in to the external services or return, and to create global variables in the Start node that can hold those pieces of the message. At the end of the flow, you then use an Assign action to compose all of those messages into the final return message format.

Click the Receive action and activate the Properties window. You will see that the Receive action already has configuration information in the Operation and Variable tabs. The Receive action's purpose is to take incoming information from the Start node and place it into a variable for later use in the flow. By default, it will take the incoming message and store it in the request variable defined in the Start node. You will rarely need to modify the Receive action.

Follow these steps to configure the split-join flow:

1. Each of the operations on the SplitJoin_WS business service needs to know the customerID, so you need to create a variable on the Start node named customerID. Right-click the Start node and select Create Variable from the pop-up menu. Set the variable name to customerID, and set the type to the int built-in type.

2. You need to populate the customerID global variable with the ID passed in from the request message. To do this, add an Assign action directly below the Receive action. The Assign action here is different from the Assign actions you are used to in other parts of OSB. The Assign action in a split-join flow will allow you to perform multiple actions, not just variable assignments. It will also allow you to delete XPath expressions, insert new XPath expressions into an existing variable, and copy and paste XPath expressions.

3. Click the plus sign in the Assign action to create a new statement. Select Assign from the pop-up menu. This will bring up the Assign Action dialog box, which allows you to specify a single Assign action.

4. Enter the expression data($request.getAllCustomerInfo/customerID) so that you retrieve just the integer value of the customer ID. Then select customerID from the Variable combo box. Your dialog box should look like the one in Figure 7-5. Click the OK button to create this Assign action.

Note You may have noticed that there is a text area underneath the list of actions in the Assign node. This text area shows you the Business Process Execution Language (BPEL) code that OSB generates to implement your Assign, Delete, Copy, Insert, and Replace actions. OSB uses a subset implementation of the BPEL 2.0 specification with some extensions. You are not directly exposed to BPEL when using OSB. OSB 3 does not let you edit this BPEL code, but it does execute this BPEL code internally. However, if you are interested in seeing the BPEL 2.0 code that OSB generates for you, open any file with the suffix .flow.

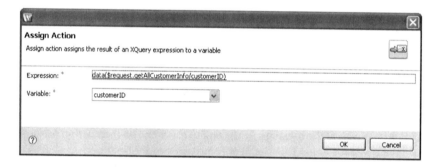

Figure 7-5. *Assigning the customer ID to the global customerID variable*

5. Next, you need to invoke the three operations—getCustomerInfo, getBillingInfo, and getOrderInfo—in parallel. For that, you need to add a Parallel action just after the Assign. When you add a Parallel action, it has two *scopes* by default. Each scope is a parallel flow (think "thread"). You can add more scopes by clicking the plus sign icon within the Parallel action. Add one more scope to the Parallel action so that you have a total of three.

6. Labeling the scopes will help to improve the readability of the Parallel action. Click the first scope to select it. Using the Properties window, set its Label property to get customer info. Repeat this process for the other two scopes to label them get billing info and get order info.

7. In the get customer info scope, add an Invoke Service action. In the Properties window for the Invoke Service action, set the Operation property to getCustomerInfo, as shown in Figure 7-6.

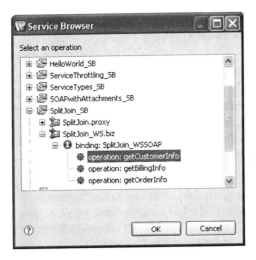

Figure 7-6. *Selecting the business service operation for an Invoke Service action*

8. From the Properties window for the Invoke Service action, create a new input variable named getCustomerInfoRequest. Make it a local variable, as shown in Figure 7-7. Notice that the Type and Namespace fields are already defined for you.

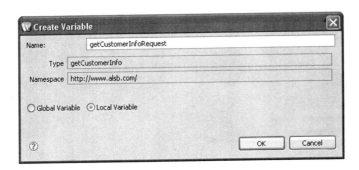

Figure 7-7. *Creating the getCustomerInfoRequest local variable*

9. Create a new output variable for the Invoke Service action. Set the name of the output variable to getCustomerInfoResponse and also make it a local variable.

10. Now that you have the input and output variables defined for the get customer info Invoke Service action, you need to set the input variable (getCustomerInfoRequest) to the correct value and retrieve the results from the output variable (getCustomerInfoResponse). Add an Assign action immediately above the Invoke Service action. This Assign action assigns the following expression to the variable getCustomerInfoRequest.getCustomerInfo. You aren't doing anything tricky here—just creating the proper request document and assigning it to the input variable.

```
<ns1:getCustomerInfo>
    <customerID>{$customerID}</customerID>
</ns1:getCustomerInfo>
```

11. From the getCustomerInfoResponse output variable, you need to retrieve the first name and last name of the customer. You need to use the firstName and lastName variables outside the Parallel action, so they must be global in their scope. Therefore, you need to create them in the Start node. Right-click the Start node of the flow and select Create Variable from the pop-up menu. Create two variables, firstName and lastName, and set their types to the built-in String type.

12. Now you are ready to retrieve the values of these variables from the getCustomerInfoResponse output variable. Add an Assign action immediately after the Invoke Service action. In the Assign node, you need to create two Assign actions. The first action assigns the XPath expression data($getCustomerInfoResponse. getCustomerInfoResponse/firstName) to the variable firstName. The second action assigns the expression data($getCustomerInfoResponse.getCustomerInfoResponse/ lastName) to the variable lastName. When you are finished, your Parallel action should look like Figure 7-8.

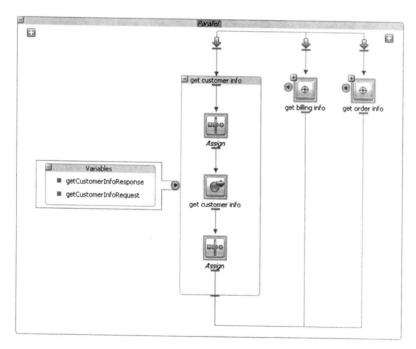

Figure 7-8. *Scope 1 completed on the Parallel action*

13. You now need to set up the other two scopes in your Parallel action. Place an Invoke Service action in each of the other two scopes: one calling the getBillingInfo operation on the business service and the other calling getOrderInfo. Place Assign actions immediately before and after each of the Invoke Service actions. Create the appropriate request and response local variables for each Invoke Service action, as you did in the previous steps.

14. In the Assign action above the getBillingInfo service invocation, assign the following expression to the getBillingInfoRequest variable:

```
<ns1:getBillingInfo>
    <customerID>{$customerID}</customerID>
</ns1:getBillingInfo>
```

15. In the Assign action above the getOrderInfo service invocation, assign the following expression to the getOrderInfoRequest variable:

```
<ns1:getOrderInfo>
    <customerID>{$customerID}</customerID>
</ns1:getOrderInfo>
```

16. The response documents for both of these service invocations can return multiple <bill> and <order> elements. You need to store these results in two global variables named billingInfo and orderInfo. Create those global variables in the Start node, as you've done in earlier steps. Be sure to set the billingInfo variable type to the BillingInfo schema type defined in the SplitJoinFlow.wsdl file, as shown in Figure 7-9. Perform the analogous steps for the orderInfo variable.

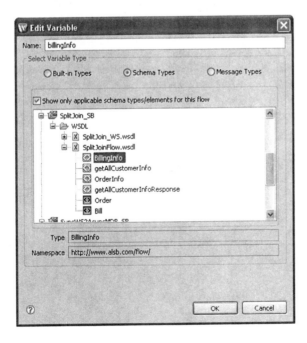

Figure 7-9. *Creating the billingInfo variable based on a schema type*

You will need to use a little XQuery to get the work done. You know that the getBillingInfoResponse variable will contain the response document from the business service. You want to transform that document into the format expected by the billingInfo variable. You need to do essentially the same thing for the orderInfo variable. The easiest way to do this is via XQuery transformations.

17. Create a new XQuery transformation in the root directory of the project and name it BillingXLA. For Source Type (be sure the XML radio button is selected), select the SplitJoin_SB/WSDL/SplitJoin_WS.wsdl/getBillingInfoResponse. Click the Next button. For Target Type, select the SplitJoin_SB/WSDL/SplitJoinFlow.wsdl/getBillingInfo type. Then click the Finish button. When WorkSpace Studio loads the new XQuery transformation, your IDE should look like Figure 7-10, without the arrows running from left to right.

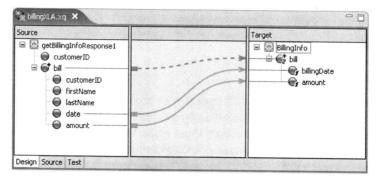

Figure 7-10. *Creating the XQuery transformation for the billingInfo variable*

18. Your next step is to create the arrows that you see in Figure 7-10. Start with the bill element on the left side. Drag and drop it onto the bill element on the right side of the window. An arrow will appear between the two elements, showing that one maps to the other. The dashed line with the arrow indicates that the XQuery will iterate over all of the bill elements. Now connect the date element to the billingDate, and also connect the amount elements, always dragging from the left and dropping on the right.

If you click the Source tab at the bottom of the XQuery transformation window, you can view the XQuery code that was generated by your actions, as shown in Listing 7-7.

Listing 7-7. *The XQuery Transformation for the billingInfo Variable*

```
declare function xf:billingXLA($getBillingInfoResponse1 as ➥
element(ns1:getBillingInfoResponse))
    as element(ns0:BillingInfo) {
        <ns0:BillingInfo>
            {
                for $bill in $getBillingInfoResponse1/bill
                return
                    <bill>
                        <billingDate>{ data($bill/date) }</billingDate>
```

```
            <amount>{ data($bill/amount) }</amount>
          </bill>
      }
    </ns0:BillingInfo>
};
```

19. In the Assign action after the getBillingInfo service invocation, add an Assign action that will invoke the billingXLA XQuery resource and bind it to the $getBillingInfoResponse. getBillingInfoResponse variable. You need to select the billingInfo variable as the destination for the assignment. When you run this, the result is that the response document from the getBillingInfo operation of the business service will be transformed into the <BillingInfo> element format that the getAllCustomerInfoResponse document is expecting.

20. Repeat steps 17 through 19 to create the XQuery transformation for the orderInfo variable (an orderXLA XQuery transformation file). The resulting XQuery from your transformation function should look like the code shown in Listing 7-8.

Listing 7-8. *The XQuery Transformation for the orderinfo Variable*

```
declare function xf:orderXLA($getOrderInfoResponse1 as ➥
element(ns1:getOrderInfoResponse))
    as element(ns0:OrderInfo) {
        <ns0:OrderInfo>
          {
            for $order in $getOrderInfoResponse1/order
            return
              <order>
                {
                  for $product in $order/product
                  return
                    <product>{ data($product) }</product>
                }
              </order>
          }
        </ns0:OrderInfo>
};
```

21. The last step in the flow is to fill the response.getAllCustomerInfoResponse variable. Add an Assign action outside the Parallel action and just above the Reply action. The Assign action needs to have a single Assign action that assigns the following expression to the response.getAllCustomerInfoResponse variable:

```
<bind:getAllCustomerInfoResponse>
    <customerID>{$customerID}</customerID>
    <firstName>{$firstName}</firstName>
    <lastName>{$lastName}</lastName>
    {$billingInfo}
    {$orderInfo}
</bind:getAllCustomerInfoResponse>
```

That completes the programming of the `SplitJoin.flow` file. Remember that, toward the beginning of this section, we mentioned that split-join flows are functionality, not services? Well, because of that, you need to wrap the flow in a business service definition before you can use it.

Wrapping the Split-Join Flow

Creating a business service for a flow is fast and simple. The proxy service creation is also straightforward.

1. Right-click the `SplitJoin.flow` file in the Project Explorer window and select AquaLogic Service Bus ➤ Generate Business Service from the pop-up menu. Name the business service `SplitJoinWrapper` and click the OK button. A business service is generated and properly configured to call the flow.

2. Create a new proxy service. Name the proxy service `SplitJoin` and base the proxy service on the `SplitJoinFlow.wsdl` file. You can accept the defaults for the rest of the proxy service creation.

3. In the Message Flow window for the proxy, add a Route node with a Routing action. Configure the Routing action to invoke the `getAllCustomerInfo` operation on the `SplitJoinWrapper` business service.

Build and deploy the `SplitJoin_WS` and `SplitJoin_SB` projects to the `osb30_book` server. When you test the proxy service, you can see in the Console window that all three operations are called on the `SplitJoin_WS` JWS, and the entire life span of the proxy service is about 5 seconds, as opposed to the 15 seconds it would have taken if it had called the back-end operations in series.

Summary

In this chapter, we've really put OSB through its paces with regard to asynchronous and parallel messaging models. You've seen how OSB can be used to service-enable low-level technologies like JMS, and how it is able to integrate with SOAP over JMS web services. The exercise using the new split-join functionality shows how parallelism can significantly reduce the execution time of a proxy service by being able to run lower-level operations in parallel. It can do all of this while presenting a more traditional (and often easier to program) synchronous interface to the service consumer.

We don't want to overlook the fact that OSB proxy services may also be implemented as asynchronous services themselves. You can define a proxy service that accepts SOAP over JMS if necessary. While that is certainly true, the vast majority of the users in the field use OSB to simplify the interfaces to complex IT systems. It is this simplification of the back-end IT systems that is at the very heart of the concept of abstraction: making complex systems easy to use. At the same time, by providing these layers of abstraction, we are continuing to leverage our existing IT investments by using the functionality we have already paid for and simply wrapping it in a reusable service.

■■■

## CHAPTER 8

Service Types and Transports

A *service type* represents a message format type. OSB supports the following service types: SOAP or XML defined by a WSDL file, SOAP without a WSDL file, and XML without a WSDL file. You can also set a messaging type of binary, text, MFL, or XML.

A *transport protocol* is a protocol that is used to transport messages from sender to receiver. JMS, EJB, and HTTP are some examples of transport protocols.

This chapter examines various combinations of service types and transport protocols.

Service Type and Transport Protocol Overview

As you've seen in previous chapters, you start creating a service by first specifying the service type that you'll need to use. Most commonly, this is a SOAP message with a WSDL service type. However, you might opt to use a different service type, depending on your specific needs. For example, if you're providing a service to clients that can't speak SOAP or WSDL, you might opt to implement an XML service type instead. If your service clients can communicate only in some proprietary binary format, you would choose the binary messaging type, and so on.

Note HTTPS is no longer a stand-alone transport type, as it was in the AquaLogic Service Bus version 2.*x*. Instead, it is now an attribute of the HTTP transport.

Once you know the service type you'll use, you then select the transport protocol. Not all transport protocols are available for every service type. Table 8-1 lists the service type and transport protocols.

Table 8-1. *Service Types and Transport Protocols*

Service Type	Transport Protocol
SOAP or XML with WSDL	DSP, JMS, JPD, HTTP, SB, WS
SOAP (no WSDL)	DSP, JMS, HTTP, HTTPS, JPD, SB
XML (no WSDL)	DSP, JMS, JPD, HTTP, HTTPS, Email, File, FTP, MQ, SB, SFTP, Tuxedo
Messaging type (Binary, Text, MFL, or XML)	JMS, HTTP, HTTPS, Email, File, FTP, MQ, Tuxedo
Transport-typed	EJB and Flow

■**Note** All service types can send and receive attachments using Multipurpose Internet Mail Extensions (MIME). However, attachments are supported for only specific transports. See Chapter 9 for a discussion of how to send SOAP messages with attachments.

SOAP with WSDL

Certainly, SOAP with WSDL is one of the most popular message types, especially in the web service world. Originally, SOAP was an acronym for Simple Object Access Protocol. Today, SOAP is generally recognized as a name only, as the old acronym no longer applies. Now, SOAP is an XML protocol for encoding and transmitting data. A SOAP message is composed of an *envelope*, which in turn is made up of a *header* section and a *body* section. Listing 8-1 shows a sample SOAP message sent to the Sync2AsyncProxy you created in Chapter 7.

Listing 8-1. *Sample SOAP Envelope*

```
<soapenv:Envelope xmlns:soapenv="http://schemas.xmlsoap.org/soap/envelope/">
    <soap:Header xmlns:soap="http://schemas.xmlsoap.org/soap/envelope/">
    </soap:Header>
    <soapenv:Body>
        <asy:submitOrder xmlns:asy="http://www.alsb.com/SyncProxy/">
            <FirstName>string</FirstName>
            <LastName>string</LastName>
            <!--Zero or more repetitions:-->
            <LineItem>
                <Product>
                    <CreditNeeded>3</CreditNeeded>
                    <Name>string</Name>
                </Product>
                <Quantity>3</Quantity>
            </LineItem>
        </asy:submitOrder>
    </soapenv:Body>
</soapenv:Envelope>
```

We won't provide a SOAP example here, because all the examples in this book, other than some of those presented in this chapter, are examples of using the SOAP protocol.

SOAP Without WSDL

At first glance, SOAP without WSDL might seem like an odd combination. Why would you ever want to use SOAP without a WSDL file to define its structure? You'll most likely need this sort of a service type when dealing with legacy SOAP clients that were written without using a WSDL file. Another use for this approach is when you want to have a single SOAP port exposed for all messages. All messages received by this single SOAP port can then be examined and routed to the appropriate web services.

Creating this type of service is simple. You need to create a proxy service and select the Any SOAP Service option for the Service Type setting, as shown in Figure 8-1. For this example, just select the defaults in the rest of the New Proxy Service wizard.

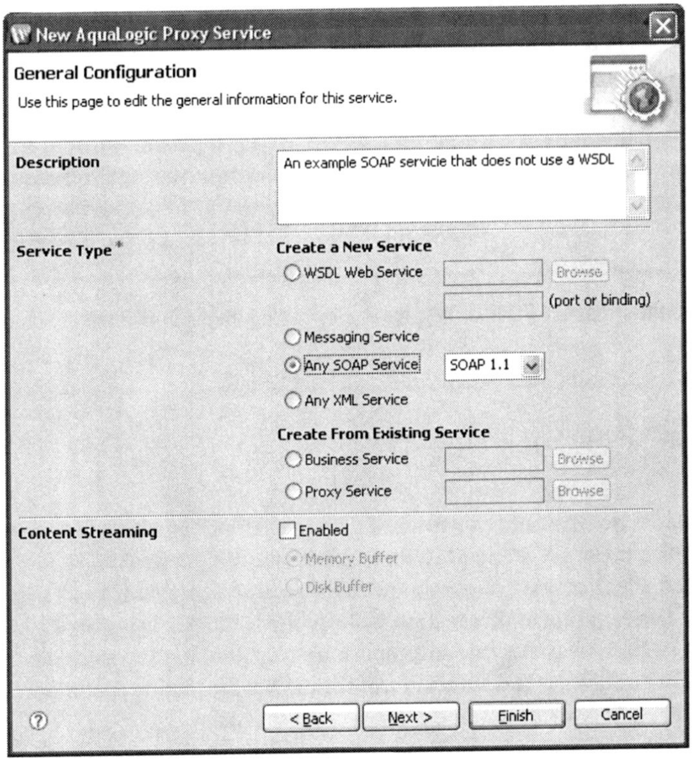

Figure 8-1. *Creating a SOAP proxy service that doesn't use a WSDL file*

Next, you need to create a simple message flow for the service. In the Message Flow window, add a Pipeline Pair node that has a single stage in the request pipeline. In that stage, add two actions:

- An Assign action, to assign the contents of the $body variable into a local variable named soapMsg (in the Properties window, set the variable to soapMsg and the expression to $body).

- A Log action with the following expression:

```
concat('Received the following SOAP Any message: ', $soapMsg)
```

No annotation should be set for this action, and its Severity property should be set to Error, so that it shows up in the OSB console and system log.

Save all your changes and publish them to the server.

Testing the service is straightforward. Bring up the test console, and you'll see that the service expects a document. Notice that the test console doesn't provide you with a default document format, with good reason: because the service will accept any SOAP document, the test console has no way of knowing which document you want to send.

To simplify testing, you'll find a sample SOAP document located in the WSDL directory of the ServiceTypes_SB project. The document is named SOAPnoWSDL.soap. Feel free to change the structure of the document to see how any valid SOAP document is accepted. The response of the proxy service is to echo whatever document was submitted.

In a nutshell, this type of service will accept *any* SOAP document you throw at it. You do need to exercise caution when using this service type. Your proxy service might end up being responsible for parsing every possible type of content for a service of this type. This structure is akin to a Java method (before version 1.5) that takes a Collection as an argument and returns a Collection; it's flexible because it *can mean anything*, and it's complex for the same reason.

■**Note** You can suppress the response from any SOAP or XML service by setting the mode element in $inbound to "request".

XML with WSDL

Although SOAP is very popular, it's not the only way to send a message. You can also use a pure XML file, and you can enforce the structure of the XML message by mapping it to a WSDL file. The key here is to create a WSDL file that doesn't rely on the SOAP protocol. Instead, it will use the HTTP POST/GET protocols. The example in this section will use the HTTP POST protocol.

A WSDL file that doesn't use SOAP is pretty uncommon, so it's worth taking a closer look at one to understand how it's put together. You can find the source file for Listing 8-2 in the WSDL directory of the ServiceTypes_SB project under the file name xml.wsdl.

Listing 8-2. *A WSDL for an XML Service That Does Not Use SOAP (xml.wsdl)*

```
<?xml version="1.0" encoding="UTF-8"?>
<wsdl:definitions xmlns:http="http://schemas.xmlsoap.org/wsdl/http/"
    xmlns:mime="http://schemas.xmlsoap.org/wsdl/mimee/"
    xmlns:alsb="http://www.alsb.com/"
    xmlns:wsdl="http://schemas.xmlsoap.org/wsdl/"
    xmlns:xsd="http://www.w3.org/2001/XMLSchema" name="XMLWSDLDefinitions"
```

```
    xmlns="http://www.alsb.com/"
    targetNamespace="http://www.alsb.com/">
    <wsdl:message name="getGreetingRequest">
       <wsdl:part name="name" type="xsd:string" />
    </wsdl:message>

    <wsdl:message name="getGreetingResponse">
       <wsdl:part name="response" type="xsd:string" />
    </wsdl:message>

    <wsdl:portType name="XMLWSDLPortType" xmlns="http://www.alsb.com">
       <wsdl:operation name="getGreeting">
          <wsdl:input message="alsb:getGreetingRequest" />
          <wsdl:output message="alsb:getGreetingResponse" />
       </wsdl:operation>
    </wsdl:portType>

    <wsdl:binding name="XMLWSDLHTTP" type="alsb:XMLWSDLPortType">
       <http:binding verb="POST" />
       <wsdl:operation name="getGreeting">
          <http:operation location="/GetGreeting" />
          <wsdl:input>
             <mime:content type="application/x-www-form-urlencoded" />
          </wsdl:input>
          <wsdl:output>
             <mime:content type="text/xml" />
          </wsdl:output>
       </wsdl:operation>
    </wsdl:binding>

    <wsdl:service name="XMLWSDLService">
       <wsdl:port binding="alsb:XMLWSDLHTTP" name="XMLWSDLHTTP">
          <http:address location="http://localhost:7001/xmlwsdl/XMLWSDLService" />
       </wsdl:port>
    </wsdl:service>
</wsdl:definitions>
```

You can see from the listing that the SOAP binding has been replaced by an HTTP binding that uses the verb POST. The getGreeting operation exists at /GetGreeting (the fully qualified location is http://localhost:7001/xmlwsdl/XMLWSDLService/GetGreeting), and it takes an input argument that is encoded in the manner used by HTTP POST. The operation returns an XML document.

Create a new proxy service with the name XMLwithWSDL, and base it on the WSDL file shown in Listing 8-2. Be sure to set the endpoint URI to /ServiceTypes_SB/XMLwithWSDL. Select the defaults in the rest of the New Proxy Service wizard.

Next, you need to create a simple message flow that gets the name from the XML document that was submitted and returns an XML document that contains the response. Figure 8-2 shows the message flow graphically.

First, you need to add a Pipeline Pair node. Create the get name stage in the request pipeline. This stage contains a single Assign action that assigns the expression $body/name/text() to the local variable name.

Next, create the create greeting stage in the response pipeline. This stage has two actions. The first action is an Assign action that assigns the value of the expression concat('Hello ', $name) to the local variable greeting. The second action is a Replace that replaces the XPath expression ./* in the variable body with the expression contents of the SOAP body element, represented by the variable $body, with the expression <response>{$greeting}</response>. Be sure to replace the entire node, not the node contents.

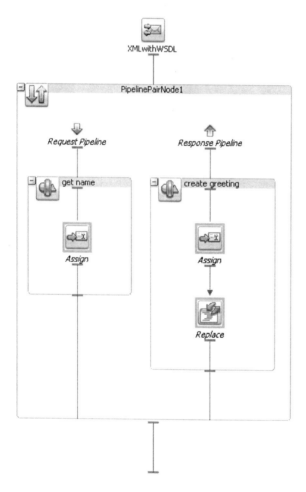

Figure 8-2. *The XMLWSDLService message flow*

Be sure to save and publish all your changes. You can use the test console to test your XMLwithWSDL proxy to ensure that it's working.

Just for fun, let's write a Java client to demonstrate how you would use such a service programmatically. This client is shown in Listing 8-3. You can find this code in the XMLwithWSDLClient_POJO project with the source code for this book.

Listing 8-3. *Java Client for the XMLWSDLService*

```java
public static void main(String[] args) {
    // Construct the XML document that we will POST
    String doc = "<?xml version='1.0'?><name>John</name>";
    String hostname = "localhost";
    int port = 7001;
    try {
        InetAddress  addr = InetAddress.getByName(hostname);
        Socket sock = new Socket(addr, port);

        //Send the header
        String path = "ServiceTypes_SB/XMLwithWSDL";
        BufferedWriter  wr = new BufferedWriter(new ➥
            OutputStreamWriter(sock.getOutputStream(),"UTF-8"));
        wr.write("POST " + path + " HTTP/1.0\r\n");
        wr.write("Host: " + hostname + "\r\n");
        wr.write("Content-Length: " + doc.length() + "\r\n");
        wr.write("Content-Type: text/xml; charset=\"utf-8\"\r\n");
        wr.write("\r\n");

        //Send the document
        wr.write(doc);
        wr.flush();

        // Read the response
        BufferedReader rd = new BufferedReader(
            new InputStreamReader(sock.getInputStream()));
        String line;
        while((line = rd.readLine()) != null)
            System.out.println(line);
    } catch(UnknownHostException ex) {
        ex.printStackTrace();
    } catch(IOException ex) {
        ex.printStackTrace();
    }
}
```

As you can see from Listing 8-3, writing the Java client requires a fair bit of knowledge about the HTTP protocol, but it's not that difficult if you have an example to work with. When you run this client, you'll see the following (raw HTTP) output as the XMLwithWSDL provides its response.

```
HTTP/1.1 200 OK
Connection: close
Date: Thu, 25 Sept 2008 20:07:41 GMT
Content-Type: text/xml; charset=utf-8
X-Powered-By: Servlet/2.4 JSP/2.0

<?xml version="1.0" encoding="utf-8"?>
<response>Hello John</response>
```

XML Without WSDL

Another service type is an XML service that doesn't use WSDL. It's similar to the SOAP without WSDL service that you defined earlier.

To see how this service type works, create a new proxy service and set its name to XMLnoWSDL. Set the Service Type setting to the Any XML Service option, set the endpoint URI to /XMLnoWSDL, and accept the rest of the default values in the New Proxy Service wizard.

To keep things simple, our message flow for this service will consist of a Pipeline Pair node with a single stage in the request pipeline. That stage will have a single action: an Assign action that will take the value of the $body variable and assign it to the input local variable.

Publish your work to the server. Now use the test console to test the XMLnoWSDL proxy. Simply enter any valid XML document into the test console, and you'll see that the service accepts it. It isn't necessary to enter the <?xml version="1.0" encoding="UTF-8"?> directive at the top of the request document to test your XML.

The XML without WSDL service type suffers from the same malady as the SOAP without WSDL service type: it's simply too flexible to be very useful. It's tempting to believe that such a service will simplify your life. Proponents might argue, "I have only one service to maintain, so it must be simpler." However, that is misleading. Although it's true that you would have only one service *interface* to maintain, who knows how many services would be implemented underneath the "cover" of this broadly defined service? To make matters worse, you have no way to control service proliferation, nor do you have any visible mechanism for handling version changes. Finally, the service contract is so broad as to be useless. The only way for service consumers to know how to make use of this service is to contact the service provider and ask for the secret XML format to use in order to get their work done. Although technically this is a service, it isn't service-oriented in any way.

Messaging Service Types

The messaging service type permits one form of message as the request and (possibly) a different message format as the response. For example, you might need a service that accepts an XML request but returns a binary file. Proxy services based on the messaging service type can give you a lot of flexibility when integrating directly with legacy systems.

■**Note** The messaging service type also supports Email, File, FTP, and Secure FTP (SFTP) transport proto-cols. However, there is one caveat here: the Email, File, FTP, and SFTP transport protocols are all "one-way" protocols, not "request-response." Therefore, if you wish to use File, FTP, or Email, you need to define the response message type as None. If you specify a return type, OSB will let you specify only HTTP, HTTPS, JMS, MQ,or Tuxedo as the transport protocol.

Message Type: Binary

As the name implies, the binary message type allows you to send binary messages. You can use a service such as this to communicate legacy or other proprietary data across the service bus. As an example, let's use the binary message type to send a binary message to an MDB over JMS for processing. To accomplish this, you need to take the following steps:

1. Create the JMS assets on the WebLogic Server. You need a JMS server, a JMS topic named BinaryFileTopic, and a connection factory named webServiceJMSConnectionFactory.

2. Create an MDB that listens to the BinaryFileTopic topic. The bean will take the binary message and write it to a temporary file.

3. Define a business service named BinaryBusinessService that knows how to route the binary message payload to the JMS topic.

4. Define a proxy service named BinaryService that accepts a binary formatted message and routes the message to the business service.

Creating the JMS Assets

As with the example of wrapping an MDB with a proxy service in Chapter 7, we have provided a script that you can use to create the JMS server for this example automatically. If you per-formed the server configuration outlined in Chapter 7, then the JMS topic BinaryFileTopic is already created and ready to go. Otherwise, follow the instructions in the section "Configuring the JMS Server in WebLogic" in Chapter 7 before continuing with this example.

Creating the MDB

Your next step is to create an MDB that will listen to the BinaryFileTopic JMS topic for binary messages. It will then save those binary messages to the local file system. You can find the source code for the MDB in the BinaryFile_MDB project in WorkSpace Studio. The important details of the MDB are shown in Listing 8-4. If you examine the @MessageDriven annotation, you can see that the JMS topic JNDI name to which the bean will listen is defined in the destinationJNDIName attribute.

Listing 8-4. *The MDB to Listen for the BinaryFileTopic (BinaryMDB.java)*

```
package com.alsb.business;
import ...
@MessageDriven(maxBeansInFreePool = "200",
```

```
                destinationType = "javax.jms.Topic",
                initialBeansInFreePool = "20",
                transTimeoutSeconds = "0",
                defaultTransaction = MessageDriven.DefaultTransaction.REQUIRED,
                durable = Constants.Bool.FALSE,
                ejbName = "binaryMDB",
                destinationJndiName = "binaryFileTopic")
public class BinaryMDB implements MessageDrivenBean, MessageListener  {
    public final static long serialVersionUID = 1L;
    private static final boolean VERBOSE = true;
    private MessageDrivenContext m_context;

    /**
     * Retrieve the BytesMessage and save that data as a file
     */
    public void onMessage(Message msg) {
        BytesMessage bm = (BytesMessage) msg;
        try {
            long length = bm.getBodyLength();
            byte[] binaryData = new byte[(int)length];
            int numRead = bm.readBytes(binaryData);
            // Create a temporary file on the local file system.
            File outputFile = File.createTempFile("mdb_", "xxx");
            log("Created the file: " + outputFile.getAbsolutePath() +
                    " with a file size of " + numRead + " bytes");
            FileOutputStream fos = new FileOutputStream(outputFile);
            fos.write(binaryData);
            fos.close();
        } catch(IOException ex) {
            ex.printStackTrace();
        } catch(JMSException ex) {
            System.err.println("An exception occurred: "+ex.getMessage());
        }
    }
    private void log(String s) {
        if (VERBOSE) System.out.println(s);
    }
}
```

The onMessage method is the entry point of every MDB. This method shows how to accept a binary message from OSB. You start by converting the input message into a BytesMessage. You then find the length of the binary message and create a byte array to hold the message contents. After you read the bytes into the array, you create a temporary file and write the bytes out to the file. You send a System.out.println to the console so that it's easy to see where the file was created. This will be handy later on when you're testing the system end to end.

Be sure to add the BinaryFile_MDB project to the osb30_book server. Once this task has completed successfully, you're ready to move to the next step: defining the business service.

Defining the Business Service

Next, you need to define a business service that represents the `BinaryMDB` you just created. This business service needs to route messages to the correct JMS topic. Follow these steps to create the business service for the binary message:

1. In the `ServiceTypes_SB` project in WorkSpace Studio, create a folder named `BusinessServices`.

2. In the new folder, create a business service named `BinaryBusinessService` and select the Messaging Service option for the Service Type setting in the General Configuration page of the New Business Service wizard. Click the Next button.

3. On the Message Type Configuration page of the wizard, set the Request Message Type setting to Binary and the Response Message Type setting to None, as shown in Figure 8-3. Click the Next button to continue.

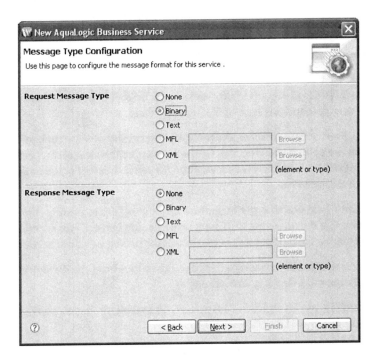

Figure 8-3. *Defining the BinaryBusinessService request and response types*

4. You need to communicate with your MDB over a JMS topic, so choose JMS for the protocol on the Transport Configuration page. The endpoint URI is composed of the JNDI name of your connection factory and the JMS topic name. Because you're connecting to a JMS server on your local machine, you can set the endpoint URI as follows, and then click Next.

    ```
    jms://localhost:7001/jms.wsConnectionFactory/jms.BinaryFileTopic
    ```

5. On the next wizard page, set Destination Type to Topic. Click the Finish button.

Your `BinaryBusinessService` is now defined and ready to be called from your proxy service.

Creating the Proxy Service

Creating a binary proxy service follows the same pattern we have used throughout this book:

1. Name the proxy `BinaryService` and select Messaging Service as the service type. Click the Next button.

2. The second page in the wizard allows you to define the request and response message types. For this exercise, you'll set the request message type to Binary. Because we're demonstrating the use of the File transport protocol (which is a one-way protocol), you must set the response message type to None. Click Next.

3. On the next page of the wizard, select the File protocol and set the endpoint URI to `file:///{drive ID}/filedir/`. Be sure to substitute the correct drive ID for your system. On a Windows system, a common endpoint URI would be `file:///c:/filedir`.

4. The next step in the wizard is to define the details of the File transport protocol. The fields with red asterisks next to them are required fields. Set the options as follows (see Figure 8-4):

   - The File Mask field is pretty straightforward. You'll leave it with the default value of `*.*` so that you can send any type of file to the service.

   - The Polling Interval field specifies the number of seconds between each polling event. When the polling event occurs, OSB will examine the directory (specified by the endpoint URI) to see if any files match the file mask. Leave it at the default setting of 60 for this exercise.

   - The Read Limit field specifies the maximum number of files to process during each polling event. The default value is 10, which you should leave. If you set this value to 0, all files that match the file mask at the time of the polling event will be processed.

   - The Sort By Arrival check box forces the selection of files from the directory based on their creation date. Leave it unchecked.

   - The Scan SubDirectories check box instructs OSB to look for files recursively in any existing subdirectories. Leave it unchecked.

   - The Pass By Reference check box tells OSB to copy the file to the archive directory and pass a reference to the file in the message itself. Leave it unchecked.

   - The Post Read Action selection tells OSB either to delete the file or to copy it to the archive directory after the message has been processed. Choose the delete action.

   - The Stage Directory field specifies where the files should be stored while they're being processed. You can leave the default `stage` directory.

   - The Archive Directory field defines a directory in the file system that will store the files after they've been processed. Of course, this has significance only if the Post Read Action field is set to Archive.

■Caution Be careful when defining your stage, archive, and error directories. Give them absolute paths so you can be sure of their location. If you have the Scan SubDirectories check box checked and you inadvertently place your archive directory within the directory specified by the endpoint URI, you can end up with an infinite loop.

- The Error Directory field specifies where messages and attachments are posted if there is a problem. You can leave the default `error` directory.

- The Request encoding field specifies the character-encoding scheme used for file requests. The default encoding is UTF-8, which you can accept.

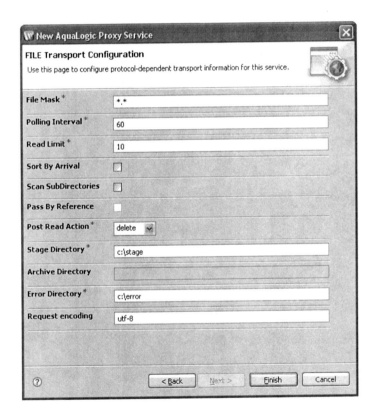

Figure 8-4. *Defining the details of the File transport protocol*

5. Be sure your configuration matches the one in Figure 8-4, and then click the Finish button to save your proxy service.

Your next step is to route requests from the proxy service to the business service.

Routing the Proxy to the Business Service

We're going to keep it simple here. Edit the message flow for your proxy service and add a Route node. Route the message to the `BinaryBusinessService`, as shown in Figure 8-5. No further actions are needed. Save all your work so far and publish the project to the server. It's testing time!

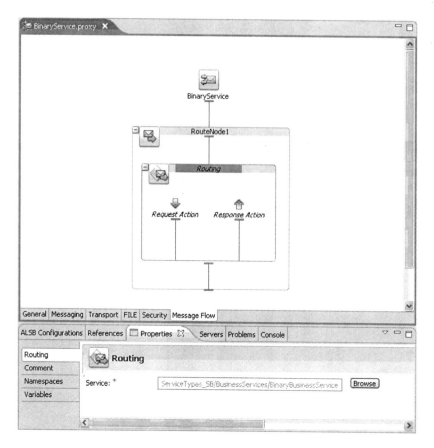

Figure 8-5. *The message flow and Route node for the BinaryService*

Creating the Directories on Your System

Be sure to create the following directories on your system:

- `C:\filedir`
- `C:\error`
- `C:\stage`

End-to-End Testing

To test a binary service, we prefer to use image files. It's much easier to notice corruption in an image, a video, or a sound file than it is to look through a text file, especially if the file is significant in size. Image files can be fairly large and still be easy to examine for errors.

■Note Binary messages cannot be directly manipulated within the message flow. If you need to manipulate binary information in a message flow, use a Java Callout action, as discussed in the "POJOs" section later in this chapter.

Start by selecting the file you wish to use for the test. Copy the test file into the directory defined by the endpoint URI for the proxy service. For this example, that means you need to copy the file into the `C:\filedir` directory on your local hard drive. Once that's done, it might take up to a minute before the proxy service polls the directory and picks up the file for processing. You'll know when the file has been processed by watching the output console for the WebLogic Server that is hosting OSB. You should see output similar to the following:

```
Created the file: C:\WINDOWS\TEMP\mdb_6801xxx with a file size of 171366 bytes
```

When you see this message, navigate to the file that the MDB just created and give it the correct file extension so that it matches the file extension of the source file (usually a JPG or PNG). When the file is appropriately renamed, open it to ensure that it arrived in good condition.

Message Type: Text

Text messages are useful when you need to exchange non-XML text information. Sample uses of this service type include exchanging plain-text files or comma-separated values. In the example in this section, you'll create a text service that uses FTP as its transport protocol. To make use of the FTP transport protocol, you'll need access to an FTP server. We use the FileZilla FTP server, available from SourceForge at `http://sourceforge.net/projects/filezilla/`. Of course, you can opt to use any FTP server you like, but you may need to modify some of the following instructions for setting up the FTP server for use by a specific account.

Setting Up Your FTP Server User Account

The installation program for FileZilla is easy to run. Once you install the FTP server and start it, you'll need to create a user account. Your proxy service will log in to the FTP server using this account. We selected this scenario for two reasons. First, it seems more realistic that the FTP server would apply some level of security when communicating business information to external entities. Second, it gives you a chance to see how to create and use service accounts in OSB.

1. To create a user account in FileZilla, select Edit ➤ Users from the FileZilla server menu.

2. In the Users dialog box, click the Add button below the Users list box. In the dialog box that appears, enter the username for the account you're creating. Name the account tester and click the OK button.

3. Now you need to set some properties for the account. Back in the Users dialog box, be sure the Enable account and Password check boxes are checked, as shown in Figure 8-6. Set the Password field to password.

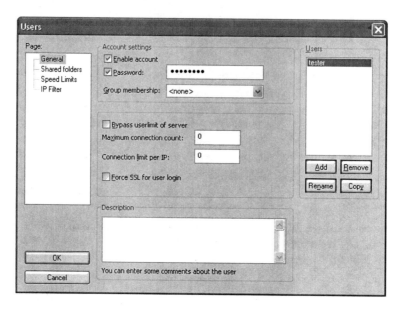

Figure 8-6. *Setting the user password in FileZilla*

4. Next, you need to define a home directory for this user account. Click the Shared folders entry in the Page list box on the left side of the Users dialog box, and then click the Add button in the Shared folders portion of the dialog box.

5. A new dialog box appears so that you can select a directory on your computer. You need to create an ftproot directory as the home directory for the tester user. Inside the ftproot directory, create another directory called ftp_in. Be sure that the tester user has full access (permissions to read, write, delete, and append files, along with create, delete, list, and add subdirectories) to both of these directories. Click OK in the dialog box for selecting a directory and in the Users dialog box to complete your setup.

Creating an OSB Service Account

Your next task is to create a service account in OSB. A service account allows you to create account names and passwords so that OSB can log in to external services and systems. In this case, you need to create a service account so that you can log in to the FileZilla FTP server using the account tester/password.

Follow these steps to create a service account:

1. Right-click the ServiceTypes_SB project and select New ➤ Service Account from the pop-up menu.

2. Name the service account FTP Account and click Next. Provide a meaningful description. Set the Resource Type setting to Static, as shown in Figure 8-7. This allows you to define a static username and password. Click the Next button.

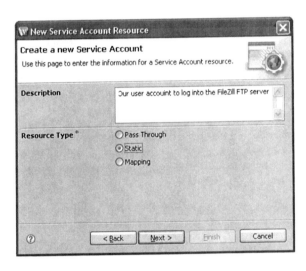

Figure 8-7. *Creating a Service Account*

3. Enter the username as tester and set the password to password. Click the Finish button.

Creating the TextFTP Proxy Service

Next, you need to create the proxy service itself, as follows:

1. Create a new proxy service in the ServiceTypes_SB project. Name the service TextFTP and select the Messaging Service option for the Service Type setting. Click the Next button.

2. Set the Request Message Type field to Text and the Response Message Type field to None. Click the Next button.

3. Set the protocol to FTP, and then provide the URI of the FTP service. The URI to use is ftp://localhost:21/ftp_in. Click the Next button.

Caution The endpoint URI of an FTP transport protocol is pretty darned picky. If the URI contains a directory name, then the URI *must not end* with a /. If the URI does not refer to a directory, then the URL *must end* with a /.

4. On the FTP Transport Configuration page, select the "external user" radio button for the User Authentication setting. The Service Account field appears. Click the Browse button and select the FTP Account service account you created in the previous section from the list of Service Accounts. Your settings should match those shown in Figure 8-8. Most of the configuration settings are the same as those for the binary message type, described previously. The following settings are added:

- Checking the Remote Streaming check box causes the file to be streamed directly from the remote server at the time of processing. If you enable this, you need to set the Archive Directory field to a directory on the remote server, relative to the FTP user directory.

- The Transfer Mode field describes the FTP mode used to transfer the files. If you know you are transferring only text files, then ASCII is fine. However, if you are transferring binary files, select the Binary option.

- The Download Directory field contains the directory on the local OSB machine where the FTP files will be downloaded. It's best to enter an absolute file path here. If you enter a relative file path, the files will be stored at the path relative to the Java process that started the WebLogic Server.

- The Timeout field defines, in seconds, the amount of time to wait for a socket connection to the FTP server before failing.

- The Retry Count field defines how many times OSB should retry the file transfer if there is a timeout on the socket connection.

5. Click the Finish button to create the proxy service.

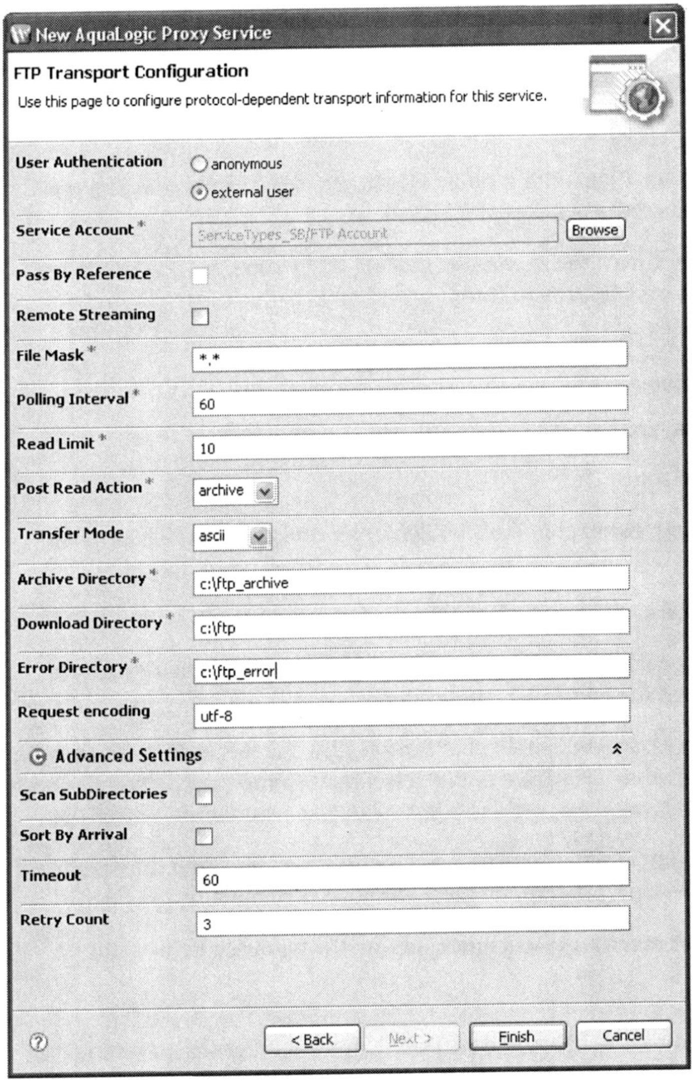

Figure 8-8. *Defining the FTP transport protocol details*

Next, you'll create a simple message flow for this proxy service. Add a Pipeline Pair node to the Start node, and then add a stage to the request pipeline. Name the stage show text info.

In the show text info stage, you'll create two new variables to demonstrate where to get the most pertinent information. The contents of the text file are held in the $body variable. You can extract just the text by using the expression $body/text(). Create the following actions in the show text info stage:

- Add an Assign action. Give it the variable textContents and the expression $body/text().

- Add a Log action. Give it the expression concat('Text contents are: ', $textContents). The Annotation property should be set to none, and the Severity property should be set to Error.

- Add another Assign action. Give it the variable fileName and the expression $inbound/ctx:transport/ctx:request/tp:headers/ftp:fileName.

- Add another Log action. Give it the expression concat('File name is: ', $fileName). Set Annotation to None and Severity to Error.

Testing the Text Message Service

Testing this service can take several forms:

- You can use the test console.

- You can use an FTP client, connect to the FileZilla server, and put a text file onto the FTP server.

- You can just make a local copy of a text file in the C:\ftproot directory.

We prefer the second approach because it more closely simulates how this service will operate in the real world. To run the test, follow these steps:

1. Create a new directory where you'll hold your sample files. For this example, name the temporary directory /ftptemp. Navigate to the new directory and create a couple short text files. We created files named a.txt and b.txt, with just a few words in each file.

2. Open a command prompt and navigate to the /ftptemp directory. Enter the command ftp. This starts the FTP client program on most Windows machines.

3. Connect to the FTP server on your local machine with the following command:

   open 127.0.0.1

4. You will be prompted for a username and password, in turn. Enter tester for the username and password for the password.

5. After you receive the "Logged on" message, type in the following command to change your upload directory on the FTP server to the ftp_in directory:

   cd ftp_in

6. Type in the FTP command mput *.txt (mput stands for "multiput," which allows you to send multiple files to the FTP server).

7. The FTP client prompts you to confirm each file (a.txt and b.txt, in this example). Press Y to confirm each file.

8. After the files are sent, you can type the commands close and quit to close the FTP connection and quit the FTP client.

In the OSB output console, you should see the results of the Log action that you defined for your proxy service. The output should look similar to the following:

```
<Sept 24, 2008 2:08:33 PM PDT> <Error> <OSB Logging> <Oracle-000000>
<[PipelinePairNode1, PipelinePairNode1_request, show text info, REQUEST]
Text contents are: This is the file a.txt END>
<Sept 24, 2008 2:08:33 PM PDT> <Error> <OSB Logging> <Oracle-000000>
<[PipelinePairNode1, PipelinePairNode1_request, show text info, REQUEST]
File name is: ftp_in/a.txt>
<Sept 24, 2008 2:08:33 PM PDT> <Error> <OSB Logging> <Oracle-000000>
<[PipelinePairNode1, PipelinePairNode1_request, show text info, REQUEST]
Text contents are: This is the file b.txt END>
<Sept 24, 2008 2:08:33 PM PDT> <Error> <OSB Logging> <Oracle-000000>
< [PipelinePairNode1, PipelinePairNode1_request, show text info, REQUEST]
File name is: ftp_in/b.txt>
```

Notice that the name of the file also includes the directory in which it resides on the FTP server. You'll need to account for this if the name of the file is important to your processing requirements. We won't bother to write a business service for this proxy service. The usage of the text data should be a trivial exercise for you by now.

Message Type: XML

There's no difference between an XML with no WSDL and the XML message type. However, you might use this message type for the following reasons:

- If XML is needed in the request or response, but not both.

- If you want to declare the schema of the XML message.

If XML is needed in both the request and response, then you should use the XML without WSDL service type, described earlier.

Message Type: MFL

MFL stands for Message Format Language. You can use MFL any time you need to process data that is formatted in some method other than XML. MFL allows you to define data format types, and then apply those types to messages that are sent and received from OSB. Some examples are COBOL copy books, comma-separated values, and EDI documents.

In the exercise in this section, you'll create a proxy service that is invoked by an e-mail message. The e-mail message will contain a formatted text message. The proxy service will read the e-mail and convert the formatted text message from its original format into a different text format that is expected by the business service. You'll also create a matching business service that will be invoked via FTP, building on some of the work you did in the previous example.

There are many moving parts in this exercise, so it will help if you keep an overview in mind of the various artifacts that you need to create and the steps you need to perform. Use the following list as a mental guide for the rest of this section:

- Install an e-mail server on your machine and create an e-mail account named proxy@mydomain.com.

- Create a service account to the e-mail server.

- Create a user account on the FTP server named customerftp. Assign the root directory of this user to D:\ftproot or C:\ftproot, whichever is appropriate for your environment. Be sure you manually create the ftproot/customerftp directory, or FileZilla might complain later about not being able to create the file.

- Create a service account to the FTP server.

- Create an MFL file that defines the data format that will be e-mailed to your proxy server.

- Create an MFL file that defines theformat of the file the business service will send to the FTP server.

- Create an XQuery transformation file that converts Email MFL format into the FTP format.

- Add both MFL files and the XQuery to the ServiceTypes_SB project.

- Create a proxy service based on the CustomerEmailFormat MFL resource and tell the proxy to poll the e-mail account for messages.

- Create a business service based on the CustomerFTPFormat MFL resource and tell it to send the data as a file to the FTP server.

- Write a message flow for the proxy service that uses the XQuery transformation and invokes the business service.

- Test the whole thing, end to end.

Simple, isn't it? Let's get started.

Setting Up the E-Mail Server and Client

You'll need an e-mail address that the proxy service can use when it checks to see if it has received an e-mail. Because it's unlikely that your system administrator will want you monkeying around with your company's real e-mail server, you'll set up your own e-mail server. For this, you'll use the Java Email Server, an open source project from SourceForge. You can download this file from the following URL:

http://sourceforge.net/project/showfiles.php?group_id=38473

To install the e-mail server, just open the ZIP file and extract the contents (preserving the directory structure) into a new directory. Once the files are in place, navigate into the directory where you extracted the files and edit the user.conf file. Add the following lines to the end of this file:

```
user.proxy@mydomain.com=password
userprop.proxy@mydomain.com.forwardAddresses=
user.mailclient@mydomain.com=password
userprop.mailclient@mydomain.com.forwardAddresses=
```

This creates a new e-mail user named proxy with a password of password. Don't change the values in the mail.conf file.

Tip If you have trouble running the e-mail server, you should check the mail.conf file first. However, the defaults are fine for most developer machines.

Next, you need an e-mail client so that you can send e-mail messages to proxy@mydomain.com to invoke the service. You'll use a simple e-mail client that will send e-mail to your proxy service. You can find the code in the MailClient_POJO project in WorkSpace Studio.

As mentioned earlier, your service will accept a formatted text message. If you take a look at the e-mail client that sends the formatted text message, you'll see in the body of the e-mail that the message has the following format:

```
[first name]\t[last name]\t[middle initial]\t[customer id]\r
```

The \t represents a tab. This is simply a tab-delimited message format. You could just as easily have used commas or another text character instead of the tab character. The important point is to understand how the body of the e-mail is formatted.

Creating the MFL Files

MFL is a notation that allows you to define arbitrary message formats, such as the tab-delimited format you'll use in this exercise. Your next steps are to create MFL files. You'll first build an MFL file that matches the tab-delimited format that will be e-mailed to your proxy service. You'll then build a second MFL file that represents the data format that will be sent to the FTP business service.

Follow these steps to create the e-mail format MFL file:

1. Right-click the ServiceTypes_SB project and select New ➤ MFL from the pop-up menu. Name the MFL file CustomerEmailFormat.mfl. Double-click the CustomerEmailFormat.mfl file to open it.

2. In the Format Builder application, select File ➤ New from the menu bar. You see the interface change and you have the opportunity to name the new message format. Change the message format name to CustomerEmailFormat and click the Apply button.

3. Right-click the envelope icon in the left pane of the Format Builder window and select Insert Field.

4. Name the field firstName and be sure the Optional check box is *unchecked*. The field type is a String value. This field will occur only once. The field is terminated by the \t delimiter, and the code page is UTF-8. Be sure to click the Apply button to save your changes to the new field.

5. Repeat steps 3 and 4 for the lastName and MI fields.

6. The last field you'll create is the CustomerID field. It's similar to the other fields in all respects, except one: the delimiter value is set to \r\n\r\n\r\n\r\n (that is, four pairs of \r\n characters). Your CustomerID field definition should look Figure 8-9.

■**Caution** The order of the fields shown in the Format Builder is critical. If your order is different, simply click and drag the fields in the left navigation pane to put them into the correct order.

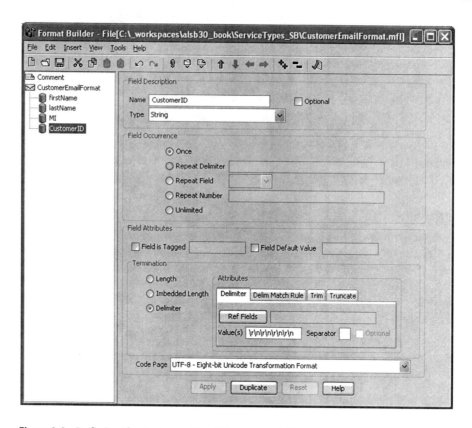

Figure 8-9. *Defining the CustomerEmailFormat.mfl file*

7. Save the CustomerEmailFormat.mfl file.

Next, you'll create the CustomerFTPFormat.mfl file, which defines the file format expected by the FTP server. This format has the following structure:

[ID]\t[Name]\r

As you can see, the format required by the FTP server is significantly different from the format you receive in the e-mail. A little transformation is in order to make this communication work. To further complicate matters, the FTP format requires that the ID field be a numeric field, while the e-mail format defines it as a `String` field. The game is afoot!

Create a new MFL file in the project and name it `CustomerFTPFormat.mfl`. Create the ID and Name fields, following the same procedure you just used with the `CustomerEmailFormat.mfl` file. The only difference is that the ID field must be defined as Numeric. Be sure the ID field is terminated with the `\t` character, and the Name field is terminated with `\r`. Your ID field definition should look like Figure 8-10. Save this file.

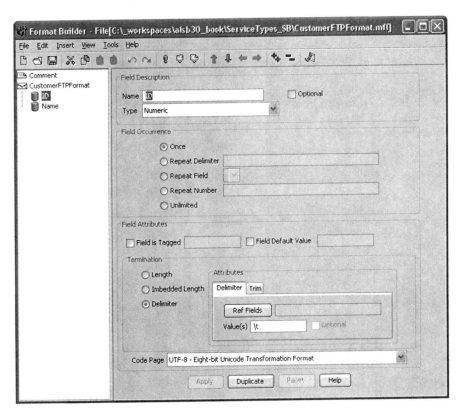

Figure 8-10. *Defining the CustomerFTPFormat.mfl file*

Sometimes when using the Format Builder, the changes it makes to the MFL files are not immediately recognized by WorkSpace Studio. Just to be sure that all of the resources are in sync in the IDE, click the `ServiceTypes_SB` project to select it, and then press the F5 key.

So far, you have defined your input and output formats. Now you need to define an XQuery resource that will perform the transformation of the data from the input format (`CustomerEmailFormat.mfl`) to the output format (`CustomerFTPFormat.mfl`).

Creating the XQuery Transformation for Converting Formats

You will use an XQuery transformation to create the rules for converting from one format to the other.

1. Create an XQuery transformation by right-clicking the ServiceTypes_SB project and selecting New ➤ XQuery Transformation from the pop-up menu. Set the file name to customerMFLTransform and click the Next button.

2. In the Source Types page of the New XQuery Transformation wizard, you specify the source of the XQuery transformation. Because MFL is a non-XML format, select the Non-XML radio button above the list box on the left side of the dialog box. Expand the path Typed/ServiceTypes_SB/CustomerEmailFormat and select CustomerEmailFormat. Set the Parameter Name setting for this data type to customerEmailFormat, as shown in Figure 8-11, and then click the Add button. Click the Next button to continue.

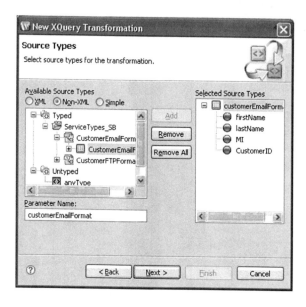

Figure 8-11. *Selecting the XQuery source type*

3. Next, you select the target type. Once again, select the Non-XML radio button. Then expand the Typed/ServiceTypes_SB/CustomerFTPFormat.mfl node so that you can select and add the CustomerFTPFormat object.

4. Click the Finish button.

You'll now see the customerMFLTransform.xq file in WorkSpace Studio. By default, you should see the design view, as shown in Figure 8-12.

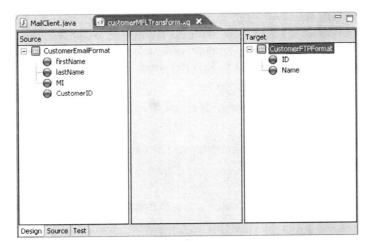

Figure 8-12. *XQuery transform design view*

As you've seen in previous chapters, the design view of the XQuery transformation editor is a powerful tool that allows you to work graphically and generate XQuery scripts. You need to do two things in this transformation. First, you'll map both the last name and first name from the source format to the Name field of the target format. Along the way, you'll ensure that the Name field of the target format ends up as [lastName], [firstName]. Adding the comma will help for human readability. Second, you'll map the CustomerID from the source to the ID field of the target, converting it from a String to a Numeric along the way.

5. Click the lastName field and drag it onto the target's Name field, then release the mouse button. A green arrow will appear, visually linking the two fields.

6. Click and drag the firstName field from the source onto the Name field of the target and release the mouse. Your XQuery transformation should look like Figure 8-13.

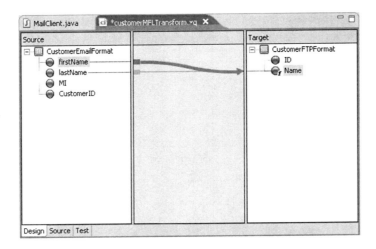

Figure 8-13. *Mapping the name fields to the target*

7. You need to do a little extra formatting in the Name field of the target format. Click the Source tab at the bottom of the window to see the raw XQuery text that has been generated so far. There is a single XQuery function declaration. In that function, look for the text between the <Name></Name> tags. That text should be as follows:

```
<Name>{
concat($customerEmailFormat/lastName, $customerEmailFormat/firstName)
}</Name>
```

8. You want to add a comma and space between the last name and the first name. Modify this line of code as follows:

```
<Name>{
concat($customerEmailFormat/lastName, ', ' $customerEmailFormat/firstName)
}</Name>
```

9. Switch back to the design view. Now you want to map the CustomerID source field into the ID field of the target format. If you click and drag, as you did before, you'll get the following error message:

```
ERROR: The datatype of the source node: [CustomerID]
and the target node [ID] are incompatible.
```

That's because you can't map a String into a Numeric. The XQuery transformation tool isn't able to make a judgment call on this kind of transformation, but *you* know that the String version of the CustomerID field will always be a numeric value, so you need to create this mapping yourself.

10. Go back into the source view of the transformation and add the following line of code just below the opening <CustomerFTPFormat> tag:

```
<ID>{ $customerEmailFormat/CustomerID/text() }</ID>
```

11. Switch back to the design view, which should look like Figure 8-14. Notice the little *f* characters on the icons next to the ID and Name attributes of the target. They indicate that the mapping uses one or more XQuery functions and is not a straight copy of the data in the fields.

12. Save the XQuery transformation file.

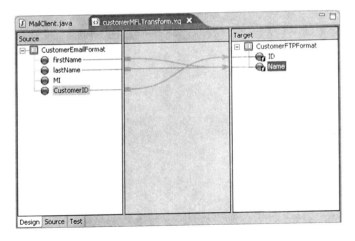

Figure 8-14. *The complete XQuery transformation*

Creating E-Mail and FTP Server Service Accounts

Next, you need to create two new service accounts: one to log into the e-mail server to retrieve the e-mail and one to connect to your FTP server using a different login name.

1. In the ServiceTypes_SB project, create a new service account named ProxyEmailAccount. Set the Resource Type setting to Static. Set the username to proxy@mydomain.com and the password to password. Click the Finish button to save this service account.

2. In the ServiceTypes_SB project, create a new service account named CustomerFTPAccount. Set Resource Type to Static. Set the username to customerftp and the password to password.

3. Create a new subdirectory in your ftproot/ directory named customerftp.

4. Open the FileZilla server interface and create a new user named customerftp with a password of password. Assign this account to the home directory ftproot/customerftp with full privileges to that directory.

These are all the service accounts you need for this exercise.

Creating the MFLEmail2FTP Proxy Service

You're now ready to create your proxy service.

1. In the ServiceTypes_SB project, create a new proxy service. Name the proxy MFLEmail2FTP. You can optionally provide a description of the service (remember that this is a best practice when creating real-world services), and select the Messaging Service option for the Service Type setting. Click the Next button.

2. Select MFL as the request message type as MFL and select the `CustomerEmailFormat`. For the response message type, select None. Click the Next button.

3. Select the Email protocol. Set the endpoint URI to use the POP3 port of 110, not the SMTP port, because you're reading e-mail via POP3 in this exercise. Figure 8-15 shows these settings. Click Next to continue.

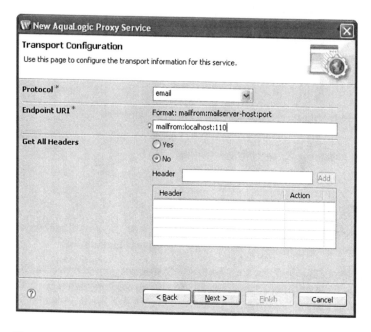

Figure 8-15. *Configuring the Email protocol*

4. On the Email Transport Configuration page of the wizard, set the options as follows (see Figure 8-16):

- For the Service Account setting, select the `ProxyEmailAccount`, so that your proxy service will be able to log in to the e-mail server to retrieve the e-mail messages.

- The Polling Interval setting defines, in seconds, how often the proxy service will connect to the e-mail server to check for new e-mail. Leave the default of 60 seconds.

- The Read Limit specifies the maximum number of e-mail messages to process each time the proxy service connects to the e-mail server. Leave the default of 10.

- The Post Read action should be delete, which specifies that the e-mail messages that are read will then be deleted.

- Set the Attachments combo box to ignore, because you aren't interested in any e-mail attachments.

- The IMAP Move Folder setting is the directory used when processing. This folder is used only if the Post Read Action field is set to move.

- The Download Directory setting specifies the directory into which the e-mail messages are downloaded when they are about to be processed. The default is fine for this example.

- The Archive Directory setting specifies the directory where the e-mail messages are archived if Post Read Action is set to archive.

- The Error Directory setting specifies where the e-mail messages are stored if there is an error processing them. Again, the default directory is fine.

- The Request Encoding setting specifies the encoding scheme used to encode the e-mail messages. This is used to ensure that the proxy server parses the e-mail messages using the correct character encoding scheme. Leave the default of ISO-8859-1.

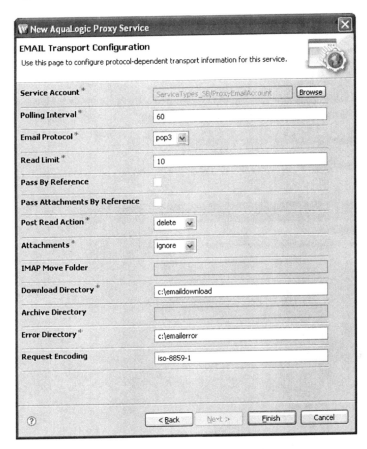

Figure 8-16. *Configuring the e-mail transport details*

5. Click the Finish button. The basics of the proxy service are now defined.

Creating the MFL Business Service

You must now create a business service that will accept a text message using the CustomerFTPFormat.

1. In the BusinessServices folder of the project, create a business service with the name MFLBusiness and select Messaging Service for the Service Type setting.

2. Set the request message type to MFL and select the CustomerFTPFormat MFL resource. Be sure that the response message type is set to None; otherwise, you won't be able to use the FTP transport protocol. Click Next.

3. For the transport protocol, select FTP and leave the load-balancing algorithm at the default value of round-robin. Add an endpoint URI of ftp://localhost:21. Accept the remaining default values and click the Next button.

4. In the next page of the wizard, set the options as follows (see Figure 8-17):

   • For the User Authentication setting, choose external user.

   • For Service Account, select CustomerFTPAccount.

   • Set the Prefix for destination File Name field to customer.

   • Set the Suffix for destination File Name field to .text.

   • For the Transfer Mode setting, choose binary, simply because it allows a greater variety of character encodings to be transferred.

   • For Request Encoding, leave the default of UTF-8.

5. Click the Finish button.

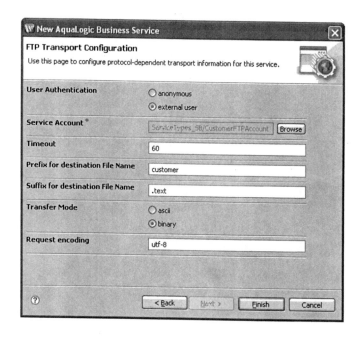

Figure 8-17. *Setting the FTP transport configuration*

Defining the Proxy Service Message Flow

Next, you define the message flow for your MFLEmail2FTP proxy service. Add a Pipeline Pair node to the message flow. In the request pipeline, add a stage and name it get Email Info. This stage is not necessary to the function of the proxy service, but we wanted to demonstrate where you find some of the important information about the e-mail message.

Edit the get Email Info stage and create some Assign actions. First, you'll create Assign actions to get the firstName, lastName, and CustomerID from the e-mail message. Click the Expression link for each Assign action, and then select the Variable Structures tab on the right side of the Expression Editor. Open the $body (request) node and the nested CustomerEmailFormat node, and *voilà!* You can see the structure of the MFL file represented in the format to which you should now be accustomed, as shown in Figure 8-18. You don't need to worry about parsing; OSB takes care of all those boring details.

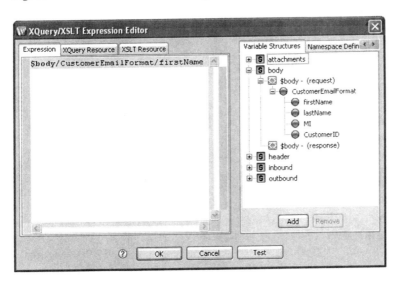

Figure 8-18. *Accessing MFL data is easy within the body variable.*

Click the firstName node and paste it into the Expression Editor's text area. Assign the value of that expression to a variable named firstName. Do the same for the lastName and CustomerID fields, assigning them to local variables.

The To and From fields of the e-mail are accessed through the $inbound structure. Figure 8-19 shows the exact location of this information. If you need to know the date of the e-mail or if you make service-routing decisions based on who sent the e-mail, the $inbound variable is a rich source of information.

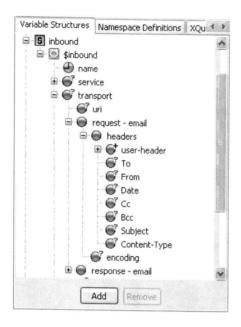

Figure 8-19. *The $inbound structure holds the rest of the commonly needed e-mail information.*

Just for completeness, create two new local variables and assign their values based on the From and Date fields of the $inbound structure. Add a few log statements that output this information at the severity error level, so you can see the debug information on the OSB console as you run your tests.

Next, you need to add a Route node to the Pipeline Pair node to route the request to the MFLBusiness service. Edit the Route node and add a Replace action to the Request Actions section. Define the XPath as "." in the variable body. Click the Expression link, and in the Expression Editor, click the XQuery Resource tab. Click the Browse button to select the specific XQuery resource you wish to use. In this case, the resource is the CustomerMFLTransform resource you defined earlier.

In the Bind Variables section, the console is asking you to bind the customerEmailFormat variable (this is an external variable defined in the CustomerMFLTransform.xq file you created earlier) to the local variable that contains that data. That information happens to be at $body/CustomerEmailFormat, so enter that as the binding.

You want to replace the node contents, not the entire body node, so select that radio button in the Replace action's Properties window, as shown in Figure 8-20. With this step complete, save everything and publish your changes to the server. It's time to test your service.

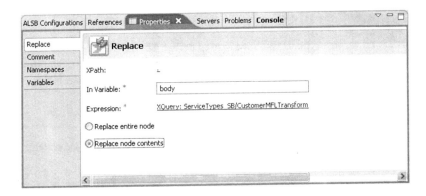

Figure 8-20. *Replace node for the MFLBusiness message flow*

Testing the MFL Service

Before you test your new MFL service, you need to be sure that your e-mail server is running. If you installed the Java Email Server, as suggested for this exercise, you need to run the `mail.bat` file in the `bin/` directory. Ensure that the e-mail server starts properly before proceeding.

To make life a little simpler, a `MailClient` program in the `MailClient_POJO` project will send a properly formatted e-mail to the `proxy@domain.com` e-mail account. Open the source file for `MailClient.java` in Workspace Studio and right-click in the source code. Select Run As ➤ Java Application from the pop-up menu, and the client will send an e-mail message. You might need to wait up to two minutes to see the proxy service receive the e-mail message and the `MFLBusiness` service fire off the FTP event.

Next, check the file that was sent to the FTP server (look in the `ftproot/customerftp` directory). You should see a file with a highly decorated name, similar to the following:

```
customer7145345159564708646--7d2b9710.1192b84e7a3.-7fb7.text
```

Open the file to ensure that it's a properly encoded, tab-delimited file whose content looks like the following:

```
75          Doe, John
```

What you've no doubt noticed after completing this exercise is the amount of coding and complexity involved in getting it to work. Although it's pretty cool to see this beast run, this level of complexity is completely counter to good SOA practices. There's a *reason* why e-mail and FTP are considered legacy connection mechanisms. Although it's good to know you have this level of flexibility with OSB, you should never connect a system of this complexity directly to your main ESB. Instead, you can use specific instances of OSB to act as an adapter to these legacy systems, converting these file formats into proper XML Schema objects and exchanging the data via web services.

Transport-Typed Service

Through the transport-typed service type, OSB allows you to define EJBs as business services. In the example in this section, we'll demonstrate how a SOAP proxy service can invoke a stateless session bean (the only kind of EJB you can invoke from OSB) to calculate the amount of tax on a given price.

Note You can also use the "flow" transport for a transport-typed service. We discussed this type of transport in Chapter 7, in the section about split-join flows.

EJB As Service Type

Using an EJB as a business service requires the following steps:

1. Create and deploy the stateless session bean (TaxCalculator in this example) to the WebLogic Server.

2. Create a business service that knows how to invoke the EJB.

3. Create a proxy service that returns the requested information (the tax for any amount given to it in this example).

4. Create the message flow that routes the proxy message to the EJB, and then returns the requested information (calculated tax amount) via the proxy service.

Creating the TaxCalculator Bean

The easiest way to get the Tax_EJB project is to import the project from the source code that comes with this book. If you want to create the EJB from scratch, you will need to create a new WebLogic EJB project in WorkSpace Studio. In the src directory of the project, create a package named com.alsb.ejb, and then create a WebLogic session bean inside that package. Name the bean TaxCalculator and edit the source code so that it looks like the code in Listing 8-5. Really, all you need to do is to add the calculateTax method as shown in the listing. Be sure to add the Tax_EJB project to the OSB server list in the Servers window.

Listing 8-5. *The TaxCalculator Bean*

```
package com.alsb.ejb;

import javax.ejb.SessionBean;
import weblogic.ejb.GenericSessionBean;
import weblogic.ejbgen.RemoteMethod;
import weblogic.ejbgen.Session;
import weblogic.ejbgen.JndiName;
import weblogic.ejbgen.FileGeneration;
import weblogic.ejbgen.Constants;

/**
 * GenericSessionBean subclass automatically generated by Workshop.
```

```
 *
 * Please complete the ejbCreate method as needed to properly initialize
 * new instances of your bean and add all required business methods.
 * Also, review the Session, JndiName and FileGeneration annotations
 * to ensure the settings match the bean's intended use.
 */
@Session(ejbName = "TaxCalculator")
@JndiName(remote = "ejb.TaxCalculatorRemoteHome")
@FileGeneration(remoteClass = Constants.Bool.TRUE,
    remoteHome = Constants.Bool.TRUE,
    localClass = Constants.Bool.FALSE,
    localHome = Constants.Bool.FALSE)
public class TaxCalculator extends GenericSessionBean implements SessionBean {
    private static final long serialVersionUID = 1L;

    /* (non-Javadoc)
     * @see weblogic.ejb.GenericSessionBean#ejbCreate()
     */
    public void ejbCreate() {
    }

    @RemoteMethod(transactionAttribute=Constants.TransactionAttribute.SUPPORTS)
    public double calculateTax(double taxableAmount) {
        return taxableAmount * 0.08d;
    }
}
```

The majority of the file is annotation. This greatly simplifies EJB development because you can now generate the boilerplate EJB code from the annotations in the implementation file.

As you can see in the source code, the tax rate is defined at 8 percent. The method returns 8 percent of the taxableAmount argument. No effort is made to qualify the taxable amount (that is, it will calculate negative numbers also) simply because this is demo code.

You will need to export the Tax_EJB project as an EJB JAR file. Name the JAR file Tax_EJB.jar. Let's move on to building the business service.

Creating the Business Service

Just like any other EJB client, OSB needs a client JAR file to connect to an EJB. Fortunately, the Tax_EJB.jar file that you exported in the previous section also contains the necessary client files. You first step will be to copy the Tax_EJB.jar file from the Tax_EJB project and paste it into the ServiceTypes_SB project.

In the ServiceTypes_SB project, you need to create a business service named TaxCalculator in the BusinessServices folder. In the New Business Service wizard, select the Transport Typed Service option for the Service Type setting and click the Next button. The Protocol field should default to EJB. An EJB endpoint has the following structure: ejb:<provider>:<jndi remote home name>. For the endpoint URI, use the following:

ejb::ejb.TaxCalculatorRemoteHome

You have the luxury of leaving the `<provider>` field blank because you're calling an EJB on the local machine. If you need to invoke a remote EJB, then you must create a JNDI provider and use it in the URI. Click the Next button to continue.

The next page of the wizard, shown in Figure 8-21, is pretty cool. Click the Browse button for the Client Jar field and select the JAR file you added earlier in this exercise. Like magic, the metadata defined in the JAR file is populated into the appropriate fields in the window! This is because OSB interrogates the JAR file resource to discover the important aspects of the EJB.

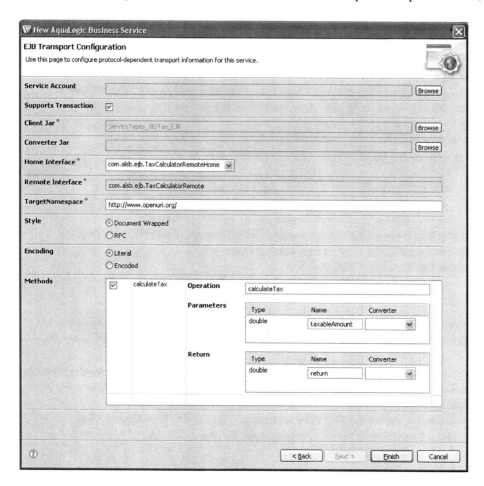

Figure 8-21. *Defining the EJB invocation details*

By default, the Style setting is Document Wrapped and the Encoding setting is Literal. These options provide the greatest level of interoperability.

In the Methods section of the page, change the name of the parameter to `taxableAmount`. Click the Finish button to save your business service.

CREATING A JNDI PROVIDER

In our simple example, we left the provider blank in the endpoint URI, because the EJB is deployed onto the same servers as the service bus. However, in real-world deployments, you'll often need to create a JNDI provider. Here, we'll walk through creating a JNDI provider to your local machine to demonstrate the process.

JNDI providers are not specific to an OSB project. Instead, they are created in OSB configuration projects. Right-click the OSB30 Book Conf project and select New ➤ JNDI Provider from the pop-up menu. Give the resource a name (localProvider in this example). The New JNDI Provider Resource wizard allows you add a new JNDI provider.

Note the use of the T3 protocol in the provider URL. Only T3 is supported here. Set the other fields appropriately (for example, set both the username and password to weblogic if you followed the instructions in Chapter 2 for creating your OSB domain), and then click Finish to create the JNDI provider. Now you can edit the EJB protocol for the same business service that you defined in this exercise and use the localProvider that you just created. The behavior will be the same. The proper endpoint URI is as follows:

```
ejb:localProvider:ejb.TaxCalculatorRemoteHome
```

Creating the Proxy Service

To create the proxy service, begin by creating a WSDL folder in the ServiceTypes_SB project. In this new folder, create a WSDL resource named TaxProxy.wsdl. You can either copy the TaxProxy.wsdl file from the sample code that accompanies this book or simply create a WSDL file that defines a web service with a single operation: calculateTax.

Next, create the proxy service named EJBTax and set the service type as a WSDL web service, based on the TaxProxy.wsdl file that you just defined in the project. Click the Next button. Set the protocol to HTTP. Set the endpoint URI to /ServiceTypes_SB/EJBTax. Click the Finish button.

Creating the Message Flow

The last item you need to create is the message flow that routes the data from the proxy service to the business service. Open the Message Flow window for the proxy service, and create a Route node that contains a Routing action. Edit the Routing action and set it to route to the TaxCalculator business service, invoking the calculateTax operation. In the Request Action section, add an Assign action that will assign the correct value to the amount variable, as shown in Figure 8-22. Set the value to a local variable named amount. Assign the value of the following expression:

```
$body/alsb:calculateTaxRequest/alsb:taxableAmount/text()
```

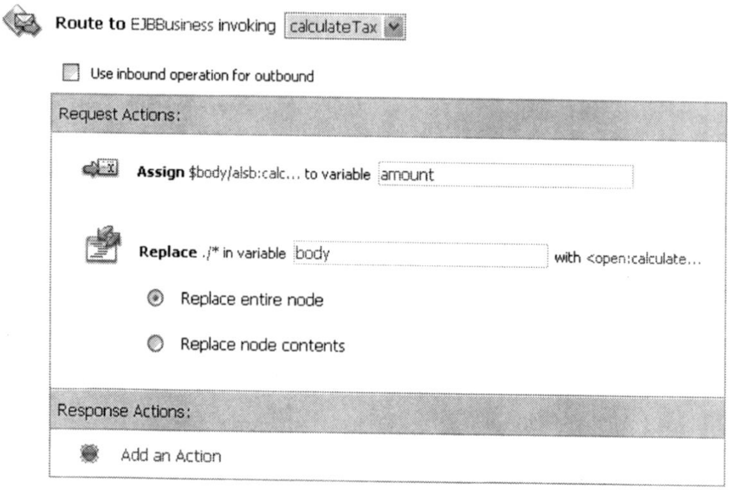

Figure 8-22. *Route node for the EJBBusiness message flow*

Next, you need a Replace action to replace the contents of the entire SOAP body element contained in the $body variable with the following expression:

```
<open:calculateTax>
    <open:taxableAmount>{$amount}</open:taxableAmount>
</open:calculateTax>
```

Once you paste in the preceding expression, OSB will complain about not knowing the value of the open prefix. You need to define the open namespace in OSB. To define the namespace, click the Expression link to open the Expression Editor. Click the Namespace Definitions tab on the right side of the window, and then click the Add button. Add a namespace with the prefix of open and the URI of http://www.openuri.org/. The final expression is shown in Figure 8-23.

■**Caution** Remember that namespaces are defined by their text value, not by their labels. Therefore, it's critical that you get the string values correct. We spent 20 minutes debugging this simple transformation just because we had originally omitted the trailing slash and defined the namespace as `http://www.openuri.org` instead of `http://www.openuri.org/`!

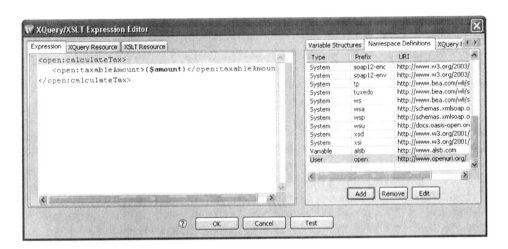

Figure 8-23. *Adding a user-defined namespace*

After you complete the Routing action, including the creation of the user-defined open namespace, save all your work and publish to the server. Test the service by entering different amounts into the test console to see the responses.

Why Use EJBs?

There are a lot of EJBs in the world. Odds are pretty good that if your company uses Java EE 5, you have legacy EJBs that implement business logic. It might make sense for you to wrap these EJBs in web services to make them more easily accessible to your enterprise. OSB allows you to connect to these assets without recompiling them or otherwise having to modify them, thereby reducing the level of effort to publish the functionality of these EJBs.

However, there's a downside to this strategy, or at least a subtle and insidious danger. EJBs are usually not written with services in mind. Entity EJBs usually contain little abstraction from the data source, and primarily function as a mechanism to mediate between data consumers and the database. Even stateless session beans, implementing the Façade pattern to hide the complexity of underlying EJB interdependencies, are rarely written to service-oriented standards. Publishing them directly as services might reduce the level of abstraction and loose coupling in your ESB. Low-level implementation details contained in common EJB interfaces can have a dire effect on an enterprise-level service bus.

Although it's *possible* to write service-oriented EJBs, it's rare that an EJB is written to that level. By their very nature, EJBs are designed to implement IT and business concepts close to the physical level. Usually, you'll find it necessary to create proxy services at a greater level of abstraction. These proxy services act more as an adapter for the EJBs. It's these low-level proxy services that can then participate in the overall SOA.

POJOs

Another feature of OSB, introduced in version 2.5, is the ability for a Java Callout action to invoke Java code directly. This approach uses what are colloquially known as POJOs, which are simple Java classes without the overhead associated with EJBs and JWS.

The benefit of using POJOs is that they are technically simple to create and have little overhead, at least compared to EJBs. The drawbacks of POJOs are the same as the benefits. Because they have little overhead, there's no thread management (as you would have in a Java EE 5 container), and their very simplicity means that without some sort of IT governance, anyone who can write even the simplest Java code can create resources for your service bus. Use POJOs with caution.

An important restriction to using a POJO in OSB is that only static methods are recognized by the service bus. The parameters that you pass to the POJO can be any arbitrary Java objects that are stored intact in variables (in a java-content XML element that points to the Java object cached in the system) and passed from Java callout to Java callout. However, there's nothing to stop you from instantiating Java objects or threads from within the POJO itself. This is similar to using an EJB—the Java EE 5 specification states that you may not create threads within an EJB, but it's still possible to do it. Similarly, Oracle strongly discourages the creation of threads and object instantiation within a POJO.

Okay, with all the legal disclaimers aside, let's hammer out a POJO to see just how easy it is. Listing 8-6 shows the source code for a simple POJO that, like the previous EJB exercise, calculates the 8 percent tax of any amount that you give it. Now this is easy code!

Listing 8-6. *A Sample POJO*

```
package com.alsb.pojo;

public class TaxPojo {
   /**
    * OSB can only call static methods in a POJO.
    *
    * @param taxableAmount
    * @return The additional tax to be paid
    */
   public static double calculateTax(double taxableAmount) {
      double taxRate = 0.08;
      return taxableAmount * taxRate;
   }
}
```

You can find this code in the ServiceTypes_SB project in WorkSpace Studio. If you wish to create your own POJO project, simply follow these steps:

1. Create a new Java project in WorkSpace Studio. Name it Tax_POJO.

2. Add a source code folder to the project. Traditionally, this is named src.

3. Create a package in the source code folder called com.alsb.pojo.

4. Create a new Java class in the com.alsb.pojo package. Name the class TaxPojo and use the code in Listing 8-6 to define the class.

5. You need to create a JAR file for the TaxPojo project. Right-click the TaxPojo project and select Export from the pop-up menu.

6. In the Export dialog box, select JAR file from the list of file types you can export. Click the Next button.

7. Select the file name and the destination of your JAR file. We prefer to put them in the root directory of our projects.

8. Click the Finish button.

This builds the JAR file for the POJO project. Next, you need to copy it into the ServiceTypes_SB project.

Now you will create a proxy service called TaxPojo. Select the Message Type option for the Service Type setting and click the Next button. Select Text for both the request message and the response message and click the Next button.

Set the protocol to HTTP and the endpoint URI to /ServiceTypes_SB/TaxPojo. Accept the default values for the rest of the New Proxy Service wizard and save the proxy service. Next, you need to create a message flow for the proxy.

Add a Pipeline Pair node to the message flow. In the request pipeline, create a calculate tax stage. Create a return tax due stage in the response pipeline. Edit the calculate tax stage.

In the calculate tax stage, add an Assign action that assigns the value of the $body/text() expression to the taxableAmount local variable.

Next, add a Java Callout action below the Assign action. Click the Method field's Browse button and select the TaxPojo.jar file from the project. You will be prompted to choose the method you want to use. Since there is only one method available, choose that one. Click the Finish button.

Now you need to fill in some simple data to connect the Java Callout action to the POJO. Set the expression for the method to $taxableAmount and the result value to taxDue. The Properties window for your Java Callout action should look like Figure 8-24.

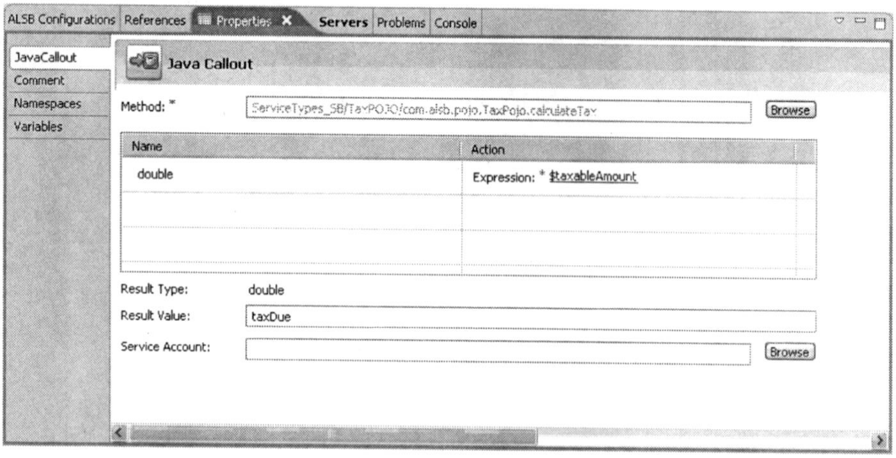

Figure 8-24. *The calculate tax Java callout*

Next, edit the return tax due stage in the response pipeline. Because you didn't route to a service, the Pipeline Pair node simply echoes the request document back to you, but you can place a Log action in this stage so that you can see the results of the POJO invocation. Use the following expression in the Log action:

```
concat('Tax due is ', $taxDue)
```

Save all your work and publish everything to the OSB server. When you test the service, you *just enter a number* in the large text area. There is no XML involved in this invocation. Look in the server console to see the log output and verify that the POJO executed properly.

In the real world, you probably wouldn't use a POJO to calculate a tax. In the United States, tax rates vary at the federal, state, and local levels, depending on the product. Most countries have similarly complex rules and calculations for their taxes. However, there are some applications where a POJO makes sense. If you have logic that's better expressed in Java code than it is in a database or in XQuery, POJOs are a perfect match.

Summary

As you've seen in this chapter, OSB provides myriad ways of connecting to and communicating with external systems. It provides an excellent mechanism for performing intelligent routing and data transformation. We've gone into great detail here and exercised almost every major capability of the service bus. At this point, you should have a solid understanding of the primary capabilities of OSB, and therefore a good idea of where you could use OSB within your architecture.

■■■

## CHAPTER 9

Advanced Messaging Topics

O SB 3 introduces some new messaging capabilities. It includes built-in support for the Web Services Reliable Messaging specification (WS-ReliableMessaging). You can now "throttle" web services and set priorities based on the caller. You can also manage service endpoints pools more effectively. This chapter covers these topics, as well as how to send SOAP messages with attachments.

Web Services Reliable Messaging

Web Services Reliable Messaging (WSRM) is a specification for a protocol that is able to deliver messages reliably between distributed applications, even if a hardware or software failure occurs. The WSRM specification is codeveloped by BEA, IBM, Microsoft, and TIBCO, so it has broad industry support.

In OSB 3, WSRM is implemented as a message transport. The reliable messaging policies can be defined directly in your WSDL file, or you can apply the policies outside the WSDL file. We prefer the latter approach, because it helps to keep the WSDL file simpler and easier to understand, while giving you more flexibility to change how you manage the WSDL by applying different contracts to it. As an example, we'll demonstrate how to create a reliable messaging service using the latter approach.

Setting Up the Reliable Messaging Service

You can find the sample code for this exercise in the WSRM_SB project. However, you'll find that OSB makes WSRM so simple to implement that you can easily type in the majority of this exercise. The only exception may be the basic WSDL file, which is shown in Listing 9-1.

Listing 9-1. *The ReliableMessagingProxy.wsdl File for the Sample Reliable Service*

```
<?xml version='1.0' encoding='UTF-8'?>
<definitions name="ReliableMessagingProxyDefinitions"
    targetNamespace="http://www.alsb.com/"
    xmlns="http://schemas.xmlsoap.org/wsdl/"
    xmlns:xs="http://www.w3.org/2001/XMLSchema"
    xmlns:alsb="http://www.alsb.com/"
    xmlns:soap="http://schemas.xmlsoap.org/wsdl/soap/">
```

```xml
<types>
    <xs:schema attributeFormDefault="unqualified"
        elementFormDefault="qualified"
        targetNamespace="http://www.alsb.com/"
        xmlns:order="http://www.alsb.com/order/">
        <!-- This is a utility element, so we can safely
             define it completely in this WSDL -->
        <xs:element name="CustomerName">
            <xs:complexType>
                <xs:sequence>
                    <xs:element name="firstName" type="xs:string" />
                    <xs:element name="lastName" type="xs:string" />
                </xs:sequence>
            </xs:complexType>
        </xs:element>

        <xs:element name="customerID" type="xs:int" />
    </xs:schema>
</types>
<message name="getCustomerRequest">
    <part name="customerID" element="alsb:customerID" />
</message>
<message name="getCustomerResponse">
    <part name="customerName" element="alsb:CustomerName" />
</message>
<portType name="ReliableMessagingProxyPort">
    <operation name="getCustomer" parameterOrder="customerID">
        <input message="alsb:getCustomerRequest" />
        <output message="alsb:getCustomerResponse" />
    </operation>
</portType>
<binding name="ReliableMessagingSOAPBinding"
    type="alsb:ReliableMessagingProxyPort">
    <soap:binding style="document"
        transport="http://schemas.xmlsoap.org/soap/http" />
    <operation name="getCustomer">
        <soap:operation soapAction="getCustomer" style="document" />
        <input>
            <soap:body parts="customerID" use="literal" />
        </input>
        <output>
            <soap:body parts="customerName" use="literal" />
        </output>
    </operation>
</binding>
<service name="ReliableMessagingProxyService">
    <port binding="alsb:ReliableMessagingSOAPBinding"
        name="ReliableOrderMgrProxySoapPort">
```

```
    <soap:address
        location="http://localhost:7001/esb/ReliableOrderMgrService" />
    </port>
  </service>
</definitions>
```

As you can see in Listing 9-1, this WSDL file is completely unremarkable. It makes no mention of WSRM or any policies.

Your next step is to create a proxy service named `ReliableMessaging.proxy` and base the proxy service on the WSDL file. As you move through the New Proxy Service wizard, be sure to set the protocol to WS.

When you finish the wizard, you will see the Policy tab for the proxy service, and there will be an error message stating that there must be reliable messaging policy assertions.

Applying a WSRM Policy

For this example, you will apply a predefined policy to the WSDL, as follows:

1. Click the Custom Policy Bindings radio button. You will now see the ReliableMessaging service in the list. Click the plus sign to the left of the ReliableMessaging service to expand its contents.

2. Within the ReliableMessaging service is an entry for Service Level Policies. Click the plus sign to the left of the Service Level Policies entry to create a slot for our policy.

3. Click the Insert [🖉] icon to select the policy that you want to apply to the service.

4. Click the Predefined Policy radio button to see the policies that are predefined in OSB. Select the `LongRunningReliability.xml` policy. Your window should now look like Figure 9-1.

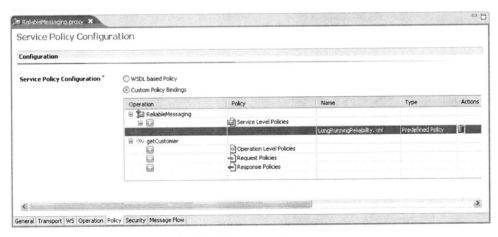

Figure 9-1. *Selecting a predefined policy for a WSRM proxy service*

5. Save all of your work.

Now you can right-click the `ReliableMessaging.proxy` file in WorkSpace Studio and select Oracle (or AquaLogic, depending on the version) Service Bus ➤ Generate Effective WSDL from the pop-up menu. This will create a ZIP file that contains the WSDL for the proxy service that OSB will publish. If you examine the `ReliableMessagingProxy.wsdl` file, shown in Listing 9-2, you will see how the original WSDL has been modified to include the necessary links to the `LongRunningReliability.xml` policy.

Listing 9-2. *The Effective WSDL for the ReliableMessaging.proxy Service (ReliableMessagingProxy.wsdl)*

```
<?xml version="1.0" encoding="UTF-8"?>
<s0:definitions name="ReliableMessagingProxyDefinitions"
targetNamespace="http://www.alsb.com/" xmlns:s0="http://schemas.xmlsoap.org/wsdl/"
xmlns:s1="http://www.alsb.com/" xmlns:s2="http://schemas.xmlsoap.org/wsdl/soap/"
xmlns:wsp="http://schemas.xmlsoap.org/ws/2004/09/policy">
  <wsp:UsingPolicy s0:Required="true"/>
  <s0:types>
    <xs:schema attributeFormDefault="unqualified" elementFormDefault="qualified"
targetNamespace="http://www.alsb.com/" xmlns:alsb="http://www.alsb.com/"
xmlns:order="http://www.alsb.com/order/"
xmlns:soap="http://schemas.xmlsoap.org/wsdl/soap/"
xmlns:xs="http://www.w3.org/2001/XMLSchema">
...
type="s1:ReliableMessagingProxyPort">
    <s2:binding style="document" transport="http://schemas.xmlsoap.org/soap/http"/>
    <wsp:Policy>
      <wsp:PolicyReference URI="policy:LongRunningReliability.xml"/>
    </wsp:Policy>
    <s0:operation name="getCustomer">
      <s2:operation soapAction="getCustomer" style="document"/>
      <s0:input>
        <s2:body parts="customerID" use="literal"/>
      </s0:input>
      <s0:output>
        <s2:body parts="customerName" use="literal"/>
      </s0:output>
    </s0:operation>
  </s0:binding>
  <s0:service name="ReliableMessagingProxyService">
    <s0:port binding="s1:ReliableMessagingSOAPBinding"
name="ReliableOrderMgrProxySoapPort">
      <s2:address location="http://localhost:7001/WSRM_SB/ReliableMessaging"/>
    </s0:port>
  </s0:service>
</s0:definitions>
```

We have highlighted the interesting sections of the effective WSDL in bold so you can see how the WSRM policy was applied. You can see how this approach simplifies the management of the service. If you needed to change the reliable messaging service, you could create and/or assign a different policy.

■**Caution** Be aware that changing the policy will affect the clients of that service. Any time you change the WSDL, you are changing the service.

Two predefined WSRM policies ship with OSB. For this example, we used the LongRunningReliability.xml policy file. The other supplied policy file is DefaultReliability.xml, shown in Listing 9-3. This policy defines an inactivity timeout of 5 minutes, and retransmission of the message every 3 seconds.

Listing 9-3. *DefaultReliability.xml Policy File*

```
<?xml version="1.0"?>
<wsp:Policy
    xmlns:wsrm="http://schemas.xmlsoap.org/ws/2005/02/rm/policy"
    xmlns:wsp="http://schemas.xmlsoap.org/ws/2004/09/policy"
    xmlns:beapolicy="http://www.bea.com/wsrm/policy"
  >
  <wsrm:RMAssertion >
    <wsrm:InactivityTimeout
        Milliseconds="600000" />
    <wsrm:BaseRetransmissionInterval
        Milliseconds="3000" />
    <wsrm:ExponentialBackoff />
    <wsrm:AcknowledgementInterval
        Milliseconds="200" />
    <beapolicy:Expires Expires="P1D" optional="true"/>
  </wsrm:RMAssertion>
</wsp:Policy>
```

Now take a look at the LongRunningReliability.xml policy file, shown in Listing 9-4. It has a much longer inactivity timeout period: 86,400,000 milliseconds, or one full day.

Listing 9-4. *The LongRunningReliability.xml Policy File*

```
<?xml version="1.0"?>
<wsp:Policy
    xmlns:wsrm="http://schemas.xmlsoap.org/ws/2005/02/rm/policy"
    xmlns:wsp="http://schemas.xmlsoap.org/ws/2004/09/policy"
    xmlns:beapolicy="http://www.bea.com/wsrm/policy"
  >
  <wsrm:RMAssertion >
```

```
    <wsrm:InactivityTimeout
        Milliseconds="86400000" />
    <wsrm:BaseRetransmissionInterval
        Milliseconds="3000" />
    <wsrm:ExponentialBackoff />
    <wsrm:AcknowledgementInterval
        Milliseconds="200" />
    <beapolicy:Expires Expires="P1M" optional="true"/>
  </wsrm:RMAssertion>
</wsp:Policy>
```

You can also define your own policies if the predefined policies don't meet your needs. Simply create a new WS-Policy file (by right-clicking in a folder or project and select New ➤ WS-Policy File from the pop-up menu) and modify it as desired. Then apply it to the proxy service by clicking the WS Policy radio button instead of the Predefined Policy button when selecting policies.

Service Throttling

Service throttling is the term used to describe OSB's ability to restrict the message flow to a business service. It may sound odd to deliberately restrict the rate of messages to a business service, but you might want to do this for a couple reasons:

- The back-end business service may be able to only process messages serially or with limited concurrency before the service begins to degrade rapidly due to overload. This is the case with certain telecommunication switches and some legacy systems. If your back-end system can support only a limited number of connections, you will want to use the service throttling feature so it does not get overloaded.

- You may want to provide a tiered service to your service consumer. For example, imagine that you provide a credit-checking service to your customers. Your first-tier customers can make 100 service calls every minute, and for that level of service, you charge a flat fee each month. Your second-tier customers are allowed to make 20 service calls every minute, and they pay a lesser fee.

Without service throttling, you would need to write code that enforces these limitations. With OSB, you can do this simply through configuring the business service.

Setting Up the Service Throttling Service

To demonstrate how service throttling works, we will walk through the process of creating a simple web service that takes 30 seconds to process each customer request. It will display a message that shows the request number and the customer ID of each request that it receives. It contains no real business logic; it just processes messages as it receives them. You can find this web service in the SerialService_WS project in the source code that accompanies the book.

We want to wrap some business logic around the web service to reflect the fact that we give a higher priority to some of our customers and their service requests. For our purposes, all customers with an ID of 10 or lower are high-priority customers, and we process their requests before the requests of lower-priority customers.

To begin, create a new OSB project and name it ServiceThrottling_SB. As usual, the next step is to define a business service that calls the web service in the SerialService_WS project. Name the business service SerialService and base it on the WSDL file that you can consume from the following URL:

```
http://localhost:7001/SerialService_WS/SerialService?wsdl
```

Accept the default values for the rest of the business service.

Next, create a proxy service named SerialService and base this proxy service on the business service you just created. You will need to modify the message flow of this proxy service to recognize the high-priority customers from the regular customers, as described next.

Assigning Priorities in the Message Flow

The message flow for the SerialService proxy service begins with a Pipeline Pair node that contains a single stage, which in turn contains a single Assign action that assigns the value of the expression $body/alsb:CustomerRequest/alsb:customerID to the variable customerID.

After the Pipeline Pair node, add a conditional Branch node. Name the conditional Branch node Decide Priority, and set the XPath expression to . (a period) and the In Variable property to customerID. This tells the conditional Branch node to simply use the contents of the customerID variable when it performs its tests.

Inside the conditional Branch node, add a Branch node and name it high priority. In the high priority branch, set the Operator property to <= and the Value property to 10. Your conditional Branch node should now have two branches: Default and high priority. In each branch, add a Route node that contains a Routing action that routes the messages to the ServiceThrottling_SB/SerialService business service. Be sure to check the "Use inbound operation for outbound" check box.

So far, both branches should be identical, since they both route to the same business service. Now you are able to define the priority of the messages by adding a Routing Options action to each of the Request Action actions. Here, you can specify the priority for each message. Configure the Routing Options action for the high priority branch as shown in Figure 9-2, setting the Priority property to 1000. Configure the Routing Options action for the Default branch in the same way, except set the Priority property to 99 (or any value less than 1000).

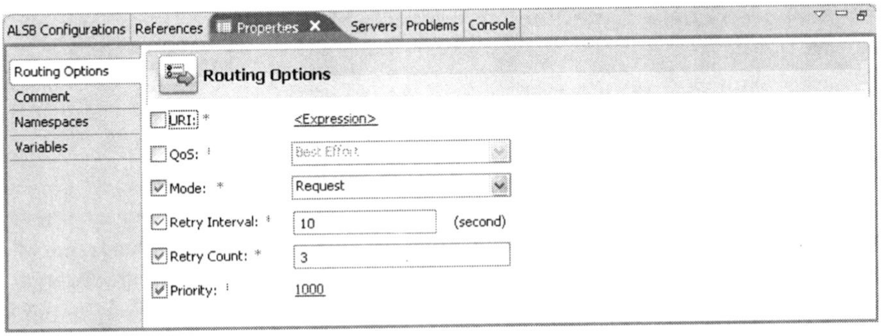

Figure 9-2. *Configuring the high-priority routing options*

Your final message flow should look like the one shown in Figure 9-3.

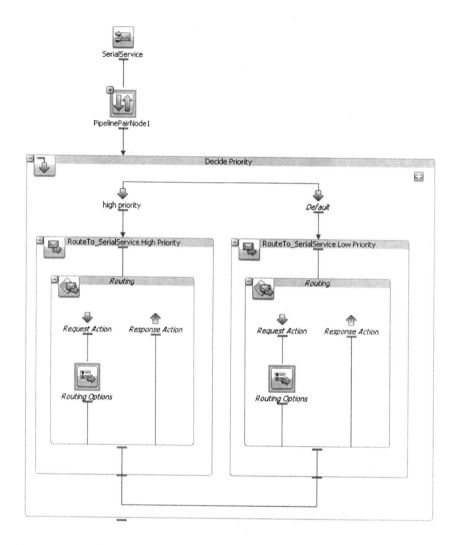

Figure 9-3. *The finished conditional branching for the proxy service*

Save and publish your work to the server.

Configuring the Business Service for Service Throttling

One more step that you need to perform before you can test the ServiceThrottling_SB project is to configure the SerialService business service from the OSB web console. This is one of the few tasks that must be done in the web console, rather than in the WorkSpace Studio environment. This is because configuring throttling is considered to be an operations activity, rather than a development activity.

In the web console, navigate to the `SerialService` business service and click the business service to see its details. Click the Operational Settings tab, as shown in Figure 9-4. Check the Enabled check box to enable throttling for this business service. Then set Maximum Concurrency to 1, Throttling Queue to 10 messages, and Message Expiration to 600000 msecs, as shown in the figure. Activate your changes, and you are ready to test this service.

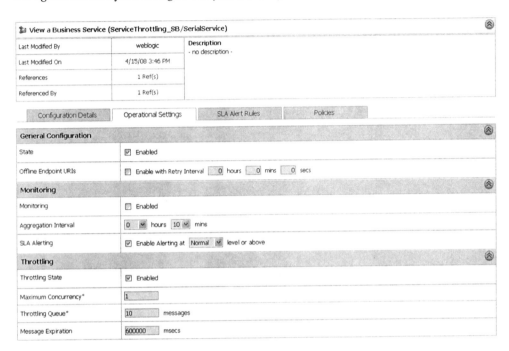

Figure 9-4. *Specifying the Throttling settings in the web console*

Testing the Service Throttling Service

You need to create a client program to call your proxy service, because the test console simply won't perform fast enough for your needs. You can find the client code located in the `ServiceThrotttlingClient_POJO` project.

■Tip Little's law states that *concurrency = average response time × average throughput*. See `http://en.wikipedia.org/wiki/Little%27s_law` for more details.

Listing 9-5 shows the client program. You can see how the client makes a total of seven calls to the proxy service, passing in different customer information with each service invocation.

Listing 9-5. *Client Program for Testing Throttling and Prioritization*

```java
public class Client {
    private static CustomerRequestType customer[] = {
        new CustomerRequestType(100, "James", "Jesse"),
        new CustomerRequestType(101, "Robert", "Dalton"),
        new CustomerRequestType(102, "Harold", "Lloyd"),
        new CustomerRequestType(7, "Lucille", "Ball"),
        new CustomerRequestType(103, "Soupy", "Sales"),
        new CustomerRequestType(104, "Elvis", "Presley"),
        new CustomerRequestType(2, "Bob", "Hope"),
    };

    public static void main(String[] args) {
        SerialService svc = new SerialServiceLocator();
        try {
            SerialPortType port = svc.getSerialService();
            for (int i = 0; i < customer.length; i++) {
                System.out.println("Processing customer " + i);
                port.processCustomer(customer[i]);
                try {
                    Thread.sleep(1000);
                } catch (InterruptedException ex) {
                    ex.printStackTrace();
                }
            }
        } catch(ServiceException ex) {
            ex.printStackTrace();
        } catch(RemoteException ex) {
            ex.printStackTrace();
        }
    }
}
```

Run the `Client.java` file as an application. You will see the following output in the Console window:

```
Starting to process request 1 from customer 103
Completed processing the request 1 from customer 103
Starting to process request 2 from customer 101
Completed processing the request 2 from customer 101
Starting to process request 3 from customer 7
Completed processing the request 3 from customer 7
Starting to process request 4 from customer 2
Completed processing the request 4 from customer 2
Starting to process request 5 from customer 104
Completed processing the request 5 from customer 104
Starting to process request 6 from customer 100
```

```
Completed processing the request 6 from customer 100
Starting to process request 7 from customer 102
Completed processing the request 7 from customer 102
```

The message order may be slightly different in your case, but it should follow the same pattern. The Client.java program sends seven service invocations very quickly. Usually, one of the lower-priority requests will be processed first, simply because it gets picked up from the message queue before any other messages have arrived. However, the second and third messages to be processed will always be the higher-priority messages from customers 2 and 7, and then the rest of the lower-priority messages will be processed.

Service Pooling

The term *service pooling* is used to more succinctly describe the management of service endpoints, including their failover logic. Service pooling is really a set of configuration items that you can use to easily manage endpoint URIs of business services. You have already seen how you can define multiple endpoints for a business service and how to load-balance the service calls over those endpoints. So far, our exercises have had only a single endpoint, so the load-balancing algorithm really didn't have anything to balance. However, in production situations, you will often have multiple endpoints for each business service, and while load balancing is important when dealing with multiple service endpoints, it is not sufficient on its own.

For example, imagine a business service with three endpoints that uses the round-robin load-balancing algorithm. As long as each endpoint is working properly, OSB will simply route each service call to the next endpoint in the list, wrapping around to the first endpoint after the last endpoint in the list has been called. But what happens if one of the endpoints fails for some reason? Perhaps the machine that hosts the endpoint is not running, or the network for that endpoint has a failure. If an endpoint fails, it's not very efficient to keep it in the list of endpoint URIs for the business service. It's also not very practical to ask a person to monitor the failures on the endpoints and manually manage the list of endpoints.

Fortunately, OSB allows you to specify some rules for the automatic removal of endpoints when they fail, along with rules (via configuration settings) regarding when to add failed endpoints back into the list of active endpoints. There are two main areas where this configuration information is specified for a business service: the Transport Configuration tab and the Operational Settings tab of the OSB web console.

Configuring the Transport for the Business Service

The Transport Configuration tab of the business service, shown in Figure 9-5, has three settings that can help with endpoint failures:

Retry Count: By default, this field is set to 0, meaning that no retries will be made on a failed service. As a result, if an endpoint fails to execute the service, no retries are made, and the error is propagated back to the caller. If the retry count is set to 1 or greater, the load-balancing algorithm will retry the service on the next appropriate endpoint. Naturally, if the next endpoint also fails, then no more retries are attempted, and the business service will return the failure to the caller. Also, if only one endpoint is defined, all calls are routed to that endpoint, regardless of any load-balancing settings.

Retry Iteration Interval: This field describes the delay, in seconds, before the next attempt is made to retry a service after all existing endpoints have been tried. For example, imagine that the business service has three endpoint URIs defined for it, and the Retry Count field is set to 3. If endpoint 1 fails, then the first retry will be on endpoint 2. The retries are made immediately after a failure. If endpoint 2 fails, then the second retry is immediately made against endpoint 3. If endpoint 3 fails, then the third retry will wait for the amount of time specified by the Retry Iteration Interval setting before proceeding to execute on the very first endpoint in the list. This field defaults to 30 seconds.

Retry Application Errors: This field allows you to configure the business service to differentiate between network errors and application errors. Usually, you will want to perform retries on nonapplication errors (that is, network and hardware errors) because nonapplication errors are often temporary in nature—network outages are often very short-lived, servers get restarted in a few minutes, and so on. Application errors, on the other hand, are usually much longer-lived. An example of an application error is when the request document is malformed and cannot be processed by any endpoint. By default, application errors are retried, but this setting makes very little sense. You should set Retry Application Errors to No.

Tip Set the Retry Application Errors setting to No as a matter of habit, unless you know of a good reason to retry this category of errors.

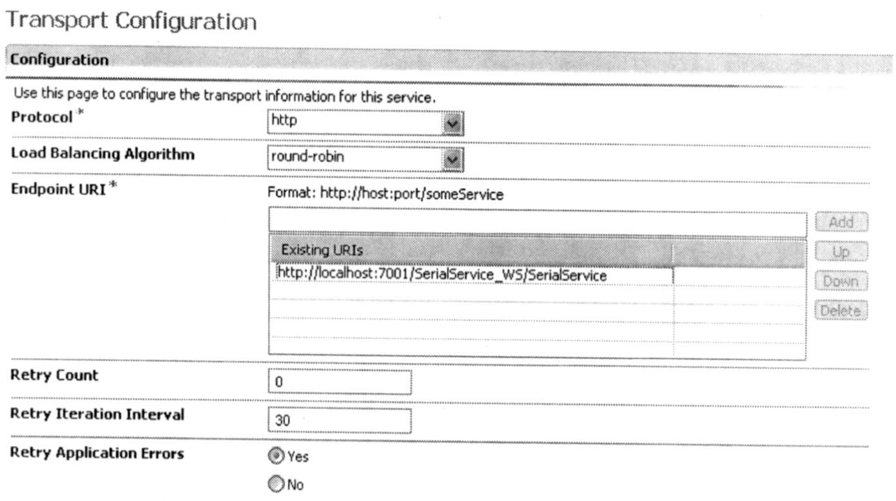

Transport Configuration

Configuration
Use this page to configure the transport information for this service.

Protocol *	http
Load Balancing Algorithm	round-robin
Endpoint URI *	Format: http://host:port/someService

Existing URIs

http://localhost:7001/SerialService_WS/SerialService

Add
Up
Down
Delete

Retry Count	0
Retry Iteration Interval	30
Retry Application Errors	⦿ Yes
	◯ No

Figure 9-5. *A sample Transport Configuration window for a business service*

These settings provide some control over error handling, but they are still pretty simplistic. Imagine having three endpoints defined in a business service, and one of those endpoints has a critical hardware failure. If the business service is being invoked hundreds or thousands of times each minute, it doesn't make much sense to have one-third of all of the requests fail and have to be retried. Web service failures take a long time to return to the caller—much longer than a success takes.

It would make more sense if you could somehow automatically remove an endpoint from the pool of services. Of course, this capability brings its own problems. If a service endpoint fails because you are restarting a server, you would like to have some way to add that endpoint *back* into the list of service endpoints once the server is able to handle requests again. You want the best of both worlds, and OSB 3 provides that, through the Operational Settings tab in the web console.

Configuring the Operational Settings of the Business Service

In the General Configuration category of the Operational Settings tab of the OSB web console (see Figure 9-4, earlier in this chapter), you'll see an item named Offline Endpoint URIs. By enabling this configuration setting, you can then specify that endpoints that have previously failed can be retried after a certain time interval. When we say "retried" here, we mean that the endpoints are simply returned to the list of active endpoints of the business service. No checking is done to see whether or not the endpoint is really back up. It is simply returned to the list of endpoints for the business service after the specified interval has passed.

How would you use this? Well, it depends on your specific needs. One example would be if your production environment is highly reliable (as production environments usually are), but once a week you take servers down for planned maintenance. The time that each server is offline is usually about one hour. In this scenario, it would make sense to enable the Offline Endpoint URIs setting.

SOAP with Attachments

It's possible to send a SOAP message with one or more attachments. This is similar to attaching a file to an e-mail message. SOAP with Attachments supports any arbitrary MIME type. Typically, attachments are defined in the WSDL file, as you will do in the exercise in this section. However, no special considerations are required when defining the WSDL for the proxy service, because attachments can be considered orthogonal to the message content and data types.

■**Note** It's best practice to declare all expected or optional attachments to operations in the WSDL file.

Setting Up the SOAP with Attachments Service

We will begin by creating a simple JWS that takes an attachment and saves it to the local file system. You can find the source code for this in the SOAPwithAttachment_WS project. Listing 9-6 shows the WSDL file for the web service. The most interesting parts of the WSDL file are highlighted in bold. To define attachments in your WSDL, you need to change the message that will carry the attachment and the soap:operation that handles the message. In this case, only the <input> message of the operation is concerned with the attachment. However, you can also have an operation return (that is, <output>) a message with an attachment.

Listing 9-6. *The SOAPwithAttachment.wsdl File for the JWS*

```
<?xml version="1.0" encoding="UTF-8"?>
    <wsdl:definitions xmlns:soap="http://schemas.xmlsoap.org/wsdl/soap/"
        xmlns:tns="http://www.alsb.com/SOAPwithAttachment/"
        xmlns:wsdl="http://schemas.xmlsoap.org/wsdl/"
        xmlns:xsd="http://www.w3.org/2001/XMLSchema"
        xmlns:mime="http://schemas.xmlsoap.org/wsdl/mime/"
        name="SOAPwithAttachment"
        targetNamespace="http://www.alsb.com/SOAPwithAttachment/">
    <wsdl:types>
        <xsd:schema targetNamespace="http://www.alsb.com/SOAPwithAttachment/">
            <xsd:element name="submitAttachmentResponse" type="xsd:string" />
            <xsd:complexType name="SubmitAttachmentRequestType">
                <xsd:sequence>
                    <xsd:element name="fileName" type="xsd:string" />
                </xsd:sequence>
            </xsd:complexType>
            <xsd:element name="submitAttachmentRequest"
                        type="tns:SubmitAttachmentRequestType" />
            <xsd:element name="zipFile" type="xsd:base64Binary" />
        </xsd:schema>
    </wsdl:types>

    <wsdl:message name="submitAttachmentRequest">
        <wsdl:part name="submitAttachment" type="tns:SubmitAttachmentRequestType"  />
        <wsdl:part name="zipFile" type="xsd:base64Binary" />
    </wsdl:message>

    <wsdl:message name="submitAttachmentResponse">
        <wsdl:part element="tns:submitAttachmentResponse"
            name="submitAttachmentResponse" />
    </wsdl:message>

    <wsdl:portType name="SOAPwithAttachmentPort">
        <wsdl:operation name="submitAttachment">
            <wsdl:input message="tns:submitAttachmentRequest" />
            <wsdl:output message="tns:submitAttachmentResponse" />
        </wsdl:operation>
    </wsdl:portType>

    <wsdl:binding name="SOAPwithAttachmentSOAP"
        type="tns:SOAPwithAttachmentPort">
        <soap:binding style="rpc"
            transport="http://schemas.xmlsoap.org/soap/http" />
        <wsdl:operation name="submitAttachment">
            <soap:operation
                soapAction="http://www.alsb.com/SOAPwithAttachment/submitAttachment" />
```

```
        <wsdl:input>
            <mime:multipartRelated>
                <mime:part>
                    <soap:body parts="submitAttachment" use="literale" />
                </mime:part>
                <mime:part>
                    <mime:content part="zipFile" type="application/zip" />
                </mime:part>
            </mime:multipartRelated>
        </wsdl:input>
        <wsdl:output>
            <soap:body parts="submitAttachmentResponse" use="literal" />
        </wsdl:output>
    </wsdl:operation>
  </wsdl:binding>

  <wsdl:service name="SOAPwithAttachment">
      <wsdl:port binding="tns:SOAPwithAttachmentSOAP"
          name="SOAPwithAttachmentSOAP">
          <soap:address location="http://localhost:7001/ ➥
SOAPwithAttachment_WS/SOAPwithAttachment" />
      </wsdl:port>
  </wsdl:service>
</wsdl:definitions>
```

This service has one operation that takes a message that contains a `String` file name and a MIME attachment as the arguments. The operation then returns the name of the newly created local file. You'll use this to send the name of a ZIP file, plus the file itself, to the web service. The web service will then save the attachment to the local file system (in the root directory of the `C:` drive).

In general, we have used a document-style binding in the examples in this book. However, when sending messages with attachments, you need to use an RPC-style document. This is due to the fact that a document-style service limits each `<message>` to only a single `<part>`. If you're sending attachments to a message, you need to define that attachment as additional parts in a message, so RPC is really the only viable approach.

Next, you need to create a business service that calls the web service. Name the business service `SOAPwithAttachment` and be sure to create it in the `BusinessServices` folder. Base the business service on the WSDL of the JWS. You should be able to see that dynamic WSDL at the following URL:

```
http://localhost:7001/SOAPwithAttachment_WS/SOAPwithAttachment?WSDL
```

If you are coding the business service yourself, just save the attachment as a file with the given name. You can see the fully coded business service in the `SOAPwithAttachment_WS` project.

Next, create a proxy service named `SOAPwithAttachment` in the project folder. You'll base this proxy service directly on the `SOAPwithAttachment` business service. Accept all default values for the proxy service, and then save it.

The test console is insufficient for testing services with attachments. As a result, you need to create a client for your proxy service in Java code. You'll use this client to test your service and ensure that the attachment is passed through the proxy service to the business service and ultimately saved as a file on the local hard drive.

The client code relies on the existence of a test.zip file in the root directory of the C: drive. You can create any ZIP file and simply save it as C:\test.zip to meet the needs of your client. We like using ZIP files for attachments for two reasons:

- They are commonly used as attachments in the real world.

- You can easily tell if a ZIP file is corrupted because it won't open.

Your client project is located in the WorkSpace Studio project named SOAPwithAttachmentClient_POJO. Run SOAPwithAttachmentClient.java as an application. Assuming that everything worked, you should now find a testX.zip file in the root directory of your C: drive. Open this file and confirm that the contents match the contents of the original test.zip file.

Working with Attachments

Now that you have a proxy service that can accept attachments, it's time to explore what you can do with these attachments in the proxy service. The possibilities are almost limitless, but we'll confine ourselves to some of the more basic tasks that demonstrate how you interact with attachments in a proxy service.

In WorkSpace Studio, open the SOAPwithAttachment.proxy file (in the SOAPwithAttachment_SB project) and view the message flow for this proxy service. The message flow should contain only two nodes: a Start node and a Route node. Click the Start node and add a Pipeline Pair node. In the request pipeline, add a new stage and name it examine attachment.

You're going to add a few logging statements so you can see the type of metadata that's associated with attachments. Start by adding an Assign action to the examine attachment stage. This action should assign the expression fn:count($attachments/attachment) to a variable named numAttachments. The $attachments structure contains all the attachments that are associated with a message. Each child attachment has a specific structure. The structure and the meaning of the fields are shown in Table 9-1.

Table 9-1. *Attachment Metadata*

Field	Description
Content-ID	The MIME type ID for the content. This is reported to be a globally unique value, but we find it tends to be the part name from the <mime:content part="" .../> section of the <soap:operation> declaration in the WSDL file. If you run this example, you'll see that the Content-ID value is file.
Content-Type	The MIME type for the content. This is represented as major type or subtype. In your WSDL file, you declared the attachment to be an application/zip. Your debugging statement will show it as an application/octet-stream.
Content-Transfer-Encoding	The encoding for the attachment. This is sometimes empty.
Content-Description	A text description of the content. This is sometimes empty.
Content-Location	A locally unique URI that identifies the attachment. This is sometimes empty.
Content-Disposition	How the attachment is to be handled. This is sometimes empty.
body	The attachment data.

Figure 9-6 shows a set of actions in the examine attachments stage that loop through all the attachments of a message.

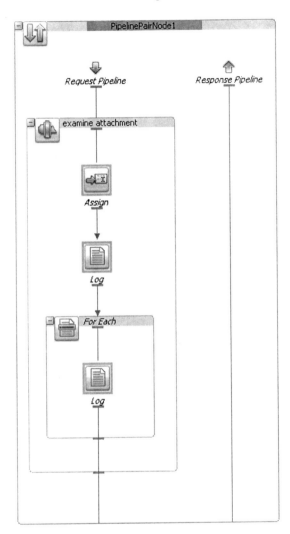

Figure 9-6. *An example of looping through the attachments of a message*

The Log action nested in the For Each action contains a single statement that sends all the attachment information to the test console of OSB, where you can read it. This rather complex statement follows:

```
concat('Attachment ', string($index), ' of ', string($totalAttachments),
 fn:codepoints-to-string(10),
 'Content-ID: ', $attach/ctx:Content-ID, fn:codepoints-to-string(10),
 'Content-Type: ', $attach/ctx:Content-Type, fn:codepoints-to-string(10),
 'Content-Transfer-Encoding: ', $attach/ctx:Content-Transfer-Encoding,
fn:codepoints-to-string(10),
```

```
'Content-Description: ', $attach/ctx:Content-Description,
fn:codepoints-to-string(10),
'Content-Location: ', $attach/ctx:Content-Location, fn:codepoints-to-string(10),
'Content-Disposition: ', $attach/ctx:Content-Disposition,
fn:codepoints-to-string(10),
'body: ', $attach/ctx:body, fn:codepoints-to-string(10))
```

By the way, you use the fn:codepoints-to-string(10) function to print a newline character to the console to make the text output more legible.

Note The <body> element in the $attachment variable contains the attachment. Binary attachments are represented as a <binary-content> XML element that points to the attachment buffered in the system. XML and text attachments are represented as XML and text, respectively, and can be manipulated directly with XQuery or XSLT. Binary attachment data can be manipulated only by passing the binary data to a Java callout for processing.

Summary

This chapter completes the suite of chapters on messaging topics that began with Chapter 6. What is clear from the examples in this chapter is the ease with which services can be controlled through configuration. WSRM is accomplished by defining XML policy files completely outside the WSDL file that defines the service. Service throttling gives you greater control over the message traffic, limiting the flow of messages as necessary and giving you another tool to provide better service by prioritizing messages. Service pooling gives you control over the management of business service endpoints—a must for managing an SOA in the real world, where unpredictable network errors do occur.

Lastly, the ability to attach files to messages gives you the flexibility to pass files along with services. This is sometimes a better approach than using FTP to transmit files between systems, especially when coupled with WSRM to reliably transmit the files. Consider the skills and techniques you've learned in this chapter as your graduating exercise in the school of SOA messaging.

## CHAPTER 10

Reporting and Monitoring

Although reporting and monitoring are discrete capabilities of the service bus, they're closely related. Monitoring is the ability to collect runtime information, while reporting is focused on delivering message data and alerts. But there's some overlap between monitoring and reporting. For example, you can monitor the number of alerts that have been reported. Monitoring is focused on operational information: the general health of the service bus, how many alerts have been generated and of what type, the status of SLAs, and the gathering of related statistics. A simple way to differentiate between monitoring and reporting is this: monitoring is strategic; reporting is tactical.

Monitoring

The Monitoring Dashboard is the default view of the service bus console. You can see this on your service bus by pointing your browser to `http://localhost:7001/sbconsole`. Click the Server Health tab to see the details of the OSB servers and log messages, as shown in Figure 10-1. The Server Snapshot portlet gives you a quick pie chart showing the health of each server. Because your domain contains only a single server, the entire pie chart represents this single server. It should be colored all green to indicate that your single server is running just fine. If you were running a cluster of service bus servers, the pie chart would be divided among the different servers.

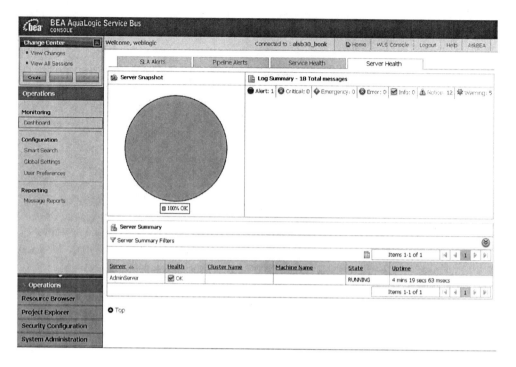

Figure 10-1. *The Monitoring Dashboard*

To the right of the Server Snapshot is the Log Summary section, which shows the number and severity of all alerts entered into the alert log within the last 30 minutes. (You need to define alerts before they appear here, as described in the "Defining the Service Level Agreements" section later in this chapter.) The Server Summary portlet at the bottom of the main browser window shows a more detailed, server-specific status, including the cluster and machine names of each server.

Within these three Dashboard portlets, you can click the information that appears and drill down into greater detail. This information is provided by the WebLogic Diagnostic Framework.

Typically, an operator looks at these Dashboard portlets and is aware of a problem when an alert is generated. The window automatically refreshes after every minute, but the interval is configurable. When an alert is generated, the operator will drill down into details for the service or server, including detailed performance-reporting windows.

As long as all your services are working as expected, the Dashboard portlets are quite boring. To jazz things up a bit, you need to create a web service whose performance you can control programmatically. You also need to create some SLAs so that your web service can violate those agreements, and you need to throw some alerts into the Dashboard portlets. To achieve this, you'll create two web services that contain various operations. These web services will contain a built-in delay mechanism. You need to be able to set the delay value from your client so you can be sure to violate your SLAs at will. Finally, you'll create a client program that can invoke your web services to help you test various scenarios and to illustrate the monitoring capabilities of OSB.

Creating the Temperamental Web Service

Listing 10-1 shows the source code for the TemperamentalCreditService.java web service. This service provides five different operations. Each operation will respond back to the caller within a semi-random timeframe. The time delay is specified using the setDelay() method. You can find this code, along with a second JWS named TemperamentalCustomerService.java, in the TemperamentalService_WS project in the source code that accompanies this book. Compile and deploy this project to get started.

Listing 10-1. *The TemperamentalCreditService*

```java
package com.alsb.temperamental;
import javax.jws.*;
import javax.jws.soap.SOAPBinding;
import weblogic.jws.WLHttpTransport;
import weblogic.jws.WSDL;

@WebService(targetNamespace="http://www.alsb.com",
    serviceName="TemperamentalService", name="TemperamentalService")
@WLHttpTransport(serviceUri="credit ",
    portName="TemperamentalSoapPort")
@WSDL(exposed=true)
@SOAPBinding(parameterStyle=SOAPBinding.ParameterStyle.WRAPPED)
public class TemperamentalCreditService {
    /** The amount of time (in seconds) the web service will delay */
    private static int DELAYINSECONDS = 0;

    @WebMethod
    public String variableCreditCheck(String arg0) {
        delay();
        return arg0 + DELAYINSECONDS;
    }

    @WebMethod
    public String variableOpA(String arg0) {
        delay();
        return arg0 + DELAYINSECONDS;
    }

    @WebMethod
    public String variableOpB(String arg0) {
        delay();
        return arg0 + DELAYINSECONDS;
    }

    @WebMethod
    public String variableOpC(String arg0) {
        delay();
```

```
      return arg0 + DELAYINSECONDS;
   }

   @WebMethod
   public String rapidCreditCheck(String arg0) {
      return arg0;
   }

   @WebMethod
   public int setDelay(int delayInSeconds) {
      DELAYINSECONDS = delayInSeconds;
      return DELAYINSECONDS;
   }

   private void delay() {
      try {
         Thread.sleep(DELAYINSECONDS * 1000);
      } catch(InterruptedException ex) {
         ex.printStackTrace();
      }
   }
}
```

The code itself is straightforward. Near the end of the listing is the setDelay() operation we mentioned earlier. This operation allows the service test client to set the delay (in seconds) that it wants each of the other operations to use. The other operation, delay(), sleeps the thread for the specified number of seconds. The methods variableCreditCheck(), variableOpA(), variableOpB(), and variableOpC() delay for whatever amount of time is specified. Only the rapidCreditCheck() operation ignores the delay and returns immediately. We'll use this operation later to show how you can failover between services.

The second web service is the TemperamentalCustomerService. However, because its implementation is remarkably similar to that of the TemperamentalCreditService, we won't bother to list it here.

Creating the Temperamental OSB Project

Your next step is to create a project named Temperamental_SB in WorkSpace Studio. In this project, you need to create two business services (TemperamentalCredit and TemperamentalCustomer) based on the WSDL files of each of the JWSs in the TemperamentalService_WS project. If you successfully compiled and deployed the business services in the previous step, you can get the WSDL files of the services at

http://localhost:7001/TemperamentalService_WS/credit?WSDL

and

http://localhost:7001/TemperamentalService_WS/customer?WSDL

Once you have the business services created, you need to create proxy services named `TemperamentalCredit` and `TemperamentalCustomer` based on their business service counterparts. Be sure to set the URLs for the proxy services to `/esb/TemperamentalCredit` and `/esb/TemperamentalCustomer`, respectively.

Because you based the proxy services directly on the business services, there is no need to modify the message routing of the proxy service; OSB has configured the message flow for you. Be sure to publish the `Temperamental_SB` project to the server.

Defining the Service Level Agreements

Creating an SLA is almost an art form. Often, you'll hear people talk about setting SLAs to detect failures. This is certainly a good idea, but if you create SLAs only to detect failures, you're doing your customers a disservice! We believe it's even more important to create SLAs that show successful service calls that are approaching their performance limit. For example, if your service must be able to respond to a service request in less than 2 seconds, and normally responds to these requests in 0.8 second, you should consider using multiple SLAs: one for the failure condition (that is, > 2 seconds) and others to help alert your operations team when the service time begins to exceed its normal time (that is, > 1 second and possibly > 1.8 seconds). The purpose of the SLA is not only to notify you of a failure, but to serve as a tool to help you *prevent failures*.

SLAs are based on alerts. Alerts are composed of an alert destination and one or more alert rules. To help you understand the capabilities of OSB monitoring, and following the true nature of this book, let's dive right in and create a few SLAs for our `Temperamental_SB` service.

Creating an Alert Destination

You begin by creating an alert destination in the project. Name the alert destination `Console` and set the SNMP Trap and Reporting fields to No. You can configure alerts to be sent to an SNMP trap, a report, an e-mail address, a JMS queue, or a combination of any of these destinations. By default, all alerts are also sent to the console.

With your alert destination created, publish the `Temperamental_SB` project to your server. Now, let's continue to the next step in SLA creation.

Enabling Monitoring

You create an SLA from the web-based administration console for OSB. Using your web browser, navigate to the following URL:

```
http://localhost:7001/sbconsole
```

Click the `TemperamentalCredit` proxy service, and then select the Operational Settings tab. Before you can create an alert rule, you need to enable monitoring of the service. Click the Create button in the Change Center, and then check the Enabled check box in the Monitoring section, as shown in Figure 10-2.

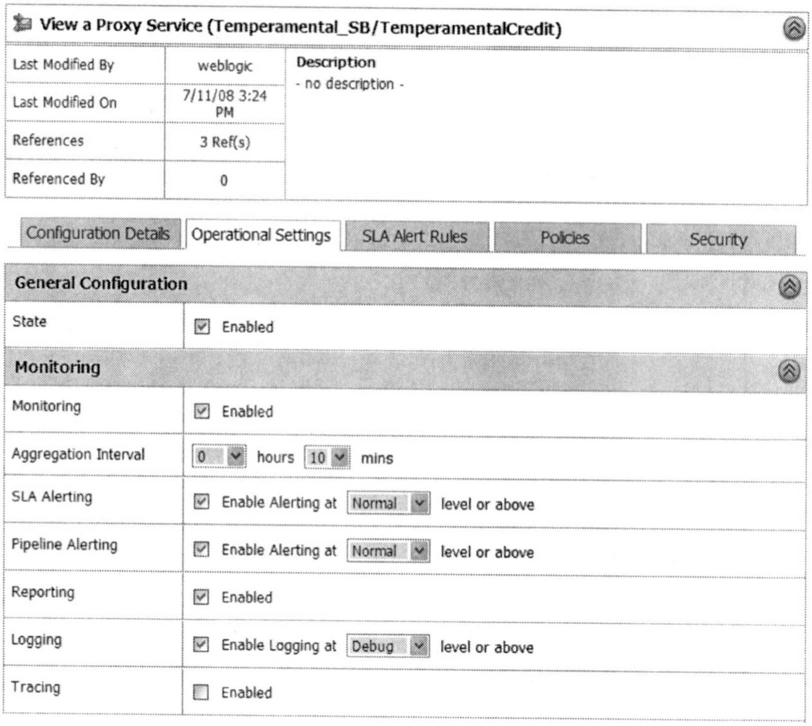

Figure 10-2. *You must enable monitoring on a service-by-service basis.*

The other settings in the Monitoring section allow you to control monitoring for the service:

Aggregation Interval: This setting defines the moving window of time over which the statistics for the service are aggregated. The window moves forward every minute.

SLA Alerting, Pipeline Alerting, and Logging: These settings allow you to specify whether or not the alerts or log events are to be tracked, and if enabled, the minimum severity which is deemed important. For now, leave these enabled and their severity set to their default values.

Reporting: This setting allows you to decide whether or not you want to report on this service.

Tracing: This setting allows you to specify if you want runtime tracing of the service enabled. Tracing is used when troubleshooting problems with a service.

With monitoring now enabled, click the Update button to save your changes on this tab.

Creating the Credit Check Failure Rule

To create an alert rule, click the SLA Alert Rules tab in the OSB administration console, and then click the Add New button. Your first alert will be to report on failures of the variableCreditCheck() maximum response time. For this operation, a failure occurs if the maximum response time exceeds 20 seconds.

Name the new rule `Credit Check Failure`. Give the alert a brief summary and description, and select the `Temperamental_SB/Console` destination you created earlier, as shown in Figure 10-3.

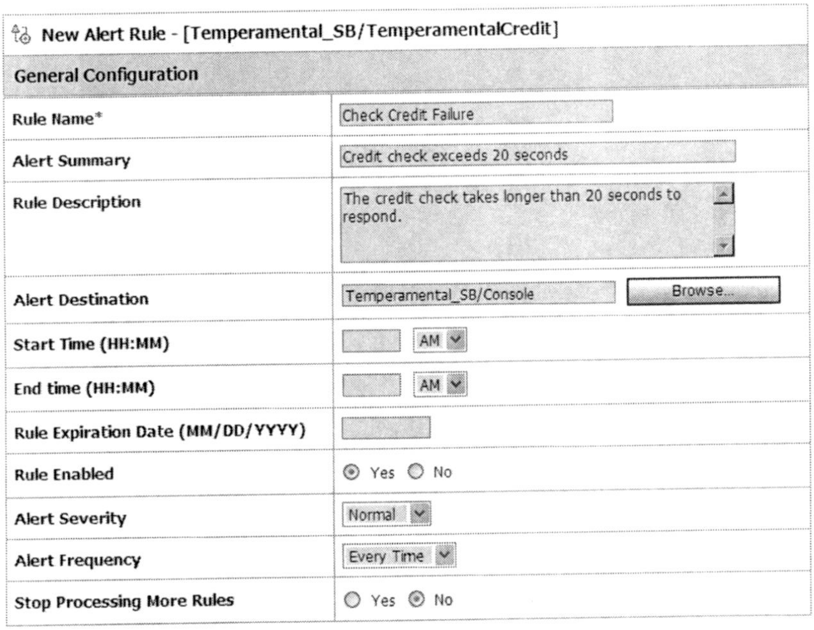

Figure 10-3. *Creating an alert rule*

■**Tip** Name your alerts carefully. If your alert is specific to an operation in the web service, then we recommend that you put the operation name into the name of the alert. However, if the alert applies to the entire service, there's no need to include the service name in the alert, because the Alert History table in the SLA Alerts tab of the Monitoring Dashboard will show the name of the service.

The other settings on this page control the alert as follows:

Start Time, End Time, and Rule Expiration Date: These fields allow you to specify when you want the rule to apply. For example, you might set the rule to apply from midnight to one minute before midnight each day until Jan 1, 2100 (effectively forever). You might want to monitor performance for only part of each day as part of your SLA. This would allow you to be concerned with the performance during working hours, or hours that are important to the consumers of your services. Similarly, providing an end date for the monitoring might make sense if your service consumer is concerned about the performance for only a limited number of days (that is, during a sales promotion or similar activity).

Rule Enabled: This field allows you simply to turn the rule on or off, as needed. Because monitoring does consume extra clock cycles on the servers, some organizations run with the monitoring turned off for maximum efficiency. Some organizations monitor services only when they are first introduced into production. After those new services have run without any problems for a week or so, these organizations relax or eliminate their monitoring. There is no right way to monitor your services. It all depends on your specific needs.

Alert Severity: This field allows you to specify the severity level of the alert. You may choose from Normal, Warning, Minor, Major, Critical, and Fatal.

Alert Frequency: This field allows you to define when the alert is fired, either Every Time or Once when Condition is True.

Stop Processing More Rules: For this field, select Yes if the alert is so bad that you want all further rule processing to stop. Normally, you leave this field set to No.

Click the Next button to move to the Alert Rule Conditions Configuration window. Here, you can define the conditions that trigger the alert. These rules are completely customizable. Before you configure your alert rule conditions for this example, let's take a walk through the types of conditions you can detect in OSB, summarized in Table 10-1.

Table 10-1. *Alert Expressions*

Type	Subtype	Description
Count	Success Ratio (%)	Test against the percentage of successful service calls and operations.
Count	Failure Ratio (%)	Test against the percentage of failed service calls and operations.
Count	Message Count	Test against the number of messages sent across services and operations.
Count	Error Count	Test against the number of messages that have errors.
Count	Validation Error Count	Test against the number of messages that have validation.
Count	Operation.<operation name>.Message Count	Test against the number of messages routed to a specific operation.
Count	Operation.<operation name>.Error Count	Test against the number of errors generated from a specific operation.
Count	<flow element>.Message Count	Test against the number of messages sent to a specific flow element.
Count	<flow element>.Error Count	Test against the number of errors generated from a specific flow element.
Count	WSS Error Count	Test against the number of Web Service Security–related errors.
Minimum	Response Time	Test against the minimum response.
Minimum	<flow element>.Response Time	Test against the minimum response time for all invocations of this flow element.

Type	Subtype	Description
Minimum	Operation.<operation name>.Response Time	Test against the minimum response time to a specific operation.
Maximum	Response Time	Test against the maximum response.
Maximum	<flow element>.Response Time	Test against the maximum response time across all invocations of the specified service.
Maximum	Operation.<operation name>.Response Time	Test against the maximum response time to a specific operation.
Average	Response Time	Test against the average response.

A flow element subtype is one of the following:

- A request pipeline in a Pipeline Pair node

- A response pipeline in a Pipeline Pair node

- A Route node

For example, if you were looking at the Count type for a service that contains a Pipeline Pair node named Pipeline1, you would see the subtypes Pipeline1.request.Error Count and Pipeline1.response.Error Count in the combo box.

As you can see from Table 10-1, you can test against a considerable number of conditions. What and how to test are highly specific to your services and the SLAs that your organization wants to meet.

Let's continue to create the Credit Check Failure alert rule. For this rule, select Maximum from the combo box on the left. In the next combo box, select Operation.variableCreditCheck. Response Time. In the third check box, select the > (greater-than) comparator. Finally, in the text box, enter **20000** to represent 20 seconds. Your window should look like Figure 10-4. When all this information is correct, click the Add button to create the simple expression.

Caution It's important to remember that the values for alert rule condition expressions are specified in milliseconds. For example, it's easy to create rules such as Operation.foo.Response Time > 2000 and Operation.foo.Response Time < 3. Obviously, the rule itself is invalid. If you find that some of your alerts aren't firing off as expected, take a closer look at the time values you've specified for each rule.

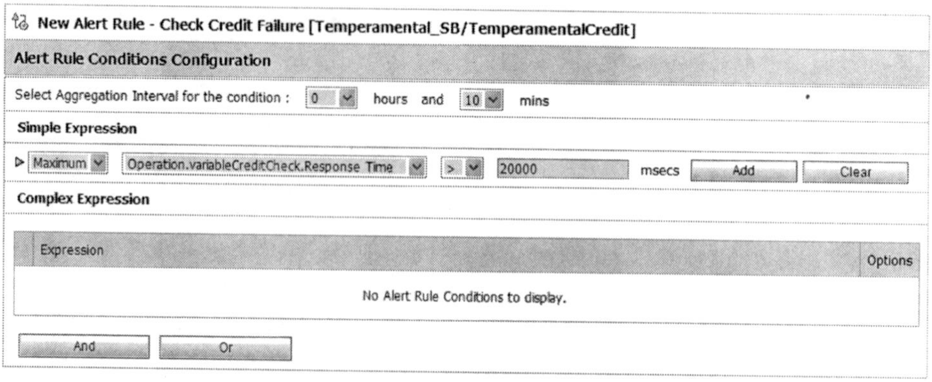

Figure 10-4. *Defining conditions for an alert rule*

Click the Last button, and then the Save button to tell OSB that you're finished with this expression. Congratulations, you've just created your first alert rule.

At this point, you have a single alert that will fire upon a fatal condition becoming true. If this happens, your whole pie chart will turn black (the color of a fatal alert). To make things more interesting, you need more alert types to be fired, and that means you need more alert rules defined in the system.

Creating the OpA Warn Rule

Your next alert rule will be to create a warning if the maximum response time is greater than 2 seconds but less than 3 seconds. This requires you to create a complex statement. Fortunately, the process for creating a complex statement is simple.

Navigate back to the SLA Alert Rules tab for the TemperamentalCredit proxy service and click the Add New button to create a new alert rule. Name the alert OpA Warn to indicate that the nature of the alert is a warning on the OpA operation performance. Set the Alert Destination field to the destination you created earlier, set the Alert Severity field to Warning. and click the Next button.

Now you're ready to create your complex expression. Complex expressions are merely two or more simple expressions linked together via a conjunction (And or Or). Begin by creating two simple expressions. The first expression is to test for the maximum response time of OpA to be > 2000. Click the Add button, and then create the second simple expression: max OpA response time < 3001. Click the Add button again so that both simple expressions are now listed in the Complex Expression section of the window.

Notice that the Last button at the bottom of the window is grayed out. That's because you have two simple expressions defined, but you haven't connected them with an And or Or conjunction to create a single complex expression. Click the check boxes next to each expression, as shown in Figure 10-5, and then click the And button. *Voilà!* You've created a complex expression.

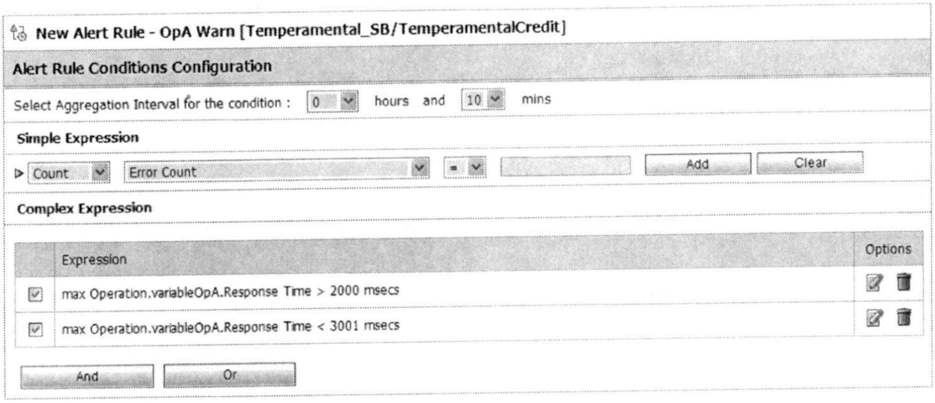

Figure 10-5. *Creating a complex expression for an alert rule*

If you look carefully at the complex expression in Figure 10-6, you'll notice there are parentheses around the newly created expression. It should also be obvious that you can now add more simple expressions and combine them into complex expressions. You can also combine multiple complex expressions into expressions of even greater complexity. There's no limit to the complexity of the expressions you can create here. Of course, evaluating expressions takes time, so it's best to keep your expressions as simple as possible.

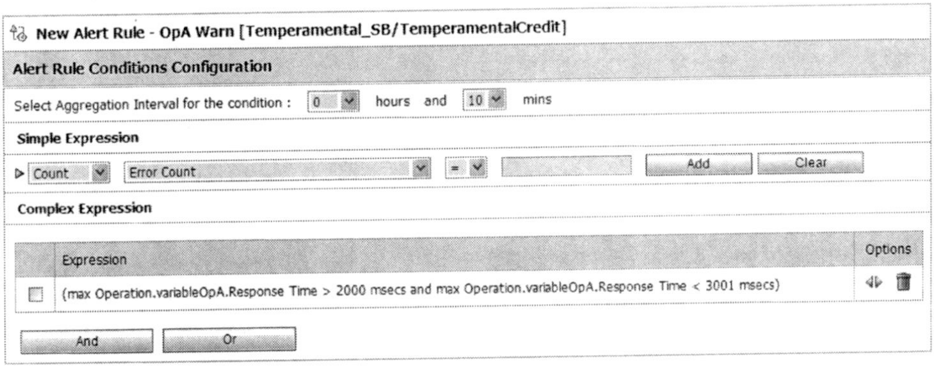

Figure 10-6. *A fully formed complex expression for an alert rule*

Adding the Remaining Alert Rules

You have two more alert rules to create for the TemperamentalCredit service. Table 10-2 provides a summary of the rules. You've already created the first two rules in the table; you'll need to add the other two to keep your monitoring display in sync with the rest of this example.

Table 10-2. *TemperamentalCredit Alert Rules*

Name	Expression
Credit Check Failure	Maximum Operation.variableCreditCheck.Response Time > 20000
OpA Warn	Maximum Operation.OpA.Response Time > 2000 and < 3001
OpB Minor	Maximum Operation.OpB.Response Time > 3000 and < 5001
OpC Major	Maximum Operation.OpC.Response Time > 5000 and < 10001

Additionally, you need to create two rules for the TemperamentalCustomer service, as shown in Table 10-3. Don't forget to enable monitoring of the TemperamentalCustomer proxy service, just as you did for the TemperamentalCredit proxy earlier in this example.

Table 10-3. *TemperamentalCustomer Alert Rules*

Name	Expression
customerOpACritical Critical	Maximum Operation.variableOpA.Response Time > 9999 and < 20001
getVariableCustomerFatal Fatal	Maximum Operation. getVariableCustomer.Response Time > 20000

Save all your work so far and activate your changes. It's time to create your service client to invoke these services and cause your newly created alerts to fire!

Note You can also create alerts for business services, not just proxy services.

Coding the Proxy Client

Your proxy client, shown in Listing 10-2, works like most of the POJO clients you've created so far. In WorkSpace Studio, open the TemperamentalServiceClient_POJO project. Within the project, open the build.xml Ant script and execute the all target. When that target completes, execute the run.wsclient target to run the LoadTestClient against the proxy services.

Listing 10-2. *LoadTestClient.java*

```
package com.alsb.temperamental;
import com.alsb.www.*;

public class LoadTestClient {
    private static final String customerUrl =
        "http://localhost:7001/esb/TemperamentalCustomer?WSDL";
    private static final String creditUrl =
        "http://localhost:7001/esb/TemperamentalCredit?WSDL";
    private static TemperamentalCreditService_PortType creditPort = null;
    private static TemperamentalCustomerService_PortType customerPort = null;
```

```java
public static void main(String[] args) {
    runMonitoringTest();
}

/**
 * Perform the necessary housekeeping to connect to the proxy services
 */
private static void loadServiceReferences() {
    try {
        System.out.println("Opening the credit service as " + creditUrl);
        TemperamentalCreditServiceProxy creditProxy =
            new TemperamentalCreditServiceProxy();
        creditPort = creditProxy.getTemperamentalCreditService_PortType();

        System.out.println("Opening the customer service as " + customerUrl);
        TemperamentalCustomerServiceProxy customerProxy =
            new TemperamentalCustomerServiceProxy();
        customerPort = customerProxy.getTemperamentalCustomerService_PortType();
    } catch (Exception ex) {
        ex.printStackTrace();
    }
}

private static void runMonitoringTest() {
    try {
        loadServiceReferences();
        System.out.println("Invoking the methods...");
        // Generate a warning on Op A
        creditPort.setDelay(2);
        creditPort.variableOpA("foo");
        // Generate a minor alert on Op B
        creditPort.setDelay(3);
        creditPort.variableOpB("foo");
        // Generate a major alert on Op C
        creditPort.setDelay(6);
        creditPort.variableOpC("foo");
        // Generate a fatal alert
        creditPort.setDelay(25);
        creditPort.variableCreditCheck("William Smith");
        // Generate a critical customer alert
        customerPort.setDelay(12);
        customerPort.variableOpA(2);
        // Generate a fatal customer alert
        customerPort.setDelay(25);
        customerPort.getVariableCustomer(2);
    } catch (Exception ex) {
        ex.printStackTrace();
```

```
            }
        }
    }
```

The code is simple. The runMonitoringTest() method simply calls each of the proxy services that you're monitoring, after setting the appropriate delay value. After you've run the LoadTestClient, there will be a number of alerts visible in the Dashboard view of the OSB console, as shown in Figure 10-7.

■Note It will take about a minute or so to run through all of the service calls in the LoadTestClient.java program, and it may take as many as 5 minutes for all of the results to show up on the Dashboard.

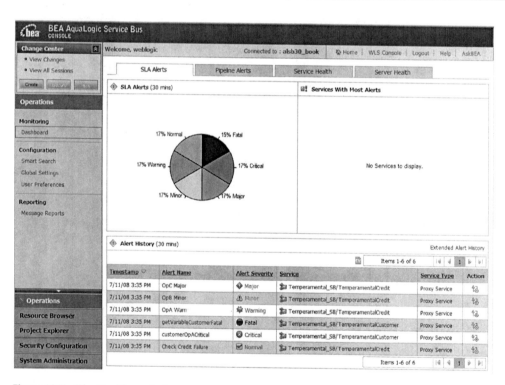

Figure 10-7. *The Dashboard after running the temperamental service tests*

Reporting

Reporting is a subset of the monitoring function of OSB. Monitoring is based on the near real-time collection of SLA and pipeline alerts. Reporting is based on the recording of parts of a message into a database. You can then either view these report entries from the OSB console or access them from an external reporting tool.

Using Report Actions

You can use a Report action in the message flow of any proxy service. You can also embed Report actions in the error handlers associated with Pipeline Pair and Route nodes. The alert information is aggregated in a database. OSB provides a reporting user interface to allow you to gather the information you need easily.

Note You can create Report actions based on alerts. However, the default report provider that ships with OSB ignores these alerts. If you want to use customized reporting alerts, you must create your own reporting provider. Furthermore, you'll also need to configure OSB to use your customized provider. The reporting provider API is a public API supported by Oracle. You can also have alerts go to the reporting system automatically.

The `Reporting_SB` project supplied with this book includes a `Report` proxy service that illustrates how you use the Report action. The `Report` proxy service is an "any XML" service, so it will accept any XML message that you want to type in. The `SampleXML.txt` file contains two different sample documents that you can use when you are testing this service.

There are two main sections of a Report action. The first is the body of the report, which contains the message data that you wish to record. The second section is for the keys by which you wish to search for the report record in the database. You can define as many keys as you would like for the message.

As a best practice, we recommend that you store the entire message in the Expression field of the report. In our Report action, we serialize the XML message into a string using the following command for the Expression field:

```
fn-bea:serialize($body)
```

OSB will automatically serialize the results of the expression. That way, you'll have all the information that was originally available when the Report action was triggered. However, if your message is very large, and all the data is stored elsewhere in your enterprise, you might wish to store only the ID in the Expression field. For example, if you're referring to a customer order, it's likely that you'll have the entire order stored in an `order` database somewhere in your enterprise. In such a case, we recommend storing only the order ID in the Report action to save space in the reporting database.

The report keys are used to search for report expressions. The keys are treated as simple text, so storing a date won't allow you to search by a date range. However, each report event is automatically assigned a date and timestamp, so you can search based on the time of the report event.

Most often, you'll create key values based on the content of the message you're reporting. In your Report proxy service, the Report action records both the id and name values of the <bar> section of the message, as shown in Figure 10-8.

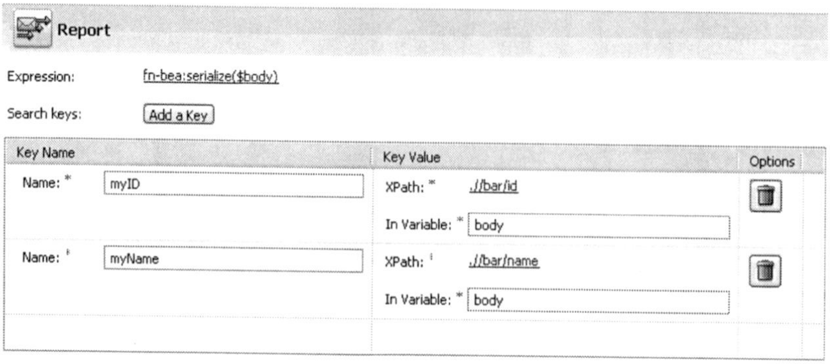

Figure 10-8. *An example of a Report action*

We recommend that you try the Report proxy service with the XML in Listing 10-3. Try varying the data values within the XML and using the test console to generate your own reporting data. That way, you'll have some data to view, as explained next.

Listing 10-3. *Sample XML File for Generating Report Events*

```
<foo>
    <bar>
        <id>1</id>
        <name>name1</name>
    </bar>
</foo>
```

Viewing Report Information

You view report information from the Operations portion of the OSB console. Under the Reporting heading, click the Message Reports link to see the Summary of Message Reports window, as shown in Figure 10-9. This window contains a table of the most recent reports. You can quickly sort the information in this table by clicking the table headers. Clicking the same header multiple times toggles the sort order between ascending and descending.

Figure 10-9. *Viewing report information*

If you're working with a large number of reporting events, simply sorting the records won't be sufficient. You can also select specific report records by entering the appropriate data in the Message Report Filters section of the window. You can use the filter to select report records as follows:

Date Range: You can filter based on the database timestamp, either by a specific date range or by selecting the most recent records within a timeframe that you can specify.

Inbound Service Name: You can search for reports based on the name of the inbound service. The inbound service name is the combination of the project name and the proxy service name, separated by a slash (/) character. You can also use an asterisk as a wildcard when searching for services by name.

Error Code: Use this field if you are looking for a specific error code. This code is automatically assigned to the reporting event (if the Report action was created in an error handler), inside the pipeline.

Report Index: You can search the keys that you've created with your Report actions. This provides a simple text-based search within the key data. There are no comparison operators for the Report Index expression. The text you enter is treated as if it had wildcards on both sides. For example, using Figure 10-9 as a reference, if you entered a value of name for the Report Index field, only records that contained the string "name" would be returned as matches. The search function is case-sensitive, so a search for myid would return zero matches, whereas a search for myID would return two matches.

If you click the link for the report in the Report Index column in the table at the bottom of the window, you will see the View Message Details window, as shown in Figure 10-10. This window is rich in detail, allowing you to see at a glance most of the information of interest. At the bottom of this window is a Detail link. Clicking this link brings up another browser window that contains the expression of the Report action.

🖹 View Message Details	
General Configuration	
Message ID	uuid:c91ab9e973f25cc1:62daeb4c:119a633c9de:-7f0e
Database Timestamp	Thursday, May 1, 2008 2:35:04 PM PDT
Time at point of Logging	Thursday, May 1, 2008 2:35:04 PM PDT
Server Name	AdminServer
State	REQUEST
Node Name	PipelinePairNode1
Pipeline Name	PipelinePairNode1_request
Stage Name	stage1
Inbound Service	
Name	Reporting_SB/Reporting
URI	/Reporting_SB/Reporting
Operation	
Outbound Service	
Name	
URI	
Operation	
Report Index	
Report Index Text	myID=2 myName=name2
Fault	
Error Code	
Reason	
Detail	
Report Body	
Detail	Detail

Figure 10-10. *Viewing the details of a report event*

Most of the View Message Details window is self-explanatory. We want to add a little detail here for the fields that are blank in Figure 10-10. The Outbound Service section is filled with data only if the Report action is contained within a Route node. It's similar in structure to the Inbound Service section above it. The Fault section is filled with data only if the Report action is included inside an error handler, whether it is a pipeline error handler or a Route node error handler. This is often a better approach to debugging errors than using the Log action, especially if you're looking for problems at runtime when the proxy service is in a production environment.

Purging Report Information

Information is like fruit—it ages quickly. The Purge Messages link in the Summary of Message Reports window (see Figure 10-9) of the OSB console provides a simple user interface for purging messages. You can either purge all messages in the reporting database or purge messages within a specific date and time range, as shown in Figure 10-11.

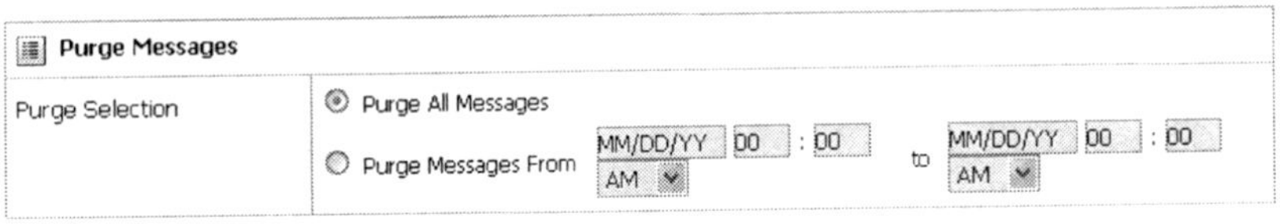

Figure 10-11. *Purging report messages*

Occasionally purging messages helps to keep your reporting data store performing at an optimal speed. It also makes managing the report records much easier.

Using Reporting Providers

A reporting provider provides both transport and storage for reporting events. If you deploy OSB in a cluster, then all the managed servers within the domain will use the reporting provider to aggregate the reporting data. By default, OSB comes preconfigured with a JMS reporting provider. The JMS reporting provider is used because it first queues the reporting record, and then dequeues and writes the records to the database. This asynchronous design improves the performance of the reporting modules within OSB. The name of the JMS server is wlsbJMSServer, and the name of the data store is wlsbjmsrpDataStore. You can find both these artifacts using the traditional WebLogic Server admin console.

You can change the data store associated with the JMS reporting provider. In a production environment, you'll probably want the report messages stored in a production-quality database, such as Oracle, Microsoft SQL Server, or MySQL. To do this, you can use the database scripts stored in the <%ORACLE_HOME%>\alsb_3.0\db\scripts\[database] directory. There's no script for MySQL, PostgreSQL, or some of the other unsupported open source databases, but if you examine the scripts for the supported databases, creating a script specific for the database you wish to use should be fairly simple.

Listing 10-4 shows the basic table structures used for OSB reporting. The MSG_GUID field is the primary key for the WLI_QS_REPORT_ATTRIBUTE table and is the foreign key for the WLI_QS_REPORT_DATA table. With this knowledge, you can create custom reports in external reporting tools such as Crystal Reports, or execute your own SQL statements directly against the reporting tables.

Listing 10-4. *The Table Definitions for the Reporting Events*

```
CREATE TABLE WLI_QS_REPORT_ATTRIBUTE (
   MSG_GUID              VARCHAR(64)    NOT NULL,
   DB_TIMESTAMP          DATETIME       DEFAULT CURRENT_ ➥
TIMESTAMP NOT NULL,
   LOCALHOST_TIMESTAMP   DATETIME       NOT NULL,
   HOST_NAME             VARCHAR(50)    NOT NULL,
   STATE                 VARCHAR(8)     NOT NULL,
   NODE                  VARCHAR(128)   NULL,
   PIPELINE_NAME         VARCHAR(128)   NULL,
   STAGE_NAME            VARCHAR(128)   NULL,
   INBOUND_SERVICE_NAME  VARCHAR(256)   NOT NULL,
   INBOUND_SERVICE_URI   VARCHAR(128)   NOT NULL,
```

```
    INBOUND_OPERATION       VARCHAR(64)     NULL,
    OUTBOUND_SERVICE_NAME   VARCHAR(256)    NULL,
    OUTBOUND_SERVICE_URI    VARCHAR(256)    NULL,
    OUTBOUND_OPERATION      VARCHAR(64)     NULL,
    MSG_LABELS              VARCHAR(512)    NULL,
    ERROR_CODE              VARCHAR(64)     NULL,
    ERROR_REASON            VARCHAR(1024)   NULL,
    ERROR_DETAILS           VARCHAR(2048)   NULL,
    CONSTRAINT PK_WLI_QS_REPORT_ATTRIBUTE PRIMARY KEY(MSG_GUID)
)


-- WLI_QS_REPORT_DATA

CREATE TABLE WLI_QS_REPORT_DATA(
    MSG_GUID        VARCHAR(64)     NOT NULL,
    DATA_TYPE       SMALLINT        NULL,
    ENCODING        VARCHAR(24)     NULL,
    DATA_VALUE      IMAGE           NULL,
    CONSTRAINT FK_WLI_QS_REPORT_DATA FOREIGN KEY(MSG_GUID)
      REFERENCES WLI_QS_REPORT_ATTRIBUTE(MSG_GUID) ON DELETE CASCADE
)
```

Finally, it's possible to run OSB without a reporting provider of any kind. You can still use the Report action in your message flows, but no data will be written. The only real reason to stop and/or remove a reporting provider is to remove the only database dependency commonly used by OSB. For most companies, this database dependency is not an issue, but if you want to run OSB without any database connections, you'll need to stop the reporting provider and possibly remove it entirely from the supporting WebLogic Server configuration.

To stop a reporting provider, you use the WebLogic Server admin console. Click the Deployments link in the left navigation bar of the console. Navigate through the list of deployed applications until you come to the JMS reporting provider (or the specific reporting provider you're using, if you aren't using the default JMS reporting provider). Click the check box next to the JMS reporting provider, and then click the Stop button. Similarly, if you wish to undeploy the JMS reporting provider, simply click the Lock & Edit button on the console's Change Center, click the check box next to the JMS reporting provider, and then click the Delete button to remove it completely from the server or cluster.

Summary

In this chapter, you learned how to create alerts in support of SLAs. You learned how to create complex rules to fire those alerts, and how to use the Dashboard to monitor the alerts and gather information about the state of your OSB deployments. Additionally, you learned how to use the built-in reporting tool to record events within a message flow, and even how you can access that raw reporting data from an external tool. What strikes us most about the tools covered in this chapter is the simplicity of their interfaces, especially when juxtaposed against their power. These tools really "open up" the service bus, so they are valuable for your operation support personnel and developers alike.

■ ■ ■

## CHAPTER 11

SOA Security

This chapter briefly explores the topic of security in SOA solutions, and then covers some of the most important security features in OSB. We will also walk through a step-by-step example that demonstrates configuring security in OSB.

Security is a huge field in and of itself. In fact, many vast fields are concerned with security in the digital age: cryptography, security protocols, network security, computer security, identity management, rights management, intrusion detection, software security, standards, malware detection and prevention, and so on.

SOA solutions build upon many layers. Well-known security algorithms, protocols, and technologies are employed in SOA products. Many details of security are handled by these other pieces. This is good, because it relieves SOA architects from needing to worry about many extremely subtle issues. For example, SOA security architects may need to choose which cryptographic encryption algorithm to use, but cryptographic algorithm design is left to cryptography experts. This chapter covers only those aspects that are most relevant to SOA deployments.

This chapter is intended for anyone interested in security: SOA architects, designers, system administrators, and system operators. We do assume some familiarity with basic security concepts and technologies, such as Public Key Infrastructure (PKI), encryption algorithms, and SSL. However, you may find this chapter useful even if you know these concepts only superficially. Knowledge of XML encryption, XML digital signatures, Web Services Security, and SAML is a big plus, but is not required. Other relevant technologies are HTTP Basic Authentication and Java Authentication and Authorization Service (JAAS). Familiarity with the security architecture of WebLogic Server is also an advantage.

Security experts can skip the first section, but we recommend you read it to get an overview of security from an SOA point of view.

An Overview of SOA Security

An SOA is in place to serve business needs. Naturally, there are many security requirements for SOA solutions. Here, we'll look at some common security goals and requirements, as well as message-level security versus transport-level security.

Security Goals and Requirements

There is no single checklist of security features that all SOA solutions must have. The actual needs depend on the business applications built on top of the SOA.

The following are some of the most common security goals:

Data confidentiality: The SOA should have the ability to ensure that sensitive data cannot be seen by unauthorized parties while in transit or while stored on disk or other media. Data confidentiality is achieved through the use of encryption algorithms.

Data integrity: The SOA should have the ability to ensure that unauthorized parties cannot modify legitimate data. Data integrity is typically achieved through digital signatures, which allow the party reading the signed content to verify that the content has not been modified in any way. More precisely, a digital signature allows the reader to detect any unwanted modifications.

Access control: Many services are available only to certain clients. A key business requirement is to be able to set policies to control who has access to sensitive data or critical services. Such policies are sometimes called access control lists (ACLs), but nowadays, they are more commonly referred to as authorization policies or access control policies.

Auditing: Security best practices dictate that systems should keep a trail of certain important operations. Keeping a secure audit log helps diagnose problems when things go wrong (usually because of some sort of accident, such as configuration errors, but also because of attempts to subvert the system). Systems may be subject to government regulations, such as the Sarbanes-Oxley Act (SOX), which mandate some form of auditing.

Privacy: Many enterprise systems handle critical consumer information (credit card numbers, Social Security numbers, addresses, and so on). Consumers demand that this data remains private. It should not be abused or leaked, either accidentally or maliciously. In some scenarios, even the interactions of a user with the system must be private; for example, users don't want their online purchase history to be disclosed. Sometimes anonymity is required; the system communicates on behalf of the users using a pseudonym or even anonymously.

Authentication: A system must be able to securely establish the identity of the entity (user or other software processes) with which it is interacting. Many of today's technologies are heavily message-oriented, meaning that systems and users interact by sending electronic messages. The party sending the message (the client) somehow sends its identity to the system receiving the message (the server). Authentication is the process whereby the client sends its identity, as well as some proof of identity or authenticator to the server, and the server uses this authenticator to verify that the client is indeed who it claims to be.

■**Note** Authentication as described so far is an asymmetrical process: the client authenticates to the server by providing an authenticator, and the server authenticates the client by verifying the authenticator and possibly looking up the client in some sort of user database. Many network protocols allow more than this. In mutual authentication protocols, such as SSL mutual authentication, the client also authenticates the server. Many systems in an SOA sometimes act as the server in a message exchange and sometimes act as the client in other exchanges.

Network security: Intranets are separated from the Internet by specialized nodes and sub-networks called *demilitarized zones* (DMZs). Firewalls on the DMZ tightly control the traffic that flows between the intranet and the Internet. Moreover, many large organizations divide their network into smaller internal networks and place restrictions on the traffic through some of these networks. A common requirement is to expose as little information about the intranet as possible to the outside world. For example, internal IP addresses are not exposed.

Along with these goals, there are other practical security requirements that are somewhat orthogonal to those in the preceding list. These requirements derive from the day-to-day tasks of conducting business. They have to do more with ease of use, flexibility, adapting to business changes, and ease of management than with basic security techniques; however, security has its impact on all of these requirements. The following are examples of such security requirements:

Operations security: Different people are in charge of different aspects of SOA operations. Some people monitor the production system. Some of them are not allowed to make any changes whatsoever to the services or other configuration; others have access to a limited set operation-related tasks. On the other hand, some administrators can control most or all of the features of SOA systems. This essentially boils down to confidentiality, integrity, auditing, and authentication, but applied to the administration and management tasks of the SOA systems themselves. Operations security should be a built-in feature of the products that comprise an SOA solution.

Separation of policy, resource configuration, and business logic: It is common wisdom today that tightly coupling specific security policies into software logic is a bad idea. The same applies to service definitions in a SOA. One reasons for this is that the service designers are usually not (and should not be) aware of all the security and business issues that weigh in on security policy. Another reason is that security policies and service definitions evolve over time, but usually on different schedules. This means that SOA solutions should separate policy management from the service life cycle.

Centralized policy management: Security policies can be complex. When designing a security policy, making the wrong decisions can result in subtle issues and even big security holes. Furthermore, few people within most organizations have the expertise or broad view to make these decisions. Therefore, security policy design is usually left in the hands of a small team of experts. Also, it is common for large numbers of services throughout the enterprise to share the same security policy. For these reasons, it is desirable to have a single policy management point. This usually comes in the form of a single tool or console for viewing and managing the policy of many services and servers scattered throughout the enterprise. This simplifies governance and reduces the likelihood of mistakes, thus cutting costs.

Centralized policy enforcement point: Just as centralized policy management makes the jobs of the security architect and administrator easier, having a small number of points in the architecture where critical security decisions take place makes the architecture simpler to design and less prone to security holes. Consider that it's easier to protect a large building if it has one entrance (with a guarded security checkpoint) than if it has a dozen entries. In the literature, this is sometimes called a *choke point.*

Bridging technologies: Enterprise computing resources are composed of a multitude of hardware/software products and business applications of differing capabilities. Not all products support the same protocols and technologies. Replacing or upgrading older systems is often not feasible. Also, an enterprise has little or no control over the products and technologies used by business partners. These are problems where an SOA can be a big help: the SOA architecture can bridge communication between systems that don't support the same features. For example, an SOA can provide a web services interface to mainframe services, while also supplying other value-added features like statistics gathering, data transformation, and logging. Or the SOA can receive internal requests over HTTPS and apply web service security packaging to those requests on their way out to trading partner services.

Secure protocol interoperability: Vendors of security technologies strive to make their products interoperable with other products, but complete interoperability between competing products—or even between versions of the same product—is often not achieved. This can be the result of ambiguity in standard specifications, bugs in the implementation, or other reasons. When designing an SOA, it is important to choose products that interoperate with other existing assets and partner systems. Standards-based solutions help in this area, but be prepared for rough spots.

Quite often, there is a tension between security and other high-level goals. Security and usability often clash. We all know how tedious it is to remember a myriad of passwords, sometimes with different password-composition rules (for example, the password must be at least eight characters long and contain uppercase and lowercase characters, digits, and special symbols). Being forced to change passwords from time to time is annoying. Two-factor authentication solutions (secure token hardware plus PIN, for example) are more secure, but a hassle when you lose the token. Configuring a personal firewall is painful even to experts.

Similarly, security and performance also clash. Even the fastest encryption and digital signature algorithms reduce throughput.

Finally, security and reliability can sometimes be at odds. The idealized central policy enforcement/management point can become a single point of failure. This is usually easier to overcome by striking a balance: the "central" policy enforcement/management point is distributed for reliability and scalability reasons. In fact, when designing any security architecture, it is necessary to strike a balance between all the competing goals.

Message-Level Security vs. Transport-Level Security

There are two main approaches to SOA security: using transport-level mechanisms or using message-level mechanisms. Transport Layer Security (TLS) is an example of a transport-level protocol. Web Services Security (WSS) is an example of a message-level security standard.

Transport-Level Security Techniques

The TLS/SSL protocol was designed to enable secure communication over the Internet. SSL is a security layer on top of Transmission Control Protocol (TCP) connections. Just as TCP offers a reliable bidirectional byte stream to upper layers, SSL offers, by extension, a secure and reliable bidirectional byte stream to upper layers. More specifically, SSL offers data confidentiality, data integrity, server authentication, and optional client authentication. SSL does not care what data is sent over its secure streams—it can be an HTTP request and its associated HTTP response, an e-mail message over SMTP, a Remote Method Invocation (RMI) request, and so on.

You can think of SSL as a secure pipe between two parties that wish to communicate; bytes pushed on one end are securely transmitted to the other end. But realize that the security guarantees apply to the data only while it's in transit over the secure pipe. Once the data reaches the other end, it is no longer protected by SSL. This is often referred to as *point-to-point security*, meaning security applies only when the data is traveling between two points—in this case, the SSL client and the SSL server. Because of this, and because SSL works on the outside as an add-on to TCP connections, SSL is often referred to as a *transport-level security protocol*.

SSL is a very robust and mature technology. It has been analyzed by many security experts over the years. Other, older transport protocols have some security features, although in many cases, they are very weak or downright unsecure. For example, SMTP and FTP allow username/password authentication, but the password is usually sent in clear text. Collectively, we call the security features of all of these protocols *transport-level security*.

Message-Level Security Techniques

Some security standards recognize the weaknesses of point-to-point security and take a different approach. Instead of sending messages over a secure channel, the messages themselves are processed by the sender to apply a security layer before sending the message over the transport protocol to its destination. The recipient applies the reverse process to validate the security preconditions and to remove the security layer before passing on the message to the upper layers. We refer to these technologies as *message-level security* techniques. S/MIME is an example of a message-level security mechanism used to protect e-mail messages. Another example that is more relevant in today's SOA world is WSS, an OASIS standard for secure web services communication.

WSS-secured messages are regular SOAP envelopes, where sensitive parts of the message (such as the SOAP body) are encrypted, and certain parts of the message (such as the SOAP body and SOAP headers) are digitally signed. On the sender side, WSS is applied before sending the message. It takes the clear-text, application-level SOAP envelope, applies cryptographic encryption and digital signature operations specified in some policy, replaces clear-text elements with encrypted elements, signs whatever must be signed, and adds its own SOAP header. This WSS SOAP header carries the digital signatures and other important information used by the recipient to verify the validity of the message and to reverse the cryptographic operations.

Message-level security technologies sit higher on the protocol stack than transport protocols. Each message is individually secured (although there are options for setting up some context, or session, that spans many messages). This is much more flexible than SSL. With SSL, every single byte of every single message that is transmitted over the secure pipe is encrypted and signed. With standards like WSS, you can decide which parts of the message are signed and which parts of the message are encrypted. Authentication information can also be added to the message. You can have the credit card SOAP header and purchase order document (SOAP body) signed, and then encrypt the credit card header. If the message travels through one or more intermediaries, or follows some workflow, all intermediate nodes will be able to read the entire purchase order (but cannot change it because any modification would break the signature); however, none of the intermediaries can get the credit card number (only the server that has access to the private key can get it). This is called *end-to-end security*.

WSS is well suited for SOA systems, and it is the only message-level security technology discussed in this book. WSS has several advantages over SSL, but it has some drawbacks as well:

- WSS is a fairly recent standard, so fewer products support WSS (whereas SSL is ubiquitous nowadays). Also, WSS may still undergo some major changes in the years to come.

- Because WSS offers many options, it is much harder to configure than SSL. Message-level security policies are complex. This makes it easier to make serious configuration mistakes.

- Modern SSL implementations interoperate well. WSS is more likely to run into interoperability issues. The WS-I Basic Security Profile goes a long way to improve the situation.

- WSS implementations have not been as thoroughly optimized for performance as SSL.

Despite these drawbacks, we expect message-level security adoption to grow over time. It supports certain scenarios that are simply not supported with SSL or other transport-level security mechanisms. It is ideal for large-scale, distributed, message-oriented enterprise applications.

How OSB Fits into an SOA Security Architecture

Now that we have covered some of the security requirements of typical SOA solutions, as well as common technologies used to implement these solutions, we will take a look at how OSB addresses many of these requirements.

Previous chapters have explained at great length what an ESB is and how OSB fits in an SOA. OSB decouples service producers from service consumers, thus making services location-independent and reducing the maintenance costs associated with rolling out new versions of services. OSB's operations and monitoring capabilities (statistics gathering, SLA support, load-balancing, throttling, endpoint management, and more) help enterprises gain more control over critical services and simplify management and operations. Universal Description, Discovery and Integration (UDDI) integration helps advertise new services and leverage existing services. OSB supports many transports, service types, and message-exchange patterns, making it an ideal product for bridging existing technologies and solving integration requirements.

OSB's security architecture is designed to solve a variety of security scenarios. The actual requirements vary a lot among organizations, as you would expect. Sometimes OSB, or any ESB for that matter, plays a key role in the enterprise-wide security architecture; other times, the security needs are primarily met by the products hosting the business services and service consumers.

DO YOU NEED OSB'S SECURITY FEATURES?

Where OSB fits with your organization, or whether it is a good fit, depends on many factors.

If the applications interconnected through the ESB exchange valuable data, such as customer information, then the overall security architecture will probably call for message confidentiality and message integrity. On the other hand, if the data is not sensitive, it is probably perfectly fine to send it over regular clear-text channels like HTTP.

If the risks and threats are fairly low, because the data is not sensitive or perhaps the endpoints and ESB are within a closely guarded network that is already protected by other technologies, then you may not need to use the security features of the ESB.

If the products that host your service consumers and service producers offer advanced security features like WSS, it may make more sense to let these endpoints handle the security requirements. That way, you may be able to build a simpler and more robust end-to-end security architecture. Because the ESB will never have access to the encryption of digital signature keys, it won't be able to read or modify the data or impersonate the client or server; that will, in turn, make it somewhat less of a target for potential attacks. On the other hand, if your assets do not all support the same technologies, and some less sophisticated endpoints need to communicate to services that expect advanced features, the ESB may bridge technologies for you.

Often, an ESB is deployed to replace and supplement an existing IT infrastructure to take advantage of the many benefits of SOA. If security policies were in place before rolling out an ESB, it is important to consider the implications of the ESB on the security architecture. For example, if a workflow application was connecting to some back-end system over HTTPS, and now messages flow through the ESB instead, it is important to decide if one or both of the legs in the communication must be over HTTPS. Similarly, if a client process authenticates to a back-end server with SSL mutual authentication, and an ESB is placed between the two, end-to-end SSL mutual authentication is no longer possible (because SSL is a point-to-point technology).

Identity Propagation

In most business applications, a back-end service needs to authenticate its clients (or service consumers), because the service is available only to certain users, because the response to the service request depends on the requester, because requests/responses are closely audited, or because of service quotas or metering. In this case, you need to address which identity should be made available to the back-end service, as well as how the identity will be securely transmitted and authenticated. This is known as the *identity propagation model*.

When requests are routed through an ESB, you need to decide first if the back-end service should still be aware of the client's identity or if it's okay for the ESB to send its identity to the back-end service (it trusts OSB to properly authenticate and authorize clients on the entry point to OSB proxy services).

If the back-end service needs to aware of the client's identity (which is usually the case), the authentication protocol used may allow end-to-end authentication. With end-to-end authentication, OSB does not play any role in the authentication process. This may be the case when using WSS authentication tokens on the message. For example, the client may send a WSS SOAP envelope that contains an encrypted WSS username/password token. If OSB does not touch the security header, then the back end can decrypt the token and authenticate the client. However, if the client uses transport-level authentication, such as HTTP Basic Authentication over HTTPS, then the OSB business service must be configured to take the username/password of the incoming client request and pass it along in the outbound request.

Another possibility is that the authentication method used in the client-to-OSB communication is different from the one used in the OSB-to-back-end leg. For example, OSB may authenticate the client with HTTP Basic Authentication, and then issue a SAML token on behalf of the client, which is sent along in the outbound request. The back-end server then validates the SAML token and establishes the client's identity based on the token. This has the advantage of not needing to share the client's password with the back-end server. Also, SAML tokens can carry other user attributes, which can be very useful in some situations.

If it's okay for the back-end service to not see the client's identity, then you configure the OSB proxy service to authenticate and authorize the client, optionally validate the request, and then route the request to the back-end service. This routing may be over a secure channel like HTTPS with SSL mutual authentication, or you can have OSB send a username/password assigned to it specifically for communicating to the back-end server (with HTTPS plus Basic Authentication or HTTP plus WSS username/password token).

As the examples here illustrate, in some cases, end-to-end authentication is possible (as with WSS); in other cases, it's not possible. Sometimes, the same technology is used in both legs (HTTPS and HTTP Basic Authentication inbound and outbound); sometimes different technologies are used (HTTPS and HTTP Basic Authentication inbound; WSS with SAML token outbound).

Finally, you need to decide whether or not OSB should actively authenticate the client. Let's consider an HTTP Basic Authentication example. HTTP Basic Authentication simply means the client sends its username/password, Base64-encoded, in a standard HTTP header called `Authorization`. You may want OSB to just look for the `Authorization` header, and take the username/password and put it in an `Authorization` header on the outbound HTTP request. Or you may want OSB to fully authenticate the user (authenticate against a user database, say Active Directory). Passing along the authenticator avoids the cost of the authentication process. (OSB keeps a time-to-live cache of subjects authenticated with username/password, so this cost can often be amortized; however, if WSS authentication is used on inbound requests, the cost can be much higher.) On the other hand, authenticating the client on entry to OSB allows you to add an authorization layer on the service bus, which may be desirable. It also allows you to bridge authentication technologies.

WS-Policy Standards

As explained earlier, separating policy from business logic is widely accepted as good practice. The World Wide Web Consortium (W3C) recognizes this and has produced a set of standards for expressing policy for web services. What exactly constitutes policy is a bit harder to define. There are authorization policies, SLA policies, quality of service policies, routing policies, encryption/digital signature policies, and so on. So, *policy* is a heavily overloaded term. The following is quoted from the W3C Web Services Policy Framework specification (`http://www.w3.org/TR/2007/REC-ws-policy-20070904/`):

> *Web Services Policy 1.5 - Framework defines a framework and a model for expressing policies that refer to domain-specific capabilities, requirements, and general characteristics of entities in a Web services-based system.*

This general-purpose foundation is extended in other specifications that define how to declare policy for domain-specific purposes. In this book (and in OSB), we use the term *WS-Policy* to refer to the W3C standard as well as specific instances of web services policies.

Caution As we've said, *policy* is an overloaded term. OSB has two types of "policies": authorization policies and WS-Policies. Authorization policies, also known as access control policies, control who can access a resource. WS-Policies describe the capabilities and requirements of a web service. Authorization policies are *not* WS-Policies. Sometimes, when there is no risk of confusion, we simply write "policy" for one or the other; which one we are talking about should be clear from the context.

The WS-Policy standard defines an associated XML schema with the namespace `http://www.w3.org/ns/ws-policy`. WS-Policies are XML documents. Listing 11-1 shows an example of a WS-Policy.

Listing 11-1. *Sign and Encrypt WS-Policy (from WS-Policy 1.5)*

```
<wsp:Policy
        xmlns:sp="http://docs.oasis-open.org/ws-sx/ws-securitypolicy/200702"
        xmlns:wsp="http://www.w3.org/ns/ws-policy" >
    <wsp:ExactlyOne>
        <wsp:All>
            <sp:SignedParts>
                <sp:Body/>
            </sp:SignedParts>
        </wsp:All>
        <wsp:All>
            <sp:EncryptedParts>
                <sp:Body/>
            </sp:EncryptedParts>
        </wsp:All>
    </wsp:ExactlyOne>
</wsp:Policy>
```

The root of every WS-Policy is the `Policy` element. Notice how some elements are from a different namespace—`http://docs.oasis-open.org/ws-sx/ws-securitypolicy/200702` in this case. These are domain-specific elements that declare something of interest—in this case, signing and encryption policies (sign and encrypt the whole SOAP body). WS-Policy calls these elements *policy assertions*. WS-Policy also defines a few elements and rules for combining multiple assertions into one WS-Policy (for example, the `<wsp:All>...</wsp:All>` construct). However, WS-Policy does not define any concrete assertions; it just defines a framework for putting these assertions together. Other standards define assertions for specific purposes: security, WSRM (covered in Chapter 9), and so on.

In OSB, WS-Policy instances are used to configure certain aspects of a service (WSS and WSRM), as well as to communicate the policy to other parties (users and other software products) that use the service. A WS-Policy can be created to declare that a service expects all its request messages to be signed and encrypted, as well as to inform clients of that service of these requirements, so they can produce the digital signature and encrypt the request before sending it. Client software can be configured to automatically consume the service's WS-Policy.

Note Of course, security architects and administrators must make sure to understand the overall security architecture and ensure all parties agree to the policies. In some contexts, it is very dangerous to sign arbitrary content. The point is that today's web service platforms can make the client engine automatically or semiautomatically apply the service's WS-Policy before transmitting service request messages.

To be useful, a WS-Policy must be assigned to a service. The W3C Web Services Policy 1.2–Attachment (WS-PolicyAttachment) specification defines how policies can be bound to a WSDL file by taking advantage of the WSDL's schema extensibility points. WS-Policy elements can be embedded in certain spots in the WSDL file to bind policies to specific operations, to individual messages (input or output of an operation), or to the whole service. WS-PolicyAttachment also defines how policies combine when multiple policies are "attached" in a single WSDL file. For more details on all these rules, see the WS-PolicyAttachment specification (http://www.w3.org/Submission/WS-PolicyAttachment/). For our purposes, it is enough to say that all the attached policies that are in scope for a specific operation are combined to produce a single logical WS-Policy, called the *effective policy*.

In OSB, you can attach policies to a WSDL file as follows:

- The policies attached to the WSDL file can be completely embedded in the WSDL (in-lined). In this case, the <wsp:Policy> element and all its policy assertions are part of the WSDL file.

- Alternatively, policies can be indirectly attached, via policy references.

Listing 11-2 shows an example of a policy directly in-lined in the WSDL file.

Listing 11-2. *WSDL with an In-Lined Policy Reference*

```
<definitions name="sample-wsdl-with-inlined-policy"
    targetNamespace="http://acme/samples"
    xmlns="http://schemas.xmlsoap.org/wsdl/"
    xmlns:wsu=
"http://docs.oasis-open.org/wss/2004/01/oasis-
200401-wss-wssecurity-utility-1.0.xsd"
    xmlns:tns="http://acme/samples"
    xmlns:soap="http://schemas.xmlsoap.org/wsdl/soap/"
    xmlns:wsp="http://schemas.xmlsoap.org/ws/2004/09/policy">
    <wsp:UsingPolicy Required="true"/>
```

```
    <wsp:Policy wsu:Id="my-policy">
        ...
    </wsp:Policy>

    ...

    <binding name="SampleBinding" type="tns:SamplePortType">
        ...
        <operation name="doFoo">
            ...
            <input>
                <soap:body/>
                <wsp:Policy>
                    <wsp:PolicyReference URI="#my-policy"/>
                </wsp:Policy>
            </input>
            <output>
                <soap:body namespace="http://acme/samples" use="literal"/>
            </output>
        </operation>
    </binding>
    ...
</definitions>
```

BEA/Oracle Proprietary Security Policy Language

OSB supports the web services security policy assertions defined by BEA/Oracle in WebLogic Server 9.2. These assertions are modeled after an early version of the WS-SecurityPolicy specification, before it was submitted to OASIS for standardization. Since then, OASIS has released the WS-SecurityPolicy 1.2 standard (WSSP 1.2), which WebLogic Server 10 supports. However, OSB does not yet support WSSP 1.2. In this book (and in OSB documentation), we call the BEA/Oracle security policy assertion language *BEA/Oracle proprietary security policy* to distinguish it from WSSP 1.2.

■**Note** OSB 3.0 does have some very limited support for WSSP 1.2 policies. You can assign a transport-level WSSP 1.2 policy to a WS-transport service. However, message-level WSSP 1.2 policies are not supported yet.

The BEA/Oracle proprietary security policy language includes four assertions:

Confidentiality: This assertion specifies that certain parts of the SOAP message are to be encrypted, as well as the encryption algorithm to be used.

Integrity: This assertion specifies that certain parts of the SOAP message are to be digitally signed, as well as the digital signature and canonicalization algorithm. It also specifies whether the signer's certificate should be included in the message and covered by the signature.

Identity: This assertion specifies that the sender must include an authentication token and optionally specifies one or more authentication mechanisms that are allowed by the recipient. The available authentication options are Username token, X.509 token, and SAML token.

MessageAge: This assertion specifies that the sender must include a message timestamp (with an expiration time) in the SOAP envelope. Typically, this timestamp is included in a digital signature. When used in this way, the timestamp and signature help the recipient prevent certain replay attacks.

Built-in BEA/Oracle Security Policies

WebLogic Server comes with a set of built-in predefined web services security policies for the most common tasks. These policies are XML files that are shipped within one of WebLogic Server's JAR files:

`Encrypt.xml`: This policy requires clients to encrypt the SOAP body with 3DES-CBC. The key wrapping algorithm is RSA 1.5. A symmetric key for the Triple Data Encryption Standard (3DES) is generated by the client and encrypted for the recipient with RSA 1.5.

`Sign.xml`: This policy requires clients to sign the SOAP body. It also requires that the client add a signed timestamp to the `wsse:Security` header. Any system header present in the message must also be signed (system headers are WSRM headers, WS-Addressing headers. and the WSS timestamp). The digital signature algorithm is RSA-SHA1. Exclusive XML canonicalization is used.

`Auth.xml`: This policy requires the client to include an authentication token in the message.

■Note WebLogic Server also ships with several WSRM and WSSP 1.2 policies.

These policies can be attached to a WSDL file using the following WS-PolicyAttachment syntax and the BEA/Oracle proprietary `policy:` URI, as shown in Listing 11-3.

Listing 11-3. *Referring to Policy Using the policy: URI*

```
<definitions name="sample-wsdl-with-inlined-policy"
    targetNamespace="http://acme/samples"
    xmlns="http://schemas.xmlsoap.org/wsdl/"
    xmlns:tns="http://acme/samples"
    xmlns:soap="http://schemas.xmlsoap.org/wsdl/soap/"
    xmlns:wsp="http://schemas.xmlsoap.org/ws/2004/09/policy">
    <wsp:UsingPolicy Required="true"/>
    ...
```

```
        <binding name="SampleBinding" type="tns:SamplePortType">
            ...
            <operation name="doFoo">
                ...
                <input>
                    <soap:body/>
                    <wsp:Policy>
                        <wsp:PolicyReference URI="policy:Encrypt.xml"/>
                    </wsp:Policy>
                </input>
                <output>
                    <soap:body namespace="http://acme/samples" use="literal"/>
                </output>
            </operation>
        </binding>
        ...
    </definitions>
```

Custom WS-Policies

We recommend using one of the built-in security policies whenever possible. However, in some cases, you will need to define your own WS-Policy:

- Whenever declaring a WSS encryption policy for encrypting business service requests; that is, whenever you want OSB to encrypt messages before sending them to a back-end service. In this case, OSB expects to find the encryption certificate of the back-end service within the policy itself, so you can't use the built-in encryption policy.

- Whenever you want to sign specific SOAP elements inside the SOAP body or SOAP headers.

- Whenever you want to encrypt specific SOAP elements inside the SOAP body or SOAP headers.

- Whenever you want to use SAML tokens.

- Whenever you want more control over which authentication tokens you want to use in your proxy service or business service. (Recall that the available authentication options are Username token, X.509 token, and SAML token.)

To define your own WS-Policy, create a WS-Policy resource in the OSB console or in WorkSpace Studio. WS-Policy resources are first-class resources in OSB, which can be imported/exported and referenced from other resources.

WS-Policies in OSB must have an Id attribute. The value of this attribute must be globally unique.

You can attach your own WS-Policy resource to a WSDL file in two ways:

- You can use the `policy:` URI with the policy ID, as in this example (where there is a WS-Policy resource named `my-policy` in project `xyz`):

  ```
  <wsp:Policy>
          <wsp:PolicyReference URI="policy:xyz/my-policy"/>
  </wsp:Policy>
  ```

- You can use an arbitrary `http` URL in the WSDL policy attachment point and declare a link between this URL and the WS-Policy resource.

So far, all the examples have assigned WS-Policies to services indirectly, via WSDL WS-Policy attachments. All proxy and business services defined from such a WSDL file automatically use the WSDL's policy. OSB 3.0 offers a way to directly assign a WS-Policy to a service, without any WSDL file changes. WorkSpace Studio and the OSB 3.0 console both have tabs for directly binding policies to services, by reference to WS-Policy resources or to built-in policies. Policies can be directly bound to service operations, the entire service, or the request or response messages of individual operations. The same rules for combining multiple policies into a single effective policy as in the WS-PolicyAttachment standard apply here. Keep in mind that these two methods of assigning a WS-Policy to a service are mutually exclusive; if there are WS-Policies attached to the WSDL file, and you decide to assign WS-Policies directly to the service, the policies attached to the WSDL file are ignored.

Abstract vs. Concrete BEA/Oracle Proprietary Security Policies

BEA/Oracle proprietary security policies have some characteristics that are not present in WSSP 1.2. BEA/Oracle security policy assertions have certain optional elements that can be used to specify certain parameters. When these elements are missing, WebLogic Server fills in the gaps. The optional elements include the following:

- The encryption certificate to be used to encrypt messages for the target service (in Base64-encoded form inside a `BinarySecurityToken` element)

- The authentication tokens accepted by the service as proof of authentication (Username token, X.509 token, or SAML token)

The OSB documentation calls policies that don't specify these optional elements *abstract* policies. Policies that specify the optional child elements are called *concrete*.

When the policy includes an Identity assertion that does not explicitly list the accepted authentication tokens, WebLogic Server determines the accepted token types based on certain parameters in server managed beans (MBeans) (`WebserviceSecurityConfigurationMBean`). These MBeans augment the policy with the missing information.

■**Note** By default, X.509 token authentication is not allowed. To turn it on, you need to make some server configuration changes. Consult the OSB security guide for more details.

If the WS-Policy of an OSB business service has a Confidentiality assertion with a `BinarySecurityToken`, OSB will use the certificate in the policy to encrypt messages routed to that business service. On the other hand, if the Confidentiality assertion does not have a `BinarySecurityToken`, WebLogic Server will look for additional configuration to find the server encryption certificate. Unfortunately, this design creates some key/certificate management complications. To avoid problems, you should use concrete Confidentiality assertions in policies assigned to business services and abstract Confidentiality assertions in policies assigned to proxy services. The encryption certificate of the target back-end services is embedded in the policy, which makes management of back-end certificates hard (this may be addressed in future releases of OSB).

WSS Scenarios

As you can probably guess by now, there are many ways you can use WSS in OSB. In this section, we briefly go over various scenarios. Keep in mind that in OSB, WSS is controlled by the WS-Policy.

To illustrate the scenarios, throughout this section, we assume a simple WSS encryption policy (the SOAP body must be encrypted). Many other options are possible.

WSS Inbound, No WSS Outbound

The proxy service has a WSS policy. The client encrypts the request with the proxy's public key, and the proxy decrypts the message. The proxy then routes the clear-text message.

No WSS Inbound, WSS Outbound

The proxy service does not have a WSS policy, but the business service does. The client sends a clear-text request to the proxy. OSB then encrypts the message with the back end's public key before routing it to the business service. The back end decrypts the message before processing it. Since the proxy does not even have a WSS policy, it's just a regular proxy service. The business service does have WSS policy, so we call it a WSS business service.

WSS Inbound and Outbound with Active Intermediary Proxy

Both the proxy service and the business service have a WSS policy. In this scenario, the proxy service plays a central role in the processing of WSS messages, so it's called an *active intermediary*. Let's look at all steps during the flow of a single message:

- The client encrypts the request with the proxy's public key and sends the request to OSB.

- The proxy decrypts the message with its private key.

- The message goes through the request pipeline.

- The Route node selects the target business service.

- OSB encrypts the outbound message with the back end's public key before transmitting the message to the back end.

- The back end decrypts the message with its private key.

In this scenario, OSB is actively doing WSS on both sides of the message path. This is obviously very computationally expensive from an OSB point of view. Note that the WSS policy on the business service does not need to be the same as the one on the proxy service.

WSS Inbound and Outbound with Passive Intermediary Proxy

Both the proxy service and the business service have a WSS policy, but this time, the proxy service does not do any WSS processing. This is called a *passive intermediary*, or *pass-through*, scenario. In this case, the message flow is like this:

- The client encrypts the request with the back end's public key and sends the request to OSB.

- The encrypted message goes through the request pipeline. Note that OSB cannot read the SOAP body; however, it may have access to clear-text SOAP headers. OSB may modify/delete these headers or add new headers.

- The Route node selects the target business service.

- OSB transmits the encrypted message to the back end.

- The back end decrypts the message with its private key.

WSS Between Client and Back End (Not Declared in OSB)

Neither the proxy service nor the business service has a WSS policy, but the client has somehow been configured to encrypt requests with the back end's public key. OSB is not aware of that; in other words, there isn't any configuration telling the OSB proxy service that the request is encrypted. Of course, the proxy request pipeline will not be able to do anything with the SOAP body, except pass it along to the back end. The back end decrypts the message and processes the request.

Passive and Active Intermediaries

Let's compare the preceding scenarios. In the first and third scenarios, we say the proxy service is an *active WSS intermediary*, because the proxy acts on the WSS policy and does some WSS processing of the request. In the fourth scenario, the proxy is called a *passive WSS intermediary*, because the proxy does not do any WSS processing or policy enforcement, even though the proxy is configured with WSS policy and advertises the WSS policy in its dynamic WSDL.

The last two scenarios are very similar. Both are passive WSS intermediaries. The difference is whether or not the proxy advertises the WSS policy in its effective WSDL.

In the first two scenarios, WSS is on only one side of the communication. This can be useful when bridging technologies. It's also useful if the ESB acts as a security gateway or concentrator.

Service Key Providers

The scenarios described in the previous section require public and private keys to encrypt and decrypt the messages. In some cases, the client encrypts the message with OSB's public key and OSB decrypts the message. In other cases, OSB encrypts the routed message with the back-end server's public key, and the back-end server decrypts the message. This means the client, OSB, and the back-end servers sometimes need to have access to private or public keys.

Public keys in PKI are always embedded within X.509 certificates. The certificate binds together the public key, the identity of the system that owns the corresponding private key, possibly some restrictions on how the key can be used, and possibly other attributes. The certificate can be issued by a certification authority (CA) or can be self-signed. The certificate has information that identifies the CA that issued it. The CA signs the entire certificate with its own key. Certificates can be distributed freely.

If we replace the hypothetical WSS policy in the examples in the previous section with a digital signature policy, then the party signing the message needs a private signing key (and accompanying certificate, of course). Digital signatures in WSS always have some way of directly or indirectly refer to the signing certificate. Sometimes the party signing the message encodes its certificate in the message (inside the WSS header); sometimes only a reference to the certificate is included in the message (such as through an issuer name, a serial number, a certificate thumbprint, or a key identifier).

The party verifying the digital signature needs to decide if it trusts the client's signing certificate. In OSB, this is done with WebLogic Server Certificate Lookup and Validation (CLV) providers. WebLogic Server's CLV providers include a *certificate registry*. As its name implies, a certificate registry is nothing more than a set of certificates—trusted certificates to be more precise. A certificate registry provider can be configured in WebLogic Server's console. You can import certificates into the registry and otherwise manage the registry from the console or through MBeans.

When a certificate registry has been configured in WebLogic Server, the server will use it when validating digital signatures to establish trust on the signer's certificate. The server will trust only certificates that are present on the registry; other certificates will be rejected. WebLogic Server can also be configured to use the CLV providers for trust decisions during SSL handshakes.

Note that if you don't configure a certificate registry, WebLogic Server (and OSB) will trust client's certificates if it can build a certificate chain from the signing certificate to one of the certificates in the server's trust keystore. This may be acceptable in some cases, but generally it is strongly recommended that you configure a certificate registry. The registry gives you much more control.

Keep in mind that those certificates corresponding to OSB's own private keys must also be trusted by the server. You must make sure those certificates (or one of the certificates in the chain of issuers) are in the certificate registry or server trust keystore. Of course, OSB's certificates must be trusted by the clients or servers OSB talks to, but that is out of the control of OSB itself.

Connection Credentials

Some OSB features (such as UDDI and JNDI providers) and several built-in OSB transports (JMS, Email, FTP, and SFTP, to name a few) rely on a poll-based messaging pattern. The transports establish long-lived connections to servers to either poll for messages to be consumed by OSB proxy services or to transmit messages destined to some back-end service.

Let's take the JMS transport as an example. Internally, JMS proxy services use long-lived connections to a JMS server to poll for messages in the request queue. When a message is present on the queue, the message is removed, and the JMS transport dispatches the message to the proxy's request pipeline for processing. This is called *asynchronous messaging*. Similarly, when OSB routes a message to a JMS business service, OSB gets a connection to the target JMS server from a pool of connections and transmits the message to the JMS server.

In the JMS transport example, in the inbound case (JMS proxy service), the long-lived connection is used to periodically check for incoming messages. In the outbound case (JMS business service), a pool of long-lived connections is used to transmit the messages (connection pooling is used for performance reasons). The important point is that in both cases, the connection is not made on behalf of a particular client request. If the connection is to be secured and OSB is supposed to present credentials to the server for authentication, then the credential must be an account assigned to OSB for that purpose—it can't be some client's identity. As mentioned, other OSB transports share this model.

OSB has a nice model for managing connection credentials. A username/password can be directly entered when configuring a UDDI registry or an SMTP server. In other cases, as in JMS, Email, FTP, and SFTP services, the user can configure a separate resource called a *service account*, enter the username/password in the service account configuration, and then have the service reference the service account.

Service Accounts

Service accounts are first-class OSB resources that solve certain security configuration needs. Service accounts are named resources that can be referenced from proxy and business services. They are created in a project or folder. OSB guarantees referential integrity to service accounts, just as with any other type of resource.

OSB has three types of service accounts:

- A *static* service account has a username/password combination, which the administrator must enter when the service account is created or updated.

- A *pass-through* service account does not have any configuration other than its type.

- A *mapped* service account has two tables: a table of remote users and their passwords and a table that maps "local" usernames to remote usernames.

These service accounts solve two distinct problems: they specify the username/password to use for connection-level authentication in asynchronous transports, and they specify the credentials used by a proxy service when routing a message to a target business service.

Connection-level authentication requires a fixed username/password to authenticate to the server when the connections are established, so static accounts are used in this case. For example, JMS proxy and business services allow you to specify an optional reference to a service account.

The second problem—let's call it the outbound authentication problem—relates to the concepts discussed earlier in the "Identity Propagation" section. If the back-end server doesn't need to know the identity of the client, a fixed username/password stored in a static service account is appropriate. More often, the back-end server will need to know the client's identity in the form of a client username/password, and in that case, a pass-through or mapped service account is required. If the proxy service gets the client's username/password somehow (through HTTP Basic Authentication or a WSS Username token), then a pass-through service account tells OSB to take that username/password and pass it along to the back end, using the authentication mechanism required by the back end.

In some complex scenarios, OSB must send a username/password to the back-end service but the proxy service authenticates the client using some mechanism other than a username/password (through a WSS SAML token, WSS X.509 token, custom transport-level or message-level token, or two-way SSL). In such cases, OSB does not have the client's username/password; therefore, a pass-through service account would not work. Mapped service accounts can be used in these situations. The mapped service account maps the client's identity—as established with the inbound authentication protocol—to a remote username (which can be the same as or different from the "local" username) and obtains the password for that remote username from the remote users table. The remote username/password combination is then used during outbound authentication.

Mapped service accounts can be used to map many clients (local username) to one or a few remote users; in other words, many-to-one relationships are allowed. If that's what your overall security architecture requires, then mapped service accounts may be what you are seeking. But keep in mind that mapped service accounts have certain limitations:

- Managing a mapped service account is difficult because it requires entering the entire local user table to remote user table, as well the remote user's password, in the OSB console, which can be impractical if either table is large.

- Mapped service accounts assume that the administrator somehow knows the remote user's password (on the target remote system). This is usually undesirable and not always the case.

- Every time the remote password is changed on the target system, the mapped service account must be updated.

Mapped service accounts can be useful in some limited scenarios. However, whenever possible, you should use some form of token authentication (for example a SAML token) instead of a mapped service account. Generating an authentication token on behalf of the client is usually better than mapping the client to a remote user/password.

One of the main advantages of service accounts is that a single service account can be shared by many services. This makes it easier to manage the credentials used for connection-level and outbound authentication.

Security Configuration Imports and Exports

One of the strengths of OSB is its user-friendly import/export functionality. OSB has some security-specific features that address import/export of security-related configuration.

When exporting resources that have username/passwords or key-alias/key-passwords (service accounts, SMTP servers, JNDI providers, UDDI registries, or service key providers),

OSB gives the administrator the option to enter a passphrase, which is used to generate a key to encrypt the username/password or key-alias/key-password. The same passphrase must be entered when importing the resources. This makes it easier to securely transfer the configuration from one OSB instance to another, or when exporting for backup reasons. The user has the option to manually exclude the resources that have sensitive information from the export step.

Another feature built into OSB import/export functionality is the ability to preserve the security configuration present on the target OSB instance when importing new versions of existing resources.

AQUALOGIC ENTERPRISE SECURITY INTEGRATION

One of the strengths of SOA is governance: the ability to easily manage the various policies associated with the enterprise computing assets. OSB can be combined with BEA/Oracle's AquaLogic Enterprise Security (ALES) to tackle the access control aspect of governance.

When the ALES Security Service Module (SSM) is plugged into WebLogic Server, access control to OSB proxy services (as well as access control to other server resources) is delegated to ALES. The access control policies themselves can be managed within the ALES administration console. ALES can be plugged into many other systems, including other application servers, web servers, Java applications, and so on.

OSB End-to-End Security Configuration

In this section, we will walk through an example of configuring OSB to enable end-to-end security. This example demonstrates how to set up security for common inbound/outbound service combinations. We will first configure WebLogic Server with a new security provider. Next, we will create a secure proxy service that requires the service request and response to be signed with a digital signature, and then create a client for the service. Finally, we will use message-level security to encrypt the body of the requests and responses.

Caution This exercise is *not* a checklist of security procedures and should *not* be used as a guideline for how to secure production systems. Many important steps have been omitted or simplified. You should consult OSB and WebLogic Server documentation to get a more complete picture.

Configuring WebLogic Server

We need to configure WebLogic Server with a new security provider. OSB will then use this security provider when it secures a web service. This involves two main steps: first, generate the needed security keystore and certificates, and then configure WebLogic Server to use those keystores and certificates.

Creating the Keystores and Certificates

To make the process of creating the keystores and certificates as simple as possible for the purposes of this example, we have developed an Ant script that does most of the heavy lifting for you. You can find the build.xml script that does this work in the Security project of the source code that accompanies this book. Just execute the all task, and the script will create everything you need for the rest of this exercise.

Here, we will analyze the script so you can better understand how it automates the process of creating keystores and certificates. With this understanding, you can then modify the script to meet your specific needs (this script should not be used as-is in a production environment).

At the top the build.xml file in the Security project, you will see a property that refers to the examples.properties file in the workspace directory (the directory that contains the various workspace projects). This file defines the location of your BEA/Oracle home directory (where you installed OSB) and the directory of your domain. It is used by many of the projects that accompany this book. Make sure those properties are configured correctly.

The second group of properties is one that you may optionally customize. We suggest that you do not customize them for the example we are implementing here, but you may wish to modify these properties when you are creating keystores for use in your own projects. For example, you will most likely want to change the names of the keystores and certificates to meet the needs of your specific projects.

The third section of properties should not need any modification. They are "utility" properties used within the build.xml Ant script. Change them at your own peril.

The first target is the all target. This target simply calls the lower-level targets in the proper order. The clean target is self-explanatory. The createServerTrustKeystore target creates the keystore that the OSB server will use to hold the certificates of trusted certificate-signing authorities (CSAs). The createClientTrustKeystore target does the same thing, only for the client's use. A keystore is really just a database of certificates and keys. We create our keystores using a 1024-byte key, which provides considerable encryption protection and will meet the needs of most production systems.

When creating the keystores, the build.xml script makes liberal use of the keytool.exe program that ships with Java. This tool is used to create the keystores and certificates. It is also used to import and export certificates to and from the keystores. Note that the createServerTrustKeystore target creates the server's keystore file and exports a certificate for the server. It also imports its own certificate into the server keystore. This process is called *self-signing*. It is basically a process whereby the keystore states that it trusts itself. Later, in the createClientTrustKeystore target, a client keystore is created, and its certificate is exported. At the end of the createClientTrustKeystore target, you will see the command that imports the client's certificate into the server keystore and the server's certificate into the client keystore. This allows the client and the server to trust certificates that are signed by each other.

The final major target in our script is copyToAdminServer. This simply copies the server keystore into the root directory of the OSB domain.

That concludes the generation of the certificates. There are a couple of other utility targets, like viewClientKeystore and viewServerKeystore, which allow you to take a look at the contents of the respective keystores.

Next, we need to configure WebLogic Server to use the certificate.

Configuring WebLogic Security

Configuring a new security provider in WebLogic Server is a fairly straightforward process. First, be sure that you have started your OSB domain. Once it is running, open you web browser to http://localhost:7001/console and log in.

Configuring Keystores

In the web console, navigate to Environment ➤ Servers and click Admin Server to see the details of the server. In the Configuration tab, click the Keystores subtab. Click the Lock and Edit button so that you can make some changes to the server. There are two types of keystores: Identity and Trust. We are going to configure both types here, so set the Keystores field to Custom Identity and Custom Trust.

Set both the Custom Identity Keystore and Custom Trust Keystore fields to alsb_trust.jks. We will use the same keystore for both the identity and trust certificates. Because our script copied the alsb_trust.jks file into the domain directory, we can simply refer to it by the file name. If the keystore were copied to another location, you would need to specify the fully qualified directory and file name to allow WebLogic Server to locate the correct file.

Lastly, set the four keystore passphrase fields to the password for the keystore: storepassword. Your Keystores tab should now match the one shown in Figure 11-1. Click the Save button.

■**Note** Normally, identity and trust keystores are stored in different files, because the protection levels applied to these files can differ significantly.

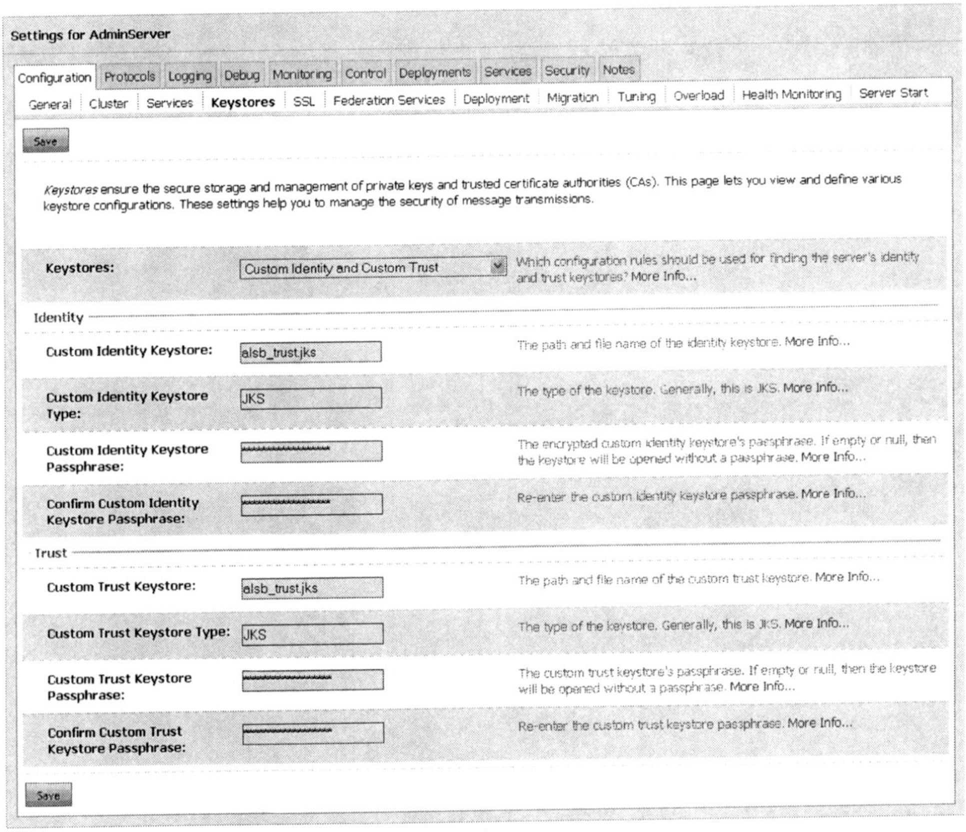

Figure 11-1. *Configuring the keystore in WebLogic Server*

Configuring SSL

Next, we will configure the server for SSL. Strictly speaking, this is not necessary. However, in a production environment, you would almost always perform this step.

Click the SSL subtab (next to the Keystores tab) in the console. Leave the Identity and Trust Locations field set to Keystores. Fill in the Private Key Alias field with the value alsbserver, and set the password fields to keypassword. Your SSL tab should look like the one shown in Figure 11-2. Click the Save button.

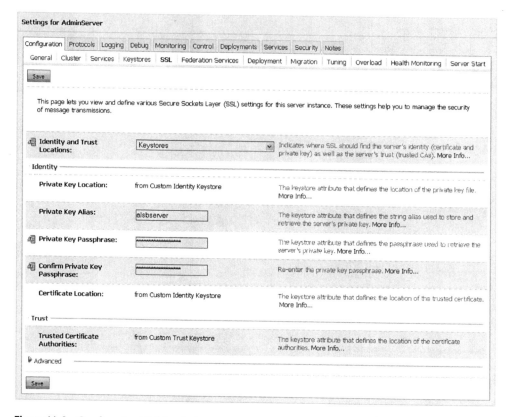

Figure 11-2. *Configuring WebLogic Server to use SSL*

Configuring the Security Realm

Our last step is to configure the default security realm to use this SSL information. In the Domain Structure section of the console, click the Security Realms link. Then click the `myrealm` security realm. Click the Providers tab, and then the Credential Mapping subtab. Click the New button to create a new credential mapper.

Set the name of the new credential mapper to `OSB.PKI.CredMapper` and select the type as `PKICredentialMapper`. Click the OK button. We created this PKI credential mapper to allow OSB to sign in and encrypt data.

Click the credential mapper that you just created. Select the Configuration tab and then the Provider Specific subtab. Set the file name field to `alsb_trust.jks` and enter `storepassword` for in the password fields. Your Provider Specific tab should match the one shown in Figure 11-3. Click the Save button.

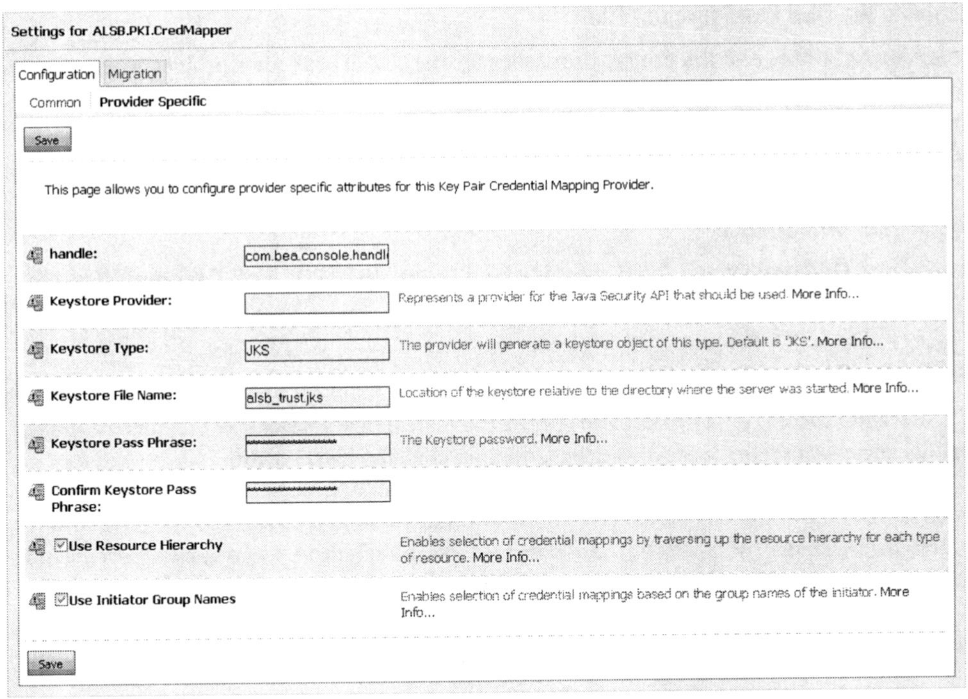

Figure 11-3. *Configuring the PKI provider-specific details*

That completes the WebLogic Server configuration. Save all of your changes and restart WebLogic Server so that the new security settings can take effect.

Now, it is time to move into OSB to get to work creating a secure proxy service.

Creating a Secure Proxy Service Using a Digital Signature

Next, we will create a secure proxy service that requires the service request and response to be signed with a digital signature. This involves the following steps:

1. Modify the OSB configuration project to make it aware of the Java keystore that will be used to implement web service security.

2. Create the OSB project that will be the home of the secure web service.

3. Create a service key provider that provides the mapping information to link the web service to the Java keystore.

4. Create the WSDL file that will be implemented by the proxy service.

5. Create an XQuery resource that will provide the functionality you want from the proxy service.

6. Create the proxy service and its message flow.

Modifying the OSB Configuration File

In WorkSpace Studio, edit the project properties for the OSB30 Book Conf project. In the Keystore File field, select the alsb_trust.jks file that you created earlier. Set the Password field to storepassword. This allows the various OSB projects in the main configuration project to access the keystore. Save your settings.

Creating the OSB Project

Create a new OSB project and call it Security_SB. Choose the OSB30 Book Conf project as the configuration project.

Creating the Service Key Provider

Right-click the Security_SB project and choose to create a new service key provider. Name the provider SecureProxyServiceKeyProvider, and then click the Next button.

Check all three check boxes (Encryption Key, Digital Signature Key, and SSL Client Authentication Key). Specify alsbserver as the key name and keypassword as the password for all three fields. Instead of typing in the alsbserver name each time, you can also just click the Browse button and select the only key from the list.

When all three keys and passwords are specified, click the Finish button. You now have a secure key provider that can be used by your web service.

Creating the WSDL

Next, we need to create a WSDL file that defines the functionality of the proxy service we are creating. We will create a simple service that takes a customer ID and returns some customer account information.

In the project, create a folder named WSDL. In the WSDL folder, create a new WSDL file named SecureMessageService.wsdl. Listing 11-4 shows the WSDL we will use. The key areas of the WSDL file that address the signing of the request/response are highlighted in bold.

Listing 11-4. *Specifying a Digital Signature Requirement in the WSDL File (SecureMessageService.wsdl)*

```
<?xml version="1.0" encoding="UTF-8"?>
<wsdl:definitions xmlns:soap="http://schemas.xmlsoap.org/wsdl/soap/"
    xmlns:tns="http://www.alsb.com/SecureMessageService/"
    xmlns:wsdl="http://schemas.xmlsoap.org/wsdl/"
    xmlns:xsd="http://www.w3.org/2001/XMLSchema"
    xmlns:wsu="http://docs.oasis-open.org/wss/2004/01/oasis- ↪
200401-wss-wssecurity-utility-1.0.xsd"
    xmlns:wsp="http://schemas.xmlsoap.org/ws/2004/09/policy"
    name="SecureMessageService"
    targetNamespace="http://www.alsb.com/SecureMessageService/">
    <wsdl:types>
        <xsd:schema
            targetNamespace="http://www.alsb.com/SecureMessageService/">
            <xsd:element name="getAccount">
```

```
            <xsd:complexType>
                <xsd:sequence>
                    <xsd:element name="customerID" type="xsd:int" />
                </xsd:sequence>
            </xsd:complexType>
        </xsd:element>
        <xsd:element name="getAccountResponse">
            <xsd:complexType>
                <xsd:sequence>
                    <xsd:element name="customerID" type="xsd:int" />
                    <xsd:element name="customerName" type="xsd:string" />
                    <xsd:element name="account" type="xsd:string" />
                </xsd:sequence>
            </xsd:complexType>
        </xsd:element>
    </xsd:schema>
</wsdl:types>
<wsp:UsingPolicy wsdl:Required="true" />
<wsdl:message name="getAccountRequest">
    <wsdl:part element="tns:getAccount" name="parameters" />
</wsdl:message>
<wsdl:message name="getAccountResponse">
    <wsdl:part element="tns:getAccountResponse" name="parameters" />
</wsdl:message>
<wsdl:portType name="SecureMessageService">
    <wsdl:operation name="getAccount">
        <wsdl:input message="tns:getAccountRequest" />
        <wsdl:output message="tns:getAccountResponse" />
    </wsdl:operation>
</wsdl:portType>
<wsdl:binding name="SecureMessageServiceSOAP"
    type="tns:SecureMessageService">
    <soap:binding style="document"
        transport="http://schemas.xmlsoap.org/soap/http" />
    <wsdl:operation name="getAccount">
        <wsp:Policy>
            <wsp:PolicyReference URI="policy:Sign.xml"/>
        </wsp:Policy>
        <soap:operation
            soapAction="getAccount" />
        <wsdl:input>
            <soap:body use="literal" />
        </wsdl:input>
        <wsdl:output>
            <soap:body use="literal" />
        </wsdl:output>
    </wsdl:operation>
```

```
      </wsdl:binding>
      <wsdl:service name="SecureMessageService">
         <wsdl:port binding="tns:SecureMessageServiceSOAP"
            name="SecureMessageServiceSOAP">
            <soap:address location="http://localhost:7001/security/SecureMessage" />
         </wsdl:port>
      </wsdl:service>
</wsdl:definitions>
```

Near the top of the WSDL file we declare two namespaces. The wsu namespace is a utility namespace. We don't reference it yet, but we will later in the exercise. The second namespace is wsp, the web service policy namespace.

You specify the need for a digital signature by using policies. The following statement tells OSB to process any WS-Policy statements found in the WSDL file:

```
<wsp:UsingPolicy wsdl:Required="true" />
```

Lastly, within the getAccount operation definition (in the soap:binding tag), we specify a wsp:Policy tag. That refers to the Sign.xml policy.

Creating the XQuery Resource

Instead of writing a JWS to provide the getAccount functionality, we are going to create an XQuery resource that does the same thing. Our XQuery will take in the getAccount element from the request and return a properly formatted getAccountResponse.

Right-click the Security SB project and select New ➤ XQuery Transformation from the pop-up menu. Name the resource Account.xq and click the Next button. The next step in the XQuery Transformation wizard allows you to specify the source type. Select the Typed / Security SB / WSDL / SecureMessageService.wsdl / getAccount element and click the Add button. Then click Next.

The next step in the wizard allows you to define the target type (that is, the return value of the transformation). Select the Typed / Security SB / WSDL / SecureMessageService.wsdl / getAccountResponse element. Click the Add button and then the Finish button. The wizard will close, and you will be returned to the XQuery transformation window.

For the Account.xq transformation, drag the name element on the left side of the window onto the greeting element on the right side of the window. This creates the basic relationship between the input and output values, but we need to customize the XQuery function a bit more so that it returns the correct getAccountResponse element format. Click the Source tab at the bottom of the window and edit the code so that it matches the code listed in Listing 11-5.

Listing 11-5. *The Account.xq XQuery Resource*

```
(:: pragma bea:global-element-parameter parameter="$getAccount1" ➥
 element="ns0:getAccount" location="WSDL/SecureMessageService.wsdl" ::)
(:: pragma bea:global-element-return element="ns0:getAccountResponse" ➥
 location="WSDL/SecureMessageService.wsdl" ::)

declare namespace xf = "http://tempuri.org/Security%20SB/Account/";
declare namespace ns0 = "http://www.alsb.com/SecureMessageService/";
```

```
declare function xf:Account($getAccount1 as element(ns0:getAccount))
    as element(ns0:getAccountResponse) {
        <ns0:getAccountResponse>
            <customerID>{ data($getAccount1/customerID) }</customerID>
            <customerName>Doe, John</customerName>
            <account>12345-6789-01234</account>
        </ns0:getAccountResponse>
};
declare variable $getAccount1 as element(ns0:getAccount) external;
xf:Account($getAccount1)
```

Save the work you have completed so far.

Creating the Proxy Service

The final step is to create the proxy service and its message flow. Right-click the Security SB
project and create a new proxy service. Name the service SecureMessage.proxy. Set the Service
Type field to WSDL Web Service and select SecureMessageService.wsdl. You can select either
the port or the binding.

In the Transport Configuration step of the wizard, ensure that the service endpoint is set
to /Security_SB/SecureMessageProxy. In the HTTP Transport Configuration step of the wizard,
leave the settings unchanged and continue. In the Operation Selection Configuration step of
the wizard, select the SOAPAction Header radio button.

After you click Finish in the wizard, the proxy service is created, but you still have a little
configuration left to do. Click the Security tab of the proxy service. Click the Browse button
and select the SecureProxyServiceKeyProvider that you created earlier. Be sure to select the
Yes radio button for the Process WS-Security Header field. Your Security tab should look like
the one shown in Figure 11-4.

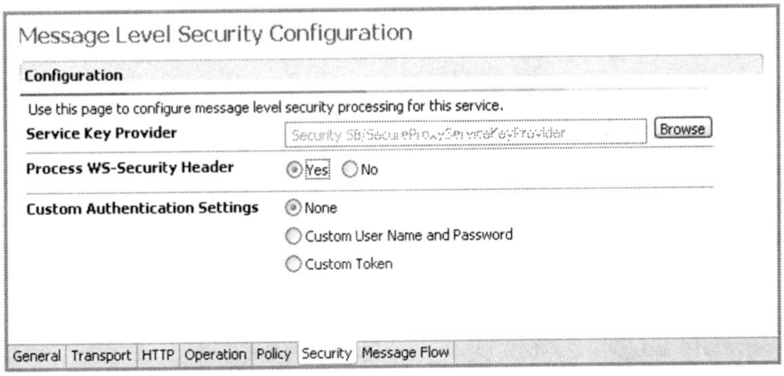

Figure 11-4. *Specifying message-level security for the proxy service*

Now we need to create the message flow that will implement the main logic of the service
and tie everything together. Our message flow is pretty simple. It contains a single Pipeline
Pair node. In the request pipeline of the Pipeline Pair node, there is a single Assign action that
assigns the expression $body/sec1:getAccount to the variable accountRequest.

In the response pipeline, there is an Assign action that assigns the return value of the XQuery resource Account.xq to the variable response. To select the Account.xq resource, click the Expression link, and then select the XQuery Resource tab in the XQuery/XSLT Expression Editor. Use the Browse button to select the Account.xq resource. For the getAccount1 bind variable, enter the value $accountRequest, as shown in Figure 11-5. Click the OK button when you are finished.

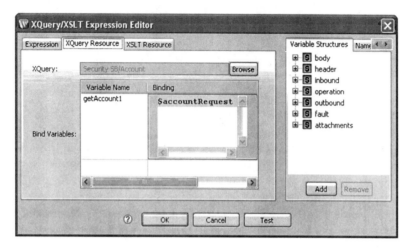

Figure 11-5. *Configuring the XQuery resource*

Under the Assign action that you just created, create a Replace action. Set the XPath to . (the period character), the variable to body, and the expression to $response. Be sure to select the Replace Node Contents radio button.

Save all of your work and deploy this project to the server. You will need the proxy service running when you create the service client.

Creating a Secure Client

We are going to create the client stubs for our service client using the clientgen Ant task provided by BEA/Oracle. We don't want to use the usual Web Service Client wizard provided by WorkSpace Studio because that wizard generates the Apache Axis web service stack. By using the clientgen Ant task, we will generate code that uses the WebLogic Server web service stack. WebLogic takes care of generating and inserting all of the additional security code for us. As you will see in a bit, that's would be a lot of work to do manually.

Begin by creating a new Java project in WorkSpace Studio. Name the project SecureClient. Be sure to add the following JAR files to the project libraries so the client will compile cleanly:

- %OSB_HOME%/wlserver10.0/server/lib/weblogic.jar

- %OSB_HOME%/wlserver10.0/server/lib/wseeclient.jar

- %OSB_HOME%/wlserver10.0/server/lib/webserviceclient+ssl.jar

■**Note** Be sure that you have the `weblogic.jar` file defined in the Global Entries of the Ant Runtime section of your preferences in order to allow the `build.xml` file to access the `clientgen` Ant task. You can set the preferences in WorkSpace Studio by selecting Window ➤ Preferences and then choosing Ant / Runtime.

Next, add a source code folder to the project and call the folder `src`. To create the client stubs using the WebLogic web service stack, run the `all` task in the `build.xml` file in the SecureClient project. Once the client stubs are created, you will need to create a package named `com.alsb.security` in the `src` folder. In this package, create a Java class and name it `SecureClient.java`.

Listing 11-6 shows the source code for the `SecureClient.java` file. Most of the source code for the client should be familiar to you now. You connect to and invoke a secure service in the same way that you invoke a nonsecure web service. However, we need to take a few extra steps before we can invoke the web service. The security-specific code that was added to allow the client to sign the request and receive a signed response is highlighted in bold in the listing.

Listing 11-6. *The SecureClient Application (SecureClient.java)*

```java
public class SecureClient {
    // Modify the file path to match the location of the
    // client_identity.jks file on your computer.
    static String clientIdentityKeystore = " client_trust.jks";

    public static void main(String[] args) {
        try {
            // Create the list credential providers
            List<CredentialProvider> credProviders = new ➥
ArrayList<CredentialProvider>();

            // Create a BinarySecurityToken credential provider.
            // This is used when digitally signing the request.
            CredentialProvider cp = new ClientBSTCredentialProvider(
                    clientIdentityKeystore, "storepassword", "jeff",
                    "keypassword", "JKS");
            credProviders.add(cp);

            // Get the service stub so we can add the security information
            SecureMessageService_Service svc =
                new SecureMessageService_Service_Impl();
            SecureMessageService_PortType port = svc
                    .getSecureMessageServiceSOAP();

            Stub stub = (Stub) port;
```

```
// Set the endpoint to the TCPMON monitor so we can see the traffic
stub._setProperty(Stub.ENDPOINT_ADDRESS_PROPERTY,
        "http://localhost:8001/Security_SB/SecureMessage");

// Associate the key-pair credentials with the web service stub
stub._setProperty(WSSecurityContext.CREDENTIAL_PROVIDER_LIST,
        credProviders);

// The client uses the server's certificate that is embedded
// in the WS-Policy file in the WSDL to encrypt the SOAP
// request. The following code shows how the client can verify
// that this certificate is valid using the TrustManager
stub._setProperty(WSSecurityContext.TRUST_MANAGER,
        new ClientTrustManager(clientIdentityKeystore));

// Make the service invocation
GetAccount account = new GetAccount();
account.setCustomerID(121);
GetAccountResponse response = port.getAccount(account);
System.out.println("Account Information");
System.out.println("====================");
System.out.println("Customer ID: " + response.getCustomerID());
System.out.println("       Name: " + response.getCustomerName());
System.out.println("    Account: " + response.getAccount());
} catch (Exception ex) {
    ex.printStackTrace();
}
}
}
```

As you can see from the code, the client side is fairly straightforward. The only real work lies in the ClientTrustManager, where we write the code that will validate the certificate returned from the server against the list of certificates contained by the client_trust.jks file. This important validation code is often omitted from most sample source code. We have included it here, in Listing 11-7, so you can get a better idea of how the validation should be performed.

Listing 11-7. *ClientTrustManager.java*

```
public class ClientTrustManager implements TrustManager {
    KeyStore keyStore = null;

    public ClientTrustManager(String keystoreFileName) {
        // Open the client keystore
        File clientKeyStoreFile = new File(keystoreFileName);
        keyStore = KeyStoreUtils.load(clientKeyStoreFile, "storepassword",
                "JKS");
    }
```

```java
/**
 * This callback method is required by the TrustManager interface. Here
 * is where we do the work to validate the certificate that is returned
 * to the client from the web service server.
 */
public boolean certificateCallback(X509Certificate[] chain,
    int validateErr) {
    boolean returnVal = false; // Default to validation failure

    if(chain == null)
        return false;

    // Check each certificate in the chain
    for (int i = 0; i < chain.length; i++) {
        try {
            // Check the validity of each certificate
            // and get its public key
            X509Certificate peerCert = chain[i];
            PublicKey key = peerCert.getPublicKey();

            // Check each alias in the client keystore
            // against each key in the certificate chain.
            Enumeration<String> aliasEnum = keyStore.aliases();
            while (aliasEnum.hasMoreElements() && !returnVal) {
                String alias = aliasEnum.nextElement();
                Certificate cert = keyStore.getCertificate(alias);
                boolean currentCertIsGood = true;
                try {
                    cert.verify(key);
                } catch (SignatureException ex) {
                    // If the key signature does not match, then this
                    // particular certificate is not valid
                    currentCertIsGood = false;
                }
                if (currentCertIsGood) {
                    // We found at least one good signature
                    returnVal = true;
                }
            }
        } catch (Exception e) {
            // Some unexpected problem occurred. Report
            // the error to the console
            // and fail the validation
            e.printStackTrace();
            returnVal = false;
        }
    }
}
```

```
        return returnVal;
    }
}
```

Before we run the client application, there is one more thing to do. We like to use a Java utility program called tcpmon, which allows us to see the TCP information as it is passed between the client and the server. You can download tcpmon from https://tcpmon.dev.java.net. Download the JAR file for tcpmon, and then just double-click the JAR file to run it. To configure a listener between our client and the OSB server, set the local port to 8001 and set the server port to 7001. You may have noticed that the SecureClient.java code includes a line that sets the endpoint to use port 8001:

```
stub._setProperty(Stub.ENDPOINT_ADDRESS_PROPERTY,
    "http://localhost:8001/Security_SB/SecureMessage");
```

If you don't want to use tcpmon, you can just change the port back to 7001. However, it is far more educational to run tcpmon and see the requests and responses as they flow back and forth.

Once you have the client file coded, right-click the code and select Run As ➤ Java Application. The client will run, and you will see the greeting on the console in WorkSpace Studio. Now take a look at the tcpmon application. See that huge amount of text in the Request and Response panes? That's the digital signature that you *didn't* need to enter because you used the WebLogic web service stack. The WebLogic web service stubs that you generated using the clientgen Ant task did all of that work for you.

At this point, you have created a web service and a service client that can digitally sign the requests and responses. This provides authentication security. The requester and responder are able to prove who they are, based on the fact that each can digitally sign a message with a certificate that the other recognizes. If you take a look at the bottom of the Response pane at the bottom of the tcpmon window, you will see the following:

```
<sec:getAccountResponse
     xmlns:sec="http://www.alsb.com/SecureMessageService/">
  <customerID>121</customerID>
  <customerName>Doe, John</customerName>
  <account>12345-6789-01234</account>
</sec:getAccountResponse>
```

The payloads of both the request and response are not encrypted. This may be fine if you don't mind potential hackers seeing this information; but what if you need to encrypt the message payloads in addition to using digital signatures? Well, that's the topic of the next section.

Using Message-Level Security

We will use message-level security to encrypt the body of both the requests and responses. Fortunately, message-level security leverages most of the work that we have already done in the previous section. It will use the same Java keystore configuration in WebLogic Server and the same service key provider defined in the proxy service. To make things a little more interesting, we will use the standard Encrypt.xml policy to encrypt the request from the client and create a custom policy to encrypt the response from the server.

Encrypting the Request with Encrypt.xml

Like the Sign.xml policy, the Encrypt.xml policy is included with OSB. You can just refer to the policy from within your WSDL file. Encrypting the request is extremely simple. Open the SecureMessageService.wsdl file in the Security SB project and modify the `<wsdl:input>` element of the `<wsdl:operation>` by adding the highlighted text shown in Listing 11-8.

Listing 11-8. *A WSDL File That Requires Encryption of the Request Message (for the getAccount Operation)*

```
<soap:binding style="document"
    transport="http://schemas.xmlsoap.org/soap/http" />
    <wsdl:operation name="getAccount">
        <wsp:Policy>
            <wsp:PolicyReference URI="policy:Sign.xml"/>
        </wsp:Policy>
        <soap:operation soapAction="getAccount" />
        <wsdl:input>
            <wsp:Policy>
                <wsp:PolicyReference URI="policy:Encrypt.xml"/>
            </wsp:Policy>
            <soap:body use="literal" />
        </wsdl:input>
        <wsdl:output>
            <soap:body use="literal" />
        </wsdl:output>
    </wsdl:operation>
</wsdl:binding>
```

Believe it or not, it's that simple. Publish the Security_SB project to the OSB server.

We will need to generate new web service stubs for our security client, based on the new WSDL file. Open the SecureClient project and delete the src/com.alsb.security.lib package. Next, run the clientgen target in the build.xml file in the SecureClient project to regenerate the client stubs. You do not need to make any changes to the SecureClient.java file, because the generated stubs take care of all of the details for you.

Run the SecureClient program again. Take a look at the Request pane of the tcpmon window, and you will see that the `<body>` of the request now contains an `<EncryptedData>` tag, instead of the clear-text request that you saw previously. The encrypted data is held in the `<CipherData>` tag.

Encrypting the Response with a Custom Encryption Policy

The approach that we used in the previous section allows us to easily encrypt the entire request message. However, what if you wanted to encrypt only part of a message? For example, if the message contained a name and a credit card number, you might want to encrypt only the credit card number. Developers often choose to encrypt a portion of the response because encrypting the entire message increases the size of the message considerably (see the next section for a discussion of the performance implications of security).

Policy files are special file types recognized by WorkSpace Studio. To create our policy file, first create a folder called WS_Policies in the Security_SB project. Right-click the WS_Policies folder and select New ➤ WS-Policy File from the pop-up menu. Name the policy file CustomEncryptionPolicy. Listing 11-9 shows the contents of our custom encryption policy.

Listing 11-9. *The Custom Encryption Policy*

```
<wsp:Policy
   wsu:Id="CustomEncryptPolicy.xml"
   xmlns:sp="http://schemas.xmlsoap.org/ws/2005/07/securitypolicy"
   xmlns:wsp="http://schemas.xmlsoap.org/ws/2004/09/policy"
   xmlns:wsu="http://docs.oasis-open.org/wss/2004/01/oasis-200401- ➥
wss-wssecurity-utility-1.0.xsd"
   xmlns:wssp="http://www.bea.com/wls90/security/policy"
   xmlns:sec="http://www.alsb.com/SecureMessageService/"
   xmlns:xsi="http://www.w3.org/2001/XMLSchema-instance">
   <sp:Strict wsp:Optional="true" />
   <wssp:Confidentiality>
      <wssp:KeyWrappingAlgorithm
         URI="http://www.w3.org/2001/04/xmlenc#rsa-1_5" />

      <!-- Require the greeting that we return to be encrypted -->
      <wssp:Target>
         <wssp:EncryptionAlgorithm
            URI="http://www.w3.org/2001/04/xmlenc#tripledes-cbc" />
         <wssp:MessageParts>
            wsp:GetBody(./sec:getAccountResponse/account)
         </wssp:MessageParts>
      </wssp:Target>
      <wssp:KeyInfo/>
   </wssp:Confidentiality>
</wsp:Policy>
```

In our experience, the most problematic part of partial encryption is getting the XPath for the element you wish to encrypt. The highlighted line in the policy file in Listing 11-9 shows the XPath that defines the element that we wish to encrypt:

```
wsp:GetBody(./sec:getAccountResponse/account)
```

Essentially, this specifies that we want to encrypt only the <account> node.

■Note The ID of the policy file (defined in the wsu:Id attribute of the wsp:Policy element) must be unique within the entire OSB domain.

Our next step is to modify our WSDL file so that is specifies the use of our custom policy for the response message. Listing 11-10 highlights the section of the WSDL file that specifies the use of the custom encryption policy.

Listing 11-10. *Specifying the Custom Encryption Policy for the Response*

```
<wsdl:binding name="SecureMessageServiceSOAP" type="tns:SecureMessageService">
    <soap:binding style="document"
        transport="http://schemas.xmlsoap.org/soap/http" />
    <wsdl:operation name="getAccount">
        <wsp:Policy>
            <wsp:PolicyReference URI="policy:Sign.xml"/>
        </wsp:Policy>
        <soap:operation soapAction="getAccount" />
        <wsdl:input>
            <wsp:Policy>
                <wsp:PolicyReference URI="policy:Encrypt.xml"/>
            </wsp:Policy>
            <soap:body use="literal" />
        </wsdl:input>
        <wsdl:output>
            <wsp:Policy>
                <wsp:PolicyReference URI="policy:CustomEncryptPolicy.xml"/>
            </wsp:Policy>
            <soap:body use="literal" />
        </wsdl:output>
    </wsdl:operation>
</wsdl:binding>
```

Build the Security_SB project and deploy it to the server. Once again, in the SecureClient project, delete the src/com.alsb.security.lib and src/com.alsb.securemessageservice packages, and then run the clientgen Ant task in the build.xml file to generate new client stubs based on the latest changes made to the WSDL. Now when you run the SecureClient application, you will see that only the <account> element in the response message is encrypted. The <customerID> and <customerName> elements are in clear text.

Performance Trade-Offs Using Security

Now that you know how to implement security in your web services, you may be tempted to make all of your web services secure. As with all things, there are trade-offs to be made. Security comes at a cost in performance. Performance is affected in two main areas:

- The size of the messages sent between the client and the server

- The amount of time it takes to sign, encrypt, and verify signatures and decrypt data

We performed some performance tests with the client and the web service both located on the same machine. We ran them on the same machine because we were interested in the effects of security on performance, not with transmission times over the wire. The machine we used was a 2GB Dell Latitude D610 laptop with a processor running at 1.8GHz.

■**Note** If you want to use the sample code provided to run your own tests, we recommend that you modify the endpoints in the clients so that they point directly to the OSB server (port 7001) instead of going through the tcpmon utility. Running the service calls through tcpmon will significantly increase the message-processing time by an order of magnitude.

In the SecureClient project, in the src/com.alsb.security package, is another test application called UnsecureClient. The UnsecureClient does everything the SecureClient application does, just without any security. We will compare this UnsecureClient with the SecureClient and measure the impact of applying the various security approaches described in this chapter.

The following sections discuss the impacts we saw on message size and execution time. Now, your mileage will certainly vary with regard to performance. The performance impact on your systems will be affected by the processor speed, number of processors. and other hardware and software considerations. The numbers we provide here are only to give you some idea of how using security may affect your systems.

Message Size

The size of the messages passed between the client and server are dramatically increased when applying the different types of security. Using the UnsecureClient application, the request message to the web service is only 232 bytes long. By simply signing the request, the message size increases to 4091 bytes. That is an increase of 3859 bytes. It is important to note that this increase in size is fixed. The size of the signature that is added to the message is in no way related to the size of the original, unsigned message. In other words, adding a 1KB signature to a web service will add a little less than 3KB to the message size.

However, when encrypting the message payload, the increase in the size of the message is a function of the size of the unencrypted message. For example, encrypting all of the request message will increase the message size from 232 bytes to 1871 bytes—an increase of 700 percent over the unencrypted size. Such a dramatic increase in message size will impact the performance of your web service simply because it has eight times the amount of information to send over the wire.

Execution Time

The increase in message size is not the only factor that will affect execution time. Execution time is also dependent on the type of encryption used. Generally speaking, the stronger the encryption, the more time it takes to encrypt and decrypt the message. On top of that, the more of the message you encrypt, the longer it will take to decrypt. If you are exchanging messages that are 5KB in size after being encrypted, you should not see much of an impact on the execution time. However, if you are exchanging messages that are 100KB in size after being encrypted, you will definitely notice a performance hit.

Let's take a look at some sample numbers using our `SecureClient` and `UnsecureClient` sample applications. Making 100 calls to the `UnsecureMessageService` takes 1.1 seconds, or roughly 0.01 second per call.

Now let's take a look at the effects of applying only the digital signature, which increases the message size by almost 4KB (to 4091 bytes per message from 232 bytes using the unsigned request and response). Making 100 calls to the signed web service takes 9600 milliseconds, or 0.09 second per service invocation. That's an increase of 800 percent in execution time. That additional time is used for creating and sending, receiving, and validating the digital signatures. However, realize that this increase in time is not linear in nature. Adding a signature really increases the overall request/response time by a flat 0.08 second. This is because the size of the signature is fixed.

If we leave the digital signatures in the request and response messages, and then also encrypt all of the request message and just the `<account>` field of the response message, and make 100 service invocations using this configuration, it will execute in 17,500 milliseconds, or 0.17 second per service invocation. So encrypting all of the request and only a small part of the response (the `<account>` field) adds 0.08 second to each call.

As we mentioned earlier, your performance metrics will vary from the numbers we've given here. These numbers are just guidelines to help you make some early, high-level design decisions about how and where to use security. As always, we highly recommend that you record your own metrics in your environment so that you are dealing with the most accurate information possible.

Summary

The challenge with securing an SOA is that most services and applications aren't stand-alone; they are already connected—with or without security. The goal is to introduce SOA or service-enable service endpoints without needing to write extensive code, incur additional maintenance costs, or leave loopholes that compromise sensitive data.

Some services and applications provide their own preferred security protocol. Leveraging these in an SOA is a challenge. For example, one application's security protocol may differ from the security protocol of the application with which it is communicating.

OSB is one of the simplest interoperable, easy-to-use, configuration-based products to help address security concerns at all levels.

Policy-based enforcement allows access to services, and OSB can act as an intermediary and a single point of enforcement for policies that can be centrally governed. The maintenance of security policies becomes much more manageable as a result.

OSB provides a configuration-driven approach that bridges multiple security protocols with minimal coding. It also provides flexible authentication for transports, including username/password basic authentication in transport headers and certificate-based authentication. Message-level encryption can also be added, including the use of security credentials in SOAP headers. SSL or HTTP can provide encryption for confidentiality.

Creating secure service-enabled processes for integration using OSB as a central security bridge makes it easy to secure new and existing services, and to manage those services on an ongoing basis.

Security is a broad topic and demands a formal strategy for proper implementation. The common patterns for using OSB as a security intermediary are using OSB for proxy inbound security enforcement and propagating user identity to the business service endpoint. In this chapter, we covered the basics of security as they apply to OSB to help you understand how to plan and implement OSB security as part of your overall security strategy.

CHAPTER 12

■■■

Planning Your Service Landscape

Designing an enterprise SOA is a formidable task. You will need patience, insight, and planning to achieve SOA. In our experience, overenthusiasm is a leading cause for SOA failure—people get excited by the promise of SOA, and then set off to achieve it without a firm understanding of SOA principles or any methodology. Although the tools that can help you to create and manage your SOA are advancing at a rapid pace, these tools cannot provide a substitute for the amount of thinking and effort required to design the SOA itself. Many of the customers we meet are eager to start designing their SOA, but almost immediately get lost in the details. Determining where to start can be a daunting task in itself.

To help architects, service designers, and developers get their bearings quickly within their SOA, we have developed a methodology called *service landscape*. The service landscape approach is based on a set of simple design principles and guidelines that will help you to successfully design and implement your SOA. It also provides you with a vocabulary with which you can quickly and effectively communicate intricate service-oriented concepts.

The purpose of the service landscape approach is to provide you with a coordinate system and a methodology to create service maps. As a byproduct, this approach will enhance your ability to communicate detailed service design information to architects and developers succinctly and unambiguously.

Essentially, service landscape provides you with a kind of global positioning system (GPS) for your enterprise architecture. In the real world, a GPS shows your location by providing you with latitude and longitude coordinates. If you understand the latitude and longitude system, and have a map that includes the surface of the earth that incorporates the coordinates, you can get a pretty good idea of your location. The more exact the coordinates and the more detailed your map, the greater the accuracy of your understanding of your position.

The problem for most people designing an SOA is that they have neither a map nor a coordinate system. In this chapter, we'll show you how to create a coordinate system and then map your enterprise services. With a little time and effort, you'll learn how to quickly create your own service maps, and you'll never feel lost again.

You'll need to keep a variety of principles in mind to successfully design your SOA, and we will cover the major ones in this chapter. We will tackle topics that at first may seem completely unrelated or irrelevant. However, by the end of the chapter, we will weave these topics together so you can get a complete view of SOA. Let's begin with the core concepts of SOA design.

Core Concepts

In this section, we will go over the fundamental concepts of the service landscape approach. Much of what we state here will make sense to you immediately and may even seem remedial in nature, but read on! We begin by reviewing commonly accepted facts, and then we will move on to combine these facts into new ways of looking at service orientation. Everything in this section of the chapter is the equivalent of four-function mathematics. Just as a complete understanding of the four basic math functions is necessary before you move on to algebra and geometry, so is a complete understanding of these core concepts necessary as a foundation for the later material in this chapter.

The SOA Coordinate System

Coordinates are just a union of one-dimensional scales. For GPS systems, coordinates use the latitude scale (how far to the north or south you are) and the longitude scale (how far to the east or west you are) to determine your position on the surface of the earth.

For the services in your SOA, you need to create a set of scales. Once you have your scales, you can join them together to create your SOA coordinate system. From there, you'll create your enterprise service maps. The scales we use for SOAs are abstraction and functionality.

THE ENTERPRISE IS THE APPLICATION

In the mid-1990s John Gage said, "The network *is* the computer." What this quote really did, aside from becoming Sun's motto, was to change our view of networks. Before John Gage uttered this sentence, the majority of software and hardware professionals did not have a holistic view of their network or how to best use it. John Gage, in a few, simple words, changed the way we look at network computing.

Leveraging John's insight into network computing, we can derive a corollary that will, we hope, change the way we look at software assets: "The enterprise *is* the application." Too often, we can't see the forest for the trees. We get so bogged down in the details of each application in our enterprise that we lose sight of the goal: our enterprises should behave like an individual organism, not some Frankenstein's monster cobbled together from disparate pieces.

It is important to think holistically about the entire enterprise. From that starting point, you can derive a system for managing various aspects of your enterprise. Start with the vision and work to make that vision real. In enterprise computing, it's not unusual to begin with the hundreds or thousands of applications in our inventory and try to make sense of them. You can never achieve vision by patching pieces together. Vision isn't discovered; it is created.

Keep the idea that the enterprise *is* the application in mind when using the service landscape methodology. This will make it easier to design and achieve the implementation of your vision.

The Software Abstraction Scale

The first scale is that of *abstraction*. Architects and developers know that abstraction is a useful tool, and we don't dispute that. However, not everything needs to be highly abstract. Some things must be literal and concrete for there to be any possibility of higher-level abstractions. We work with a natural scale of abstraction as software developers every day.

Figure 12-1 shows our software abstraction scale. It begins at the bottom with artifacts that have very little abstraction. For example, a database implementation is about as concrete or "physical" as things get in the software world. We don't mean to imply that there's no room for abstraction and good design within a database schema; certainly, database design is vitally important. The point we make is that in the grand view of enterprise software development, databases are the least abstract elements. Similarly, physical devices—routers, modems, switches, and so on—are also at the bottom of this scale.

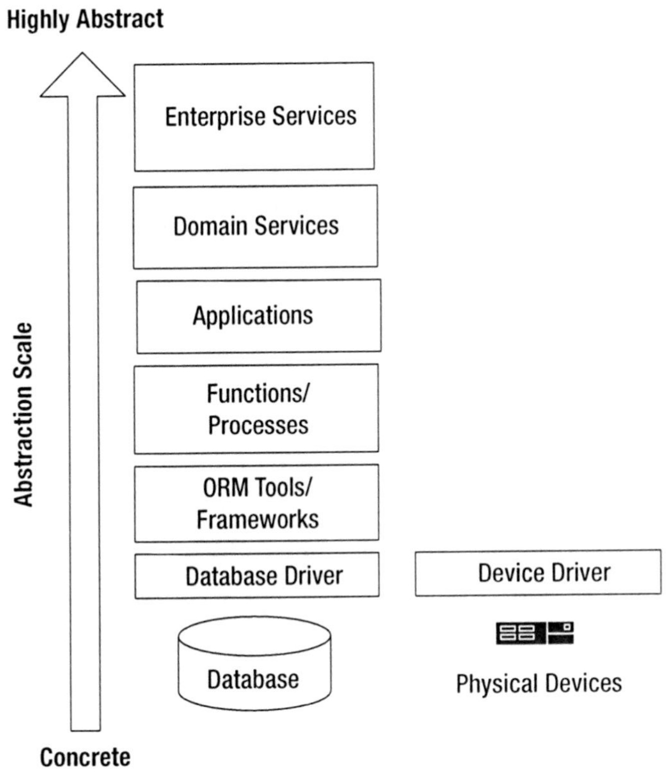

Highly Abstract

Figure 12-1. *The software abstraction scale*

Moving up a level on our abstraction scale, we have low-level software components, such as device drivers and database drivers. These components provide a level of abstraction above the devices they represent. This is an expression of the Façade design pattern, where the complexity and interdependencies of lower-level components are hidden. This is the fundamental pattern of abstraction, and we'll see it repeated in each successive level.

Next, we see object-relational mapping (ORM) tools and frameworks. This level includes software packages such as Hibernate, Kodo, and Cayenne. These tools make it easy to persist the object data within an object-oriented application. Those ORM tools are then accessed from the function/processes within a software application. Software applications, in turn, provide a greater level of abstraction, and are often the lowest level of interaction, where people other than software developers become involved. For most of the history of software, applications represented the apex of abstraction. Now we have domain services and enterprise services above that level.

An important principle is associated with the software abstraction scale: the level of functional detail in any system is inversely proportional to its level of abstraction. Figure 12-2 represents this graphically. At the lower levels of abstraction, you'll find exponentially more functional and technical implementation detail than at the higher levels of the abstraction scale. This is as it should be. For every enterprise service, there should be 5 to 20 lower-level, supporting services. If you have 100 enterprise-level services and 100 low-level implementation services, you have provided no abstraction at all! These numbers aren't hard and fast, but they are representative of the orders of magnitude that naturally occur with SOA. If you don't respect this principle (and by *respect*, we mean design and code with this principle in mind), you'll effectively destroy your abstraction scale and, of course, your SOA.

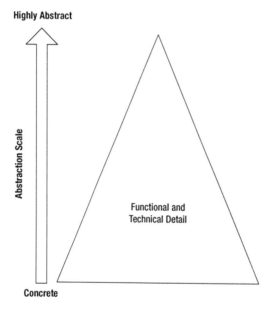

Figure 12-2. *Functional detail as it relates to abstraction*

We won't ask you to accept this pattern blindly. Let's double-check this pattern against current, successful models to see how well they match up. Let's begin with a technology we all know and love: television. Figure 12-3 shows our TV abstraction model.

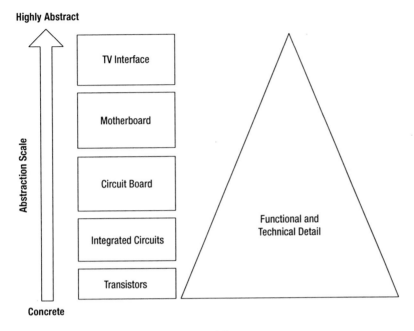

Figure 12-3. *Television abstraction model*

There's a tremendous amount of complexity and detail in any TV set. The vast majority of the details involved in presenting you—the TV viewer—with the images and sounds on your set are hidden from you. Think of TV as a service. You use a remote control to send commands to your TV. You can perform three basic functions with your TV: change the channel, adjust the volume, and turn it on and off. If you examine all those buttons on your remote control, you'll see that these are the operations that your remote control provides. Everything else on the remote control simply allows you to specify the parameters of those operations.

Those operations, in turn, are handled through a motherboard on your TV set. The motherboard aggregates circuit boards (many of them integrated so they physically appear as part of the motherboard) that perform finer-grained functions. Those circuit boards are composed of hundreds of integrated circuits, each of which is composed of millions of individual transistors. This is abstraction at its best.

Abstraction isn't a technology-specific concept. We see it in human organizations also. Even the largest companies are organized into hierarchies, as shown in Figure 12-4.

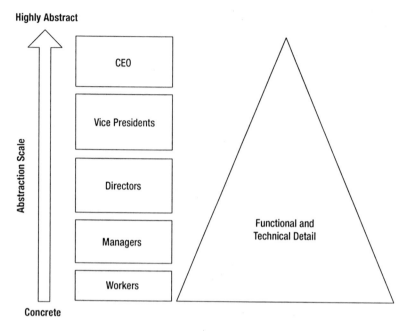

Figure 12-4. *Organizational abstraction model*

Again, we see another example of abstraction in our daily lives. The CEO cannot possibly know the technical details that each worker must know for that worker to be effective at his job. In fact, even the worker's direct manager cannot know all the details that the worker must deal with on a daily basis. The important thing to remember here is that this is a good thing (though you might question that on your next annual review). As you move down the abstraction scale, the level of detail and the amount of work increases dramatically. This is a natural organizational principle. As architects, service designers, and service developers, we must embrace this principle to design and manage our enterprise architecture successfully.

An important principle at work here is that of *knowledge dependency;* each level of abstraction "knows" about the level beneath it. A JDBC driver "knows" about (that is, it is configured to talk to) an instance of a database. Databases do not "know" about JDBC drivers. The dependency is directional.

Another important principle is that of *diminishing detail.* As you travel up the scale of dependency, the amount of technical implementation detail contained in each higher level *must be less than* the levels below it. This doesn't imply that there is less information at the higher levels of abstraction. It simply means that the amount of "low-level" technical information decreases rapidly. Components at the bottom of the scale contain a tremendous amount of technical and implementation detail because they're doing the real work. Components at the bottom know exactly what to do to make their little piece of the enterprise function correctly. Components at the top of the scale know what to do (such as process an order), but have no detailed knowledge of how that work gets done. We call this process separating the *what* from the *how.* It is an important principle of abstraction.

INTERFACES: SEPARATING THE "WHAT" FROM THE "HOW"

An important concept built into the service landscape approach is that of interfaces. The purpose of an interface is very simple: to separate the API (or programming "contract") from the code that implements the functionality. However, interfaces are not just useful for designing software applications; they are vital for designing the API of your entire enterprise.

Each service has two components to it: the interface defined by its WSDL and the implementation logic. The service landscape approach adds a new dimension to interfaces and implementation: the organizational context of the service. By categorizing services by abstraction level and functional domain, you are able to better define the scope of each service.

It's best to think of an interface as a kind of remote control that gives high-level commands. The remote control has no idea how your TV set changes channels; it is simply an interface to the TV. Best of all, you don't need to know how the TV changes channels. You don't even need to know how your remote control works. You issue commands to your remote control by pressing its buttons. Inside the remote control is implementation logic that translates your commands (the what) into actions (the how). The remote control's actions are translated into infrared (IR) signals that are sent to the TV.

In turn, the TV supports an IR interface through which it takes commands, and it also contains the implementation logic to act on those IR commands. This is the basic pattern of abstraction: interfaces are realized by implementations, and implementations use other interfaces. Keep this pattern in mind as you learn more about the service landscape methodology, because it is a founding principle of the entire approach.

Now we are able to derive the SOA abstraction scale that we will use, as shown in Figure 12-5. This scale shows four main categories of abstraction: enterprise, domain, atomic, and physical. The diagram also shows how functional detail increases as the level of abstraction decreases.

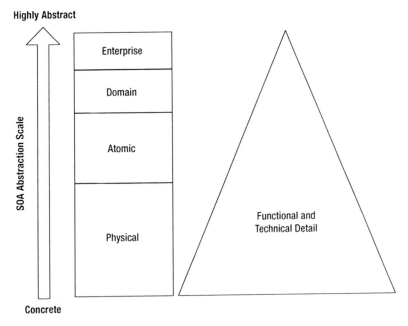

Figure 12-5. *SOA abstraction scale with the named service levels*

Let's go through the levels, starting at the bottom of the scale:

Physical: This level is used to represent the things that you cannot change (or cannot *easily* change). For example, external web services that are provided by your partners or suppliers would be categorized as being in the physical level. The services provided by Salesforce.com are another example of external functionality that belongs in this level. Commercial applications, like Siebel and SAP, are also categorized into the physical level, because you really have very little (or no) control over those applications. Even your own applications may be categorized into the physical level. It's the level where individual software systems live.

Atomic: This level is used for publishing application/system–specific services and functionality. For example, if you created an EJB application that handles order management and then wrote one or more web services to publish that application's functionality, the application itself would be categorized in the physical level, but the web services that connect to the application would be categorized into the atomic level.

Domain: This level's services aggregate and orchestrate the lower-level atomic services. This is the level of abstraction where you will first realize application independence. The domain services are used to make the lower-level atomic services behave in a rational and more business-oriented manner. This will make more sense when we add our next scale to the coordinate system.

Enterprise: This is the highest level of abstraction. We think of this level as the API for the entire enterprise. Services at this level of abstraction don't recognize the arbitrary boundaries of databases, applications, or business domains. These services can go anywhere and do anything (by making use of the domain level of abstraction). However, services at the top level of the abstraction scale *must not know* the implementation details of the hundreds or thousands of components that live further down the abstraction scale. Enterprise services "paint with a broad brush," issuing commands to the various domain-level software components and expecting timely results.

The SOA abstraction scale is not very useful alone. It's kind of like having the latitude without the longitude. It is helpful, but only marginally so. We need our next scale to work in conjunction with the SOA abstraction scale to provide real value.

THE ROOTS OF SOA

Service orientation began quietly, many years ago, under the name of *application integration*. As enterprises became more adept at creating software applications to automate their processes, there arose a need to have these applications share information with one another. Application developers began to create public application programming interfaces (APIs) to provide a controlled way to allow other applications to make use of their functionality. Looking back, we can see that these APIs were really the first step toward service orientation.

In modern IT shops, the number of applications range from the dozens to the thousands. Although each application might have distinctive features and capabilities, there always emerges a natural "clustering" of applications, based on their business function. An order management application is often tightly integrated with other applications that play supporting roles in the order fulfillment process. These clusters of applications represent the functionality required by the business. By integrating applications together, you create functionality at a higher level of abstraction.

The Functional Category Scale

Our second scale is that of categories of functionality, as shown in Figure 12-6. This scale categorizes the various functions that every enterprise must have in order to succeed.

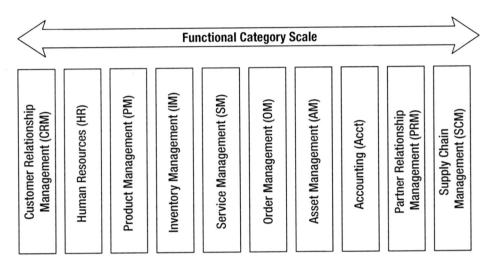

Figure 12-6. *Functional category scale*

A *functional category* is simply an area of logically related knowledge or expertise within the enterprise. Most companies are divided into categories. We commonly see companies organized into departments such as sales, marketing, human resources, IT, and so on. Functional categories are an important concept in enterprise architecture; they provide a logical demarcation between applications and their functionality. This demarcation allows us to make better decisions about how to integrate individual applications.

Each company may modify its list of functional categories. For example, the service management category applies only to companies that provide services to their customers. Telephone companies, utility companies, and financial service companies are good examples of organizations that would need a service management category. If your company sells physical products only, you don't need a service management category.

Table 12-1 lists the functional categories and provides a description for each. It's important to think of each functional category as a peer in the enterprise architecture. Human resources might not have the same priority within your organization as does managing customer relationships or billing, but it plays an important role in keeping your enterprise in compliance with government rules regarding employment, and also helps to keep your employees happy, which in turn benefits the enterprise.

Table 12-1. *Functional Categories*

Category	Description
Customer relationship management (CRM)	This category is responsible for maintaining accurate customer information. CRM systems are commonly found in this domain, as are other customer/lead tracking types of software. This is also referred to as the customer category, since the terms *customer* and *CRM* are often interchangeable when referring to services.
Human resources (HR)	PeopleSoft and related software products are often found here. For example, in pharmaceutical companies, you would find employee training records for using respirators, CPR training, and so on.
Product management (PM)	Products are a marketing concept. Marketing defines and promotes products, and this category contains the software tools to allow the marketing department to do its job.
Inventory management (IM)	Inventory is a count of physical items that are sold to customers, or in the case of service providers, are physical elements that allow the company to provide services to its customers (for example, telephone switches, line cards, and so on).
Service management (SM)	This category is used exclusively by service providers. If a company sells services (such as communication services, electrical services, natural gas, and so on), this is where those services are defined and maintained.
Order management (OM)	Here, orders from customers are collected and processed/fulfilled.
Asset management (AM)	Every organization has assets. An asset is an item used by the company or by its employees and contractors. For example, a building owned by the company is an asset; the computers used by the employees are assets, as are the furniture, vehicles, and so on.
Accounting (Acct)	Commonly referred to as "billing," this category contains the majority of the accounting systems (accounts receivable/accounts payable) used by the company.
Partner relationship management (PRM)	This category is responsible for keeping records of the various partners of the company.
Supply chain management (SCM)	This category contains information about suppliers. This is also the category where the enterprise places orders with suppliers.

With your two scales in hand, you're ready to create your coordinate system.

The Coordinate System

When you put these two scales together, you get a coordinate system for your services in your SOA. Figure 12-7 shows the coordinate system that applies to every enterprise. This will become a useful tool when you begin to create service maps. Service maps are discussed later in this chapter and the next chapter.

	CRM	HR	PM	IM	SM	OM	AM	Acct	PRM	SCM
Enterprise										
Domain										
Atomic										
Physical										

Figure 12-7. *The SOA coordinate system*

The coordinate grid is not the traditional Cartesian grid, and with good reason. At the top level, the enterprise level, we have enterprise-wide services that may access any of the lower-level domain services. Enterprise services may orchestrate domain services in any functional category. With that in mind, it is tempting to draw the coordinate system in Figure 12-7 with no vertical lines in the enterprise level, making it just one wide rectangle. However, in practice, you will find that enterprise services always have a "focus" on a specific functional category. For example, it is likely that you will define an enterprise-level service that is focused on interacting with customer information in the CRM category. Because enterprise services often have a business-domain-specific focus, we categorize our enterprise services the same way we do the domain and atomic services.

The physical level is not confined by the concept of a functional category. Small applications may be able to fit into a single functional category, but many of the larger enterprise resource planning (ERP) applications (like SAP and PeopleSoft) cross these category boundaries. Now, you could argue that these ERPs are not single applications, but are really suites of integrated applications, and you would be right. But even a single, smaller application within the ERP suite can cross these conceptual categories. This SOA coordinate system simply takes that reality into account.

As we mentioned earlier in this chapter, there are natural clusters of applications in any IT department. Upon careful examination, you'll find that this clustering falls along the lines of the functional categories. You need to formalize these clusters of applications to use the service landscape approach. To do this, you must begin to think of your architecture in terms of trees, not just simple stacks or levels. Using a tree as a conceptual model will simplify your ability to navigate through the enterprise.

Figure 12-8 shows how organizing services into a tree structure works perfectly with the concepts of interfaces, façades, and hiding technical detail and complexity at the lowest levels of abstraction. It also introduces our first service map, which shows how various services are related to each other on the SOA coordinate system. The whole point of the enterprise level is that it's designed to integrate the different domain-level service categories below it. Similarly, an individual functional category in the domain level usually contains multiple portions of application functionality, so it spans the various atomic services within its functional category.

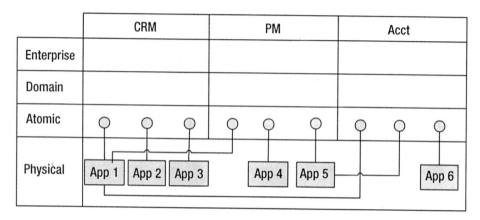

Figure 12-8. *Simple service map showing physical applications and their atomic services*

A single application at the physical level (the bottom of the diagram) will often provide functionality that is best represented in different functional categories. For example, App 1 provides atomic services in the CRM, PM, and Acct functional categories, as shown in Figure 12-8. App 5 has functionality published in both the PM and Acct functional categories.

■**Note** Services are often referred to by their functional category and the abstraction level. For example, a "customer domain" service is a service at the intersection of the domain level and the CRM functional category.

Keep in mind that this is a logical view of services. It breaks down functionality into logical categories. For example, imagine that your company uses Siebel for its CRM and order management capabilities. Furthermore, some of the customer information resides in a customer database that came to your IT shop through the acquisition of another enterprise a year ago.

As you can see in the simple service map in Figure 12-9, Siebel is a single application that implements two atomic services that logically belong in different functional categories. Siebel's customer service is mapped into the atomic level beneath the CRM domain, while Siebel's order service is mapped into the atomic level beneath the order domain. Applications routinely cross functional category boundaries. Always keep in mind that the logical view is what's important in enterprise architecture. When we lose sight of this logical view, we become lost in the details again.

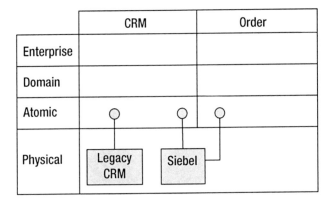

Figure 12-9. *Physical application deployment doesn't impact the logical service map.*

Communication Principles and Patterns

We now will explain three communication principles and four basic communication patterns in the service landscape approach. These principles and patterns should be clearly understood by each architect, service developer, and software engineer involved with realizing SOA. Fortunately, they're simple and easy to understand.

Communication Principle 1

Each service level knows about the level below it, but not the level above it.

Each service level acts as a façade for the level below it. For example, services in the enterprise level have no knowledge of the atomic services beneath the domain level. This "knowledge dependency principle" is a fundamental part of abstraction.

Communication Principle 2

Every service level can know about the enterprise level.

The enterprise level is the public API for the enterprise. As a result, it must be available as a resource for any component in the enterprise. This is the only time when it's permissible for a component in a level to know about a level above it.

Communication Principle 3

Web services are used between the service levels, whenever practical.

By using web services to communicate between the service levels, you create the ability to have a rationalized monitoring strategy for your enterprise. This approach also promotes reuse of services at each level by providing a standard service interface format. Certainly, all enterprise-level and domain-level services should be published as web services. However, things get a little murky at the atomic level. There are times when your atomic service may be implemented as a JDBC driver or as a piece of code that uses an HTTP POST to communicate with the application it represents.

Web services provide an enterprise standard for integration. There are many different ways to integrate disparate systems. Settling on a standard will reduce your training and maintenance costs, and enhance your operational efficiency.

Communication Pattern 1: Flow of Gravity

The Flow of Gravity pattern is the model that immediately springs to mind for most people when they imagine messages flowing through their enterprise. The arrows in the service map shown in Figure 12-10 represent the message call flow from the top downward. As the message passes through each level, there is an opportunity for the message to be transformed and enriched. This demonstrates the first communication principle, and shows how a single message invocation from an enterprise service client can span service domains and multiple application services in a manner completely transparent to the client.

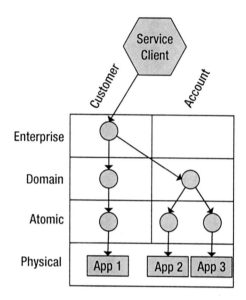

Figure 12-10. *The Flow of Gravity pattern*

Communication Pattern 2: Direct Use of Enterprise Services

The Direct Use of Enterprise Services pattern demonstrates the use of the first communication principle. As shown in Figure 12-11, the enterprise service is being invoked by a domain service, an atomic service, and an application in the physical layer. Many modern applications are now capable of invoking external web services (that is, web services that are implemented outside the invoking application). We expect this trend to continue, making this pattern increasingly common.

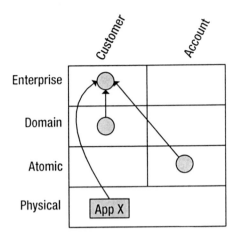

Figure 12-11. *The Direct Use of Enterprise Services pattern*

Communication Pattern 3: Indirect Use of Enterprise Services

The Indirect Use of Enterprise Services pattern, illustrated in Figure 12-12, is really a variation of the second communication pattern. Older software systems that aren't capable of using web services to integrate with other systems can still participate fully as clients of your SOA. The key is to create an adapter that can translate between the application-specific data formats and the enterprise message formats. This pattern applies only to the atomic level, because the domain level is fully web service–enabled.

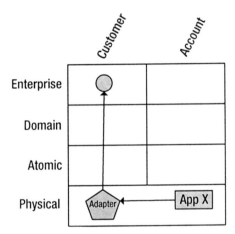

Figure 12-12. *The Indirect Use of Enterprise Services pattern*

■**Caution** One thing to beware of with Communication Patterns 1 and 2 is the possibility of putting your entire enterprise into an infinite loop. It has always been possible to do this, even with a point-to-point architecture. However, an SOA makes it easier to create infinite loops inadvertently. This is one area where your SOA governance group earns its keep. The governance groups are commonly charged with understanding the interrelationships among enterprise, domain, and application services.

Communication Pattern 4: Communications Within an Abstraction Level and Functional Group

The fourth and final pattern covers communication and integration within an abstraction level and/or a functional group. Figure 12-13 shows how this pattern allows you to leverage your existing tightly coupled systems in a positive way. Point-to-point integrations are allowed within an abstraction level and a functional group combination. Point-to-point is not a bad integration approach when used with a relatively small number of integration points. Point-to-point integration is simply not a viable enterprise strategy. This pattern is most commonly used in the physical level, although we do also see it to a lesser extent in the enterprise and domain levels. This pattern should not exist at all in the atomic level.

The number of system interactions (and therefore the number of messages or procedure invocations) in the physical level is high. Here, we routinely find very "chatty" applications—applications that are poorly suited for web service interfaces—but that's perfectly acceptable in the physical level. As long as those "chatty" applications are chatting with other applications via a high-speed point-to-point integration, they can continue to work without any modifications. This is also where the bulk of your existing point-to-point integrations exist today. With this approach, we leverage the integration work that has already been implemented (and paid for), instead of trying to rewrite it. The old rule "if it works, don't fix it" applies here with full force.

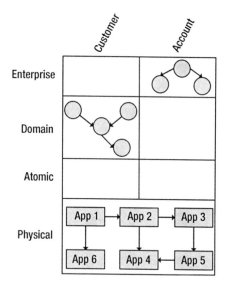

Figure 12-13. *Acceptable point-to-point integrations*

Advanced Concepts

Now that you have mastered the basic principles of the service landscape approach, it's time to move on to more advanced topics. Here, we'll talk about service and operation visibility, and loose coupling.

Service and Operation Visibility

Like Java classes in packages and methods in classes, services and service operations also have categories of visibility. Just because WSDL does not support this concept directly does not mean that your SOA governance group cannot apply this concept as a useful management tool. It does mean that you will need to document, monitor, and enforce the concept of visibility outside a WSDL file and even OSB. You may want to document the visibility in a text document, a wiki, or a full-fledged enterprise repository tool.

Service visibility is either public or private. A public service is a service that can be accessed by the abstraction level above it. For enterprise-level services, a public service can be accessed by any potential service consumer. For a domain-level public service, a public service may be accessed by any enterprise-level service. An atomic-level service that has public visibility can be accessed by a domain-level service within the same functional group.

In general, a private service may not be accessed by any service outside its abstraction level and functional group. For example, a private enterprise service can be accessed by any other enterprise-level service, but cannot be accessed by any other service consumers. A private domain service in the CRM functional category may be accessed by any domain service also in the CRM category, but not by an enterprise-level service.

Operations within a service follow similar rules. A public operation is accessible to any legal caller of the service. By *legal caller*, we mean any service consumer that would normally be allowed to call the service based on the rules and principles defined in the service landscape methodology. A private operation is one that is called only by operations within the same service. Operations can have a third visibility type: protected. A protected operation is simply an operation that can be called by service consumers within the same abstraction level and functional group. So, a protected operation in a customer domain service could be called by any other services defined in the customer domain.

Service visibility takes precedence over operational visibility. If you declare a service to have private visibility, then all of the operations within that service are treated as private. The most restrictive visibility is always used.

■**Tip** Don't go overboard with service and operation visibility. The very nature of most services and their operations dictates that they should be public. You should restrict visibility only when it makes sense. The more you restrict visibility, the more governance work you'll need to do to ensure that your visibility rules are not violated.

Loose Coupling

Loose coupling is a term that architects and developers use a lot, yet the concept is rarely applied to living code, where it matters most. Since loose coupling is vital to SOA, we will take a closer look at loose coupling in its various forms.

To begin, there are several different categories of loose coupling. Things may be loosely coupled in time (for example, asynchronous invocation). Things may be loosely coupled in definition (data types may be transformed from one format to another). Functionality should be loosely coupled with regard to implementation (for example, generic interfaces may be used to access more specific functionality, as is common in Java and C++ programming). Furthermore, entire systems may be loosely coupled with regard to physical location. DNS is a prime example of this. When you use your browser to go to www.yahoo.com, you have no idea which specific computer you are connecting with (nor do you care). You have a logical destination (www.yahoo.com), and the infrastructure of the network takes care of the details to route you to the correct computer.

While loose coupling is something we strive for in the software world, attaining 100 percent decoupling between systems is rarely useful. We add value to our enterprises when we couple information systems together. If we tightly couple the systems together, they are harder to maintain, as each system naturally changes over time. The purpose of loose coupling is to make it easier to couple systems together, yet allow those systems to be resilient (not resistant) to change.

Loose coupling is essential in SOA because unlike EAI, where you couple a dozen or so systems together into a spoke-and-hub architecture (as discussed in Chapter 1), SOA integrates your entire enterprise. Hundreds, or in some cases thousands, of ever-changing applications must interoperate.

Schema Management

Schema management is one of the often overlooked areas of SOA, especially in the early days of a company's adoption of SOA. We've frequently heard people say, "We are loosely coupled because we are using web services." In fact, the exact opposite is true. If you are just using pure web services in your enterprise, you are tightly coupling your applications in a point-to-point integration. The only difference is that your enterprise will have a "service-enabled" point-to-point integration.

Let's explore this concept with several examples. First, let's take a look at a very simple enterprise, with three portals and three web services, as shown in Figure 12-14.

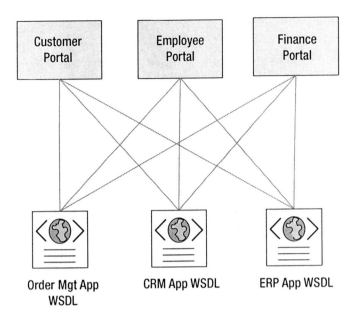

Figure 12-14. *Tight coupling using web services*

Each portal needs information from one or more operations within each of our three web services. Therefore, each portal depends on the WSDL files of each service. Keep in mind *how* each of these portals will access these web services: a developer will point a client-generation tool at the WSDL file of each web service to generate the client stubs necessary to allow the portal to call the web service. On the surface, that doesn't sound too ominous, but let's take a deep dive into the order management application's WSDL file, specifically the <service> tag, as shown in Listing 12-1.

Listing 12-1. *The <service> tag for the Order Management Application*

```
<wsdl:service name="Order_Mgt_Service">
   <wsdl:port binding="tns:OrderMgt_WSSOAP"
      name="OrderMgtSOAPService">
      <soap:address location="http://order.foo.com:8081/OrderMgt_WS" />
   </wsdl:port>
</wsdl:service>
```

The SOAP specification states that only a single <soap:address> can exist within a <wsdl:port> element. So, if you do not use OSB to mediate between the service caller and the service endpoint, you have three options for handling web services with multiple endpoints:

- The service clients must manage the list of service endpoints (and therefore the load balancing) themselves.

- You can program the service endpoints into a DNS load-balancer and have the service clients call a single, logical endpoint that will be translated into a physical endpoint by the load-balancer at runtime.

- You can use a UDDI registry to track the multiple physical endpoints, forcing the service clients to ask the UDDI registry to select the correct physical endpoint at runtime.

The first option is obviously a bad approach. You should not write load-balancing logic into your applications. It also means that the service clients will need to be updated with endpoint information whenever the endpoints for the back-end services change.

The second approach is technically viable, but usually impractical. DNS load-balancers are often maintained by the IT operations department, and they are very reluctant to tweak a DNS load-balancer every time a service is added or removed, or whenever a service endpoint is modified. Given their choice, IT operations folks want to minimize the changes to their IT infrastructure as much as possible. They have a very good reason for this: they know that every time they make a change to the fundamental IT infrastructure, they are putting the entire enterprise at risk. Furthermore, a number of DNS systems and load-balancers actually require a restart in order for the changes to take effect. A restart means an outage for the company—an event that often requires an explanation to the executive team. Making changes to a DNS system or a load-balancer represents a fairly high level of "threat" to most IT operations folk. Additionally, IT operations teams at most companies are staffed at a fraction of the size of IT development. There just aren't as many people to go around in operations. As a result, operations work is often forced into planned "maintenance windows," which are times when the IT operations technicians routinely take portions of the enterprise out of service for scheduled maintenance.

The UDDI registry approach was popular for a while. However, the drawback is that the service client must first request an endpoint from the UDDI registry (a network call), and then invoke the service endpoint. You can try to cache the endpoint information in the service client (assuming you are writing that client), but even then, you are forced to write a certain amount of middleware to handle the aging of cached data and service invocation failover.

Coupling with an ESB

Just as people often assume that using web services gives them loose coupling, they also assume that an ESB provides a greater level of loose coupling. An ESB *can* provide looser coupling between the components/applications of your enterprise, but it can also provide an equally tight coupling if you are not careful. We will explain this potential trap in detail in just a bit. First, we want to show how an ESB can provide a better model for loosely coupling your systems through mediation.

Figure 12-15 shows how the service consumers (the portals in this case) are loosely coupled to the physical deployment of the service providers. Working from the top of the diagram downward, we can see that each portal invokes services using a virtual IP (VIP) address. In this example, the VIP address is esb.foo.com. This VIP address is then translated through the normal DNS and load-balancer technology into one of the physical IP addresses listed in the IP map of the DNS/load-balancer. This approach provides loose coupling between the service consumers and the three instances of OSB.

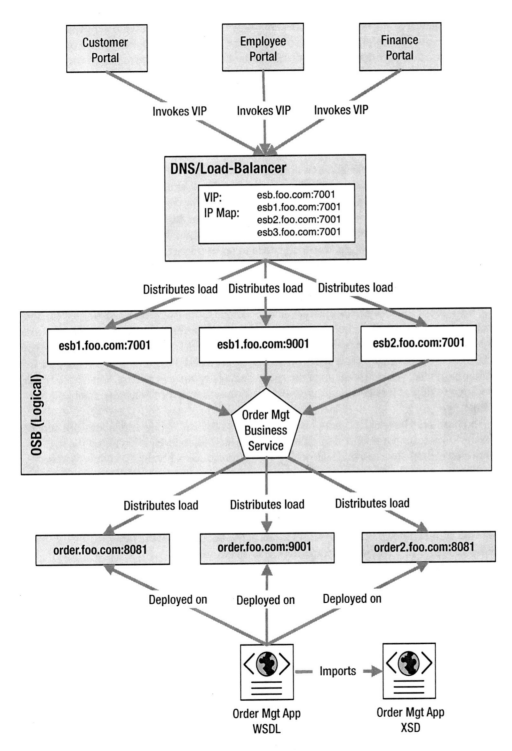

Figure 12-15. *Standard physical deployment architecture for OSB*

Each instance of the OSB has an order management business service deployed on it. Technically, you need to deploy the business service on only the administration server of a cluster. The administration server will take care of distributing the service to each of the managed nodes in the cluster. Part of the definition of the business service is a list of service endpoints where the web service is deployed (order.foo.com:8081, order.foo.com:9001, and so on). The business service now acts as a load-balancer and balances the service invocations across the three web service instances near the bottom of the diagram in Figure 12-15. Each of those web service instances, of course, supports the web service defined by the WSDL file at the bottom of the diagram.

With this architecture, you can now add new service endpoints near the bottom of the diagram without affecting (that is, recompiling) the service clients at the top. For example, imagine adding a new computer named order3.foo.com:6777 and deploying the order management application service at that endpoint. All you need to do is open the OSB console and navigate to the business service definition, modify the list of service endpoints to include the new service endpoint, and save your changes. You do not need to recompile any code. You do not create EAR files or JAR files with OSB. You just click the Activate Changes button in the Change Center, and your changes take effect immediately. This is one example of how OSB acts as a service mediator and provides you with the much sought after "business agility."

Think about the rate of change in your web service infrastructure. It will be very high in the early days of your SOA adoption. You will constantly be adding, changing, and scaling your services. If you need to scale up one or more of your services in an emergency situation (say you advertise a product during halftime at the Super Bowl and the entire planet visits your site to order products), you will want all of the speed and agility you can muster. You certainly will not want any kind of service outage, and you won't want to wait for the normal maintenance window.

You have seen how an ESB can provide you with speed and agility, which are both benefits from the loose coupling provided by OSB acting as a mediation level. What about the trap we mentioned earlier? How can this technology and approach possibly tightly couple systems?

The trap is subtle. It is initially set by the misconception that "SOA is all about reuse." The architects and developers, laboring under this misconception, decide that when they publish the order management web services through the service bus, they may as well use the same XSD that the application uses. They mistakenly believe that this constitutes the "reuse" that they hear about with SOA. Once again, let's look at the details to see the ramifications of their decisions. Figure 12-16 shows the trap after it has been sprung.

Again, remember that the three service clients will create and compile their web service stubs from the order management proxy service WSDL file hosted by OSB. The OSB proxy service WSDL file, in turn, is directly importing the XSD from the order management application. This tightly couples the schema of the proxy service to the implementation of the application. If you replace the order management application with one from a different vendor, it will likely use a complete different schema. Even if you are simply upgrading the existing application to a newer version, you run the risk of the vendor having changed schema elements and namespaces. This forces your proxy service to change, which, in turn, forces you to recompile all of your service clients. That is tight coupling in action!

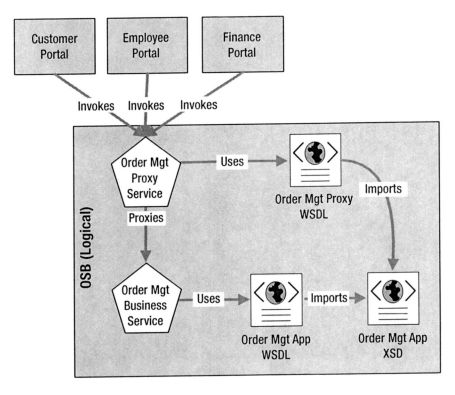

Figure 12-16. *The dependency trap is sprung!*

OSB mitigates this problem significantly by the fact that when you create a proxy service that is based on a business service, OSB automatically makes a copy of both the WSDL file and any XML Schema artifacts that it imports. However, not all ESBs are created equal, and most of them do not provide this default functionality for you, making you prey to the dependency trap.

So now you know what *not* to do. We haven't yet covered what you *should* do. Let's cover a more flexible design that avoids the dependency trap entirely. A fundamental power of OSB is the ability to translate message formats and transform data formats in messages as they pass from proxy service to business service and back again. This allows you to maintain XML document schemas, as well as WSDL files, at different levels of abstraction that map to the SOA abstraction scale we covered earlier.

Figure 12-17 shows how this simple change in architecture brings big benefits with regard to loosely coupling the schemas. There is now an order management proxy service (WSDL and XSD) that operate at the domain level, while the order management business service (WSDL and XSD) represents the atomic-level order management service.

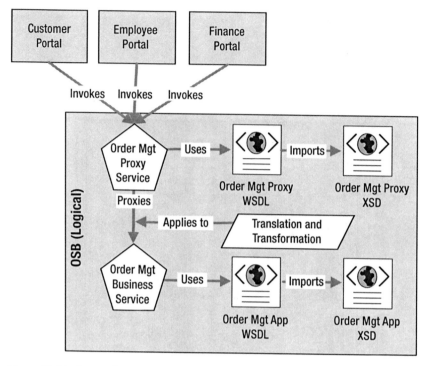

Figure 12-17. *Proper loose coupling of schemas*

This is the fundamental principle of dependency management: WSDL and XSD files should never depend on anything outside their abstraction level. By diligently observing this rule, we can build architectures that can accommodate change much more easily. In the structure shown in Figure 12-17, if you change the order management application to something completely new, you need to re-create the business service that represents the new order management application, and then update the translation and transformation rules to adapt the new schemas, message formats, and operations to what the existing proxy service is expecting. Assuming that all changes can be handled using translation and transformation, the effects of changing the order management application are completely encapsulated, and none of the service consumers is affected.

Concepts vs. Implementation

Business concepts are often tightly coupled to implementations in software applications. For example, *customer* is a core business concept, yet if you examine even a handful of your applications in your enterprise, you will find that the customer concept is implemented in each application. Where we use the word *implementation*, you can freely substitute the word *definition*. Therefore, if you have multiple software applications, you most likely have multiple definitions of core business concepts.

We must have a way to loosely couple business concepts with their various application-specific implementations. Putting together everything we have covered in this chapter, we are now ready to reap the benefits of the service landscape methodology and our architectural approaches to keeping our levels of abstraction separate.

Information Aggregation

Let's start with information aggregation, which is the process of taking data from data sources and aggregating it into larger and larger units of information that have a value greater than the sum of their parts. In this example, we will begin with focusing on three applications (in the physical level, of course) that all implement the *customer* business concept.

First is the CRM application. The CRM system stores a lot of information about the company's customers, such as the address, customer's contacts within the company, a history of each interaction (call or e-mail) with the customer, and a history of the customer account. Listing 12-2 shows a pseudo-code example of the customer schema. The plus sign (+) indicates that more than one record of that type may be stored by the application (for example, a customer may have multiple addresses).

Listing 12-2. *Customer Application Schema*

```
Id
Name
Address+
Contact+
Contact History+
Account History+
```

The second application is a contract management system. This application stores details about the legal agreements between each customer and the company. The contract information is quite rich and detailed, as you would expect. However, the customer information is minimal when compared to what is stored by the CRM system. The contract management system really does not care about (which means it does not record) the account history of the customer or the customer contact information for Sally in the shipping department of the customer company. Listing 12-3 shows the pseudo-code for this schema.

Listing 12-3. *Contract Application Schema*

```
Customer id
Name
Contract+
```

Finally, the score card application tracks how well the customer performs as far as we are concerned. It measures how often the customer pays its invoices on time and how long it has been purchasing from our company, and then assigns a "score" for the customer. This score allows our company's customer service representatives to prioritize customer orders and other customer interactions, so that we can be sure we are giving the best service possible to our best customers. Listing 12-4 shows the pseudo-code for this schema.

Listing 12-4. *Score Card Application Schema*

```
Customer id
Name
ScoreCard+
```

Our service map for these three systems and their atomic-level services would look like Figure 12-18.

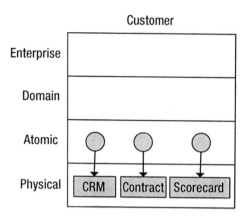

Figure 12-18. *Service map for the customer functional category so far*

There are no surprises here and no real benefit—yet. Let's take the next step and create our domain-level service, as shown in Figure 12-19. This service will have its own WSDL file and XSD (possibly more than one each, in the real world). A tree structure appears, showing how the customer domain service invokes the three atomic services below it.

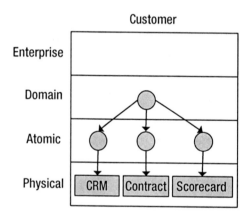

Figure 12-19. *Adding a customer domain service*

The real benefit occurs when we start to examine the customer domain schema that naturally results from the aggregation of the three atomic services, as shown in Listing 12-5. Now our customer domain service level has a much richer view of a customer than any single application does. It is also operating at a higher level of abstraction. If we replace or change one of the component applications or atomic services, we have a greater ability to control the effects of that change, without needing to modify any of the clients of the customer domain service.

Listing 12-5. *Customer Domain Schema*

```
Id
Name
Address+
Contact+
Contact History+
Account History+
Contract+
Scorecard+
```

A further benefit is that clients of the customer domain service no longer need to be aware of the existence of the lower-level applications or atomic services. They do not require accounts to log in to the applications. They do not need to understand the schema of each of the application's data structures. They only need to connect to and interact with the customer domain service, which acts as a façade over the complexity of the underlying applications.

Business Concept Leakage

At this point, it may have occurred to you that customer information does not just reside in the customer (CRM) domain. Many applications in an enterprise either store or read customer data. Let's take a look at three more applications that live in two functional categories other than CRM. Each of these applications requires some customer information in order to do its work properly.

The first application is an order entry system. This system knows how to create, search, and update orders. By necessity, it has detailed knowledge of each order, but a very limited amount of information about the customer that placed the order. Listing 12-6 shows the pseudo-code for this schema.

Listing 12-6. *Order Entry Schema*

```
Id
Customer Id
Address+
LineItem+
TotalCost
```

Our second application is the order fulfillment system. It cannot create orders, but it can take an order and determine how to fulfill that order for the customer. It contains the logic for making single or multiple shipments to a customer, when to contact a customer if there is a problem with the order, and many other process-oriented rules. Listing 12-7 shows the pseudo-code for this schema.

Listing 12-7. *Order Fulfillment Schema*

```
Order Id
LineItem+
CurrentProcessStep
```

Our third application is the accounting system. It has a fair bit of information about the customer, but with a very different focus than the CRM application has, as well as different security needs. This application will contain information about account numbers, payment history, and other sensitive information. Listing 12-8 shows the pseudo-code for this schema.

Listing 12-8. *Accounting Schema*

```
Customer Id
Order Id+
Account+
paymentHistory+
```

Just as we did with the customer domain service before, we will create an order domain service that will aggregate the services and information across both the order management application and the order fulfillment application. In this simple example, we show only the single accounting application, but in the real world, you will find that you have auxiliary applications that participate in the accounting functional category, and they would also aggregate into the accounting domain service. It starts to get really interesting when we aggregate those domain-level services up into the enterprise level, as shown in Figure 12-20.

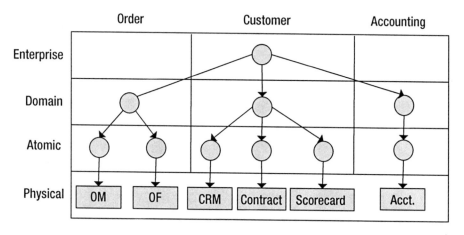

Figure 12-20. *An enterprise service that aggregates three domain-level services*

The enterprise level is the only service level that really has a complete view of what a customer is. It is also the closest in form and function to how your business thinks about a customer. Business leaders don't think about customers in terms of the applications that store the data; they think of a customer in a far more holistic way. Listing 12-9 shows an enterprise schema centered on the customer concept.

Listing 12-9. *Customer Schema at the Enterprise Level*

```
Id
Name
Address+
Contact+
```

```
Contact History+
Account History+ (CRM definition of Account here)
OrderHistory+
Account+
PaymentHistory+
Contract+
Scorecard
```

Obviously, if you take this model to its logical conclusion, you can see that the enterprise level could provide its service consumers with a 360-degree view of the customer. Of course, this principle does not just apply to customer information, but also to every bit of information in the enterprise: product-centric views that show order details, consumer geography, and so on.

Furthermore, the enterprise level is now twice removed from the applications themselves. The service and schema definitions at the enterprise level also operate at a higher level of abstraction than do the domain-level services. This gives you two opportunities to control the effects of change in your enterprise when you make a change to one of the low-level applications.

Another byproduct of this approach is that you will naturally develop a single canonical vocabulary for your enterprise, at the enterprise level. New portals can access information anywhere in your enterprise without needing to know the integration details of each application. In fact, they won't need to know the specifics of each domain. A single API to your enterprise will emerge, reducing the learning curve for many of your developers, and providing you with the much-promised speed and agility that you are looking for with SOA.

Data Reduction

In the previous section, you saw how you could, in a rational manner, manage logical views of data/information within an enterprise. There is tremendous benefit to this approach, but we must give you a caveat: *not all data in your enterprise should be available at the enterprise level.*

The basic nature of data is passive. Applications and services are active. Databases hold information, while computer programs act on that information. The combination of data and programming logic creates a software system. If you make the mistake of publishing all data fields at the enterprise level, that will force all of your functionality into the enterprise level also. That is not what we are trying to do. Just as the service landscape methodology divides data and schemas into the various tiers, it also divides service functionality along the same lines.

Let's take a look at an example, using an airline as our business. Our airline uses a CRM system that has hundreds of data fields pertaining to a customer. Publishing those hundreds of fields into the enterprise-level schema will not simplify our enterprise; it will do the opposite. Data supports functionality. If the data is needed only at a low level of abstraction, it should be paired with functionality at the same level of abstraction.

One common bit of information in a CRM system is that of customer market segment. This information is used to categorize customers into one or more groups. These customer groups are then targeted for marketing campaigns or other promotions. These groups also give clues as to how the company may treat the customers. For example, an airline's frequent-flier club members rate a little higher than the average fliers. Customers who have flown more than 100,000 miles on the airline will receive an even better level of service.

Let's assume that this bit of customer information resides in the database of the CRM application in a simple field called marketSegment. We know that understanding the customer's marketSegment value is important to the business. Should we include that information at the atomic level? Probably, because functionality at the atomic level may require that the market segment is provided as a parameter.

How about the customer domain schema? Should it also contain this data point? We would argue that this information probably does not need to exist at the domain level. Consider the fact that the CRM application defines marketSegment for its own (application-specific) purposes. Our business uses that information to identify groups of customers for marketing purposes. However, our business also uses that information (or a portion of it) to determine its SLA and its own behavior toward a customer. The way the business treats customers is not based solely on their market segment. The treatment of customers will also be influenced by how much they paid for their current ticket. If you pay full price for a ticket, the customer service representative knows about it (it's actually printed on your ticket), as does the automated reservation system. In fact, most reservation systems use this information when determining who gets bumped from a flight.

With this in mind, it's obvious that at the higher levels of abstraction, we need to know more than the marketSegment field in the CRM system to determine how we should treat our customers. We also need to know their current ticket information, their account status (are they in arrears for some reason?), and many other factors. Therefore, at the domain and enterprise levels, we need a higher level of abstraction for this information. At the customer domain level, we should instead have a new field named customerRating, whose value is calculated from the marketSegment field in the CRM system, along with the customer's membership status in our frequent-flier program and whether or not they have purchased a membership for the club/lounge that our airline provides at airports throughout the world. All of this information is then included in the calculations to render the value of the customerRating field in the customer domain schema.

A similar process of data reduction occurs at the enterprise level. However, at this level. the customerRating field would be calculated from the customerRating field at the domain level, the past flight history from the order domain, current account/billing status from the accounting domain, and so on.

The only reason we would have a customerRating field at the enterprise level is because it is important at the enterprise level. That information is used at that level. However, some data never reaches the enterprise level at all and is instead hidden by service functionality. Let's take our CRM marketSegment field as an example. Our marketing department wants to have the ability to send e-mail messages that are targeted at specific customer groups. The staff wants to be able to send an e-mail promotion to all customers who are part of the frequent-flier program but are not currently members of the Big Dog Club (the airline-specific club that has lounges in each airport). At its core, we need a service that says, "Send an e-mail to each customer who has characteristic [Frequent Flier], but does not have characteristic [Big Dog Member]." This service operation would take this form:

```
sendTargetedEmail(EmailTemplate, SelectionCriteria) : void
```

and would probably be composed of two other service operations at the enterprise level:

```
getCustomerList(SelectionCriteria) : CustomerList
sendCustomerEmail(EmailTemplate, CustomerList) : void
```

The getCustomerList(SelectionCriteria) operation would then invoke a customer domain-level operation (and possibly other domains) to find customers based on the domain-level selection criteria. There would be a translation of the selection criteria from the enterprise-level document to a new document that made sense within the context of the customer domain. The customer domain-level operation would then call the CRM atomic-level service (and possibly other atomic services) to do the search.

The results of these searches would then be aggregated as the various results were returned, up through the levels of abstraction to the originating enterprise service. You can see how this process hides the CRM-specific field of marketSegment, but still leverages it at the higher abstraction levels. The rule is that data follows the same process of abstraction that service functionality does. At the domain or enterprise level, we don't publish data that is a direct replication of the application-specific data, since doing so tightly couples these levels of abstraction. You will see an example of this in Chapter 13.

Abstracting Geography and Politics

Another challenge of enterprise architecture is dealing with geographically and politically diverse organizations. For example, your company may have software development shops and IT centers scattered around the globe. Such an organization is geographically diverse. Political diversity means that your various development organizations operate independently of any centralized architecture group. Both political and geographic diversity are quite common in today's enterprises.

Once again, the service landscape approach affords us considerable benefit in abstracting (hiding) this organizational complexity from the service consumers. Let's examine an organization that makes liberal use of its CRM system and has also taken the time and effort to implement the service landscape architecture. Our sample company (company A) then acquires and merges with a similar business (company B) on the other side of the world. Company B also maintains its own CRM system and has its own development, architecture, and IT standards.

The two companies merge together to become a unified company, but it's unified in name only. In all likelihood, the newly acquired IT shop (IT shop B) is unwilling to adopt the standards and processes of its parent company. Furthermore, the parent company is unlikely to have the *ability* or the *will* to force its standards onto company B. How can we maintain a rational architecture when large portions of the organization are unable or unwilling to adopt it?

Despite the fun and allure we all associate with grand political battles (sarcasm definitely intended), the key to success is having a flexible view of the architectural world. The solution is to "wrap" these elements of your company within levels of abstraction. When it comes to hiding political and geographic distinctions, the existence of the domain level comes to the rescue. The two distinct CRM systems that are now owned by the company are wrapped under the customer domain level. The interface to the customer domain level does not represent the fact that two different CRM systems exist underneath it, yet this same level is where the routing and business logic are encoded to make sure that the two CRM systems appear as a unified business capability to the enterprise level.

As a result, the change that we would need to ask of IT shop B is to provide some sort of remote interface that the parent company can call in order to access CRM system B. Odds are that CRM system B already has some kind of interface, so there should be little or no work for IT shop B. If the interface to CRM system B is already web-enabled, then we already have our atomic level defined. If the interface to CRM system B is EJB or some similar technology, we have the option to simply declare the EJB interface as the set of atomic services and use that interface directly from the customer domain. Another option would be to write our own atomic web service that calls the EJB interface of the CRM system B application, depending on which approach we deem to be best.

So you can see how the architecture of service landscape provides more than mere technical flexibility and agility. It provides a political and geographical agility as well. You don't need to make exceptions to the architecture to handle these common issues. The architecture is built to handle political and geographical diversity from the ground up, not as exceptions.

Architectural Transformation

Odds are that your current enterprise architecture doesn't formally recognize service domains. If your company is like the vast majority of companies, your current enterprise architecture will resemble that shown in Figure 12-21. This is commonly referred to as a *point-to-point* (P2P) integration strategy. We've also heard people refer to it as a "rat's nest" of integrations or the "accidental architecture."

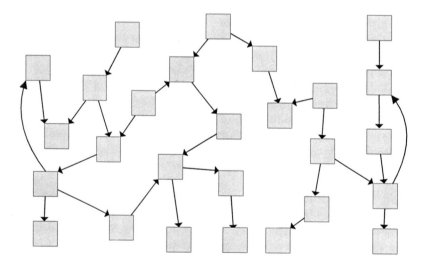

Figure 12-21. *Point-to-point integration*

Figure 12-21 shows 27 squares. Each square represents an application in the enterprise. The arrows show the dependencies between the applications. Although the figure shows only a modest number of applications (most medium-sized enterprises have well over 100 software applications running at any time), it represents sufficient complexity for our purposes.

The big question is, "How do I transform my architecture from this rat's nest to use the SOA coordinate system?"

First, it's important to recognize that your enterprise didn't implement this rat's nest overnight. It took years—even decades—to build that P2P architecture, and you won't correct it overnight. However, we have an approach that will simplify this process, allowing you to implement enterprise-wide SOA without needing to rewrite your entire enterprise.

As we write this, SOA is at a high point in its "hype cycle." SOA advocates earnestly promise that SOA will cure all your ills and make you more attractive to the opposite sex. These promoters will promise that everything you ever learned about software engineering and running an IT shop is now outdated. SOA makes it so easy that a trained monkey can do it!

If you've spent any amount of time in the software industry, you recognize this hype cycle pretty quickly. You know that the old 80/20 rule applies: about 80 percent of the hype will turn out to be exaggerations or outright lies, while the other 20 percent is the really useful stuff that you need to learn and apply immediately. The difficulty is in knowing which statements are hype and which statements are true.

Let's debunk a commonly held belief in our industry: P2P integrations are evil. In fact, there are advantages to using a P2P integration strategy. First, P2P is usually fairly quick to implement. Once you know how to communicate to the foreign software system, it's just a matter of doing the work to make the various API calls. Second, P2P is fairly easy. You don't need to be a software design expert. The foreign software system's API is already written, and there's usually nothing you can do to improve it. Just write the integration code and go home. Third, P2P is usually fast from an execution time point of view. Not a lot of translation happens in a P2P integration, thereby eliminating any translation or transformation overhead.

Of course, P2P also has some serious drawbacks. P2P systems are difficult to maintain over time, and there tends to be little abstraction in the interfaces of most of these software systems, so making any changes to them tends to affect every client that's integrated with the system. Because every little change requires significant engineering effort, a greater percentage of the IT budget goes to maintaining existing systems, and less money is spent on creating new systems or improving existing ones. This phenomenon leads directly to IT systems (and therefore the business itself) becoming lethargic and resistant to change.

So, P2P isn't evil, nor is it blessed. It's simply an integration strategy that makes sense to use in certain situations. The fact is that P2P is already present and pervasive in your enterprise. You cannot ignore it; you must deal with it. If your enterprise is like most, you have neither the time nor the money to fix it, so there's only one thing left to do: embrace it.

The approach we suggest here is simply to accept that you're going to live with large pockets of P2P for some years to come. The trick is to know where P2P is acceptable in the short term, and where you really need to buckle down and fix it. Now that we have an SOA coordinate system and a service map, we can tell you where you need to fix P2P and where you can safely ignore it for the time being. It all comes back to the functional categories. Applications within a functional category are already implemented using P2P. Because the work they do is closely related anyway, it's perfectly acceptable to allow them to remain that way. However, you must break this P2P model when it comes to integrations that cross functional categories.

Your first step is to take an inventory of all your applications and begin to categorize their functionality into the appropriate functional categories. Once that's done, you can begin a series of engineering projects to refactor the various applications so that they're appropriately represented by atomic services. Figure 12-22 shows a set of applications, represented by the squares, and their P2P dependencies. We are looking for integrations that cross functional categories. The dashed lines that cut across two of the dependencies indicate integrations that cross functional categories, such as the order application calling the CRM application.

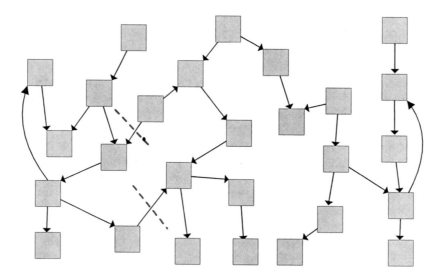

Figure 12-22. *Isolate application functionality that belongs in the same functional category.*

When you're identifying applications and atomic services, it's important that you understand the dependencies between the applications in sufficient detail to make good decisions.
Each dependency has a direction associated with it, and you must understand the direction of
each dependency. The direction of a dependency always starts with the integration logic that
uses (depends on) an interface. With this knowledge, you're able to begin to sort application
functionality into logical atomic services. Figure 12-23 shows how this is done. Only application A needs to be modified to call the new service C in the domain service level, instead of
calling application B directly.

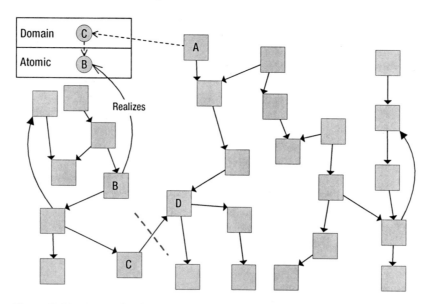

Figure 12-23. *Create the domain and atomic layers.*

Notice how application C is still directly dependent on application D. For the time being, this is acceptable. Because application D does not yet have an atomic-level service defined for it, the outgoing call from C to D is unavoidable.

Our next step is to repeat the process. Once again, we isolate application functionality services that belong in the same logical functional category, paying close attention to their dependencies. We create a second functional category. At this stage, we break the direct dependency between application C and D and refactor application C to call the newly created domain-level service in category 2.

There is no hard-and-fast rule about when to introduce an ESB, but we recommend that you introduce it as the second project (immediately after you create your first domain-level category) or as the third project (after the second domain-level category is complete). It's important to introduce the ESB fairly early in the process of creating domain-level services to reduce the amount of refactoring that must be performed for each application that invokes services in other functional categories. For example, if you examine Figure 12-24, you'll notice that application C is now dependent on the category 2 domain-level service, while application A is dependent on category 1 domain-level service. Yet a quick examination of Figure 12-25 shows that applications A and B are now dependent on the enterprise level. This implies a double refactoring of those applications (from the domain level to the enterprise level). Obviously, each of these refactoring efforts takes time and money to complete, so you want to minimize the number of such projects.

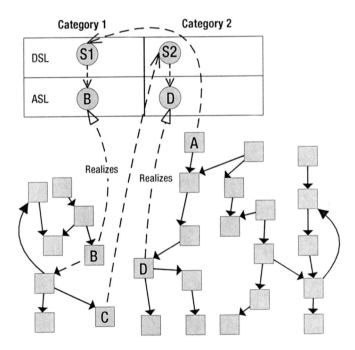

Figure 12-24. *Repeat the process for each domain.*

Of course, you might ask, "Why not start by creating the enterprise level and completely avoid the double refactoring effect?" That sounds good in principle, but we find that creating at least a domain level for a single functional category helps the architects and developers to get their minds wrapped around the new technologies and new design patterns required by SOA. We find that this helps to diffuse the attendant fears of experiencing so much change, which, in turn, increases the success rates of these early projects. Of course, if your organization is already adept with the technologies you are going to use in your enterprise and has good abstraction skills, there is nothing prohibiting you from creating an enterprise level as part of your very first project.

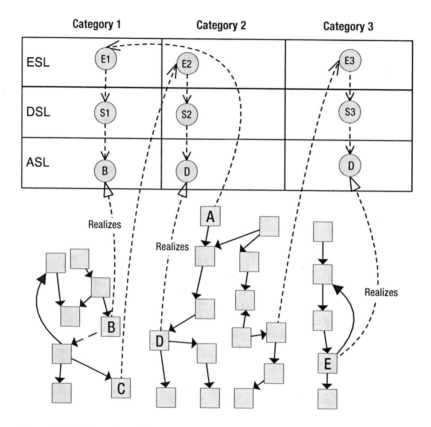

Figure 12-25. *Introduce the ESB early in the process.*

Not Just an ESB!

Keep in mind that BEA did not originally name the product AquaLogic Enterprise Service Bus, and isn't now called Oracle Enterprise Service Bus. Certainly, OSB is designed to operate under the rigors and stresses of an ESB. However, OSB is also well suited to perform in areas of your enterprise that aren't immediately evident.

For example, OSB is well suited to operate in the domain level. Just point it at the various atomic services below it and create a more abstract set of proxy services. That alone will create an entire domain level for one of your functional categories.

OSB doesn't just "speak" services, though. You can also easily connect to Java code, EJBs, and JDBC drivers. These capabilities make OSB a candidate to act as an adapter within the atomic level, allowing legacy applications to participate in your SOA by service-enabling them, even though they were never designed with services in mind.

It can be difficult to integrate an old mainframe system into your SOA. Mainframe applications are rarely designed to integrate with anything at all. They all see themselves as the center of their software universe and often don't even have a public API. One integration trick we've used in the past is to integrate at the database level. Mainframe applications commonly use a relational database management system to store data. By adding or modifying insert, update, and delete triggers, you can often push data to an outside application, such as OSB. This is especially easy in an Oracle application, because Oracle provides the capability to write triggers and stored procedures in Java. We prefer to keep our code at this level asynchronous if possible, so it doesn't interfere too much with the normal execution time of any existing triggers in the database. We usually opt to publish a database "event" over a JMS queue and have OSB receive the JMS message. We don't mean to represent this process as being overly simple, but it is possible, and it does work.

Similarly, many older systems use FTP as their messaging systems. Exchanging formatted files was probably the earliest widespread messaging system. Using OSB, you can receive or copy these files, monitoring the file transfers and even reading the data in these files to perform content-based routing.

Don't let the name fool you. OSB has a lot of functionality. Use it wherever its functionality matches the needs of your architecture. As the feature list of OSB grows with each release, you'll find more and more ways to use it.

Summary

We've gone through a lot of theory quickly in this chapter. We'll close this chapter with a quick review of the four main advantages of the service landscape methodology:

- It leverages your existing P2P architecture, minimizing the amount of change you need to make in your current applications. Fewer changes to your existing systems will translate directly into less development time and cost.

- It reduces the P2P integrations within the physical level, breaking your single large "rat's nest" of applications into nine or ten smaller and more manageable rat's nests.

- It provides you with a well-defined process that's easy to explain to technologists and businesspeople alike. Trying to get your projects funded under the banner of "SOA" is a difficult proposition. However, once you can clearly explain how you will achieve your SOA goals and break down the process into discrete projects, you'll increase your odds of success. People rarely fear what they understand.

- Organizing IT assets into a series of functional categories that make sense to most businesspeople will increase the level of alignment between your IT shop and your business leaders.

## CHAPTER 13

Implementing Your Service Landscape

In the previous chapter, you learned a lot of SOA theory very quickly. Theory is useful only when you can apply it to the real world. You need to build your SOA using real computers, software, and architecture. In this chapter, we will demonstrate how to put the service landscape methodology into practice. However, first we need to address the important topic of standards.

Standards, Standards, and More Standards

A critical factor for success in any sort of enterprise architecture is to specify standards to be used across the organization. One of the keys to having these standards adopted and put into practice is to make them easy to remember and use. The more complicated your standards are, the harder it will be to get everyone to use them.

Here, we will present some standards for naming namespaces, services, and operations, as well as for defining schema scope. Naturally, you are free to take, leave, or modify the standards we suggest to suit your needs. We want to be clear on this point: the standards that we specify here are guidelines to help you get started. If they conflict with your existing standards, you should use your current standards instead.

Naming Namespaces

Namespaces are fundamental to WSDL and XSD, so it's important to have standards around their construction. Our approach to namespaces is simple yet flexible.

First, namespaces should include the organization that generated or maintains them. We prefer to use the URL format for namespaces, as opposed to Java package names. So at Oracle, the organizational part of the namespace is always `http://www.oracle.com/`.

Next, we include the service landscape level of abstraction in which the namespace applies. So we append `enterprise/`, `domain/`, or `atomic/` to the namespace.

If we are working with the enterprise level of the abstraction scale, we can optionally append the functional category name if the service is focused on a specific business concept (and services usually are). For example, it's not uncommon to see a namespace that contains `enterprise/customer/`, which indicates that the namespace is concerned with the customer concept at the enterprise level of abstraction. If we are working with the domain level of the abstraction scale, then we *always* append the name of the functional category (for example, `domain/customer/`). If we are working at the atomic level, we always append the name of the functional category, application, and optionally any specific business concept (for example, `atomic/customer/SAP` or `atomic/customer/Siebel/contactHistory`).

To the end of the namespace, we may append a version number for the namespace, the date that the namespace was ratified by the organization, or any other information that we feel is critical.

Finally, our standards require that all namespaces end in a forward slash. Now, ending namespaces with a slash is not any better than ending namespaces without a slash. However, it is very important that your namespace standard specifies either one or the other. We can't tell you how much development and QA time has been wasted just because we were using a namespace that did not end in a slash when it should have, or vice versa. To combat this irksome problem, we simply decided that all namespaces should end in a slash. We are not exaggerating when we say that this is one of the first areas we inspect when troubleshooting our web services.

Here are some examples of namespaces:

- `http://www.oracle.com/enterprise/accounting/20080215/`

- `http://www.foo.com/domain/customer/profile/`

- `http://www.acme.com/atomic/customer/SAP/`

Naming Services

It is important to create standards for naming services within your organization. Naming standards will help developers and architects more easily find the services they are seeking. This is especially true if you are using enterprise repository software like Oracle's Enterprise Repository. Again, you want to define some naming standards that are simple yet robust.

The service naming standards used in our examples are based on the abstraction level and functional category in which the service is defined. Service names may be modified by a domain specialization, especially at the enterprise level. For example, an enterprise service may be focused on dealing with customer accounts, a specialized subset of customer-oriented services. However, even domain-level services may indicate a specialization if that is appropriate. The same is true for atomic-level services. Appending the word `Service` at the end of each service name is optional.

The formats for service names are as follows:

- `<Layer>[Specialization][Service]`

- `<Layer><Domain>[Service]`

- `<Layer><Domain><Application>[Specialization][Service]`

Here are some sample service names that follow these guidelines:

- EnterpriseCustomerService

- EnterpriseCustomerAccountService

- AtomicCustomerCRMService

- DomainCustomerService

- DomainCustomerQueryService

Naming Service Operations

Just as naming standards are important for services, they are equally important for operations. For the most part, the operation-naming guidelines are similar to the naming guidelines for modern programming languages, but with some twists that are due to the nature of WSDL. The first rule for operation names is that they start with a verb. The following are some common verbs and their implication for the rest of the operation:

- get: Gets a specific instance of an entity. Returns a single result. A null result will usually throw a fault message.

- find: Searches for information. Expects to return zero or more results.

- create: Creates new information, usually related to entities.

- update: Updates existing entity information.

- delete: Deletes existing information. This is usually used with a specific entity, not with a range of entities.

- is: Tests an aspect of information.

This list of verbs is not exhaustive. In fact, later in this chapter, you will see a couple of verbs that are not listed here.

Information volume is also included in the operation name. There are three classic volumes of information:

- List: A brief amount of information usually meant to be placed into a list of results.

- Basic/Summary: A moderate amount of information, usually about an entity.

- Detail/Complete/All: A detailed view of information. This is very often a composite view of multiple entities.

If the information volume is not specified in the name, it can be assumed that the operation will return a basic or summary amount of information.

The operation name should also contain the name of any entities that it is focused on (customer, customer account, and so on). Also, due to the nature of WSDL 1.2 (namely its lack of method overloading), we recommend that the operation name give some indication of the argument it will take and the information it will return. In general, here is a template for operation names:

```
<verb><entity | topic | return type><info-volume>By<parameterType>
```

The following sample operation names illustrate these guidelines. You will find many of these operation names in use later in this chapter.

- `findCustomerContactListByProfile`: Finds a basic amount of customer information based on the specified profile. The term *profile* is used to indicate advanced search criteria that often span applications or domains.

- `getCustomerDetailByID`: Gets a detailed view of a specific customer record, based on the customer ID. You should expect a single record to be returned, or a fault to be thrown if no customer exists with the specific ID.

- `sendTargetedMessageToCustomersByProfile`: Sends a customized message to each customer who meets the search criteria specified by the profile argument.

▪**Note** These operation-naming conventions are not always possible at the atomic level if the application provides its own web service interface. However, they should always be observed for enterprise-level and domain-level services, and for atomic services that your own company creates.

Schema Scope: Service-Specific vs. Core Concept

Not all types are created equal. Some schema types represent fundamental business concepts or entities. For example, *customer* is a core concept for most companies. `CustomerList`, `CustomerSummary`, and `CustomerDetail` each represents a different information volume (see the previous section on naming service operations) of the customer concept. Other schema types are more utilitarian in nature and are specific to your service implementations. For example, you may create a schema within a WSDL file that aggregates two core schema types in a manner that is specific to the service itself. An example of this service-specific aggregation would be an operation that returns a customer and a list of recent customer orders.

This is definitely a case where a picture is worth a thousand words, so we will limit our verbiage and show you a diagram that illustrates the point. Figure 13-1 shows two different WSDL files. The `CustomerCentricService` has an operation named `findCustomerContactListByProfile`, which takes a `CustomerProfile` as an argument and returns a `CustomerContactList`. The `CustomerContactList` and `CustomerContact` schema objects both have a service-specific scope. The `CustomerContact` type is really just a local "wrapper" for the more substantial schema types defined in the XML Schema.

The rule is pretty simple: if the schema type is required only by a single WSDL file and has little or no chance of being needed in a different WSDL file, the schema type should be declared in the WSDL file. If you believe that the schema type represents one of the core concept types for your business, you should define it in a separate XML Schema.

This approach gives you the ability to reuse common schema objects across multiple services within a specific abstraction level. If you do not take this approach, you could end up creating multiple versions of what is essentially the same data type within each service definition. This approach applies primarily to the enterprise and domain abstraction levels. In the domain level, the XSD elements can be shared by multiple WSDL files within the same functional category, but they cannot be shared among domain-level WSDL files across functional categories.

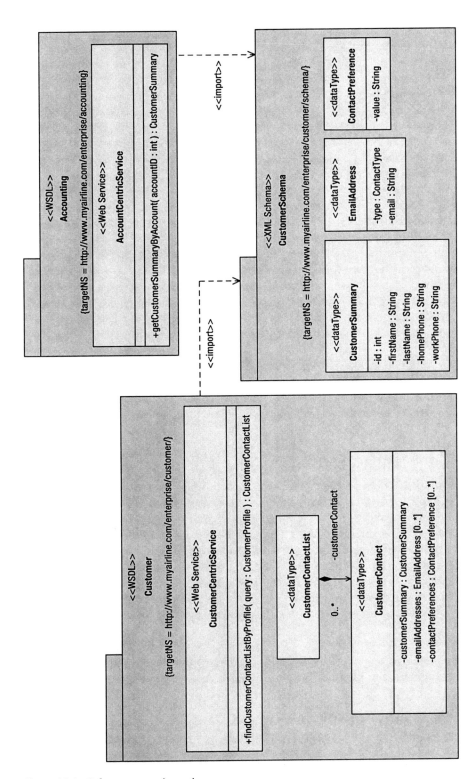

Figure 13-1. *Schema scope in action*

This approach also insulates you from creating complex schema types that are of limited reuse. For example, examine the `CustomerSummary` type in the `CustomerSchema` in Figure 13-1. Notice how it is not related to the `EmailAddress` type or the `ContactPreference` type within the schema. This is important. If we defined the `CustomerSummary` as relating to (usually as a container of) the `EmailAddress` and `ContactPreference` types, then that relationship would affect the operation in the `AccountCentricService` also. There is no business reason for the `getCustomerSummaryByAccount` operation to return contact preferences for the customer, but if we created that relationship inside the XML Schema, it would either be forced to return that information or would mislead the service consumer into believing that e-mail and contact preferences will be returned by the operation.

This does not mean that you do not create relationships between schema types under any circumstances. It simply means that you need to be aware of the ramifications of creating relationships within a schema or a WSDL file. Create the relationships between elements only where appropriate. We will illustrate this in later sections of this chapter.

By defining the scope of a schema element this way, you can then use the higher-level WSDL files to compose the lower-level schema elements in ways that make sense for each service. You gain flexibility and reusability with this approach. This runs counter to the common thinking in database design that you need to create a comprehensive data model. Remember that you are not creating a comprehensive data model when you create services. You are creating only views of information—views that should be focused on delivering just what the service consumer needs.

As we said at the beginning of the discussion of standards, feel free to use these guidelines and modify them as needed. They are not rules or "laws" of SOA; they are just some hard-won lessons from the real world. We will use these guidelines in the examples in this chapter, so you can get a better feel for how to implement them.

Where Do We Begin?

SOA development is still managed using the traditional project. We have heard some people state that SOA is the end of projects, but that doesn't make any sense at all. Projects exist to accommodate how human beings work. The pyramids were built as projects and so are space stations. SOA doesn't change that approach. The good news is that all of your company's current skills and infrastructure for managing projects remains unchanged. The bad news is you still need to answer the most difficult question in your first SOA project, "Where do we begin?"

At this point in the book, we assume that your developers, architects, and operations personnel have already gained sufficient skill with web services and basic SOA concepts, and are ready to begin the work of adopting SOA. That is the point where you usually ask, "Where do we begin?"

You implement SOA to provide value to your enterprise. So you begin with an understanding of what is important to your company. Once you understand what is important to your company, you can then make informed decisions about what services are needed and where.

The Concept-First Approach

Figure 13-2 shows a "target" of business concepts for most commercial companies. This diagram is not meant to be definitive, merely representative. Feel free to modify it to meet your specific needs.

Figure 13-2. *Business concept target*

At the center of the diagram are the core concepts that are most critical to the business. For most businesses, the core concepts are customer, orders, products/services, and billing. The concepts in the first ring that surrounds the core are less critical but still important. The concepts in the third ring are less critical than both the core concepts and the inner-ring concepts.

This does not mean that you don't service-enable all of these concepts, but it does give you a good idea of where to start: the core concepts. In all probability, customer, orders, products, and billing are at the heart of your enterprise. These core concepts are invariably the most commonly used concepts across all of your existing software applications, and they are usually the most important to your businesspeople. If you want SOA to provide value to your organization as quickly as possible, we recommend that you start by service-enabling the systems that deal with these core concepts.

An implied principle here deserves to be made explicit: you service-enable concepts, not applications. It is tempting to approach this from the other direction, by examining applications and then service-enabling them. We call this the "application-first" approach. This leads to whole projects being initiated to service-enable specific applications. At the end of those projects, money and time have been expended, but no benefit is realized by the company. This is a sure approach for killing SOA at your company.

Beginning with the "concept-first" approach is subtly different. You take a look at the concepts that are core to your company, and then identify business functionality that uses those concepts and provides benefit at the same time.

Service Mapping

For the examples in this chapter, we will continue to use the fictitious airline that we introduced in the previous chapter as our company and business model. Suppose that the airline identifies a need to allow customers to view their bills online through the company's public web site. Figure 13-3 shows a service map that can fulfill this business need. Right from the start, we know that we need a service in the enterprise level, because the service needs to access information from two distinct functional categories (customer and accounting). This brings us to our first rule of service mapping.

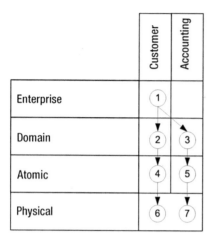

Figure 13-3. *Mapping your first service*

Enterprise Service Mapping Rule 1

If the service must cross functional category boundaries to do its job, it must exist in the enterprise level.

Or to put it another way, only enterprise services can cross functional category boundaries.

In our example, service 1 must aggregate information from the two service domains that are logically responsible for the customer and billing information, so the service in the enterprise level invokes the two services in the domain level.

This rule exists to prevent service developers from re-creating a P2P integration within the domain level (as they will be sorely tempted to do at first).

Enterprise Service Mapping Rule 2

The enterprise level cannot "skip" the domain level below it.

As this rule declares, the service in the enterprise level cannot skip over the domain level and get the information directly from the various application services. Doing so violates the fundamental principle of abstraction and will quickly render the coordinate system (and therefore your SOA) completely useless. It would be akin to putting a button on your TV remote control to change a single transistor state on a microchip in the TV.

If the enterprise level could skip the domain level, you would lose a fundamental layer of abstraction, and the enterprise level would then need to know about the physical deployment details of the atomic level. This not only increases the amount of maintenance that needs to happen each time a change is made to a physical application deployment (a server is added or deleted), but also eliminates a key layer of transformation. This forces the enterprise level to "speak" the same language as the application, increasing the coupling between the enterprise level and the application.

In our service map in Figure 13-3, each respective domain-level service makes use of the atomic level, which in turn accesses the physical level. In this case, we see that the customer domain service (2) invokes the atomic service (4), which in turn invokes the CRM application (6).

Service Map vs. Physical Deployment

The first time people see a service map they often think, "That's a lot of network hops!" They see every level in the logical model as a level in the physical world also. This is simply not the case. It is important that you understand how to translate the logical model into a physical realization. Let's take a close look at how we transform the logical model depicted in Figure 13-3.

Recall the business requirement that was used to derive our service map: we need to allow our customers to view their bills online. The enterprise level contains a customer-centric service that contains an operation (1) with the likely name of getCustomerBillingHistory. This operation is realized in OSB as a proxy service. This proxy service aggregates two other operations, one in the CRM category and the other in the accounting category. Following the CRM functional category first, the CRM domain service would contain an operation named getCustomerSummary (2) that would return a lightweight amount of data about the customer. This operation would then invoke the appropriate atomic service for the CRM system (4), which connects to the CRM application (6).

Now let's look at the accounting services. The accounting domain service would have an operation named getBillingHistory (3) whose purpose is to return billing records for a specified customer and time frame. It is rarely a good idea (and sometimes illegal) to bypass the accounting application, so the getBillingHistory domain service invokes a web service interface in the atomic level named getCustomerBillingHistory (5), a business service defined in OSB. This business service, in turn, invokes the accounting application (7) to perform the work and return the results.

This information is depicted in Figure 13-4. The dashed ellipse represents a single instance of OSB. The number of network hops is the same as it would be if you wrote some custom code to integrate the CRM system and the accounting systems directly: one hop from the client to your integration code, one hop from the integration coded to the CRM system, and one more hop from the integration code to the accounting system.

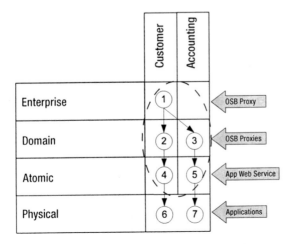

Figure 13-4. *Realizing a service map*

How would you deploy these services in the real world? What would this service map look like as a UML implementation diagram? Figure 13-5 answers that question. It shows three nodes (computers that are hosting running software) and the components of each node. We have also noted the abstraction levels to help highlight how these levels map to a physical deployment. In the real world, you would not add these level names to your deployment diagrams, because the UML tags Abstraction Layer and Functional Group assigned to each component would be sufficient to relay that information.

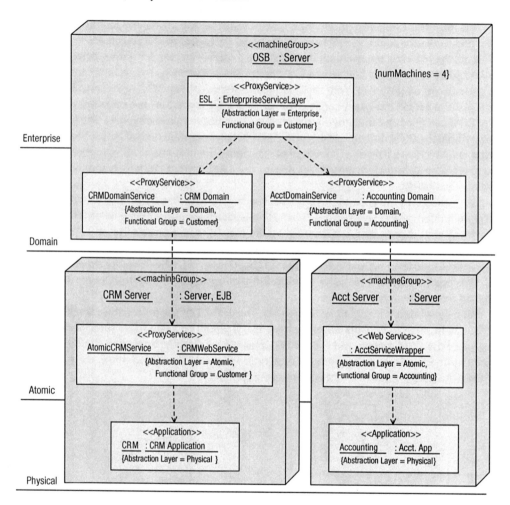

Figure 13-5. *Physical deployment architecture of the service map in Figure 13-3*

Figure 13-5 makes it plain that we have only two network hops in the entire deployment. The first hop is between the OSB server and the CRM server. The second hop is between the OSB server and the accounting server. This deployment diagram does not take into account any clustering of these servers for redundancy and failover (we wanted to keep the diagram simple and easy to read). However, if we had added a second machine for each type of server, it would not affect the number of network hops.

Of course, this is not the only possible way to deploy the service map. We could have deployed each of the proxy services onto their own servers and really increased the number of network hops. In some instances, that may make sense for you. You may need to scale up portions of the functionality by adding more computing power, too. However, the purpose of this example is to illustrate the difference between the logical view of a service map using the service landscape approach and the physical realization of the service map.

TOP-DOWN VS. BOTTOM-UP DESIGN

We have heard proponents for taking a "top-down" approach to service development, where you begin with a high-level need and then decompose the higher-level service into smaller, discrete services and so forth. The alternative approach is "bottom-up," where you take a look at the functional capabilities provided by your existing systems and begin to design the low-level services first.

We find that each of these approaches has benefits and drawbacks. When starting with a top-down approach, it can be easy to overlook existing services and capabilities in your enterprise. With a bottom-up approach, it's easy to get lost in all of the details and end up creating services that provide little abstraction over the physical systems and that don't fulfill any business need. These approaches are like tools in your problem-solving tool chest. If one is a hammer and the other is a screwdriver, which one is better? It depends on if your solution involves nails or screws. You need to use the right tool for the job at hand.

In practice, we begin by defining the business requirement. The requirement gives us the high-level problem definition. We sketch out the enterprise-level service, roughly describing its inputs and outputs. We then move to identifying the systems in the physical level that provide the functionality that we expect to use to fulfill the needs of the enterprise-level service. From there, it becomes a matter of discovering or creating atomic services and operations and domain services and operations. In essence, we use both a top-down and a bottom-up approach together. It's pretty simple and works well.

The First Project

For our first project, we have already gotten started by defining our business requirement— allow our customers to view their bills online—and developing our service map, shown earlier in Figure 13-3. We can now initiate a project that is both limited in scope (we will not service-enable entire applications, only the functionality we need) and provides business benefit. We will continue by creating the atomic services for our CRM and billing system.

Creating Atomic Services

We must identify the atomic services that we want to publish from the existing CRM and billing applications. We know from the business requirement and service map that we need to get some basic customer information from the CRM system. We then define a CRM atomic service that meets our need to return simple customer information based on a customer ID. However, while designing this service, we also feel that we can pretty safely predict the need for an operation that allows us to search for customers, based on some common criteria supported by the CRM application, so we take the liberty (and some small risk) of adding a findCustomerList operation to the service definition at this time, because we are confident we will need such functionality in the very near future.

Since XML is too space-intensive for these exercises, we will use UML notation to provide a simple view of the web service to save space. Figure 13-6 shows the service definition for the CRM atomic service.

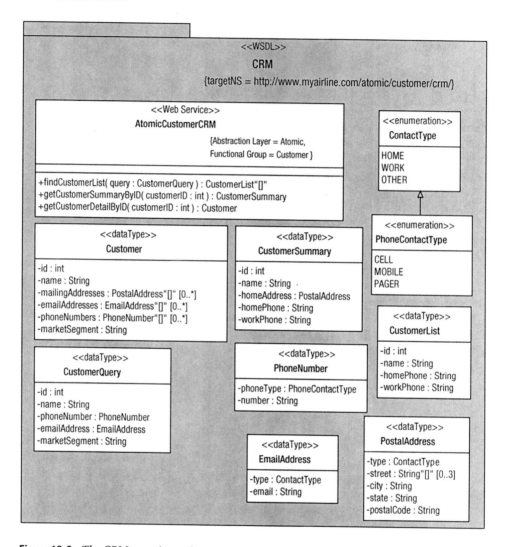

Figure 13-6. *The CRM atomic service*

The package in Figure 13-6 shows the namespace we are going to use for this atomic service: http://www.myairline.com/atomic/customer/crm/. We are following the namespace naming convention defined at the beginning of this chapter. Note that the [*application*] portion of the namespace is used only when creating atomic services.

The AtomicCustomerCRMService class at the top of the figure shows the three operations defined by the service and the various data types and enumerations defined in the <Schema> section of the web service. For the time being, this service definition will meet our needs.

A CRM application is likely to have hundreds of entities and often thousands of operations you can call. It is important to recognize that for our current project, we create only the atomic service and entities that we need to complete the project. This approach allows us to keep our design and development efforts small and focused. In turn, this increases the chance of success of the overall project, and begins to provide the much-promised benefits to the company as quickly and cheaply as possible.

Let's turn our attention to the billing application. We also need to create an atomic service for this application. We need to be able to query the billing system to get the billing records for a specific customer. It is fair to assume that the caller would like to provide some criteria to the operation, such as specifying a date range for billing events. We will incorporate that capability into our atomic service.

Using our design experience, we can also conclude that on top of showing the billing history for a specified date range, it would be useful to show the current billing status for the customer, so we add the getSummaryOfAccounts operation to the service. Again, we take some risk by adding an operation that is not clearly called for by the requirements, but we believe that such an operation will be useful in the near future. Just to be sure, we get approval from the architecture team, business analyst, or whoever else needs to approve the additional work to add and test the additional operation. The result is shown in Figure 13-7.

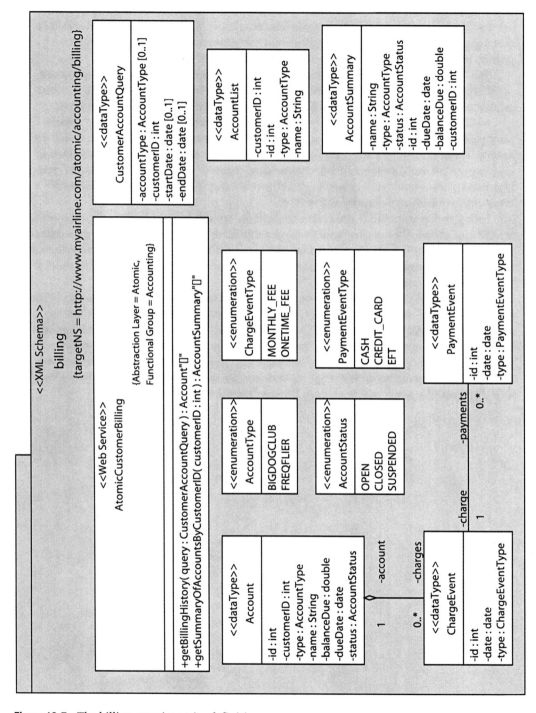

Figure 13-7. *The billing atomic service definition*

Once these atomic services are ready, we can move onto the domain-level services.

Creating Domain Services

Because our first atomic services are so simple, our domain services will also be simple. We need to define domain-level services for two domains: customer and accounting. The services at the domain level will be merely pass-through services that provide us with some loose coupling between the enterprise level and the atomic services.

For example, take a look at the customer domain service definition depicted in Figure 13-8. It looks very similar to the atomic CRM server we defined a bit earlier, but we have introduced important changes. First, of course, the domain service is defined with a completely different namespace than the atomic service uses. Second, we believe it is both better and necessary to differentiate between the customers' first and last names, whereas the CRM application just uses a single name field to capture this information. Now the CRM domain service will allow the caller to query for customer records by first name or last name, additional functionality that is not provided out of the box by the CRM atomic service.

Of course, the implementation for this query logic must reside somewhere, and the most likely spot for it is in the implementation of the customer domain service. If the caller wants to search for all customers with a *last* name of George, then the customer domain service that implements that call would call the CRM atomic service, passing in George as the search query name. At this point, we will assume that the CRM system at least formats the customers' names to <LastName>, <FirstName>, which will allow us to differentiate between the first and last names, even though they are stored in a single field. Naturally, the CRM application would return customer records with the first name of George also, and it would be the responsibility of the customer domain service to ignore the customer records with the first name of George and to pass back to the caller only the records where the last name matches the search criteria.

Similar changes are made to the accounting domain service. as shown in Figure 13-9. Not only does the accounting domain use a different namespace, but we have also changed the one of the enumeration values in the AccountStatus from OPEN to ACTIVE.

What we are demonstrating here is the ability to add significant abstraction over the underlying atomic services and applications, and provide a more business-oriented service infrastructure. By necessity, our examples are simple so they remain clear. In your own enterprise, you will go far beyond these simple examples.

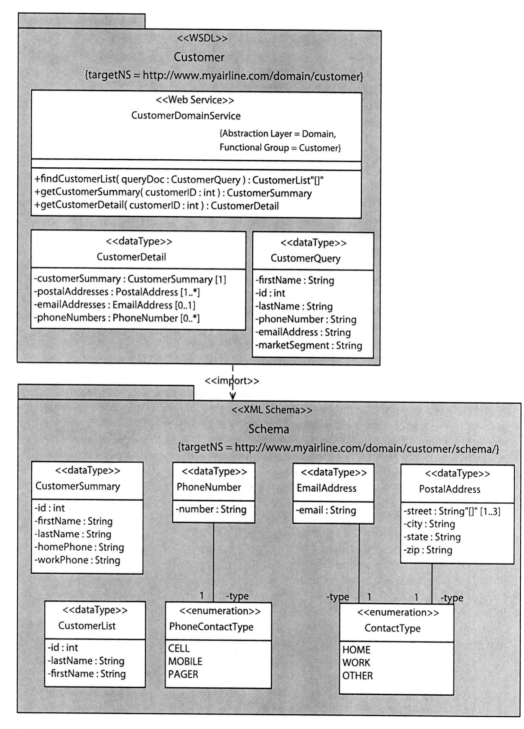

Figure 13-8. *The customer domain service definition*

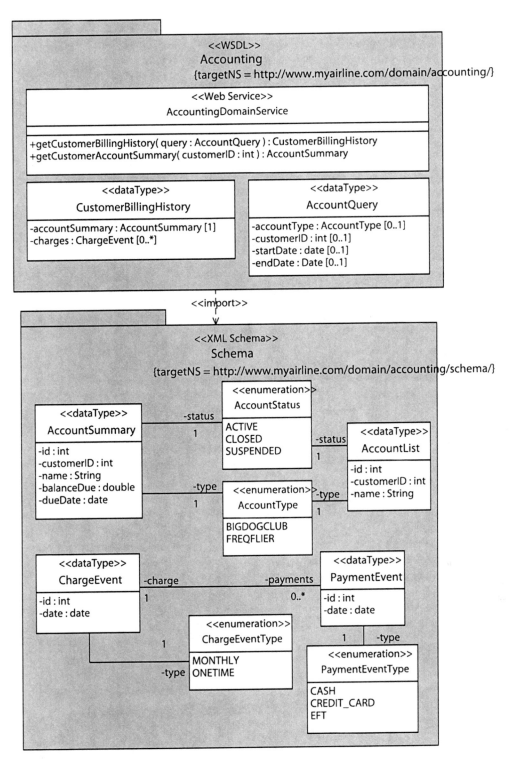

Figure 13-9. *The accounting domain service definition*

Creating the Enterprise Service

Our last step in this initial exercise is to create the enterprise-level service that will realize the entire business requirement. This definition is shown in Figure 13-10.

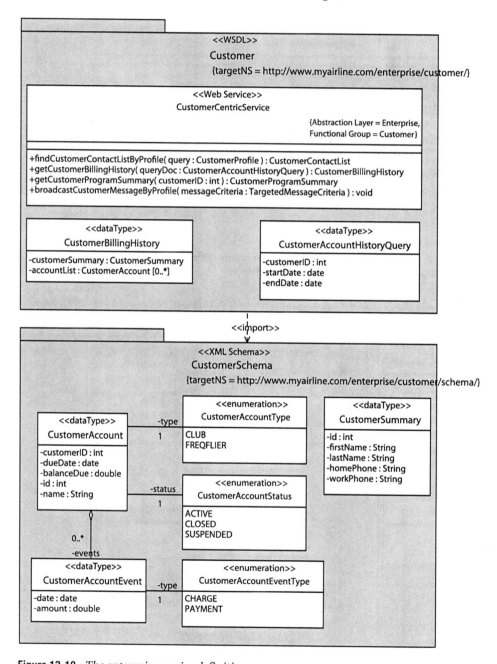

Figure 13-10. *The enterprise service definition*

In the enterprise service, we need to differentiate between customer accounts and other types of accounts. Therefore, we name our entity `CustomerAccount` and make similar changes to the supporting entity and enumerations. You will also notice that our entity model for account information does not directly reflect the entity models of the lower-level domain services. Specifically, we have merged the accounting domain entities of `ChargeEvent` and `PaymentEvent` into a single `CustomerAccountEvent`. This makes more sense to us at the enterprise level. We have also changed one of the literals in the `CustomerAccountType` enumeration from `BIGDOGCLUB` to simply `CLUB`. It is conceivable that the company may change the name of the club, and it's rarely a good idea to have enumeration literals reflect application-specific names.

Now we can take a look at how the customer self-serve portal would make use of this new service, and see the sequence of service calls that support the overall enterprise service. Figure 13-11 shows a sequence diagram with the call order. Transformations of message formats are needed at each level to account for the minor changes in message format and the complete change in namespaces.

From Figure 13-11, you can see how the complexity of the service realization is completely hidden from the portlet that initiates the call. If we make changes to the supporting applications, we have plenty of room to adapt to those changes without affecting the enterprise service definition or the calling portlet.

Also, while you can see that we started this exercise from the bottom up, by defining the atomic services first, there is nothing stopping your development teams from working in parallel. SOA and service landscape work very well with a "design by contract" approach. One developer can work on the atomic services, while another developer works on the domain services, and yet another developer works on the enterprise service. Once you have defined your service map (Figure 13-3, discussed later), defining the contracts between the various supporting services becomes easier and allows your developers to work in parallel.

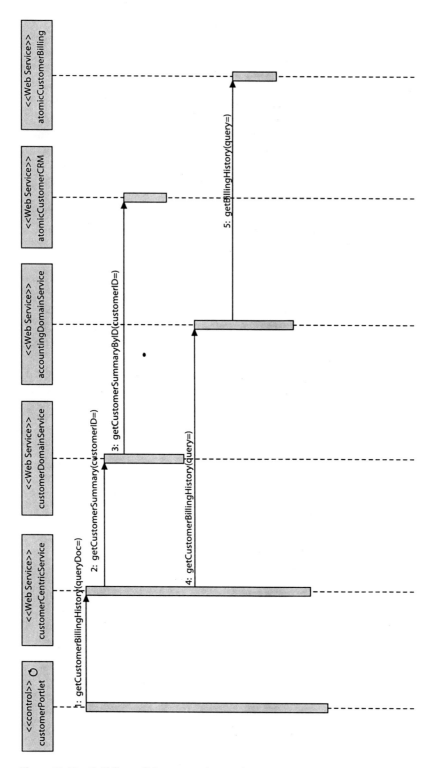

Figure 13-11. *Call flow of the enterprise service*

The Second Project

Our first serious project using the service landscape methodology has been a success. The overall project took a bit of time because we needed to build new infrastructure everywhere. Also, while we did develop an enterprise service that provides value to the enterprise relatively quickly, we don't have any service reuse. This is the nature of SOA. Your first project won't be completed any faster than your non-SOA projects, simply because you must create all of the supporting services. In fact, you first project will take a little longer than normal, because your developers and architects are learning new skills while they develop the first project.

For our second project, we want to provide new business functionality that will leverage our existing service infrastructure and build on top of it. The airline wants to allow customers, through the public portal, to see their frequent-flier miles. At the same time, the marketing department would like to be able to send out promotional e-mail to all members in good standing of the Big Dog Club. Furthermore, they want to be able to send promotional e-mail to all customers who fit one or more of the market segments defined by the current CRM application. We want to provide this functionality using SOA and service landscape principles in order to help us better manage changes to these functional requirements and our IT infrastructure over the coming years.

The First Requirement

Once again, we begin by creating a service map for the business requirement. Our first requirement for this project is as follows:

> *We want to allow customers to be able to see their frequent-flier miles.*

At this point, your service designer "radar" ought to be buzzing. The business has made a request to see something from a specific application. However, isn't it very likely that once we allow the customer to see their frequent-flier status, they will also want to be able to see the status of other programs they are involved in? Specifically, wouldn't they like to see information about their status in the Big Dog Club? If we later introduce a new program, won't the business want the customers to see their status in the new program as well? You're darned right they will! Therefore, we need to design an enterprise service that shows the status of the customers for any/all programs in which they are involved.

So our enterprise-level operation won't be called getCustomerFreqFlierStatus. Instead, we are going to start with a higher level of abstraction, getCustomerProgramSummary. It will have the ability to report on the customer status in each program. Part of that status information will also include customer billing status. The getCustomerProgramSummary operation is represented on the service map as service 1, as shown in Figure 13-12.

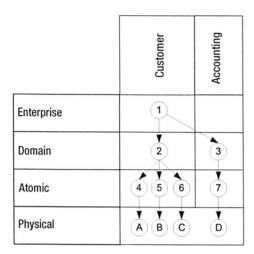

Figure 13-12. *Service map for retrieving the customer status*

We know that the only programs we currently have in operation are the frequent-flier program and the Big Dog Club. Those programs are categorized in the customer domain (service 2 in the service map). The account/billing information is represented by the accounting domain (service 3). The customer domain service is going to need to interact with the CRM, FreqFlier, and BigDogClub applications (applications A, B, and C) through their atomic services (4, 5, and 6, respectively).

Creating the Enterprise Operation

Let's start at the top this time and work our way down the service map. We know that the enterprise level needs an operation called getCustomerProgramSummary(). This operation will need to get customer program participation information from the customer domain (service 2), and current billing information from the accounting domain (service 3). Service 2 will be implemented with a new operation called getCustomerProgramSummary(), just like the enterprise-level service. However, on the accounting side, we are going to use the getCustomerAccountSummary() operation. This isn't true reuse, since we created the getCustomerAccountSummary() operation in the first project but never used it. However, in this second project, we get all of the development speed benefits from using this existing service simply because we don't need to create it.

The domain-level getCustomerProgramSummary() operation that we'll create needs to aggregate the results from calls into the CRM, FreqFlier, and BigDogClub atomic services and return the results to the enterprise-level service. The enterprise-level service will then be responsible for rationalizing the results from the two domain services (that is, figuring out which account summary goes with which program summary).

Figure 13-13 shows the changes we need to make to the enterprise CustomerCentricService. To support the single new operation, we are going to reuse the CustomerSummary data type by returning it as part of the new CustomerProgramSummary data type. We will also add a ProgramSummary type, which will simply wrap a CustomerLoungeProgram or a FrequentFlierProgram data type.

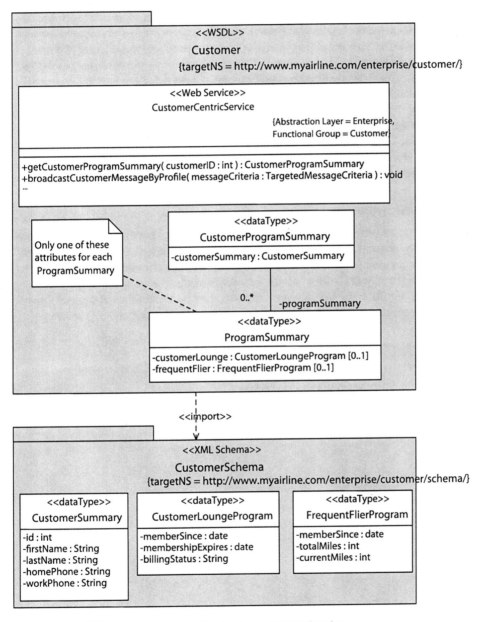

Figure 13-13. *Additions to the enterprise CustomerCentricService*

Does that last sentence concern you? It looks like we are taking application-specific information and data structures and applying them at the enterprise level. That must violate the abstraction principles we have been working toward, right?

The answer is no, it does not violate the abstraction principles. The programs CustomerLoungeProgram and FrequentFlierProgram are both enterprise-level *concepts* when they are modeled here. The information they represent is of interest to the business. Even if we were to rewrite the BigDogClub and FreqFlier applications or replace them both completely with a commercial software package, the business still needs those business concepts and related services to exist somewhere in the enterprise. They are part of our company's service offering to our customers. This is why we have used more generic "business-oriented" names in the enterprise-level schema and have not used the application-specific names.

The data model shown in Figure 13-13 is fine for our purposes. Our airline has only two programs in use at the moment, and we cannot reasonably predict the addition of too many more programs or services that we will offer to the customer. If the company does add one or two more programs, we would just extend the existing model. Companies that provide dozens or more services, or even just a few services that are short-lived, would want to design a different schema to support their specific needs.

Creating the Domain Operations

Next we come to the customer domain service definition. We need to define the program concept in the domain schema here also. As you can see in Figure 13-14, the design approach for handling various customer programs does not differ between the domain and enterprise levels. However, the domain level "knows" about the two programs the company currently has: FreqFlier and BigDogClub. The domain level invokes the atomic services of each of those applications and transforms the return results into the application-neutral ProgramSummary schema.

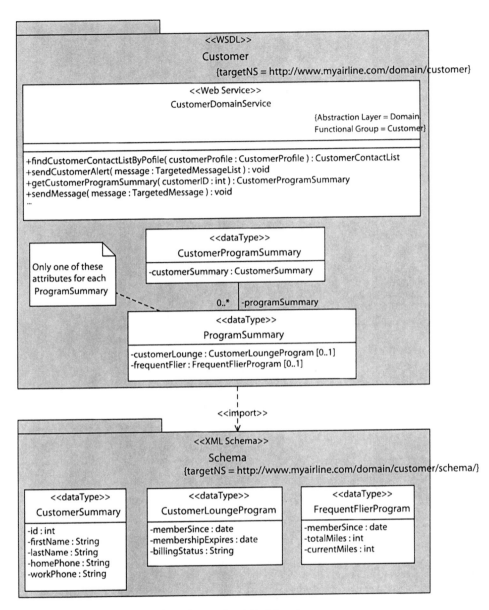

Figure 13-14. *The customer domain service definition changes*

Creating the Atomic Operations

As shown in Figure 13-15, the FreqFlier atomic service is deliberately simple for our example. The bulk of the information that is important to the caller is precalculated from the set of FlightEvent records associated with the FreqFlierID. We don't model how credit card offers and hotel stays may also affect the overall availableMiles for the customer, but it doesn't take a lot of imagination to see how that type of information could be incorporated into the application.

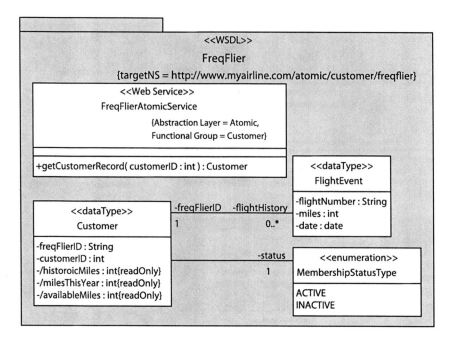

Figure 13-15. *The FreqFlier atomic service definition*

Lastly, we need to define the atomic services for the BigDogClub application. Figure 13-16 shows the very simple atomic service definition. It has a single operation that takes the customerID as an argument and returns the appropriate Client record.

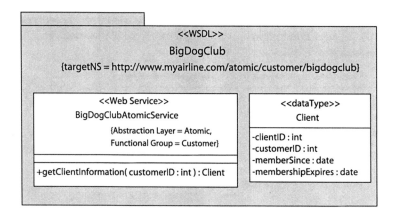

Figure 13-16. *The BigDogClub atomic service definition*

Let's see how all of this works together in a sequence diagram. Figure 13-17 shows the service invocation flow in detail. From reviewing the flow, it should be obvious how the various services and schemas are transformed as the information moves between abstraction levels.

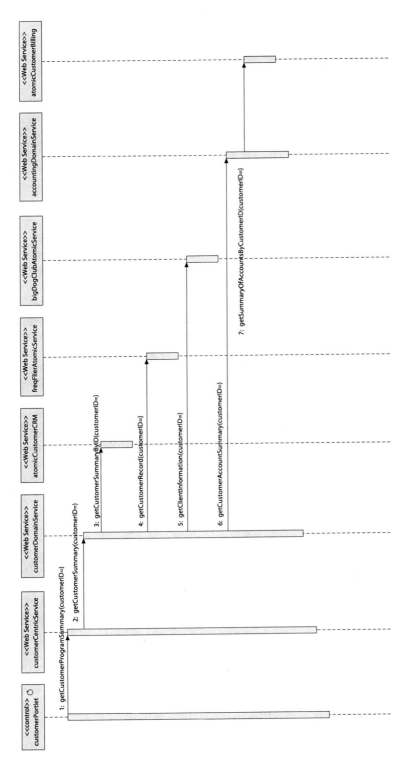

Figure 13-17. *The service call flow*

You can see how each service invocation has the opportunity to translate the messages into the format required by the lower-level service interfaces. Note that operations 3, 4, and 5 all require the `customerID` value as an argument. Those three operations are great candidates for running in parallel when invoked by the `CustomerDomainService`.

The Second Requirement

Now we're ready to tackle the second business requirement:

> *We want to be able to send promotional e-mail to all customers who fit one or more of the market segments defined by the current CRM application. However, the customer must be able to opt out of receiving our promotional e-mail.*

Once again, is your designer radar buzzing? Sure, the marketing department wants to be able to e-mail customers in a specific market segment. Isn't it likely that the company will want to e-mail customers that fit any kind of profile? Perhaps we will want to e-mail all customers in the frequent-flier program or who belong to the Big Dog Club also? Once again, we need to plan for the future a bit when we create our service map for this requirement. Going one step further, it's entirely reasonable that marketing may want to be able to contact customers using technologies other than e-mail. Why not include text messages to mobile phones or even generate automated phone calls to customers?

We also need to allow the customer to opt out of receiving e-mail containing promotional materials. Some people don't want companies to market to them through e-mail, and we must design for this contingency.

It's easy to go overboard when defining new functionality, but in this case, we know that our competitors are allowing their customers to sign up for updates on flight information through e-mail, text messages, and automated phone calls. We know that we need to do the same to be competitive. However, for this project, we don't have the time or the money to implement all of those contact methods. That's okay. We can still design a service framework that will support the expanded functionality in the future with minimal changes.

Creating the Enterprise Operations

The service operation at the enterprise level should not be `emailCustomer` or something that specific. Instead, we need to step back a moment and think about what we are trying to do.

What the marketing department really wants to do is to contact a specific subset of customers that match some arbitrary criteria and send to that subset of customers a targeted message. You can bet that marketing will also want that message personalized (for example, to use the individual customer's name and other customer-specific information in the message). If we incorporate the ability to send flight information to customers who have signed up for receiving that information, it becomes clearer that what we are really doing here is sending alerts to customers who match a specific profile. With this information in mind, we can better visualize the enterprise-level operation: broadcastCustomerMessageByProfile. We can safely assume that this will be an asynchronous operation also, since sending messages to potentially thousands of customers is going to be a time-consuming task. Now that we have a high-level understanding of the service operation we are going to create, let's flesh out the rest of the service map, as shown in Figure 13-18.

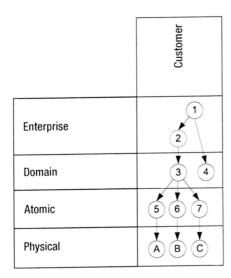

Figure 13-18. *The service map for the second requirement*

The broadcastCustomerMessageByProfile operation (operation 1 on the service map) performs several distinct steps. First it needs to find customers based on some search criteria. If you examine Figure 13-19, you will see how we model this search criteria at the enterprise level. We create a TargetedMessageCriteria data type that contains the CustomerProfile and ProgramProfile types. This allows us to search for customers based on core customer attributes (last name, e-mail address, and so on) and/or by the programs in which they participate (currently, frequent-flier and/or Big Dog Club) or even by a flight number. We anticipate our customers being able to sign up for notification when their flights are delayed, so we need to select them by flight number also.

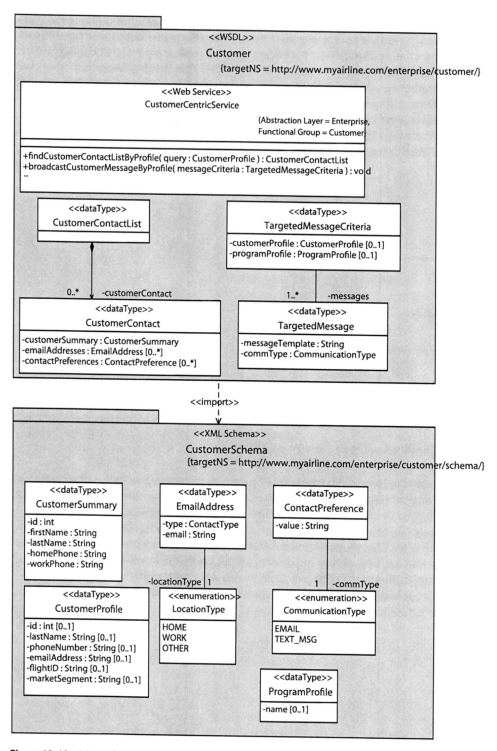

Figure 13-19. *More changes to the enterprise level*

One thing to note in Figure 13-18 is that service operation 2 has a dashed line around it. We use this notation to show that the operation is private to the `CustomerCentricService` in the enterprise level. We introduced the concept of operation visibility in Chapter 12. Just like methods in Java or C++, service operations can be defined as having public, private, or protected visibility. This concept does not exist in WSDL, but it is a necessary concept for SOA governance and enterprise architecture. Just because a service has an operation defined does not mean that you intend for that operation to be called from outside the service or abstraction level.

Operation 2 on the service map is `findCustomerContactListByProfile`. It will return a list of customers and their contact information, including the newly added `ContactPreference` and `CommunicationType` data types in the `CustomerCentricService` schema. This method takes care of retrieving a list of customers who meet the specified search criteria. In a moment, you will see that this operation is really just a lightweight proxy for the `findCustomerContactListByProfile` operation in the `CustomerDomainService`. We have taken a liberty here and separated this search functionality from the parent `broadcastCustomerMessageByProfile` function. We did this because we believe that this searching capability will be used by other operations within the enterprise level. Also, in the foreseeable future, we may want to expand the search capability to include information from functional categories other than customer. For example, it's quite conceivable that we may want to search for customers whose account information fits a certain profile. For these reasons, it makes sense to create this search capability as a private operation in the enterprise level.

Once the `broadcastCustomerMessageByProfile` operation gets the search results, it invokes the `sendCustomerAlert` operation in the `CustomerDomainService`. The `sendCustomerAlert` operation takes care of formatting the individual messages and sending them out via e-mail.

Since OSB can send e-mail messages, we have designed this service map to use OSB's e-mail capability. However, if we were to later expand this service to also send SMS messages to cell phones, we would most likely amend the service map to add the atomic (if we write the service) or physical service for SMS messages, and then provide a domain service that wraps those atomic services appropriately. But which functional category would the SMS and voice message services belong to?

There are two main schools of thought on this subject. The first is that we are communicating with customers, so those services should belong to the customer functional category. The second school argues that sending e-mail messages or making phone calls does not strictly apply to customers, but may also be used with partners and suppliers. This line of thought leads to adding a new functional category to the service landscape, one with the name infrastructure or miscellaneous, to act as a catch-all for every bit of additional functionality.

Additionally, a third approach exists. Keep in mind that applications themselves rarely fit nicely into the functional category concept. We may have built an SMS messaging application in-house, or more likely, we are using external services to handle the SMS and voice messaging. Companies like StrikeIron offer both of these services. If we wanted to be able to access that functionality from different domains, we could easily put atomic services in each domain that needs to access the functionality. However, duplicating the atomic services is redundant and adds maintenance overhead whenever the service interface changes. Bear in mind that all of service landscaping is taxonomy for services. There is nothing stopping us from categorizing an atomic service as belonging to both the customer and partner functional categories. In Figure 13-20, we represent the external SMS and voice services in the physical level as applications D and E. We can then publish atomic services that represent applications D and E in both the customer and partner domains. Of course, we could repeat this pattern for every domain that needs to access functionality specific to those applications.

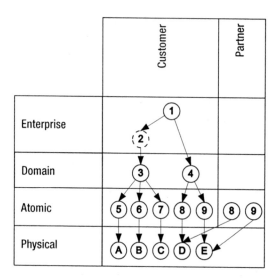

Figure 13-20. *Modifying the service map to add the SMS and voice-messaging capability*

There is a trade-off here. If you categorize the same atomic services in multiple functional categories, you save development and maintenance time, but you run the risk of complicating the tree of service relationships that the service landscape approach strives to simplify. A slightly modified solution to this problem would be to define two new services, 10 and 11, and distinct atomic services that replace services 8 and 9 in the atomic level of the partner category, and manage them separately from atomic services 8 and 9 in the customer category.

At first blush, it may seem redundant to create several copies of the same atomic services in each domain, and there is validity to that argument. However, consider for a moment the amount of development time and effort it would take to create an atomic service to represent an external service, such as our SMS and voice-messaging services. First, we would register a business service in OSB that represents the external services, then we create a proxy service that directly represents the business service, and we are finished. The entire process would take minutes. As with all engineering trade-offs, you need to make the right choice for your particular situation.

Creating the Domain Operations

The customer domain service operations for the service map shown in Figure 13-18 are relatively straightforward. Operation 3 (findCustomerContactListByProfile) performs a search for customers who meet the specified criteria. Service operation 4 (sendCustomerAlert) is responsible for sending out the e-mail messages. It does not call any other services (yet). The pertinent operations and data types are shown in Figure 13-21.

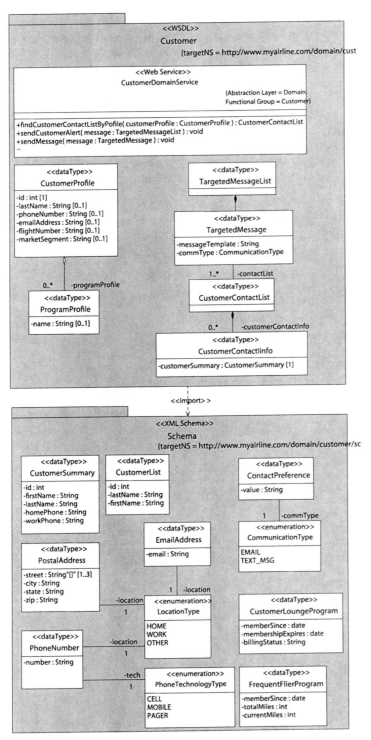

Figure 13-21. *Customer domain service operations to support the second requirement*

Creating the Atomic Operations

The bulk of the work for this project occurs in the CRM application and its atomic services. We need to add the capability to track customer preferences regarding how we contact them. This takes the form of the CustomerAlert data type and related functionality. The CustomerAlert data type allows customers to specify how they want to be contacted with promotional e-mail. If a CustomerAlert record exists for a customer, it means that customer has opted to receive promotional e-mail messages. If no record exists, the customer has opted out and does not wish to receive any e-mail messages.

Figure 13-22 shows enumerations for the TechnologyType and the AlertType. We've added the SMS TechnologyType and FLIGHT AlertType, which we will cover shortly, in the "Adding a New Capability" section.

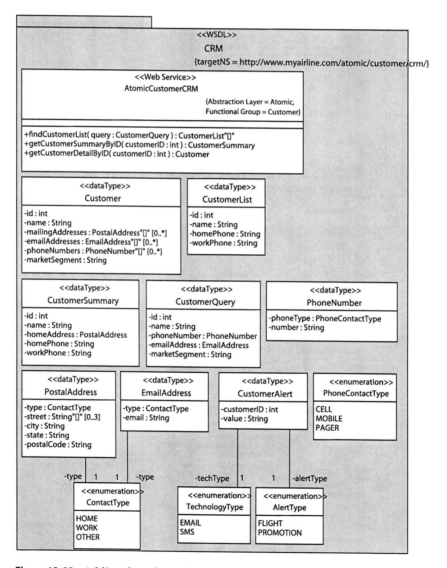

Figure 13-22. *Adding the rules to the CRM application*

Lastly, keep in mind that the value field of the `CustomerAlert` contains the e-mail address where the customers wish to receive their messages, which may be different from the e-mail address in the customer records in the CRM system.

Correlating Searches

These services are returning a lot of information. The customer domain service will make queries to the CRM, BigDog, and FreqFlier systems. It then must correlate the results from these three different service calls into the `CustomerContactList` return type. You may want to keep the searches simple at first, allowing the searcher to perform queries on a single data point only.

Imagine trying to perform a more complex query, such as to find all customers in the frequent-flier program who live in Texas. Now you need to add some additional logic into the system to correlate the search results from various systems and rationalize them into a single result set. That's a heck of a lot of work. It requires you to build a fair bit of logic and functionality that approximates a query engine.

You can do this type of work with OSB, but it involves writing a significant amount of XQuery or XSLT code. It's much faster and easier to use a query engine that is designed specifically for the task of rationalizing related data. Oracle provides just such a tool, known as BEA AquaLogic Data Services Platform (ALDSP). ALDSP is designed to query databases, flat files, and web services. It provides an easy-to-use interface for mapping disparate results into a single, rational format.

If you employed a query engine like ALDSP, you would use it to create a domain-level service that either invokes the atomic services directly or bypasses those atomic services and connects directly to the databases that support those applications—or perhaps a hybrid of those two approaches.

Adding a New Capability

Because of the work that we have done so far, we are just a short step from adding a new capability to our project: the ability to notify customers if their flight is going to be delayed or changed. The bulk of the infrastructure is already in place. We just need to add a new enumeration type to the `AlertType` in our CRM application (see Figure 13-22) and modify the user interface to allow the users to choose "flight" as a topic for their alerts.

We also can add the ability to send SMS messages in addition to e-mail messages. We do this by modifying the `TechnologyType` enumeration in Figure 13-22 to include the SMS option. Again, we need to make some minor changes to the customer portal to allow the customers to specify the technology type(s) they want to use for the alert.

If we add SMS as a delivery option, we must find a way to send SMS messages (OSB does not support SMS out of the box). Of course, we can always code this functionality ourselves, but that takes time and testing. Another option would be to use an external service provider, like StrikeIron, to handle the technical parts of the service for us. This has the advantage of being immediately available (that is, we don't need to write the SMS messaging service), which will save us time and money.

How would you categorize the SMS service provided by StrikeIron? It is a web service, and we're pretty sure there is some application sitting behind that service. Does that make the StrikeIron service an atomic service?

The fact that the SMS service provided by StrikeIron is maintained by StrikeIron and completely out of our control means that the SMS service really belongs in the physical level of the service landscape. Just because it is a web service doesn't mean it belongs in the atomic level or domain level.

Furthermore, it would be perfectly acceptable for the domain level to call the SMS service directly. There is no concrete need to write an atomic service over the external SMS service in the physical level. However, there is a good argument for writing an atomic service "wrapper" for the StrikeIron SMS service (and other external services). Like many external service providers, StrikeIron requires that you pass in some authentication information with your service call. That is low-level, detailed information that we don't necessarily want our domain service to need to provide. If we put that kind of information in our domain service, we're hard-coding the domain to this vendor-specific service, and that works against our overall agility goals. Since the StrikeIron SMS service will take bulk messages, it will execute relatively quickly, and creating an atomic level wrapper over it will not add noticeable overhead.

Figure 13-23 shows a sequence diagram of our service map, with the SMS capability included. Note that each type of search is represented as an option in the diagram. This is done to show that we are supporting only simple queries based on a single data point: market segment or program participation, for example.

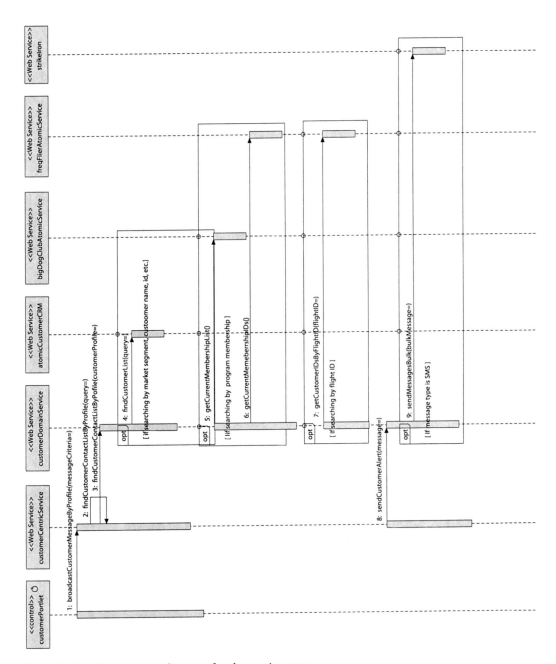

Figure 13-23. *The sequence diagram for the service map*

Summary

We went into a lot of detail in this chapter. The intent was to show, unambiguously, how to go about implementing IT systems using the service landscape approach. As you can see from our work in this chapter, the service landscape methodology, plus good designer "radar," will help you to work beyond fine-grained requirements and to achieve the flexibility that your company wants from the IT department.

We hope that you have learned the basic steps of implementing the service landscape approach. It's not hard or tricky. It does not require super-human intelligence or an army of specialists. It is a straightforward approach to managing IT capabilities and the changes that inevitably occur to the software applications that provide those capabilities.

CHAPTER 14

■■■

Versioning Services

Change is inevitable. That's a basic fact of life, and SOA doesn't change that. SOA promises to make your company and IT systems more tolerant of change—more agile. You need to do your part by understanding the different types of changes that can occur, and then developing and enforcing governance policies to manage changes in your services. Managing change is not just a technology problem; it's also a governance problem that requires the full participation of the people responsible for SOA governance.

Tools do play a role in governing the *service life cycle* of services. Your particular strategy will be influenced by the tools you have available to manage changes to services. For example, if you're writing web services without using OSB, or any other tools, you might opt to track your services using a simple text document. That's not a very robust solution, but it's perfectly acceptable, especially when you have a small number of services. At the other end of the tooling spectrum, if you have a service registry or service repository, you would want to leverage the capabilities of those tools to track different versions of the same service and dependencies between services, and allow the service client either to specify the specific service characteristics it's looking for or allow developers to reliably discover the most recent version of the service.

However, not everyone has a service registry or service repository. Because you're reading this book, it's a pretty safe bet that you *do* have OSB. Therefore, we'll focus on scenarios that leverage OSB.

Before we jump into strategies for managing changes in your service offerings, we need to spend a little time explaining what we mean by "change" when it comes to services. People often jump directly to various versioning strategies without first understanding the problem space. By understanding the basic principles of the service life cycle, you'll be able to apply that knowledge to any supporting tool set that you might use, whether it's OSB or a service registry or repository. Let's start at the beginning.

What Is a Service?

Let's step back from the technical world of web services for a moment and take some time to clarify our definition of a service. We'll examine some of the services we use on a daily basis: real-world services that can help us to define the term *service*. This discussion will yield three principles that apply to all types of services. We'll then be able to use these principles as guidance when we look at web services specifically.

One service that we use every day is an electrical service. Here in the United States, residential electrical service comes in two forms: 110-volt AC and 220-volt AC. Ninety-five percent of the appliances in our homes use the 110-volt service, while only a select few use the 220-volt service (primarily electric stoves and some electric water heaters and clothes dryers). The actual voltage that's delivered to a US home varies somewhat. The 110-volt service can be between 105 and 120 volts, depending on local conditions. Controlling this variation in voltage is part of the quality of service that the electric company promises in its contracts. Both 110-volt and 220-volt services have standard interfaces (that is, the plugs and sockets) that are incompatible. You cannot plug a 110-volt device into a 220-volt receptacle unless you (as the service client) break your agreement with the electrical provider (and state and federal laws) and alter the 110-volt plug to connect to the 220-volt plug somehow. Because 220-volt service is deadly to human beings, those foolish enough to attempt such a feat are rarely allowed the opportunity to reproduce.

Telephones represent another commonly used service type. You can buy a telephone from virtually any phone producer, plug it into the phone receptacle in your home, and it will work just fine. Again, the phone service defines a standard physical interface (the RJ-11 phone jack) combined with standardized transport protocol (tone dialing and analog signals) to deliver the service to your home and the local telephone device that you've chosen to use.

Another real-world service is a postal service. If you follow the defined protocol for how a postal address is formatted (street, city, state, and ZIP code) and the placement of the addresses (sender's address in the top-left corner, recipient's address in the middle), and apply the correct postage, you can send a letter or package with a high level of confidence that it will reach the intended recipient. The postal service even provides error-handling mechanisms in case something goes wrong. For example, if the recipient is no longer at the address, the current person at the address can simply write "return to sender" on the package, and the postal service will return it to the sender.

We could go on with this list for a long time. You receive service at restaurants, bookstores, car dealerships, home contractors, public transit organizations, airlines and their reservation desks, and so on. We all know what a service is, yet for some reason, when we think specifically of web services and SOA, the definition of a service begins to get complex. Throw that thought out of your head.

Services really are simple. The implementations behind the services are often complex; they are supposed to be complicated. A large part of the benefit of any service is hiding the complexity from the service consumer. When we order a meal at a restaurant, we want to pay money to receive food. It's that simple. We don't want to know about the difficulties involved with running a restaurant. We don't want to know about labor laws or the tax code. We don't want to know about the highly complex supply chain that reliably provides the materials for our meal to the restaurant. We pay for simplicity. Don't lose sight of the simplicity; it is the key to your success in this area.

From this position, we can draw a conclusion about a general service concept that will provide value to us in the web services world: *implementation is unimportant to the service consumer.* When we purchase a meal at a restaurant, we don't care how they create the meal, as long as the meal meets our expectations. If we order a steak cooked rare with a baked potato, and they deliver a Happy Meal, they have not met our expectations. Similarly, if they deliver the items, but they aren't prepared as ordered (perhaps the steak is overcooked), the restaurant has not met our expectations for the service. If they deliver what we ordered, cooked the way we ordered it, then we don't really care *how* they did it. In fact, we probably don't have any way to know the details of the preparation of the food, or who supplied the raw food materials. So, we come to our first rule of services:

Implementation is not part of the service.

Obviously, implementation is important to delivering a service, but implementation resides purely in the domain of the service provider. The service consumer should be completely ignorant of the implementation. The minute you break this rule, you begin creating tightly coupled systems. Continuing the food service analogy, if we asked for meat from a specific ranch and a potato from a specific farm, the restaurant might well refuse our request. If it was willing and able to comply, it might need to charge us extra to cover its additional costs to meet our expectations. Furthermore, we could not go to any other restaurant and have any hope of it being able to meet those same expectations when we walk through the door. By placing constraints on the implementation of a service, we have tightly coupled ourselves to that particular restaurant/service.

Based on what we've learned so far, we can draw another conclusion and derive our second rule of services:

Everything that requires client knowledge is part of the service.

What should a client know about a service? Well, the client ought to know what services the service provider makes available. You can't order a rare steak and baked potato at McDonald's and reasonably expect to get it. Therefore, services must be published or somehow be made available to potential service consumers. Next, client expectations must be met. Back at our restaurant, if we order a rare steak and baked potato but our meal is served cold, the restaurant has failed to meet our expectations. Similarly, if we order ice cream, we expect it to be cold and in the form of a solid or semisolid mass. Bring us a bowl of melted ice cream and there will be trouble.

Meeting client expectations is a fundamental part of any service. Therefore, a service must be defined by an agreement between the service provider and a service consumer (also known as the *client*). The agreement covers both what will be delivered and how it will be delivered. For example, we know we'll get a rare steak with a baked potato at temperatures that both meet our need for warmth and meet federal requirements for sanitation (that is, cooked at 160+ degrees to kill any organisms on the meat). Furthermore, we know how it will be delivered to us: the server will pick it up in the kitchen and deliver it to our table, and will perform this task in a "reasonable" amount of time. Therefore, we can derive our third principle:

Services are governed by contracts.

Contracts define what the service does and how the service is delivered to the client, along with any time constraints on either the service provider or the service client. Contracts are really the star of the services show. A contract governs a service. This includes the intent of the service, operations and faults, semantics, invocation style, policies, quality of service, security, timeliness, and pre/post conditions. The contract also defines how the service is delivered, including the transport protocol (HTTP, JMS, and so on), the wire protocol (SOAP), and the invocation model (synchronous or asynchronous).

■Note Do not confuse the *contract* with the *WSDL*. A WSDL file is a contract, but the current specification of a WSDL file doesn't address many of the characteristics that also belong in a contract. When we use the term *contract* in this chapter, we mean a contract as used in our three principles, not just a WSDL file.

Let's take a look at the electrical service for a second. You move into a new house and you call the electric company and order service for your home. Imagine your surprise when an electrical technician appears on your doorstep with a truckload of batteries! Your expectation was that the service would be delivered over the existing wiring, not through some device that would take up half of your basement. Also, when you ordered electrical service, you specified when you wanted the service activated (it's dangerous to move furniture in the dark). If you ask for service to begin on the first of the month, you certainly expect those lights to come on when you flip the switch. Similarly, once the service is activated, you expect it to stay activated, barring some unusual circumstance, such as a severe storm. Timeliness is an important attribute of services.

Additionally, a service contract may define what happens if the service fails to meet your expectations for whatever reason. In the case of the electrical service, you might be compensated for a service outage if the service provider makes a mistake of some sort, whereas events that qualify as "acts of God" always exempt the service provider from any culpability.

To recap, here are our three principles of services:

- Implementation is not part of the service.

- Everything that requires client knowledge is part of the service.

- Services are governed by contracts. Contracts define what the service does and how and when the service will be delivered.

At this point, we can define a service as follows:

A service is a facility that provides the client with some benefit, such as food or electricity, or some capability, such as communication or access to information. Services act on behalf of the client, allowing the client to give commands through the service interface while being protected from the implementation details.

That's what a service is. It is simple. It is something that human beings understand with ease.

Now that you know what a service is, it's time to look at service orientation and what it means to you.

Service Orientation

If you think about it, a well-designed web service is object-oriented by nature. A well-designed service *acts* on behalf of the service client. We see this principle on object-oriented systems all the time. Poorly designed services often arise because they weren't implemented using object-oriented principles. For example, let's look at a poorly implemented service that doesn't follow good object-oriented design practices, illustrated in Figure 14-1.

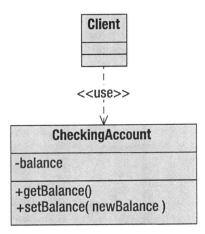

Figure 14-1. *An example of poor service design*

In this example, you can see that there's little encapsulation of the implementation details from the client. The client can see the balance in his checking account, which is a good thing, and can set the balance in his checking account, which may be a bad thing. The client can simply ignore the current balance and send through a command to set a new balance to some astronomical number. Instead of acting on behalf of the client, this kind of design places all the required business logic on the client. Remember our earlier discussion about the restaurant? Part of the reason we pay money is because the restaurant hides all the complexity of food preparation from us. We ask the restaurant to give us a meal and it does. That kind of simplicity should also exist in your services. Let's take another crack at this design and see if we can improve it. Figure 14-2 shows the modifications.

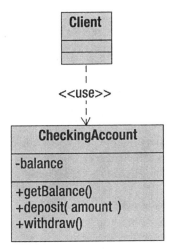

Figure 14-2. *An improved service design*

In this second version, you see how the system provides a service to the client. The client acts on the service by interacting with the service using operations that insulate the client from the necessary implementation logic. The `CheckingAccount` service takes action on behalf of the client, allowing the client to deposit money, withdraw money, and check his balance. All the logic regarding withdrawing more than is available can now be encapsulated within the `CheckingAccount`, where it should be. The service also provides commands that make sense (`withdraw` and `deposit` instead of `setBalance`) for the service.

Once you get comfortable with designing services, you'll see that many of the object-oriented design skills apply equally well to service orientation. In fact, we would go so far as to say that if your object-oriented design skills are good, then your service design skills will be just as good. Service orientation is simply object orientation at the enterprise level.

What Is Versioning?

Versioning arose from source code control (SCC) systems as a mechanism for controlling change within the many files that comprise a software application. The value of an SCC system is the ability to "go back in time" to an earlier version of a single file or a group of files. You usually go back to previous versions to figure out what you messed up in the current version. "That code was working fine in the last version" is usually the first thing a developer says before he uses the SCC system to get a previous version of the code and compare files using a "differencing" tool.

SCC systems are also great tools for team development, helping to keep all the developers on a development team in sync with the correct versions of the source code files. This became a critical feature once software programs grew so large that teams of developers were needed to complete a project. The need for SCC was further increased when development teams became geographically dispersed.

Finally, SCC systems provide the capability to archive source code, allowing corporations to protect their development investment. SCC systems are critical tools in modern software development. Through these tools, the concept of a *version* became universal in the software industry.

The concept of a version might not be specific to software development, but it certainly has a vise-like grip on the thinking of most software professionals. We commonly apply versions to our various files, both the source code and the executable code. We even apply the concept of a version where it really has no place: have you heard the term *wife 2.0*?

Remember that versioning rose to prominence as a byproduct of change-management tools. Specifically, versions are used to name a specific instance of a changing artifact, usually a file or a set of files. *Therefore, we're only concerned with defining versions for artifacts that change.* If the implementation changes, you can use SCC to manage (or at least track) those changes. As long as the change to the implementation doesn't affect the contract, the change can be managed wholly within the SCC system. Versioning still applies at this level—the implementation code.

Outside the software industry, the concept of "version" is far less prevalent. In the publishing industry, there are sometimes second and third (or more) editions of a book. Sometimes those editions contain changes beyond fixing mere typos; sometimes they're just reprints of popular books that have sold out of the previous edition, and no significant changes are included. In most industries, the mental model of the "version" isn't used. Instead, each product stands on its own. Newer products are released to replace earlier products in the same family. For example, the Lexus ES 300 was superseded by the ES 330, which in turn was superseded by the ES 350. There is a general concept of a product family and a loose concept of a version of these cars, but for all practical purposes, they are completely different, stand-alone products.

Do We Version Services or Operations?

Let's make the argument here and now that the use of a "version" to manage change in an SOA has little or no usefulness. It simply does not apply. This also explains why so many people have worked so hard and for so long to figure out a way to apply the version concept to web services, with little or no success. It's like working hard to give the ability of flight to pigs. Even if you could figure out some way to do it, you would need to ask yourself, "Does this really help anything?" The answer is "no." In the rest of this section, we intend to prove conclusively that applying the change-management approach of versioning to web services is as useful as adding wings to pigs.

We need to look at services in a new light. Just as we needed to adjust our mental models as we got our minds wrapped around procedural programming, event-driven programming, object-oriented programming, messaging, and so on, we need a new mental model for managing changes to services. If you were an expert at procedural programming and started to learn object-oriented programming, you quickly found that your procedural mental model simply was not sufficient to cope with the new concepts of object orientation. Similarly, our EJB, J2EE, C#, and .NET views of the world are insufficient to understand service orientation. As a result, we are forced to abandon these antiquated mental models and focus our energies on understanding services and how we manage them in a new way.

Changing your mental model is easier said than done. We don't profess to have all the answers here, but we do have a number of questions that will help you to begin the construction of a new mental model for service versions. These questions must not be philosophical in nature. They must be finite, pointed, and answerable. Mental models are a mechanism by which we're able to understand reality. Object orientation is a reality that has existed in this universe since the beginning. Only when we learned to construct our mental models of object orientation were we able to use object orientation as a tool.

The real point of interest for change management occurs at the contract level. There are a lot of moving parts at this level, and we must agree on what we're managing. For example, are we managing versions of the overall service, or do we want to manage changes at the service operation level? What about the data types defined in a web service? Do we care if we change a data type that is an argument to an operation? Is changing such a data type really a change to the operation? The versioning of web services appears to be a vastly complex issue.

If you examine Java, you'll see that Sun Microsystems performs coarse-grained versioning by being able to deprecate individual methods, but it tracks the version numbers at the class level. This is further enforced by most SCC systems. You may change an operation, but the version is associated with the file, not the operation. This is because SCC systems are file-oriented, with no concept of operations or methods.

■**Note** WorkSpace Studio, based on the Eclipse IDE, integrates with SCC systems to allow you to easily manage changes to your source code.

Versioning Operations

We find that when most people talk about versioning web services, what they really mean is versioning the operations of a web service.

Let's start with some basic questions. Suppose you've defined a brand-new web service with a single operation. The operation is named `getGreeting`, and it takes a string argument that contains the name of the person. The operation returns a string greeting. The UML notation for this operation would be the following:

```
public getGreeting(String name) : String
```

Obviously, because this web service is new, it's version 1.0. (We'll get into version numbers later on; bear with us for now.) Next, you decide to make a small change to this operation. You decide that the operation should take two arguments: a first name and a last name. So you redefine the operation to become the following:

```
public getGreeting(String firstName, String lastName) : String
```

Have you created a new version of the operation, or have you simply removed the old operation and created a brand-new one? The answer is important, so take a moment to think about it. Has the operation been changed or replaced?

You might argue that the operation has been changed because it has the same name as before. There's some logic to such a position. Let's test that logic a bit. At the heart of any operation is the fact that it *does* something. It might do something big, or it might do something small, but it does *something*; otherwise, you wouldn't waste your time writing the operation in the first place.

An operation is defined by what it does *and* by its name *in the context of* a service. In the first getGreeting example, the operation takes a `String` argument and returns a `String` greeting. The second getGreeting operation takes two `String` arguments and returns a `String` greeting. They are two different operations, even though they share the same name. This should be patently obvious simply from the fact that you must create and maintain each of these operations.

Now imagine that you also have a different operation defined as follows:

```
public sayHello(String name) : String
```

It turns out that the sayHello operation does the exact same thing as the getGreeting operation does. Would you say that the sayHello operation is a different version of the getGreeting operation, or a different operation that performs the same function? Naturally, you would say that the sayHello operation was a different operation, even though the operations perform the same function. The two operations are simply redundant. They are not different versions of each other.

So, you can safely conclude that the name of the operation itself is incidental and doesn't define the operation in a meaningful way, at least with regard to versions. Therefore, naming strategies such as getGreetingV1(String name) and getGreetingV2(String firstName, String lastName) are exercises in futility and shouldn't be pursued as realistic strategies.

Similarly, the argument that "operation names are important in the context of the overall service" is equally specious. If names don't sufficiently represent operational relationships within a service definition (WSDL), then they surely cannot represent those relationships across different service definitions.

Let's go back to the restaurant analogy. A restaurant provides food and beverages to its customers. If we were to look at a restaurant through WSDL glasses, we might say that the operations of a restaurant, from the customer's point of view, are as follows:

```
getProducts() : ProductList
submitOrder(ProductList) : Bill
payBill(PaymentInfo) : Receipt
```

These are all operations within an overall Food service. Now let's assume that our favorite restaurant has bought the tire company next door. The owner of the newly combined restaurant/tire company believes that there's a strong market for customers who need to eat while they wait for their new tires to be installed. Unfortunately, the owner's Food service has a Product definition (the ProductList document is composed of Product objects) that is tightly coupled to food items. So, he needs a new version of the Product object that can represent both food items and tires. However, he has invested a lot of money and time in creating his current food-oriented systems and in training his staff how to use it.

"I know," he says to himself, "I'll just create a new version of Product and ProductList, along with new getProducts() and submitOrder() operations that can handle both food items and tires. I'm a genius!"

Besides being the company owner, he is also a handy software developer. He sets about creating new document types and new operations in his web service, thereby creating a new version of his service. He creates document types called NewProduct and NewProductList that can represent both his product types, and hopefully any other new products that he might choose to sell in the future. Similarly, he adds the operations submitNewOrder() and getNewProducts() to his web service.

Are submitNewOrder() and getNewProducts() newer versions of their submitOrder() and getProducts() counterparts? No, they are new operations that provide expanded service capabilities to the customers. Conceptually you might think of them as newer versions of old capabilities, but as far as WSDL and your web services server are concerned, they are entirely different operations. It's impossible to apply a version to operations without creating new operations. That leaves us with applying versions to the service itself.

Versioning Services

At first, versioning services appears to make sense, because there's a close correlation between a file and a web service. Because versioning works well with source code, it should work well with web services also. Let's continue our restaurant/tire company scenario and see how that pans out.

Selling tires is a lot like selling a meal. Customers can select the tires they want from a "menu" of tires. However, tires come in different sizes, and you don't want to sell the customer tires that are the wrong size. Furthermore, tires are usually installed onto a vehicle at the time of purchase. Meals are not installed; they are simply delivered.

At first, our restaurateur considers "overloading" the getProducts() method with a version that takes a TireSize argument, as in getProducts(TireSize): ProductList. However, he quickly realizes that WSDL 1.2 doesn't allow method overloading, so this approach is impossible. He then considers creating a getTireProductList(TireSize): TireProductList operation. Similarly, he considers creating a submitTireOrder(TireOrder) operation. Adding these two operations to his existing FoodService would work, but his gut instincts tell him it would be the wrong approach. He is mixing different concerns within his FoodService. "Tires," he reasons, "are really part of a different business domain. They have nothing to do with food." As a result, he creates a TireService to handle these automotive tasks. Once again, the concept of a version doesn't apply. The real solution is to create an entirely new service.

The versioning concept has taken a bit of a beating so far, but it's not out of the running yet. There are two other scenarios to explore; perhaps versioning will yet prove to be useful. In this next scenario, our entrepreneur expands his tire service to include oil changes. He creates a new operation in his TireService called changeOil(CarInfo). This new operation shares no information with the other operations in TireService. He implements this service quickly and continues to be a successful businessperson.

Here's the question: when he added the changeOil operation and the CarInfo data type, did he create a new version of the service? If you say "yes," can you explain why? Let's examine this in more detail.

Certainly, there are existing clients for his getTireProductList and submitTireOrder operations. If he called the older service "version 1.0" and the changed service "version 1.1," would the current service clients care? Of course the clients wouldn't care (as long as the service endpoints have not changed). As far as his current clients are concerned, they are still working with the original service. The fact that new capabilities have been added is of no concern to them.

What about the new clients—the ones who will use the new changeOil operation and possibly the older operations? Will these new clients care which "version" they're using? Again, the answer is "no." The only person who cares about this change is our business owner who is writing the implementation. He cares, as does his SCC system. Remember the rule: implementation is not part of the service. If we apply that principle here, then we can see that the "version" again doesn't apply because the clients are unaffected by the change.

That brings us to the last scenario. What happens when we make a change to an existing operation or data type in a service that *will* affect the current service clients? Is that change reason enough to introduce "versions" to your web services? To answer this question, we need to examine the effects of such a change in detail.

In this case, our business owner makes a change to the CarInfo data type, adding a required field that must be set to a specific range of values and for which there is no default. This change will affect every client of the changeOil(CarInfo) operation. Now he has a choice to make: he can either update every client of the changeOil(CarInfo) operation to submit the new version of CarInfo or he can create a new "version" of the service.

Let's start with the first option. To do this, you must know every client instance of the changeOil operation in the TireService, and you must have the capability to change them all and deploy them at the same time you deploy your modified version of the changeOil service. If you're fortunate enough to find yourself in these circumstances, then you must ask yourself, "Why would I version this service?" If you have the ability to change all the clients at the same time you change the service, what's the point of having a "version" of the service? The answer is simple. There's no reason to "version" a service under these circumstances, because the previous "version" of the service is immediately decommissioned.

Now let's turn our attention to the much more interesting second option. With this option, you don't know where all your service clients are. Similarly, even for the service clients that you do know, you might be unable to make the necessary changes to that client. Perhaps you've lost the source code, or perhaps the service client is owned and operated by a customer who refuses to upgrade her client. Either way, you're forced to continue to run the original service operation to meet your obligations with your current service client and introduce a new operation within the service that uses the new data type.

This brings us back to versioning operations. As we discussed in the previous section, you cannot "version" operations; you can only add and delete them. It turns out that the same rule applies to data types. The core question is this: does adding or deleting operations and data types within a service result in a new version of the service or a completely new service?

To begin with, our business owner cannot maintain a new "version" of the `CarInfo` data type in the same WSDL file. The newer version of `CarInfo` must reside in a different XML namespace than the current `CarInfo` data type, or its name must be changed so that there are no naming conflicts within the WSDL file. Therefore, he would end up maintaining multiple (read: different) definitions of the `CarInfo` data type. If he is adding new operations and data types to his service, then his existing service clients won't be affected by the change, and applying a versioning strategy to the service is a waste of time. If he is changing the existing operations and data types, then that affects all of his existing service clients. Those clients will need to be updated to the new service definition, which for all intents and purposes is really a version 1.0 of an entirely new service.

We argue that all this is a waste of time. The new version of `changeOil` isn't a new version at all. It's an entirely new service operation. If you treat changes to existing services as the creation of an entirely new service, the level of complexity for maintaining these services is reduced, and you won't need to engage in any operation-naming shenanigans.

You can see why there's such confusion around versioning operations or services: it's the changes to the operations (or the data types upon which the operations depend) that concern us and the service clients. However, now that you've walked through the issues in detail, you can easily answer the question we posed at the top of this section: do you version services or operations? The answer is neither!

Constrained by Reality

Despite our best wishes, the realities of web service technologies intrude upon us. First and foremost is that WSDL files are an imperfect service-expression mechanism. As a result, we're accustomed to some versioning scenarios in the traditional source code world that don't work with web services—namely, extension or inheritance. For example, take the `getGreeting(String name) : String` operation. In a traditional object-oriented language, you could add a second method with a different signature—for example, `getGreeting(String firstName, String lastName) : String`. In the object-oriented world, there's no conflict because the method signatures are different, and that's enough for the compiler to understand your intent. When you check the source code back into SCC, your source file version would change from 1.0 to 1.1 (or something similar, depending on the numbering strategy employed by the SCC system).

XSDs do have the core object-oriented concept of extension (and restriction for that matter), but they don't run on a smart compiler. Services live at service endpoints—distinct URIs that are remarkably intolerant of the simple object-oriented concept of method overloading. This has significant ramifications. It means that if you want to deploy the `getGreeting(String firstName, String lastName) : String` operation, you must define it on a different web service endpoint than the `getGreeting(String name) : String` operation.

What about the clients? The clients depend on these contracts. If you were implementing an EJB system, you would have the benefit of having a pretty good idea of who the clients are. However, in the world of SOA, it's quite likely that over time, your services will acquire clients that were completely unknown at the time that the service was created. This is another design decision point: do you try to track your service clients to help manage changes to your service landscape? If you do, you have an opportunity to notify the people who run the client applications so that they can maintain their client software as your service matures over time.

Ask yourself this: can you guarantee with absolute certainty that you will always know exactly who the clients of your services are? Amazon has a public web service that allows you to write a client that will pass an ISBN to the web service and receive the price of the book, the title, and so on. If Amazon changed that service interface, how could it possibly know how many distinct service clients are calling it? Perhaps Amazon could change the service interface, so that along with the ISBN you could give it your e-mail address. That way, its system could keep track of who was using its service, so it could send you an e-mail message when it makes a significant change to the service. If there was a business case to support such a process, maybe Amazon would do so. Overall, such a strategy seems convoluted and contrived. When you need to put this much effort into making reality fit your view of how reality should be, it's time to find a new reality.

If Not Versions, Then What?

At this point, we have made our case against service versioning. It's a wrong-headed idea. However, we still need a strategy for dealing with the inevitable changes in our services! Once again, let's look to the real world for a better approach.

Consider how car-rental companies work. Here's a typical scenario:

Customer: "I'd like to rent the cheapest car you have."

Agent: "Great. Let me get that booked for you."

The agent looks at her computer screen, performs the usual rental-agent voodoo, and then looks at the customer again.

Agent: "I'm sorry; we are all out of our compact cars. However, I can *upgrade* you to a mid-size car at the same rate as the compact car. Would that be okay?"

Notice that the agent didn't offer a different *version* of a car; it was an *upgrade*. Upgrades are usually "new and improved" or "better than" their predecessor. Think of the things you can upgrade in your life. You can upgrade your cable TV service to the "Platinum" or "Gold" level from your current "Bronze" level. You can upgrade your DSL to a faster speed. You can trade in your old car for this year's model (another form of an upgrade). Newer is better in the advertising world *and* the IT world. No one is talking about replacing their current web-enabled systems with older client-server solutions or mainframes. The past is dead in the IT world. Long live the future!

Let's go back to our getGreeting(String name) operation and look at it with new eyes. When this operation was first implemented, it adequately met the requirements. However, over time, the requirements changed. Requirements always change. Eventually, the requirements changed sufficiently to warrant the development of the new service operation getGreeting(String firstName, String lastName). This new getGreeting operation is an upgrade over the previous one.

IT people need to consider themselves as businesspeople first, and technical experts second. The IT business is to deliver services (think products) to its customers (the line of business, partners, suppliers, and so on). With this view of the world, things start to make more sense, especially when your strategy is to provide new and better products for your customers to use.

For example, an automobile company produces new vehicle models every year. As much as it would like to, it cannot force its customers to upgrade to the new models. In fact, it will continue to produce machine parts to service the vehicles it produced in prior model years. However, as time moves forward, the automobile company begins to sunset the production of the machine parts for the very oldest (or least popular) models, eventually ceasing their manufacture completely. Try finding a carburetor for a Ford Model T sometime. You can find it, but it isn't made by Ford Motor Company anymore.

The service-oriented IT shops work the same way. They produce services (again, think "products") to meet the needs of their customers. As time moves forward, new and improved services will be made available to the IT customer base. Just like the automobile company, as much as the IT shop would like to force its customers to upgrade to the newest services, it simply must maintain the previous services until it becomes feasible to retire them. The time to retire a service is determined by the level of demand for that service and the cost of maintaining that service. It's a business decision made in the same manner that the other lines of business make on a daily basis. If IT determines that a service needs to be retired due to cost, but a single line of business still relies on it, then that line of business might need to resort to hiring a custom programmer to maintain the service on its behalf, just like a Model T owner might need to hire a machinist to manufacture a new carburetor if he wants to keep driving that Model T!

Notice with this new mental model of "upgrade," we don't seem to be fighting reality anymore. It parallels the real world and behaves in a more natural fashion. That is not to say that transitioning to this new view of the world will be easy. Many procedural programmers never understood the need for event-driven or object-oriented programming models. Similarly, many people will cling to the idea that web services must be versioned, especially when we see so much discussion about it in today's press. In our mind, those arguments are meaningless. The new view of the world has arrived.

As any salesperson will tell you, you cannot rely solely on customers to buy the product that's best for them. This applies to the IT department and its products as well. The IT department needs its own "salespeople": experts in the IT products that can give advice and guide customers to the right products and services. The "right" products and services are those that will best meet the customers' needs now and into the foreseeable future.

Imagine for a moment that you're relatively ignorant about today's networking technology. Your roommate has a wireless-B router and you would like to connect to it. So you go to your local electronics store and ask the sales associate there to help you pick a wireless-B card for your computer. If the sales associate is unskilled, she may direct you to the aisle where you'll find wireless-B adapters at a bargain price. However, if the salesperson is more skilled, she will ask you a few questions first. The conversation might go like this:

Customer: "I need a wireless-B adapter for my computer."

Salesperson: "Great. We have some on sale for a very good price today because they're being discontinued."

Customer: "They're being discontinued?"

Salesperson: "Yes. Hardly anyone uses wireless-B technology anymore. The predominant technology is wireless-G. It's much faster than B and far more common in airports and coffeehouses. Plus, it's backward-compatible with wireless-B routers."

Customer: "Are they very expensive?"

Salesperson: "They run about $50. They're half the price of the new wireless-N technology cards. Wireless-N is 12 times faster than wireless-G and it has 4 times the range. Those adapters cost around $120."

Now you have some very good information to use to make a decision that's right for you. Perhaps, as a poor college student, you're better off buying a wireless-B adapter from the discount bin for $9.99. Or it might be that $50 is well within your price range, and now you get the benefit of using your wireless laptop at many more places. Perhaps you're a big iPod junkie and download music and videos on a daily basis. In this case, the wireless-N is the right purchase for you. It's the responsibility of the salesperson to help customers identify the product that's right for them.

The process is exactly the same at a service-oriented IT shop. There must be a salesperson who knows the IT product line well. Like the different wireless adapters, the services offered by the IT shop also have a life cycle. Some are brand new and more expensive, while others might be dirt cheap but at the end of their life. IT must employ these sales experts to ensure that its customers are informed enough to make good decisions.

Now, it might seem crazy to have a salesperson in an IT shop. These folks don't need to be sales professionals per se. More often than not, they will be architects who can advise customers as to the services that would best meet the customer's needs. The architects will know which services are deprecated (at the end of their life), which ones are current, and which ones are either brand new or are in development. You can see that it's critical to know where each service is in the service life cycle.

The Service Life Cycle

The service life cycle is fairly straightforward, as illustrated in Figure 14-3. Services begin life as soon as planning begins.

- A *planned* service has a name and a general description of its purpose.

- Assuming that the service is approved for development, it moves into the *development* stage.

- When development is complete, it's *released* into the IT department's service portfolio. A *service portfolio* is simply the group of services that are currently offered to customers.

- As the service ages (that is, it becomes less and less useful), the IT department might release an upgrade to the service. When the upgrade is released, the older service becomes *deprecated*. A deprecated service is still in production and is still available for customers to use, but it isn't recommended that any new service consumers use the service.

- The last step in the cycle is to *retire* the service. A retired service is removed from the production environment and is no longer offered by the IT department.

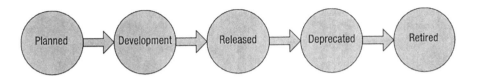

Figure 14-3. *The service life cycle*

Naturally, the steps in the service life cycle can be modified by each IT department to better meet the needs of its company. For example, your company might want to insert a *funded* stage between planning and development. Alternatively, your company might opt to create a *quarantined* stage between the deprecated and retired stages to ensure that the service really is no longer in use before it's completely retired. You can customize the service life cycle to meet your needs.

Because it's important to know the stage of each service in the service life cycle, you must record that information for later retrieval. There are a number of ways to record service life cycle information; the method you choose will be influenced by the tools you have at your disposal. Before deciding on where to store the information, let's first consider where you would like to find this information. Using our wireless networking scenario as a guide, we strongly suggest that this information be available at design time. That means that the current life cycle stage of the service should be easily found in your service catalog.

In addition, it might be useful to provide this information during runtime to the service clients. This means either providing the life cycle stage as metadata in a service registry or as header information in the SOAP message itself. How the client handles this information is the business of the client and not something that we, as service providers, should dictate. However, we always want to give our service clients the most opportunity to receive critical information about our services, so we highly recommend making this information available at runtime.

Some life cycle stages deserve additional metadata to be truly effective. For example, if the service is in the development stage, you should also include the planned release date of the service. Obviously, that date might change, but the planned release date will be important information to potential consumers of that service. Similarly, a service in the released stage should provide the date of its release. A deprecated service should record the planned date of its retirement, and retired services should record the actual date they were retired.

In the real world, services represent business functionality. Rarely does a business function disappear completely. Usually it's upgraded. Therefore, when a service is deprecated and marked for eventual retirement, you'll usually have its replacement planned, in development, or released into production. You might even have several different upgraded versions of a service in production at the same time. Wireless-B adapters were still big sellers when the wireless-G adapters were first introduced. In terms of our service life cycle, both of those products were in the released stage at the same time, but every wireless salesperson could tell you that wireless-G was the successor of wireless-B. You need the same ability with your services. Therefore, you need an additional bit of metadata that points to a newer service that supersedes the service in question.

Let's take a look at some examples of this information. Imagine that you need to retrieve customer information to fulfill the needs of a service you're creating. Your current service portfolio information is held in a database. You search the database for services that contain the word "Customer" in hopes of finding a service that will meet your needs. Your search returns several records, as noted in Tables 14-1 through 14-3. Beginning with Table 14-1, you can see immediately that the service is still available, but it has been deprecated on July 2008. You can also see from the metadata that the successor to the service is also named `getCustomerInfo` and exists at `http://esb.mycorp.com/customer2`.

Table 14-1. *Multiple Services Representing the Service Life Cycle in Action*

Tag	Value
Service name	`getCustomerInfo`
URI	`http://esb.mycorp.com/customer`
Life cycle stage	Deprecated
Life cycle date	July 2008
Successor	`getCustomerInfo`
Successor URI	`http://esb.mycorp.com/customer2`

Next, we examine the successor URI, as shown in Table 14-2. From the life cycle stage, you can see that the service is in production and was released on June 2008; perfect! But wait; you can also see that this current service already has a successor defined for it. You need to examine the record of this successor service before you make any final decisions about which service to use.

Table 14-2. *The Current getCustomerInfo Service Metadata*

Tag	Value
Service name	`getCustomerInfo`
URI	`http://esb.mycorp.com/customer2`
Life cycle stage	Released
Life cycle date	June 2008
Successor	`getCustomerInfo`
Successor URI	`http://esb.mycorp.com/customer3`

Table 14-3 shows the metadata for the `getCustomerInfo` service that's in development. If you intend to release your service on or after July 2009, you should seriously consider using this service instead of the `getCustomerInfo` service that is currently operational. If this service doesn't meet your timeline needs, then you need to use the service that's currently in operation.

Table 14-3. *The Future getCustomerInfo Service Metadata*

Tag	Value
Service name	`getCustomerInfo`
URI	`http://esb.mycorp.com/customer3`
Life cycle stage	Development
Release date	July 2009
Successor	None
Successor URI	

As you can see, maintaining standard metadata about each service in your portfolio is critical to your success in SOA. You not only need to know what the service does, but you also need to understand where it is in its life cycle and when the IT department intends to change the life cycle status. You also need to know how this service relates to other services, at least with regard to the upgrade path of the service.

The Future of IT

We would like to invite you to take a walk with us into the future of IT, and the future of business in a service-oriented world. In this future world, service orientation is the norm, not the exception. Services are fundamentally understood by all IT professionals to the point where they're taken for granted, similar to how we regard compiler technology today. In our service-oriented IT shop, the IT professionals' foremost thought is to keep the customer happy. Customers are other departments within their enterprise. Additionally, the IT professionals view their partners and suppliers as customers whenever those partners and suppliers need to make use of the enterprise architecture.

Our service-oriented IT department creates new products (that is, services) that are either currently needed by its customers or will be needed in the near future. This IT shop will even engage in some speculation and create products that it believes its customers *might* need in the immediate future. Its job is to meet and exceed the needs of its customers.

The customers (other departments in the company or the company's partners and suppliers) will often "shop" for the products that they need. Therefore, the IT department must be able to provide a menu of products and services that it can offer to its customers, along with an idea of the associated costs. Customers need to know what they're buying and how much it will cost them to make sound purchasing decisions.

Additionally, the customers have the option of using services provided outside the IT department. Application service providers (ASPs) have evolved to become commercial service providers (CSPs)—companies that make their living by selling service-oriented products to customers. These CSPs are able to leverage the costs of developing services across multiple customers, just as product companies do today. Service customers within an enterprise now have choices about where they'll get their services. For some services, the CSPs are a cheap, fast, and reliable solution. For services that are specific to their business, customers might opt to use services developed by their internal IT department.

As a result, some IT departments will disappear altogether. The enterprise simply won't require them. If CSPs can provide all the functionality needed by the enterprise, then maintaining an IT shop won't make financial sense. However, for the majority of larger enterprises, their need to differentiate themselves from their competitors will force them to become agile, combining atomic services provided by the CSPs with custom services developed in-house into processes and higher-level services. Only a small number of companies will need to employ highly specialized developers and architects to create completely new services.

That last paragraph might worry you. We don't predict the end of the software profession, only another evolutionary change in our industry. There was a time in computing history when large armies of keypunch operators were required to enter software commands on punch cards, which were used to program mainframe computers. The advent of compilers and interpreters (along with an increase in the power of the computers themselves) put an end to that job description. However, no one laments the loss of keypunch operators today. The people who worked as keypunch operators moved on to other jobs. They adapted to a new reality. Similarly, with outsourcing in many of today's companies, software profession-als are adapting to a new marketplace. Service orientation brings its own share of changes. Low-level coding will become commoditized. Service creation, orchestration, and opti-mization will arise as a new frontier.

Summary

Change is inevitable. You can fight against it, but history teaches us that such efforts are largely a waste of time. The Luddites of the world don't make history, except as curiosities and historical footnotes. To rail against change is to make yourself a dinosaur and doom yourself to extinction. The key to success is the ability to adapt—to thrive in chaos while your competi-tors drown in it. SOA won't just change your IT shop; it will change your company, your marketplace, and the way the world does business.

■■■

## CHAPTER 15

Performance: Tuning and Best Practices

Within an SOA framework, OSB provides connectivity, routing, mediation, management, and some process orchestration capabilities. The design philosophy for OSB is to be a high-performance and stateless (nonpersistent state) intermediary between two or more applications. However, given the diversity in scale and functionality of SOA implementations, OSB applications are subject to a large variety of usage patterns, message sizes, and quality of service (QoS) requirements.

This chapter is intended to provide general tuning guidelines and best practices to achieve optimal performance and scalability for different usage scenarios.

Factors That Affect OSB Performance

Before diving into performance tuning and best practices, it is important to understand some of the main factors that influence OSB performance:

Message size: Message sizes determine network latency, memory requirements, and parsing/transformation costs. Throughput falls with increasing message size for a given scenario. Using content-streaming mode in OSB may help scale better with message size.

Design requirements and complexity: XML processing is typically expensive compared to core OSB runtime performance. Hence, the numbers of transformations, routing decisions, service callouts, and so on have a major impact on the cost of a proxy service.

Underlying transport: OSB performance and scalability characteristics derive directly from those of the inbound and outbound transports. Different transports, such as HTTP and JMS (persistent and nonpersistent), have different network representations, QoS levels, and I/O overheads.

Reliability requirements: In most cases, the greater the reliability requirement, the greater the performance penalty to achieve that level of reliability. Reliability is determined by various characteristics of a proxy, such as transaction support and delivery guarantees (best effort or once and only once).

Security policies: OSB supports a large combination of network and message-level security paradigms. Associated costs vary significantly with the selected paradigm.

Hardware: Hardware characteristics such as CPU architecture and storage media performance play an important part in determining throughput and latency.

Tuning an OSB Instance

We use the term *tuning* to selectively refer to those optimizations that can be achieved by simply changing the value of a parameter. Changes to proxy service design are covered in the "Best Practices for OSB Proxy Design" section later in this chapter.

An OSB instance can be tuned at the following levels:

- Java Virtual Machine (JVM)

- Operational parameters

- Transport (WebLogic Server and OSB)

JVM Memory Tuning

The selection of a garbage collection (GC) algorithm has a significant impact on throughput and variance in response times (latency). A throughput-oriented collector provides the best throughput and average latency, but it also causes greater variation in latencies. To avoid occasional spikes in latency, it is better to use a concurrent generational garbage collector. JRockit (real-time) also supports an algorithm called deterministic GC, which provides the lowest variance in response times with a slightly lower throughput.

Here are some sample JRockit memory-tuning flags for JVM version 27.3 or higher:

```
-XgcPrio:throughput -XXtlasize:min=16k,preferred=32k
```

And here are some sample Sun VM memory-tuning flags for JDK version 1.5:

```
-XX:PermSize=256m -XX:MaxPermSize=256m -XX:NewSize=512m -XX:MaxNewSize=512m
```

Tuning Operational Parameters

The following are some guidelines for tuning operational parameters:

Domain mode: Always create a domain in the production mode for optimal performance.

WebLogic Server logging: Set all WebLogic Server logging levels to Error or the highest level possible. Also, increase the rotation file size to 5000. This reduces I/O contention associated with debug messages. Log levels can be set on the WebLogic Server console by navigating to Home ➤ Summary of Environment ➤ Summary of Servers ➤ AdminServer ➤ Logging ➤ General (under the Advanced section), as shown in Figure 15-1.

Figure 15-1. *Tuning WebLogic Server logging through the WLS console*

Connection backlog buffering: In the WebLogic Server console, click the Configuration tab, and then click the Tuning link to see the settings for tuning the server, as shown in Figure 15-2. You can tune the number of connection requests that a WebLogic Server instance will accept before refusing additional requests. The Accept Backlog parameter specifies how many TCP connections can be buffered in a wait queue. This fixed-size queue is populated with requests for connections that the TCP stack has received but the application has not accepted yet. The default value is 300. This parameter should be set to a high value when dealing with a large number of concurrent clients.

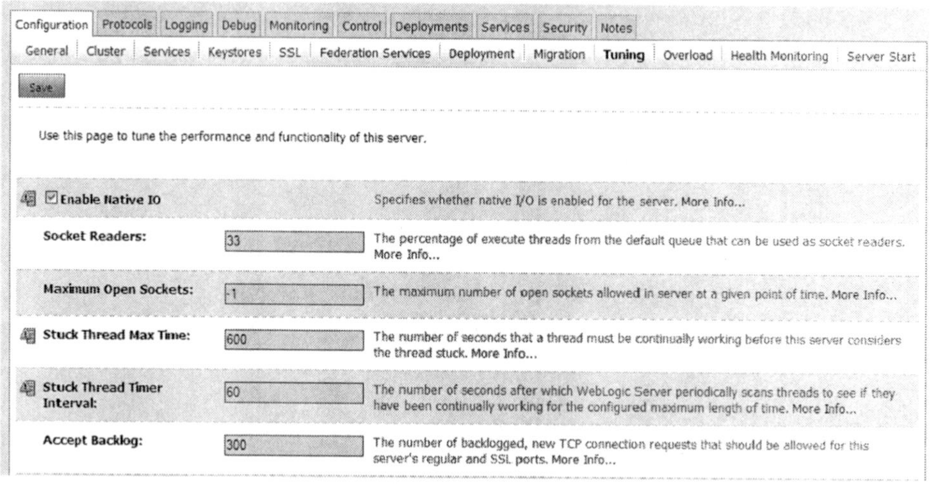

Figure 15-2. *Setting the Accept Backlog parameter in the WebLogic Server console*

Log actions: The next configuration section is found in the OSB console. Open your web browser to http://localhost:7001/sbconsole and log in with the username weblogic and password weblogic. Click the Operations header in the left navigation pane of the web browser, and then select the Global Settings link under the Configuration subheading. Log actions add an I/O overhead. Logging also involves an XQuery evaluation, which can be expensive. Writing to a single device can also result in lock contentions. You can enable and disable logging through the Logging check box, as shown in Figure 15-3.

Figure 15-3. *Disabling OSB logging for all services in a domain using the OSB console*

OSB monitoring: The out-of-the-box monitoring subsystem has a very low overhead and can scale well to a large number of services, as well as to multiple nodes in a cluster. However, when dealing with thousands of services or a large-scale cluster deployment, being selective about enabling monitoring can help reduce network traffic. Monitoring can be enabled or disabled at the domain level, as shown in Figure 15-3. Monitoring can also be enabled or disabled on a per-service basis.

OSB tracing: Tracing is disabled by default, but can be enabled on a per-service basis. Ensure that tracing is turned off for performance-sensitive services. To turn tracing on or off for a proxy service, select the proxy service using the OSB web console (selecting either the Resource Browser or Project Explorer link) and click the Operational Settings tab.

Proxy service runtime data caching: OSB caches proxy service runtime metadata using a two-level cache with static and dynamic sections. The cache introduces a performance trade-off between memory consumption and compilation cost. Caching proxy services increases throughput but consumes memory otherwise available for data processing. The static section is an upper-bound least recently used (LRU) cache that is never garbage-collected. When a proxy service is bumped from the static section, it is demoted to the dynamic section, where the cache can be garbage-collected. You can tune the number of proxy services in the static portion of the cache by setting its size using the system property `com.bea.wli.sb.pipeline.RouterRuntimeCache.size`. The default value is 100. You can increase this number when there are more than 100 latency-sensitive services on a single cluster, provided that there is sufficient memory for runtime data processing.

OSB Transport Tuning

Many transports are supported by OSB, including HTTP, JMS, EJB, File, FTP, MQ, and others. This section deals with tuning the most commonly used transports.

HTTP

Turn off HTTP access logging (enabled by default). In the WebLogic Server console, navigate to Servers ➤ AdminServer and select the Logging tab. On that tab, select the HTTP category, which contains the check box to enable/disable HTTP access logging, as shown in Figure 15-4. If this logging is enabled, any access to an HTTP endpoint results in two lines written to the access logs, which is in an I/O overhead. Also, the WebLogic Diagnostic Framework (WLDF) subsystem optimistically indexes the logs, taking up some CPU cycles.

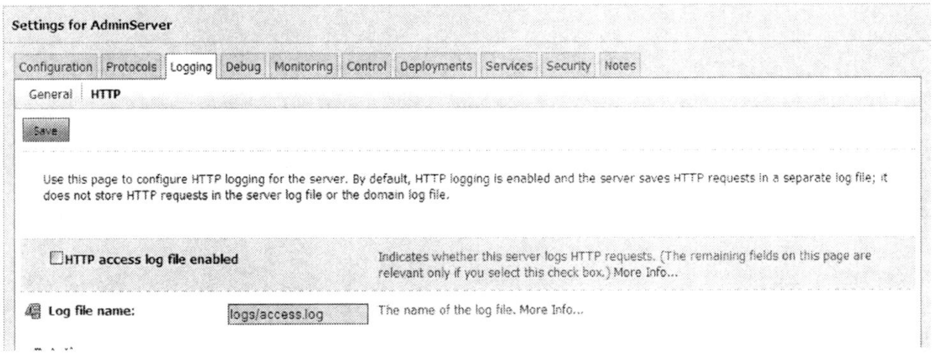

Figure 15-4. *Disabling HTTP access logging in the WebLogic Server console*

JMS

Ensure that the correct persistence level is set for JMS destinations:

- For nonpersistent scenarios, explicitly turn off persistence at the JMS server level by unchecking the Store Enabled flag (in the Advanced section of the General tab for the JMS server on the WebLogic Server console), as shown in Figure 15-5. It is also possible to override the persistence mode at the JMS destination level.

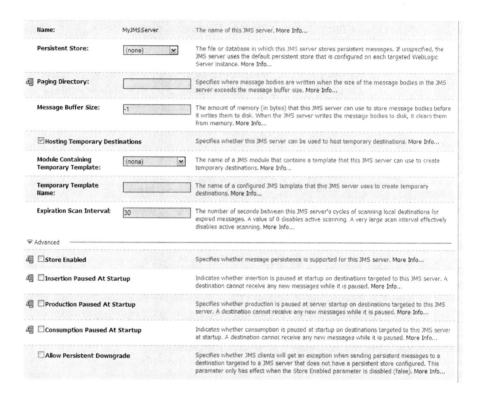

Figure 15-5. *Configuring a nonpersistent JMS server using the WebLogic Server console*

- For persistent JMS scenarios, typically a file store performs better than a JDBC store (chosen through the Persistent Store setting for the JMS server, shown in Figure 15-5). If there are multiple JMS servers involved, ideally, you would create each store on a separate disk for the lowest I/O contention.

When benchmarking with more than 16 client threads calling a JMS-based proxy service, use a dispatch policy with a maximum threads constraint. Set the maximum threads constraint to be equal to the number of clients. Typically, do not go beyond six threads per CPU. If a dispatch policy is not defined, the default number of active listener threads per JMS proxy is 16.

File, FTP, and MQ (Poller-Based Transports)

Latency and throughput of poller-based transports depend on the frequency with which a source is polled and the number of files or messages read per polling sweep. These settings are available when you configure the transport for a proxy service, as shown in Figure 15-6.

Create a Proxy Service (test/FileProxy)	
FILE Transport Configuration	
File Mask*	* *
Polling Interval*	5
Read Limit*	25
Sort By Arrival	☐
Scan SubDirectories	☐
Pass By Reference	☐

Figure 15-6. *Tuning the File transport using the OSB console*

The default polling interval for the File and FTP transports is set to 60 seconds. Use a smaller polling interval for high-throughput scenarios where the message size is not very large and the CPU is not saturated.

The read limit determines the number of files or messages that are read per polling sweep. This defaults to 10 for the File and FTP transports. Set this value to the desired concurrency.

Setting the read limit to a high value and the polling interval to a small value may result in a large number of messages being simultaneously read into memory. This can cause an out-of-memory error if the message size is large.

Best Practices for OSB Proxy Design

The following are some suggested best practices for OSB proxy design:

Place routing information in the SOAP header or the transport header when you have a choice. When designing an SOA framework, it is recommended that routing decisions be based on SOAP headers or transport headers (for non-SOAP payloads). OSB uses partial parsing to process SOAP headers without parsing the body section. Transport headers are easily accessed without parsing the payload. Thus, you can scale better with increasing message size by storing information in headers.

Use a Replace action to transform entire contents of a context variable (such as $body). Use a Replace action to complete the transformation in a single step. If the entire content of $body is to be replaced, leave the XPath field blank and select "Replace node contents," as shown in Figure 15-7. This is faster than pointing to the child node of $body (such as $body/Order) and selecting "Replace entire node." Leaving the XPath field blank eliminates an extra XQuery evaluation.

Figure 15-7. *Transforming the contents of a context variable*

Use $body/*[1] *to represent the contents of* $body *as an input to a transformation resource.*
OSB treats $body/*[1], as shown in Figure 15-8, as a special XPath that can be evaluated
without invoking the XQuery engine. This is faster than specifying an absolute path pointing to the child of $body. A general XPath like $body/Order must be evaluated by the
XQuery engine before the primary transformation resource is executed.

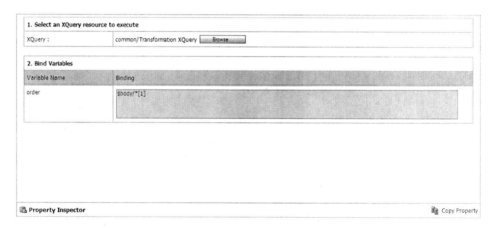

Figure 15-8. *Optimal representation of the contents of $body*

Avoid creating many context variables that are used just once within another XQuery.
Context variables created using an Assign action are converted to XMLBeans, and then
reverted to the native XQuery format for the next XQuery. Multiple Assign actions can be
collapsed into a single Assign action using a FLWOR expression. Intermediate values can
be created using let statements. Avoiding redundant context variable creation eliminates
overhead associated with internal data-format conversions. This benefit must be balanced
against visibility of the code and reuse of the variables.

■**Note** FLWOR (pronounced "flower") is an acronym for the keywords For, Let, Where, Order by, Return. The XQuery specification defines a FLWOR as a feature that supports iteration and binding of variables to intermediate results. A FLWOR expression is similar to a SQL query in its structure.

Use OSB as WSS enforcement point only when message-level security is required. As discussed in Chapter 11, typically WSS has higher overhead associated with encryption and processing than network-level security paradigms like SSL with Basic Authentication. There are certain scenarios where OSB does not act as a security enforcement point and is a passthrough intermediary in the larger security architecture. In such scenarios, WSS can be used as the security paradigm with no security policies configured for the OSB service for optimal end-to-end performance.

Use EJB transport primarily when loose coupling is desired. The EJB transport in OSB is designed to offer a loosely coupled and message-oriented interface using WSDL. A WSDL-based SOAP message must be bound to a Java interface using the standard JAX-RPC binding. This binding has a translation cost, which is acceptable when the back-end EJB represents a reusable service. However, the translation cost may be regarded as high when making multiple short calls to one or more EJBs in a single proxy. A Java Callout action may be a better solution to access an EJB in a more tightly coupled but low-overhead mechanism.

Standardize XML representation when switching between Java Callout and XML manipulation actions (Assign, Insert, and Replace). Minimize conversions from an XML data type to "XML as text" and vice versa. If a subsequent action requires an XML data type, return an XMLBean from a Java callout instead of a `String`.

Set the appropriate QoS level. Do not use the XA or Exactly Once setting for QoS unless a reliability level of once and only once is required and is possible (for example, it's not possible if the client is an HTTP client). XA adds to both CPU and I/O costs for all components involved in the global transaction. OSB can invoke a back-end HTTP service asynchronously if the QoS is set to Best Effort, as shown in Figure 15-9. Asynchronous invocation allows OSB to scale better with long-running back-end services. It also allows publishing over HTTP to be truly fire-and-forget.

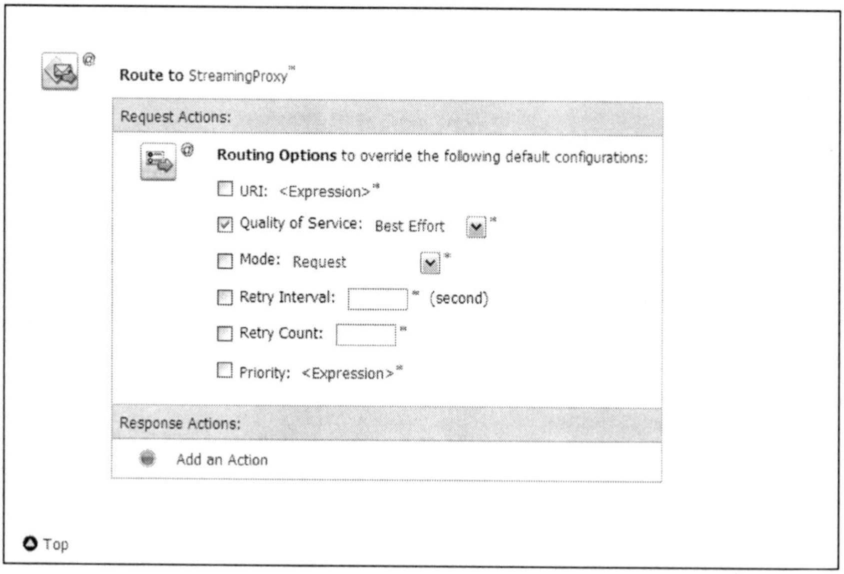

Figure 15-9. *Setting QoS using routing options*

Use Logging Last Resource (LLR) optimization through JDBC data sources for two-phase transactions. LLR is a performance enhancement option that enables one non-XA resource to participate in a global transaction with the same ACID guarantee as XA. In many cases, a global transaction becomes a two-phase commit (2PC) transaction because it involves a database operation (using JDBC) and another nondatabase operation, such as a message queuing operation (using JMS). In such cases, the LLR Optimization transaction option can significantly improve transaction performance by eliminating some of the XA overhead for database processing and by avoiding the use of JDBC XA drivers, which typically are less efficient than non-XA drivers. If OSB initiates a transaction that involves a database, it is possible to replace XA with LLR to achieve the same level of reliability. For more information about LLR, see the WebLogic Server documentation at http://edocs.bea.com/wls/docs92/jta/llr.html.

XQuery and XPath Optimizations

OSB uses XQuery and XPath extensively for various actions like Assign, Replace, and Routing Table. The XML structure ($body) shown in Listing 15-1 is used to explain XQuery and XPath tuning concepts.

Listing 15-1. *Sample SOAP Payload*

```
<soap-env:Body>
   <Order>
     <CtrlArea>
         <CustName>Mary</CustName>
     </CtrlArea>
```

```
           <ItemList>
        <Item name="ACE_Car" >20000 </Item>
        <Item name=" Ext_Warranty" >1500</Item>
        .... a large number of items
    </ItemList>
    <Summary>
        <Total>70000</Total>
        <Status>Shipped</Status>
        <Shipping>My Shipping Firm </Shipping>
            </Summary>
     </Order>
</soap-env:Body>
```

The following are some guidelines for optimizing XQuery and XPath:

Avoid the use of double forward slashes (//) in XPaths. $body//CustName, while returning the same value as $body/Order/CtrlArea/CustName, will perform a lot worse than the latter expression. // implies all occurrences of a node, regardless of the location in an XML tree. Thus, the entire depth and breadth of the XML tree must be searched for the pattern specified after a //. Use // only if the exact location of a node is not known at design time.

XPaths should be indexed where applicable. An XPath can be indexed by simply adding [1] after each node of the path. XQuery is a declarative language, and an XPath expression can return more than one node; it can return an array of nodes. For example, $body/Order/CtrlArea/CustName implies returning all instances Order under $body and all instances of CtrlArea under Order. Thus, the entire document must be read in order to correctly process this XPath. If you know that there is a single instance of Order under $body and a single instance of CtrlArea under Order, you could rewrite the XPath as $body/Order[1]/CtrlArea[1]/CustName[1], which implies returning the first instances of the child nodes. Thus, only the top part of the document needs to be processed by the XQuery engine, resulting in better performance. Proper indexing is the key to processing only what is needed.

Caution Indexing should not be used where the expected return value is an array of nodes. For example, $body/Order[1]/ItemList[1]/Item returns all Item nodes, but $body/Order[1]/ItemList[1]/Item[1] returns only the first item node. Another example is an XPath used to split a document in a for action.

Extract frequently used parts of a large XML document as intermediate variables within a FLOWR expression. An intermediate variable can be used to store the common context for multiple values. Here are sample XPaths with common context:

```
$body/Order[1]/Summary[1]/Total,
$body/Order[1]/Summary[1]/Status
$body/Order[1]/Summary[1]/Shipping
```

These can be changed to use an intermediate variable:

```
let $summary := $body/Order[1]/Summary[1]
$summary/Total, $ summary/Status, $summary/Shipping
```

Using intermediate variables may consume additional memory, but it eliminates redundant XPath processing and hence reduces the load on the CPU.

Scalability Considerations for an ESB

Scalability is a very important aspect of any SOA deployment. The SOA fabric connects all critical systems of an enterprise and is hence subjected to the cumulative load of multiple individual systems. In an SOA environment, scalability can be defined along the following dimensions:

- *Vertical*: Ability of a single bus instance to scale to multiple CPU cores

- *Horizontal*: Ability of the bus to scale to multiple clustered instances

- *Number of services*: Ability of the bus to support a large number of services

- *Message size*: Ability of the bus to handle large payloads

- *Number of users*: Ability of the bus to scale to a high concurrency

It is critical that an "enterprise-class" service bus be able to scale along these dimensions with low impact to performance.

OSB leverages the clustering capabilities of the underlying WebLogic Server to scale horizontally. Being a stateless engine, OSB can scale easily to multiple nodes of a cluster with minimal or no loss in performance. OSB can support thousands of services on a single cluster. The streaming capabilities of OSB allow it to scale with increasing message size without compromising significantly on performance. The underlying WebLogic Server "socket-muxer" technology provides high scalability with increasing number of concurrent clients.

Handling Large Messages with Content Streaming

OSB supports the streaming of content through the service bus and also supports streaming transformations. For reliability reasons, however, the content is buffered in a serialized format, either in memory or on disk. Despite the buffering of content, streaming offers significant advantages in terms of memory footprint and garbage collection costs. There are also reductions in CPU cost for certain use cases that benefit from partial parsing.

Content streaming is enabled by simply selecting the Enabled check box during proxy service definition, as shown in Figure 15-10.

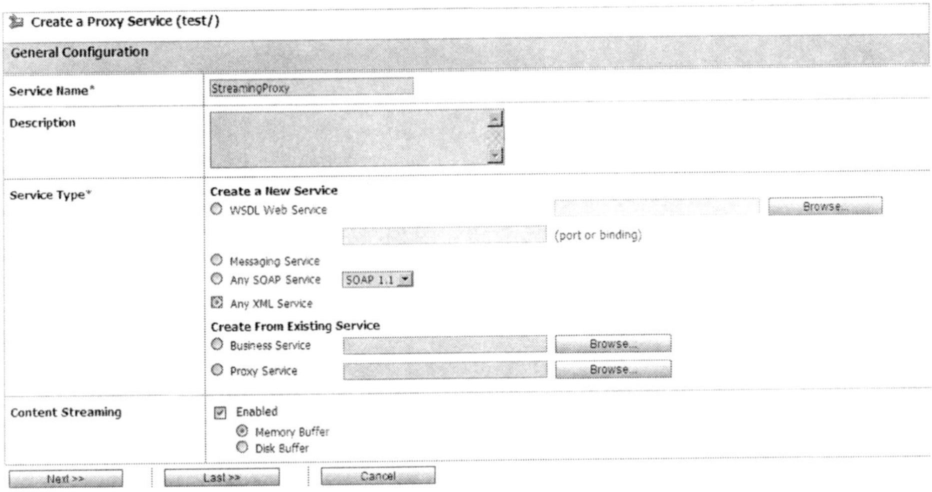

Figure 15-10. *Enabling content streaming for a proxy service*

The following are some of the best practices related to streaming content:

Enable streaming for pure content-based routing scenarios. Read-only scenarios such as content-based routing can gain significantly from enabling streaming. OSB leverages the partial parsing capabilities of the XQuery engine when streaming is used in conjunction with indexed XPaths. Thus, the payload is parsed and processed only to the field referred to in the XPath. Other than partial parsing, an additional benefit for read-only scenarios is that streaming eliminates the overhead associated with parsing and serialization of XML-Beans.

Enable streaming if there is an out-of-memory error when transforming large messages. The output of a transformation is stored in a compressed buffer format either in memory or on disk. Using a compressed buffer format has a significant CPU penalty. Hence, when running out of memory is *not* a concern, streaming with compressed buffering should be avoided.

Use a hybrid approach for multiple reads with streaming. The gains from streaming can be negated if the payload is accessed a large number of times for reading multiple fields. If all fields read are located in a single subsection of the XML document, a hybrid approach provides the best performance. The hybrid approach includes enabling streaming at the proxy level and assigning the relevant subsection to a context variable. The individual fields can then be accessed from this context variable. For example, the fields Total and Status from the XML sample in Listing 15-1 can be retrieved from a fully materialized subsection Summary:

```
Assign "$body/Order[1]/Summary[1]" to "summary"
Assign "$summary/Total" to "total"
Assign "$summary /Status" to "status"
```

Flow-Control Patterns Using OSB

Thus far, we have assumed that default performance and scalability bottlenecks are factors of OSB tuning and proxy design. However, a real-world deployment is more complex, since an OSB instance is hosted on a specific hardware configuration and interacts with other systems. Thus, OSB is part of a larger system, and the objective of tuning is to optimize the overall system performance. This involves not only tuning OSB as a stand-alone application, but also using OSB to implement flow-control patterns such as throttling, request-buffering, caching, prioritization, and parallelism.

■**Note** The term *flow control* in this context refers to the ability to change and manage the load on downstream systems. This term should not be confused with the term *flow* in an orchestration context, where it refers to the path of a request through the system.

A System's View of Performance

In most SOA deployments, OSB is part of a larger system, where it plays the role of an intermediary between two or more applications (servers). Also, within the bounds of a single OSB instance, the software requires multiple system resources such as CPU, memory, and so on. The OSB service, hardware resources, and external systems can be thought of as components of a larger system, as illustrated in Figure 15-11. The throughput of such a system can only be as high as the throughput of the slowest component. This component is referred to as the *system bottleneck*.

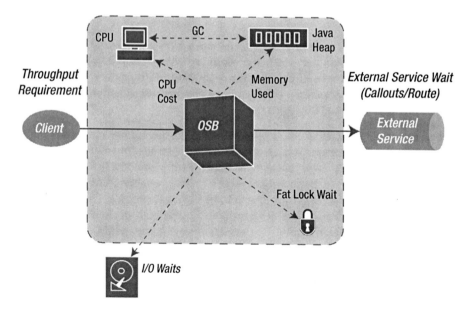

Figure 15-11. *A performance-centric system's view of an OSB instance*

A typical OSB configuration involves a client invoking an OSB proxy, which may make one or more service callouts to intermediate back-end services, and then route the request to the destination back-end system before routing the response back to the client. This configuration is illustrated in Figure 15-12. In such a scenario, the bottleneck could be the client, the OSB instance, intermediate back-end services, or the destination back-end system. Tuning starts with correctly identifying the system bottleneck, as tuning other systems may not improve overall performance.

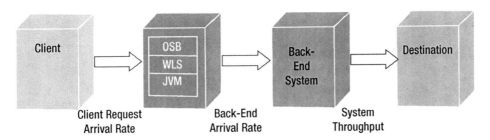

Figure 15-12. *High-level view of flow of requests within an OSB system*

Throttling and Prioritization

Throttling is the ability to control the maximum load applied to downstream systems. A dam is a real-world example of throttling. As illustrated in Figure 15-13, the flow of water in controlled to protect downstream systems from floods, as well as use make optimal use of the water.

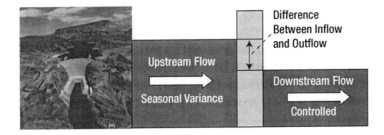

Figure 15-13. *Impact of throttling on the flow of water*

Throttling adjusts the load to the throughput capabilities of a system instead of adding hardware to handle the additional load. Thus, downstream (back-end) systems need to scale to a lower capacity, which in turn results in reduction of hardware and software costs. Another impact of throttling is that downstream resources are better utilized over the duration of the day, as shown in Figure 15-14.

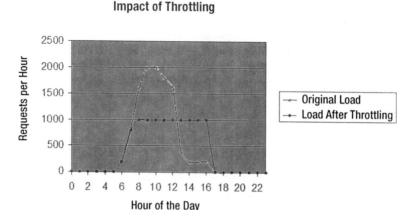

Figure 15-14. *Load characteristics of a throttled system*

Using OSB, you can implement throttling in three ways:

- The requests can be throttled on the inbound side by the use of Work Manager-based policies. A dispatch policy can be specified as part of the transport configuration of a proxy service. The dispatch policy can refer to an existing Work Manager. In order to throttle the requests, a maximum threads constraint must be associated with this Work Manager. The value of this constraint controls the maximum threads available for a proxy service deployment. In effect, this controls downstream concurrency and throughput.

■Note A Work Manager is a logical entity that applies certain constraints to a WebLogic Server deployment. Work Managers can be defined in the WebLogic Server console. One or more proxy services can be associated with a Work Manager using dispatch policies. For more information about Work Managers, see the WebLogic Server documentation at http://edocs.bea.com/wls/docs103/config_wls/self_tuned.html.

- You can limit the maximum number of concurrent calls to the outbound or back-end service by applying throttling policies to the OSB business service, via the Operational Settings tab on the OSB web console, as shown in Figure 15-15. This approach controls the downstream concurrency after the requests have been processed by the proxy service.

Figure 15-15. *Enabling outbound throttling for an OSB business service*

- If a higher level of reliability is desired, you can use persistent JMS as a secure and transactional store for buffered requests.

For all of these throttling approaches, a priority value can be associated with a message. While each approach has a different way to locate the priority value, all of them have the ability to expedite the processing of higher-priority messages.

Parallel Execution Using Split-Join

Parallel execution is a common paradigm used to reduce latency while consuming higher system resources. If a set of tasks includes tasks that have no dependency on one another, they can be executed in parallel. This is very useful for latency-sensitive use cases.

Executing multiple tasks in parallel increases CPU consumption. Hence, parallelism provides no benefits when the CPU is already saturated. In OSB, parallel tasks do not participate in the parent transaction and hence need to be idempotent. For details on making parallel calls with split-joins, see Chapter 7.

Summary

OSB is a powerful tool that adds great flexibility in the design of numerous SOA mediation and integration patterns. While the guidelines discussed in this chapter are relevant to the vast majority of patterns and deployment architectures, it is important to empirically validate the behavior of the system under load before going into production.

CHAPTER 16

■■■

Administration, Operations, and Management

Design and development are only part of the OSB life cycle. Modern IT shops usually deploy their software into distinct environments. Commonly, these environments can be classified as development, testing, staging, and production (this list is by no means definitive, but it is representative). This process is complicated by the fact that the software deployed in each environment is often tied to local software assets that are part of the environment, not part of the software itself. OSB provides capabilities to ease these operational challenges. In this chapter, we will discuss administration, operations, and management capabilities of OSB.

Deployment

Deployment is the process of installing software onto servers. For OSB, it is the process of moving one or more projects and configurations onto a server or a cluster of servers. When you move software from one environment to another, problems often arise because external resources, such as database names and URIs, differ between environments.

For example, imagine moving an OSB project from a development environment into a staging environment. In the development environment, the business services had only single endpoints associated with them. In the staging environment, the business services will have multiple endpoints. Nothing else has changed—just the endpoints for each business service. This is a very common scenario and one that should be automated. You don't want your system administrators typing in endpoints by hand. That information should reside in a script somewhere for rapid, reliable, and repeatable results. Through OSB, you can create such scripts to automate the deployment process.

OSB uses the WebLogic Scripting Tool (WLST). This scripting language is based on the Jython scripting language. The developers of the OSB have provided public APIs that are easily accessible using WLST. These APIs are designed not only to make it easier to deploy OSB projects between environments, but also to include a tremendous amount of administrative function-ality. If you are in charge of maintaining OSB instances in various environments, including production environments, you need to make it a point to learn WLST and the public OSB APIs.

We will use an example to demonstrate how to write and run these scripts. We will create a production environment, and then take our sample project from our osb30_book domain into our osb30_prod domain. While our example will cover moving a project from only one environment to another, the principles are exactly the same when you are moving projects among any number of environments.

Creating a Production Domain

First, we need to create our production OSB domain. Create the production domain in the same parent directory in which you created the osb30_book domain in Chapter 2. Keeping all of your domains in the same parent directory is a good practice. It makes them easy to find, especially if you have multiple administrators.

Run the Configuration wizard. You can find this tool on the Start ➤ Programs ➤ BEA Products ➤ Tools menu (if you are using Windows). Alternatively, you can find the script file that runs the Configuration wizard in the <%BEA_HOME%>\wlserver_10.0\common\bin directory. Run the config.cmd file if you are on a Windows platform or the config.sh file if you are on a Unix platform.

Once you have the Configuration wizard running, follow the wizard's steps and specify the values defined in Table 16-1. If a page appears in the Configuration wizard but you don't see its name in Table 16-1, just click the Next button to move to the next page in the wizard.

Table 16-1. *Domain Creation Values for the OSB30_prod Domain*

Page	Name	Value
Welcome	Create a new WebLogic Domain	Select
Select Domain Source	Generate a domain	Select
Select Domain Source	WebLogic Server (Required)	Checked
Select Domain Source	Workshop for WebLogic 10.2	Checked
Select Domain Source	Oracle Service Bus	Checked
Configure Admin	User name	weblogic
Configure Admin	User password	weblogic
Configure Admin	Confirm user password	weblogic
Configure Server Start	Development Mode	Select
Configure Server Start	BEA Supplied JDKs	Sun SDK
Customize Environment	Yes	Select
Configure the Administration Server	Listen Port	7101
Configure JDBC Sources	For Each Data Source	Set the DBMS port to 9193 and the DBMS name to weblogic_prod_eval (do this for all three JDBC data sources)
Run Database Scripts	Run Scripts	Select
Create WebLogic Domain	Domain name	osb30_prod
Create WebLogic Domain	Domain location	d:\domains (or the parent directory where you previously installed the osb30_book domain)

Do not choose to start the admin server in the last step of the wizard. You will need to do a little manual configuration of this domain, so you can run it and the osb30_book domain's server at the same time on your machine. Specifically, you will need to change the DEBUG_PORT setting to a value other than the default 8453, since that port will be used by the osb30_book domain. To do this, find and edit the setDomainEnv.cmd file (setDomainEnv.sh for Unix users) in the \bin subdirectory of the osb30_prod domain. Search for the string 8453 and replace that value with the value 8553 (using our standard practice of adding 100 to the port number for the osb30_prod domain). Save the file.

You can now start the osb30_prod domain by running the startWebLogic.cmd script in the osb30_prod domain directory. If the osb30_book server is not running, start that server now also.

For the example, we will move the HelloWorld project into our new osb30_prod domain. Since the HelloWorld project depends on the HelloWorldService web service, we will need to ensure that the web service is also deployed on our new domain. This is a simple matter in WorkSpace Studio. Ensure that you are using either a J2EE [JMD1]perspective or an Oracle Service Bus perspective (so that the Servers tab appears at the bottom of the IDE). Right-click the Servers tab, create a new server to represent the osb30_prod domain, and assign the HelloWorld web service project to the osb30_prod server.

Exporting a Project

We will export the HelloWorld project from the osb30_book domain and import it into the osb30_prod domain. In WorkSpace Studio, find the project named Administration, open that project, and look in the ExportImport folder. This folder includes a set of files that will allow you to export the HelloWorld project from the osb30_book domain and import the project into the osb30_prod domain. Table 16-2 provides a quick overview of the files and how they are used.

Table 16-2. *Files for Exporting and Importing a Project*

File	Description
build.xml	This is the Ant build script that contains the instructions for exporting and importing projects among OSB servers. This is really boilerplate code, because all of the customization is held in other files.
customize.xml	This is a sample customization file that can be created when exporting projects or resources from a server environment. You will often modify this file after an export to configure the environment variables before you perform the import step. This file is not always needed.
export.properties	This is a property file used by Ant to specify the connection information when connecting to the osb30_book server, along with additional information about the project you are going to export and whether or not to use a passphrase on the exported file.
export.py	This is the Jython script that contains the commands for exporting projects and resources.
import.properties	Like the export.properties file, this file contains connection information and some other details to be used when importing the project into the osb30_prod server.
import.py	This is the Jython script that will run when you import the project.

Your first step is to edit the export.properties and import.properties files to match your environment. Listing 16-1 shows the export.properties file. The bulk of the fields should be self-explanatory.

Listing 16-1. *The export.properties File (in the ExportImport Folder)*

```
###################################################################
# OSB Admin Security Configuration                                #
###################################################################
adminUrl=t3://localhost:7001
exportUser=weblogic
exportPassword=weblogic


###################################################################
# OSB Jar to be exported                                          #
###################################################################
exportJar=export.jar


###################################################################
# Optional passphrase and project name                           #
###################################################################
passphrase=aqualogic
project=HelloWorld_SB


###################################################################
# Optional, create a dummy customization file                    #
###################################################################
customizationFile=customize.xml
```

Two fields in the export.properties file are worth a closer look:

passphrase: This variable is used only if you want to use a password to protect the file you are going to export from OSB. It's purely optional.

customizationFiles: This variable allows you to specify the name of the customization file that will be generated by the export process and used by the import process, if you are editing the import.properties file. The customizationFile variable is also optional. If you do not specify a file name, no file will be generated.

To perform the export, be sure that the osb30_book server is running and open the build.xml file in WorkSpace Studio. Run the export target of the build.xml file. Your console should display a series of messages similar to those in Listing 16-2.

Listing 16-2. *The Output of the Export Ant Task*

```
Buildfile: C:\_workspaces\OSB30_book\Administration\ExportImport\build.xml
export:
     [echo] exportscript: export.py
     [java] Initializing WebLogic Scripting Tool (WLST) ...
     [java] *sys-package-mgr*: skipping bad jar,
'C:\BEAHome\OSB30\wlserver_10.0\server\lib\webserviceclient.jar'
     [java] Welcome to WebLogic Server Administration Scripting Shell
     [java] Type help() for help on available commands
     [java] Loading export config from : export.properties
     [java] Connecting to t3://localhost:7001 with userid weblogic ...
     [java] Successfully connected to Admin Server 'AdminServer' that belongs
to domain 'OSB30_book'.
     [java] Warning: An insecure protocol was used to connect to the
     [java] server. To ensure on-the-wire security, the SSL port or
     [java] Admin port should be used instead.
     [java] Location changed to domainRuntime tree. This is a read-only tree
with DomainMBean as the root.
     [java] For more help, use help(domainRuntime)
     [java] OSBConfiguration MBean found
     [java] HelloWorld_SB
     [java] Export the project HelloWorld_SB
     [java] OSB Configuration file: export.jar has been exported
     [java] [Project HelloWorld_SB]
     [java] EnvValueCustomization created
     [java] [com.bea.wli.config.customization.FindAndReplaceCustomization@
1bb4e04]
     [java] OSB Dummy Customization file: customize.xml has been created
BUILD SUCCESSFUL
Total time: 6 seconds
```

Importing a Project

With the export complete, you are ready to import the project into the osb30_prod environment. When you do this in a real environment, execute the appropriate setDomainEnv script again. However, our two sample domains are similar enough that we don't need to reexecute the script. Simply run the import target of the build.xml file to import the HelloWorld project into the osb30_prod server.

The import process will run as smoothly as the export process did. When the import completes, open a web browser and browse to the OSB console for the osb30_prod server at http://localhost:7101/sbconsole. Navigate to the HelloWorld project, and take a look at the Configuration Details page, as shown in Figure 16-1. Do you see the problem here?

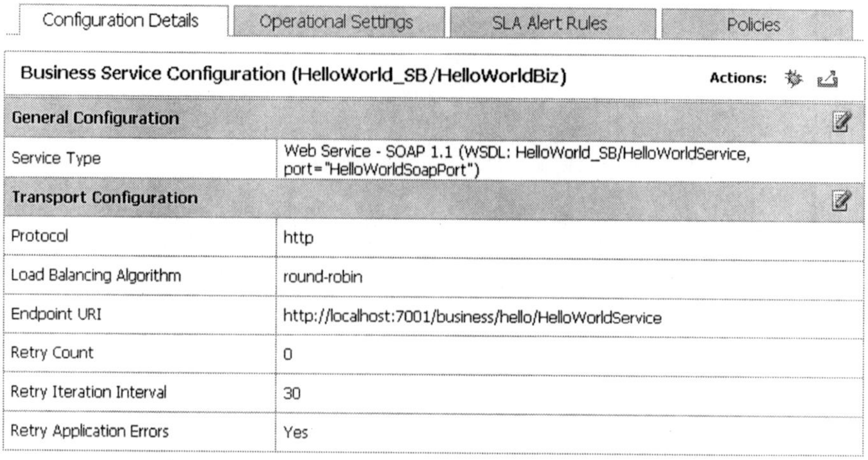

Configuration Details	Operational Settings	SLA Alert Rules	Policies

Business Service Configuration (HelloWorld_SB/HelloWorldBiz)		Actions: ⚙ ↗
General Configuration		✎
Service Type	Web Service - SOAP 1.1 (WSDL: HelloWorld_SB/HelloWorldService, port="HelloWorldSoapPort")	
Transport Configuration		✎
Protocol	http	
Load Balancing Algorithm	round-robin	
Endpoint URI	http://localhost:7001/business/hello/HelloWorldService	
Retry Count	0	
Retry Iteration Interval	30	
Retry Application Errors	Yes	

Figure 16-1. *Endpoint URI is pointing to the wrong port!*

When the project was imported, it used the endpoint URI that applies to the osb30_book server (port 7001). You need to update the endpoint URI to use port 7101, which is the port used by the osb30_prod server. You must alter the export.py file so that it looks for environment variables that contain the string localhost:7001 and replaces that string with the value localhost:7101. Listing 16-3 shows an excerpt from the export.py file.

Listing 16-3. *Excerpt from the export.py File*

```
#==============================================================================
# Exports a project
#==============================================================================
def exportAll(exportConfigFile):
    try:
        print "Loading export config from :", exportConfigFile
        exportConfigProp = loadProps(exportConfigFile)
        adminUrl = exportConfigProp.get("adminUrl")
        exportUser = exportConfigProp.get("exportUser")
        exportPasswd = exportConfigProp.get("exportPassword")

        exportJar = exportConfigProp.get("exportJar")
        customFile = exportConfigProp.get("customizationFile")

        passphrase = exportConfigProp.get("passphrase")
        project = exportConfigProp.get("project")

        connectToServer(exportUser, exportPasswd, adminUrl)

        OSBConfigurationMBean = findService("OSBConfiguration", ➥
"com.bea.wli.sb.management.configuration.OSBConfigurationMBean")
        print "OSBConfiguration MBean found"
```

```
        print project
        if project == None :
            ref = Ref.DOMAIN
            collection = Collections.singleton(ref)
            if passphrase == None :
                print "Export the config"
                theBytes = OSBConfigurationMBean.export(collection, ➥
true, None)
            else :
                print "Export and encrypt the config"
                theBytes = OSBConfigurationMBean.export(collection, true, ➥
 passphrase)
        else :
            ref = Ref.makeProjectRef(project);
            print "Export the project", project
            collection = Collections.singleton(ref)
            theBytes = OSBConfigurationMBean.exportProjects(collection, ➥
passphrase)

        aFile = File(exportJar)
        out = FileOutputStream(aFile)
        out.write(theBytes)
        out.close()
        print "OSB Configuration file: "+ exportJar + " has been exported"

        if customFile != None:
            print collection
            customList = ArrayList()
            query = EnvValueQuery(None, ➥
Collections.singleton(EnvValueTypes.WORK_MANAGER), collection, false, ➥
None, false)
            customEnv = FindAndReplaceCustomization('Set the right Work ➥
Manager', query, 'Production System Work Manager')
            customList.add(customEnv)

            # Uncomment the next three lines to update the server and port
            # to the OSB30_prod environment correctly
            #query = EnvValueQuery(None, ➥
Collections.singleton(EnvValueTypes.SERVICE_URI), collection, false, ➥
'localhost:7001', false)
            #customEnv = FindAndReplaceCustomization('Update to the correct ➥
server and port number', query, 'localhost:7101')
            #customList.add(customEnv)

            print 'EnvValueCustomization created'
            print customList
            aFile = File(customFile)
            out = FileOutputStream(aFile)
```

```
        Customization.toXML(customList, out)
        out.close()

    print "OSB Dummy Customization file: "+ customFile + ➡
" has been created"
    except:
        raise
```

■**Note** There have been some changes to the API used in the scripting language between OSB 2.6 and OSB 3.0. Some classes have been removed (for example, TypeIds), and some classes have physically changed their JAR files. The examples in this book are all up-to-date for OSB 3.0.

Two critical commands are highlighted in Listing 16-3:

EnvValueQuery(): This is not just a command in a script; it is the Java constructor for the EnvValueQuery class, which is found in the package com.bea.wli.config.env. This class allows you to specify the type of information you are seeking. In our example, we were looking for endpoint URIs. OSB does not differentiate between endpoint URIs and any other URIs. By passing in EnvValueTypes.SERVICE_URI, you can confine the search to URIs within the system. If you passed a null value here instead, you would end up searching all types of environment values.

■**Tip** Using EnvValueQuery() in export.py, you can look for other specific types of data. If you examine the Javadoc for the com.bea.wli.sb.util.EnvValueTypes class, you will see a long list of data types you can search—everything in OSB from e-mail alert destinations to Work Managers is searchable.

FindAndReplaceCustomization(): This method takes three arguments: a description of the customization, the query that contains the information you want to replace, and the new string value.

The purpose of the export.py file is to specify the types of information that will need to be customized when the project is deployed into a new environment. These customizations are stored in the customize.xml file that the export.py script creates. As a result, you will need to have an export.py file for every project (or possibly a set of related projects) in your service bus. For example, if you had a set of related projects that were deployed at the same time, you would create a single export.py script to handle them.

Now that you understand what the export.py script is doing, the resulting customize.xml file, shown in Listing 16-4, should make sense. The second customization looks for the string localhost:7001 among all of the URI resources in the configuration file and replaces it with the string localhost:7101, which is exactly what we want.

Listing 16-4. *The Resulting customize.xml File*

```
<?xml version="1.0" encoding="UTF-8"?>
<cus:Customizations xmlns:cus=http://www.bea.com/wli/config/customizations ➡
xmlns:xsi="http://www.w3.org/2001/XMLSchema-instance" ➡
xmlns:xt="http://www.bea.com/wli/config/xmltypes">
  <cus:customization xsi:type="cus:FindAndReplaceCustomizationType">
    <cus:description>Set the right Work Manager</cus:description>
    <cus:query>
      <xt:envValueTypes>Work Manager</xt:envValueTypes>
      <xt:refsToSearch xsi:type="xt:LocationRefType">
        <xt:type>Project</xt:type>
        <xt:path>HelloWorld_SB</xt:path>
      </xt:refsToSearch>
      <xt:includeOnlyModifiedResources>false</xt:includeOnlyModifiedResources>
      <xt:searchString xsi:nil="true"/>
      <xt:isCompleteMatch>false</xt:isCompleteMatch>
    </cus:query>
    <cus:replacement>Production System Work Manager</cus:replacement>
  </cus:customization>
  <cus:customization xsi:type="cus:FindAndReplaceCustomizationType">
    <cus:description>Update to the correct server and port number ➡
</cus:description>
    <cus:query>
      <xt:envValueTypes>Service URI</xt:envValueTypes>
      <xt:refsToSearch xsi:type="xt:LocationRefType">
        <xt:type>Project</xt:type>
        <xt:path>HelloWorld_SB</xt:path>
      </xt:refsToSearch>
      <xt:includeOnlyModifiedResources>false</xt:includeOnlyModifiedResources>
      <xt:searchString>localhost:7001</xt:searchString>
      <xt:isCompleteMatch>false</xt:isCompleteMatch>
    </cus:query>
    <cus:replacement>localhost:7101</cus:replacement>
  </cus:customization>
</cus:Customizations>
```

As you can see from the lines in bold in Listing 16-4, you could easily modify the contents of the customize.xml file to meet your specific needs for searching and replacing text (or simply setting values without searching when appropriate), as you move from one environment to the next.

When you import the OSB project into the osb30_prod server, the import.py script will read in the customize.xml file and use it as a template for making changes to the OSB project when the project is imported. The customize.xml file acts to keep the export process and the import processes loosely coupled. Commonly, you take advantage of this loose coupling by creating a customize.xml file for each of your environments. For example, you might copy the generated customize.xml file and save it under multiple file names (such as helloworld_prod.xml, helloworld_stage.xml, and so on). Saving customize.xml under multiple names allows your administrators to independently modify the environment variables for each deployment environment. Modifying the Ant script and the `import.py` file to take a specific customization file is then a small matter, which would allow your administrators to use commands like `ant import helloworld_prod.xml`.

Ideally, you will need only a single `import.py` file in your entire enterprise, because it simply acts on the commands in the customization file. The `import.py` file really does not need any modification. With a little scripting work up-front, you can automate the entire deployment process.

OSB Domains and Clusters

A *domain* is a logical grouping of WebLogic Servers. Each domain has a single *admin server* and zero or more *managed servers*. The admin server is created when you create the domain. A *managed server* is any WebLogic Server that is not an admin server; the only difference between a managed server and an admin server is that the admin server has a number of additional administration applications deployed on it. In this book, you have created two domains: osb30_book and osb30_prod. Each of those domains contains a single admin server.

A *cluster* is a logical grouping of managed servers that all perform the same functionality. Clustering allows the administrator to manage all of the individual servers in the cluster as a single unit. Each cluster belongs to a single WebLogic domain and is composed of one or more managed servers.

Throughout this book, we have used single-server domains. This is the common approach when developing OSB services. However, in a production environment, running OSB in a cluster of servers is usually necessary. You use clustering in a production environment for several reasons:

- The amount of network traffic is too much for a single server to handle.

- The computational load is too much for a single server to handle.

- You want failover and high availability. If a server goes down in the cluster, the remaining servers in the cluster can continue to operate.

■**Note** The admin server does not represent a single point of failure in a cluster. If the admin server fails, the managed servers continue to run and service requests as usual.

Figure 16-2 shows a typical physical deployment diagram for an OSB domain with a cluster. The figure contains a lot of information, so let's go through it in detail.

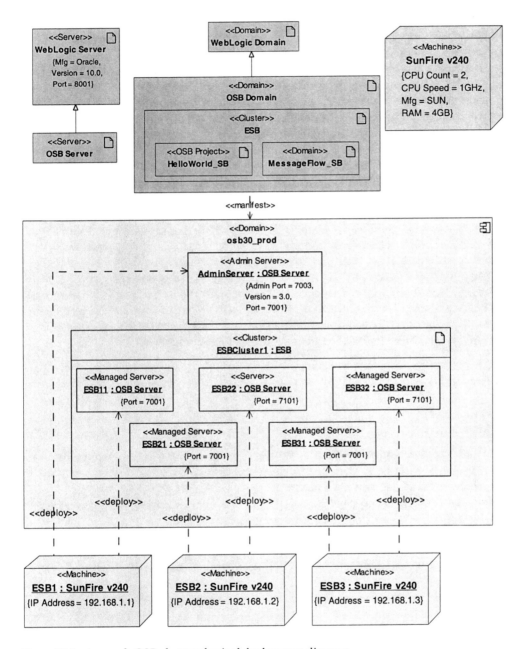

Figure 16-2. *A sample OSB cluster physical deployment diagram*

In the top-left portion of the diagram, you can see the artifacts for the WebLogic Server and the OSB server. The OSB server is just a specialized version of the WebLogic Server that contains additional applications specific to the needs of OSB.

In the top-middle of the diagram is an artifact that represents a WebLogic domain. Immediately beneath it is an artifact that represents an OSB domain, which is a specialized version of the WebLogic domain. The OSB domain contains a cluster named ESB, and the ESB cluster contains two OSB projects: the HelloWorld_SB and the MessageFlow_SB projects. This nesting notation specifies that anywhere you see the ESB cluster, the HelloWorld_SB and MessageFlow_SB projects will be deployed.

On the top-right portion of the diagram is the node specification, which defines some technical details of the type of machines used in the physical deployment of the system. When you match this node with the node instances at the bottom of the diagram, you get a clear picture of the types of computers used in the production environment. In most production environments, you will need to define multiple node elements if you are deploying onto different machine (computer) types.

The largest box in the diagram is the osb30_prod domain instance. This is an instance of the OSB domain artifact. Inside the domain are an admin server and a cluster. Within the cluster, you can see the individual managed servers. Each of these managed servers will be running instances of the HelloWorld_SB and MessageFlow_SB projects.

For the service clients, it is very important that the ESB performs as a single entity. You don't want your service clients to be aware of the fact that there is an OSB server running on the machine named ESB3. You also don't want your service clients to need to worry about the different ports used by each OSB managed server. Instead, you want your clients to be able to reference the ESB through a single, logical DNS name. That DNS name should then use a standard DNS load-balancing algorithm to distribute the calls among the various managed servers in the cluster. For example, the primary DNS alias should be a name like esb.mycorp.com. In our example, that DNS name would be a proxy for the following servers:

```
192.168.1.1:7101
192.168.1.2:7001
192.168.1.2:7101
192.168.1.3:7001
192.168.1.3:7101
```

Notice that the IP address of the admin server is not in the list. In a clustered environment, the admin server really exists just to manage the managed server. You do not deploy applications to the admin server in a cluster.

By using a DNS alias, you gain the operational freedom to add, move, and delete servers from the domain and cluster without affecting your service clients.

At this point, you are ready to create a cluster on your computer. In this example, we will create a new domain for our cluster. You can modify an existing domain and configure it for a cluster, but this is a painstakingly detailed process. Simply creating a new domain is much easier.

We will also show you how to create a software load-balancer server for the cluster, which will be able to emulate the effects of a hardware load-balancer. You use the software load-balancer only when working in development environments where you do not have access to a hardware load-balancer. The software load-balancer is a single point of failure. However, a software load-balancer is useful when you want to test the cluster and failover aspects of your OSB domain.

Creating a Cluster

Here are the steps for creating the clustered environment, including the software load-balancer:

1. Using the Configuration wizard, create a new domain that supports WebLogic Server, Workshop for WebLogic 10.2, and OSB.

2. Specify the username and password as weblogic and weblogic.

3. Select Production mode, and select one of the listed JDKs.

4. When asked if you want to customize any settings, click Yes.

5. Keep the default AdminServer name, and listen on port 7001.

6. Add a managed server named ESB1. Set its listen port to 7101. Add a second managed server named ESB2, and set its port to 7201. Add a third and final managed server named LoadBalancer, and set its listen port to 7301.

7. Add a cluster named ESB_Cluster. Keep the default multicast address and port. Set the cluster address to localhost:7101,localhost:7201.

8. Assign the ESB1 and ESB2 managed servers to the cluster.

9. Click the "Create HTTP proxy for cluster ESB_Cluster" check box and select LoadBalancer as the proxy server.

10. Add a machine named MyComputer (select the Unix tab if you are working on a Unix box). Keep the default Node Manager listen address and the default Node Manager listen port of 5556.

11. Add the AdminServer, ESB1, ESB2, and LoadBalancer servers to the MyComputer machine.

12. Accept the defaults for the JDBC data sources.

13. Run the database scripts, and be sure they all ran successfully.

14. Accept the defaults for the JMS file stores.

15. Accept the default values when reviewing the domain.

16. Name the domain osb30_cluster, and place it with the other domains you have created for this book.

17. At the end of the Configuration wizard, *do not check* the Start Admin Server check box. You must start the admin server manually the first time so you can provide the username and password in the console. This is because we are running this domain in production mode. Click the Done button.

18. In the osb30_cluster folder, run the startWebLogic script. This will create the server folder for the admin server.

19. Once the admin server is running, open the folder osb30_cluster/servers/AdminServer. Create a folder named security. In the security folder, create a file named boot.properties. Edit the boot.properties file so that it contains these two lines:

```
username=weblogic
password=weblogic.
```

That's it. You have created a domain with a cluster of two managed servers, plus a software load-balancer. The managed servers aren't running yet, but we will address that in a moment.

CONFIGURING SERVER MEMORY

You are welcome to create more managed servers if you like. You are constrained only by the amount of RAM available on your computer. On a 2GB machine, you could easily run an administration server and a single managed server. Trying to run a second managed server on a 2GB machine is tricky and will require you to modify the memory settings on your servers. You do not need to perform the steps outlined in this sidebar unless you are going to try to fit an additional managed server onto your machine. For example, you may be able to run two managed servers in a cluster on a 2GB laptop, but you would need to constrict the memory requirements of the servers severely.

You can control the memory requirements of your OSB servers by editing the setDomainEnv script in the bin directory of your domain. The following code snippet shows how to reduce the primary server arguments from 512MB to 384MB:

```
@REM Reduced stack and heap size from the default 512m to 384m to ➥
run the cluster on a single machine.
set MEM_ARGS=-Xms384m –Xmx384m
```

The next instruction in the setDomainEnv script specifies how much permanent memory the JVM should set aside. This memory is used to store objects that the JVM will need throughout its entire life cycle. Finding the correct part of the setDomainEnv script can be a little tricky, because you will see several different commands that include the MaxPermSize argument for each JAVA_VENDOR. It's usually easiest just to change all of the MaxPermSize instances in the script. The default MaxPermSize value is 128MB, but you can get away with a value as low as 96MB:

```
if "%JAVA_VENDOR%"=="Sun" (
    set MEM_ARGS=%MEM_ARGS% %MEM_DEV_ARGS% -XX:MaxPermSize=128m
)

if "%JAVA_VENDOR%"=="HP" (
    set MEM_ARGS=%MEM_ARGS% -XX:MaxPermSize=128m
)
```

If you are running OSB on a machine that is larger then 2GB, feel free to create additional managed servers for your cluster. Similarly, if you have access to several different machines on a network, you can create additional managed servers on other computers, which is the true purpose of clustering.

Introducing the Node Manager

When you were creating the osb30_cluster domain, the Configuration wizard asked you about the port that the Node Manager used on the machine you configured. The Node Manager is a utility that runs on every computer that hosts a managed server. The admin server communicates to the Node Managers on each machine when it needs to start or stop a managed server, and the local Node Manager executes the commands it receives from the admin server.

You need to run the Node Manager on your computer. The easiest way to do this is to open a command prompt. First, run the setDomainEnv script in the osb30_cluster\bin directory. This will set all of the environment variables properly for the Node Manager. Next, start the Node Manager by executing the command startNodeManager on the command line. If your domain exists on more than one computer, you will need to start a Node Manager on each computer in your domain.

When the Node Manager starts up, you will see output at the end of the startup sequence where the Node Manager displays its configuration settings, as shown in Listing 16-5.

Listing 16-5. *Configuration Settings of a Node Manager*

```
Node manager v10.0.0.0

Configuration settings:

NodeManagerHome=C:\BEAHome\osb30\WLSERV~1.0\common\NODEMA~1
ListenAddress=
ListenPort=5556
ListenBacklog=50
SecureListener=true
AuthenticationEnabled=true
NativeVersionEnabled=true
CrashRecoveryEnabled=false
JavaHome=C:\BEAHome\osb30\JDK150~1\jre
StartScriptEnabled=false
StopScriptEnabled=false
StartScriptName=startWebLogic.cmd
StopScriptName=
LogFile=C:\BEAHome\osb30\WLSERV~1.0\common\NODEMA~1\nodemanager.log
LogLevel=INFO
LogLimit=0
LogCount=1
LogAppend=true
LogToStderr=true
LogFormatter=weblogic.nodemanager.server.LogFormatter
DomainsFile=C:\BEAHome\osb30\WLSERV~1.0\common\NODEMA~1\nodemanager.domains
DomainsFileEnabled=true
StateCheckInterval=500

Domain name mappings:

wl_server -> C:\BEAHome\osb30\wlserver_10.0\samples\domains\wl_server
osb30_cluster -> C:\Domains\ osb30_cluster
osb30_prod -> C:\Domains\ osb30_prod
osb30_book -> C:\Domains\ osb30_book
...

<May 15, 2008 10:54:12 AM> <INFO> <Secure socket listener started on port 5556>
```

You can customize these settings by editing the nodemanager.properties file in the BEA_HOME\wlserver_10.0\common\nodemanager directory. The nodemanager.properties file is created for you the first time you run the Node Manager application. Also in that directory is the nodemanager.domain file, which contains a list of OSB domains that the Node Manager can handle. As you can see, the Node Manager is specific to a BEA_HOME, not to a domain.

For our example, we need to modify the nodemanager.properties file slightly. Specifically, we need to set the StartScriptEnabled property to true. This tells the Node Manager to use a script to start the managed servers and to ignore any settings defined for the servers in the WebLogic Server console. You will need to restart the Node Manager to load these property settings.

Controlling Managed Servers

With the Node Manager running, you can now open your browser and point it to the WebLogic console at http://localhost:7001/console. Navigate to the Clusters window (you can use the Domain Structure portlet on the console and select Environment ➤ Clusters), and select ESB_Cluster. You should now be viewing the Settings for ESB_Cluster window.

Among the set of tabs at the top of this window is a tab named Control. Click this tab to see a list of managed servers in the cluster, as shown in Figure 16-3.

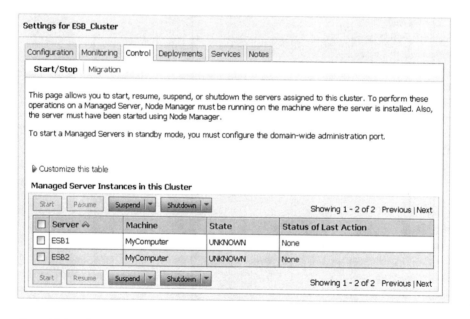

Figure 16-3. *The Settings for ESB_Cluster window*

Starting Managed Servers

Since this will be the very first time you start these managed servers, we recommend that you start them individually and wait for each server to start successfully before you start another server. It may take several minutes for the managed server to start. This is due to the fact that the very first startup for each server will involve a lot of data transfer between the managed server and the admin server. In the future, you will be able to start both servers simultaneously (and they will start faster, too).

To start the managed servers from the Control tab of the Settings for ESB_Cluster window, select the check boxes next to each server name and click the Start button.

You can also start managed servers from the command line. Simply navigate to the `bin` directory of the domain, run the `setDomainEnv` script, and start each managed server with the command `startManagedWebLogic <ServerName> <AdminServerURL>`. For example, you would start the ESB1 managed server with the command `startManagedWeblogic ESB1 http://localhost:7001`.

Starting the Load-Balancer

Before moving on, you will need to start the `LoadBalancer` server also. Using the Domain Structure portlet in the WebLogic Server admin console, select the Environment link, then the Servers Link, and then click the LoadBalancer link. This will take you to the Setting portlet for the `LoadBalancer` server. Click the Control tab to see the current status of the `LoadBalancer` server. Start the `LoadBalancer` server.

Deploying to a Cluster

One of the benefits of using a cluster is that it simplifies the management of software deployment. You can deploy OSB projects to the entire cluster simultaneously. Whenever you deploy an application to the admin server for the domain, the admin server automatically updates all of the managed servers.

Caution An OSB domain can support only one cluster. If you need multiple OSB clusters, you must create an OSB domain for each cluster.

For this exercise, we will deploy the `HelloWorld_WS` and `HelloWorld_SB` projects to the cluster. For previous examples, we created a server in the WorkSpace Studio IDE, but now we will more closely approximate the deployment process for a production environment. The first step is to create the appropriate deployable files from each of the projects.

Exporting the Deployable Files

We will begin with the `HelloWorld_WS` project. In WorkSpace Studio, right-click the project and select Export from the pop-up menu. JWS projects should be exported as WAR files (in the Web folder of the Export wizard). Name the WAR file `HelloWorld_SB.war`. Be sure that you select the `HelloWorld_WS` web module in the Export wizard also.

You will follow a similar process for the `HelloWorld_SB` project, except that you will export it as Resources as a Configuration JAR (in the Oracle Service Bus folder of the wizard). Export only the `HelloWorld_SB` project and name the export file to `HelloWorld_SB_sbconfig.jar`. Alternatively, you can open the `build.xml` file in the `DeployCluster` folder of the `Administration` project and execute the `export` target of the Ant script.

You now have the files that you would normally deliver to your QA and production teams, outside the development environment.

Deploying the WAR File

Deploying the HelloWorld_WS.war file to the cluster follows the traditional WebLogic approach for deploying web applications. Open a browser to http://localhost:7001/console, and then click the Deployments link. Create a change in the Change Center, and then click the Install button. Select the HelloWorld_WS.war file and click the Next button. Click the "Install this deployment as an application" button, and then click the Next button. You will now be given an option to deploy this web service to the cluster, as shown in Figure 16-4. Click the Next button, and then the Finish button to deploy the web service to the cluster. Activate your change in the Change Center.

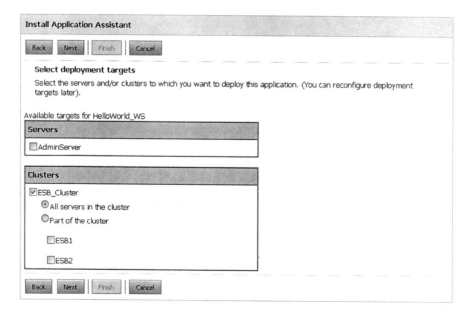

Figure 16-4. *Deploying a web application to a cluster*

The final step is to find the HelloWorld_WS deployment in the list of deployments in the admin console. You should see that it has a status of Prepared. Click the check box next to the web service, and then click the Start button. This will activate the web service so that is will start servicing all requests.

You can verify the deployment by opening your browser to http://192.168.1.102:7301/business/hello/HelloWorldService?wsdl. If you see the WSDL, you know that the web service has been deployed successfully.

Notice that we are using port 7301 in this URL. That is the port number used by the LoadBalancer server. The LoadBalancer's HTTP proxy service is forwarding the WSDL requests between the ESB1 and ESB2 servers.

Deploying the JAR File

Deploying the HelloWorld_SB_sbconfig.jar file uses a different process. Previously, we used a WLST script to import the JAR file. There is another way to do the same work that is often a better approach: use executable Java code. For this clustered project, we want to define multiple endpoints for the business service that will point to the HelloWorld_WS instances on the ESB1 and ESB2 servers, not the admin server.

You will notice that there is no import.py file in the DeployCluster folder. That is because the import logic is in the ImportProject.java file (in the src/com.osb.admin folder). There are two important methods in this class:

importFile: This method imports the HelloWorld_sbconfig.jar file into the OSB30_cluster domain. The code in this method is fairly straightforward. First, it creates a session for importing the file. This is done by creating both a SessionManagementMBean object and an OSBConfigurationMBean object. The importing is then performed with the OSBConfigurationMBean object. Whenever you want to make changes to an OSB configuration, you need both of these objects.

customizeProject: This method accesses the HelloWorld_SB project that was imported into the domain server and then modifies the URL endpoints of the HelloWorldBiz business service. The Ref class is used to provide a reference to the project and the business service. Listing 16-6 shows the customizeProject method. As in the importFile method, we create a SessionManagementMBean and an OSBConfigurationMBean. We then use the OSBConfigurationMBean to retrieve information about the business service.

Listing 16-6. *The customizeProject() Method*

```
private void customizeProject() {
    String projectName = (String)configProps.get("project");
    Ref projectRef = Ref.makeProjectRef(projectName);
    Ref businessServiceRef = Refs.makeBusinessSvcRef(projectRef, "HelloWorldBiz");

    try {
        // Create a session
        String sessionName = createSessionName();
        sm.createSession(sessionName);

        // Obtain the ALSBConfigurationMBean instance that operates on the
        // session that has just been created. Notice that the name of the
        // MBean contains the session name.
        ALSBConfigurationMBean ALSBSession = (ALSBConfigurationMBean) domainService.
            findService(ALSBConfigurationMBean.NAME + "." + sessionName,
                    ALSBConfigurationMBean.TYPE, null);

        URITableType uriTable = (URITableType)
            ALSBSession.getEnvValue(businessServiceRef,
                EnvValueTypes.SERVICE_URI_TABLE,
                null);

        URITableElementType newUri = uriTable.addNewTableElement();
        newUri.setURI("http://localhost:7201/business/hello/ ➥
HelloWorldService");
```

```
            // Let's also distribute the weight between the existing and
            // new URLs such that the existing one is used twice as much
            newUri.setWeight(1);
            URITableElementType existingUri = uriTable.getTableElementArray(0);
            existingUri.setURI("http://localhost:7101/business/hello/ ➥
HelloWorldService");
            existingUri.setWeight(2);

            QualifiedEnvValue env = new QualifiedEnvValue(businessServiceRef,
                EnvValueTypes.SERVICE_URI_TABLE, null, uriTable);

            EnvValueCustomization cust = new EnvValueCustomization(
                "adds a second url for a business service",
                Collections.singletonList(env));
            ALSBSession.customize(
                Collections.<Customization>singletonList(cust));
            // Activate changes performed in the session
          sm.activateSession(sessionName, "description");
      } catch(NotFoundException ex) {
            ex.printStackTrace();
      } catch(Exception ex) {
            ex.printStackTrace();
      }
   }
}
```

This listing shows how to retrieve the entire URITableType for the business service. You can then manipulate the URI table information, adding a new URI and modifying the existing URI to meet your needs. The code also shows how to set weight values for each URI. However, the weight values have meaning only if the load-balancing algorithm is set to random-weighted.

With this sample code, it's easy to imagine creating more sophisticated programs that can control the deployment details for a variety of services and resources. With a little work, you could modify this code to read endpoints in from a property file or a database of configuration information. It's even possible to connect to a UDDI registry and read some or all of the needed configuration information. Being able to do this configuration work in Java code opens up many possibilities!

To run the ImportProject.java program, just right-click the source code and select Run As ➤ Java Application from the pop-up menu. This will load the HelloWorld_SB_sbconfig.jar file into the admin server. Once the admin server has the project loaded, it will distribute the HelloWorld_SB project to both the ESB1 and ESB2 managed servers in the cluster.

Testing the Deployment

You can test the deployment using the test console. When you use the test console on the admin server of a cluster, you actually test the managed servers. Open the test console, and test the HelloWorld proxy service. You will need to perform several tests before you see the round-robin load-balancing take place.

After each test, take a look at the Invocation Trace section in the test console. In the `RouteToHelloWorldBiz` section, take a look at the added $outbound section to see the URI that was used for the test. Each time you test it, you will see the URI alternate between `localhost:7101` and `localhost:7201`. Each server gets two service invocations before the round-robin algorithm moves on to the next server in the cluster.

You can test the HTTP proxy server by making a modification to the `HelloWorldClient` program that we used in Chapter 3. The main change is to use the URL that points to the HTTP proxy server, as shown in Listing 16-7.

Listing 16-7. *The Modified HelloWorldClient Program*

```
public static void main(String[] args) {
    try {
        HelloWorldProxy proxy = new HelloWorldProxy();
        proxy.setEndpoint("http://localhost:7301/esb/HelloWorld");
        HelloWorld service = proxy.getHelloWorld();
        String greeting = service.getGreeting("Test");
        System.out.println("Greeting returned was: " + greeting);
    } catch(RemoteException ex) {
        ex.printStackTrace();
    }
}
```

As you can see, the HTTP proxy server on port 7301 is providing *location transparency* for our service client. The `HelloWorldClient` application has no knowledge of the physical location of the OSB servers. Location transparency allows you to scale your OSB server instances to as many as you need, without affecting any of your service clients.

Summary

A full treatise on the administration of any system, especially one as flexible and mature as OSB, could fill an entire book on its own. In this chapter, we covered some of the most important aspects of administration that are not easily discovered by reading the product documentation. This chapter answered the most common questions we encounter in the field by explaining how you can script the deployment process and configure OSB for production-level loads and load-balancing. With the information presented in this chapter, you are ready to put OSB into production in a reliable and scalable manner.

CHAPTER 17

■■■■

Custom Transports

You can extend the capabilities of OSB in several ways beyond those it has straight out of the box. The simplest way is to use the Java Callout action to invoke a POJO, as described in Chapter 8. In this chapter, we'll discuss how you can extend OSB's capabilities by adding custom transports beyond the standard transports that come with OSB, such as HTTP and JMS.

OSB comes with a set of interfaces for creating a custom transport, called the Transport Software Development Kit (SDK). You can use these interfaces to create a transport that fits into OSB as naturally as any of the standard transports. In fact, the transports that come with OSB are built using this very same Transport SDK! A custom transport can even have a transport configuration page that is presented to the user as one of the steps in creating a proxy or business service. The later sections of this chapter will cover the Transport SDK in detail.

Introduction to Custom Transports

Before we talk about the custom transports, let's review the standard transports that come with OSB 3 and later, listed in Table 17-1. This list will likely grow with future releases of the product.

Table 17-1. *Standard Transports*

Transport Name	Description
HTTP(S)	HTTP is the most common transport used by web services, employing the standard HyperText Transport Protocol used in the Web. HTTPS is just HTTP over SSL, a relatively efficient way to encrypt messages so that third parties cannot eavesdrop to get access to confidential information.
JMS	Using the JMS transport is an easy way to transmit messages reliably. JMS messages can also be transactional, providing "exactly once" quality of service (discussed later in the chapter, in the sections "Inbound Message Processing" and "Outbound Message Processing").
MQ	The MQ transport is for transmitting messages over IBM's WebSphere MQ using the native MQ libraries. It provides access to all of the WebSphere MQ headers. It has better performance than the JMS transport over WebSphere MQ.
File	The File transport is used for processing messages to or from files in a locally mounted file system. This is commonly used for large messages.
FTP	The FTP transport has similar use cases as the File transport, but is used for files in a remote file system, accessible via an FTP server.

Continued

Table 17-1. *Continued*

Transport Name	Description
SFTP	The SFTP transport is similar to the FTP transport in that it can read or write files from a remote file system, but it uses an encrypted, secure protocol that runs over SSH.
Email	The Email transport is used for processing e-mail messages, via POP3, IMAP (inbound), or SMTP (outbound).
EJB	The EJB transport is an outbound-only transport for invoking EJBs, either locally in the same server running OSB, or in a remote server.
WS	The WS transport supports WSRM, a standard protocol for reliably transmitting messages, even in the event of server or network failures.
DSP	The DSP transport is an outbound-only, optimized transport for communicating with ALDSP.
JPD	The JPD transport is an outbound-only, optimized transport for communicating with WebLogic Integration (WLI).
SB	The SB transport is an optimized transport used by other BEA products (such as ALDSP and WLI) to communicate with OSB. It can also be used between OSB domains.
Tuxedo	The Tuxedo transport is for communicating with Tuxedo systems, supporting all the standard Tuxedo buffer types (such as VIEW, FML, CARRAY, and so on) and even conversions between the typed buffers and standard XML messages.

You can mix and match different transports within a proxy service; that is, a proxy service can have one transport for receiving an inbound message and a different transport (or transports) to send outbound messages. For example, you can web service–enable an EJB or Tuxedo service by having a proxy that takes HTTP inbound and then invokes the EJB or Tuxedo service on outbound, after doing the appropriate transformations.

Why Build a Custom Transport?

Many people will have no need to build a custom transport. The standard transports provide support for a wide range of transport scenarios, satisfying most needs. However, you might need to build a custom transport to work with a proprietary communication mechanism, a transport not yet supported by OSB, or even a new protocol over one of the existing transports.

The following are some examples of new transports:

- Raw sockets, perhaps with text or XML messages (see "The Sample Socket Transport" section later in this chapter)

- CORBA or IIOP protocol for communicating with CORBA applications

- Variations on FTP, such as FTP over SSL (FTPS)

- A proprietary transport used by an organization in its existing applications

Alternatively, you can use the Transport SDK to support a specialized protocol over one of the existing transports. Examples of this include the following:

- Messages consisting of parsed or binary XML over HTTP

- Support for new web service standards over HTTP

- Request-response messaging over JMS, but with a different response pattern than supported by the OSB JMS transport

One of the prime reasons for using the Transport SDK is to support a specialized transport a company already employs for communication among its internal applications. Such a transport might have its own concept of setup handshake, header fields, metadata, or transport-level security. You can create an implementation of the transport for use with OSB that allows configuring individual endpoints—inbound, outbound, or both. You can map the metadata and header fields nicely to context variables available in a proxy service pipeline.

Creating a new OSB transport using the Transport SDK can be a significant effort. The Transport SDK provides a rich, full-featured environment, so that a custom transport has all the usefulness and capabilities of the transports that come natively with OSB. But such richness brings complexity. For certain cases, you should consider easier alternatives.

If you need the extension merely to support a different type of message format sent or received over an existing protocol, it might be possible to use the existing transport and use a Java Callout action to convert the message. For example, suppose you have a specialized binary format (for example, ASN.1 or a serialized Java object) being sent over the standard JMS protocol. An alternative to consider is to define the service using the standard JMS transport with the service type as a messaging service with binary input and output messages. Then, if the contents of the message are needed in the pipeline, you can use a Java Callout action to convert the message to or from XML.

Tip Implement a custom transport when you need to communicate over a completely different transport mechanism, or when using a different protocol over an existing transport. If you just need to support a new message format over an existing transport, instead of creating a custom transport, try creating a messaging proxy with a binary format and using a Java Callout action to interpret the message.

How Does a Custom Transport Fit into OSB?

A custom transport built with the Transport SDK is a first-class citizen. It can do anything that other standard transports can do. You can configure both proxy services and business services using the custom transport (or the custom transport can support just proxy services or just business services), as illustrated in Figure 17-1. The transport provider decides which—or all—of the service types to support. (For example, it might not make sense to support SOAP services or binary services). Business services defined using the custom transport can be used in Route, Publish, or Service Callout actions.

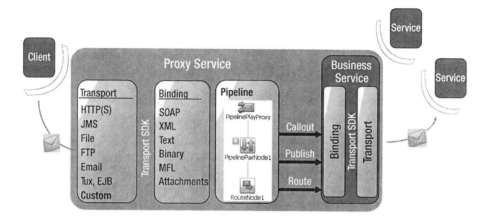

Figure 17-1. *Where transports fit in at runtime*

The life of a message in OSB starts in the inbound transport and ends with the outbound transport. The transport used by a proxy has some mechanism to listen for new messages and then feed the incoming messages into the OSB runtime. At the other end, when the processed message is being sent out to a business service, the last stop in the processing is the business service transport, whose responsibility is to deliver the message. The runtime APIs in the Transport SDK form the interface, or glue, between the transport and the rest of the OSB runtime system.

The wizard used to create a proxy or business service includes a generic transport configuration page, followed by a configuration page specific to the chosen transport. The Transport SDK includes APIs for declaring the user interface (UI) fields that can be filled out when declaring a service using a custom transport (details will be covered in the section "Implementing Transport Provider User Interface Classes"). The system automatically creates the transport-specific configuration page based on the transport's configured UI fields. A custom transport adds a new choice to the list of possible transports in the generic window, and then provides a unique transport-specific window for configuring a service that uses the custom transport.

For example, Figure 17-2 shows the configuration window for the socket transport—the sample custom transport that comes with OSB (details of the sample socket transport are given in the next section). You won't see this in your standard installation of OSB. This page will be available only after you install the sample transport.

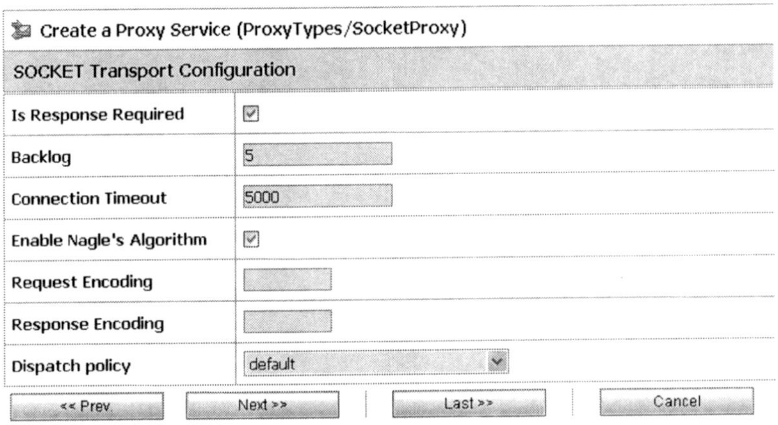

Figure 17-2. *Socket Transport Configuration window*

A wide variety of UI elements are available to use in a custom transport configuration window. Notice how the Socket Transport Configuration window in Figure 17-2 includes check boxes, pull-down lists, and fill-in-the-blank–type fields. Browsing through the windows for the other transports will give you a good idea of the available UI elements.

The result of using these UI elements is that a custom transport configuration window looks like the other windows in OSB. The transport provider can do full validation on the fields to make sure good values have been entered. No one will know that this comes from a custom transport rather than a standard transport, except for the transport provider.

The preceding discussion covers the design environment in the console-based UI, but the same is true for the WorkSpace Studio IDE. The same Transport SDK APIs that declare UI elements for the console are used to dynamically create a UI in WorkSpace Studio. In other words, the transport provider implements one set of APIs that give metadata descriptions of the configuration fields, and that metadata is rendered one way for the browser-based console and in a different way in WorkSpace Studio.

Figure 17-3 shows the configuration window for a proxy service using the socket transport as it appears in WorkSpace Studio. Notice how this is just another rendering of the same data that appears in the browser-based window in Figure 17-2. Again, you won't see this in the standard installation of OSB. The option to use the socket transport appears only after the socket transport is packaged as an Eclipse plug-in and deployed to WorkSpace Studio.

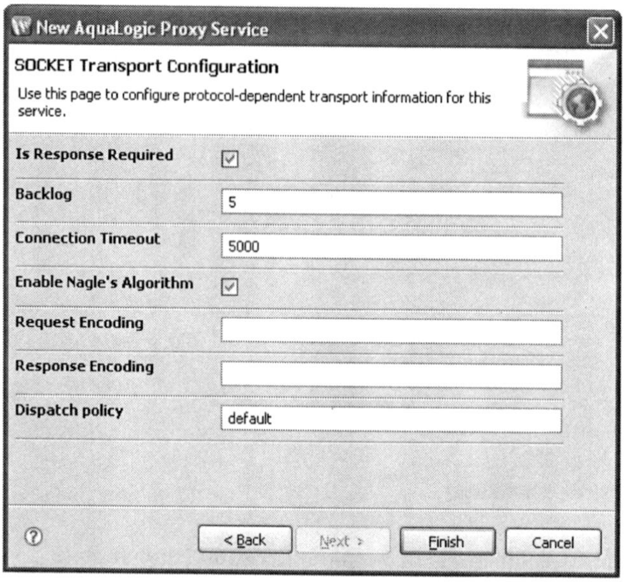

Figure 17-3. *Socket Transport Configuration window in the IDE*

■**Caution** Proxy and business services that use custom transports can be exported like any other resources. However, if you import them into another OSB domain that doesn't include the custom transport, you'll get validation errors and the import will fail.

There are many options to consider when designing a custom transport. A transport can support just inbound (proxy services), just outbound (business services), or both. It can support one-way messages or request-response exchanges. It can enforce transport-level security. Inbound transports can achieve "exactly once" semantics by beginning and committing transactions, while outbound transports can participate in a transaction. A transport can even define a custom message format for holding the message, and provide transformations to convert the message into a format OSB can understand (for example, XML) when needed.

If you don't understand all the options discussed in the previous paragraph, don't worry. We'll be discussing these topics and more in later sections of this chapter.

Components of a Custom Transport

Here's a quick glimpse at the components you'll need to create as part of a custom transport. We'll go into this in much more detail, but this section will provide an overview of what needs to be built.

You'll need a deployment unit, such as an EAR file, for deploying all the code for your custom transport to WLS. You'll use standard WLS application deployment tools to deploy your file. The deployment unit will contain the following:

Design-time code: This code defines the UI and configuration of services using custom transport. The OSB console will call this code when a new service is created or updated. This includes methods to validate the configuration data.

Runtime code: This code is used to receive or send messages. The receiving code delivers the message to the OSB runtime system along with any metadata or transport headers, while the sending code gets messages from OSB for delivery to the external service.

XMLBean classes and schemas: These define how your custom transport is configured, and the metadata and headers used by your transport. These XML configuration files are a key part of a custom transport.

Registration code: This code will register your transport provider with the OSB transport manager on application deployment life-cycle events, such as server startup.

The Sample Socket Transport

The easiest way to learn how to develop a new custom transport is by looking at an example. OSB version 2.5 and later comes with a sample custom transport that implements a simple socket mechanism for talking to services using raw TCP/IP. This transport is called the socket transport. In this section, we'll describe this sample transport, how to build and install it, and how to use it in OSB proxy and business services. We'll use the sample socket transport in examples in the following sections.

Capabilities of the Socket Transport

You can probably imagine many different interesting transports that could have been chosen to form a sample custom transport. Why make a sample transport communicate over something as simple as plain TCP/IP sockets? That simplicity is exactly the answer! The sample transport can focus on demonstrating how to use the interfaces of the Transport SDK without getting bogged down with complex transport logic, such as how to perform CORBA calls, interact with MQ interfaces, map some proprietary message format to XML, and so on.

The socket transport is a basic transport that can send and receive text messages (including XML) over sockets. Messages are terminated by a blank line (more explicitly, by two sets of carriage-return, line-feed characters). Because the message is terminated by a blank line, there's no need for a message header describing the length of the message, and the message can be streamed in and out of the service.

You can use the socket transport with service types compatible with text messages—namely, Any XML—and messaging services with messages that are either text or XML (with or without a schema). You can't use the socket transport with SOAP-based services (though you can use it with a WSDL service whose binding type is plain XML).

The socket transport has some configuration attributes for the underlying socket usage, such as Nagle's Algorithm, an option that can help optimize the TCP/IP traffic. These attributes are somewhat gratuitous. They are included just to have something to configure in the transport-specific pages. In addition, the socket transport has some metadata and transport headers associated with each message—again, mostly for the purpose of demonstrating how to support those features.

When you do a full installation of OSB, you'll get the sample socket transport installed in the OSB `samples` directory, as indicated in Figure 17-4. The files included with the sample include scripts for compiling and deploying the sample, configuration and schema files, and Java programs to help test OSB services that use the socket transport. All source files are included.

Figure 17-4. *Location of the sample transport*

Building and Installing the Sample Transport

At the top level of the sample transport directory is a README.TXT file that gives instructions on how to build, deploy, and test the socket transport. We'll go through those steps here. We'll describe these steps in terms of Windows commands, but the steps are equivalent on Unix platforms.

Before you can deploy the sample socket transport, you'll need an OSB domain. We'll assume you've already created an OSB domain using the standard Domain Configuration wizard. For simplicity, put the location of your domain directory into a variable DOMAIN_DIR. Also, put the location of the sample-transport directory into another variable SAMPLE_DIR.

The first thing you need to do is to set the appropriate environment variables. The build and deploy scripts use these. Execute the following commands:

```
cd  %DOMAIN_DIR%\bin
setDomainEnv
```

Now you're ready to build the sample socket transport. Simply execute the Ant build script:

```
cd %SAMPLE_DIR%
ant build-jar
```

If everything builds correctly, you'll get a message "Build Successful," with the time taken to do the build. The output will look something like the condensed output shown in Listing 17-1 (some of the output has been omitted for brevity). Notice how at the end of the script execution, the transport EAR file is placed in the servicebus\lib directory.

Listing 17-1. *Output from Building the Sample Socket Transport*

```
D:>cd %DOMAIN_DIR%\bin

D:>setDomainEnv
D:>cd %SAMPLE_DIR%

D:>ant build-jar
Buildfile: build.xml

build-jar:
     [echo] -------------------------------------------------
     [echo] |              Socket transport build starting    |
     [echo] -------------------------------------------------
    [mkdir] Created dir: D:\WL_HOME\alsb_3.0\samples\servicebus\
sample-transport\build

create_directories:
     [echo] >>>>>> create_directories >>>>>>
    [mkdir] Created dir: D:\WL_HOME \alsb_3.0\samples\servicebus\sample-transport\
build\classes
    [mkdir] Created dir: D:\WL_HOME \alsb_3.0\samples\servicebus\sample-transport\
build\help
    [mkdir] Created dir: D:\WL_HOME \alsb_3.0\samples\servicebus\sample-transport\
build\ear
    [mkdir] Created dir: D:\WL_HOME \alsb_3.0\samples\servicebus\sample-transport\
build\eclipse
     [echo] >>>>>> Done create_directories >>>>>>

xbean:
```

```
schema_compile:
     [java] Time to build schema type system: 1.352 seconds
     [java] Time to generate code: 0.311 seconds
     [java] Time to compile code: 5.019 seconds

compile:
     [echo] >>>>>> compile >>>>>>
     [echo] debug = on, optimize = off,     deprecation = off

compile.i18n.catalogs:
     [echo] >>>>>> compiling i18n catalogs >>>>>>
                                              :
                                              :


fixup.i18n:
     [echo] >>>>>> Done compiling i18n catalogs >>>>>>
                                              :
                                              :


create_jar:
     [copy] Copying 48 files to D:\WL_HOME\alsb_3.0\samples\servicebus\
sample-transport\build\help
      [jar] Building jar: D:\WL_HOME\alsb_3.0\samples\servicebus\sample-transport\
build\sock_transport.jar

create_ear:
                                              :
                                              :
      [ear] Building ear: D:\WL_HOME\alsb_3.0\servicebus\lib\sock_transport.ear

create_plugin:
                                              :
                                              :
      [zip] Building zip: D:\WL_HOME\alsb_3.0\samples\servicebus\sample-transport\
build\eclipse\Socket_Transport_3.0.0.0.jar

create_test_client_jar:
                                              :
                                              :
     [echo] -------------------------------------------------
     [echo] |            Socket transport build completed     |
     [echo] -------------------------------------------------

BUILD SUCCESSFUL
Total time: 18 seconds
```

Now that you've built the socket transport, you can deploy it to the running OSB domain. However, the deploy script needs information about the running domain in order to deploy the transport EAR file. This requires editing the build.properties file, shown in Listing 17-2, to add information about the domain.

Listing 17-2. *build.properties File*

```
# What we get from the env.
root.dir=${basedir}

# Compiler options
optimize=off
debug=on
deprecation=off
build.compiler=modern
# javac.lint.flag=-Xlint -Xlint:-path
javac.lint.flag=

# Weblogic home
bea.home=${env.BEA_HOME}
wl.home=${env.WL_HOME}
qs.install.dir=${env.ALSB_HOME}
modules.dir=${bea.home}/modules
env.INSTALLDIR=${wl.home}/server

# If you need to use an external weblogic home
# bea.home=${env.BEA_HOME}
# wl.home=${env.WL_HOME}

### Weblogic Server information  ###
wls.hostname=localhost
wls.port=7001
wls.username=weblogic
wls.password=weblogic
wls.server.name=AdminServer
```

The WebLogic Server information section (shown in bold) now requires filling out. You'll need to specify the hostname and port where your OSB domain is running, the administrator's username and password, and the managed server name. If your OSB domain is running in a cluster, you'll need to run the deploy script for every managed server in the cluster. Luckily, if you're running on your own local machine with the default settings, the values in that section should already be set appropriately.

Tip Before you deploy the sample socket transport, make sure you've already started your OSB domain.

With the `build.properties` file now describing how to access your running OSB domain, you can simply deploy the built EAR file. Make sure you're still in the `sample-transport` directory and execute the following command:

```
ant deploy
```

This step deploys the socket transport to the server environment, which includes making the configuration pages available in the console. However, you still need to deploy the transport to the WorkSpace Studio environment. (The earlier build step created the Eclipse plug-in, but none of the steps deploy the plug-in to WorkSpace Studio.) Fortunately, this is quite simple to do. You merely copy the already built plug-in to the Eclipse `plugins` directory. You can do this through the copy from a Windows Explorer window, or you can make a copy from the command line by executing the following command (making sure you are in the `samples` directory).

```
copy build\eclipse\Socket_Transport_3.0.0.0.jar %ALSB_HOME%\eclipse\plugins
```

That's it. You've now built the sample socket transport and have deployed it to both the server and WorkSpace Studio! The next time you start WorkSpace Studio, the transport will be automatically loaded.

■**Tip** If you want to make changes to the socket transport and try out your changes, you can simply re-execute the Ant build command, and then restart your server. There's no need to execute the deploy step a second time. In fact, doing so will cause problems with the deployed EAR file.

Using the Sample Socket Transport

Now that you've built and deployed the sample socket transport, let's take it out for a test drive. We'll describe these steps in a Windows environment, but these are readily translatable into a Unix environment.

The first thing you need is a running service using sockets for OSB to access. Just such a service comes with OSB. The sample socket directory has a `test` subdirectory that contains source for a socket server and a socket client. As part of building the sample transport, you've already built these two programs. You can now run them.

The command to run the test server is as follows:

```
java -classpath .\test\build\test-client.jar -Dfile-encoding=<char-set> ↩
    -Drequest-encoding=<char-set> com.bea.alsb.transports.sample.test.TestServer ↩
    <port> <message-file-location>
```

The choice of encoding character sets is optional (it defaults to UTF-8, which is close enough to plain-old ASCII). The `message-file-location` is also optional. The server always gives a fixed, canned response, drawn from the message file. If you don't provide the `message-file-location`, the server will just use the standard message, which is good enough for our purposes.

```
<?xml version="1.0" ?>
<project name="sock-transport" default="build-jar" basedir="."/>
```

Now open a command-line window. In that window, type the following commands to start the server. This will start the server listening on port 8100 (use a different port if that one is already in use on your machine).

```
cd %SAMPLE_DIR%

java -classpath .\test\build\test-client.jar ➥
    com.bea.alsb.transports.sample.test.TestServer 8100
```

Before you try to access this server from OSB, make sure everything is working. Let's invoke this service from the test client:

```
java -classpath .\test\build\test-client.jar -Dfile-encoding=<char-set> ➥
    -Drequest-encoding=<char-set> com.bea.alsb.transports.sample.test.TestClient ➥
    <host-name> <port> <thread-ct> <message-file-location>
```

You can do similar simplifications when running the test client as you did for running the test server. So, open another command-line window, and type these commands to have the test client talk to your running test server:

```
cd %SAMPLE_DIR%

java -classpath .\test\build\test-client.jar ➥
    com.bea.alsb.transports.sample.test.TestClient localhost 8100 1
```

In the command-line window, you should get output like the following:

```
D: >java -classpath .\test\build\test-client.jar
com.bea.alsb.transports.sample.test.TestClient localhost 8100 1
<Sun Jun 08 23:16:04 PDT 2008> ----> host = localhost
<Sun Jun 08 23:16:04 PDT 2008> ----> port = 8100
<Sun Jun 08 23:16:04 PDT 2008> ----> threadCt = 1
<Sun Jun 08 23:16:04 PDT 2008> ----> file-encoding = utf-8
<Sun Jun 08 23:16:04 PDT 2008> ----> sock.getPort() = 8100
<Sun Jun 08 23:16:04 PDT 2008> ----> sock.getRemoteSocketAddress() = ➥
    localhost/127.0.0.1:8100
<Sun Jun 08 23:16:04 PDT 2008> ----> sock.getLocalSocketAddress() = /127.0.0.1:4637
<Sun Jun 08 23:16:04 PDT 2008> ----> sock.getInetAddress() = localhost
<Sun Jun 08 23:16:04 PDT 2008> ----> sock.getLocalPort() = 4637
<Sun Jun 08 23:16:04 PDT 2008> Sent a message to the server on thread: Thread-0
<Sun Jun 08 23:16:04 PDT 2008> ----> response for thread: Thread-0= ➥
    <?xmlversion="1.0" ?> <project name="sock-transport" default="build-jar" ➥
    basedir="."/>
```

Note how the response for the thread is exactly the same as the canned response the server gives, as described earlier. The server command-line window should have output like the following:

```
D: >java -classpath .\test\build\test-client.jar
com.bea.alsb.transports.sample.test.TestServer 8100
<Sun Jun 08 22:26:57 PDT 2008>Started listening on socket:0.0.0.0/0.0.0.0
on thread:main
<Sun Jun 08 22:28:24 PDT 2008>Connection established for: /127.0.0.1 on
thread:main
<Sun Jun 08 22:28:25 PDT 2008>Request is:I am a Rimbaud with a leather jacket,
If my poetry aims to achieve anything, it's to deliver people from the limited
 ways in which they see and feel-- the Lizard King -----JM
```

That odd bit of text is the canned request the test client has sent to the server. Evidently, the developer who created the sample was a fan of Jim Morrison of the Doors, whose music was generally regarded as being much better than his poetry.

This is all well and good, but you haven't done anything to demonstrate your transport working with OSB. It's time to create an OSB proxy service and business service that use the socket transport.

To begin, open the OSB console and click the Create button in the Change Center to start a new session for your work. Then perform the following steps:

1. Create a new project and name it SocketTest.

2. In this new project, create a business service resource named SocketBS. For the Service Type setting, select Any XML Service, and go to the next page.

3. If the socket transport was deployed correctly, you should now see "socket" in the Protocol drop-down list. Select it.

4. Add an endpoint URI to be that of your running test socket server. Enter the URI tcp://localhost:8100 and click the Add button. The default retry values are fine, so go on to the next page.

5. This next page is the socket transport configuration page. This is the screen that was automatically created by OSB. Because all the default values are fine, go on to the next page.

6. Save your business service.

The summary of the SocketBS business service should look like Figure 17-5.

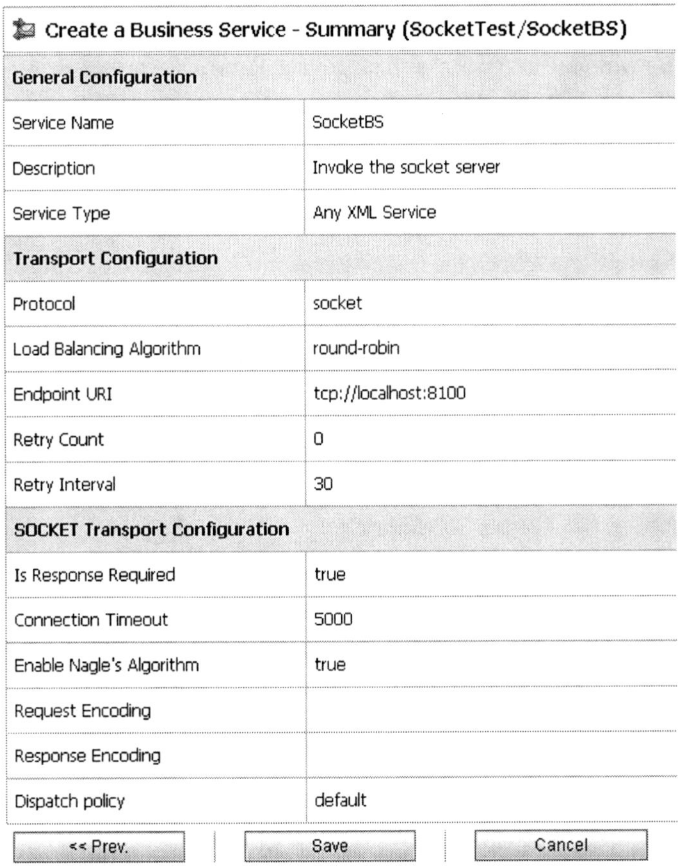

Figure 17-5. *SocketBS business service summary*

You could activate your session and test this business service. But, while you're in the session, go ahead and create a proxy that invokes this business service.

1. In the SocketTest project, create a proxy service resource named SocketProxy. Use the option to create this service from the business service SocketBS.

2. Select "socket" from the Protocol drop-down list. Set the endpoint URI to tcp://7100. So, while your test server is listening on port 8100, your intermediary proxy will be listening on 7100.

3. Just accept the rest of the default values on the following pages until you've finished creating the proxy service, and save it.

4. Because you created the proxy service from a business service, the pipeline has already been initialized with a Route node that has a Routing action that routes to SocketBS.

5. Activate the session.

You've now created both the business service for accessing your test server and a proxy service to act as an intermediary. Let's test each of these.

Back in the Project Explorer window for the SocketTest project, launch the test console for the SocketBS. Enter any legal XML snippet, such as <MySocketTest/>, and hit Execute. You should see the same canned response in the response document that you saw earlier when you tested the server from the test client:

```
<project  name="sock-transport" default="build-jar" basedir="."/>
```

Now go back to the OSB console and launch the test console for the proxy SocketProxy. Follow the same steps to test SocketProxy as you did for SocketBS. You'll get the same response.

Finally, just to complete the whole cycle, bring up the command-line window where you ran the test client. Let's rerun that test client again, but this time specifying port 7100 rather than port 8100:

```
D: >java -classpath .\test\build\test-client.jar
com.bea.alsb.transports.sample.test.TestClient localhost 7100 1
<Sun Jun 08 23:21:06 PDT 2008> ----> host = localhost
<Sun Jun 08 23:21:06 PDT 2008> ----> port = 7100
<Sun Jun 08 23:21:06 PDT 2008> ----> threadCt = 1
<Sun Jun 08 23:21:06 PDT 2008> ----> file-encoding = utf-8
<Sun Jun 08 23:21:06 PDT 2008> ----> sock.getPort() = 7100
<Sun Jun 08 23:21:06 PDT 2008> ----> sock.getRemoteSocketAddress() = ➥
    localhost/127.0.0.1:7100
<Sun Jun 08 23:21:06 PDT 2008> ----> sock.getLocalSocketAddress() = /127.0.0.1:4368
<Sun Jun 08 23:21:06 PDT 2008> ----> sock.getInetAddress() = localhost
<Sun Jun 08 23:21:06 PDT 2008> ----> sock.getLocalPort() = 4368
<Sun Jun 08 23:21:06 PDT 2008> Sent a message to the server on thread: Thread-0
<Sun Jun 08 23:21:06 PDT 2008> ----> response for thread: Thread-0= ➥
<?xml version="1.0" ?> <project name="sock-transport" default="build-jar" ➥
    basedir="."/>
```

What's happening here is that the test client is talking to the OSB proxy on port 7100, over the socket transport. The OSB proxy is forwarding the message on to the test server on port 8100, again using the socket transport on the outbound side. The socket transport is being successfully used on both the inbound and outbound sides!

Building a Custom Transport

In this section we'll dive into the details of what needs to be done to build a custom transport. We'll draw heavily from the sample socket transport discussed in the previous section, so refer to that section as necessary. We'll cover the standard stuff that every transport needs to implement, and later get into advanced topics whose usage can vary by transport.

Overview of the Transport SDK Interfaces

Before we get too deeply into the bits and bytes of building a transport, we want to give you a high-level overview of the main Transport SDK interfaces that are used to build a transport. More information about these classes is available in the Javadoc API documentation.

Class TransportManagerHelper: A utility class that provides information about the OSB domain, accesses features of the domain such as security information or dispatch policies, and most important, can get an instance of the TransportManager.

Class ServiceInfo: Information about a configured service (proxy or business service), including the transport configuration and binding type.

Interface TransportManager: The key interface a service provider uses to interact with OSB. This includes methods to register a new transport provider and to pass an incoming message into the OSB pipeline.

Interface TransportProvider: The key interface a service provider must implement. There are both design-time–oriented methods (for example, methods for creating, updating, and deleting service endpoints that use this transport) and runtime methods (for example, methods sending an outbound message). OSB calls some of the methods to query the capabilities of the provider.

Interface SelfDescribedTransportProvider: An interface that extends TransportProvider and can be used for transports whose endpoints are "self-described," meaning that they define their own WSDL or schema interface based on the endpoint configuration. A transport provider can optionally implement this interface if it supports services that are self-typed.

Interface TransportCustomBindingProvider: Another interface that the TransportProvider implementation class can optionally implement if it wants to control some of the settings in the effective WSDL for the service, such as the URI identifying the transport or the modified URL of the service. (See the "Custom Transport WSDL Support" section later in this chapter.)

Interface TransportProviderFactory: The extension point to plug custom OSB transports into WorkSpace Studio. The provider implements this interface to provide an alternative way of registering a transport provider when running in WorkSpace Studio. (See the "Registering the Transport Provider in WorkSpace Studio" section later in this chapter.)

Interface EndPointOperations: Contains data that is passed to the TransportProvider when it needs to do an operation on a service endpoint, such as create, update, delete, suspend, or resume.

Interface TransportWLSArtifactDeployer: A transport provider can optionally implement this interface if it needs to interact with WLS management as part of deploying a service endpoint; for example, if it needs to deploy an EJB, a JWS, or some other WLS artifact as part of activating a service.

Interface ServiceTransportSender: An object of this type is passed to the outbound transport when sending a message to contain the data and metadata associated with the message.

Interface TransportEndPoint: Represents a service endpoint; that is, the transport portion of a proxy service (inbound endpoint) or a business service (outbound endpoint).

Interface Source: Messages are passed through the runtime system via classes implementing the Source interface. These classes are containers for representing the content of a message. The common denominator of all sources is that they must provide an input stream to their contents and be able to write their contents to an output stream. There are many standard sources, including StreamSource, ByteArraySource, StringSource, XmlObjectSource, DOMSource, MFLSource, SAAJSource, MimeSource, MessageContextSource, and AttachmentsSource. You can also define your own custom Source object.

Interface Transformer: If you do define your own custom Source object, you can also provide transformers that can convert your Source class to any of the other standard Source classes, without needing to go through a stream.

Class RequestHeaders, ResponseHeaders: Along with the Source representing the message, these classes contain transport header information associated with the message.

Class RequestMetaData, ResponseMetaData: These extend the headers to provide additional metadata associated with the message.

Interface InboundTransportMessageContext, OutboundTransportMessageContext: The transport provider implements these interfaces to bring together all the information associated with a message under one object. This includes the Source for the payload of the message, the headers, the metadata, and other information associated with the message.

Interface TransportSendListener: The callback object that the outbound transport uses to deliver a response message into the pipeline.

Interface TransportUIBinding: The transport provider implements this interface to provide all the information for rendering the provider-specific transport configuration screen. This also includes the methods for validating the entered configuration data.

Class TransportUIFactory: A utility class for creating various UI elements to be included on the transport configuration screen. These include text box, check box, select drop-down, password entry, browser text box (for selecting OSB artifacts such as a service account), text area, and dynamic table.

The preceding list includes the main classes and interfaces of the Transport SDK. There are several more classes, which are essentially value objects for grouping together a bunch of information into one interface. These consist mainly of getter- or setter-type methods for accessing or setting their information. Information about these classes is available in the Javadoc API documentation.

Another set of classes worth mentioning are classes that aren't documented in the Javadoc API documentation. These are the XMLBean classes (of type `XmlObject`) that are generated from the XML schema file `TransportCommon.xsd`. You'll find this file in `BEA_HOME/alsb3.0/lib/sb-kernel-api.jar`. XMLBean technology is used heavily in OSB. For more information about this technology, see `http://xmlbeans.apache.org/`. Although there isn't Javadoc API documentation for these interfaces, the documentation for these XMLBean classes is in the `TransportCommon.xsd` schema file.

`EndPointConfiguration`: The generic configuration for a service endpoint. This contains the configuration data that applies to all transports. A custom transport provider defines its own schema for the additional configuration necessary for endpoints using the transport. This additional XML configuration data is assigned to the `provider-specific` element within `EndPointConfiguration`.

`RequestHeadersXML`, `ResponseHeadersXML`: The base type for request and response headers. Custom transports extend these schemas to define their own headers.

`RequestMetaDataXML`, `ResponseMetaDataXML`: The base type for request and response metadata associated with a message. Custom transports extend these schemas to define their own metadata.

`TransportProviderConfiguration`: An XMLBean providing configuration information about the transport; for example, whether it supports inbound (proxies), outbound (business services), or both.

We'll describe how to create all these XMLBeans in the upcoming sections "Transport Provider Configuration XML File" and "Transport Provider Schemas."

Overview of Tasks

Here are the tasks to implement a custom transport. This is a roadmap for the following sections.

1. Create your custom transport provider configuration XML file.

2. Create schemas for your custom transport. This includes schemas for your service endpoint configuration, for your request and response headers (if any), and for your request and response metadata.

3. Implement the custom transport UI classes.

4. Deploy service endpoints using the custom transport.

5. Implement the message-processing runtime classes.

6. Register the custom transport provider.

Transport Provider Configuration XML File

Part of the behavior of a transport provider is described via a simple XML file named TransportProviderConfiguration. This is a convenient place to declare behavior and properties of the transport without needing to code Java methods. The schema for this file is shown in Figure 17-6.

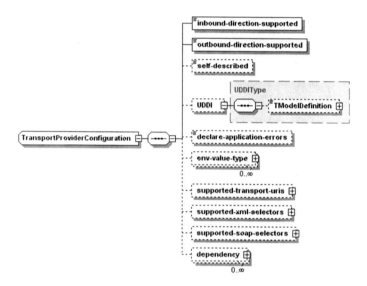

Figure 17-6. *Transport provider configuration schema*

Notice that the configuration XML file has only two required elements: inbound-direction-supported and outbound-direction-supported. All of the other elements are optional. You can safely ignore those other elements until you have the first blush of your transport working, and then come back to them to fill in some additional capabilities of the transport.

inbound-direction-supported *and* outbound direction-supported: Declare whether the transport supports inbound (proxies), outbound (business services), or both.

self-described: Declares whether the endpoint configuration defines its own structure or schema. The EJB transport is an example of such a transport. Rather than being defined by a WSDL file, the EJB transport generates its own WSDL by introspecting the target EJB.

UDDI: A place for a transport to declare a UDDI tModel definition for the transport. OSB can publish proxies to a UDDI registry. The published proxy has information describing its interface, including identifying the transport used by the service. The transport is identified by pointing to the tModel for the transport. OSB will publish all the transport tModels when you configure the UDDI registry to be used by OSB.

declare-application-errors: Declares whether a transport can distinguish application errors from other types of errors like communication or connection errors. This allows the user to select an option to suppress retries on application errors. (See the "Runtime Endpoint Management" section later in this chapter for more information.)

env-value-type: Declares the environmental values that are used in the endpoint configuration for the transport. These are values that may change from one environment to the next or values that should be preserved when reimporting a configuration JAR file, such as operational or security values. (See the "Declaring Environmental Attributes" section later in this chapter for more information.)

supported-transport-uris: Declares the set of transport identification URIs supported by this transport that may appear in WSDL files. This should be specified only for transports that support WSDL service types. This helps OSB identify the possible transports when parsing WSDL files.

supported-xml-selectors *and* supported-soap-selectors: Declare the set of WSDL operation selection algorithms supported by the transport for XML or SOAP messages, respectively. By default, the transport provider is assumed to support the full set of operation selection choices: Transport Header, WS-Addressing, SOAP Header, SOAP Body, and SOAP Action for SOAP WSDL services; Transport Header and Payload Type for XML WSDL services. If your transport doesn't support this entire set (perhaps it doesn't support transport headers), you can list the selection set you do support, and those will be the only ones offered in the UI. If your transport doesn't even support WSDL-type services, you can ignore this element.

dependency: Declares the set of other values or references in the service definition that when updated, should cause the endpoint to be redeployed. Normally, when the service is updated without modifying the endpoint configuration, or when a dependent resource (such as the referenced WSDL) is updated, the endpoint is not redeployed. But a transport can use this element to declare to which parts of the service definition, or to which dependent resource types, it is sensitive (for example, if it needs to put the dependent WSDL or schema into the generated EAR file for deployment).

The sample socket's configuration is given in Listing 17-3. Notice that it supports both inbound and outbound, and provides a tModel definition.

Listing 17-3. *Provider Configuration XML for the Socket Transport*

```
<?xml version="1.0" encoding="UTF-8"?>
<ProviderConfiguration xmlns="http://www.bea.com/wli/sb/transports">
  <inbound-direction-supported>true</inbound-direction-supported>
  <outbound-direction-supported>true</outbound-direction-supported>
  <UDDIMapping>
    <TModelDefinition>
      <tModel tModelKey="uddi:bea.uddi.org:transport:socket">
        <name>uddi-org:socket</name>
        <description>Socket transport based webservice</description>
        <overviewDoc>
          <overviewURL useType="text">
            http://www.bea.com/wli/sb/UDDIMapping#socket
          </overviewURL>
        </overviewDoc>
        <categoryBag>
          <keyedReference keyName="uddi-org:types:transport"
                          keyValue="transport"
```

```
                                tModelKey="uddi:uddi.org:categorization:types"/>
        </categoryBag>
      </tModel>
    </TModelDefinition>
  </UDDIMapping>
</ProviderConfiguration>
```

So, how does this information get into the running transport? This XML file is included in the final EAR file that you build. Listing 17-4 shows how this XML file is parsed and how an XMLBean is created to contain this information. This code is extracted from the SocketTransportProvider class.

Listing 17-4. *SocketTransportProvider getProviderConfiguration Method*

```
/**
 * @return the XML document for the static properties for this provider
 * @throws TransportException
 */
public TransportProviderConfiguration getProviderConfiguration()
  throws TransportException {
  try {
    URL configUrl =
      this.getClass().getClassLoader().getResource("SocketConfig.xml");
    return ProviderConfigurationDocument.Factory.parse(configUrl)
      .getProviderConfiguration();
  }
  catch (Exception e) {
    SocketTransportUtil.logger.error(e.getLocalizedMessage(), e);
    throw new TransportException(e);
  }
}
```

Transport Provider Schemas

A transport needs to provide XML schemas for several items. It must have a schema for its endpoint configuration describing what information must be configured for a service endpoint. This schema is completely up to the transport provider. It may also have schemas for metadata and headers that accompany request or response messages using the transport. These last four schemas extend base schemas defined in TransportCommon.xsd.

The endpoint configuration schema for the socket transport is given in Figure 17-7. The fields in this schema should look familiar. You saw those fields when you were configuring your socket transport proxy and business service earlier.

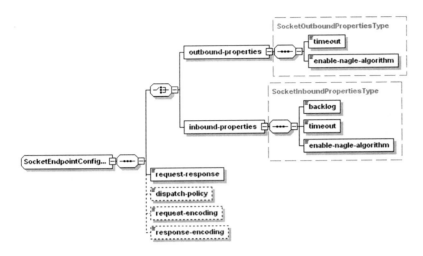

Figure 17-7. *Socket transport endpoint configuration schema*

Headers are typically just name/value pairs. They are part of the information communicated with a message, though they're separate from the message payload. Don't confuse headers with the SOAP header for SOAP messages. Transport headers come from the transport, not from the SOAP message. Good examples of headers are HTTP headers and JMS properties. The main point of having a schema for transport headers is that it provides a way to define the list of standard headers. These are presented to users when they use the Transport Headers action in the pipeline. You can still use headers that aren't a part of the transport; they're just considered user-defined headers.

The socket transport defines some headers, primarily for the sake of demonstrating the use of headers. These aren't really natural for socket communication. Only the request message is defined as having headers. The schema to declare socket transport request header is shown in Figure 17-8.

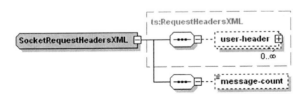

Figure 17-8. *Socket transport request headers schema*

Transport metadata is a superset of transport headers. In addition to the transport headers, it contains other metadata associated with a message. This metadata provides a context for the message. Unlike headers, this is not typically data that's carried along with the message. It might be configuration data or data about the message. Figure 17-9 shows how the socket transport defines its request metadata.

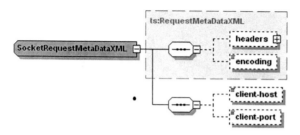

Figure 17-9. *Socket transport request metadata schema*

Notice how the socket request header schema and the request metadata schema extend the corresponding base schema from TransportCommon.xsd, namely RequestHeadersXML and RequestMetaDataXML.

OSB uses this metadata schema to define part of the contents of the message context variables $inbound and $outbound. These variables have an XML section (for example, at $inbound/transport/request) that conforms to the request metadata schema, and another section ($inbound/transport/response) that conforms to the response metadata schema. So, for example, if you log $inbound in your socket transport proxy, you get XML looking like Listing 17-5. (Some groups in the listing have been collapsed so you can focus on the request metadata.)

Listing 17-5. *$inbound for the Socket Transport*

```
- <endpoint name="ProxyService$SocketTest$SocketProxy" xmlns=...>
      <service />
    - <transport>
          <uri>tcp://7100</uri>
          <mode>request-response</mode>
          <qualityOfService>best-effort</qualityOfService>
        - <request xsi:type="sock:SocketRequestMetaDataXML">
            - <tran:headers xsi:type="sock:SocketRequestHeadersXML">
              <sock:message-count>5</sock:message-count>
              </tran:headers>
              <tran:encoding>utf-8</tran:encoding>
              <sock:client-host>127.0.0.1</sock:client-host>
              <sock:client-port>4513</sock:client-port>
          </request>
        + <response xsi:type="sock:SocketResponseMetaDataXML">
      </transport>
    + <security>
  </endpoint>
```

Now, we must once again address how these schemas get turned into usable data structures that affect how the socket transport actually works. First, you must compile the transport schema into Java classes representing the associated XMLBeans. This is done via the schema_compile step in the Ant build file. This uses the XMLBeans schema compiler to generate Java classes from the XML schema. A Java class is generated for each type defined in the schema. These Java classes implement the XmlObject interface (part of the XMLBeans standard). This has an attribute XmlObject.type that gives the SchemaType for the XmlObject: a Java object representing the associated schema.

Methods are defined on the TransportProvider for returning these schema objects. Recall that the transport provider must implement the TransportProvider interface. For example, the socket transport provider has a class, SocketTransportProvider, implementing this interface. The relevant methods are shown in Listing 17-6.

Listing 17-6. *Providing the Various Schema Types for the Socket Transport*

```
/**
 * @return the XML schema type for the endpoint configuration for this
 *         provider
 */
public SchemaType getEndPointConfigurationSchemaType() {
  return SocketEndpointConfiguration.type;
}
/**
 * @return the XML schema type of the request message for this provider
 */
public SchemaType getRequestMetaDataSchemaType() {
  return SocketRequestMetaDataXML.type;
}
/**
 * @return the XML schema type of the request headers for this provider. If
 *         provider does not support request headers, return null.
 */
public SchemaType getRequestHeadersSchemaType() {
  return SocketRequestHeadersXML.type;
}
/**
 * @return the XML schema type of the response message for this provider
 */
public SchemaType getResponseMetaDataSchemaType() {
  return SocketResponseMetaDataXML.type;
}
/**
 * @return the XML schema type of the response headers for this provider. If
 *         provider does not support response headers, return null.
 */
public SchemaType getResponseHeadersSchemaType() {
  return SocketResponseHeadersXML.type;
}
```

Implementing Transport Provider User Interface Classes

One of the elegant capabilities of a custom transport is its ability to integrate with the OSB UI in a natural way. Services using the custom transport have a special console page for configuring transport-specific information. This is why custom transports are considered first-class citizens and are indistinguishable from transports supplied with OSB.

The classes that provide this UI integration also work with the OSB WorkSpace Studio plug-in. A transport provider implementing the classes described in this section can also be packaged as an Eclipse plug-in and be a first-class citizen in the WorkSpace Studio design environment. The classes are agnostic toward the presentation technology, so the UI will be rendered using HTML for the browser-based console or using the Eclipse Standard Widget Toolkit (SWT) for WorkSpace Studio.

To provide this UI integration, the transport provider implements a class supporting the TransportUIBinding interface. This is the key class for defining the UI for the custom transport. It declares what kinds of service types the transport supports, describes what its URL should look like, lists the fields that should be given to the user to fill out to describe a service endpoint, validates the user's entry, and translates the user's entry into a transport endpoint configuration (the XMLObject described earlier in the "Transport Provider Schemas" section). We'll go through these steps.

Let's first review the steps to take to create a proxy service (creating a business service is similar). This will help us to relate the implementation tasks to what's happening in the console UI. To create a proxy service, you go through the service creation wizard, which has these pages:

1. The General Configuration page, where you name your service, declare its service type, and fill in some other information

2. The generic Transport Configuration page, where you select a transport and provide transport configuration data that applies to all transports, such as the endpoint URI

3. The transport-specific Transport Configuration page, where you provide configuration that's specific to the transport provider selected in step 2

4. The Summary page where you confirm your configuration and save the service

The implementation of the TransportUIBinding comes in at pages 2, 3, and 4. In addition, the service type from step 1 impacts the later pages and is used in the validation.

The first thing to implement is the method isServiceTypeSupported(). In step 1, you pick a service type, such as WSDL, messaging, any SOAP, and so on. However, not all transports support all service types. OSB will call your transport with the chosen service type, and your transport can say whether it's supported. Then the drop-down list of transports in step 2 will show only the transports that support the chosen service type.

For example, the socket transport's implementation of this method is given in Listing 17-7 (with some code eliminated for brevity). If your transport provider supports all service types, you can simply return true for this method.

Listing 17-7. *Socket Transport isServiceTypeSupport Implementation*

```
/**
 * Returns true if the message type is either TEXT or XML. Socket transport
 * supports XML and TEXT message types only for both the request and the
 * response messages.
 */
public boolean isServiceTypeSupported(BindingTypeInfo bindingType) {
  try {
    BindingTypeInfo.BindingTypeEnum type = bindingType.getType();
    /**
     * If the binding is mixed, request type should exist and it should be
     * either TEXT or XML type and if there is any response type,
     * it must be either TEXT or XML.
     */
    if (type.equals(BindingTypeInfo.BindingTypeEnum.MIXED)) {
      /* ... Return false if there is an unsupported type,
             Else return true. */
    }
    /**
     * Binding type must be either ABSTRACT_XML or XML.
     */
    return type.equals(BindingTypeInfo.BindingTypeEnum.ABSTRACT_XML)
      || type.equals(BindingTypeInfo.BindingTypeEnum.XML);
  } catch (TransportException e) {
    SocketTransportUtil.logger.error(e.getLocalizedMessage(), e);
    return false;
  }
}
```

There are a couple other ways that the page in step 2 is tailored by the custom transport. The custom transport provides the sample format for the endpoint URI. It also provides the starting URI value, which is typically the prefix of the given URI. This information is returned in the value object TransportUIGenericInfo and is returned by the method getGenericInfo(). This is also where you declare whether your transport supports WS-I compliance.

The socket transport's implementation of this method is provided in Listing 17-8. This has been simplified a little from the real implementation, which pulls the actual string values from an i18n file so that they can be localized for different languages.

Listing 17-8. *Socket Transport getGenericInfo*

```
public TransportUIGenericInfo getGenericInfo() {
  TransportUIGenericInfo genInfo = new TransportUIGenericInfo();
  if (uiContext.isProxy()) {
    genInfo.setUriFormat( "tcp://port" );
    genInfo.setUriAutofill( "tcp://9999" );
```

```
    } else {
      genInfo.setUriFormat( "tcp://socket-ip-address:port" );
      genInfo.setUriAutofill( "tcp://localhost:8888" );
    }
    return genInfo;
  }
```

Before you leave the page in step 2, you must validate the URI (or URIs for a business service) that the user has entered. This is done with the method validateMainForm(). To understand this method, you need to understand how fields are represented on the console UI pages.

A generic class TransportEditField represents an editable entry field on a console page. There are many types of UI fields, but they all have some common characteristics, including a label, whether it is a required field, whether it is an advanced field (appears in the advanced portion of the configuration page), whether it is disabled, and so on. The actual entry field is of type TransportUIFactory.TransportUIObject. There are many of these types of UI objects, including the following:

- TextBox: A single-line text area

- TextArea: A multiline text area

- BrowserTextBox: A selection text box driven by a pop-up chooser window

- CheckBox: A simple Boolean check box

- Select: A drop-down list

- SimpleTable: A fixed table of values

- DynamicTable: A dynamic table of values

- ExpandableTable: A table of values that can grow as data is entered

- Password: A text box where the values are not shown

For a complete list, see the Javadoc for TransportUIFactory.

Now, we can discuss how the validateMainForm() method can validate the URI in the generic Transport Configuration page. This method takes an array of TransportEditFields representing the fields on the page. However, it's more convenient to grab just the URI field by first turning this array into a map, and then map the field name into the corresponding TransportUIObject. You can then get the TransportUIObject for the URI field, extract the URI values from this field, and check them for syntactical correctness. Listing 17-9 shows how the socket transport validates the URI field, which is a different validation for proxies and business services (the simpler proxy check is suppressed for brevity).

Listing 17-9. *Socket Transport validateMainForm*

```
public TransportUIError[] validateMainForm(TransportEditField[] fields) {
  Map<String, TransportUIFactory.TransportUIObject> map =
    TransportEditField.getObjectMap(fields);
```

```
    List<TransportUIError> errors = new ArrayList<TransportUIError>();
    if (!uiContext.isProxy()) {
      List<String[]> uris = getStringValues(map, TransportUIBinding.PARAM_URI);
      for (String[] uristr : uris) {
        try {
          URI uri = new URI(uristr[0]);
          if (!(uri.getScheme().equals("tcp") && uri.getHost() != null &&
            uri.getPort() != -1)) {
            errors.add(new TransportUIError(TransportUIBinding.PARAM_URI,
              "Invalid URI"));
          }
        } catch (URISyntaxException e) {
          errors.add(new TransportUIError(TransportUIBinding.PARAM_URI,
            e.getMessage()));
        }
      }
    } else {
      /* Do a similar check for proxy URLs, they should be of form "tcp:<port>" */
    }
    return errors == null || errors.isEmpty() ? null :
      errors.toArray(new TransportUIError[errors.size()]);
}
```

You're now ready to go on to step 3, the transport-specific Transport Configuration page. The fields on this page are completely prescribed by the transport. The transport provides the list of fields to show on the page via the method getEditPage(). This method is given the EndPointConfiguration for the service (or a default one if the service is being created for the first time) and the BindingTypeInfo for the service. It must return an array of TransportEditFields to be shown on the screen, with their values pulled from the EndPointConfiguration.

In the socket transport version of the getEditPage() method (shown in Listing 17-10), it's convenient to build up the array of TransportEditFields using a List, and then at the end, convert this list back to an array. Look back at the Socket Transport Configuration page shown in Figure 17-2 and compare that with this code. The code has been simplified, as shown, for brevity.

Listing 17-10. *Socket Transport getEditPage*

```
public TransportEditField[] getEditPage(EndPointConfiguration config,
                                        BindingTypeInfo binding)
    throws TransportException {
    List<TransportEditField> fields = new ArrayList<TransportEditField>();
    SocketEndpointConfiguration sockConfig = null;
    if (config != null && config.isSetProviderSpecific()) {
      sockConfig = SocketTransportUtil.getConfig(config);
    }
```

```java
/* Add requestResponse checkbox */
boolean requestResponse =
  sockConfig == null || sockConfig.getRequestResponse();
TransportUIFactory.CheckBoxObject checkbox =
  TransportUIFactory.createCheckbox(null, requestResponse, true);
TransportEditField editField =
  TransportUIFactory.createEditField(REQUEST_RESPONSE, REQUEST_RESPONSE_LABEL,
    REQUEST_RESPONSE_TOOLTIP, false, checkbox);
fields.add(editField);
/*
 * If it is a proxy, add the Backlog field.
 * But in either case, get the timout and enableNagleAlgorith values.
 */
long timeout = 5000;
boolean enableNA = true;
if (uiContext.isProxy()) {
  int backlog = 5;
  if (sockConfig != null) {
    SocketInboundPropertiesType inboundProperties =
      sockConfig.getInboundProperties();
    backlog = inboundProperties.getBacklog();
    timeout = inboundProperties.getTimeout();
    enableNA = inboundProperties.getEnableNagleAlgorithm();
  }
  TransportUIFactory.TextBoxObject textBox =
    TransportUIFactory.createTextBox(backlog + "", 20);
  editField = TransportUIFactory.createEditField(BACKLOG, BACKLOG_LABEL,
      BACKLOG_TOOLTIP, false, textBox);
  fields.add(editField);
} else {
  if (sockConfig != null) {
    SocketOutboundPropertiesType outboundProperties =
      sockConfig.getOutboundProperties();
    timeout = outboundProperties.getTimeout();
    enableNA = outboundProperties.getEnableNagleAlgorithm();
  }
}

/* Add the Connection Timeout TextBox field */
/* Add the Enable Nagle's Algorithm checkbox field */
/* Add the Request Encoding TextBox field */
/* Add the Response Encoding TextBox field */
/* Add the Dispatch policy SelectObject (drop-down list) field */

return fields.toArray(new TransportEditField[fields.size()]);
}
```

A transport might want to change the transport configuration page depending on what data the user has entered. One of the attributes of a TransportUIObject is whether there is an event associated with it. This acts like a callback mechanism, allowing the transport provider to change the UI fields, perhaps by adding or deleting fields or by enabling/disabling fields. This is done with the UpdateEditPage() method.

Again, examples make this simpler to understand. In the socket transport, you should only be able to set the Response Encoding field if there is a response; that is, if Is Response Required is checked. Hence, checking and unchecking the Response Required check box causes the Response Encoding field to be enabled and disabled. The socket transport's UpdateEditPage() method demonstrates this, as shown in Listing 17-11.

Listing 17-11. *Socket Transport UpdateEditPage*

```
public TransportEditField[] updateEditPage(TransportEditField[] fields,
                                            String name)

    throws TransportException {
    /** update the values only for REQUEST_RESPONSE field. */
    if (!REQUEST_RESPONSE.equals(name)) {
      return fields;
    }
    /** RESPONSE_ENCODING field should be enabled only when REQUEST_RESPONSE
      * is true.*/
    Map<String, TransportEditField> fieldMap =
      TransportEditField.getFieldMap(fields);
    TransportEditField editField = fieldMap.get(REQUEST_RESPONSE);
    TransportUIFactory.CheckBoxObject selectObject =
      (TransportUIFactory.CheckBoxObject) editField.getObject();
    boolean b = selectObject.ischecked();
    fieldMap.get(RESPONSE_ENCODING).setDisabled(!b);
    return fields;
}
```

The service definition page also supports validating the entered data. This provides an opportunity for the transport provider to give friendly diagnostics on this page before going on with the rest of the service definition. This is done via the validateProviderSpecificForm() method, which is given the array of TransportEditFields and returns an array of TransportUIError diagnostics.

The socket transport doesn't do any validation of the entered data, so we won't bother showing the code for the function. However, this is not the best practice; doing validation here is useful. For example, the socket transport should validate that the data entered for a socket timeout is an integer (not just a random string of characters), and should probably check to ensure it is a nonnegative integer at that. It should probably also validate that any character encoding entered is legitimate. The socket transport does none of these checks, although it will catch entering string data into the Timeout field at a later stage, in an unfriendly manner! We'll leave adding this validation code as an exercise for the reader.

The last thing that happens before you leave this page is that all the data entered into the UI fields must be converted back to the provider portion of the endpoint configuration. This is the XMLObject for the provider-specific configuration, which should match the transport provider schema described earlier. This is done via the getProviderSpecificConfiguration() method. This is another place to catch errors, but doesn't allow for returning friendly diagnostic messages.

You can think of this as the inverse to the getEditPage() method, taking an array of TransportEditFields and returning an XMLObject for the provider-specific configuration. Just note this difference: getEditPage() gets the outer EndpointConfiguration object, which has both the generic transport information as well as the provider-specific information.

An abbreviated version of the socket transport getProviderSpecificConfiguration() method is shown in Listing 17-12.

Listing 17-12. *Socket Transport getProviderSpecificConfiguration*

```
public XmlObject getProviderSpecificConfiguration(TransportEditField[] fields)
  throws TransportException {

  SocketEndpointConfiguration socketEndpointConfig =
    SocketEndpointConfiguration.Factory.newInstance();
  Map<String, TransportUIFactory.TransportUIObject> map =
    TransportEditField.getObjectMap(fields);
  socketEndpointConfig.setRequestResponse(
    TransportUIFactory.getBooleanValue(map, REQUEST_RESPONSE));

  if (uiContext.isProxy()) {
    SocketInboundPropertiesType socketInboundPropertiesType =
      socketEndpointConfig.addNewInboundProperties();
    socketInboundPropertiesType.setBacklog(
      TransportUIFactory.getIntValue(map, BACKLOG));
    socketInboundPropertiesType.setEnableNagleAlgorithm(
      TransportUIFactory.getBooleanValue(map, ENABLE_NAGLE_ALGORITHM));
    socketInboundPropertiesType.setTimeout(
      TransportUIFactory.getIntValue(map, TIME_OUT));
  } else {
    /* Do the same for outbound properties for a business service */
  }

  String reqEnc = TransportUIFactory.getStringValue(map, REQUEST_ENCODING);
  if (reqEnc != null && reqEnc.trim().length() != 0) {
    socketEndpointConfig.setRequestEncoding(reqEnc);
  }
  String resEnc = TransportUIFactory.getStringValue(map, RESPONSE_ENCODING);
  if (resEnc != null && resEnc.trim().length() != 0) {
    socketEndpointConfig.setResponseEncoding(resEnc);
  }

  String dispatchPolicy =
    TransportUIFactory.getStringValue(map, DISPATCH_POLICY);
  socketEndpointConfig.setDispatchPolicy(dispatchPolicy);
```

```
        return socketEndpointConfig;
    }
}
```

Wow! That was a lot of work just for step 3. Luckily, that is the hard part of the transport UI the UI work. That involves the last pagbinding work. There's only one more small task to do before you're completely finished with e of the service creation wizard, the final summary.

In the final summary, a portion of the page gives a read-only view of a subset of the transport provider's specific configuration. The transport provider can select which fields should be present in the summary (all of them or a subset). A general rule of thumb is to show the fields whose values differ from their defaults, and perhaps the most critical fields.

The transport provider gives the list of fields to show in the getViewPage() method, which returns an array of TransportViewField objects. The interesting data in a TransportViewField is just the label and the value, so it's a simplified version of a TransportEditField. getViewPage() is similar to getEditPage(), except that the returned information is simpler and doesn't need to be complete. So, without further ado, let's show the simplified form of the socket transport's version of this method in Listing 17-13, and be finished with implementing transport provider UI classes.

Listing 17-13. *SocketTransport getViewPage*

```
public TransportViewField[] getViewPage(EndPointConfiguration config)
    throws TransportException {
    List<TransportViewField> fields = new ArrayList<TransportViewField>();
    SocketEndpointConfiguration socketEndpointConfiguration =
        SocketTransportUtil.getConfig(config);

    /* Add requestResponse field */
    TransportViewField field =
        new TransportViewField(REQUEST_RESPONSE, REQUEST_RESPONSE_LABEL,
            socketEndpointConfiguration.getRequestResponse());
    fields.add(field);
    /*
     * If it is a proxy, add the Backlog field.
     * But in either case, add the timeout and enableNagleAlgorithm fields.
     */
    if (uiContext.isProxy()) {
        SocketInboundPropertiesType inboundProperties =
            socketEndpointConfiguration.getInboundProperties();

        field = new TransportViewField(BACKLOG, BACKLOG_LABEL,
            inboundProperties.getBacklog());
        fields.add(field);

        /* Add the Connection Timeout field from inboundProperties */
        /* Add the Enable Nagle's Algorithm field from inboundProperties */
```

```
    } else {
      /* Add the Connection Timeout field from outboundProperties */
      /* Add the Enable Nagle's Algorithm field from outboundProperties */
    }

    /* Add the Request Encoding field */
    /* Add the Response Encoding field */
    /* Add the Dispatch policy field */

    return fields.toArray(new TransportViewField[fields.size()]);
}
```

Deploying Service Endpoints Using the Custom Transport

Now that you have the UI for configuring the custom transport, it's time to deploy the service
endpoint. The transport provider must implement the support for deploying the service endpoint, making it active for sending and receiving messages. This includes initiating any listeners
for incoming messages.

The methods for deploying and managing endpoints include operations create,
update, delete, suspend, and resume. There are two sets of these methods: those in the basic
TransportProvider interface that every transport must implement, and those in the optional
TransportWLSArtifactDeployer interface. We'll describe the difference between these two sets
of methods.

The methods in TransportWLSArtifactDeployer are for deploying WebLogic Server entities
such as EAR or WAR files using the WebLogic configuration domain MBean. These methods are
called only in the admin server, because by using the domain MBean, the entities will automatically be propagated out to the cluster by WebLogic Server. Furthermore, because WebLogic Server
persists the deployment of these entities, the methods in TransportWLSArtifactDeployer are
called only upon activation of a session that has made changes to a service using the transport.
These methods are not called at server startup.

However, the endpoint management methods in the base TransportProvider interface
are called in every managed server in the cluster *and* in the admin server (though they typically wouldn't do anything in the admin server). These methods are called upon activation of
a session that has made changes to a service, and they're also called at server startup for every
deployed service. These methods are for dynamically creating and starting an endpoint in
a managed server.

Because it's more common to deploy endpoints via the methods in the TransportProvider
interface, we'll focus our initial attention on those methods.

Deploying an endpoint is a two-stage process. OSB first invokes the transport's method to
do the operation (create, update, delete, suspend, or resume). It does this across all the changed
services, and after they have all been completed, it calls activationComplete(). For example,
if 20 services are created, OSB invokes the createEndpoint() 20 times, once for each service
transport endpoint during the first phase, and then invokes the activationComplete() method
for each service transport endpoint during the second phase.

During the first phase, the transport should do as much work as possible to deploy the
endpoint and catch any errors that might exist in the runtime environment. If any phase 1 call
to an endpoint operation results in an error, all the changes are backed out by OSB issuing the

opposite call (compensating action) to undo the previous actions, and the session activation fails. During the second phase, with the call to activationComplete(), there's no opportunity to report an error.

The challenge in deploying an inbound endpoint is to do as much as possible during that first phase to set an endpoint, but without actually starting to process messages. You should start processing messages only once the activationComplete() call has occurred. Your call to create an endpoint might actually get backed out before activationComplete() is called, so you don't want to start processing messages until that second phase completes.

OSB calls each endpoint operation with a value object containing data associated with the operation. The following attributes are common to all operations:

Type: The type of the operation; that is, CREATE UPDATE, DELETE, SUSPEND, or RESUME

Ref: A reference to the associated service

ScratchPad: A map that can be used as a temporary holding place until activationComplete() is called

Compensating flag: A Boolean determining whether the operation is undoing a previous action due to the session activation being rolled back

The only operational-specific data that extends this is on the create and update operations. Following are the extra attributes for the create operation:

EndPointConfiguration: The transport endpoint configuration data with both the generic and provider-specific portions

New flag: A Boolean determining whether this is a new endpoint being created or an existing endpoint being reloaded on server startup

Enabled flag: A Boolean determining whether the endpoint should initially be in the enabled or suspended state

The extra attributes for update are just the EndPointConfiguration and the Enabled flag described in the preceding list.

The transport provider is responsible for keeping track of all its endpoints. It must be prepared to return a collection of the endpoints when its getEndPoints() method is called. Hence, the create/update/delete operations should manage this collection.

Listing 17-14 shows the socket transport implementation of the create and update operations.

Listing 17-14. *Socket Transport Create and Update Endpoints*

```
public TransportEndPoint createEndPoint(
  EndPointOperations.Create createContext) throws TransportException {
    if(TransportManagerHelper.isAdmin() && TransportManagerHelper.clusterExists())
        return null;
  Ref ref = createContext.getRef();
  createContext.getScratchPad().put(ref.getFullName()+ENABLED,
                                    createContext.isEnabled());
  SocketTransportEndPoint socketTransportEndPoint =
    new SocketTransportEndPoint(ref,
```

```java
        createContext.getEndPointConfiguration(), this);
    endPoints.put(ref, socketTransportEndPoint);
    return socketTransportEndPoint;
}

public TransportEndPoint updateEndPoint(EndPointOperations.Update update)
    throws TransportException {
    if(TransportManagerHelper.isAdmin() && TransportManagerHelper.clusterExists())
        return null;
    Ref ref = update.getRef();
    SocketTransportEndPoint oldEp = endPoints.get(ref);
    /** oldEP can be null, when the socket transport is restarted and existing
     * configuration is updated.
     */
    if (oldEp != null) {
        update.getScratchPad().put(ref.getFullName()+UPDATE_OLD_ENDPOINT, oldEp);
    }
    endPoints.remove(ref);
    update.getScratchPad().put(ref.getFullName()+ENABLED, update.isEnabled());
    SocketTransportEndPoint endPoint = new SocketTransportEndPoint(ref,
        update.getEndPointConfiguration(), this);
    endPoints.put(ref, endPoint);
    return endPoint;
}

public void activationComplete(EndPointOperations.CommonOperation context) {
    Ref ref = context.getRef();
    EndPointOperations.EndPointOperationTypeEnum type = context.getType();
    SocketTransportEndPoint endPoint = endPoints.get(ref);

    if(TransportManagerHelper.isAdmin() && TransportManagerHelper.clusterExists())
        return;

    try {
        if (EndPointOperations.EndPointOperationTypeEnum.CREATE.equals(type)) {
            if ((Boolean) context.getScratchPad().get(ref.getFullName()+ENABLED)) {
                endPoint.start();
            }
        } else
        if (EndPointOperations.EndPointOperationTypeEnum.UPDATE.equals(type)) {
            SocketTransportEndPoint oldEP = (SocketTransportEndPoint) context
                .getScratchPad().get(ref.getFullName()+UPDATE_OLD_ENDPOINT);
            if (oldEP != null) {
                oldEP.stop();
            }
```

```
      if ((Boolean)context.getScratchPad().get(ref.getFullName()+ENABLED)) {
        endPoint.start();
      }
    } else
        /* Handle Delete/Suspend/Resume cases */
  } catch (Exception e) {
    String msg = SocketTransportMessagesLogger
      .activationFailedLoggable(ref.getFullName()).getMessage();
    SocketTransportUtil.logger.error(msg, e);
  }
}
```

Notice that the socket is not actually started in the create or update method. Instead, that's deferred to the activationComplete() method (and is only done there if the endpoint is enabled). That's how endpoint management is supposed to work. The actual enabling of the endpoint to start processing messages shouldn't happen until the activationComplete() method. By the way, for the socket transport, this start method is where a listening thread is created for a proxy (it's not used for the socket transport business service).

Now, let's go back and explain a little more about the TransportWLSArtifactDeployer interface. The object that you register with TransportManager.registerProvider() implements the TransportProvider interface, but it may also optionally implement the TransportWLSArtifactDeployer interface. You would do this if you wanted to deploy WebLogic Server artifacts, such as EAR files, JMS destinations, and so on.

The create, update, delete, suspend, and resume methods in TransportWLSArtifactDeployer parallel the ones in the base TransportProvider interface. One significant difference is that the methods in TransportWLSArtifactDeployer are given a reference to the WebLogic Server DomainMBean. They can use this MBean to deploy artifacts to WebLogic Server.

Prior to calling the methods in TransportWLSArtifactDeployer, the OSB configuration system makes sure that a WebLogic Server edit session is created. Hence, all configuration updates done via the MBean will be done in an edit session. This ensures they will all happen atomically, and will happen only if the OSB session activates successfully.

When the transport provider's object implements TransportWLSArtifactDeployer in addition to TransportProvider, both sets of endpoint methods are called. For example, if a session has created a service using the custom transport, OSB will first call makeWLSChangesOnCreate() (from TransportWLSArtifactDeployer) on the admin server, then call createEndpoint() (from TransportProvider) on the admin server, and then call createEndpoint() on each of the managed servers in the cluster. The transport provider needs to determine which of these calls to implement and which to ignore.

Implementing Transport Provider Runtime Classes

Having worked our way through what it takes to configure and deploy a custom transport for a service, we can now take a look at the primary function of a transport—how it transports messages. It's time for the rubber to meet the road as we show you how to process messages in a custom transport.

Let's divide and conquer again. To keep this manageable, let's divide the message processing into the following steps. These are listed from the point of view of a transport provider interacting with the OSB runtime:

- Delivering an inbound request

- Receiving an inbound response

- Receiving an outbound request

- Delivering an outbound response

However, before we can discuss message processing by the custom transport, we need to digress and talk about how messages are represented in the Transport SDK. There are two parts to this: how transport headers and metadata are represented, and how the actual message payload is represented. Both of these are put into a normalized form, so that OSB can handle them in a unified way. However, the solutions for each are much different.

Transport Headers and Metadata Representation

OSB supports the notion of transport headers (information that's transmitted with the message at the transport level, but is not part of the message payload) and metadata (attributes associated with the message but that aren't formal transport headers). For example, the HTTP transport has HTTP headers such as Content-Type and Content-Encoding, and has metadata such as queryString and clientAddress.

Every transport provider must implement a Java class that extends the abstract class RequestHeaders, and another Java class that extends the abstract class RequestMetaData (or more precisely, RequestMetaData<T extends RequestHeaders>). Similarly, it must have Java classes for ResponseHeaders and ResponseMetaData. These classes act as POJO containers for the custom transport headers and metadata.

You might recall that in the earlier section "Transport Provider Schemas," we mentioned that the transport provider must provide a schema for the request headers and another one for the request metadata (ditto for response). We also described how to create XmlObject classes for these schemas. So, if we have XmlObject classes to hold this data, why do we need POJO Java objects?

The answer is performance. Working with POJOs is much faster than working with XmlObjects. OSB is optimized to always work with headers and metadata via their POJO representation whenever possible. The only time that this data must be represented as XmlObjects is if the user manipulates the headers or metadata via XPaths, XQueries, or XSLTs in the pipeline. For example, the use of the Transport Headers action goes directly against the POJO representation rather than the XmlObject representation, so it's much faster.

To have the best of both worlds, the transport provider supplies the message metadata (which contains the headers) in POJO form, but also supplies methods for converting between the POJO form and the XmlObject form. The methods to convert to XmlObject are the toXML() methods on the classes extending RequestHeaders and RequestMetaData (ditto for response). To go from the XML form to the POJO form of metadata, the transport provider must implement the createResponseMetaData() and createRequestMetaData() methods in the InboundTransportMessageContext and OutboundTransportMessageContext interfaces, respectively.

RequestHeaders and RequestMetaData are abstract classes, but the only abstract methods in them are their toXML() methods. So, the purpose of having a transport-specific extension of these classes is twofold: to implement the toXML() method and to extend these classes to add additional headers or metadata attributes, respectively.

To make things even easier, a transport provider doesn't even need to implement the toXML() methods. There is a concrete implementation of RequestHeaders and RequestMetaData that has the toXML() methods implemented by introspecting the schema for the headers and metadata, respectively. These are called DefaultRequestHeaders and DefaultRequestMetaData. Hence, all a transport provider needs to do is to extend these classes if they have specific headers or specific metadata. If a transport has no specific headers, it can use the DefaultRequestHeaders class without extension. Similarly, if a transport has no metadata associated with requests, it can use the DefaultRequestMetaData without extension.

There are equivalents to all the preceding classes for responses.

Looking at the socket transport's implementation should make this clearer. The socket transport arbitrarily defines a single request header called message-count (this is kind of a misuse of transport headers, but is included for demonstration purposes). Its request metadata extends the standard metadata by adding the fields client-host and client-port. It doesn't define any response headers, but does define response metadata to include service-endpoint-host and service-endpoint-ip.

Hence, the socket transport defines classes SocketRequestHeaders, SocketRequestMetaData, and SocketResponseMetaData. Each extends the DefaultXXX equivalent. Notice that SocketResponseHeaders is missing. Because there are no response header fields, the socket transport can just use the default implementation. Listing 17-15 shows the implementation of SocketRequestHeaders, and Listing 17-16 shows the implementation of SocketRequestMetaData.

Listing 17-15. *SocketRequestHeaders*

```
public class SocketRequestHeaders extends
  DefaultRequestHeaders<SocketRequestHeadersXML> {
  /*message-count element specified in the schema, whenever a new header
  element is added their get/set type methods can be added here. */

  private static final String MESSAGE_COUNT = "message-count";

  public SocketRequestHeaders(RequestHeadersXML headers) throws
    TransportException {
    super(SocketTransportProvider.getInstance(), headers);
  }

  public long getMessageCount() {
    return (Long) getHeader(MESSAGE_COUNT);
  }

  public void setMessageCount(long messageCount) {
    setHeader(MESSAGE_COUNT, messageCount);
  }
}
```

Listing 17-16. *SocketRequestMetaData*

```
public class SocketRequestMetaData
  extends DefaultRequestMetaData<SocketRequestMetaDataXML> {
  private int port = Integer.MIN_VALUE;
  private String hostAddress;

  public SocketRequestMetaData(SocketRequestMetaDataXML rmdXML)
    throws TransportException {
    super(SocketTransportProvider.getInstance(), rmdXML);
    if(rmdXML != null) {
      if(rmdXML.isSetClientHost()) {
        setClientHost(rmdXML.getClientHost());
      }
      if(rmdXML.isSetClientPort()) {
        setClientPort(rmdXML.getClientPort());
      }
    }
  }
  public SocketRequestMetaData(String requestEncoding) throws TransportException {
    /*not calling super.(TransportProvider provider, RequestHeaders hdr,
    String enc) because it does not create new headers if hdr is null.*/
    super(SocketTransportProvider.getInstance());
    setCharacterEncoding(requestEncoding);
  }

  protected RequestHeaders createHeaders(TransportProvider provider,
                                          RequestHeadersXML hdrXML)
    throws TransportException {
    return new SocketRequestHeaders(hdrXML);
  }

  public SocketRequestMetaDataXML toXML() throws TransportException {
    SocketRequestMetaDataXML requestMetaData = super.toXML();
    // set socket transport specific metadata.
    if (hostAddress != null) {
      requestMetaData.setClientHost(hostAddress);
    }
    if (port != Integer.MIN_VALUE) {
      requestMetaData.setClientPort(port);
    }
    return requestMetaData;
  }

  public void setClientHost(String hostAddress) {
    this.hostAddress = hostAddress;
  }
```

```
public void setClientPort(int port) {
  this.port = port;
}

/**
 * Validates and parses the given XmlObject to SocketRequestMetaDataXML.
 * @param xbean
 * @return SocketRequestMetaDataXML of the given XmlObject.
 * @throws TransportException
 */
public static SocketRequestMetaDataXML getSocketRequestMetaData(
  XmlObject xbean) throws TransportException {
  if (xbean == null) {
    return null;
  } else if (xbean instanceof SocketRequestMetaDataXML) {
    return (SocketRequestMetaDataXML) xbean;
  } else {
    try {
      return SocketRequestMetaDataXML.Factory.parse(xbean.newInputStream());
    } catch (XmlException e) {
      throw new TransportException(e.getMessage(), e);
    } catch (IOException e) {
      throw new TransportException(e.getMessage(), e);
    }
  }
}
}
```

Message Payload Representation

Now that we've described how to represent the metadata associated with a message, we turn our attention to representing the message itself. The Transport SDK provides ways to represent the message data that can be simple for most use cases or can be flexible for optimizing other use cases. A transport provider can use one of the standard classes for holding its data (say, if it's in the form of a byte array, a string, or a simple input stream), or it can use its own native representation, if that makes sense for the transport.

At the heart of the message representation is an interface called Source. This is the basic interface that all classes representing message content must support. The Source interface consists of two methods:

- InputStream getInputStream(TransformOptions options) returns the contents of this source as a byte-based input stream.

- void writeTo(OutputStream os, TransformOptions options) writes the contents of this source to a byte-based output stream.

A Source has two methods for getting at the underlying message: a pull-based method getInputStream, and a push-based method writeTo. The methods in the Transport SDK that pass a message around, either from a transport into the binding layer or vice versa, use a Source object.

A wide range of use cases can simply take advantage of one of the standard, simple Source classes that comes with OSB. For example, if a transport provider naturally gets the incoming message in the form of a byte array, a string, or an input stream, it can easily create a ByteArraySource, a StringSource, or a StreamSource, respectively. The transport provider can then leave to the binding layer the task of parsing the message into the form given by the service type (for example, SOAP, XML, text, and so on).

The StreamSource deserves a little extra explanation. For a typical Source, you should be able to call either of the methods for getting at the underlying data multiple times. For example, the runtime might call the getInputStream() method once to get the underlying message data, consume the returned stream, and then call it a second time to get the underlying message data via a stream a second time. However, a special marker interface, SingleUseSource, extending Source, declares that the underlying data can be consumed only once. The StreamSource implements this SingleUseSource.

With a source that implements SingleUseSource, rather than just Source, OSB will internally buffer the contents of the source so that it can reuse the data from this buffer (for example, for retrying of a message after a failure). For example, a stream coming from a socket or an HTTP connection can be read only once—it cannot be reset back to the beginning as can a byte array or string. Hence, such a stream will be encapsulated in a StreamSource, so that OSB will know to buffer the contents.

For transports that get their data in a more structured form (rather than just a raw sequence of bytes), other standard sources come with OSB. These generally follow the pattern of having one or more constructors that create the Source class from the underlying structured data, and a get method for directly getting the underlying structured data:

- ByteArraySource is a byte-based Source based on a byte array.

- StringSource is a text-based Source based on a string object.

- StreamSource is a single-use Source based on an InputStream.

- XmlObjectSource is an XML-based Source based on an XmlObject.

- DOMSource is an XML-based Source based on a DOM node.

- MFLSource is an MFL-based Source whose underlying content is represented by XmlObject and an MFL resource.

- SAAJSource is a SOAP-based Source based on a SAAJ javax.xml.soap.SOAPMessage.

- MimeSource is a MIME-based Source composed of MIME headers, and another Source for the content. The serialization representation of a MIMESource is a standard MIME package.

- MessageContextSource is a Source representing a message and its attachments, each of which is another untyped Source. The serialization of this Source is always a MIME multipart/related package.

The last few Sources in this list are for handling messages with attachments, something that few transports will need to handle. For example, within OSB, only the HTTP, SB and Email transport support messages with attachments.

> ■**Note** Don't confuse the `Source` object representation with the service type. The two are somewhat related, but are independent. However, the `Source` object representation should be at least compatible with the service type.

The OSB binding layer (look back at Figure 17-1) is responsible for converting content between the `Source` representation used by the transport layer and the message context used by the OSB runtime. How that conversion happens depends on the service type (its binding type) and the presence of attachments.

When attachments aren't present, the incoming `Source` represents just the core message content. The incoming `Source` from the transport is converted to a specific type of `Source`, and then the underlying content can be extracted. For example, for XML-based services, the incoming `Source` is converted to an `XmlObjectSource`. The `XmlObject` is then extracted from the `XmlObjectSource` and used as the payload inside the $body context variable. SOAP services are similarly converted to `XmlObjectSource`, except that the extracted `XmlObject` must be a SOAP envelope so that the `<SOAP:Header>` and `<SOAP:Body>` elements can be extracted to initialize the $header and $body context variables.

Following are the most natural `Source` types used for the set of defined service types:

- SOAP: `XmlObjectSource`

- XML: `XmlObjectSource`

- Text: `StringSource`

- MFL: `MFLSource`

For binary services, no `Source` conversion is done. Instead, the `Source` object is stored in a private repository, and a special `<binary-content/>` XML snippet that references the data is used as the payload inside $body. The pipeline sees only the XML snippet that refers to the binary data, not the binary data itself. However, the binary data is available to Service Callout, Routing, Publish, and Java Callout actions.

A transport provider is free to implement its own *XXX*Source object representing its particular message representation. At a minimum, this must implement the basic methods for streaming the data (after doing appropriate conversions). The main advantage of creating such a custom `Source` object is that if both the inbound and outbound transport recognize this type of `Source` object, and the message is not touched in the pipeline, the message representation will never need to be converted.

Along with implementing a custom *XXX*Source object, a transport provider can register transformations that can convert from this custom representation to one or more of the standard representations. This can provide an optimal way to go from a custom representation to, for example, an `XMLObject` representation. This is done when the transport provider is registered with the transport manager: `TransportManager.registerProvider()`.

Let's give a more concrete example. Suppose your custom transport supports some form of binary XML representation. You could define a `BinXMLSource` class, with get and set methods for accessing the underlying binary XML (`BinXML`). The stream methods would need to convert from the `BinXML` representation to standard text XML. The binding layer could get this stream of text XML and parse it to an `XmlObject`. But this is inefficient, because the `BinXML` is already parsed and structured. So, suppose there is a more direct method for going from a BinXML representation to an XMLObject representation. Then you would also register a transformer that can convert between those two representations. In this way, you could eliminate the overhead of going from binary XML to text XML, and then parsing the text XML back into an XmlObject.

When your custom transport is invoked on outbound with a Source object, it can first test whether the Source object is an instance of BinXMLSource. If so, it can directly call the get method to get the BinXML representation and send it out. If the Source object isn't already a BinXMLSource, it can use the master transformer—TransportManager.getTransformer()—to convert from the given Source object to a BinXMLSource. OSB creates this master transformer as being the transitive closure of all the built-in and registered transformers.

Inbound Message Processing

We're finally ready to discuss how messages actually get processed. We'll first discuss how the inbound transport passes a request message into the pipeline and how it receives the response to send back out. The next section will discuss the analogous processing for outbound messages.

How an inbound service endpoint initially gets a message from the outside world is transport-specific and is outside the use of the Transport SDK. It might have a listener on some kind of communication channel, it might poll for input, or it might rely on WebLogic Server services to deliver a message to it somehow. But however it receives a message, the transport must deliver the message to the OSB runtime. To do this, the transport provider must implement a class supporting the InboundTransportMessageContext interface. This class serves multiple purposes: it packages up all the information associated with the inbound message (for example, endpoint information, metadata associated with the message, and the actual message payload); it serves as a callback for the response, to receive the response metadata and payload; and it serves as a factory for creating ResponseMetaData objects, either from scratch or from an XML representation.

With a message in hand, the inbound transport provider attaches to the message any metadata that came with the message and the endpoint that received the message, putting all that information into the InboundTransportMessageContext object. It then invokes TransportManager.receiveMessage(), passing this InboundTransportMessageContext object and some transport options. In the typical case, the TransportManager will invoke the following methods on the provider's InboundTransportMessageContext:

- getEndpoint() to find out the endpoint delivering the message

- getMessageId() to get a message identifier (ideally unique) associated with the message

- getRequestMetaData() to get the metadata associated with the message

- getMessage() to get the Source object containing the message data, either a standard Source that comes with OSB or a custom Source

At this point, the runtime has all the information about the incoming request message. It then can invoke the pipeline and do the proxy service processing on the message. When everything is complete and it's ready to deliver a response, it calls the following methods on the provider's InboundTransportMessageContext:

- `createResponseMetaData()` to create the object to hold the response metadata

- `setResponseMetaData()` to set the response metadata

- `setResponsePayload()` to set the source object containing the response message data

- `close()` to signal the provider that processing is complete and it can send the response message back to the client

The call to `close()` is the final call. When the inbound transport provider receives this call, it not only sends the message back to the client, but it can also clean up any resources associated with the message.

■Note The call to `close()` typically comes from a different thread than the one that issued the call to `TransportManager.receiveMessage()`. This is the fundamental callback mechanism to invoke the inbound response processing from the proxy service response thread. It's only after receiving this call that the provider should access the response metadata or response payload.

The other parameter to `TransportManager.receiveMessage()` is the value class `TransportOptions`. This class has a number of properties that are mostly self-explanatory. A couple of the properties need further explanation. The property QoS represents quality of service, and can be either `EXACTLY_ONCE` or `BEST_EFFORT`. You should use `EXACTLY_ONCE` only when a transaction is associated with the incoming message. OSB will use this value to set the QoS element in the message context variable $inbound, which is available in the pipeline, and controls the default quality of service used for outbound calls.

Another property closely related to QoS is `ThrowOnError`. This tells the runtime to throw an exception if an error is encountered during the request processing. If this is unset and an error is encountered in the request pipeline, the runtime won't return with an exception, but will instead invoke the various response methods on the provider's `InboundTransportMessageContext` object, terminating with the `close()` call. The provider will recognize this as an error because the `ResponseCode` property in the `ResponseMetaData` will be set to `TRANSPORT_STATUS_ERROR` rather than `TRANSPORT_STATUS_SUCCESS`. This property affects only errors that are found during the request pipeline processing. Errors found during response pipeline processing always result in `setResponse()` and `close()` calls being made on the provider's `InboundTransportMessageContext` object.

Typically, `ThrowOnError` is set only if the QoS is set to `EXACTLY_ONCE`. In this way, when an error is encountered during request processing, the inbound transaction can be aborted. For certain transports, this can be done without returning a response and can allow the transaction to be replayed (for example, JMS).

One other property of `TransportOptions` worth mentioning is Mode. This can be either `REQUEST_ONLY` or `REQUEST_RESPONSE`. If the Mode is `REQUEST_ONLY`, the runtime won't make the calls to the response methods on the provider's `InboundTransportMessageContext` object. It will call the `close()` method only at the end of message processing.

So, you can see that the properties described earlier affect the sequence of methods called on the provider's `InboundTransportMessageContext` object. Although the methods relating to getting the inbound request message will always be called, the methods relating to setting the outbound response message might not be called, depending on `TransportOptions` and possible error conditions. For example, the transport provider should be prepared to have the `close()` method called without a call to set the response payload.

To give an example of this inbound processing, let's look at the socket transport. The socket transport has an implementation of `InboundTransportMessageContext`, called `SocketInboundMessageContext`. A subset of this class is shown in Listing 17-17. Parts (including most of the simple get methods) have been omitted for brevity.

An interesting method to look at is the constructor of the class, which initializes all the fields that the transport manager will later query, such as the endpoint, the message ID, the request metadata, and the message payload. The get routines are then just mostly returning these instance variables. The `getRequestPayload()` method takes the incoming message, which is in the form of a `String`, and simply turns it into a `StringSource`.

The other interesting method to look at is the `close()` method. The transport manager calls this method after setting the response metadata and response message payload. The `close()` method is responsible for sending the response back to the client. At the end of the `close()` method, all processing for this invocation is complete.

Listing 17-17. *Simplified SocketInboundMessageContext*

```
public class SocketInboundMessageContext
  implements InboundTransportMessageContext {
  private SocketTransportEndPoint endPoint;
  private Socket clientSocket;
  private String msgId;
  private String msg;
  private SocketRequestMetaData requestMetadata;
  private SocketResponseMetaData responseMetaData;
  private Source responsePayload;
  private static int count = 0;

  /**
   * Constructor of SocketInboundMessageContext. Initializes the field
   * variables, reads the message from the input stream and it is set.
   */
  public SocketInboundMessageContext(SocketTransportEndPoint endPoint,
                                     Socket clientSocket, String msgId,
                                     String msg) throws TransportException {
    this.endPoint = endPoint;
    this.clientSocket = clientSocket;
    this.msgId = msgId;
    this.msg = msg;

    String requestEncoding = endPoint.getRequestEncoding();
    if(requestEncoding == null) {
      requestEncoding = "utf-8";
    }
    requestMetadata = new SocketRequestMetaData(requestEncoding);
    ((SocketRequestHeaders)requestMetadata.getHeaders()).setMessageCount(++count);
```

```java
    requestMetadata.setClientHost(clientSocket.getInetAddress().getHostAddress());
    requestMetadata.setClientPort(clientSocket.getPort());
  }

  /**
   * @return returns the source reading the inbound message or null if
   *         there is no body of the request.
   */
  public Source getRequestPayload() throws TransportException {
    if (msg == null) {
      return null;
    }
    return new StringSource(msg);
  }

  /**
   * @return empty (new) metadata for the response part of the message, e.g.
   *         headers, etc. Used for initializing the inbound response
   */
  public ResponseMetaData createResponseMetaData() throws TransportException {
    SocketResponseMetaData responseMetaData =
      new SocketResponseMetaData(endPoint.getResponseEncoding());
    return responseMetaData;
  }

  /**
   * @return metadata for the response part of the message, e.g. headers, etc
   *         initialized according to transport provider-specific XMLBean. Used
   *         for initializing the inbound response
   */
  public ResponseMetaData createResponseMetaData(XmlObject rmdXML)
    throws TransportException {
    SocketResponseMetaDataXML xmlObject =
      SocketResponseMetaData.getSocketResponseMetaData(rmdXML);
    if (xmlObject != null) {
      return new SocketResponseMetaData(xmlObject);
    }
    return null;
  }

  /**
   * sets the response metadata of the message.
   */
  public void setResponseMetaData(ResponseMetaData rmd)
    throws TransportException {
    if (!(rmd instanceof SocketResponseMetaData)) {
      throw new TransportException(
```

```java
        SocketTransportMessagesLogger.invalidResponseMetadataType(
          SocketResponseMetaData.class.getName()));
  }
  responseMetaData = (SocketResponseMetaData) rmd;
}

/**
 * sets the response payload of the message.
 */
public void setResponsePayload(Source src) throws TransportException {
  responsePayload = src;
}

/**
 * Sends the response back to the client.
 */
public void close(TransportOptions transportOptions) {

  OutputStream outputStream = null;
  try {
    /** If message pattern is one way, return immediately.*/
    if (endPoint.getMessagePattern()
      .equals(TransportEndPoint.MessagePatternEnum.ONE_WAY)) {
      return;
    }
    /** Write the response back to the client. */
    String reqEnc =
      endPoint.getSocketEndpointConfiguration().getRequestEncoding();
    if(reqEnc == null) {
        reqEnc = "utf-8";
    }
    outputStream = clientSocket.getOutputStream();
    if (responsePayload != null) {
      TransformOptions options = new TransformOptions();

      options.setCharacterEncoding(reqEnc);
      responsePayload.writeTo(outputStream, options);
    } else {
      SocketTransportMessagesLogger.noResponsePayload();
    }
    /** write \r\n\r\n at the end. */
    outputStream.write(SocketTransportUtil.D_CRLF.getBytes(reqEnc));
    outputStream.flush();
  } catch (Exception e) {
    /* Log an error */
  } finally {
    try {
```

```
      // closing the socket stream.
      clientSocket.close();
    } catch (IOException ignore) {
    }
  }
  }
 }
}
```

To complete the picture, let's discuss where the SocketInboundMessageContext object is created. This occurs in the SocketTransportReceiver class. This class has a listener on the configured port, and spawns off a worker thread when a new incoming message is available. A lot of socket-specific work is done in this class. The basic idea is that a worker thread is created to read the message from the socket and pass it, along with the associated metadata, to the transport manager. Listing 17-18 shows the simplified version of that worker thread.

Listing 17-18. *WorkerThread Handling the Inbound Message*

```
static class WorkerThread implements Runnable {
  private Socket clientSocket;
  private SocketTransportEndPoint endPoint;
  private int timeout;
  private boolean enableNagleAlgorithm;

  public WorkerThread(Socket clientSocket, SocketTransportEndPoint endPoint,
                      int timeout, boolean enableNagleAlgorithm) {
    this.clientSocket = clientSocket;
    this.endPoint = endPoint;
    this.timeout = timeout;
    this.enableNagleAlgorithm = enableNagleAlgorithm;
  }

  public void run() {
    try {
      /** set the socket properties. */
      clientSocket.setSoTimeout(timeout);
      clientSocket.setTcpNoDelay(!enableNagleAlgorithm);

      String msgId = new Random().nextInt() + "." + System.nanoTime();
      InputStream inputStream = clientSocket.getInputStream();

      /** read the incoming message */
      String msg = ;/* Message from input stream. Details omitted */

      /** if it's one way close the connection. */
      if (endPoint.getMessagePattern()
        .equals(TransportEndPoint.MessagePatternEnum.ONE_WAY))
```

```
        try {
          // closing the input stream only because we didn't open any output
          // stream.
          clientSocket.getInputStream().close();
        } catch (IOException e) {
          SocketTransportUtil.logger.error(e.getLocalizedMessage());
        }
      }
      final SocketInboundMessageContext inboundMessageContext =
        new SocketInboundMessageContext(endPoint, clientSocket, msgId, msg);

      /** send inbound context to SDK, which sends it to the pipeline */
      TransportManagerHelper.getTransportManager()
        .receiveMessage(inboundMessageContext, null);

    } catch (Exception e) {
      /* log an error */
    }
  }
}
```

Outbound Message Processing

Outbound messages are sent on behalf of a business service. Outbound processing is the inverse of inbound processing. In this case, the OSB runtime delivers the outgoing request message to the transport provider, and the transport provider delivers the response message (if any) back.

The transport manager delivers the outgoing request message by calling the sendMessageAsync() method on the provider's implementation of the TransportProvider interface. We discussed the TransportProvider interface in earlier sections; this is the one method that is used for runtime message processing (the other methods are used at design and deploy time). This method is invoked with three parameters:

- TransportSender is a container for the request message, metadata, endpoint information, and credentials.

- TransportSendListener is the callback object for sending the response message.

- TransportOptions is a value class containing properties affecting how the message should be sent.

The TransportSender parameter can be one of two subclasses. However, for custom transports, it's always a ServiceTransportSender, so we won't bother describing a NoServiceTransportSender (it's used internally within OSB). The transport provider can pull all the data for the outgoing request message from the ServiceTransportSender. This consists of the message payload, the RequestMetaData associated with the message, the endpoint destination for this message, and the security credentials for the message.

The TransportOptions parameter can affect how the provider should send out the message. The following properties can affect how the message is sent:

- Mode is one way or request/response.

- OperationName, for SOAP services, is the name of the invoked operation.

- QoS is the quality of service, which potentially affects whether the operation is transactional.

- URI is a URI that can override the one configured in the endpoint (the pipeline can change this value).

Tip The outbound transport can ignore several properties in TransportOptions, such as RetryCount, RetryInterval (retries are all handled by the transport manager), and ThrowOnError (outbound can always raise an exception; this only applies to inbound).

So, now the transport provider, having all the data associated with the message and the options for sending the message, can send out the request message in the manner specific to the transport. That is pretty straightforward.

What gets a little trickier is providing the response message back to the OSB runtime (or at least signaling the OSB runtime to do response processing when there is no response). The rule for outbound transport providers is that the response must come back on a different thread than the request. In other words, the call to TransportProvider.sendMessageAsync() should return prior to giving the response, and the response should be given on a different thread by calling one of the two methods in TransportSendListener.

Creating a new thread for the response might be an inherent part of the transport; that is, the response might just naturally come in on a different thread (for example, a JMS listener). However, if the message is one way or the response doesn't naturally come in on a different thread, the transport must allocate a new thread for the response processing. You can allocate this thread using TransportManagerHelper.schedule(), which can optionally be given a dispatch policy if the business service endpoint configuration contains one.

The outbound transport provider also must implement a class supporting the OutboundTransportMessageContext. The only requirement for this class is that it be a container for response message payload and associated metadata (including the URI and message ID). These can be null in the case of a one-way message. The OutboundTransportMessageContext is passed back to the TransportSendListener method.

Note that the TransportSendListener has two callback methods: onReceiveResponse() and onError(). As their names suggest, the outbound transport should call onReceiveResponse() in the successful case, and onError() in the error case.

So, in total, there are three ways for the outbound transport to initiate response processing in the OSB runtime: calling onReceiveResponse() in a new thread, calling onError() in a new thread, or raising a transportException in the original thread (from TransportProvider.sendMessageAsync()). The outbound transport should raise the transportException if it had problems in even sending out the request message (for example, due to having a connection problem).

It is useful to understand how the transport manager handles retries. When retries are configured (either because multiple endpoint URIs are configured for the business service or the retry count is greater than zero), they might or might not be used depending on the quality of service, on the transactional status, and on how the error was reported. The transaction status could be Tx Null (there is no transaction), Tx Okay (there is a good transaction), or Tx Rollback (there is a transaction, but it is marked as rollback only due to the error). Table 17-2 describes the combinations.

Table 17-2. *Retry Semantics*

QoS	Error Mechanism	Tx Null	Tx Okay	Tx Rollback
BEST_EFFORT	transportException	Retry outbound in request pipeline.	N/A. Transaction suspended by the transport manager.	N/A. Transaction suspended by the transport manager.
BEST_EFFORT	onError()	Retry outbound in response pipeline.	N/A. Transaction suspended by the transport manager.	N/A. Transaction suspended by the transport manager.
EXACTLY_ONCE	transportException	Retry outbound in request pipeline.	Retry outbound in request pipeline.	No retries. Error handler in request pipeline.
EXACTLY_ONCE	onError()	No retries. Error handler in response pipeline.	No retries. Error handler in response pipeline.	No retries. Error handler in response pipeline. Request rolled back.

So, to summarize, the sequence of events for an outbound transport is as follows:

1. TransportProvider.sendMessageAsync() is called by the transport manager.

2. The transport provider extracts the endpoint data, message payload, metadata, and possibly the credentials from the ServiceTransportSender.

3. The provider examines the options in TransportOptions.

4. The provider sends out the request message using a transport-specific mechanism.

5. If necessary, the provider creates a new thread using TransportManagerHelper.schedule().

6. The provider gets the response message using a transport-specific mechanism.

7. The provider creates an OutboundTransportMessageContext object to contain the response message and associated metadata.

8. The provider invokes one of the callback methods in TransportSendListener on the new thread.

One special case needs mentioning: the case of a proxy service invoking another proxy service. We call this a *colocated call*. In this case, the transport provider's sendMessageAsync() method is invoked, but the supplied endpoint is an inbound endpoint, rather than an outbound endpoint; that is, a proxy service rather than a business service. A transport provider would typically bypass the whole transport mechanism and directly invoke the targeted proxy.

The Transport SDK makes this easy, by supplying a CoLocatedMessageContext class. The transport provider can extend this class by simply adding the methods for creating the request metadata. The sample socket transport demonstrates this simple concept in its implementation of SocketCoLocatedMessageContext, which can be copied verbatim.

Now, let's take a look at the socket transport's outbound implementation. The socket transport puts the majority of the implementation of the outbound transport into its class implementing the OutboundTransportMessageContext: the SocketOutboundMessageContext class. Hence, the sendMessageAsync() implementation merely creates and invokes this object. The code for this method is given in Listing 17-19.

Listing 17-19. *SocketTransportProvider sendMessageAsync*

```
public void sendMessageAsync(TransportSender sender,
                             TransportSendListener listener,
                             TransportOptions options)
  throws TransportException {
  /** whether the the other endpoint is inbound */
  boolean isInbound = false;

  if (sender instanceof ServiceTransportSender) {
    isInbound = ((ServiceTransportSender) sender).getEndPoint().isInbound();
  }

  if (!isInbound) {// other endpoint is an out-bound
    SocketOutboundMessageContext socketOutboundMessageContext =
      new SocketOutboundMessageContext(sender, options);
    socketOutboundMessageContext.send(listener);
  } else { // other endpoint is an inbound.
    SocketCoLocatedMessageContext socketCoLocatedMessageContext =
      new SocketCoLocatedMessageContext((ServiceTransportSender) sender,
        options);
    socketCoLocatedMessageContext.send(listener);
  }
}
```

So, the heart of the outbound socket transport implementation is in the SocketOutboundMessageContext class, whose implementation is given in Listing 17-20. It's rather long, but the points to consider are how the send() method makes a connection and sends the outbound request, using the Source for the outbound request; how it uses the TransportManagerHelper.schedule() method to create a new thread to get the response; and how it invokes the TransportSendListener methods to return that response. Some details have been omitted for brevity.

Listing 17-20. *SocketOutboundMessageContext*

```
public class SocketOutboundMessageContext
  implements OutboundTransportMessageContext {
  private TransportSender sender;
```

```java
private TransportOptions options;
private String msgId;
private EndPointConfiguration config;
private InputStream responseIS;
private SocketResponseMetaData responseMetadata;

/**
 * Initializes the field variables.
 */
public SocketOutboundMessageContext(TransportSender sender,
                                    TransportOptions options)
  throws TransportException {
  this.msgId = new Random().nextInt() + "." + System.nanoTime();
  this.sender = sender;
  this.options = options;
  if (sender instanceof ServiceTransportSender) {
    this.config =
      ((ServiceTransportSender) sender).getEndPoint().getConfiguration();
  } else {
    throw new TransportException(
      SocketTransportMessagesLogger.illegalTransportSender());
  }
}


public ResponseMetaData getResponseMetaData() throws TransportException {
  return responseMetadata;
}


public Source getResponsePayload() throws TransportException {
  return responseIS == null ? null : new StreamSource(responseIS);
}


public URI getURI() {
  return options.getURI();
}


public String getMessageId() {
  return msgId;
}


/**
 * Sends the message to the external service, schedules a Runnable which sets
 * the response metadata, and reads the response from the external service.
 */
public void send(final TransportSendListener listener)
  throws TransportException {
  String address = options.getURI().toString();
```

```
    try {
      String host = null;
      int port = 0;
      try {
        URI uri = new URI(address);
        host = uri.getHost();
        port = uri.getPort();
      } catch (URISyntaxException e) {
        new TransportException(e.getMessage(), e);
      }
      SocketTransportMessagesLogger.ipAddress(host, port);
      final Socket clientSocket = new Socket(host, port);

      SocketEndpointConfiguration socketEndpointConfiguration =
        SocketTransportUtil.getConfig(config);
      SocketOutboundPropertiesType outboundProperties =
        socketEndpointConfiguration.getOutboundProperties();
      clientSocket.setTcpNoDelay(!outboundProperties.getEnableNagleAlgorithm());
      clientSocket.setSoTimeout(outboundProperties.getTimeout());

      String reqEnc = socketEndpointConfiguration.getRequestEncoding();
      if (reqEnc == null) reqEnc = "utf-8";

      // Send the message to the external service.
      OutputStream outputStream = clientSocket.getOutputStream();
      TransformOptions transformOptions = new TransformOptions();
      transformOptions.setCharacterEncoding(reqEnc);
      sender.getPayload().writeTo(outputStream, transformOptions);
      outputStream.write(SocketTransportUtil.D_CRLF.getBytes(reqEnc));
      outputStream.flush();
      SocketTransportMessagesLogger.flushed();

      PipelineAcknowledgementTask task =
        new PipelineAcknowledgementTask(listener, clientSocket,
          socketEndpointConfiguration);
      TransportManagerHelper
        .schedule(task, socketEndpointConfiguration.getDispatchPolicy());
    } catch (Exception e) {
      /* log the error */;
      throw new TransportException(e.getMessage(), e);
    }
  }
}

/**
 * This task does the acknowledgement work of the outbound to the pipeline.
 */
class PipelineAcknowledgementTask implements Runnable {
```

```java
        private TransportSendListener listener;
        private Socket clientSocket;
        private SocketEndpointConfiguration epc;

        public PipelineAcknowledgementTask(TransportSendListener listener,
                                           Socket clientSocket,
                                           SocketEndpointConfiguration epc) {
            this.listener = listener;
            this.clientSocket = clientSocket;
            this.epc = epc;
        }

        /**
         * It reads the response sent from the external service, sets the headers,
         * and invokes the pipeline.
         */
        public void run() {
            try {
                // if the end-point is one-way, don't read the response.
                if (!epc.getRequestResponse()) {
                    SocketTransportMessagesLogger.oneWayEndpoint();
                    listener.onReceiveResponse(SocketOutboundMessageContext.this);
                    return;
                }
                String resEnc = getResponseEncoding();
                responseMetadata = new SocketResponseMetaData(resEnc);
                InetAddress inetAddress = clientSocket.getInetAddress();
                responseMetadata.setEndPointHost(inetAddress.getHostName());
                responseMetadata.setEndPointIP(inetAddress.getHostAddress());

                // Read the response from the external service.
                /* CODE FOR READING THE MESSAGE HAS BEEN OMITTED */
                String msg = omittedStuff();
                responseIS = new ByteArrayInputStream(msg.getBytes(resEnc));
                listener.onReceiveResponse(SocketOutboundMessageContext.this);
            } catch (Exception e) {
                listener.onError(SocketOutboundMessageContext.this,
                    TransportManager.TRANSPORT_ERROR_GENERIC, e.getLocalizedMessage());
            } finally {
                try {
                    clientSocket.close();
                } catch (IOException e) {
                }
            }
        }
    }
}
```

Registering the Transport Provider

One last implementation job remains: you need to get the custom transport implementation hooked into the OSB runtime.

Deploying the Custom Transport to WebLogic Server

Earlier, we discussed packaging all the pieces of the custom transport into a deployable EAR file. You can deploy the custom transport into an OSB domain using any of the standard mechanisms of WebLogic Server:

- Use the WebLogic administration console.

- Use WebLogic Server programmatic APIs.

- Add an entry to the OSB domain `config.xml` file, as shown in Listing 17-21.

Listing 17-21. *Deployment Entry to Add to config.xml to Deploy a Custom Transport*

```
<app-deployment>
    <name>My Transport Provider</name>
    <target>AdminServer, myCluster</target>
    <module-type>ear</module-type>
    <source-path>$USER_INSTALL_DIR$/servicebus/lib/mytransport.ear</source-path>
    <deployment-order>1234</deployment-order>
</app-deployment>
```

However, you still need to register the custom transport with the transport manager.

Registering the Custom Transport with the Transport Manager

You register your custom transport with the transport manager by using the method `TransportManager.registerProvider()`. You can call this method from the `postStart()` method of the `ApplicationLifecycleListener` for the EAR file. The socket transport provides a simple example, as shown in Listing 17-22, which can be copied verbatim.

Listing 17-22. *Socket Transport ApplicationListener*

```
public class ApplicationListener extends ApplicationLifecycleListener {
  /**
   * After an application is initialized, this method is invoked by the Deploy
   * framework. Socket transport is registered with TransportManager.
   */
  public void postStart(ApplicationLifecycleEvent evt)
    throws ApplicationException {
    try {
      TransportManager man = TransportManagerHelper.getTransportManager();
      SocketTransportProvider instance = SocketTransportProvider.getInstance();
      man.registerProvider(instance, null);
    } catch (Exception e) {
```

```
        /* Log an error */
    }
  }
}
```

■**Caution** You cannot unregister the transport provider or undeploy the custom transport EAR file. As you do development, and you want to update the custom transport, you can update the EAR file and then restart the server.

Registering the Transport Provider in WorkSpace Studio

Registering the transport provider in WorkSpace Studio is a little different. Rather than using an application listener class that is automatically invoked when loaded, the transport provider implements one extra, very simple interface: TransportProviderFactory. The key method in this interface is registerProvider(TransportManager tm). The OSB transport subsystem in WorkSpace Studio will call the transport provider's implementation of this method at startup, passing a reference to the TransportManager. The transport provider implementation can then register the transport with the transport manager.

You may be wondering how the transport subsystem knows where to find the implementation class. A reference to the implementation class for this interface is put into the plug-in XML file that configures the WorkSpace Studio plug-in. So, by looking at the plug-in XML configuration files, the transport manager in WorkSpace Studio can find all of the transport plug-ins, and can call their registerProvider methods.

Examples of the plug-in XML configuration file and the implementation of the TransportProviderFactory for the socket transport are shown in Listings 17-23 and 17-24. Notice that registerProvider method keeps track of whether the provider is being used in WorkSpace Studio or in the server environment. This can be useful for a transport to know so that it doesn't try using WebLogic Server APIs while not running on the server.

Listing 17-23. *Socket Transport Configuration plugin.xml File*

```xml
<?xml version="1.0" encoding="UTF-8"?>
<?eclipse version="3.2"?>
<plugin>
    <extension point="com.bea.alsb.core.transports"
          id="socket"
          name="Socket Transport">
      <transport transport-provider=
              "com.bea.alsb.transports.sock.SocketTransportProviderFactory"/>
    </extension>
    <extension point="org.eclipse.help.toc">
      <toc file="/help/en/toc.xml" primary="true"/>
    </extension>
    <extension point="org.eclipse.help.contexts">
      <contexts
```

```
            file="/help/en/contexts_socketTransport.xml"
            plugin="Socket_Transport"/>
    </extension>
</plugin>
```

Listing 17-24. *Socket Transport TransportProviderFactory Implementation*

```
Package com.bea.alsb.transports.sock;
import ...;

public class SocketTransportProviderFactory implements TransportProviderFactory {
    private static boolean isOffline = false;

    public static boolean isOffline() {
        return isOffline;
    }
    public void registerProvider(TransportManager tm) throws TransportException {
        isOffline = true;
        SocketTransportProvider instance = SocketTransportProvider.getInstance();
        tm.registerProvider(instance, null);
    }
    public String getId() {
        return SocketTransportProvider.ID;
    }
}
```

Advanced Custom Transport Topics

The previous sections described how to build a transport provider that can work with OSB.
You can work through those steps to get a functioning custom transport. But after getting the
basics down, you may want to add some features and capabilities to your custom transport to
provide a better experience for users.

Using the Transport Provider in WorkSpace Studio

There are a couple of special considerations for running the transport provider in WorkSpace
Studio. Since WorkSpace Studio is solely for designing services, the only part of the transport
provider that is used is the UI classes (described earlier in the section "Implementing Transport Provider User Interface Classes"). This includes the methods for describing the UI fields
and the various validation methods. Excluded are any methods for activation or deploying
a transport, as well as any of the actual runtime classes for processing messages.

   As we mentioned, the same interfaces are used in both the console and WorkSpace Studio
environments, even though the rendering technology is different. However, it may be necessary
to have some differences in the implementation, such as when the creation of the UI widgets
involves calls to the server environment. For example, dispatch policies may be displayed in
a drop-down list that is populated by a call to the server to get the list of all available policies.
This can be difficult when not running on the server.

As we discussed earlier, the transport provider can record whether or not it is running on or the server by seeing whether the EAR file application listener method or the TransportProviderFactory registerProvider method is called. It can then use that information to have slightly different implementation of the UI widgets, making sure that when running in offline mode, it doesn't try to make calls to the WebLogic Server routines.

The transport provider can actually run in three possible modes:

Online mode: The transport provider runs on the OSB server with full access to all server functions.

Offline mode: The transport provider runs outside the OSB server (for example, on Work-Space Studio) with no access to server functions.

Offline with remote server mode: The transport provider runs outside the OSB server, but with remote access to the OSB server; that is, via remote MBean calls.

Both of the offline modes cover when the transport provider is running in WorkSpace Studio, but if the transport provider has server-dependent logic in its UI routines, it can do a slightly better job by offering the offline with remote server mode. This is an option when WorkSpace Studio is connected to a running instance of WebLogic Server. So, some server functions can be preserved even in this offline mode by going through Java Management Extensions (JMX) to remote MBeans.

To get access to the remote MBeans, you use a JMXConnector. When running in the offline with remote server mode, this is supplied in the TransportUIContext that is given to TransportUIBinding. It can be extracted from the context with a call like this:

```
jmxConnector =
        (JMXConnector) uiContext.get(TransportValidationContext.JMXCONNECTOR);
```

So, continuing with the example of creating a UI widget for the user to enter the dispatch policy, the implementation could have tests for the mode in which it is operating and handle each mode differently, as follows:

Online mode: Populate a drop-down list with the set of Work Managers in the local server, using TransportManagerHelper.getDispatchPolicies().

Offline mode: Since there is no way to get a list of available policies, put up a text box for the user to manually enter the dispatch policy.

Offline with remote server mode: Populate a drop-down list with the set of Work Managers in the remote server via the JMX connector, using TransportManagerHelper.getDispatchPolicies(jmxConnector).

Other differences in the WorkSpace Studio environment are the packaging of the transport provider and how it registers with the transport manager. The registration was covered in the earlier section "Registering the Transport Provider in Workspace Studio." To deliver the transport provider as an Eclipse plug-in, it should be packaged as a JAR file with the following directory structure:

- `plugin.xml` is the root of the plug-in JAR.

- `/lib/your_transport.jar` contains the transport classes and resources.

- `/META-INF/Manifest.mf` is the standard manifest for the Eclipse plug-in.

- `/help` is the location of help resources if they are provided for the transport.

The easiest way to create this structure is to follow the build steps for the sample socket transport. You can copy the build steps from the socket transport's `build.xml` file.

Declaring Environmental Attributes

A typical pattern for OSB is to develop proxy and business services in one environment (such as a development environment) and later move them to other environments (such as a test or production environment). Certain service configuration attributes are specific to each environment. These attributes may need to be altered when going from one environment to another. But, more important, when redeploying an updated version to an environment, these attributes should be preserved.

A variation of this issue comes from moving artifacts from WorkSpace Studio to the runtime environment. Developers working in WorkSpace Studio focus on the main design of the services: the transformation, the transports, the logic, and so on. They are less concerned about runtime issues, such as security settings and operational characteristics.

OSB provides the capability to preserve security and operational settings when deploying services from one environment to another, including from WorkSpace Studio to the runtime server. OSB distinguishes three kinds of special configuration attributes.

True environment values: Settings that are truly specific to the server environment, such as URLs.

Operational values: Settings that an operator may set to help manage the system, such as SLA alerts.

Security values: Settings that the administrator may configure to handle the security requirements of a particular environment, such as service account references.

Some of these settings may be part of a transport endpoint configuration, though that is somewhat uncommon for the operational values. Hence, to work well with this OSB capability, the transport provider needs to support optionally preserving these three types of attributes when a new configuration JAR is imported.

Toward this objective, the transport provider advertises which of the endpoint configuration attributes are in these categories. This is declared in the `TransportProviderConfiguration` XML file. The transport provider lists the attributes, giving their name, their category (`environment`, `security`, or `operational`) and whether the attribute is a simple value (such as a string or integer) or has a more complex structure.

The way this works is that when an configuration JAR file is imported, and one of the preserve options is selected, the transport manager will use the methods `getEnvValues()` and `setEnvValues()` on the `TransportProvider` to preserve the appropriate settings. The transport provider should return attributes of all three types on the `getEnvValues()` for the given services endpoint configuration, and be prepared to receive all of these values on a call to `setEnvValues()`. The transport manager will get all of the old environment values for a service about to be overwritten with a new version in a configuration JAR. It will filter this list depending on the categorization of the environment values and the options selected by the user on input. It will overwrite the old service with the new service coming from the configuration JAR, and then reinstate the filtered set of values with a call to setEnvValues().

■**Caution** The terminology is a little confusing. At the low levels of the code, all of the attributes that could possibly be preserved are called env-value types. But at the user-visible level, they fall into three categories: environment, security, and operational values. So the term *environment* is used differently at the internal low level and as seen by the user.

Listing 17-25 shows a sample XML snippet listing some attributes that should be preserved for different scenarios.

Listing 17-25. *Example of the Three Types of env-value Declarations*

```
<env-value-type>
    <name>ServerName</name>
    <display-name>Name of the Server</display-name>
    <description>Give the managed servers name</description>
    <simple-value>true</simple-value>
    <category>environment</category>
</env-value-type>
<env-value-type>
    <name>ServiceAccount</name>
    <display-name>Service Account</display-name>
    <description>Credentials for accessing the server</description>
    <simple-value>false</simple-value>
    <category>security</category>
</env-value-type>
<env-value-type>
    <name>maxThreads</name>
    <display-name>Maximum concurrency</display-name>
    <description>
        Maximun number of threads that should be used to access the server
    </description>
    <simple-value>true</simple-value>
    <category>operational</category>
</env-value-type>
```

Runtime Endpoint Management

OSB 3 introduced some new features for runtime endpoint management. Two of these features require support from the transport provider, but that support is optional. Transports that do not provide this support will work fine, but will not have these endpoint management features.

The following sections discuss the features for runtime endpoint management that require some work on the part of the transport provider.

Application Error Handling

One runtime endpoint management feature concerns special handling for application errors. In general, the user can configure a business services with retries, and OSB will retry requests that result in errors. But for some services, it is desirable to suppress such retries if the service returns an application error (such as a SOAP fault), rather than an error from being unable to communicate with the service.

To take advantage of this feature, the transport provider must be able to distinguish application errors from other communication errors. If it can do so, it should declare that it supports application errors in its `TransportProviderConfiguration` XML, in the `declare-application-errors` element (see Figure 17-6). If this declaration is present, the OSB UI will know to offer the option to suppress retries of application errors.

To return an application error, the transport provider uses a special error code string: `BEA-380001` or `TransportManager.TRANSPORT_ERROR_APPLICATION`. If the error is being raised in the request pipeline, this should be set in the `TransportException`. If the error is being returned in the response pipeline, this error code string should be passed to the `TransportSendListener.onError` method.

Connection Error Handling

Another endpoint management feature is for taking a URL endpoint offline after a connection failure. This is an optional feature that the person configuring the business service can choose to use. If the business service has multiple URL endpoints for load-balancing and failover purposes, and one endpoint becomes unavailable (say, the server is down), this option will suppress trying to use that URL endpoint for a configurable period of time or until the operator puts it back online.

Unlike with the feature for handling application errors, the transport provider doesn't need to declare support for this feature. The transport provider only needs to recognize errors that indicate the service is unavailable (as opposed to possibly a transient problem or a problem with a specific message, like a security authorization failure). When such an error is encountered, another special error code string is used to report it: `BEA-380002` or `TransportManager.TRANSPORT_ERROR_ CONNECTION`. This error code is returned in the same way as the application error code, in the `TransportException` in the request pipeline or through the `TransportSendListener.onError` method in the response pipeline.

Custom Transport WSDL Support

There are some special considerations for transport providers that support WSDL-typed services. (If your transport does not support WSDL-typed services, you can skip this section.)

First, let's quickly review the parts of a WSDL file that are pertinent to this discussion. The `portType` section of a WSDL file provides an abstract description of the request and response messages for the various operations of the WSDL file. The `binding` section describes how those abstract descriptions should be packaged and represented.

OSB classifies WSDL bindings into two general categories: SOAP binding and plain XML binding. A SOAP binding WSDL file has a `soap:binding` section (not too surprising). An XML binding is defined in a standard way only for HTTP services, using an http:binding section. OSB extends this notion to define a plain XML binding when the transport is not HTTP as a BEA binding: bea:binding.

Both the SOAP binding and the BEA binding have an attribute that identifies the transport being used. The SOAP binding element and the BEA binding element in a WSDL file look like the following.

```
<soap:binding style="rpc" transport="[Transport IdentifierURI]"/>
<bea:binding transport="[TransportIdentifierURI]"/>
```

This TransportIdentifierURI identifies the transport used in the WSDL file. The following are examples of a SOAP binding over the JMS transport and a BEA binding (plain XML) over the SB transport.

```
<soap:binding style="rpc" transport="http://www.openuri.org/2002/04/soap/jms/"/>
<bea:binding transport="http://www.bea.com/transport/2007/05/sb"/>
```

OSB has a capability to generate the "effective WSDL" for a service. This means you could start out with a WSDL file for one kind of transport—perhaps one not even having a service or port section—and use it to create an OSB service using a different type of transport. OSB will generate the WSDL that matches the configured service, putting in the correct transport identifier URI and completing the WSDL to contain a single service and port section.

So what does all of this have to do with custom transports? A custom transport that supports WSDL-typed services needs to provide a couple of bits of information:

Supported transport URIs: It is convenient for it to list all of the transport URIs that it supports, so that when a service is created from a WSDL file, OSB can default the transport provider correctly. To identify the transport URIs supported by a transport, you add the list to the TransportProviderConfiguration XML using the supported-transport-uris element (see Figure 17-6). If no list is supplied, OSB will use the default URI for the transport (described next).

Transport identifier URI: The custom transport can help fill out the transport identifier URI in the generated effective WSDL. When filling in the transport identifier URI in the effective WSDL, OSB will get this value from one of the following places (in decreasing precedence).

- The transport provider implementation class can also implement the TransportCustomBindingProvider interface. In this case, OSB will call the method getIdentifierURI in this interface, passing a Ref to a service, and the transport provider can give the specific transport identifier for that service. This is the finest granularity of control.

- If the transport provider always uses the same transport identifier, it can simply declare it in the provider XML. The supported-transport-uris element has a subelement default-transport-uri. OSB will use this value in the effective WSDL for services using this transport.

- Finally, if the transport provider does neither of the preceding, OSB will default the transport identifying URI to one of the following form: http://www.bea.com/transport/2007/05/<transport_id>.

Service endpoint address URL: The custom transport can determine the service endpoint address URL for the effective WSDL. In the port section of the effective WSDL of a service is the URL address of the service endpoint. By default, this is simply the proxy or business service URL. If that URL needs to be modified (for example, it needs to be extended with the OSB server's host and port), the transport provider can implement the getEndPointAddress method in the TransportCustomBindingProvider interface. OSB will then consult with this method when generating the effective WSDL for a service using the transport to get the endpoint URL.

Custom Transport Online Help

Custom transports can optionally supply online help pages, further making them appear as natural components of OSB. This feature provides a way for the custom transport to give detailed help information about the transport's endpoint configuration properties. If the transport does not implement this feature, a generic transport help page will be displayed when the user clicks the help link.

OSB Console Online Help

To supply online help in the OSB console, the transport provider implements an additional interface CustomHelpProvider in the class that implements the TransportUIBinding. This interface has only one method to implement: getHelpPage, which returns a Reader object that streams an HTML help page. The contents of this page can be packaged as a resource in the transport provider's EAR file and loaded via the transport application class loader. When the user clicks the help link for the transport configuration page, the console will call this interface and stream the results back to the user's browser for display.

Listing 17-26 shows the implementation of the CustomHelpProvider interface for the sample socket transport. This implementation can be used nearly verbatim in your custom transport.

Listing 17-26. *Socket Transport Implementation of CustemHelpProvider*

```java
public class SocketTransportUIBinding
    implements TransportUIBinding, CustomHelpProvider {
    ...
  public Reader getHelpPage() {
    String helpFile = "help/en/contexts_socketTransport.html";
    ClassLoader clLoader = Thread.currentThread().getContextClassLoader();
    InputStream is = clLoader.getResourceAsStream(helpFile);
    InputStreamReader helpReader = null;
    if(is!=null)
      helpReader = new InputStreamReader(is);
    else
      /* Log a warning - no help available */
    return helpReader;
  }
}
```

If the help for the custom transport is simple, it can be presented in the single page returned from getHelpPage, and no other work is required. However, if it is desirable to have more advanced help, say with graphic images or additional linked pages, then a little more is involved. To provide the additional help files, you can embed a web application in the transport provider EAR file. Then the initial help page returned from getHelpPage can simply redirect the user (via a link) to the extended help in the transport web application. Of course, the initial page could redirect the user to additional help anywhere—even to some wholly separate online help location.

The sample socket transport follows this pattern. The initial help page returned from getHelpPage has little more than a link to /help_socket/help/en/example.html. Then in the socket transport EAR file, there is a web app subdirectory, with context root help_socket. This has additional help content resources, including HTML pages, images, and CSS files. See the sample socket implementation files for more details.

WorkSpace Studio Online Help

The same help files can also be used to provide help in WorkSpace Studio, but the packaging is a little different. If you look back at the plugin.xml file in Listing 17-23, you'll see two additional Eclipse extension points that are used to plug a transport provider's help into the WorkSpace Studio help system.

One extension point is org.eclipse.help.toc and gives a table of contents file, toc.xml. A toc.xml file defines the key entry point into the HTML content files by mapping a topic label to a reference to the root help HTML file. The topic label appears in the hierarchical table of contents, and a user can click the label to link to the associated help HTML file.

The toc.xml file also defines where the transport documentation should exist in the overall table of contents structure using bottom-up composition. In this case, there is an anchor in the higher-level OSB help file identified as postTransports. The transport's help is merged into the upper-level table of contents at this entry point.

The other extension point is at org.eclipse.help.contexts and gives the contexts.xml file (contexts_socketTransport.xml for the socket transport). The contexts.xml file provides context-sensitive help. This form of help is delivered when a user triggers context help (for example, by pressing the F1 key on a Windows system) while viewing the transport configuration page. The context ID in the context.xml file is the same as the transport provider ID. Thus, the user can get to the transport provider help through the general table of contents or by asking for help while viewing the transport provider's transport configuration page.

The actual detailed help content resources, including HTML pages, images, and CSS files, are contained in the help/en/* subdirectories of the transport JAR file. For example, the socket transport's root help page help/en/example.html is referenced from its toc.xml and contexts_socketTransport.xml files. That root help page, in turn, references other files in help/en and image files in help/en/wwimages.

Summary

As you've seen in this chapter, there are quite a few things to consider when implementing a custom transport. We discussed why you would build a custom transport and when it is appropriate to do so (and when you can avoid doing so). We introduced the sample socket transport, which is an excellent starting point for creating a custom transport, and we used it to provide examples of how to implement the various aspects of a custom transport. We gave an overview of the Transport SDK interfaces, describing which interfaces you'll invoke and which interfaces you'll implement to build a custom transport. We covered each of the steps involved in implementing a functioning custom transport, including creating the various XML and schema files, implementing the UI and deployment classes, executing the actual message processing, and registering the provider.

Finally, we covered several advanced topics for putting the finishing touches onto a custom transport. Though not required, these features may enhance a custom transport. We discussed including support for WorkSpace Studio, declaring attributes that are environment-specific, working with the OSB endpoint management features, customizing effective WSDL files, and providing custom transport online help. Once you've implemented all those steps, a custom transport will be a first-class transport in OSB, indistinguishable from the out-of-the-box transports.

Using this information, you can build new custom transports tailored for your company's business, allowing even greater integration of your company's services via OSB.

■■■

## CHAPTER 18

How Do I . . . ?

Although this book covers the details of using OSB, we've found over the years that there are a set of commonly asked questions by our customers about specific uses of OSB. They range from the simple to the unusual. In this chapter, we'll provide answers to the most commonly asked questions. Furthermore, we've picked out a few questions that might be uncommon, but that demonstrate just how flexible OSB is in practice. The questions are broken down into different categories, to help you find the answers. Some questions cross these categorical boundaries. Where appropriate, we've given credit to the folks who answered the original questions.

Be sure to visit http://www.otn.com or http://www.dev2dev.com. Those sites contain thousands of tips, code samples, and technical articles on OSB and other Oracle products. They are invaluable resources for developers and architects.

Security

Here are some questions and issues that commonly come up regarding security.

Is OSB certified by a security assessment?

Yes, OSB is certified by Federal Information Process Standard (FIPS) 140-2, which certifies the user access, cryptographic, and SSL capabilities of the product. Additionally, the product is in process for Common Criteria certification at Evaluation Assurance Level (EAL) 4, the highest security level attainable for an ESB product.

Thanks to Suman Cuddapah for this tip!

Are there any sample clients that can be used to test a web service on OSB using HTTPS with Basic Authentication?

Listing 18-1 provides a sample HTTPS client. Thanks to Nadim Samad for this solution.

Listing 18-1. *A Sample HTTPS Client*

```
import tests.util.HTTPHelper;
import tests.util.Credentials;
import tests.util.SecurityTestUtils;
import java.security.KeyStore;
import java.security.PrivateKey;
```

```
import java.security.KeyStoreException;
import java.security.NoSuchAlgorithmException;
import java.security.cert.Certificate;
import java.security.cert.X509Certificate;
import java.security.cert.CertificateException;
import java.util.List;
import java.util.ArrayList;
import java.io.IOException;
import java.io.FileInputStream;
import weblogic.xml.crypto.wss.provider.CredentialProvider;
import weblogic.wsee.security.bst.ClientBSTCredentialProvider;

public class InboundHTTPSClient {
    public static void main (String args[]) {
        System.setProperty("weblogic.security.TrustKeyStore", "CustomTrust");
        System.setProperty("weblogic.security.CustomTrustKeyStoreFileName",
            "C:\\bea\\user_projects\\domains\\tranSecTestDomain\\TestTrust.jks");
        System.setProperty("weblogic.security.SSL.ignoreHostnameVerify","true");
        System.setProperty("keystores.path",
            "C:\\bea90_1027\\user_projects\\domains\\tranSecTestDomain");
        InboundHTTPSClient ihttpsc = new InboundHTTPSClient();
        try {
            ihttpsc.testInboundHttpsWithClientCert();
        } catch (Exception e) {
            e.printStackTrace();
        }
    }

    public void testInboundHttpsWithClientCert() throws Exception {
        String iserviceName = "transport/inbound/https/clientCert/proxy";
            HTTPHelper httpHelper = new HTTPHelper();
            String requestMsg = "<bea>Oracle Bobble Dreams</bea>";
            Credentials cred = loadCredentials();
            System.out.println("cred: " + cred.toString());
            // send 5 requests
            HTTPHelper.HttpResponse httpResponse;
        for (int i = 0; i < 1; i++) {
            httpResponse = httpHelper.doRequest("POST", requestMsg,
                "https://fifa:7002/" + iserviceName, cred, 100, null);
            System.out.println(httpResponse.getBody());
        }
    }

    private Credentials loadCredentials() throws Exception {
        String ks_path = "C:\\bea90_1027\\user_projects\\ ➥
domains\\tranSecTestDomain\\client_keystore.jks";
        KeyStore ks = getClientKeyStore(ks_path, "password");
```

```
        Certificate clientCert = ks.getCertificate("transport-test-key");
        PrivateKey clientKey = (PrivateKey) ks.getKey("transport-test-key",➥
"password".toCharArray());
        Credentials cred = new Credentials();
        cred.useClientKeySSL(true);
        cred.setClientKey(clientKey);
        cred.setClientCerts(new Certificate[] {clientCert});
        return cred;
    }

    public static KeyStore getClientKeyStore(String ks_path, String ks_password)
        throws KeyStoreException, NoSuchAlgorithmException, IOException,
            CertificateException {
        FileInputStream fis = new java.io.FileInputStream(ks_path);
        KeyStore ks = KeyStore.getInstance("JKS");
        ks.load(fis, ks_password.toCharArray());
        fis.close();
        return ks;
    }
}
```

Administration

This section covers questions related to OSB administration.

How do I import a WSDL file (or other resource type) from a URL?

This tip applies to using the web console interface. Perform the following steps to import a WSDL file from a URL:

1. Use the OSB console to create a change in the Change Center.

2. Navigate to the project into which you want to import the WSDL file. Open the folder in the project where you want to store the WSDL file.

3. In the Create Resource field, select the Resources from URL item under the Bulk heading. This displays the Load Resources page.

4. In the URL/Path field, enter the URL of the WSDL file.

5. In the Resource Name field, provide a name for the WSDL file you're going to import.

6. In the Resource Type field, select the resource type you're importing.

7. Click the Next button, review, and accept the import information.

8. Be sure to activate your changes in the Change Center.

How do I run multiple instances of the PointBase database on a single machine?

When developing on a single machine, you sometimes need to run multiple domains. The PointBase database that ships with WebLogic Server and OSB defaults to use port 9093. There will be a conflict if you are running multiple domains on the same computer. You can easily change the PointBase port used by a server by editing the setDomainEnv.cmd (or .sh) script in the bin/ directory of your domain. Look for this line:

```
set POINTBASE_PORT=9093
```

and change the port number to an unused port on your computer. Remember that you'll also need to change any JDBC drivers in your domain to point to the new port number!

Thanks to James Bayer for this tip.

How do I set up an OSB server as a Microsoft Windows service?

A script was provided with OSB version 2.1 to do this. That script is no longer included with OSB 2.5. The following listings show how to install OSB 2.5 (and WebLogic Server 9) as a Windows service. You can download the code for all these scripts from the Source Code/Download area of the Apress web site at http://www.apress.com.

Listing 18-2 is the low-level script file that does the heavy lifting in this process. You don't need to call this script directly. Instead, you would call install AdminSrvrSvc.cmd (see Listing 18-3) to install the admin server as a Microsoft Windows service, or you would call install MgdSrvr1Svc.cmd to install managed server 1 as a Windows service. Notice that the managed server scripts apply to individual managed servers, requiring you to modify Listing 18-4 for each managed server in your OSB cluster.

Thanks to John Graves for this solution!

Listing 18-2. *The installSvc.cmd File*

```
@rem ***************************************************************************
@rem This script is used to install WebLogic Server as a Windows Service.
@rem
@rem To create your own start script for your domain, simply set the
@rem SERVER_NAME variable to your server name then call this script from your
@rem domain directory.
@rem
@rem This script sets the following variables before installing
@rem WebLogic Server as a Windows Service:
@rem
@rem WL_HOME     - The root directory of your WebLogic installation
@rem JAVA_HOME   - Location of the version of Java used to start WebLogic
@rem               Server. This variable must point to the root directory of a
@rem               JDK installation and will be set for you by the installer.
@rem               See the WebLogic platform support page
@rem               (http://e-docs.bea.com/wls/platforms/index.html) for an ➥
up-to-date list of
@rem               supported JVMs on Windows NT.
@rem PATH        - Adds the JDK and WebLogic directories to the system path.
```

```
@rem CLASSPATH   - Adds the JDK and WebLogic jars to the classpath.
@rem
@rem Other variables that installSvc takes are:
@rem
@rem WLS_USER       - admin username for server startup
@rem WLS_PW         - cleartext password for server startup
@rem ADMIN_URL      - if this variable is set, the server started will be a
@rem                  managed server, and will look to the url specified (i.e.
@rem                  http://localhost:7001) as the admin server.
@rem PRODUCTION_MODE    - set to true for production mode servers, false for
@rem                  development mode
@rem JAVA_OPTIONS - Java command-line options for running the server. (These
@rem                  will be tagged on to the end of the JAVA_VM and MEM_ARGS)
@rem JAVA_VM        - The java arg specifying the VM to run.  (i.e. -server,
@rem                  -client, etc.)
@rem MEM_ARGS       - The variable to override the standard memory arguments
@rem                  passed to java
@rem
@rem jDriver for Oracle users: This script assumes that native libraries
@rem required for jDriver for Oracle have been installed in the proper
@rem location and that your system PATH variable has been set appropriately.
@rem
@rem For additional information, refer to the WebLogic Server Administration
@rem Guide (http://e-docs.bea.com/wls/docs90/adminguide/startstop.html).
@rem *************************************************************************

@echo off
SETLOCAL

rem set DOMAIN_NAME=OSB
rem set SERVER_NAME=ESB_PROD2
rem set WLS_USER=weblogic
rem set WLS_PW=weblogic

set WL_HOME=C:\bea\weblogic91
call "%WL_HOME%\common\bin\commEnv.cmd"

@rem Check that the WebLogic classes are where we expect them to be
:checkWLS
if exist "%WL_HOME%\server\lib\weblogic.jar" goto checkJava
echo The WebLogic Server wasn't found in directory %WL_HOME%\server.
echo Please edit your script so that the WL_HOME variable points
echo to the WebLogic installation directory.
goto finish

@rem Check that java is where we expect it to be
:checkJava
```

```
if exist "%JAVA_HOME%\bin\java.exe" goto runWebLogic
echo The JDK wasn't found in directory %JAVA_HOME%.
echo Please edit your script so that the JAVA_HOME variable
echo points to the location of your JDK.
goto finish

:runWebLogic

if not "%JAVA_VM%" == "" goto noResetJavaVM
if "%JAVA_VENDOR%" == "BEA" set JAVA_VM=-jrocket
if "%JAVA_VENDOR%" == "HP"  set JAVA_VM=-server
if "%JAVA_VENDOR%" == "Sun" set JAVA_VM=-server

:noResetJavaVM
if not "%MEM_ARGS%" == "" goto noResetMemArgs
set MEM_ARGS=-Xms32m -Xmx200m

:noResetMemArgs

@echo on

set CLASSPATH=%WEBLOGIC_CLASSPATH%;%CLASSPATH%

@echo **************************************************
@echo *  To start WebLogic Server, use the password    *
@echo *  assigned to the system user.  The system      *
@echo *  username and password must also be used to    *
@echo *  access the WebLogic Server console from a web  *
@echo *  browser.                                       *
@echo **************************************************

rem *** Set Command Line for service to execute within created JVM

@echo off

if "%ADMIN_URL%" == "" goto runAdmin
@echo on
set CMDLINE="%JAVA_VM% %MEM_ARGS% %JAVA_OPTIONS% -classpath \"%CLASSPATH%\"
-Dweblogic.Name=%SERVER_NAME% -Dweblogic.management.username=%WLS_USER% ➡
-Dweblogic.management.server=\"%ADMIN_URL%\" ➡
-Dweblogic.ProductionModeEnabled=%PRODUCTION_MODE% ➡
-Djava.security.policy=\"%WL_HOME%\server\lib\weblogic.policy\" ➡
weblogic.Server"
goto finish

:runAdmin
@echo on
```

```
set CMDLINE="%JAVA_VM% %MEM_ARGS% %JAVA_OPTIONS% -classpath \"%CLASSPATH%\"
-Dweblogic.Name=%SERVER_NAME% -Dweblogic.management.username=%WLS_USER% ➥
-Dweblogic.ProductionModeEnabled=%PRODUCTION_MODE% ➥
-Djava.security.policy=\"%WL_HOME%\server\lib\weblogic.policy\" ➥
weblogic.Server"

:finish
rem *** Set up extrapath for win32 and win64 platform separately
if not "%WL_USE_64BITDLL%" == "true" set EXTRAPATH=%WL_HOME%\server\native\win\32;➥
%WL_HOME%\server\bin;%JAVA_HOME%\jre\bin;%JAVA_HOME%\bin;➥
%WL_HOME%\server\native\win\32\oci920_8

if "%WL_USE_64BITDLL%" == "true" set ➥
EXTRAPATH=%WL_HOME%\server\native\win\64\;%WL_HOME%\server\bin;➥
%JAVA_HOME%\jre\bin;%JAVA_HOME%\bin;%WL_HOME%\server\native\win\64\oci920_8

rem *** Install the service
"%WL_HOME%\server\bin\beasvc" -install -svcname:"Oracle Products ➥
 %DOMAIN_NAME%_%SERVER_NAME%" -javahome:"%JAVA_HOME%" ➥
-execdir:"%USERDOMAIN_HOME%" -extrapath:"%EXTRAPATH%" ➥
-password:"%WLS_PW%" -cmdline:%CMDLINE%

ENDLOCAL
```

Listing 18-3. *Installing the OSB Admin Server As a Windows Service*

```
echo off
SETLOCAL
set CLASSPATH=C:\bea\WEBLOG~1\servicebus\lib\sb-public.jar; ➥
C:\bea\WEBLOG~1\servicebus\lib\sb-internal.jar; ➥
C:\bea\WEBLOG~1\integration\common\lib\wlicommon.jar; ➥
C:\bea\WEBLOG~1\integration\common\lib\qs_p13n_system.jar; ➥
C:\bea\WEBLOG~1\servicebus\lib\xbus-core.jar; ➥
C:\bea\WEBLOG~1\server\lib\wlxbean.jar; ➥
C:\bea\WEBLOG~1\server\lib\xquery.jar; ➥
C:\bea\WEBLOG~1\server\lib\binxml.jar; ➥
C:\bea\WEBLOG~1\common\lib\log4j.jar; ➥
C:\bea\WEBLOG~1\servicebus\lib\uddi_library.jar; ➥
C:\bea\WEBLOG~1\servicebus\lib\uddi_client_v3.jar; ➥
C:\bea\patch_weblogic910\profiles\default\sys_manifest_classpath\➥
weblogic_patch.jar;C:\bea\JDK150~1\lib\tools.jar; ➥
C:\bea\WEBLOG~1\server\lib\weblogic_sp.jar; ➥
C:\bea\WEBLOG~1\server\lib\weblogic.jar; ➥
C:\bea\WEBLOG~1\server\lib\webservices.jar; ➥
C:\bea\WEBLOG~1\servicebus\lib\version.jar; ➥
C:\bea\WEBLOG~1\common\eval\pointbase\lib\pbclient51.jar; ➥
```

```
C:\bea\WEBLOG~1\server\lib\xqrl.jar; ➥
 C:\bea\WEBLOG~1\integration\lib\util.jar;


set JAVA_HOME=C:\bea\jdk150_04
set JAVA_VENDOR=Sun
set DOMAIN_NAME=WM_ESB_DOMAIN_1
set USERDOMAIN_HOME=D:\APPS\WM_ESB_DOMAIN_1
set SERVER_NAME=WM_ESB_SRVR_ADMIN
set PRODUCTION_MODE=true
JAVA_OPTIONS=-Dweblogic.Stdout="D:\APPS\WM_ESB_DOMAIN_1\stdout.txt"➥
 -Dweblogic.Stderr="D:\APPS\WM_ESB_DOMAIN_1\stderr.txt"
set MEM_ARGS=-Xms40m -Xmx250m


call "C:\BEA\weblogic91\server\bin\installSvc.cmd"


ENDLOCAL
```

Listing 18-4. *Installing a Managed Server As a Windows Service*

```
echo off
SETLOCAL
set CLASSPATH=C:\bea\WEBLOG~1\servicebus\lib\sb-public.jar; ➥
C:\bea\WEBLOG~1\servicebus\lib\sbinternal.jar; ➥
C:\bea\WEBLOG~1\integration\common\lib\wlicommon.jar;➥
C:\bea\WEBLOG~1\integration\common\lib\qs_p13n_system.jar; ➥
C:\bea\WEBLOG~1\servicebus\lib\xbus-core.jar; ➥
C:\bea\WEBLOG~1\server\lib\wlxbean.jar; ➥
C:\bea\WEBLOG~1\server\lib\xquery.jar;C:\bea\WEBLOG~1\server\lib\binxml.jar; ➥
C:\bea\WEBLOG~1\common\lib\log4j.jar; ➥
C:\bea\WEBLOG~1\servicebus\lib\uddi_library.jar; ➥
C:\bea\WEBLOG~1\servicebus\lib\uddi_client_v3.jar; ➥
C:\bea\patch_weblogic910\profiles\default\sys_manifest_classpath\➥
weblogic_patch.jar;C:\bea\JDK150~1\lib\tools.jar; ➥
C:\bea\WEBLOG~1\server\lib\weblogic_sp.jar; ➥
C:\bea\WEBLOG~1\server\lib\weblogic.jar; ➥
C:\bea\WEBLOG~1\server\lib\webservices.jar; ➥
C:\bea\WEBLOG~1\servicebus\lib\version.jar; ➥
C:\bea\WEBLOG~1\common\eval\pointbase\lib\pbclient51.jar; ➥
C:\bea\WEBLOG~1\server\lib\xqrl.jar; ➥
C:\bea\WEBLOG~1\integration\lib\util.jar;
set JAVA_HOME=C:\bea\jdk150_04
set JAVA_VENDOR=Sun
REM Modify the DOMAIN_NAME, USERDOMAIN and SERVER_NAME as appropriate
set DOMAIN_NAME=WM_ESB_DOMAIN_1
set USERDOMAIN_HOME=D:\APPS\WM_ESB_DOMAIN_1
set SERVER_NAME=WM_ESB_SRVR_1
set PRODUCTION_MODE=true
```

```
JAVA_OPTIONS=-Dweblogic.Stdout="D:\APPS\WM_ESB_DOMAIN_1\stdout.txt"↪
 -Dweblogic.Stderr="D:\APPS\WM_ESB_DOMAIN_1\stderr.txt"
set ADMIN_URL=http://SYDBIZSO2:7001
set MEM_ARGS=-Xms40m -Xmx250m
call "C:\BEA\weblogic91\server\bin\installSvc.cmd"

ENDLOCAL
```

What happens to "in-flight" processes when I update a proxy service?

The fact that OSB is configuration-driven instead of code-driven leads to some interesting questions. If you change a proxy service while it is running (that is, in the middle of receiving requests and sending responses), what happens?

The answer is simple. If a proxy service is in the middle of a request or response when it's updated, it's cached as a copy of the proxy service until the transaction is complete. The newer version is immediately activated and starts to handle all new requests. The cached copy handles all current work until all current (also known as *in flight*) work is completed. Once all the current work is complete, the cached version of the proxy service is removed from memory.

Messaging and Protocols

This section is devoted to messaging topics and issues with transport protocols.

How do I see the low-level web service messages from my client?

Sometimes it's very useful when debugging to be able to see the messages that your client is sending and receiving. If you are using a POJO client, you can simply pass in the following command-line argument to Java:

```
-Dweblogic.wsee.verbose=*
```

If you are starting your client with an Ant script, use the `<sysproperty>` element inside a `<java>` tag, as follows:

```
<java fork="yes" classname="${package.name}.Client" failonerror="true">
    <sysproperty key="weblogic.wsee.verbose" value="*"/>
    <classpath refid="clientrun.class.path"/>
</java>
```

How do I retrieve a SOAP header using XQuery?

If you want to add an `appinfo` field to your SOAP header so you can use the data for reporting, use the following code:

```
<SOAP-ENV:Header xmlns:soapenv="http://schemas.xmlsoap.org/soap/envelope/"
xmlns:SOAP-ENC="http://schemas.xmlsoap.org/soap/encoding/"
xmlns:xsi="http://www.w3.org/2001/XMLSchema-instance"
xmlns:xsd="http://www.w3.org/2001/XMLSchema"
```

```
xmlns:SOAP-ENV="http://schemas.xmlsoap.org/soap/envelope/">
<MyHeader xmlns:myns="http://foo.com/soaplatform/">
   <myns:appinfo>TESTAPPLICATION</myns:appinfo>
</MyHeader>
</SOAP-ENV:Header>
```

Perform the following steps:

1. Add a user-defined namespace for myns with the value of http://foo.com/soaplatform/.

2. Use the XQuery $header/MyHeader/myns:appinfo/text() to retrieve the text value of the header.

Thanks to Deb Ayers for this answer.

How do I get the HTTP URL parameters?

Use the $inbound/ctx:transport/ctx:request/http:query-string element to get all the arguments in the URL. For an example of how to do this, see the next question.

How do I accept HTTP/POST information from a web form?

You can create a proxy service in OSB that can be invoked by an HTML form. This might sound odd, but it is a good example of using OSB to integrate non–web service systems. Listing 18-5 shows the HTML code that will HTTP/POST form data to a proxy service in OSB.

Listing 18-5. *The HTML Form That Will POST Data to an OSB Proxy Service*

```
<!DOCTYPE HTML PUBLIC "-//W3C//DTD HTML 4.01 Transitional//EN">
<html>
<head>
<meta http-equiv="Content-Type" content="text/html; charset=ISO-8859-1">
<title>XML HTTP POST Example</title>
</head>
<body>
<h1>Use this form to post a message to the XMLWSDL service</h1>
<form name="GetGreeting" action="http://localhost:7001/HTTPPOSTProxy/">
<textArea rows="20" cols="60" name="payload">Foo</textArea>
<button name="Submit" type="submit">Submit</button>
</form>
</body>
</html>
```

Create a proxy service called HTTPPOSTProxy based on the Any XML Service setting for the service type. Set the endpoint URI to /HTTPPOSTProxy (so that it matches the action URI of the HTML form). In the message flow of the proxy service, add a Pipeline Pair node with a single stage that contains three actions.

The first action is an Assign action that assigns the value of the following expression to the variable queryString:

```
$inbound/ctx:transport/ctx:request/http:query-string
```

The second action is also an Assign action that assigns the value of the following expression to the variable payload:

```
fn:substring-before(fn:substring-after($queryString, 'payload='), '&Submit')
```

As you can see, this expression simply extracts a substring from the queryString variable between the payload= and &Submit markers in the queryString variable.

The third and final action is a Log action so that you can see the value of the payload field that is HTTP/POSTed to the proxy service. The Log action should have the following expression:

```
concat('queryString = ', $queryString, ' payload = [', $payload, ']')
```

This will clearly show you the entire contents of the queryString that was posted to the proxy service, and the fully parsed value of the payload field.

How do I calculate the content length of an inbound HTTP request?

You can't get this information directly, or even exactly. John Shafer offers the following solution.

There's no easy way to calculate content length on your own, especially if attachments are involved. Note that $attachments uses an XML representation, whereas a transport-level message containing attachments will be represented as a multipart MIME package, so the lengths will differ by quite a bit. Also, if you have any binary attachments (that is, non-XML or nontext), that content isn't even part of $attachments, so any length calculation based simply on the serialization of $attachments will be *way* off.

Even if attachments aren't involved and you update your formula using the fn-bea:serialize() method, your following formula doesn't take into account the <SOAP:Envelope xmlns:SOAP="..."> wrapper. Also, the formula will calculate only character length, not byte length. For example, although UTF-8 uses a single byte for encoding US-ASCII characters, characters in other languages might require two or even three bytes when encoded in UTF-8 for transport. Of course, other nonuniversal encodings such as ISO-8859-1 are single byte by definition.

In any event, if you're looking for only a rough estimate, aren't using attachments, and are willing to deal with a character-based length rather than byte-based, the following tweaked formula might be a reasonable estimate:

```
fn:string-length(fn-bea:serialize($header)) +
fn:string-length(fn-bea:serialize($body)) + 90
```

The 90 is an estimate of the character length of the start and end <SOAP:Envelope> elements, including the SOAP namespace declaration.

Of course, none of this applies if you aren't dealing with SOAP.

How can I get the WSDL/Policy/MFL/Schema/Proxy via HTTP?

You can retrieve many of the resource types directly from the OSB server by using HTTP instead of needing to use the service bus console. The general pattern for the URL is as follows:

```
http://[hostname]:[port]/sbresource?[Resource Type]/[Project Name]/[Resource Name]
```

The [Resource Type] section of the URL may be any one of the following values:

- BIZ

- MFL

- POLICY

- PROXY

- SCHEMA

- WSDL

The URL must be UTF-8 encoded. If the resource is stored in a directory, then the directory structure needs to be declared explicitly in the URL also.

For example, in the Hello World project in Chapter 4 of this book, we defined a WSDL resource in the WSDL folder of the project. The name of that WSDL resource is set to HelloWorld. To retrieve this WSDL, you would use the following URL:

```
http://localhost:7001/sbresource?WSDL/Hello+World/WSDL/HelloWorld
```

If you wanted to see the WSDL for the proxy service, you would use the following URL:

```
http://localhost:7001/sbresource?PROXY/Hello+World/ProxyServices/HelloWorld
```

Many thanks to Gregory Haardt for this tip!

How do I update the EJB client JAR resource of an EJB transport business service?

When you update the client JAR of an EJB business service, you need to update OSB with the new client JAR. The process is simple, though it might not be obvious. To update the business service in OSB, you simply click the link of the EJB client JAR resource.

How do I map a URL context root to a service?

Sometimes you might want a proxy service to be identified by part of a URL, and have the remainder of the URL act as a command. This allows you to create simple web-based services without the need for WSDL files, XSDs, and the like. This is similar in nature to taking the REST approach to web services. In this example, you'll create a proxy service that looks for commands encoded into the URL and prints those commands to the standard output. The format for the URL to invoke this service is as follows:

```
http://[host]:[port]/[Service context]/[Commands]
```

You'll create a proxy service and bind it to the /REST/CommandHandler context root. When the proxy is invoked, it will examine the remainder of the URL to discover the command and associated parameters. Figure 18-1 shows the start of a RESTful proxy service creation. When creating a service like this yourself, be sure to select the Messaging Service setting for the service type.

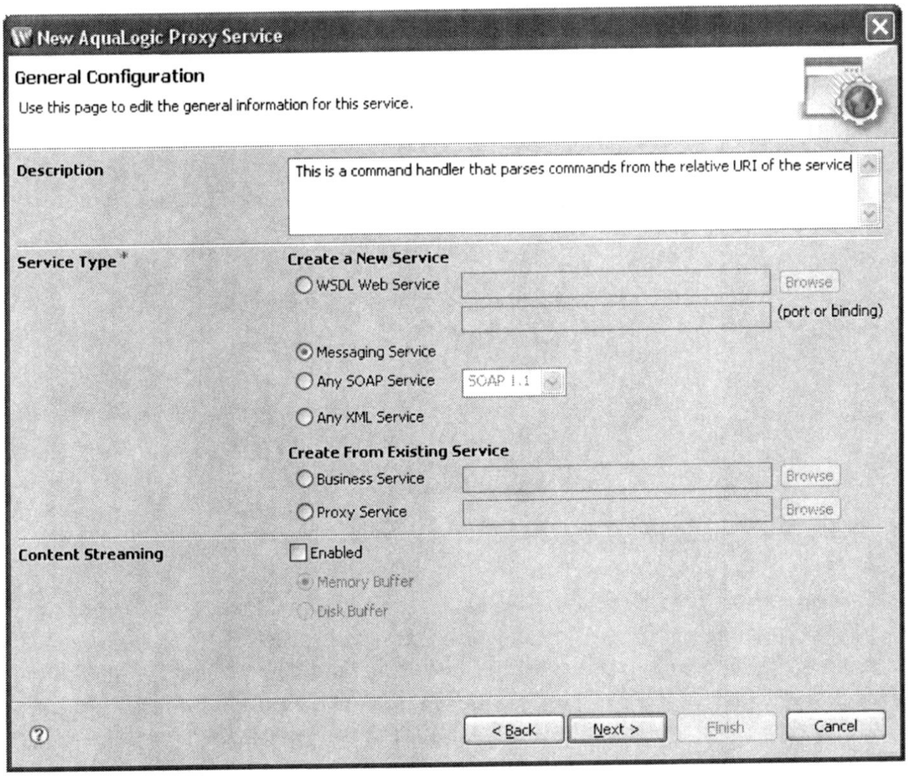

Figure 18-1. *Defining a RESTful proxy service*

The key to creating a service such as this is to set the request message type to None (you're only parsing the URL) and the return type to XML, as shown in Figure 18-2. By specifying XML as the return type, but not specifying a specific XML schema element, your service is free to return any XML value.

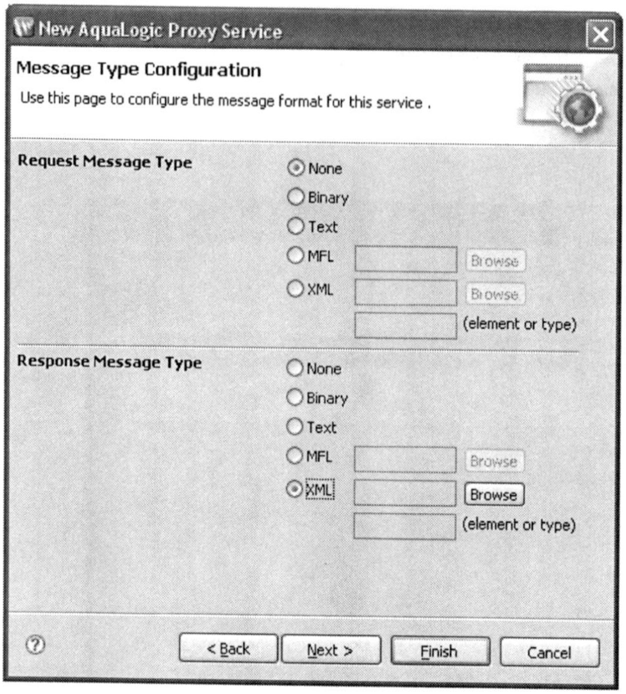

Figure 18-2. *Setting the request and response types*

Click the Next button and leave the endpoint URI set to /REST/CommandHandler for this example. Click the Next button. Accept the defaults for the rest of the New Proxy Service wizard.

You'll implement the proxy service's message flow using a simple Pipeline Pair node with a single stage in the request and the response pipelines. The request stage simply gathers the command and params values from the relative URI, found in the $inbound/ctx:transport/ctx:request variable.

The first Assign action assigns the results of the following expression to the command variable:

```
fn:tokenize(data($inbound/ctx:transport/ctx:request/http:relative-URI), '/')[1]
```

The second Assign action assigns the results of the following expression to the params variable:

```
fn:tokenize(data($inbound/ctx:transport/ctx:request/http:relative-URI), '/')[2]
```

Lastly, add a Log action at the end of the request pipeline so that you can see the values that were passed in with the request. The expression of the Log action can be as simple as follows:

```
concat('Command: ', $command, ', Params: ', $params)
```

The response stage is equally simple. In this stage, you'll construct an arbitrary XML response that contains the command and the parameters that were extracted from the original URL. The step is to assign your XML structure, including the command and params variables to the xmlResponse variable. You use the concat function to assemble a string version of your XML, then you use the fn-bea:inlinedXML function to turn the string into an XML variable:

```
fn-bea:inlinedXML(
concat('<Response><Command>', $command, '</Command><Params>',
$params, '</Params></Response>')
)
```

The next two actions are straightforward. You replace the XPath expression of . (a period) of the body variable with the expression $xmlResponse. Be sure to select the "Replace node contents" radio button. Then log the $xmlResponse so you can see what's going on when you test this service.

One thing to note: because this service has a request type of None, you cannot use the OSB test console to test this service. Instead, you'll use a web browser where you can specify any arbitrary URL. You can send commands with parameters in the URL; for example:

```
http://localhost:7001/REST/CommandHandler/Foo/Bar=4;happy=1
```

The CommandHandler will identify Foo as the command and Bar=4;happy=1 as the parameters. You can find the code for this in the REST project if you download the OSB sbconfig.jar file from the Source Code/Download area of the Apress web site at http://www.apress.com.

Many thanks to Stuart Charlton for this tip!

XML, XQuery, and XSLT

Many questions about using OSB successfully are really questions about XML, XQuery, and XSLT technologies. OSB is built on these technologies. Here are some of the most common questions we've encountered in the field.

How can I convert XML into a string using XQuery?

OSB provides an extension to XQuery to perform this function. fn-bea:serialize($arg-xml) converts an XML variable into an XML string.

How can I convert a string value into an XML variable using XQuery?

OSB provides an extension to XQuery that performs this function. fn-bea:inlinedXML($arg-string) converts a string argument into an XML variable that you can then use in conjunction with other XQuery and XPath statements.

How do I get the namespace of an XML node?

XQuery provides a function for this explicitly:

```
fn:namespace-uri($node-with-namespace-containing-version)
```

Closely related to this question is the following question.

How do I get the version number from the namespace?

It's common practice to include some version information embedded into the namespace. For example, the following namespace uses the release date of October 15, 2008 to indicate its version number:

```
http://www.openuri.org/acmeworld/schemas/2008/10/15/Financial
```

The XQuery statement to extract the version number simply splits the namespace string using two nested substring operations, as follows:

```
fn:substring-before(fn:substring-after(xs:string(fn:namespace-uri(➥
$node-with-namespace-containing-version)),"/schemas/"),"/Financial")
```

This returns the string 2008/10/15. Thanks to Mike Wooten for this tip.

How do I test for a null?

Handling null values in XQuery is simple, but not intuitive to those who are new to the language. Beginners often try to use expressions such as Eq NULL or is null in their tests. The correct way to test for null values in XML tags is to use one of the following expressions:

```
not exists(column)
```

or

```
empty( column )
```

Thanks to Michael Reiche for this tip.

Miscellaneous

Here are some general tips that just don't fit into any other category.

How do I get rid of the Work Manager warnings when starting OSB?

When starting the service bus, you might see a series of errors on the console, such as the following:

```
<Jan 5, 2007 11:20:51 AM PST> <Warning> <WorkManager> <BEA-002919> <Unable to
find a WorkManager with name weblogic.wsee.mdb.DispatchPolicy. Dispatch policy
weblogic.wsee.mdb.DispatchPolicy will map to the default WorkManager for
the application bea_wls9_async_response>
```

If you're like us, you hate to see extraneous errors. This error is caused by the fact that a default installation of OSB doesn't have any Work Managers defined. The solution is simple: define a Work Manager using the WebLogic console. Log into the WebLogic console (not the service bus console), create a Work Manager with the name weblogic.wsee.mdb.DispatchPolicy, and these warning messages will cease. Be sure to target the Work Manager to the machine(s) in the domain.

How do I read from a database?

In OSB version 2.5 and later, it's possible to have OSB read information from a database. It's easy to overlook this feature, because it doesn't use an action. Instead, it uses an XQuery function to access the database.

The following XQuery line demonstrates how to use OSB to read from a data source defined in the host WebLogic Server. The `'jdbc.mySQLDS'` argument is the JNDI name of the data source defined in WebLogic Server. The `'total'` argument is the name of the tag used to encapsulate the result of the query. The last argument is the SQL statement that will execute.

```
fn-bea:execute-sql('jdbc.mySQLDS', 'total', 'select count(*) from company')
```

Executing the preceding SQL statement returns the following value (assuming you have a table named company in your MySQL database):

```
<total>
<COUNT_x0028__x00210__x0029_>122</COUNT_x0028__x00210__x0029_>
</total>
```

The `<COUNT_x0028__x00210__x0029_>` tag is the translation of the count(*) portion of the SQL expression, using XML safe encoding. This is fairly ugly, but using a modified SQL statement can fix it. For example, change the expression to the following:

```
fn-bea:execute-sql('jdbc.mySQLDS', 'total', 'select count(*) as count from company')
```

This yields the following result:

```
<total>
<COUNT_>122</COUNT>
</total>
```

This looks much cleaner.

How do I get a list of disabled services?

When you're dealing with numerous web services in your environment, it becomes impractical to examine individual services manually to see whether they are enabled. Fortunately, the Smart Search feature in the OSB console makes finding disabled services a breeze (see Figure 18-3).

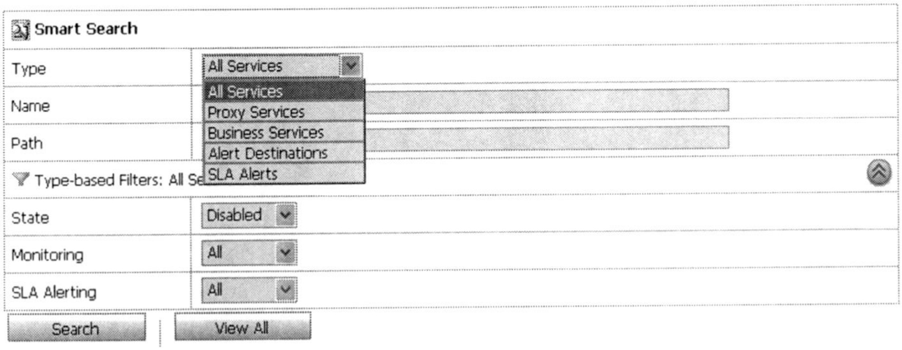

Figure 18-3. *The Smart Search feature*

You can access the Smart Search feature from the Operations section of the Dashboard. Thanks to Gaston Ansaldo for this tip.

What is an EJB Converter JAR?

The EJB transport (introduced in OSB 2.5) supports the notion of converter classes. These classes help map parameter and return value types to Java classes that can be mapped to XML. Prior to OSB 2.6, these converter classes had to be packaged in the EJB client JAR—the same JAR containing the client stubs.

We received feedback from users that they didn't like having to package the converter classes in with their EJB client JAR files. The EJB client JARs are typically produced by EJB tools. People don't like needing to unjar this JAR, add the converter classes, and rejar them. That's cumbersome. By having a separate EJB converter JAR entry, you can package your converter classes separately. In addition, the EJB converter JAR can be used on several EJB business services. So, this is a usability improvement.

Summary

We hope that this chapter will save you a lot of time and trouble in your career using OSB. When you come across a question in the field, look here first. With luck, you'll find your answers so quickly that your question will never exist long enough to become a problem. Obviously, we can't answer every question related to OSB in a single chapter, but these questions represent the most common questions we encounter, especially with people who are new to OSB. If you cannot find an answer to your question here, search the Web, especially the Oracle Technology Network (OTN) web site at http://www.oracle.com/technology, for a more exhaustive list of questions and the most up-to-date answers.

Index